Bible Commentary
by
E. M. Zerr

Volume III
Psalms—Isaiah

© **Truth Publications, Inc. 2018.** All rights reserved. No part of this book may be reproduced in any form without written permission from the publisher. Printed in the United States of America.

ISBN 10: 1-58427-183-3

ISBN 13: 978-1-58427-183-3

Truth Publications, Inc.
CEI Bookstore
220 S. Marion St., Athens, AL 35611
855-492-6657
sales@truthpublications.com
www.truthbooks.com

Foreword: The E.M. Zerr Bible Commentaries

Cecil Willis
Reprinted From *Truth Magazine* XX:26 (June 24, 1976), pp. 3-5

The Cogdill Foundation, which publishes *Truth Magazine*, has obtained exclusive publication rights to the six volume *Bible Commentary* written by Brother E.M. Zerr. . . .

Information About E.M. Zerr

Brother Zerr was quite well-known among a group of very conservative brethren, but he may not have been known among brethren in general. Hence, a little information concerning him is here given. Edward Michael Zerr was born October 15, 1877 in Strassburg, Illinois, but his family soon thereafter moved to Missouri. He was the second of six children born to Lawrence and Mary (Manning) Zerr. Brother Zerr's father was reared as a Catholic, but after he married Mary Manning, he obeyed the gospel. At the age of seventeen, young Edward was immersed into Christ in Grand River, near Bosworth, Missouri.

In June, 1897 young Brother E.M. Zerr received a letter from A. L. Gepford asking him to go to Green Valley, Illinois, and to preach in his stead. His first sermon was entitled, "My Responsibility as a Preacher of the Gospel, and Your Responsibility as Hearers." In the years between delivery of this first sermon on July 3, 1897, and the delivery of his last sermon on October 25, 1959, Brother Zerr preached about 8,000 sermons, from California to Connecticut, and from Washington to Arizona. It is noteworthy that his last sermon was built around Matt. 13:44, and was entitled "Full Surrender." Brother Zerr preached the gospel for a little over 60 years.

Among the brethren with whom Brother Zerr was most frequently associated, it was then common to have protracted periods of concentrated Bible studies, commonly referred to as "Bible Readings." Young Brother Zerr attended a three month "Bible Reading" conducted by the well-known teacher, A.M. Morris, in 1899. During this study which was conducted at

Hillsboro, Henry County, Indiana, Brother Zerr stayed in the home of a farmer named John Hill. After leaving the John and Matilda Hill farm, "E.M." began correspondence with their daughter, Carrie. The following year, while attending a "Bible Reading" conducted by Daniel Sommer in Indianapolis, "E.M." and Carrie were married, on September 27, 1900. The newlyweds took up residence in New Castle, Indiana, where their four children were born, one of whom died in infancy.

In 1911, Brother A.W. Harvey arranged for Brother Zerr to conduct a "Bible Reading" which continued for several months at Palmyra, Indiana. These "Bible Readings" usually consisted of two two-hour sessions daily. Young Brother Zerr's special ability as a teacher was soon recognized, and he continued to conduct such studies among churches of Christ for 48 years. Edward M. Zerr died February 22, 1960, having been in a coma for four months following an automobile accident at Martinsville, Indiana. His body was laid to rest in the little country cemetery at Hillsboro, Indiana, near the church building in which he had attended his first "Bible Reading."

Brother Zerr's Writings

In addition to his oral teaching and preaching, Brother Zerr was a prolific writer. He was a regular contributor to several religious periodicals. Brother Zerr also composed the music and lyrics of several religious songs. Two of these, "The True Riches," and "I Come to Thee," may be found in the widely used song book, *Sacred Selections.*

One of the books written by Brother Zerr is entitled *Historical Quotations,* and consists of the gleanings from 40,000 pages of ancient history and other critical sources which he read over a period of twenty years. These quotations are intended to explain and to confirm the prophetic and other technical statements of the Bible. Another book, a 434 page hard-cover binding, consists of a study course containing 16,000 Bible questions. This book, *New Testament Questions,* has at least 50 questions on each chapter of the New Testament. A smaller book, *Bible Reading Notes,* consists of some of the copious notes which Brother Zerr made in connection with the "Bible Readings" which he conducted. But the crowning success of his efforts was the writing of his six volume commentary on the whole Bible.

These six volumes were published between 1947 and 1955. Brother Zerr has the unique distinction, so far as is known to this writer, of being the only member of the church to write a commentary on the entire Bible. Many other brethren have written excellent and valuable commentaries on various books of the Bible, but no other brother has written on the entire Bible.

Foreword

The writing of this commentary consumed more than seven years of full-time labor. In order that he might devote himself without interruption to this herculean effort, Brother Zerr was supported by the Newcastle church during this seven year period. It is unfortunate, in this writer's judgment, that other competent men have not been entirely freed of other duties that they might give themselves to such mammoth writing assignments. Through *Bible Commentary*, Brother E.M. Zerr, though dead since 1960, will continue to do what he liked best to do—conduct "Bible Readings" for many years to come. The current printing is the fifth printing of the Old Testament section (four volumes) of the commentary, and the sixth printing of the New Testament section (two volumes).

Many Christians spend but little money on available helps in Bible study. Some own perhaps only a *Cruden's Concordance*, a Bible dictionary of some kind, and then *Johnson's Notes*. It would be interesting to know how many copies of B.W. Johnson's *The People's New Testament Commentary With Notes* have been sold. If I were to hazard a guess, it would be that at least 1,000,000 copies of this superficial commentary have been sold. *Johnson's Notes* contains the printing of the entire New Testament text in both King James Version and the English Revised Version (the predecessor to the American Standard Version), and his comments, all contained in two volumes. In fact, a single volume edition also is available. Thus one is buying two copies of the New Testament, and B. W. Johnson's *Notes*, in one or two volumes. So necessarily, *Johnson's Notes* are very brief.

If brethren somehow could be made acquainted with Brother Zerr's *Bible Commentary*, it is possible that it could be as widely used as has been *Johnson's Notes*, first published in 1889. Brother Zerr printed very little of the Bible text in his commentary. He assumed you would have your own Bible nearby. To have printed in the commentary the entire Bible would have required at least three other volumes. While it would have been helpful to have the Bible text printed by the comments, this unnecessary luxury would have been very expensive, since we all have copies of the Scriptures already. Furthermore, Brother Zerr intended that one be compelled to use his Bible, in order that his commentary never supplant the Sacred text.

A Word of Caution

I am sure that Brother Zerr, were he yet living, would advise me to remind you that his *Bible Commentary* is only that of a man, though a studious man he was. In fact, in the "Preface" to this set of books, just such a word of warning is sounded by Brother Zerr. The only book which we recommend without reservation is the Bible! But Bible commentaries, when viewed merely as the results of many years of study by scholarly men, can be very helpful to one.

Brother Zerr spent his life-time working among those brethren who have stood opposed to "located preachers" and to "Bible Colleges." However, he has not "featured" these distinctive views in his *Bible Commentary*. If one did not know of these positions held by Brother Zerr, he might not even detect the references to them in the commentary. However, I want to call such references to your attention. Along with the opposition to "located preachers," Brother Zerr also held a position commonly referred to as "Evangelistic Oversight." This position declares that until a congregation has qualified elders appointed, each congregation should be under the oversight of some evangelist. With these positions, this writer cannot agree. References to these positions will be found in his comments on Acts 20:28; Eph. 3:10; 3:21; 4:11; 1 Tim. 5:21; 2 Tim. 4:5, and perhaps in a few other places that do not now come to memory. Brother Zerr also took the position that a woman should never cut or even trim her hair. His comments on this position will be found at 1 Cor. 11:1-16.

But aside from a very few such positions with which many of us would disagree, Brother Zerr's *Bible Commentary* can be very helpful. Some restoration period writers of widely used commentaries held some rather bizarre positions regarding the millennium. Brethren scruple not to use *Barnes' Notes*, in spite of his repeated injection of Calvinism, and *Clark's Commentary*, in spite of his Methodist teaching.

Brother Zerr's *Bible Commentary* is far superior to *Johnson's Notes*. Though there are some extraordinarily good volumes in the well-known Gospel Advocate commentaries, there also are some notoriously weak volumes in this widely used set. Viewed from the point of consistent quality, Brother Zerr's *Bible Commentary* is superior to the Gospel Advocate set. Some brethren whom I consider to be superior exegetes of the Word have highly recommended Zerr's *Bible Commentary* and have praised the splendid and incisive way in which he has handled even those "hard to be understood" sections of God's Word.

Our recommendation regarding E.M. Zerr's six volume commentary can be paraphrased from the words of a well-known television commercial: "Try it; you'll like it!"

Bible Commentary

PSALMS 1

General remarks. This book holds a place of unusual interest in the Bible. By one classification it is distinguished from the law (Luke 24: 44), and by another it is referred to as a part of the law (John 10: 34). It contains various forms of speech; poetical, musical, historical and prophetical. Many "authorities" divide it into 5 books, with other tabulations regarding the several verses in each book. This information is all interesting and useful, but is too detailed and technical to be given space in a commentary like this. For the benefit of the readers who might be interested, I shall cite some authors: Schaff-Herzog Encyclopedia; Smith's Bible Dictionary; Oxford Cyclopedic Concordance; Two Thousand Hours in the Psalms, by Dr. Marion McH. Hull. Wherever, in my judgment, any of the Psalms require some special notice as per the information cited above, I will point it out. Otherwise I shall comment on the verses of the chapters in the order as contained in the A. V. of the Bible, as I have done in the preceding volumes of the commentary.

Verse 1. In this verse we see the entire scope of human conduct classified under three heads; walking, standing and sitting. It would be impossible literally or physically to do all of them at the same time, hence we should look for the figurative sense of the words. *Blessed* is from ESHER and is rendered "happy" by Strong, Young and Moffatt. *Walketh* is from HALAK and has a variety of applications both figurative and literal. Perhaps its most outstanding thought is to "frequent a place." *Counsel* has been translated from ETSAH and Strong defines it, "advice." The whole statement means one who follows the advice of the *ungodly*. The last word is from RASHA, which Strong defines, "morally wrong; concretely an (actively) bad person." *Standeth* is from AMAD and defined by Strong as follows: "A primitive root; to stand, in various relations (literally and figuratively, transitively and intransitively)." *Way* is from DEREK and defined, "A road (as trodden); figuratively a course of life or mode of action, often adverbially."—Strong. In the A. V. it has been rendered by conversation 2 times, custom 1, journey 23, manner 8 and way 1692. The thought is of a man who does not "stand for" the manner of sinners. *Sitteth* is from a word that has been rendered by dwell 434 times. *Seat* is from MOSHAB and Strong gives "session" as a part of his definition; Moffatt renders it "company." *Scornful* is from LUWTS and Strong defines it, "to make mouths at, i.e. to scoff." A man who cannot deny the truthfulness of God's Word will try to weaken its force by making light of it.

Verse 2. The preceding verse describes a man who is good negatively, this one will consider a man who is good affirmatively. To *delight* in the law of the Lord means more than merely enduring it. A man might accept it with a passive approval because he has no reason to dispute it, but he should also accept it as a chief source of joy. Jesus taught the same principle in Matt. 5: 6. *Meditate* means to think seriously and respectfully over the law even when one cannot have the text before his eyes. The Bible is so full of precious material that a man can read enough of it in a few moments preceding his day's activities to keep his mind busy all day. *Day and night* comprehends the entire period of time which might seem to leave no opportunity for any necessary attention to the body. The expression is figurative, meaning that at all available moments whether in the day or night, one should be thinking of the law.

Verse 3. *Rivers of water* is a significant phrase. The first word is from PELEG which means, "a rill (i.e. small channel of water, as in irrigation)." —Strong. It is from another Hebrew word meaning, "to split (literally or figuratively)." It refers to places where two streams meet and the soil between them is always moist, therefore fruitful. Both fruit and foliage need nourishment and the life-giving liquid is ever present because of the condition brought about by the two streams. However, the moisture saturating the ground near the tree would be of no value did the tree not reach out and drink of it. Likewise the happy man of God is enabled to thrive because he does his part by reaching for the life-giving source in the stream of God's truth. *Whatsoever he doeth* is based on the condition that he delights in the law of the Lord and constantly meditates therein. The *prosperity* assured him is of a spiritual nature, not that any special providence is to be expected as a reward for his study of the Word.

Verse 4. *Ungodly* is defined in the comments at v. 1. Chaff is light and passive in the presence of wind. It is used to compare the wicked men because they are of such little weight or consequence that God's blast will separate them from the righteous. See the same thought in Matt. 3: 12.

Verse 5. *Stand* is from a different original from that in v. 1. Here it means to endure or withstand a test. *The judgment* does not refer especially to that of the last day. It means any time that a test accounting is to be made. Whenever that is done the ungodly will fail to "pass" the test of truth. The last clause is practically the same in thought as the preceding one. An assembly of righteous people would expel an ungodly man from its midst. That agrees with the principles of government regulating the church in the New Testament. (1 Cor. 5: 5-8; 2 Th. 3: 6.)

Verse 6. *Knoweth* means to recognize or own. *Way* means a course of action in one's life. God will own or accept the life of a righteous man by accepting and saving the man. On the other hand, the course of life followed by an ungodly man is objectionable, and the Lord will reject it in that he will let the man perish.

PSALMS 2

Verse 1. This whole chapter is a prophecy concerning Christ. The reader should not be confused by the present or past tense of the verb, for that is the prophetic style. God knows the future as well as he does the present and indicated that fact by inspiring the prophets to write of future events as if they had already taken place. *Heathen* means "a foreign nation," and here refers to the Gentiles in the time of Christ and his disciples. *Rage* is defined by Strong "to be tumultuous," and refers to the disorderly assemblages in which the enemies of Christ conspired to injure his cause. *Imagine* means to meditate and plan to oppose the works of the disciples of the Lord. *Vain thing* is from a Hebrew word that means emptiness. It denotes that the malicious purposes of the foes of the Lord were to come to nought. This prophecy was quoted by the disciples as recorded in Acts 4: 25, 26.

Verse 2. *Lord* and *his anointed* mean God and Christ. The *kings* refers to the rulers in the time of Christ and his followers who plotted against their work. Herod and Pilate were among them and are named in Acts 4: 27.

Verse 3. *Their bands* and *their cords* refers to the hold that God and his Son rightfully had on the rulers of the world. They (heathen) plotted to revolt against the divine legislation.

Verse 4. *Laugh and derision* are practically the same in meaning. The thought is that God will look upon his enemies with contempt. He will regard their attempts at overthrowing his counsel as of too little consequence to deserve serious attention.

Verse 5. God will look with contempt upon the doings of his enemies, yet that will not end the matter. They will be made to feel the sting of his wrath finally.

Verse 6. David uses the pronouns promiscuously as to the 1st, 2nd, or 3rd person. In this verse he uses the 1st person and is speaking for God the Father. In spite of the plots of the heathen, God will (have) set his king (Christ) upon the holy hill of Zion of Jerusalem.

Verse 7. David is the speaker in the first clause in which he is introducing a decree about to be quoted. That decree was made by the Father concerning the Son, and the rest of the verse is the language of the Son, repeating the decree of God. It may well be worded with parenthetical explanations thus: "The Lord (God) hath said unto me (Christ), thou art," etc.

Verse 8. *Me* refers to God, making a prediction in the form of an invitation to the Son. The *heathen* refers to the nations of the world who were to embrace the Gospel and become members of the kingdom of Christ.

Verse 9. The expressions in this verse are figurative and are intended to give the idea of God's firm rule. A king holds a rod or scepter in his hand while on the throne, indicating his right and ability to rule. A rod of iron would denote a rule that is firm and enduring. A potter's vessel is fragile and would shatter into many pieces if struck. The ease and certainty with which a man would break this vessel into many pieces is used to compare God's success in demolishing the heathen in their wicked attempts at overthrowing the divine authority.

Verse 10. This is an admonition to the rulers of the world to give attention to the prediction about to be made.

Verse 11. *Fear* and *trembling* have practically the same meaning, which is to have deep reverence for the Son of God. On that condition one would have right to rejoice in that he might expect the favor of the Son.

Verse 12. *Kiss the son* means to do homage to him. The writer is prophesying that kings and other rulers who would not incur the anger of the Son of God must do him homage. If they will do so and put their trust in him they will be happy.

PSALMS 3

Verse 1. Many of the Psalm of David were prompted by his experiences. The present one was suggested by his difficulties with Absalom. The *increase* of the enemies is recorded in 2 Sam. 15: 12.

Verse 2. This verse is verified in 2 Sam. 16: 8. *Selah.* This word occurs 70 times in the Psalms and 3 times in Habakkuk. I shall give the definition of it here and the reader is requested to make note of it for reference to save space in commenting on it at the various places. "A pause or musical note."—Young. "Suspension (of music), i.e. pause."—Strong. It has the same force in musical compositions as our "hold" or "bird's-eye," and the punctuation marks in language compositions. We do not pronounce the "hold" when singing nor the period and other marks when reading. They are observed but not pronounced, and that should be done when reading the Psalms. Just observe the significance of the term but do not pronounce it. Moffatt's translation does not even contain the term in the text.

Verse 3. David was always a firm believer in God. His example should be an encouragement for us.

Verse 4. *Holy hill* is a figurative reference to the throne of God.

Verse 5. This verse is a brief but beautiful statement concerning the watchful care that God had over David. In his waking or slumbering hours the vigilance of the Lord sustained him.

Verse 6. Numbers do not count when arrayed against the true man of God. Paul expressed the same thought in Rom. 8: 31.

Verse 7. David was thinking of God's past victories over the enemy. In view of that record he called upon Him to come to his rescue now. *Cheek bone* or jaw is a vital part of the human body, and to be able to attack one at that place would indicate having the mastery.

Verse 8. All salvation must come from the Lord. It is true that such a blessing will be on his *people* only, but it is true also that all men have the opportunity of becoming a part of the people of the Lord.

PSALMS 4

Verse 1. *God of my righteousness.* David meant that his life of righteousness was according to the will of God. No man's life can truly be said to be righteous unless it is approved of God. *Enlarged me* means that God helped him out of distress.

Verse 2. David wrote as if God spoke to the sons of men. He rebuked them for their shameful attitude toward the Lord's glory. They were charged with seking after *leasing* which means falsehood.

Verse 3. *Set apart* is a definition of "sanctified." No arbitrary miracle ever was or ever will be done by the Lord to sanctify a person, but when one turns from his sins and accepts God's terms of pardon he is then in a sanctified state. Such an individual will be assured of having his prayers heard according to the will of God.

Verse 4. *Awe* means such respect for God that a man fears to do wrong. Instead of plotting to sin, he will meditate on the goodness of God and will *be still* or calm in the consciousness of the peace that comes from serving God.

Verse 5. Animal sacrifices were right under the law when properly offered. However, the most acceptable sacrifice one can make is a life that is generally righteous. Such a life entitles one to lean with *trust* or faith on the Lord.

Verse 6. The desire to find something really good is a righteous one. In behalf of such inquirers David asked the Lord to show the light of his countenance. A similar thought is to be gathered from Matt. 5: 6.

Verse 7. This means that David's gladness because of the Lord's countenance was great. It exceeded that of people who had been blessed with temporal prosperity.

Verse 8. This verse is the same in thought as Ch. 3: 5.

PSALMS 5

Verses 1, 2. David was a praying man and many of his prayers were very earnest and in the form of supplications. In this prayer he recognized God as his King also. That was significant, for there are men who would profess to lean upon God for purposes of divine aid, but look to some man for guidance in their manner of life.

Verse 3. This shows a devoted life, for David began the day's activities with prayer to God.

Verse 4. David ascribed the purest of principles to the Lord. He not only takes no pleasure in wickedness but will not permit evildoers to dwell with him.

Verse 5. *Stand* is from a word that has "withstand" as one definition. It means the foolish shall not withstand the searchlight of God's eyes. *Workers of iniquity* must be considered as a whole to understand what God hates. He loved the world to the extent that he gave his only begotten Son as a sacrifice to save sinners. But it is the works of iniquity that he hates. He hates sin but loves the sinner.

Verse 6. *Leasing* is falsehood and all liars shall be cast into the lake of fire. (Rev. 21: 8.) God abhors the bloody man in the same sense he hates the *workers of iniquity* in the preceding verse.

Verse 7. The mercy of God only would admit an erring mortal to come into the house of the Lord. *In thy fear* means in reverence for God only would David presume to offer worship toward the holy temple.

Verse 8. It would not be so difficult to live righteously were it not for the opposition of enemies; for that reason David prayed for divine guidance. He also longed for a pathway that was correct. This is a parallel in thought with Matt. 6: 13.

Verse 9. In this verse David described his enemies. *No faithfulness in their mouth* means they were inconsistent in their speeches. *Inward part* refers to their thoughts about David. *Open sepulchre* would be one into which a man might fall alive and be swallowed. It was not considered a literal death. The open sepulchre (mouth) would expose the unsuspecting person to the tongue which would kill the victim with its poisonous flattery.

Verse 10. David lived in a dispensation where force was lawful in defense of religion. He therefore prayed for the destruction of his enemies. This prayer was explained by the last clause of the verse. Those who opposed David had rebelled against God. David was an official person under God, and enmity against him was enmity against God. That principle has always been true regarding God's legal representatives. (1 Sam. 8: 7; Luke 10: 16; Rom. 13: 4.)

Verse 11. This is a fine thought and characteristic of David. He would have people rejoice, not merely because they were victorious over their enemies, but because the victory came through trusting in God.

Verse 12. This verse is much like the one preceding with regard to its thought. It promises the blessing of God upon the righteous.

PSALMS 6

Verses 1, 2. In the preceding Psalm David prayed for divine help through the day. In this one he prayed for the help of God as he approached the night. He was weary with the cares and vexations of the day and felt the need of support for his body.

Verse 3. Not only did his body feel the strain of the ordeal, but his inner being was vexed. He longingly asked how long he would be compelled to suffer thus.

Verse 4. *Return* did not mean that the Lord had forsaken David. He meant to pray for a *return* or repetition of the blessings of God.

Verse 5. *In death . . . in the grave.* These phrases must be considered together to get the thought intended by the writer. It is true that the body knows nothing while in the grave, for it is the part of man that dies and decays.

Verse 6. David was dreading the night that was upon him; the nights were often sleepless and passed in tears.

Verse 7. David's weeping over the insults of his enemies caused his eyes to become sore.

Verse 8. Later, God answered the prayer of David and gave him courage to oppose his enemies, bidding them to depart from him.

Verse 9. Many terms of respect for God are repeated in the Psalms. It indicates the fervent devotion David maintained toward God. *Supplication* and *prayer* are mentioned in the same verse. There is not much difference, but the former is more urgent than the latter.

Verse 10. This verse was encouraged by the Lord's answering of David's prayer. *Let them return* means for them to turn back to their own proper place and be ashamed for having persecuted David.

PSALMS 7

Verse 1. The Psalms of David were composed on various occasions and there might sometimes have been much time between them. If the reader will keep this in mind the seeming frequency of the repetitions will not appear so strange. Here we read again of David's plea for God to deliver him from the hand of his enemies.

Verse 2. *None to deliver* would be the case did the Lord not save him. *Tear my soul.* One definition of the last word is "vitality," and refers to the man as a whole. The thought of David was that his enemies would wish to injure him completely.

Verses 3, 4. *If* was used in these verses with the sense of a denial, or as a condition on which David would agree to submit to the following experiences.

Verse 5. The *soul* that David meant was his life. If he had been guilty of the wrongs named in the preceding verses, then he admitted he should be tormented.

Verse 6. But David did not admit being guilty, therefore he called upon the Lord to pour out his anger on the enemies.

Verse 7. The righteous judgment of God would cause the people to assemble before him. For that reason David prayed the Lord to *return* or renew his favors to them.

Verse 8. A righteous man will not object to the judgment of God. David called upon the Lord to judge him according to the merits of his works.

Verse 9. *Wickedness of the wicked* was what David prayed to be ended. That agrees with the comments made at ch. 5: 5.

Verse 10. God will save only the upright. David's righteousness was the basis for his expecting the defense from God.

Verse 11. *With the wicked* is not in the original. The statement is simply that God is angry every day. The thoughts in the text and the comments at ch. 5: 5 will indicate what it is at which God is angry. The intensity of the Lord's *anger* is clear from the definition of the word in Strong's lexicon thus: "a primitive root; properly, to foam at the mouth, i.e. to be enraged."

Verse 12. There are pronouns for both God and the wicked. If the wicked man does not turn from his wickedness, God will whet his sword of judgment and use it.

Verse 13. If the enemies continue to persecute the righteous, God will use his instruments of death on them.

Verse 14. *He* is the wicked man who takes delight in persecuting the righteous. *Travaileth with iniquity* means he is in pain with desire to commit iniquity.

Verse 15, 16. A wicked man may become the victim of his own device. See the case of Haman in Esther 5: 14; 7: 10.

Verse 17. *According to his righteousness* means because of his righteousness. David was a very musical man and used that form of praise often.

PSALMS 8

Verse 1. *Lord* occurs twice and is from different originals. The first is from YEHOVAH and Strong defines it, "(the) self-Existent or Eternal; Jehovah, Jewish national name of God." The second is from ADOWN and defined, "sovereign, i.e. controller (human or divine." The phrase means that the Being who always existed was acknowledged as the one to rule over David and his brethren. No wonder, then, that His name was praised above everything else in the universe.

Verse 2. This verse states a general fact, but was especially meant as a prediction that was fulfilled in Matt. 21: 16. *Babes and sucklings* was used figuratively, meaning that praise would come from those who were least expected to be able or inclined to do so. To *still* means to overcome another. By bringing praises from such humble sources, the enemy would be put to shame.

Verse 3. David was here meditating on the same subject he wrote about in the noted 19th Psalm. He was filled with admiration at the greatness of a Creator who could make such wonderful things by the power of his hand.

Verse 4. David was overwhelmed at the thought that human beings like him would be given such great attention from the Lord of all creation.

Verse 5. *Little lower than the angels* referred to man's nature being subject to death while the angels could not die. Notwithstanding his mortal body, man had been given *glory and honor* above that of the angels. It will be described in the following paragraph.

Verses 6-8. This refers to the time when God placed mankind over the works of creation. Please read Genesis 1: 26-28.

Verse 9. This is identically like the first verse of the chapter. For that reason Dr. Marion Hull calls this an envelope psalm. That means the verses between the first and last ones describe the truth expressed by the first and last ones.

PSALMS 9

Verse 1. David would be expected to praise the Lord. The special thought is that his praise was with his whole heart. That degree of devotion was always required by the Lord. (Deut. 6: 5; Matt. 22: 37.) David had a practical reason for praising God, which was the marvelous works of his creation.

Verse 2. *Glad and rejoice.* The first word describes the state of mind, and the last one indicates that some outward expression was to be made of it. That expression took the form of singing and suggests the statement in James 5: 13.

Verse 3. David had many enemies and spoke of them frequently. *Turned back* means they were repulsed by the presence of God.

Verse 4. *Right . . . cause.* Had David's cause not been right the Lord would not have maintained it for him against his enemies.

Verse 5. The *heathen* were the people outside the congregation of Israel who were idolaters. God rebuked them by destroying their idols. This was already true historically to some extent. But it was also a prophecy of the complete overthrow of idolatry among the Jews after the captivity.

Verse 6. The thought in this verse is much like that of the preceding one. It is largely prophetic, looking to the complete overthrow of the enemies of God's people.

Verse 7. The Lord as an independent being will endure forever. He also will continue to withstand his foes for the eternal throne has been made ready for judgment.

Verse 8. The judgments of God are always right. This is true whether we are considering his edicts of punishment for the wicked, or the favorable ruling for the righteous who have been done injustice at the hands of the wicked.

Verse 9. The assistance the Lord renders to the oppressed may be said to be negative and positive. The negative consists in overthrowing the oppressor, and the positive consists in offering a haven to the unfortunate victims.

Verse 10. To *know his name* as David was considering it meant to realize the power of that name over the workers of iniquity. However, to get the benefit of the holy name it is necessary that they have sought after the Lord; this idea is taught in the New Testament. (Matt. 7: 7.)

Verse 11. God as a spirit is everywhere. There was a special sense in which he dwelt in Zion or Jerusalem. That was the location of the temple and the ark at which the national religious exercises were done.

Verse 12. *Inquisition* means inquiry. When blood has been shed unlawfully, God will look into the matter and will punish the guilty.

Verse 13. David had been threatened with death more than once. God had saved him from it and so had lifted him up *from the gates of death.* But he still felt the need of the mercy of the Lord to help him in his many trials.

Verse 14. *Daughter of Zion* was a figurative name for Jerusalem. David wished to express his praise of God in the gates of his capital city.

Verse 15. The heathen were the nations foreign to the people of Israel. They had devised plots against God's people but had perished in their iniquity.

Verse 16. God was *known* or recognized by the righteousness of his judgments. They were different from the popular ones of the world. By the divine operations the wicked were trapped in their own schemes. *Haggion* is defined by Strong as "a musical notation." It is therefore a term to be observed but not pronounced. *Selah* is explained by my comments at ch. 3: 2.

Verse 17. The word *hell* in the Old Testament is always from SHEOL and that word is also translated by grave and pit. Its figurative meaning is "oblivion" or "forgetfulness." It is true that the wicked will finally be cast into the lake of fire otherwise termed "hell" in the New Testament. David was making a more general use of the word and coupling it with the idea of the nations that forget God. The persons who forget God will themselves be forgotten by Him.

Verse 18. God will forget the wicked people and thus consign them to the figurative pit of forgetfulness. But the needy will not be forgotten, which is a statement made in contrast with what will happen to the wicked in v. 17. *Not perish forever* is significant. The poor may have to suffer for a time, but they will finally be remembered and cared for by the Lord.

Verse 19. David was still concerned about the success of unworthy men. He prayed for them to be judged in the presence of the Lord.

Verse 20. Many heathen rulers acted as if they were superior and in no danger of defeat. David would have God bring them to realize their own littleness.

PSALMS 10

Verse 1. David was an inspired man when he wrote his portions of the Bible. Whenever he reported the occurrences of his day he told the truth. And, like Job, he had many personal tribulations from his enemies and was authorized by the Lord to write about them for the information of the reader. In keeping with this idea he made frequent complaints of his experiences. In some of them it might seem that he was dissatisfied with the care he received from God. We should observe that he was often giving a description of those circumstances as they appeared to him "as a man" (see Job 38: 3 with my comments). But in giving a "write-up" of his feelings and experiences he was an inspired scribe. Let the reader constantly keep these thoughts in mind studying this book and he will be saved much confusion. So here we have an example of the conditions just described. David felt that God was too far from him for his comfort while his enemies were so near.

Verse 2. David's fine character was often manifested by his consideration for others. In this verse he was worried because of the troubles of the poor, and prayed that the persecutors might be trapped in their own wicked devices.

Verse 3. The desires of a wicked man would logically be favored by riches if improperly used. For that reason such a man would be friendly with an enterprise of covetousness. even though such would be abhorred by the Lord.

Verse 4. *Countenance* means the face in general, because that is the part of a man's body where his thoughts are usually indicated. One of the most active emotions is pride and in order for a proud man to "save his face" in his wickedness, he will shun the presence of God.

Verse 5. David was describing a man who combined pride with other forms of wickedness in his life. The *ways* or conduct of such a man would always be grievous to the Lord. One reason such a person ignores the righteous judgments of God is his determination to persecute those whom he regards as his enemies. *Puffeth* means to scoff which is a coward's method for opposing that which he cannot meet otherwise.

Verse 6. Wealth and other worldly advantages have the effect of making wicked men vain. They form conclusions of their own importance that make them feel secure.

Verse 7. *Cursing* means a wishing for some evil thing to come upon another. The one doing the cursing will even try to carry out his evil wishes by using deceitful dealings. *Under his tongue* means that his language is prompted by vain motives.

Verses 8, 9. Almost this entire psalm is a description of a wicked man, and the details of his wickedness are many. In this paragraph he is described as a coward who will not meet his victim face to face, but crouches in hiding places and waits for the opportune time to strike. This wicked man seems to have special designs against the poor and that was the chief reason why David abhorred him.

Verse 10. *Humbleth himself* does not refer to his state of mind, for such an evil person would not have that sentiment. It refers to the posture of his body in crouching down like a huge cat, waiting to spring at his unsuspecting prey.

Verse 11. The temporary success of an unrighteous man sometimes leads him to conclude that God had not observed his actions: that he had forgotten to notice what had been going on in the conduct of the evil character.

Verse 12. David would have the Lord bring the wicked man to his senses. *Humble* is from a word that also means to be afflicted. God was asked to relieve all such.

Verse 13. *Contemn* means to treat with disrespect. David asked why the wicked man was suffered to treat God in that manner. By his apparent success he was prompted to conclude that he was in no danger of punishment from God. *Thou wilt require it* means the unrighteous man did not expect to be required to answer to God for his sins.

Verse 14. David acknowledged that God had seen the things of which he was complaining. He also cited the good example of the poor who put their trust in God.

Verse 15. *Break thou the arm* was figurative and meant for God to crush the devices of the wicked. *Till thou find none* means till there was no more wickedness left after God had searched it out and had overthrown the evildoers.

Verse 16. *Lord* means one who rules or controls. David ascribed the authority of a king to the Lord of Heaven, and declared that he should so rule forever. He predicted the final overthrow of the *heathen* or foreign nations.

Verses 17, 18. David's confidence in the goodness of God to the poor was indicated by his positive declaration that he would do so. We should therefore not regard this paragraph in the light of a dictation.

PSALMS 11

Verse 1. David was having many troubles; in spite of them, however, he had full confidence in the Lord. With such a trust to cheer him he rejected the suggestion to flee as a bird would to the mountain for refuge.

Verse 2. That was not because he did not realize the seriousness of his difficulties. He thought of his enemies as those who were poised with their weapons in position for discharge. He knew that he would not escape if the enemy had his way.

Verse 3. *Foundations* is from SHA-THAH and defined thus: "a basis, i.e. (figuratively) political or moral support."—Strong. In this verse David was giving a picture of the utter helplessness of the righteous were it not for some *foundation* or basis of support on which to rest.

Verse 4. In reference to the thought expressed in the preceding verse, David announced the existence of a sure foundation. It consisted in the fact that the Lord has a throne in the heavens and that he is occupying it. That would constitute the surest of all bases for support. From that high abode the cause of everyone will get a just hearing and the wrongs of all evil men will be punished. *Eye* and *eyelids* are used in the same sense. The meaning is that God sees all that men do and will give them the deserts of their deeds whether good or bad.

Verse 5. *Trieth* means to put to the test. This is done to the righteous in order to verify the good esteem already had of them. But a violently wicked man is so evidently wrong that God does not consider it necessary to make a test of him.

Verse 6. The wicked will actually suffer the penalty of eternal fire after the final judgment. The terms of this verse, however, are used figuratively, referring to the utter defeat of all those who oppose the works of God.

Verse 7. The first clause of this verse is more than a mere repetition of words. There is a logical connection between the words. The reason the Lord loves righteousness is the fact that he is righteous himself. By that same token, if a person does not love righteousness it is because he is not righteous himself. *Countenance* means the face as a whole, and represents the mental expression of the person. *Behold* means to look at with interested pleasure. The Lord will take such a look at an upright man. See this same thought expressed at Isa. 66: 2.

PSALMS 12

Verse 1. We must take this verse in a comparative sense, for we know that there have always been some godly and faithful men. But the percent of them is and was so small that David felt the need of divine help.

Verse 2. *Speak vanity* means to say things that are empty and without sound thought. *Double* heart is a figure meaning a heart that is not sincere; one that will cause its owner to say one thing today and another tomorrow.

Verse 3. Flattery is a form of falsehood in that is seeks to make an impression that is not out of sincerity. The Lord will cut off all such speaking in the end. *Speaketh proud things* denotes a boasting of accomplishment beyond the facts.

Verse 4. These boastful persons relied on the power of their speech to accomplish their purposes. They boastfully claimed full control of their lips and said that no one could be *lord* over them.

Verse 5. God is always considerate of those who are oppressed. That is especially true if the oppression comes from the proud and double-tongued. *Puffeth at him* refers to the man who would attack the poor for the purpose of ensnaring them. God will protect the one who is being thus attacked by placing him in a safe position.

Verse 6. *Pure* means unmixed, and the words of the Lord have that quality. Nothing can literally be purified more than once. *Purified seven times* is a figurative term used for emphasis on the quality of the words of the Lord.

Verse 7. God will see that his words are preserved indefinitely, from that day or *generation* to the end. Jesus said about the same thing in Mark 13: 31.

Verse 8. When vile men are suffered to be in the ascendency the wicked ones will strut about all over the place. Their presence will be encouraged by the support of the vile rulers, which proves the objectionable character of such overseers. The opposite will be the case if righteous men are placed in authority.

PSALMS 13

Verse 1. Again we should remember that David was writing of his experiences in trials "as a man." See my comments at ch. 10: 1. It seemed at times that the Lord had forgotten him; that was because one's suffering makes the time seem long.

Verse 2. *Counsel in my soul* refers to his meditations over his sorrows. He feels as if his enemies had the advantage over him.

Verse 3. This is a fervent prayer for help from God. David's eyes had become heavy from sorrow and felt the dreariness that comes from much weeping. His condition was so grievous that gloom was overshadowing him like the shades near the river of death. That is why he prayed for light to brighten his eyes.

Verse 4. David's chief concern was the thought of being overcome by his enemies. He could have endured any amount of discomfort that would come in the natural course of events. The thing that he prayed to avoid was the triumph of his enemies over him.

Verse 5. David was not in utter despair. At times he would seem to give way to his grief, then suddenly he would recall his faith in God's mercy. When he did that, he again rejoiced because he expected salvation from the Lord.

Verse 6. Having considered anew the bountiful assistance received from God he was influenced to praise him. And he used the form of expression so usual with him, that of singing the praises.

PSALMS 14

Verse 1. *Fool* is from NABAL and Strong defines it, "stupid; wicked (especially impious)." *No God* is the doctrine of an atheist. No one but a stupid person would make such a statement. It is not merely saying he does not believe there is a God; that would be bad enough. But the atheist affirms a negative. To declare that there is no God is the same as stating that the speaker has seen every nook and cranny of the universe and found that there is no God. Otherwise, if there was a single bit of space that he had not seen, there might be a God there. But since it is impossible for any man to have seen every inch of space in the universe, the affirmation of the atheist is ridiculous; therefore the term fool is a proper one for such a character. The last part of the verse is an additional comment of David on the kind of men who would assume the position of an atheist. There is absolutely no good in such persons.

Verse 2. Much of the language in the Bible coming directly from God and about him, sounds as if he were a man. The statement of Paul in Rom.

6:19 should be a familiar one to all Bible students. It will serve as a key to many otherwise difficult passages. God is infinite and is capable of using language as high as his thoughts (Isa. 55: 8, 9), but man could not understand it. Therefore the language of Heaven is made to conform to the habits and mental capacity of man. This verse speaks of God as making the same investigation as a man would make under the circumstances. When even one human being appeared so corrupt that he would deny the existence of God, perhaps it would be well to take a look at the race in general.

Verse 3. When the Lord made the investigation he found that the race as a whole had become corrupt. All rules have exceptions and we know this one had, for the Bible itself records the names of some good men. We think of Abel, Noah, Abraham, Jacob, Joseph, Job and many others. When these are considered as they are scattered out over the centuries they look like a small minority. But that very fact gives emphasis to the statement of the verse as to rules and exceptions.

Verse 4. The distinction between the *workers of iniquity* and *my people* agrees with the remarks concerning a rule and its exceptions in the preceding verse. The question about the lack of knowledge is really a charge that the knowledge is lacking. That lack of knowledge, however, was without excuse. The 19th psalm, also the statement of Paul in Rom. 1: 20, 21, indicates there were many evidences of the existence of God. Their ignorance was wilful, then, and due to their failure to consider the evidences as was charged later against the Israelites in Isa. 1: 3.

Verse 5. When God saw his righteous people in trouble at the hands of these unbelievers he defended them against their oppressors. That caused the wicked ones to be afraid of the Lord's judgments; or it put them *in great fear*.

Verse 6. These unbelievers could not defeat the Lord who is the refuge of the poor and oppressed. They therefore made their attack directly against the people.

Verse 7. *Captivity* is from SHEBIYTH and Strong defines it, "exile; concretely, prisoners; figuratively, a former state of prosperity." The word actually refers to a condition that existed previously, and *bringing back the captivity* means to bring the people back to the state of good fortune that was enjoyed before the captivity. That good fortune could have consisted in either temporal or spiritual blessings. Many prophecies in the Bible have a twofold application. The one in this verse has first a reference to the return of the Jews from Babylonian captivity. Its second application is to the Jewish nation in the return from disbelief in Christ to a state of belief in him (Rom. 11: 26).

PSALMS 15

Verse 1. The *tabernacle* and *holy hill* of the Lord are the same and refers to the house of God. For the present purpose it is likened to the home of a citizen. David introduces his description of an acceptable guest by asking a double question. *Abide* is from GUWR and Strong defines it, "a primitive root; properly to turn aside from the road (for a lodging or any other purpose). i.e. sojourn (as a guest)." *Dwell* is from SHAKAN and defined, " a primitive root [apparently akin (by transmutation) to shakab through the idea of lodging]; to reside or permanently stay (literally or figuratively)."—Strong. A p e r s o n might be regarded good enough to admit as a temporary guest who would not be good enough as a permanent occupant. But according to David a man would not be worthy of even temporary lodging unless he came up to the qualifications described in the following verses.

Verse 2. A man does not literally speak with his heart, but he should speak from his heart. If he cherishes the truth in his heart his outward conduct will likely be righteous. This was taught by Jesus in Matt. 15: 19.

Verse 3. *Backbiteth* means to slander one at his back. *Taketh up a reproach* means to act as a repeater of a reproach. It is as bad to repeat a slander as it is to start one. The civil law of the land will punish a man who helps to circulate a reproach as well as the one who starts it. It is about the same in prinicple as to receive stolen goods because it makes such a man a party to the offense.

Verse 4. *Contemn* means to regard with disrespect. A vile person is one who is filthy either morally or physically. All such should be held beneath the notice of the man who is good enough to enter the house of God.

David puts the *vile* person in contrast with one who *fears the Lord*. That is an important thought and shows that a man who has respect for God will not be vile in his life. *Sweareth . . . changeth not*. This means that after a man has made a promise to do a certain thing, he will make his word good even though he learns that he will be the loser in the transaction.

Verse 5. *Usury* in the Old Testament is from three different Hebrew words that have practically the same meaning. I shall quote the one definition from Strong that represents the word in its various passages: "Interest on a debt." Common usage in our day makes it mean excessive interest, but it had no such qualification in the law of Moses. It is true that some passages refer to usury as an oppression on the poor, but it was the fact that any usury or interest was charged at all that constituted the oppression. Of course we should understand the law to apply to the taking of interest from their brethren. They were permitted to exact usury from strangers, for they were not under any obligations of special compassion toward the foreigners. One qualification a man must have to admit him as a guest was that he did not charge usury on his money. Another was that he would never be bribed into opposing an innocent man. This would especially apply in a case where he was acting as a judge between others. David closed this psalm with about the same thought he expressed at its beginning. *Never be moved* means he will never fall.

PSALMS 16

Verses 1, 2. David makes another prayer for divine preservation. *Goodness extendeth not to thee*. The second word is not in the original. The clause means that David's life of goodness was of no personal benefit to God. He will soon tell us who were to be benefitted by him if he lived a righteous life. Notwithstanding, because of his example lived for the ecouragement of others, he claimed assistance from God.

Verse 3. This verse tells for whose benefit David maintained his good life; it was the excellent saints of the Lord.

Verse 4. In this verse David brings up the subject of false gods. He predicts many sorrows for those who worship such gods. The latter part of the verse disclaims any fellowship with the above-mentioned characters.

Verse 5. *Portion* is from a word that has the sense of allotment or ration. The richest ration anyone could have would be the Lord, and David claimed to have received it. No heir could complain of the manner in which an inheritance was settled if he received such a liberal portion as that.

Verse 6. *Lines* has the same force as *portion* in the preceding verse. It is defined in Strong's lexicon thus: "a rope (as twisted), especially a measuring line; by implication a district or inheritance (as measured)." Sometimes when an inheritance of land is being divided one heir may think the line is not drawn in the proper place; that he is being deprived of some of the good land. David used the circumstance as an illustration and said he was satisfied with the places allotted to him. That was because the "boundary line" had been drawn in such a place that his portion included the Lord, the richest spot in the universe.

Verse 7. David *blessed* or praised the Lord for his helpful counsel or instruction. *Reins* refers to the mind and David meant he could meditate profitably in the night hours on the counsel the Lord had given him in the day. This is the idea expressed in ch. 1: 2 and my comments thereon.

Verses 8-10. I am grouping these verses in one paragraph because they compose one of the most important prophecies in the whole Bible; on the resurrection of Christ. We know it is on that subject, for Peter so applied it in the first discourse of the Christian Dispensation, recorded in Acts 2: 25-31. The prophecy was written by David, but in using the 1st personal pronoun he was speaking for Christ, and we should think of him as the speaker while we read this interesting passage. Furthermore, in thinking of Christ as the speaker, we should understand that when he uses the 2nd or 3rd personal pronouns he means God the Father. The word *hell* is from SHEOL here and means the unseen world or abode of the soul after death. The soul or spirit of Christ went into that place at death, and his body went to the grave.

There is another application made of this prophecy in 1 Cor. 15: 4. "According to the scriptures" had to mean this passage in the Psalms, for it is the very one that Peter quoted almost verbatim and applied it to that subject. It is also the only prophecy in the Old Testament that spoke specifically of the resurrection of Christ. But it may be asked how the "third day" idea got into the passage. It is in the statement that the flesh of Christ was not to remain in the grave long enough to begin to decay. According to John 11: 39 a body will start decaying in 4 days. Three days, then, would be as long as a body could remain dead and not *see corruption*. And so this noted prophecy, written hundreds of years before it was fulfilled, gives us another proof that the Bible was not written by uninspired men. The detail that Christ not only was to rise from the dead, but was to do so after the 3rd day and before the 4th, forms an evidence that will forever baffle those who scoff at the Word of God.

Verse 11. David now came back to his personal line of thought to speak of his confidence in the Lord and what he expected to gain by his service to Him. In the first place, God will show him the proper way of life, and that will finally lead him up to the divine presence. In that holy place there is fulness of joy. It will be at the right hand of Jehovah where the pleasures will continue forever.

PSALMS 17

Verse 1. *Feigned lips* means lips that merely pretend to honor God by praying to him. David was always sincere and never tried to keep anything back, even when he was guilty of a great wrong. (2 Sam. 12: 13.)

Verse 2. *Sentence* means judgment and *equal* means that which is just. The verse indicates that David was relying on the judgment of God; that it would be just.

Verse 3. *Shalt find nothing* was David's way of inviting the test of the Lord. He believed he would be found acceptable in God's sight were he put to the test.

Verse 4. David had escaped the destruction his enemies had plotted against him. That was done by following the *word of thy lips*, or by heeding the counsel of God.

Verse 5. David prayed to be kept in the paths of God in order that he might not stumble. This same thought is expressed in Psalms 37: 23 and 119: 133.

Verse 6. David always had faith in God and believed it would avail him much to pray toward the divine throne. He made another approach, therefore, and asked to be heard.

Verse 7. A person's right hand would not be more able, physically, than his left in accomplishing a purpose. It is referred to figuratively, meaning the righteous power and method of the individual.

Verse 8. This verse is all figurative, *apple* meaning something that is very near of kin. If God would so regard David, he would certainly keep him from the harm intended by his enemies.

Verse 9. *Deadly enemies* were those who would destroy David had they the opportunity. He prayed for God to keep him from the grasp of such foes. They were round and about him constantly and hence the protection of the Lord was always needed.

Verse 10. *Fat* is from CHELEB and Strong defines it, "from an unused root meaning to be fat; fat, whether literal or figurative; hence the richest or choice part." These enemies of David were rich and were allowing their wealth to blind them to the regard they should have for others.

Verse 11. The enemies had surrounded David's pathway, seeking to interfere with his progress. *Eyes bowing down* means the enemies had their eyes on the lower plain of life thinking to drag David down to it.

Verse 12. A lion is like all of the cat family in that he crouches in hidden places, waiting to spring upon his helpless prey.

Verse 13. David wished his enemy to be disappointed in his plans. The defeat was to consist in the very thing he had planned against David by being himself cast down. *Which is thy sword* was said in the sense of a comparison. If God would reverse the plan of the enemy by giving him the very thing he had intended against David, that would be the most effective sword God could use against the evil plot.

Verse 14. *Which are* is like the same words in the preceding verse and means "by." The thought is that David was praying God to rescue him from worldly men and to do it by his (God's) hand. *Portion in this life* means such men will find their only joy in this life, none can be expected for the next. Jesus taught the same idea in Matt. 6: 2, 5, 16. *Belly thou fillest* refers to the temporal prosperity that God had provided for their people. They having many children to help enjoy their temporal blessings, that gave the occasion to have an abundance so that the youngest of the family would find a remainder of the wealth left after their father was gone.

Verse 15. *Behold thy face in righteousness* means David would not expect to behold the face of God unless he lived a righteous life in this world. Such a life would finally end in death, but it would not be "an eternal sleep." He believed there would be a resurrection at which he and all other righteous persons would awake in the likeness of the Lord. This is taught also in the New Testament. (1 John 3: 2.)

PSALMS 18

Verses 1-50. I have made one paragraph of this whole chapter because it is practically identical with 2 Samuel 22. Detailed comments are made on the chapter which is at the regular place in volume 2 of this commentary and will not be repeated here. The reason for giving the comments at the other place is the fact that it came in more direct connection with the history belonging to it. I will call attention to one special circumstance in the differences between the two chapters. The statements that are placed as a heading here are included in the text in 2 Samuel 22. When the collection of the Psalms of David was made into one book, the one he wrote at the time of his conflicts with Saul and other enemies was brought and included in the document. Since the two occurrences of the psalm are alike, the reader of the commentary would have no advantage offered him were I to repeat the comments in this place. I therefore urge him to see my remarks in the other place.

PSALMS 19

Verse 1. The original for *heavens* is defined by Strong as follows: "from an unused root meaning to be lofty; the sky (as aloft; the dual perhaps alluding to the visible arch in which the clouds move, as well as to the higher ether where the celestial bodies revolve." From the definition it can be seen that the word is a descriptive one and the regions to which it is applied are so named because they partake of the description. Thus the sky (1st heaven), the region of the planets (2nd heaven), and the abode of God (3rd heaven) are so named because they all are especially characterized by the leading definition of the word, "to be lofty," either materially or otherwise. With only 3 exceptions the word "heaven" in the Old Testament comes from the Hebrew words SHAMAYIM or SHEMAYIM whether singular or plural. The first is used 393 times and the second 38 times. Hence the context alone can determine whether the 1st, 2nd or 3rd heaven is meant in given cases. See Gen. 1: 20; 22: 17 and 1 Ki. 8: 30 for instances, respectively, of these heavens. The connection in the present verse shows that the 1st and 2nd heavens are meant. *Declare* is from CAPHAR which Strong defines as follows: "to score with a mark as a tally or record, i.e. (by implication) to inscribe, and also to enumerate; intensively to recount, i.e. celebrate." The clause means that the splendor of God is inscribed or written in the region of the planets. *Firmament* is from RAQIYA and Strong defines it, "an expanse, i.e. the firmament or (apparently) visible arch of the sky." This region is also a part of the 1st heaven but is noticed here by itself because of an additional characteristic, that of being expansive as well as lofty. One meaning of *sheweth* is to manifest or expose. *Handywork* is from two Hebrew words that combine to mean "the work of God's hand." The clause means that the work of God's hand is made manifest by the appearances in the sky. Without doubt the 19th Psalm is a citation to one of the strongest, most unanswerable lines of evidence proving the existence of the Supreme Being. Let us study the entire chapter with profound respect.

Verse 2. The word for *day* is so rendered 1167 times and the definition in Strong's lexicon includes all the phases of the period; whether that portion from sunrise to sunset, or only from sunrise to sunset. So the connection in each case must determine the application of the word. In this verse it is used in contrast with *night*, therefore it means the time between sunrise and sunset. That is very significant because the sun is visible in the day while the stars are visible in the night. *Unto* has the sense of to or after; *day after day*, etc., not that one day shows something to another.

The thought is that from day to day the declaration of God's glory is known by the evidences in the heavens as mentioned in verse one.

Verse 3. *There is* and *where* are not in the original. The verse means that the declaration of the glory of God is made without audible speech or specific language. In other words, when a man looks up at the sun and stars he should be filled with awe by the silent tribute to the power and wisdom of the Creator. David had expressed this very thought in Ch. 8: 3, 4. A group of atheists were overheard discussing the existence of God. A bystander-interrupted to ask: "Gentlemen, do you say there is no God?" Upon receiving an affirmative reply he pointed up toward the myriad of stars twinkling overhead and asked: "Who made all of those?" Profound silence was their only response.

Verse 4. The antecedent of *their* is the declaration of evidences of the preceding verses. *Line* means the collection of evidences of the glory of God. That line or collection extends throughout the *earth* or the globe, and to the end of the *world* or inhabitants of the globe. *In them*, meaning in the collection of the evidences, hath *he* (God) set a *tabernacle* for the sun. A tabernacle is usually thought of as a portable structure. It does not necessarily mean that, and one part of Strong's definition is, "dwelling place." The idea is that the sun has a fixed position in the collection of the heavens; that agrees also with what men have learned about astronomy. The sun is stationary and other bodies move around it.

Verse 5. A *bridegroom* all prepared for the great event, and a man prepared for the test of a race are used to compare the dignity of the sun in its powerful shining.

Verse 6. This verse might seem to contradict the comments made at v. 4, but it does not. The sun itself is in a fixed position, but the light rays of it *go forth* from one end of heaven to the other. This disproves the speculation that there are other worlds outside the realm affected by the sun. That is also proved by the last clause of the verse; that is, nothing exists beyond the reach of the sun's rays. The *heat* of the sun extends so far that *there is nothing hid* from it which shows that the solar system contains everything that belongs to the creation of material things.

Verse 7. Having devoted 6 verses to the creation of the material world, David takes up the subject of God's Word in its various phases. *Law* is a general reference to the rule of God for the conduct of man. It is perfect in its ability to convert a soul, which would mean that no human law is needed to be added to it. *Testimonies* has special reference to the words of the Lord that have been tested and proved to be true. They will add wisdom to those who are simple or uninstructed.

Verse 8. *Statutes* means the set ordinances of God. They are just and right so that they cause the heart to rejoice instead of dreading the Lord. *Commandment* specifically refers to personal action and gives instructions and warnings to the (mental) eyes. It is *pure* which means it is not mixed with any human weakness.

Verse 9. *Fear* has two phases of meaning; one to dread, the other to respect the Lord, the latter is its meaning here. It is *clean* in the sense of being free from elements of decay; that is why it endures forever. *Judgments* refers to the verdicts or decisions of God. The full definition of this word is quoted at Ex. 21: 1 in the first volume of the commentary. The decisions of the Lord are always according to truth and hence are altogether righteous.

Verse 10. The value of spiritual things cannot be fully estimated by temporal things. The best that can be done, therefore, is to compare them with such values; things that we prize and enjoy. Gold was one of the most precious metals known in olden times. The first occurrence in this verse is from a word that is defined in the lexicon, "something gold-colored." In the second instance the word *fine* is not in the original as a separate word. *Gold* is from a different Hebrew word from the one above and is defined, "pure (gold); hence gold itself (as refined)."—Strong. The statement in comparison is interesting. David first compared the Word of God to things that looked attractive, then intensified it by naming the article that not only looked desirable but was of genuine worth. In other words, the things of God not only look good to the man who will give them his attention, but upon closer inspection they will be found to be of real value. *Honeycomb* by itself is not sweet, hence the comparison must be seen by a closer study of the words. The first use of the word *honey* is from an original that means the entire product that we call by that name, including the comb. The word *honeycomb* is from two Hebrew words and means extracted honey. Of course we would understand that the per cent of sweetness in the extracted product would be greater than it would be in the whole article including the comb.

Verse 11. The antecedent of *them* is the Word of God with its various classifications. *Warned* means, "to enlighten (by caution)."—Strong. To be warned of danger should not be the only purpose of the law of God and it is not. The next part of the verse states the affirmative benefits; they consist in *great reward*.

Verse 12. This verse has reference to the life of a human being passed in a world where innumerable temptations abound. No man fully realizes the multitude of weaknesses that exist in his flesh; no one but the Lord knows. Such is the meaning of the question, *who can understand his errors?* Recognizing this fact, David asked the Lord to cleanse him from the errors that he could not see but which can be seen by the Lord. Of course it must be understood that such a favor from God will not be extended to a man unless his life otherwise is in keeping with the law. The same teaching regarding the continuous favor of the cleansing for a righteous person is given in 1 John 1: 7.

Verse 13. *Presumptuous* sins are the opposite of the ones described in the preceding verse. Those were committed ignorantly while these are committed in the spirit of arrogance. It would be bad enough were a man to give way to that kind of sin even occasionally. But David was concerned lest such sins should get the *dominion*, which means the rule over him. If he were free from such a life he would then be upright. *The great transgression*. No special significance can be attached to the definite article. The original expression means anything great in the way of transgression. The statement as a whole means that if David would be kept from presumptuous sins he would be clear of much unrighteousness.

Verse 14. It will be noticed that David specified his thoughts and words, but said nothing directly about his deeds. That was not an oversight, for the thoughts of the heart are the source from which actions spring. Jesus taught that in Mark 7: 20-23. It is also taught in Philippians 4: 8 which the reader should see. If a man will keep his thoughts pure he will likely not have much trouble with his actions.

PSALMS 20

Verse 1. David is the author of this psalm but he wrote it as a song or prayer to be offered by the people. They were to appeal to God in behalf of their king who was about to contact his enemies in battle. This view of the situation will explain why the 2nd or 3rd person was used, although David was composing the passage.

Verse 2. The *sanctuary* was the holy place and it was in Zion, a place in the city of Jerusalem. God was officially located there, wihch made it a source of help.

Verse 3. David had made many sacrifices to God, and the people were to ask that the sacrifices be remembered.

Verse 4. The prayer at this point should be considered as being conditional. The desires and advice of the king should be granted as far as they were acceptable to the Lord

Verse 5. *Thy salvation* means the salvation of David their king in his struggles for success over his enemies. Such results would bring rejoicing to the people and they would be encouraged to *set up banners* which means raising the flag of triumph.

Verse 6. *Anointed* means the king who had been anointed over the people of Israel. Having given special instructions that David be anointed king over his people (1 Sam. 13: 14; 16: 1, 12), he would certainly protect him in his struggles.

Verse 7. *Trust* is not in the original but is justified by *remember* later on in the verse. *Some* is from a word that is defined by Strong, "these or those." The antecedent is the heathen with whom the king was about to engage in battle. They depended for success on their (war) *chariots;* the Israelites depended on *the Lord our God*.

Verse 8. *They* refers to the same heathen mentioned in the preceding verse. They were destined to fall before the might of the king of Israel.

Verse 9. This is a prayer of the people. They were interested in two beings; those beings were God and David. They asked for the victory for their king, then he would be able, as a victorious king, to help his people when they called upon him.

PSALMS 21

Verse 1. Please read my comments on Ch. 20: 1. The people are still represented as praying for their king and they have confidence that the Lord will grant him much cause for rejoicing.

Verse 2. The people acknowledged that their king had been given his heart's desire. That was because his desire was pleasing to God. We would expect that of a man who was after God's own heart. (1 Sam. 13: 14.)

Verse 3. *Preventest* means to assist, for it is used in connection with God's blessings and goodness. *Pure gold* means refined gold, and it is called pure because that term means unmixed.

Verse 4. *He* means the king and *thee* means the Lord. *Ever and ever* was used figuratively, meaning that David was to die in peace, not by the sword of war.

Verse 5. *His glory* means the glory of their king. It was great because it was accomplished through the salvation from the Lord. *Honor* means splendor and *majesty* means dignity and power.

Verse 6. *Blessed for ever* was and is still true of David. Although he is dead his name is still honored throughout the earth. The *countenance* or face of God was favorable toward David, therefore he was made exceeding glad.

Verse 7. David trusted in the Lord, not in the might of war chariots as did the heathen. (Ch. 20: 7.)

Verse 8. *Thine* refers to king David. The people believed their king would be able to *find out* or manage his enemies. *Right hand* had a figurative as well as literal meaning. David was destined to win out against his enemies because the things he was doing with his hand were right.

Verse 9. *As a fiery oven* means as if they were cast into such an oven. The comparison is made to the wrath of God against the enemies of David.

Verse 10. *Their fruit* means the fruit of this body. *Their seed* means the same as the fruit and the statement was added for emphasis.

Verse 11. *They* still means the enemies of *thee* who is David. The verse means to declare that the plans of the enemies were too great for them to carry out.

Verse 12. *Turn their backs* refers to the retreat of the enemies. The cause of their flight will be the sight of the weapon of war (the bow and arrow) in the hand of David's army. *Upon thy strings* denotes that the end of the arrow will be attached to the string ready to be discharged against the foe.

Verse 13. The psalm or prayer closes with a tribute of praise for the Lord. *Thine own strength* means that God is strong in his own might and not in that of another.

PSALMS 22

Verse 1. This psalm as a whole is a prophecy of Christ. The proof for that statement is in the chapter itself. Christ quoted the first clause verbatim when he was on the cross, and other verses in the chapter plainly identify it to have been written with Christ and his times in view. (Matt. 27: 46; Mark 15: 34.) Christ realized that the sustaining strength of God had been taken from him for the time.

Verse 2. The form of speech indicates that David was writing about his own personal troubles. It is true that he was having just the experiences of which he complained. He might not have realized that in describing those experiences he was giving a prophetic picture of those to be shared by his most illustrious son in the centuries to come. His ignorance of that would not affect the truth of the prophecies since he wrote by inspiration. In fact, it was taught by Jesus and the apostles that many of the writers of the Old Testament did not know "what it was all about" when they penned their documents. (Matt. 13: 17; 1 Pe. 1: 10, 11; 2 Pe. 1: 20, 21.)

Verse 3. *Inhabitest* is used in the sense of dwelling in a certain place or in some special surroundings. The verse means that God continually dwells in the midst of the praises of his people Israel.

Verse 4. *Fathers* refers to the ancient ancestors of the race. The history shows that in proportion as they put their trust in the Lord they were delivered from the grasp of their enemies.

Psalms 22: 5-21

Verse 5. Trusting in God was manifested when the people made their prayer unto him. *Not confounded* means they were not disappointed or confused.

Verse 6. The use of *worm* and *man* is for comparison only since David was not only a man, but an important one. But he was like the worm in that his body was subject to decay. Please see my comments on Job 25: 6 in the 2nd volume of the commentary.

Verses 7, 8. This paragraph is specifically a prophecy of Christ. It was fulfilled in Matt. 27: 42, 43.

Verse 9. A nursing babe could not literally have the sentiments of hope. It means that God was the source of all hope for the newborn infant. The argument is that since God was the one who brought the infant into being, it was reasonable to expect Him to see that he would succeed in life.

Verse 10. *Cast upon thee* denotes that from the first moment of his life, David was dependent on God for his continued existence.

Verse 11. Since God was the one who brought David into the world, he was the one to whom the prayer for protection should be made.

Verse 12. We know that *bulls* is used figuratively since it was men who were opposing David. Moffatt renders the word by "a brutal horde." The verse has the force of a prophecy pointing to Christ when on the cross, which the following verses show beyond any doubt.

Verse 13. *Gape* means literally to open the mouth as if in yawning. The verse refers to the time when the "brutal horde" stood round the cross and opened their mouths in mockery at Jesus. They were compared to a lion because of their desire to destroy the victim of their hatred.

Verse 14. *I* represents Christ describing his condition while on the cross. The expressions are figurative, of course, and give a picture of a human being that is fast approaching death. The whole body would be entering a state of dissolution as if the organs were melting and running together like wax.

Verse 15. This verse is practically the same in thought as the preceding one. It describes the physical condition of one who is dying. That would be especially true where the condition was not caused by any active disease, but by the slow ebbing of the forces of life through nervous exhaustion.

Verse 16. *Dogs* is used figuratively, referring to the wickedest of men. It applied specifically to the soldiers who executed the Roman sentence and drove the nails through the hands and feet of Jesus.

Verse 17. *Tell* means to count or number. It was the rule to break the bones of the legs of one crucified, near the end of the day. It was unlawful to let a body remain on a tree overnight (Deut. 21: 22, 23), yet the mere fact of crucifixion would not ordinarily produce death before the end of the day. In order to hasten death the legs were broken, and the shock would put an end to the life that had already been weakened. For some reason not directly told us, Jesus died before the executioners got to the cross, making it unnecessary to break his legs. Instead of doing that, they pierced his side. That act opened the cavity near the heart where the blood had gathered after death, but it did not break any bone. The apparently whimsical act of the soldiers fulfilled, the prediction made here. It also carried out the antitype of the restriction about the Jewish passover that the bones of the lamb must not be broken (Ex. 12: 46). *Stare upon me* was fulfilled in John 19: 37.

Verse 18. The physical reason for not dividing the garment of Jesus among the soldiers was the character of its making. It was woven "without seam" and hence could not be divided without destroying its use. They settled the matter by casting lots, thus fulfilling another prophecy. (John 19: 23-25.)

Verse 19. This and the rest of the verses is a combining of descriptions of David's experiences with thoughts pertaining to Christ. David still felt the need of the Lord in overcoming his personal enemies.

Verse 20. *My darling* is in the 3rd person. Inspired writers often used that person in referring to themselves (Num. 12: 3; Josh. 1: 1, etc.). The word is from an original that means someone who is precious and valued very highly. David wished to be delivered from the power of wicked men. He also predicted a like desire on the part of Jesus.

Verse 21. *Heard me from the horns*, etc. This means when David prayed to be delivered from the horns of the unicorn (a species of wild ox that was strong and vicious) the Lord heard his prayer.

Verse 22. Again we have the direct proof that Christ is being prophesied for the verse is quoted in Heb. 2:12. In that connection the name of Jesus is given which identifies the subject of the verse beyond any doubt.

Verse 23. *Fear the Lord* means to respect him, for the ones fearing him are the same ones expected to indicate their respect by their praise.

Verse 24. To *despise* means to overlook or think lightly of. God does not thus treat his servants when they cry to him in their afflictions.

Verse 25. This verse is plainly applicable to both David and Christ. As a prophecy of Christ it would read, *my* (Christ's) *praise shall be of thee* (God) *in the great congregation* (the church). *Pay my vows* as it pertains to David refers to his obedience to the law of Moses. As it pertains to Christ it means he is willing to do his part of God's plan of salvation. (Heb. 10: 5-9.)

Verse 26. This verse coincides with one of the sayings of Jesus. Matt. 5: 5 pronounces a blessing on the meek. The Holy Spirit evidently had this in mind when it directed David to write the statement.

Verses 27, 28. This prediction was fulfilled when the kingdom of Christ was established throughout the world. (Rom. 10:18; Col. 1:23.)

Verse 29. This verse predicts that all classes of people, the *fat* (prosperous) as well as those in the *dust* (the poor) would bow before the Lord. The last clause means that no man can save his own soul, and that is the reason all classes would come to the Lord for salvation.

Verse 30. This is a prediction that Christ was to have a seed that would be spiritual and that it would be greater than the fleshly seed of David. The fulfillment of this prediction is indicated in John 3: 1-5 and 1 Pe. 2: 9.

Verse 31. *That shall be born* is a prophecy of those who would be born again and become a part of the spiritual seed of Christ.

PSALMS 23

Verse 1. David had been a shepherd when a boy (1 Sam. 16: 11; 17: 34, 40), and had many experiences that he used as illustrations in his writings. This psalm is almost wholly drawn from that subject. The expressions are largely figurative, and the phases of his experiences will be used either in comparison or contrast or both, as the nature of the cases may suggest. He had been a shepherd over literal sheep, now he is a sheep himself and the Lord is his shepherd. It was his duty as a shepherd to see that proper nourishment was provided for his flock. Accordingly he felt assured that his shepherd would not let him *want*. That word is from CHACER and Strong defines it, "a primitive root; to lack; by implication to fail, lessen." Young and Moffatt also render it by lack. So it does not mean that God's people will always obtain their desires or wishes, but they will be supplied with their actual needs as sheep of the Lord's pasture.

Verse 2. *Lie* is from RABATS and is defined thus: "a primitive root; to crouch (on all four legs folded, like a recumbent animal)."—Strong. It does not mean to be prone, with the body extended as if from exhaustion. But it describes an animal in a posture of comfort and contentment. *Green pastures*. The first word is from an original that means "young and tender," hence very desirable food. When an animal lies down in the pasture (not where the pasture was), it proves that there was enough provision for him and some to spare. When *waters* are used figuratively they represent the state of mind or the surroundings of the individual concerned. If the condition is one of unpleasantness, then we will see such terms as "troubled waters" or "waters of affliction." If the condition is of the other kind, we will see such terms as David used here; *still waters*. The direct thought is that the divine shepherd will always give the sheep of his pasture such complete care they will be happy and contented.

Verse 3. A shepherd was supposed to provide food to *restore* or nourish the bodies of his sheep. He did so by placing them in the pastures described in the preceding verse. The spiritual Shepherd provides spiritual food for the *souls* of his sheep. This consists of the instruction found in the Word of God. A careful shepherd will seek a safe path in which to conduct his sheep to the places of good pasture. It is natural for a sheep to follow wherever his master leads, whether the path goes into a wild and dangerous thicket, or into the good fields of tender grass. David's shepherd always led him in the *paths of righteousness*, which means the right paths. An earthly shepherd would be concerned about his reputation as a reliable man to have charge of a flock. If he had no other motive, yet he would not knowingly mislead the flock, for that would injure his good name as a dependable shepherd. Likewise David's shepherd would lead him in the right paths *for his name's sake*. Dr. Marion Hull renders this by, "on account of his reputation," and Strong's lexicon justifies the translation. God is said to be free from all evil. He certainly would not stain such a good name by leading his flock unrighteously.

Verse 4. A sheep is a timid animal. In passing from one pasture to another it might be necessary to walk down the slope near a stream, dividing the present location from some pasture land beyond. There are usually some trees and other growing things that would cast a shadowy appearance around. The trusting sheep keeps close to his master with confidence. It was likewise with David and his confidence in the Shepherd of his soul. The valley of death did not hold any dread for him. Though the pathway leading downward was shaded by the dimness of approaching death, he was confident it would finally bring him over safely to the brighter fields of eternal verdure on the other side of the valley. A shepherd carries a rod or stick for the purpose of defense against any unfriendly creature, and a staff or walking cane for the support of his body. (1 Sam. 17: 40.) The Word of God was both rod and staff for David.

Verse 5. In the verse David drops the illustration of the shepherd to some extent. Instead of likening himself to a sheep he thinks of being a man. As a man he thinks of his troublesome enemies who have been opposing him in every way possible. It would be something of a triumph to have provisions of life made for him even under favorable circumstances. It would be a greater one to have it done in the presence of his enemies. Such a fact not only would tend to arouse the envy of the enemies, but would actually prove God's power by making the provision in spite of the enemies. All of this would have special significance with a man whose chief secular business of life was to be a "man of war," and to "shed blood abundantly." Victory over his enemies would be one of his most cherished desires. In ancient times when a man was to be given an important position of power and satisfaction, he was anointed by having oil poured over his head (1 Sam. 10: 1; 16: 13; 1 Ki. 1: 39; 2 Ki. 9: 3, 6). The practice was afterward used as a figure in cases where some person was given any great favor. *Cup* is from an original that means "lot." *Runneth over*. The 2nd word is not in the original. The 1st is from a Hebrew word that means "satisfaction." The clause means that his lot was wholly satisfactory.

Verse 6. *Goodness* is from an original that means "good things," and *mercy* is from one that is defined "kindness." *Follow me* is properly rendered and indicates that the favors will come after David has gone forward in serving the Lord. To be a permanent occupant of the house of the Lord would be a greater favor than merely entering it for a short time. Such a blessing would be the lot of the man complying with the conditions set forth in this psalm.

Before leaving this interesting psalm I will make a few more general remarks. The second but more important application of the prophecy is to Christ. It will be well for the student to go through the entire chapter again with Christ specifically in mind. It will then be possible to see and hear him on the cross as he quotes the 1st verse of the preceding chapter. Then coming directly to the present one again, hear Christ as he speaks of his Father in the relationship of his shepherd who was at the very instance of his crucifixion preparing (through it) a table or spiritual feast (salvation) for *me*, meaning his church. Then he can be heard saying, *death, I will fear no evil*, in the language of the psalm. Or, if we listen for his own words in the fulfillment we will hear him saying, "Father, into thy hands I commend my spirit." And, true to the prophecy, he afterward entered his Father's heavenly mansion above, there to abide forever.

PSALMS 24

Verse 1. This is quoted in 1 Cor. 10: 26. *Fulness* is from a word that means "everything in it." Since all belongs to the Lord, we are expected to make such use of it as will be pleasing to

Him. That is the reason for connecting the thought of the inhabitants of the world directly with the first statement.

Verse 2. *Seas* refers to the stationary bodies of water, and *floods* is from a word that means the rivers. (see Josh. 24: 2, 3.) The Lord created all of these things and has the right of control over them.

Verse 3. The psalmist again writes in language tht could apply to man in general, but he will come to special consideration of Christ before the chapter is ended. *Hill* and *holy place* refers to the sanctuary of the Lord. The question means to inquire who is worthy to enter that place.

Verse 4. This verse answers the question of the preceding one. *Clean hands* are hands that do clean or righteous acts, because they are prompted by a pure or unmixed heart. *Vanity* means thoughts that are useless. *Sworn deceitfully* denotes that the one guilty had made on oath that was not from the heart and was thus deceitful.

Verse 5. A person who is free from such wrongs not only will be permitted to come into the house of the Lord, but will be blessed with *righteousness* from the Lord. That means he will be given the reward coming to a life of righteousness.

Verse 6. *Generation* as used here means a race or species of persons who seek the Lord. It was especially true of Christ, and that entitled him to the favor indicated in v. 3. *O Jacob* is a brief form of "O God of Jacob." As Christ was preeminently entitled to "dwell in the house of the Lord forever" (ch. 23: 6), or to receive the favor named in v. 3 in this chapter, the writer plunges next into one of his most important prophecies of Christ which will be seen in the following paragraph.

Verses 7-10. This is a prophecy of the ascension of Jesus and the reception that was accorded him. It is figurative, of course, and represents a call upon his celestial city to open its gates to the conquering king. A short time ago he left the city for a sojourn in the world of mankind. He met the enemy of souls in battle and came off the victor. He was suffered to become the victim of murderous hands and was put to death. But even death did not hold him in its grasp, because his own Shepherd was with him and brought him forth again to die no more. His great mission into yonder's world was accomplished and he was returning to the Eternal City as the greatest conqueror the universe ever knew or was destined ever to know. Now the gates of the city were bidden to admit this *King of glory*. He entered and was seated at his Father's right hand, where he is now reigning as King of kings and Lord of lords.

PSALMS 25

Verse 1. To lift up the soul means to pray with the soul to God.

Verse 2. *Not be ashamed* means not to be debased by the defeat from his enemies. We should keep constantly in mind the fact that David was actively at war most of the time. That made him many enemies among the heathen. Besides this, he had been given the kingdom in preference to Saul which brought him the enmity of Saul's family.

Verse 3. The thought is significant that David considered the service to God as a just condition for escaping confusion. On the other hand, if a man transgressed the law of God he was worthy to be made ashamed.

Verse 4, 5. As a man in distress David prayed the Lord to show him the right way of life. As an inspired man he pointed out that way himself (ch. 37: 23; 119: 133).

Verse 6. God never forgets, as David knew. The statement is a form of request for God to renew his favors of the past.

Verse 7. David was always open and fair with the Lord. He never tried to shield himself in wrong, but humbly and frankly came to the Lord for pardon. Such is the meaning of this verse, and not that God would remember a man's sins against him after having forgiven them.

Verse 8. If sinners do not know better than they are doing it is not through any neglect of God. He is upright and therefore will teach them if they will learn.

Verse 9. This gives the key to the reason some are uninformed. If a man is meek or humble he will even seek for information from God.

Verse 10. The paths or steps the Lord requires his people to follow are really merciful in their effects. The way of the transgressor is hard when the end thereof is considered. Also the path the Lord advises is *truth* which means it is according to truth. But in order to profit by this arrangement a person must keep the *covenant* (agreement) and the testimonies (proven truths) of the Lord.

Verse 11. *Name's sake.* For explanation of this see my comments at ch. 23: 3.

Verse 12. To fear the Lord in the favorable sense is to respect him. The man who does so will be taught in the right way, that being the kind of way a God-fearing man would choose.

Verse 13. The inner man can be at ease regardles of outward conditions. Such will be the case with a man who fears God. His seed or descendants will not literally possess this globe on which we live, but they will enjoy the blessings of it.

Verse 14. *Secret* is from a word that Strong defines in part as "intimacy." In other words, those who fear the Lord will be "taken into a sacred nearness with Him." He will impart his covenant to them.

Verse 15. *The net* refers to the snares that David's enemies placed in his pathway. They were hidden from human eyes, but the Lord sees them and will snatch his faithful followers from the danger.

Verse 16. In the desolation brought on David by his enemies, he made his appeal to God, and was always confident of receiving a hearing.

Verse 17. The troubles were *enlarged* which means they were growing. God alone was able to overcome the forces of his enemies.

Verse 18. The *affliction* and *pain* were not necessarily of a physical nature. David was not concerned about mere temporal discomfort. He desired above all other things to be contented in mind. At the same time he realized his weaknesses of the flesh and made his usual plea for the pardon of his sins.

Verse 19. The chief sources of David's worries were his enemies. The mention of them identifies the character of troubles that he has been praying about to God.

Verse 20. *Be ashamed* means to be confused by the treatment from his enemies. David prayed for the saftey of his soul. He trusted the Lord with all his highest interests and desires.

Verse 21. David realized that his conduct would need to be right before he could expect the favor of God. Hence he asked consideration for his *integrity* or loyalty. *Wait on thee* means he was ever ready to serve the Lord.

Verse 22. David was not selfish. While praying for personal favors he did not forget his people. He had shown that kind of charity right while he was distressed over the sufferings they were experiencing. (2 Sam. 24: 17.)

PSALMS 26

Verse 1. *Judge me* indicated he was ready to be examined as to his conduct and then humbly submit to whatever decision the Lord would make against David. He was confident of the result should the Lord make such a test of him. That was because he had walked in his *integrity* or innocence. To *slide* means to slip or waver. David's trust in God gave him confidence against the pitfalls along the way.

Verse 2. The confidence felt by David was so great that he would willingly submit to an examination for the purpose of *proving* or testing him. That is the attitude of all persons who are sincere in their professions. If a man evades the attempts to investigate him he shows evidence of being wrong knowingly. This idea is taught in John 3: 19, 20. There is not much difference between *reins* and *heart*, and they may ordinarily be used interchangeably. But when the two are employed in the same sentence the first refers especially to the mind as the director of a man's actions, and the second has more application to the feelings or emotions of the mind. David invited an examination of his entire inner being.

Verse 3. It was not the sentiment of dread or terror that prompted David to walk according to truth. He was drawn along his pathway of life by the *lovingkindness*, which means the same as just "kindness," of God.

Verse 4. In ch. 1: 1 David has expressed his disapproval of those who *sat* with the wrong kind of persons. In this psalm he affirms he has not done so himself. The *dissemblers* were men who practiced hypocrisy in their plans.

Verse 5. *Congregation* also means company, and David hated all such associations. He had the same idea that is expressed in 1 Cor. 15: 33.

Verse 6. *Wash mine hands* is a figurative reference to Deut. 21: 6-8. An innocent man had the right to practice that, and David claimed to be innocent. It also is related to Ex. 30: 18-21, which is why he added *so will I compass thine altar.*

Verse 7. Having prepared himself according to the law, David was ready to make an offering. Not of an animal, however, but of a devotional service to God in appreciation for his *wondrous works.*

Verse 8. *Habitation* means abode or a place to stay. *House* is from BAYITH and has been rendered in the Authorized Version by house over 1900 times, also by such words as court, door, family, home, household, palace, place and temple. The clause means David loved to spend time in the Lord's temple. The reason given for it was the fact that God's honor dwelt there. We will find many instances where David expressed his pleasure in the Lord's house.

Verse 9. *Gather* means "remove," and "soul" means his life. David prayed that sinners might not be permitted to take his life. The last clause was more specific as he prayed to be delivered from bloody men; those who delighted in shedding blood.

Verse 10. These bloody men were using their hands to perform mischief. When *right hand* is used figuratively and for a good purpose, it means that the person uses his hand to do right things. When used in the sense of this verse, *right hand* means his stronger and more experienced hand. The person uses his greatest ability to perform something to earn a bribe.

Verse 11. *Walk in mine integrity* means to walk innocently, and in such a manner as to retain a good reputation. *Redeem* as used here has the sense of "preserve," and was said in view of the dangers threatened against David by his many enemies.

Verse 12. *Even* means level or plain. It has the same idea as was set forth in the work of John the Baptist. (Luke 3: 4, 5; Isa. 40: 3, 4.) *Congregations* refers to any of the groups or assemblies where David might be present. In all such places he would bless or praise the Lord.

PSALMS 27

Verse 1. *Light* refers to instruction and it leads a man into the paths of salvation. With such provisions David had no one to fear. He drew the strength of his life also from the Lord and hence need not be afraid of any man. (Rom. 8: 31.)

Verse 2. *Enemies* and *foes* mean also the same, but there is a slight difference in degree. The first has the sense of a competitor without any necessary personal feeling of enmity. The second means those who hate another. *Eat up my flesh* means they wanted to do him bodily harm. God intervened and caused them to fail in their designs against David.

Verse 3. Numbers do not count when arrayed against the Lord or those in his service. Even in war the Lord can give the victory by the use of small numbers. The experience of Gideon could be cited as a proof (Judges 7: 7).

Verse 4. Of course David would not expect to be in the temple constantly, any more than Christians can be in an assembly at all hours. But he wanted to be always in position to enter the house of God to receive its spiritual benefits.

Verse 5. A pavilion is a covering and shelter. In times of trouble God will cover his faithful servants with strong protection. In the secret or intimacy of the sacred house of the Lord there is shelter from the storms of life. A *rock* is a sure foundation, and God will be a rock of support for his loved ones.

Verse 6. To lift up the head means to have a feeling of triumph when it is said with reference to personal enemies. A man might have various reasons for coming to the house of God with an offering. David's success over his enemies gave him one of his chief motives for such devotion, and it was accompanied with songs of praise.

Verse 7. A prayer formed in the mind would be known by the Lord and would be given proper attention. In times of great distress, however, a man would be inclined to make his prayer audible. That was what David did in this verse and it expressed an earnest desire for the help of God.

Verse 8. The first 3 words of this verse are not in the original. The true thought is a view of the dictates of the heart of David. In the time of his troubles his heart (sentiments or feelings) urged him to seek the face of the Lord (in prayer). In response to the urge of his heart he sought the Lord by prayer and song.

Verse 9. No man can literally see God's face and live (Ex. 33: 20). The expression used so frequently by David partakes of some of the figurative meanings of the word. It is from PANIM and has been rendered in the Authorized Version by anger 3 times, countenance 30, edge 1, face 356, favor 4, forefront 4, forepart 4, form 1, former time 1, front 2, heaviness 1, looks 2, mouth 1, old time 1, person 20, presence 75, prospect 6, sight 40, state 1, time past 1, times past 1, upside 2. With such a field of meanings we know that we should not be too technical in applying the word. It would be reasonable to conclude that David wished to receive the spiritual smile of the Lord. He felt the need of such an influence while combatting the enemies.

Verse 10. There is no evidence that David ever had any trouble with his parents. The idea was that he regarded the Lord as being more dependable than even his own flesh-and-blood relations. Such comparison to one's blood relatives is found elsewhere in the Bible (Proverbs 18: 24).

Verse 11. *Plain path* is one that can be easily seen and followed. *Mine enemies* is rendered in the margin by, "those which observe me." A footnote in the American Standard Version renders it, "them that lie in wait for me." Young translates it, "my beholders." From these various translations we can arrive at the thought intended by the psalmist. He knew he was being watched and did not want to make a mistake in his life. For that reason he asked for instructions that could be easily understood.

Verse 12. David never expected or asked to be spared having enemies in this life. He evidently understood that a godly man is bound to have opposition. That doctrine is also found in the New Testament (2 Tim. 3: 12). What he often prayed for was to be supported so that his enemies could not overcome him. One of the bitterest kinds of enemies is a false witness. A man could better be attacked by a physical assailant than by a man who would make a false report about him. The physical opponent would be visible and a man could know whom he was meeting; but a liar would be using his cowardly weapon in the absence of his victim.

Verse 13. The first 3 words have none in the original. The connection, as well as David's trust in the Lord which has been expressed in so many places, indicates that he was making a positive statement. He meant to say that he actually did believe in seeing the goodness of the Lord.

Verse 14. This verse is an exhortation addressed to himself to wait on the Lord. That means to trust the Lord and be ready to do his bidding. If he will do that the Lord will strengthen him.

PSALMS 28

Verse 1. *Cry* is a strong word for pray, and David was earnest in his prayer to God. *Be not silent* does not mean that he expected an audible voice from God. It means for God not to overlook his cry. *Down into* the pit means down to a state of great depression and forgetfulness.

Verse 2. Lifting the hands at a time of prayer was a practice to indicate respectful appeal to God. (1 Tim. 2: 8.) *Supplications* is an urgent form of prayer. *Holy oracle* is a term applying to the temple as the spiritual headquarters of God.

Verse 3. *Draw me not*, etc., means for God not to class David with these wicked men. They were hypocrites; saying one thing and thinking another.

Verse 4. This whole verse is a prayer for God to punish the wicked persons in a way worthy of their unrighteous deeds.

Verse 5. *Works of the Lord* refers to the things that the Lord has created. *Operation of his hands* means the management of those created things. These wicked men disregarded the whole subject, which was the chief basis for David's criticism of his enemies. *Not build them up* means the Lord will not uphold such characters.

Verse 6. *Blessed* usually means "happy," and when applied to God it means he is to be praised because he gives happiness to others. He had given it to David in answer to his supplications.

Verse 7. *Strength* would enable David to perform the service desired by the Lord, and *shield* would protect him in the performance of it. This help came to David because he trusted in the Lord. As an expression of his appreciation for the favors, David praised God with songs.

Verse 8. The antecedent of *their* is indicated by the last word of the verse. His *anointed* refers to the people whom God had chosen.

Verse 9. *Save thy people* should not be interpreted as an indication of partiality. It is true that David prayed only for the Lord's people to be saved for no others have the promise of salvation. But the subject will appear clear and just when we remember that all people have the opportunity of being among God's people as far as personal salvation is concerned. David prayed that all of them should be fed and lifted up, which meant they were to be taught and upheld.

PSALMS 29

Verse 1. This chapter as a whole is a psalm of praise. It is a call for all people to give the Lord the credit for all *glory and strength*.

Verse 2. *Due unto his name* requires that men not merely admit some glory for the Lord; they should give all that is justly his; it must be a wholehearted service. There is nothing really more beautiful than a holy service to God. It will be such a service if conducted according to the Lord's directions. That is what David meant by *the beauty of holiness*.

Verse 3. We should not think of the *voice* of the Lord in an audible sense as used in this and several verses following. It is true that every sound, whether the "still small voice" of the meekest living creature, or the mightiest peal of thunder and the roar of the ocean's stormy billows, all come from the God of all creation. But David is describing God's voice in the sense of his intelligent supervision over all the various domain itemized in the passage. Let us read this and the several verses following and think of the majesty of the Word of God. The mighty ocean, covering over half of the earth's surface and thousands of feet in depth, indicates the force of God's word when he said, "Let the waters under heaven be gathered together unto one place (Gen. 1: 9).

Verse 4. *Full of majesty* means it is full of magnificence and glory. Because of this the psalmist declares the voice of God is powerful.

Verse 5. The cedar was noted for its size, strength and beauty. Referred to figuratively it stood for power of influence and demanded the attention and respect of other things in nature. But the voice of God was mightier than all of these things credited to the cedar.

Verse 6. *Them* refers to the cedars of the preceding verse. They would not literly *skip* or dance around. The figure means that even as important things as these noted plants of the mountains will respond jubilantly to the voice of their Creator.

Verse 7. *Divideth flames*. Human artists can carve and form the various materials of the earth because they are adapted to their capacity. The great Artist of the universe can "hew, split, square, quarry, engrave," materials as flames of fire. The quotation is from Strong's definition of the original word for *divideth*.

Verse 8. *Kadesh* was the place where the Israelites murmured at the report of the spies (Num. 13 and 14). At that place God took charge of the situation and sentenced the congregation to wander in the *wilderness* 38 years longer, thus giving another demonstration of the power of his voice.

Verse 9. The *hind* was a timid animal and at the sound of thunder would give birth to its young. Since this was done away from and independent of man, it formed one of the evidences of the existence of God mentioned in Job 39: 1. *Discovereth the forests* means he has power over them and strips them of their foliage. All appearances in the temple reflect the glory of God.

Verse 10. In Gen. 1: 2 the spirit of God moved or hovered over the face of the waters. His voice then handled those waters according to his will and he still has complete control of them. To sum up, the Lord is King or ruler over everything, and will continue to rule throughout the existence of all things.

Verse 11. A Being so powerful as the one described above can do great things for his people. He will do so by giving them the peace that no other could provide.

PSALMS 30

Verse 1. To *extol* means to elevate by praise. It was appropriate for David to be so disposed toward God for he had received that favor himself. A detail was added regarding the sense in which David had been elevated; his foes had not been allowed to rejoice over him.

Verse 2. *Lord* and *God* are from different originals. The first is from JEHOVAH and means the self-Existent One. It was the Jewish national name of God. The second is from ELOHIYM and its outstanding meaning is one who rules. Taken together, the two words mean to state that the supreme, uncreated, and eternal Being is the rightful ruler over all. No wonder, then, that David so often cried unto him for help. To *heal* does not always refer to disease, but frequently means to relieve from any form of distress.

Verse 3. David had been in danger of death by the hand of his enemies. In rescuing him from evil designs he had really been saved from the grave. *Pit* is from an original that has been properly translated, but David used it figuratively. Had he been suffered to be overcome by his enemies it would have been his ruin.

Verse 4. In gratitude for the many favors from the Lord, David called on all his saints to praise him in song, and as a memorial service to His great holiness.

Verse 5. This verse has some contrasting terms to give force to the thought. The anger of the Lord is but for a moment compared with his favor which lasts a life-time. This translation is supported by the Revised Version, Moffatt's Translation and by Dr. Hull. Other contrasts are between weeping and joy, night and morning. The lesson is that we can afford to submit to the discipline that comes from God for the sake of the happy results that will follow.

Verse 6. *Prosperity* refers to the state of security that David felt through the protection from God. He was so assured that he believed he would never *be moved*.

Verse 7. This verse uses words figuratively. *Mountain* means the highest hopes. As long as David had the favor of God his hopes were "high as a mountain." In times of great trouble he felt that the face of God had been hid from him.

Verse 8. When David was discouraged over the pressure of troubles from the enemy, he prayed to God with the strongest form of petition which was *supplication*.

Verse 9. David believed that death would end all of his activities for the Lord. After he had gone down to the *pit* (grave) he could be of no further service. Therefore, if his enemies were suffered to take his blood it would be in vain as far as the cause of the Lord was concerned.

Verse 10. David was a normal man and wished to live for the sake of life itself. Yet we are pleased to learn that he also wished to live for the sake of what good he could do. In that way he was like Paul in Philippians 1: 21-25. Since David needed to live in order to render this service, he prayed for God to be his merciful *helper*.

Verse 11. When *dancing* is used figuratively it means leaping for joy. *Sackcloth* was worn in times of distress or danger. God had helped David out of his difficulties and he expressed it by using the contrasting terms of this verse.

Verse 12. *Glory may sing praise* refers to the motive that a good man would have in praising God. It means he would sing praises unto the Lord in order to express the glory he believed to be due to Him.

PSALMS 31

Verse 1. *Deliver me in thy righteousness* is about the same as saying, "thy will be done." Such deliverance as would be righteous would be all that David would expect from the Lord. *Never be ashamed* means never to be confused.

Verse 2. *Bow down thine ear* is equivalent to saying, "give a listening ear." A *rock* indicates strength and would provide a good basis for support. A *house* would indicate a defense because it would be a shelter.

Verse 3. A *fortress* is a place that has been fortified against attack. *Name's sake lead me*. For explanation of this see my comments at Ch. 23: 3.

Verse 4. All public or official men dread a secret enemy more than all other kinds. One man lurking in ambush, waiting to spring unexpectedly at his victim, is more difficult to cope with than a score of men in the open. David was aware that he had many such enemies conspiring and plotting against him. But while he had evidence of their existence and activities he could not always discern them; hence he sent the plea to God for defense against his private foes.

Verse 5. This verse might be taken as a prophetic statement, referring to the one made by Christ in Luke 23: 46. But a similar one was made by

Stephen in Acts 7:59. The clearest explanation is that it was a coincidence. But we should not overlook a very informative idea that is suggested in all three of the statements. The men asked the Lord to receive their spirit which shows that something was taken out of the body or was to leave it. That disproves the theory of materialists of every grade who maintain that every part of man is mortal and all there is of him goes to the grave at death.

Verse 6. All *vanities* are wrong and all *lying* is to be condemned. When the two evils are combined in one person it forms a character that would certainly be hateful to as humble and candid a man as David.

Verse 7. Among human beings it is required that one have a like experience before he can sympathize with another in trouble. It is not so with the Lord for his knowledge is infinite. That was why David could rejoice in the hope of divine mercy.

Verse 8. *Large room* means the Lord had made plenty of room for him to escape from his enemies and to counteract their schemes against David.

Verse 9. *Soul* means the inner part of a man and *belly* means the body. It is a strong statement of David's trials, meaning that his enemies had given him afflictions that affected him "soul and body."

Verse 10. Iniquity is sometimes translated by, "punishment of iniquity." Moffatt renders the word here by "punishment." The verse means that David was being punished by his enemies. The punishment was so great that his strength of body was being spent and he was required to call upon the Lord for help.

Verse 11. David was a fighter by disposition and not afraid of the strongest of foes who would offer him physical combat. But he was made to feel depressed when his enemies treated him with contempt. The very ones who were nearest to him and who should have given him the most cordial respect, were the ones who evaded him like cowards. However, that should be considered in favor of him. When those who know a good man the best will avoid a personal contact, it is an indication that they realize their inferiority and are too low in principle to admit it.

Verse 12. This verse is a continuation of the treatment David was receiving from his cowardly foes, which was described in the preceding verse.

Verse 13. In describing the activities of his enemies, David unconsciously predicted the actions that were plotted against Christ. *Took counsel against me* was done in Matt. 26: 14-16; Luke 22: 3-6. But David frequently had such plotting against his life by Saul and also by his own family relatives.

Verse 14. David never lost his faith in God, although he was very much concerned many times about what was going to be the next move of his enemies.

Verse 15. *Times are in thy hand* means he was in the hand of the Lord at all times. On that basis David felt he had the privilege of calling on Him for deliverance.

Verse 16. *Face to shine* denotes that David wanted the face of God to be favorable toward him. The attribute of the Lord that would prompt him to help was his mercy.

Verse 17. *Ashamed* occurs very frequently in the Bible. It has a varied meaning, but we would not go wrong were we always to think of it as meaning to be confused, disappointed or humbled. This will explain why David used the word twice in this verse; once about himself and once about his enemies. *Silent in the grave* was David's way of wishing the destruction of his enemies.

Verse 18. All lying should be condemned, but the kind that David had in mind here was *grievous*. That is from a word that means hard or cruel. The foes of David not only wished him harm, but were eager to make his life as miserable as possible.

Verse 19. *Laid up* means reserved. *Goodness* does not refer primarily to character, but to the good things that the Lord has to give. He reserves them for the ones who respect and serve him. God has *wrought* or brought about these good things for those who trust in him, and he has done so in the sight of other human beings.

Verse 20. The first clause of this verse means that God will take his faithful servants into his confidence and shield them from harm. *Pride* is often the result of envy. David had many foes who envied him his standing with God and in revenge wished to injure him. *Pavilion* means a covering or protection from danger.

Verse 21. *Strong city* has reference to a fortified one. David likened the favor of God's care over him to the security of that kind of a city. When he *blessed* the Lord he meant to ascribe all blessings to Him.

Verse 22. *In my haste* referred to those times when David's persecutions almost caused him to despair. One definition of the word is "distraction." But even in such times he looked to the Lord in earnest prayer and was heard. In the most trying hours of distress David never forgot to appeal to the divine throne for help.

Verse 23. This is an exhortation for all of God's people to love him in order to secure the presevation that can come from that source only. *Plentifully rewardeth* means that the proud or haughty person will get the full deserts of his deeds.

Verse 24. An old saying is, "God helps those who help themselves." That idea is set forth in the exhortation to the saints. If they will gird up their courage the Lord will add to their heart's desire.

PSALMS 32

Verse 1. This verse is cited in Rom. 4: 7, 8. Sinless perfection is not expected of man in this life and blessedness is nowhere based on it. But God has always had some system whereby a man could obtain the forgiveness of his sins and thus be permitted to have the divine blessing. *Sin be covered* means it is put out of sight by the plan of atonement that is in force at the time.

Verse 2. This verse is about the same in thought as the first one. To impute means to hold it against one. If a man complies with the law of pardon that he is under, the Lord will not hold his iniquity against him. *Guile* is a special kind of sin, meaning something in the nature of deceit. However, if a man comes up to the terms of forgiveness that God lays down to him, it will indicate his sincerity and show him to be free of guile.

Verse 3. Until David came to the throne of grace with his prayer for divine mercy, he was not at ease in mind over his condition. The last half of the verse is figurative and intended to indicate his dissatisfied feeling.

Verse 4. *Moisture* and *drought* are opposite terms and are used by David to indicate his feelings when the troubles of life beset him. *Selah* is punctuation mark in language and a pause in music, and is explained at Ch. 3: 2.

Verse 5. In this verse we have *sin, iniquity* and *transgressions.* The first two mean practically the same and are not quite as strong as the third. It is from an original that means to commit a sin with the attitude of rebellion against some constituted authority. David made full confession of all his faults and was forgiven.

Verse 6. The quality of godliness is due to the attitude toward God, hence that kind of a man would be disposed to pray to Him. *Mayest be found* does not indicate that God sometimes is unwilling to be sought. But he will be found only when men have sought him after the proper manner and in the right frame of mind. *Floods of great waters* means the waves of troubles that come over men in this life. The floods will not come nigh *him,* referring to the man who has sought and found God.

Verse 7. *Hiding place* does not mean a place of secrecy for a wicked person, but means a shelter for David because he had trusted in the Lord. *Compass with songs* denotes that God would surround David with the conditions that would cause him to give a song of deliverance.

Verse 8. *I* stands for the Lord who is answering the prayer of David. *Guide thee with mine eye* refers to the oversight that God always has for his people. There is an eye watching over the righteous and looking out for the welfare of those who desire counsel in the uncertain ways of the world.

Verse 9. This verse is also the language of God giving admonition to man. The beast requires some mechanical means to guide him, but man should use his reasoning faculties and apply the instructions that come from the Lord.

Verse 10. Righteous men often have sorrows, but they are not the sorrows of penitence like the experiences of the wicked. Mercy shall *compass* or surround the man who puts his trust in the Lord.

Verse 11. *Glad* and *rejoice* are about the same practically. The first refers especially to the state of mind and the second to the expression of it. *Shout* is a stronger word than *rejoice.* It is defined in Strong's lexicon, "to creak (or emit a stridulous [shrill] sound)."

PSALMS 33

Verse 1. The first definition of the original for *comely* is "suitable." The expression is significant and agrees with a principle that is taught throughout the Bible. Praise is a term connected with the services offered to God. It is suitable or consistent for the *upright* to offer the service of praise to God. It is out of place for the wicked to pretend that they wish to praise the Lord.

Verse 2. It is a well-known truth that David's specialty in the field of religious exercises was the musical instruments of various kinds; so this verse is in true form. The *harp* was the national instrument of the Hebrews. It was a stringed instrument and was played on with a plectrum, an attachment worn on the finger. The *psaltery* also was a stringed instrument and specially used to accompany the voice. *Ten strings* is only a detail of the kind of instrument David meant when he said to praise the Lord with the psaltery, the word *and* not being in the original.

Verse 3. *Skilfully* with a *loud noise* means to play correctly as to the proper strings plucked, and also to make it emphatic. It was to accompany a new song.

Verse 4. The *works* of the Lord pertain to his dealings with men, hence they could properly be said to be according to truth. This, then, has reference to the intellectual activities of the Lord instead of his mechanical ones, which agrees with the first clause of the verse on the subject of the *word of the Lord*.

Verse 5. God loves a man who is righteous; and that means he will be just in his dealings with his fellowmen. And there is an example to follow, for the earth is full of the *goodness* or good things of the Lord.

Verse 6. This refers to the week of creation. "And God said" were the words that were used and the only means by which the Creator brought the things into existence. This is affirmed in Heb. 11: 3 in conenction with the subject of faith.

Verse 7. This refers to God's control of the sea.

Verse 8. *Fear* and *awe* are used in the same sense. They mean to have deep respect for God for his wonderful works of the universe.

Verse 9. See my comments at verse 6.

Verse 10. A heathen nation may plan to oppose the interests of God but they will be overthrown. The Egyptian nation intended to destroy the Israelites but met defeat itself in the death of all its men in the march, including their king.

Verse 11. God can see the end from the beginning. Because of that he can give counsel or advice that will prove to be correct in the coming ages.

Verse 12. The Jewish nation is specifically the one meant in this verse. In an extended sense it is true that any nation that acknowledges God (the self-Existent One) as its Lord (ruler) will be in more favor. This principle was taught to the Babylonian king (Dan. 4: 17).

Verse 13. The Lord as a personal Being is in heaven and from there he can see all of the actions of men.

Verse 14. This is practically the same as the preceding verse. *Habitation* is a place where a person habitually dwells. God's spirit is everywhere, but his person is on his throne in the Eternal City.

Verse 15. God is the maker of all the hearts of men. The one who makes a piece of mechanism would certainly understand all about its working. If it did not perform in the way he expected he should understand what was wrong. On that basis the Lord understands the failures of the hearts of men since he *fashioned* all of them.

Verse 16. Numbers alone will not count when arrayed on the wrong side. Gideon won in the conflict with the Midianites although he had but 300 men. But they were supported by the Lord and that outweighed all other considerations. Paul had this idea in mind in Rom. 8: 31.

Verse 17. We know that David did not discount the actual usefulness of the horse, for he had seen him in action in many a battle. We must look for some comparison that he had in mind. He meant that the mere strength of the animal would not take care of a dangerous situation, any more than would numbers of men as per the comments on the preceding verse.

Verse 18. This verse should be considered in the light of the two preceding ones. If a man so conducts himself that the eye of the Lord is upon him for good, he need not be afraid of a million men on as many strong horses.

Verse 19. Even when death by famine threatens a servant of God, he is able to provide food for him by miracle if necessary. (See the cases in 1 Ki. 17: 6, 16.)

Verse 20. In the Old Testament *soul* comes from NEPHESH and its first definition in Strong's lexicon is, "a breathing creature." It could be used for the entire creature or for only the inner part of him, and the connection will determine how it is used in given cases. Since the present verse speaks of an action requiring an intelligent attitude toward the Lord, the inner man is evidently meant. To *wait for the Lord* means to rely on the Lord for help.

Verse 21. The word for *heart* has some of the same meaning as that for soul, but has more special reference to the emotional part of man. That explains why the heart would *rejoice in Him.*

Verse 22. *Mercy* often has the idea of leniency toward those deserving stern treatment because of evil conduct. It also means kindness and pity in times of distress or other need and is so used here.

PSALMS 34

Verse 1. To *bless* generally means to make happy when used with regard to man-to-man treatment. When used toward God it means to praise him as the source of happiness.

Verse 2. For *soul* see my comments at Ch. 33: 20. To *boast* in a good sense means to make a strong claim of having some favor.

Verse 3. Since *magnify* means to enlarge, and since man cannot actually enlarge the Lord, the clause means to enlarge our praises of the Lord. The second clause is practically the same in thought, meaning to hold the name of the Lord above all others. The verse also expresses the idea of a united action on the part of the people.

Verse 4. God *heard* David when he *sought* for him, which shows that prayer is one method of seeking the Lord. Professed children of God who never pray do not indicate much eagerness to find him. David profited by his searching for the Lord who delivered him from the fears that were thrown round him by his enemies.

Verse 5. *They* refers to persons in general; that is, all they who looked unto the Lord *were lightened*, meaning they were made to be cheerful and not *ashamed* or confused. If people would turn to the Lord for help in times of fear or other trouble they would find the consolation not to be had elsewhere.

Verse 6. *This* poor man does not refer to any certain person. It is a general reference to some supposed instance among the ones called *they* in the preceding verse.

Verse 7. God dwells in heaven in the everlasting city, but accomplishes his purposes by the use of means. One of those means is the ministration of angels according to this verse. The same is taught in Heb. 1: 14.

Verse 8. *Taste and see*, etc., is the same idea expressed by the apostle in 1 Peter 2: 3. Sometimes children will refuse certain articles of food offered to them, and will give as a reason that they "do not like them." Then the parent will probably tell them that if they would only taste the foods they would find out that they would like them. It is likewise so with the children of God in many instances. They imagine they would not relish the things offered to them when they have not even had the interest, perhaps, to taste and see.

Verse 9. To *fear the Lord* means to reverence him. *Want* means to lack or actually have need. People often desire or long for things they do not need. The real needs of mankind will be supplied by the Lord for all who prove to be worthy.

Verse 10. *Young lions* comes from one Hebrew word. In their lack of judgment they sometimes are hungry for the very nourishment that nature has provided for them. Such a circumstance was used by David to illustrate the professed children of God who do not seek the Lord in the appointed way. Those who do seek properly will not *want* (lack) any *good* thing.

Verse 11. As a father would talk to his children, so David exhorted the nations under him to fear or reverence the Lord.

Verse 12. This verse was not worded as an inquiry, for every man desires the things named. It was another way of calling for the attention of all such to a suggestion about to be made as to how a man may obtain his desire.

Verse 13. The first item in the method of obtaining the genuine good things of life is to guard one's language. This idea is also to be seen in James 1: 26.

Verse 14. The first clause is identical in thought with Isa. 1: 16, 17. Repentance not only requires that one cease his life of sin, but he must also take up an active life of good works. *Seek* and *pursue* are different only in degree of meaning. The second means not only to be eager for peace but to run after it.

Verses 15, 16. These verses are made to form one paragraph because they form one verse almost verbatim in 1 Pe. 3: 12. Words should be understood by the connection in which they are found. We know that in the general sense the eyes of the Lord are everywhere (Prov. 15: 30), regardless of whether men are evil or good. But the context here shows the expression is used in a special sense and means that the eyes of the Lord are favorable toward the righteous. Because of this attitude the Lord will give a favorable ear to the *cry* or prayer of those who are good. *Face* includes the whole countenance and everything that would be used in giving attention. It means that if a man's life is continually one of *doing evil* the Lord will not honor his prayers. That does not mean that a sinner cannot turn to the Lord for mercy. If he will *depart from evil* (v. 14) and show signs of repentance the Lord will hear him.

Verse 17. *The righteous* has no words in the original, but the connection in this and the preceding verses justifies their use. God will be merciful to the righteous.

Verse 18. *Lord is nigh* should be understood in the light of the comments on v. 15. If a man is *contrite*, which means he is penitent and humble, the Lord will be near him with assistance.

Verse 19. *Afflictions* do not refer especially to physical diseases. The word means adversities in general, including persecutions by enemies. The New Testament teaches that righteous persons will have such afflictions (2 Tim. 3: 12). The Lord in his own way will care for all such.

Verse 20. David was an inspired writer and wrote many prophetic statements. This verse refers to the circumstance that the legs of Jesus were not broken on the cross as were those of the thieves. (John 19: 36.)

Verse 21. The judgment to come on the wicked does not always come literally in this life. The unrighteous men who do not repent will be slain with eternal death after the judgment of the last day.

Verse 22. *Redeemeth the soul* is significant. The bodies of God's servants may suffer persecution and finally be put to death by the tormentors, but the soul is beyond the power of man to destroy. (Luke 12: 4, 5.) *Desolate* means to be under punishment for guilt of sin, and the righteous will escape that lot.

PSALMS 35

Verse 1. *Plead* is from an original that means not only to advocate, but to grapple with the cause of another for his benefit. David called upon the Lord actually to take charge of his controversy with the enemy.

Verse 2. *Shield* and *buckler* were articles worn in warfare. David used them figuratively in asking God to fight for him against his enemies.

Verse 3. The articles mentioned in the preceding verses were for defense. The *spear* is a weapon of attack and David used the word in a figurative sense also. I do not mean that he did not want literal protection against the enemy, but he expected God to use his miraculous power to give him the help these instruments would do in the hands of a man in literal warfare, only in a more perfect manner and degree of success.

Verse 4. *Confounded* and *shame* are practically the same in effect. Strictly speaking, the first means to be defeated and the second means to be humiliated because of the defeat. *Soul* is used of the man in general, for these enemies were not especially concerned with the spiritual lot of David; they were after him bodily. *Hurt* is used in the same sense as the words about the soul.

Verse 5. There were two reasons why David compared his enemies to chaff. One was to express their worthlessness and the other was to indicate their destruction. Matt. 3: 12 gives a good description of the lot awaiting the chaff. Since *angels* are instruments in God's hands to carry out his purposes (Heb. 1: 14), we may understand why David mentioned them.

Verse 6. The use of *dark and slippery* is to indicate that the enemies would be hindered in their purposes against David. *Persecute* means to pursue and defeat the enemies in their persecutions of David.

Verse 7. It means they had no just cause for opposing David. The *net* meant a trap and the *pit* meant it was hidden so as to take David unawares. *Digged for soul* is explained by my comments at v. 4.

Verse 8. The enemy had formed a plot for David and he prayed God that the enemy might be caught in his own trap. Such a fate was endorsed by Solomon (Prov. 26: 27), and Haman actually had that experience. (Est. 7: 10.)

Verse 9. David was more concerned in his soul than his body. In spite of persecutions, if God assisted him he believed it would be well with his soul.

Verse 10. *Bones* is from ETSEM and Strong defines it, "a bone (as strong), by extension the body." David meant that his whole being was engaged in praise for the Lord for his many good deeds unto the unfortunate.

Verse 11. If a man lives righteously the only kind of testimony that can be against him is falsehood. Naturally, then, such charges would concern some form of misconduct of which he *knew not.*

Verse 12. *Spoiling* is from SHEKOWL which Strong defines by "bereavement," and that makes the thought clearer. It shows the nature of those who are so wicked as to return to a man some evil for his good.

Verse 13. Sackcloth was worn in times of grief or anxiety. Instead of returning evil for good, when David's enemies were in trouble he grieved for them and showed his concern by clothing himself with sackcloth. Paul told Christians to "weep with them that weep" (Rom. 12: 15). This sentiment was further expressed by David in the form of *prayer* and *fasting.* *Prayer returned* means his prayer was not appreciated by those for whom it was offered. In other words, the selfish spirit of ingratitude was all that David received for his unselfish interest in the welfare of his enemies.

Verse 14. David had treated his enemies in distress as he would a friend or nearest relative, but his kindness was not appreciated.

Verse 15. In return for the kindness of David in their adversity, when a like misfortune came to him they rejoiced. The *abjects* were the low characters who secretly plotted against David. To *tear* him meant they reviled him at his back.

Verse 16. They were *hypocritical mockers* in that they pretended to be David's friends, but secretly wished to devour him as a vicious beast would have done.

Verse 17. For explanation of *my darling* see the comments at ch. 22: 20

Verse 18. Wherever a large gathering of the people might be, David would utter forth his gratitude for the goodness of God.

Verse 19. David never did ask to be upheld in anything that was wrong. He only prayed that his enemies not be allowed to rejoice over him in their wrong-doing. To *wink with the eye* is a gesture of contempt as if they would humiliate him with scorn.

Verse 20. David's enemies not only did nothing in behalf of peace, but were active in devising plots against peaceful citizens of the land.

Verse 21. *Aha, aha,* was another expression of ridicule and fun-making. *Hath seen it* refers to the misfortunes of David, and his enemies were outwardly glad because of his troubles.

Verse 22. *Keep not silence* means for the Lord not to fail to help David.

Verse 23. This is similar to the preceding verse. It is a supplication for divine help. *God* and *Lord* are used in one sentence, which indicates a difference in meaning. The first is from an original that means a Being to be worshiped. The second is from a word that means a ruler. The combined thought is that God should be worshiped and obeyed as supreme Ruler.

Verse 24. *Judge* means to pronounce a verdict, and to do so according to the facts in the case. David believed he had been righteous in his conduct and therefore was not useasy as to the judgment that God would form. In that case his enemies would have no ground for rejoicing over him.

Verse 25. David could not bear the thought of giving his enemies something to gloat over. The mere fact of having some kind of unpleasant experience would not have troubled him so much, but he did not want his enemies to claim credit for it.

Verse 26. *Ashamed* and *confusion* are practically the same and are used together for the purpose of emphasis. They mean for the enemies to be defeated in their plots against David. *Shame* means a feeling of humiliation, and *dishonor* has the sense of disgrace. All of these conditions were what David wished to come on his enemies because they *magnified* or boasted themselves against him.

Verse 27. We should like the spirit of this verse. David was not interested merely in his own welfare, but wished the Lord to receive due credit for it. The people he expected to take such an attitude were those who were in sympathy with him in his righteous service to God.

Verse 28. *Thy righteousness* had special reference to God's righteous dealings with man. *Thy praise* meant the praise that David believed to be justly due the Lord.

PSALMS 36

Verse 1. The pronouns are a little indefinite as to person, but they both refer to *the wicked*. In their *transgressions* (which means rebellion), they deny having any fear of God in their hearts.

Verse 2. The wicked man coaxed himself into thinking that he was all right. That kind of conduct led him on until his iniquity became hateful.

Verse 3. It is significant that the wicked man *left off* both wisdom and doing good at the same time. The wisest man in this world is one who knows to do good.

Verse 4. The antecedent of *he* is the *wicked* man of v. 1. In the hour when he is reclining he plans on the mischief he wishes to do on the morrow. *Setteth himself in a way* denotes that he becomes "set in his ways" of unrighteousness. Paul taught that we should "abhor that which is evil (Rom. 12: 9)," but the man whom David was considering did not do that. Of course such a man would not hesitate to devise evil plans.

Verse 5. *Heavens* and *clouds* are used to indicate the extent of God's mercy and faithfulness. There is no limit to the mercy of God on his part. Man limits it by his refusal to meet the terms on which divine mercy is offered.

Verse 6. In a number of verses the psalmist expressed his adoration for the qualities of the Lord by some comparisons. He used some of the things of the material creation for his figures. A *mountain* is lofty and great, and the sea has great depth; so is the goodness of God. Both *man* and *beast* owe their existence to the preserving might of their Creator.

Verse 7. Strong defines the original word for *excellent* by "valuable." The term, then, means something more than a mere sentiment. When God extends his kindness to the children of men, they receive something that is of actual assistance in life.

Verse 8. *Fatness* literally means richness, and when used figuratively means that rich blessings are to be had in the house of the Lord. A *river* is abundant in volume, continuous in supply, pure in quality. For these reasons it is used to compare the pleasures flowing from the throne of God. (Rev. 22: 1.)

Verse 9. A *fountain* has about the same meaning as a river when used as an illustration. It is continuous and bountiful. The light that comes from God is infinite, yet it is adapted to the needs of man, shedding light across his pathway.

Verse 10. *Know thee* means the people who recognize and honor the Lord. They are the kind that have the right to the favors of God. This thought is indicated by the term near the end of the verse; the *upright in heart*.

Verse 11. *Let not the foot* means not to let the proud enemies walk or move against David. *Remove me* would indicate an attempt to interfere with David's relation of favor with the Lord.

Verse 12. *There* implies the place where the evil men had been cast down by the Lord. That is, after the wishes of David that he had just expressed had been granted, these workers of iniquity would be in that condition.

PSALMS 37

Verse 1. It seems a little strange for David to give us this advice, after he has said so much about those evildoers and manifested so much concern over them. It will be well to read the comments at ch. 10: 1 in connection with the above remarks. But this verse is good advice, for after all these wicked men are not to be envied.

Verse 2. This verse does not teach that the wicked will be put out of existence as materialists claim. It means they will soon come to the end of their wicked plans.

Verse 3. *Doing good* is put before *being fed*, which is the same principle taught by Christ in Matt. 6: 33. It is taken for granted that if a man really does *trust in the Lord* he will do his part in acquiring the necessities of life.

Verse 4. The promises of God are generally made conditional. Here we are taught that a man will get his *heart's desire* if he will *delight* in the Lord. That is true, for a man who has that regard for the Lord will not have unrighteous desires.

Verse 5. This verse has much the same thought as the preceding one. *Commit thy way* literally means to roll one's burdens on the Lord. The New Testament teaches this idea in 1 Pe. 5: 7. Then after committing one's way on the Lord he should not regret his action but should *trust in Him*. *Shall bring it to pass* means that all desires that are according to the will of the Lord will be brought to pass.

Verse 6. A beautiful object will look the more attractive if in the light. Likewise the righteous life of a man of God will shine all the more when *brought forth* in the divine light.

Verse 7. This verse is about the same in thought as the first one. To *rest in the Lord* means to be contented in him and not be worrying at the success of the wicked.

Verse 8. *Anger* is the violent action of the temper and *wrath* is the anger settled down into a steady heat; both degrees should be brought under control. A man should not "lose his temper" over the success of wicked persons.

Verse 9. The success of *evildoers* will be brought to an end in God's own way. *To wait upon the Lord* means to trust and obey him. Those who do so shall inherit the earth as the New Testament also teaches in Matt. 5: 5; 2 Pe. 3: 13.

Verse 10. *Wicked shall not be* as far as his activities in wrong are concerned.

Verse 11. This verse repeats the statement in v. 9. It should be understood that no actual possession of this earthly globe is meant. But the righteous people on the earth shall appreciate the good things produced thereon, and later will be given a place on the new earth referred to in v. 9.

Verse 12. *Plotteth* and *gnasheth* are used to indicate the intensity of evil men in their designs against good men.

Verse 13. The Lord is never frivolous, but to *laugh* means to look with belittling on the plots of wicked men. God is able to see the end of such a wicked career.

Verse 14. The *sword* and *bow* were used as weapons of war, but the wicked men used them as instruments of cruelty against the helpless. *Upright conversation* means righteous conduct. An evil man would want to "get even" with a righteous one and could do so only by slaying him.

Verse 15. The thought in this verse is that evil workers will fail in their plans in the end. Their weapons will be destroyed or be turned against themselves. This will again remind us of the lesson about the pit and gallows. (Prov. 26: 27; Est. 7: 10.) The same idea is expressed by saying, "Evil works its own rebuke."

Verse 16. His *little* is better for two reasons. He obtained it by the proper means, and a righteous man will appreciate what he has and make proper use of it.

Verse 17. *Arms* is from an original that has a figurative as well as literal definition. It is here used in the first sense and means "force." The forces of the wicked will finally be brought to naught.

Verse 18. *Lord knoweth* is used in the sense of approval. *Inheritance* means the reward that the upright man will receive from the Lord, never to fade away.

Verse 19. *Not be ashamed* means they will not be confused or disappointed in times of distress. The Lord will remember them and supply their needs.

Verse 20. *The fat of lambs* is used as a sacrifice to God. The wicked will not be literally burned up as the fat is done, but they will be consigned to the wrath of God and their evil works shall utterly perish.

Verse 21. Two opposite kinds of conduct are described in this verse, and the characteristic of the one emphasizes that of the other. If the wicked man should repay what he had borrowed it would be only what strict justice would require. The righteous man goes farther than the demands of justice. He shows mercy by giving to the needy who would not be able to repay. (See Luke 14: 12-14.)

Verse 22. *Blessed of him* means blessed by the Lord. Those who are righteous come under this benefit and shall *inherit the earth*. For explanation of this phrase see comments at v. 9.

Verse 23. *Good* is not in the original and should not be in the translation. The predestinarians teach that if a man is good it is because God decreed it that way before he was born, and that his own choice had nothing to do with it. They claim this verse teaches that theory. But God has ordered or pointed out the steps he wishes all men to take and has left it to them to make the choice or decision as to whether they will walk in that way. If they do, then they become good men. David understood this subject, for in ch. 119: 133 he states that the steps are ordered through the word of God. When a man walks in the steps advised in the Word the Lord *delighteth in his way* according to the statement of the verse.

Verse 24. If a good man falls it will be through the human weakness and not any fault of the way ordered by the Lord. In that case he will be lifted up by the divine help. This is like the doctrine in 1 John 1: 7. It is not the man who never makes a mistake who will be saved, for there is no such a man. But the man who gets right up and "tries again" is the one whom the Lord will help.

Verse 25. Critics have tried to array this verse against the facts of life and against other parts of the Bible, but it is a strained application of the passage. Almost any rule has some exceptions, and the exception really emphasizes the rule. It should be noticed that the righteous were not *forsaken*, which is a stronger word than saying they had never been reduced or inconvenienced. A good man may have to endure some hardships, but the Lord will take care of him in the end. There is another thought that is overlooked. David did not profess to have seen everything that ever took place, he was only telling what he had not seen. We should be careful not to make a statement of scripture mean more than the writer intended.

Verse 26. This verse will shed some light on the preceding one. That same righteous man is said to be lending to the less fortunate. To do that he would need to have more than his own life required, which indicates financial success. That would justify a reflection on the other verse, that the righteous man considered was the industrious one. Such a person would logically not need to go begging for bread when he had enough and to spare, so that he could supply the needs of others. In this connection the student should read Matt. 6: 33.

Verse 27. *Forever* means to the end of the age, and it is applied here to the span of life usually allotted to man. If he will follow the laws of God, to depart from evil and do good, he will have the assurance of the best things of life.

Verse 28. *Judgment* means justice or the rights belonging to upright persons. The saints of the Lord deserve his attention, and since He loves justice he will see that his people receive it. *Preserved forever.* They may suffer death at the hands of enemies, but their soul can no man touch to destroy; God will preserve it forever. *Seed* is used in the sense of fruit or product, and that which was brought about by the wicked shall be destroyed when the final lot of all actions is manifested.

Verse 29. This verse is to be understood in the same sense as v. 27.

Verse 30. Righteousness will not give intelligence to a man whom nature has denied. But such a man will speak the wisdom that God gives him in his Word.

Verse 31. This verse confirms the comment made in the preceding one. Such a man will not *slide* or slip out of the way.

Verse 32. In times when physical persecutions were tolerated by the government this verse would have a literal application. Otherwise it would refer to the moral and spiritual destruction that could be brought upon the righteous. That is why Christians are warned to be on their guard. (1 Pe. 5: 8.)

Verse 33. *Him* refers to the righteous man of the preceding verse and *his* means the wicked. A righteous man may have to suffer some hardships, but when he is judged or put to the test God will deliver him.

Verse 34. *Wait on the Lord* means to trust him and look to him for all needed help. In order to have the right to such favors, however, one must *keep his way* which means to do the *way* the Lord wishes him to. *Inherit the land* is explained at v. 9. When that blessing comes to the righteous they will realize that the wicked are *cut off* or denied such favors.

Verse 35. *Bay* is from an original that means "native," and *green* means a new plant that had sprung up and made a big showing at first because it did not have the "shock" of transplanting. The wicked man was compared to this tree on account of his threatening boasts of power, thinking to make others come and cower under him. The word *power* is from ARIYTS and Strong defines it, "fearful, i.e. powerful or tyrannical." In the Authorized Version it is rendered mighty 1 time, oppressor 3, terrible 13.

Verse 36. This verse is a comment on the preceding one. A tree that is making a big showing because of special advantages will likely soon die. It is the same with the boastful man in his wickedness and terrorizing over others. Such a character is doomed to final defeat.

Verse 37. *Mark* and *behold* were David's words for calling attention to the good man. It is significant that peace was to come to that man in the *end*. He might have many trials in course of his journey but when the "last mile of the way" has been traveled he will have peace. The "end of a perfect day" is not as important as the perfect end of a day. Paul taught this idea in Acts 20: 24.

Verse 38. *End of the wicked* means the wicked shall be cut off in the end. It is the opposite of the lot of the righteous that was described in the preceding verse.

Verse 39. The final success of the righteous is accounted for by the fact that his salvation is of the Lord. The weakest man who is righteous will win out over the wicked, for the strength of the Lord will hold him up.

Verse 40. God will not save the righteous on the basis of their merit or because they have "earned" it. It will be in reward for their trust in Him.

PSALMS 38

Verse 1. God suffers his faithful servants to be tested by the persecutions of the enemies. David did not mean to ask the Lord to relieve him of all unpleasantness. His idea was to ask for a modification of it.

Verse 2. David likened the troubles suffered to come on him to the arrows of the Lord. He did not mean that God directly afflicted him, but he suffered the enemy to wound him with the arrows of persecution.

Verse 3. David had always considered himself human and subject to the same weaknesses as other men. He believed that one's faithfulness to God needed to be tested in order to fortify him against his natural tendency to sin. That test at times was so severe that he described it figuratively by its effect on his body.

Verse 4. *Gone over mine head* means his *iniquities* had overwhelmed him. This means his afflictions, for iniquities often has that application.

Verse 5. It is well for us to make frequent reference to 1 Sam. 13: 14. The reason David was a man after God's own heart was his frankness and willingness to admit his sins and other weaknesses. He manifested almost what we might term was an "inferiority complex" in regard to his moral and spiritual worth. That is why we have so many verses along here in which are the severe criticisms of himself.

Verse 6. All of the things complained of in this verse pertain to the mind or inner man. David was greatly worried over the trials he was having.

Verse 7. *Disease* is not in the original and is not necessary. *Loins* has a general meaning and refers to the sources of strength in various parts of the body. The verse means that David was practically reduced in strength by reason of his many trials.

Verse 8. This verse is similar in thought to the last one above. There is no evidence that David had any special physical affliction, but his many trials and persecutions had the effect of prostrating him.

Verse 9. The second half of this verse explains the first. David believed his complaints were known to the Lord, and that was why he made his desire known to Him.

Verse 10. These are strong statements, intended to express the depressed state of David's mind over his troubles.

Verse 11. *Sore* is a figurative term to designate the hard lot that had come upon David. *Stand aloof* refers to the shock it was to his friends and relatives.

Verse 12. The private foes of David have been his most dreaded problem. It would be so with any of us. There is some chance of wrestling with an antagonist who will come out openly with his challenge, but it is hard to deal with a sneaking coward.

Verse 13. See the comments on the previous verse. This offers the same thoughts in different words. If an enemy keeps his operations out of hearing of his victim he might as well be deaf. Or, he might as well be dumb since he could not have known when to speak against his foe.

Verse 14. This verse should take the comments of v. 13.

Verse 15. David was practically deaf to the activities of his enemies because of his finite knowledge. But God can see and hear everything and thus would know all about the plots of the enemies against David. For that reason he turned to the Lord for help and believed that his services to the God of heaven and earth would avail.

Verse 16. David's greatest dread regarding his personal misfortunes was about the attitude of his enemies toward him in his condition. He knew they would rejoice at any calamity that would come to him, and that was what he desired the Lord to prevent.

Verse 17. *Ready to halt* is rendered "on the verge of a collapse" by Moffatt. The thought is that his trials were at that very moment about to overwhelm him. They would do so, he feared, unless God helped him.

Verse 18. Here is another reference to his sin. See the comments at vs. 3, 5.

Verse 19. Usually those who are unrighteous are in the majority; it was so in the case of David's enemies. As they were *multiplied* that gave them the strength that comes from numbers. Such strength, however, will not avail when God enters the situation, hence David made his appeal to Him.

Verse 20. It would be taken for granted that those who would return evil for good to a man would be his adversaries. That was not the information David intended to impart in this verse. The significant idea is the motive he assigned to them; that it was because he followed that which was good. It has been the general history of mankind that a wicked person will dislike one who is good.

Verses 21, 22. David expected his enemies to continue their persecutions against him, therefore he was earnestly praying to God for relief. *Make haste* is a phrase that refers to David's feeling of eagerness rather than to the action of God.

PSALMS 39

Verse 1. David expressed the sentiments of this verse in ch. 19: 14. He knew the relation between a man's words and his action. That is why he resolved to *bridle* his mouth. This thought is expressed in James 3: 3.

Verse 2. *Even from good* means that even when the facts would have been in his favor he refrained from "talking back." This restraint caused his troubles to burn in him, yet for the better effect he practiced control of his mouth.

Verse 3. There is a limit to human endurance. The proper control of the tongue does not require that a person should never speak out against a wrong. *The fire burned* refers to the heat in his heart while he was thinking over the injustices heaped upon him by his enemies. The fire at last broke out in the form of speech by his tongue. But it was not in rashness nor undue haste, for he mused over the situation a while first. This is like the teaching in the New Testament (Jas. 1: 19), "let every man be . . . slow to speak, slow to wrath."

Verse 4. David did not expect the Lord to name the day on which he would die. *Make to know* meant to help him realize the shortness and uncertainty of this life.

Verse 5. This verse is about the same in thought as the preceding one. It expresses the same idea concerning which David prayed to God, which is to the effect that man's life, at best, is brief. This will remind us of James 4: 15.

Verse 6. This verse is a general reference to the actions of men. They are more interested in this life than in the one to come. They act as if they would live here forever to enjoy the riches they have accumulated. It is foolish for a man thus to spend his days in that way, for he will not stay here always, nor does he know just who will get to use the riches he has spent his life to produce. This thought also is offered in the New Testament (Luke 12: 20).

Verse 7. *What wait I for* means there is no reason to look further than to the Lord for help. There is no hope worth cherishing not based on the promises of God.

Verse 8. *All my transgressions* does not necessarily mean a confession of any specific sins. It is an acknowledgement that any humble servant of God should make.

Verse 9. *I was dumb* means David did not have a word of criticism to offer against the dealings of God with man.

Verse 10. This verse is merely a plea for the mercy of God in his treatment of the children of men. While David used the personal pronoun *I*, he was speaking for the human race as a whole as the following verse will show.

Verse 11. Here we see the writer speaks of *man* in general which shows he did not have anything special in mind about his own experiences under the discipline of God. But the chastisement coming from the Lord will expose the vanity of man's earthly pretentions and desires. It will make them appear as flimsy as the moth that shines brilliantly in the light at the moment and in the next is gone out of sight.

Verse 12. This is another application to God for his mercy and guidance. *Stranger with thee* means David was here for a time only and would soon pass away. He wished to pass the few years of his life on this earth under the care of the Lord.

Verse 13. *Go hence* means to go from here. *Be no more* means he will not be living on the earth any more after death.

PSALMS 40

Verse 1. *Waited* is from an original that Strong defines (figuratively), "to expect." The verse means that David had hope in the Lord. If a person hopes for a thing he will be patient in waiting for it. This thought is given in Rom. 8: 25.

Verse 2. *Pit* and *miry clay* are figurative, meaning the lowly condition David's foes were forcing upon him. The *rock* was the foundation of truth on which God placed his feet along the pathway of life.

Verse 3. *A new song* denoted that David was enabled to sing with renewed spirits; that he could offer a song of rejoicing. God was so gracious to him that he was able to sing praises because of his triumph over his enemies. This was so much in evidence that others could realize it and were induced to respect the Lord.

Verse 4. Trust in the Lord is set over against being proud. We thus see that pride can be manifested in more than one way. Another contrast that is indicated is between trust in God on the one hand, and turning to lies on the other. Any statement that questions the faithfulness of God is a falsehood.

Verse 5. This verse simply teaches that the wonderful works of God are "too numerous to mention."

Verses 6-8. This paragraph is a prophecy of Christ and is quoted in Heb. 10: 5-7. David was writing by inspiration and with his prophetic eye he could see Christ as he came into the world to become the supreme sacrifice for sin. An extended explanation of this prophecy will be found in its proper place in the New Testament.

Verse 9. This verse is less definite than the preceding paragraph. It is prophetic of the work of Christ, and also describes the activities of David in the congregation of Israel over which he was king.

Verse 10. This also has the twofold application noted in the preceding verse. Both David and Christ imparted their knowledge of God to the people.

Verse 11. David came back to his personal needs, and, as he had so often done, prayed for the mercies of God.

Verse 12. *Evils* and *iniquities* are used in the same sense, referring to the afflictions that David was suffering. They had been caused by his enemies and were severe enough to "break his heart."

Verse 13. David feared he would be overwhelmed by his trouble unless the Lord gave him speedy assistance.

Verse 14. *Ashamed and confounded* means to be humiliated and defeated.

Verse 15. *Desolate for a reward* denoted that David's enemies were to find no way out of their humiliation. *Aha, aha* is a term of ridicule.

Verse 16. David prayed for the favor of God to come on certain persons. It was on condition, however, that they reverence and serve Him.

Verse 17. *Poor and needy* did not refer to temporal possessions, for David had a sufficiency of those things and to spare. It was said with reference to his human weaknesses as if he would have said, "I need thee every hour." *Make no tarrying* is an expression of earnestness in pleading for divine help.

PSALMS 41

Verse 1. So much of the activity of mankind is for the gaining of the things of this world that selfishness has become one of the most outstanding traits. Because of that fact we observe that David has very frequently referred to the fine but rare practice of helping the poor. So this is another verse to show how the Lord considers the subject and how he will treat the persons concerned.

Verse 2. This verse expresses the same thoughts as the first verse. God has such tender regard for the poor that he will bless the man who has a like regard.

Verse 3. *Make* is from HAPHAK which Strong defines, "a primitive root; to turn about or over; by implication to change, overturn, return, pervert." It means that when the merciful man is on a bed of sickness, the Lord will take care of him.

Verse 4. David had been good to the poor and therefore had reason to expect the favor of God. His confession of sin did not refer to any specific act that we know of here. The humble servants of God are always willing to acknowledge their weakness.

Verse 5. David prayed for the death of his enemies. That was a military age when physical force was often used against an antagonist. However, he never believed in using any unlawful means to defeat even his personal enemies. He wished to have the result come through the Lord, hence his frequent prayer on that subject.

Verse 6. This means that when David's enemy asked for a visit with him it proved to be in hypocrisy. *Speaketh vanity* means that the conversations the enemy had were empty and not sincere. The real motive he had was to catch something from David about which he could spread some gossip.

Verse 7. This verse describes the kind of opposition that was waged against David. The enemies would *whisper* or hold secret counsel against him, plotting some way to injure him.

Verse 8. When David would appear to be hurt by the action of his enemies, they would pretend to believe they had conquered him.

Verse 9. This is another passage with twofold application. The personal experiences of David were so much like those that came to Jesus that occasionally the circumstances were described in language that could be used as a prophecy. David's close personal associates often proved to be his personal enemies, and took advantage of their confidential relationship with him to injure him. (As an example of such a fact see the case of Absalom in 2 Samuel 15.) This passage is quoted by Jesus in John 13: 18 where he applies it to himself and Judas.

Verse 10. *Raise me up* meant to help David against his enemies, and as it applied to Jesus it meant to bring him up from the grave. *Requite them* means to punish the enemies according to their just deserts.

Verse 11. Both with David and Christ, when God came into the situation, what seemed to be a triumph for the enemies was turned into their defeat.

Verse 12. *Integrity* is another word for steadiness in an innocent life. As a reward for such a life God upheld David and gave him assurance of his continued favor.

Verse 13. *Everlasting* means "agelasting" or endless. God always was in existence and hence there could be found no end to his existence in either direction, past or future. That is the meaning of the expression *FROM everlasting TO everlasting*. *Amen and amen* is a phrase intended as a very emphatic sanction of truths just expressed.

PSALMS 42

Verse 1. A *hart* is a male of the deer family. It is a timid creature and will flee from any indication of danger. In its fright and excitement it will become exhausted and long for water. David used the circumstance to compare his thirst for the Lord. Jesus pronounced a blessing on those who have such an appetite (Matt. 5: 6).

Verse 2. This verse is an emphasis on the preceding one. David longed for the spiritual presence of God.

Verse 3. Of course this is figurative, meaning his life had consisted very much of lamentations over the mistreatment from his enemies.

Verse 4. Many of the men who were his enemies had previously gone into the house of God. Now that something had turned them against David he felt the sting of their enmity all the more because of indications of their insincerity.

Verse 5. This verse is an effort to David to rouse himself from his despondency and think of the goodness of God. He had been helped many times before, so now why allow himself to be so discouraged?

Verse 6. This verse is more along the line of the preceding one. *Land of Jordan* means the land made famous by the noted river. David recalled the multitude of wonders that God had wrought in that land and took renewed courage by trusting in Him.

Verse 7. Waters and floods and other like terms are used to compare the trials to which man is often subjected. David was not criticizing God, yet he believed that the afflictions his enemies were suffered to pour upon him was due to the will of God and for some good reason.

Verse 8. This is another effort at self-cheer over the final goodness of God. *Daytime* and *night* are opposite terms and used to indicate completeness of divine favor.

Verse 9. This talking-to-himself sort of discussion was a form of exhortation intended by David to get himself out of the mire of despondency. It was also for the purpose of advice for those who would read his writing.

Verse 10. David compared the thrusts of his enemies to the wounds caused by a sword. He was always greatly grieved when the reality of God was questioned.

Verse 11. See my comments at v. 5 for application to this verse.

PSALMS 43

Verse 1. The word for *nation* also means race or people and is so used in this place. The reference is to them as individuals and not as an organized group, for David was a member of the Jewish nation himself and would not wish to be separated from it. But many of his fellow citizens were his personal enemies and worked against him secretly. He prayed for God to deal with them as they deserved.

Verse 2. *God of my strength* denotes that David could feel strong only in God. Paul taught the same truth in 2 Cor. 12: 10; Eph. 6: 10. The verse contains another effort to bestir himself and shake off his feeling of despair.

Verse 3. David expressed confidence in the Word of God and prayed for more of it to be sent forth. He wished to be led by it according to the idea he expressed elsewhere. (ch. 119: 133). *Holy hill* and *tabernacle* refers to the temple which was the place where God's name was recorded. It was the place where the national worship was conducted and where the spiritual interests of the people of God were centered.

Verse 4. Both of the altars were at the temple and the sacrifices and incense were offered thereon. David looked to that service for help in times of spiritual need. While in that vicinity he engaged in praise service in connection with the musical instruments that he had originated.

Verse 5. This verse is in the same mood as many others of David's utterances, and upon which I have already made frequent comments. I will add, however, that while he wrote from the standpoint of his personal experiences, he was an inspired writer and issued his instructions for the benefit of his readers. Hence his many exhortations to rely on the goodness of God and trust him for his grace.

PSALMS 44

Verse 1. The *hearing* that David mentioned had a figurative meaning. He was referring to the events that occurred many years before he was born. When people accepted and observed the sayings of God's Word they were said to be hearing it. This principle is what is meant in Heb. 2: 1, for the things that "we have heard" had been said long before that day, and had been transmitted to the future generations in the writings of the apostles of Christ.

Verse 2. *Heathen* and *people* denoted the nations living in Canaan when the Israelites reached the land. *Plantedst them* means God settled his own people in the land.

Verse 3. This does not mean that the children of Israel did not have to use the sword, for they did. But that would not have conquered the heathen without the help of God. *Light of thy countenance* means that God's face was toward the Israelites for their good and prompted him to fight for them.

Verse 4. God's right to be ruler over all was the idea David meant to express in this verse. Clothed with such power and might he could decree that *Jacob* (the Israelites) be delivered, and their enemies be put to shame.

Verse 5. David's confidence of victory over his enemies was based on his trust in the Lord. Lack of such faith caused the people to murmur when the spies formed their evil conclusions about the land. (Num. 13 and 14.)

Verse 6. This verse repeats the sentiments of the preceding one, with a specification on the negative side. It does not mean that no weapons were to be used, but that such weapons would succeed only when used in the service of God.

Verse 7. This verse starts with *but*, which verifies the comments I have made on the preceding one. Instead of relying on his material weapons for victory, David ascribes it to the help from the Lord.

Verse 8. *Boast* is not used in a bad sense. It is true the word usually has the idea of vanity and display. But it also may be used as an expression of gratitude, and of recognition of the true value of the things one possesses. It is used in that sense by David in this verse. For *selah* see my comments at ch. 3: 2.

Verse 9. From here on through several verses the psalmist seems to have reversed his feeling of triumph through the Lord. He complained of the misfortunes that he and his people had suffered at the hands of the enemies. Again it should be remembered that he wrote "as a man," yet was directed in his expressions by the Lord so that they became prophetic of the experiences that God's people will be suffered to receive in the future. (See comments at ch. 10: 1.)

Verse 10. *Turn back* means to retreat from enemy. *Spoil for themselves* refers to the act of taking their possessions from them.

Verse 11. This means that the people of God had been given over to the enemy for slaughter. In attacking a flock of sheep, some would escape the immediate destruction by the wolves of the heathen, but would be scattered out over that territory and would be exposed to the dangers of future attacks.

Verse 12. This verse is a figurative reference to a bad bargain for the purpose of comparison. If an article should be sold for a price far below its true value it would be said that it was "just given away." Of course such a transaction would not leave the "seller" any profit.

Verse 13. If the people were neglected by their master, the witnesses would take it as a victory for themselves and would give forth expressions of ridicule.

Verse 14. A *byword* as used here means that the enemies considered themselves superior to the Israelites and formed their witty sayings in the manner that would hold the victims in contempt. A *shaking of the head* was a gesture of fun-making of the unfortunate people of God.

Verse 15. An experience like that just described would affect a man of God with a feeling of humiliation. David was given that feeling by the treatment imposed on him.

Verse 16. Actual physical contact did not always take place between David and his enemies. A reproaching voice from them tortured him about as severely as if he had been attacked bodily.

Verse 17. Let the reader please keep in mind the remarks at ch. 10: 1 and v. 9 in this chapter. Constancy to God in spite of afflictions is the leading idea of the verse considered in this paragraph.

Verse 18. A true servant of God will not waver nor step aside from the pathway of duty because of persecutions. He will press on in the good and the right way regardless of the mistreatment from the enemy.

Verse 19. A *dragon* was some kind of monster and meant death to those who were so unfortunate as to be thrown into its vicinity. It was used here to illustrate the rough treatment from the enemy that manifested his characteristics.

Verse 20. the proviso *if* in this verse refers to what might have been the misdeeds of God's people. They were sometimes guilty, and when they were the dealings they got from the Lord was a just punishment. But at other times their afflictions were suffered to come on them as a test of their faith. Such afflictions were administered through the agency of the enemy.

Verse 21. Outward actions can be seen and known by any person of ordinary intelligence. Only God can know the hidden motives of the heart. That is why he not only can see and punish the stretching out of the hands (a visible gesture) to a strange god, but he knows if his people forget the name of the true God wihch would be *the secret of the heart* mentioned in this verse.

Verse 22. Unknown to the psalmist, his prophetic eye was lifted to see some events of the far-off future. The events, however, were to be similar to the ones he had just been writing about, in that they pertained to some persecutions heaped upon God's servants in the days of the apostles. Paul quotes this in Rom. 8: 36 and applies it to the experiences that he and other Christians were having. No one man could literally be *killed all the day long*. The meaning is that he was in danger constantly.

Verse 23. This verse is a plea for the mercy of God. It is similar to many other passages which we have been considering.

Verse 24. This is more along the same line. When the enemy gets forward with his program of persecutions, it would seem that God was hiding his face from the scene.

Verse 25. The terms in this verse are used figuratively and refer to the state of humiliation to which the enemy had brought God's people.

Verse 26. David did not make any special claim for help on the basis of merit, but asked for it on the ground of mercy.

PSALMS 45

Verse 1. *Inditing* is from RACHASH and Strong defines it, "a primitive root; to gush." Dr. Hull renders it, "bubbling over." The thought is that David was so full of the great subject that his heart was overflowing. He was eager to recite the *things* or sentences he had *made* (formed) concerning the king. He was so enthused over the subject that he felt as if he could speak with as much ease as an able scribe could write it, which is why he compared his tongue to the pen of such a writer.

Verse 2. The pronouns are in the 2nd person but refer to David. This is a clear and specific example of a fact described previously, that an inspired man could write by the dictation of the Spirit, yet write about himself as if he were another. See the comments at ch. 10: 1. In the present verse David was considering the many favors he had received from God.

Verse 3. Much of the fighting was done with the sword. To gird it on the thigh meant to make ready for action, and the verse was worded in view of the assurance David had of success in his conflicts.

Verse 4. It is well to observe that *truth and righteousness* formed the basis of his expected success. Happy is the man whose triumphs are always a result of that kind of motive.

When the *right hand* is said to do things it means the things being done by the hand of the person are right. Thus the activities of such a person would result in practical teaching for others. This teaching would consist of the terrible things that were to be feared or respected.

Verse 5. The success of the conflicts with the enemy is the subject of this verse.

Verses 6, 7. Again the Spirit saw such a likeness between David's personal experiences or circumstances and those to happen to Christ, that a noted prophecy of the latter was dictated to the psalmist. This paragraph is quoted in Heb. 1: 8, 9 and applied to Christ. He is here referred to by the name of God because that is the family name and he is a member of the divine family. It is a prophecy of the eternal character of his kingdom, and the same that is predicted in Dan. 2:44. A scepter is a sort of baton or rod that a king on the throne holds, somewhat after the manner of a judge's gavel. It indicates authority to call a session to order and then preside. In the present case the scepter was held rightfully because the ruler not only loved righteousness but had hated wickedness. *Oil of gladness* is a figurative expression. In ancient times it was a custom to pour olive oil on the head of a person who was to become a ruler or other important public servant. Olive oil was the sole material for artificial light, and the pouring of it over the head of a prospective ruler signified that he was endowed with the light of truth so that he could administer his office efficiently. When oil is referred to figuratively it means the person is showered upon with special favors resulting in his feeling of gladness.

Verse 8. Having worded his statements in such a manner that they had more specific application to Christ, David continued to apply them in that direction. Unknown to him (as a man), he wrote several verses that are highly figurative and describing the honor and splendor that would be given to King Jesus. The figures are drawn from the attention that was anciently given to persons of high rank. The spices named indicated a station in the life generally enjoyed by those being regarded with high esteem among the people. Ivory is a valuable substance and was used extensively in works of art where beauty and strength were desired. No building was literally made all of it but much of some of them was overlaid and paneled with the material. That was especially true of the residences of kings and other persons of high rank. (See 1 Ki. 10:18; 22:39.) The furniture of such buildings was sometimes also covered with ivory according to Amos 6:4. To leave a building so appointed, in whose wardrobes was an abundance of garments filled with the odor of these precious spices—to leave all that and go out among the lower ranks of the people would indeed be a condescension. That is why a certain religious hymn, composed in view of the humbleness of Jesus, starts with the words *out of the ivory palaces.* That hymn is correct for those words are a part of this marvelous group of verses on the prophecy of Christ.

Verse 9. This is another figurative verse, comparing the honor to be due the King of Kings to the splendor heaped upon royal persons in ancient times.

Verse 10. This verse pictures the attractions of the king's palace as being so great that any daughter would prefer it to the accommodations provided by her own people.

Verse 11. The daughter who will show a preference described in the preceding verse, will be honored by the king and will be considered beautiful by him. Transferring the thought to the time of Christ, persons who will prefer to be part of the bride of Christ over their earthly relations will be honored by Him. (See Matt. 10:37.)

Verse 12. Tyre was an important city in a foreign country. Bringing a *gift* was a custom in ancient times by which one person recognized another person or kingdom. (See comments at Gen. 32:13; 1 Sam. 10:27.) The practice is referred to here to indicate the respect that was to come to the individual of whom David is writing.

Verse 13. It is indicative of the high estate of a king that his family can be equipped with the gorgeous raiment. Such a state was predicted for the king in the mind of the Spirit as he directed David in this wonderful chapter.

Verse 14. This verse continues along the same line as that in the preceding one. *Needlework* was a leading finery of old times and indicated a state of delicate dignity.

Verse 15. *Gladness* and *rejoicing* are practically the same in meaning.

The first refers especially to the state of one's mind and the second is the outward expression of it. The companions of the king's daughter will come into the palace possessed with such sentiments because of the favorable surroundings.

Verse 16. This verse could not apply literally to Christ for he had no descendants. (Isa. 53:8 and Acts 8:33.) But he was to have spiritual seed who were to be made *princes.* This was fulfilled when his disciples became kings according to 1 Cor. 4:8; 1 Pe. 2:9; Rev. 5:10.

Verse 17. The perpetuity of Christ's reign is clearly predicted here. *For ever and ever* has the same application as Dan. 2:44.

PSALMS 46

Verse 1. *Present help* means the assistance that does not wait for some convenient time in the future. It comes to the aid of one at the very time of his trouble.

Verse 2. Genuine confidence in the Lord will not shrink at sight of any apparent calamity. Regardless of all charges threatened by the enemy, God will protect his own.

Verse 3. Most of this verse is on the thought of the preceding one. *Selah* is explained at Ch. 3:2.

Verse 4. Rivers have always been regarded as important creations, both for diversion and as a necessity. A river was used to water the first garden (Gen. 2:10), the Nile River supported the land of Egypt (called "Sihor" in Isa. 23:3), and the city of Babylon was adorned by the great Euphrates. Now we have David prophesying the most important of all rivers, the one to gladden the city of God in the Life Beyond. (See Rev. 22:1, 2.)

Verse 5. The presence of God would assure any city of protection against harm.

Verse 6. The *heathen* refers to all people who are not citizens of the Lord's city. It does not necessarily mean they are idolaters. When such people realize the might of God's voice they are put to shame and caused to rage in their defeat.

Verse 7. A *host* may signify any large group of men. It is generally used, however, to mean the organized army of warriors of a nation. David was a man of war and very logically thought of God from that standpoint.

It would mean sure protection to have the Commander in Chief of heaven on one's side. *God of Jacob* means the God whom Jacob served.

Verse 8. Strong defines the original for *desolations* as "*consternation.*" The idea is that God's great works all over the earth had filled the *heathen* with astonishment. The heathen are the people referred to in v. 6.

Verse 9. Wars have been conducted from David's time until now and the Lord knew it would be so. We do not believe that an inspired man would contradict facts. The latter half of the verse shows he means that God ended or defeated the wars aimed against the righteous people who were worshiping the true Lord of the earth.

Verse 10. David was speaking for God in this verse. *Be still* means not to be troubled, just as Jesus calmed his disciples in John 14: 1. God assured his servants that he would overcome the heathen and would be exalted in all the earth.

Verse 11. This verse does not present any new thoughts. The psalmist concludes the chapter as he began it, calling for praises unto the Lord.

PSALMS 47

Verse 1. Clapping the hands was a physical expression of what was in the mind. God had shown his power over the enemy and the people had reason to rejoice.

Verse 2. *Terrible* means to be dreaded by the enemy and reverenced by the people of God.

Verse 3. God will use his own people as instruments to bring the nations of the world under defeat because of their wickedness.

Verse 4. *Jacob* was the father of the 12 tribes of Israel and hence the name is often used to signify the nation as a whole. God willed that his people should have the good things of the world, to make a proper use thereof. That is why it was said that he chose the inheritance for them.

Verse 5. A *shout* was an indication of triumph in battle (Ex. 32: 18), therefore the term was used in that sense in this verse.

Verse 6. A shout for victory should be followed by a song of praise to the leader in the battle, for it is he who made the victory possible.

Verse 7. *King* is used in its strongest sense. The word frequently is used with reference to secondary rulers. That is why Jesus is called King of kings. The same thought is meant by the word here as used of God. There is no ruler or power in the earth who is as great as our God. *With understanding* means to use intelligent expressions in praising God; not merely making a noise. The same idea was meant when Paul instructed Christians to sing "with the understanding," or, in such a manner that the hearers could understand what was being sung. (1 Cor. 14: 15.)

Verse 8. *Throne of his holiness* means that God's throne is one from which a holy reign is administered, such as that always issuing from God.

Verse 9. *Shields of the earth* means the protection provided the people of the earth is from the *God of Abraham*, the God whom Abraham worshiped. *Together* is from YACHAD and Strong defines it, "properly a unit, i.e. (adverbially) unitedly." Since the *shields* or protection had been assured to the people of God, they were unitedly trusting in the divine help and were assembling together without fear. The same thought is expressed in Micah 4: 4, which is a prophecy of conditions to be enjoyed in the kingdom of Christ. It is what is meant by the oft-repeated expression that "we may assemble to worship God without fear of molestation."

PSALMS 48

Verse 1. The *city* referred to is Jerusalem and the *mountain* is the government of God which is holy.

Verse 2. This verse pertains to the same subject as the preceding one. *Situation* is from an original that means "elevation." It does not refer to it from a physical standpoint, but from the high honor that God had brought unto it. *Mount Zion* was that part of the city where David had his headquarters and aften called "city of David."

Verse 3. The people came to recognize the institution of the Lord as one to offer protection to the righteous.

Verse 4. *The kings* meant the prominent persons of the earth; especially those who would have harmed God's people had they not been afraid.

Verse 5. When these would-be enemies saw the safety provided for the people of God they were *troubled*. That was because they realized they would be the loser should they attempt any harm to the righteous.

Verse 6. *Pain . . . travail* means the pains accompanying childbirth. According to Gen. 3: 16 it was the decree of God that women should experience some pain in bearing children. After the sin of Eve these pains were to be increased. Any unnatural means, therefore, used to try to avoid these pains is an attempt to set aside the will of God. These pains are characterized with such terrible keenness of body and such dreadful disturbances of mind, that the situation is used to compare other conditions of unusual distress.

Verse 7. In 1 Ki. 22: 48 is an account of this very fact. The great merchandising projects of man are nothing when subjected to the power of God.

Verse 8. David meant he had seen demonstrations of the power of God, as well as having heard about it. See comments at ch. 3: 2 on meaning of *Selah*.

Verse 9. Kindnes that is prompted by love is more to be desired than that performed merely from a sense of duty. All of God's acts of kindness are thus prompted.

Verse 10. This means that wherever the name of God had reached, it had been given the praise of men. *Right hand* means the things that are done by the hand of God are right.

Verse 11. *Judah* refers to the nation and *Zion* means the capitol in Jerusalem.

Verses 12, 13. This paragraph is a challenge to the world to inspect the institutions of the Lord. The people are invited to take notice of all the strong points and then report it to their generations after them. The inplication is that when the world realizes the perfection of God's great works it will make them have deep respect.

Verse 14. The name *God* is from an original form that especially means supreme ruler. A Being who could provide such a bulwark as that described in the preceding paragraph is worthy to rule. Such ruling would be a safe guidance throughout life.

PSALMS 49

Verse 1. This is a call of admonishing for the world to respect the God of Israel.

Verse 2. No man is so low that the mercy of God will not come down to him. No one is so high as to be above needing the Lord. The rich in worldly goods are as nothing without God. The poor in material wealth may find true riches in the things that God provides for all his faithful servants.

Verse 3. The *wisdom* and *understanding* that David meant he would use would come from God. On such matters he proposed to meditate. (See ch. 1: 2.)

Verse 4. This verse is quoted in Matt. 13: 35 and applied to the teaching of Jesus. It would be appropriate for David to connect his poetic and prophetic sayings with praises on musical instruments for they were his specialty. But the central idea was a prediction of the revealing through the teaching of Jesus of hitherto unknown truths.

Verse 5. *Wherefore* means "why," and David was expressing confidence that he need fear no evil effects from his enemy. That was true even when such evils were *of my heels*, which means they were so near as to be "at his heels."

Verses 6, 7. The worthlessness of worldly riches for the soul is the subject of this paragraph. Could money be used to save the soul of men it would have been unnecessary for Christ to die.

Verse 8. This verse will seem plain by noting that the antecedent of *it* is *wealth* in the preceding paragraph. And *ceaseth* is from CHADAI which Strong defines, "A primitive root; properly to be flabby, i.e. (by implication) desist; be lacking or idle." The meaning of the verse is that wealth would be for ever unable to ransom a man's soul; either before or after death of the body.

Verse 9. Man's body dies in spite of his wealth while the soul continues to exist. That proves that material wealth is not good enough to save the soul from the judgment of God.

Verse 10. All classes of humanity are subject to death. *Brutish* is from an original that means, "subject to consumption or decay," and is a characteristic of mortal man. When the human being succumbs to the universal rule of death, all his wealth must be left behind and hence cannot benefit him after death. Paul gives us this same truth in 1 Tim. 6: 7.

Verse 11. It would be no particular wrong for a man to call his land by his own name. The point David was making was on the motive that caused him to do so. He seemed to think that future generations would make no change in their property, and that the personal name of a former owner would always be appropriate.

Verse 12. In many respects man is honored above the beasts. But in the matter of physical death he is no better than the beasts of the field.

Verse 13. The generations that follow the above foolish men do not profit by their experience. Instead, they *approve their sayings;* that is, they act and speak just as their forefathers did.

Verse 14. Mortal man is as frail as the sheep of the pasture in the presence of death. The *upright* means those whose faith in God causes them to fashion their lives in view of a better existence to come. Such shall have dominion or have the advantage over the ones who live for this world only.

Verse 15. This is one of the Old Testament passages that teach belief in another life after this fleshly one. The soul of man does not go to the *grave* as we use that word. In the Old Testament the word SHEOL is used to signify both the place for the body after death, and the unseen state of the soul. It corresponds to HADES in the Greek New Testament. The present verse, therefore, means that God will bring the soul out of the unseen state at the general resurrection. *Selah* is explained at ch. 3: 2.

Verse 16. The lesson in this verse is that we should not envy others when they become rich. Their wealth and other apparent advantages will do them no good at last.

Verse 17. This verse verifies the comments on the preceding one. It also agrees with the statement of Paul in 1 Tim. 6: 7.

Verse 18. The worldly-rich man enjoyed his goods *while he lived.* Other men also congratulated him on his success.

Verse 19. The rich man will go the same way his fathers went. *Never see light* means he will never come back to earth to live. (Job 7: 9, 10.)

Verse 20. A man may be flooded with all these worldly honors while in this life. But if he does not use them according to *understanding* he will be no better than the beasts when the time comes from him to die.

PSALMS 50

Verse 1. The original for *God* means a supreme ruler, and that for *Lord* means the self-existent One. Both are applied to the same Being and it is affirmed that he hath spoken. *Called* means that all people of the earth are commanded to hear the divine voice from morning until night.

Verse 2. *Zion* was that part of Jerusalem where the temple was located. The government of God on earth was administered from that place. *Perfection of beauty* indicates that real beauty in its perfect form shines from that source. It is about the same thought as expressed by "beauty of holiness" in ch. 29: 2.

Verse 3. *Shall come* means that God will be in evidence. The *fire* refers to the fiery judgments that he will send on the earth.

Verse 4. *Heavens* and *earth* are used figuratively; that is, God's call was universal.

Verse 5. There was a general call to all inhabitants of the earth (v. 4), but this is a special call to the professed people of God. *Covenant by sacrifice* refers to the great institution of national service, the central item of which was the sacrifices of animals and the shedding of their blood. (See Heb. 9: 22.)

Verse 6. This verse is similar in thought to ch. 19: 1.

Verse 7. It was true that God had a covenant with his people which required material sacrifices. However, such services were not enough unless the general conduct was right. Israel had often lapsed into a mere formality with their altar service and that was displeasing to God. In other words, the ritualistic features of the covenant could not be depended upon to make up for their shortcomings in personal life. This thought will be prominent in the next several verses.

Verse 8. God was not going to charge his people with failure to offer the sacrifices or burnt offerings. They had not been short in such performances.

Verse 9. *I will not take,* etc. God was not calling for more gifts of this kind for they had brought their quota along that line.

Verses 10, 11. The covenant of sacrifices in the first place was not for the purpose of supplying a need for the Lord. The very creatures that were being offered in sacrifice had already been the possessions of the Lord.

Verse 12. Even if God were in personal need of anything, he would not look to man to supply it. The very things that man could present were the creation of God.

Verse 13. God is a spirit and has no bodily use for the food of animals. It was not for such use that animal sacrifices were ordained.

Verse 14. With this verse the psalmist begins to show what it is that God desires in addition to the material sacrifices. Generally speaking it consists in the spiritual devotions out of a pure heart.

Verse 15. If God's people are consistent in their professed service, they may call upon Him with the assurance that he will hear and bless them.

Verse 16. God does not ask unrighteous persons to proclaim his Word. If a wicked person preaches the statutes of the Lord they will still be the truth. And those who hear and accept it will be blessed. But the wicked speaker will get no reward from God.

Verse 17. When a wicked man presumes to preach the word of the Lord it is from the wrong motive. Were he moved by the right purpose he would not himself remain a wicked man. But in his inconsistency the Lord regards him as having cast the truth away.

Verse 18. The preceding verses made general charges of the one-sided lives of the people. Some specific accusations will next be made, such as theft and adultery.

Verses 19, 20. Deception and evil speaking are charged against them.

Verse 21. The longsuffering of God had been mistaken for approval of their evil lives. The time for their chastisement finally came and God was rebuking them.

Verse 22. The full severity of God's judgments had not as yet been heaped upon the people but they were warned to repent or such treatment would come.

Verse 23. Sincere praise will redound to the glory of God. Hence it is that the Lord promised salvation to those who ordered their *conversation* or manner of life according to the divine will.

PSALMS 51

General remarks. This remarkable psalm was composed in connection with the sad affair of David and Bathsheba. The student should now read carefully the 11th and 12th chapters of 2 Samuel which will give him the historical setting. There was every indication of genuine repentance on the part of David. Furthermore, not only did he fully repent and make unreserved acknowledgment of his sin to the prophet, but God fully pardoned him. That is, he was spared all personal or bodily punishment for it, though he was required to undergo some bitter experiences and losses as a result of his sin. And while he was forgiven his sin upon repentance and confession, as good a man as David would naturally feel humiliated by the circumstance. We know that when God "forgives" he also "forgets," and that the frequent pleas in this psalm do not indicate that David needed more than once to be forgiven for the same transgression. Instead, we should regard the repeated expressions as parts of one great supplication before the throne of God for mercy, in answer to which he was fully pardoned and reinstated in the favor of Jehovah.

Verse 1. David believed that mercy from God toward a guilty man would have to be on the ground of lovingkindness and not on the merit of man. Hence we often read such expressions as the ones in this verse.

Verse 2. *Wash* was used figuratively because there was no physical ceremony to be performed in the case. The Mosaic system did have much to do in the way of literal cleansing. All figurative expressions are based on literal facts or actions, or at least on the possibility of such facts. David had such as that in his mind when he composed this verse and several to follow in the chapter.

Verse 3. *Ever before me* is rendered by Moffatt, "never out of my mind." David knew that God forgets when he forgives, but that did not prevent him from remembering the awful affair himself.

Verse 4. *Against thee only* should not be interpreted to mean that the persons involved had not been sinned against. Bathsheba had been violated and her husband had been killed at the instigation of David. The original for *only* has a meaning that is equivalent to "chiefly." God is the creator of all things and persons in the universe. For that reason, any injury done to things or persons is the same as being done to Him. David used the expression in view of that fundamental truth.

Psalms 51: 5-17

On that basis, also, God would be considered *justified* when he condemned a guilty man.

Verse 5. This verse is relied upon by the advocates of "Adamic sin" or "inherited depravity." By that is meant that human beings come into the world in a state of sin, having received it from the mother at the time of conception, she having received the same condition from her mother, and so on back to Adam and Eve. The doctrine is not only contrary to the general teaching of the Bible, but is not taught by this verse, as a critical study of the words will show. The words *I was shapen* are from CHIL and Young translates it, "To be formed, brought forth." Strong defines it, "A primitive root; properly to twist or whirl (in a circular or spiral manner), i.e. (specifically) to dance, to writhe in pain (especially of parturition [childbirth]) or fear." *Conceive* is from YACHAM and Strong's first definition is, "a primitive root; probably to be hot." It is the word for "warm" in Eccl. 4: 11 where the warmth is caused by the nearness of one body to another, not by one body being enclosed by another. A child being warmed in the arms of his mother would thus be "warmed" in the sense of the present verse. With this critical information, considered in the light of the general teaching of the Bible, the meaning of the verse is clear. It shows that the conditions described by David were dated at and after his birth. That will disprove the doctrine that the stain of sin is attached to a person before he is born. We are not told why David mentioned this subject in connection with his own conduct. However, we have no right to assume what his purpose was and then build up a human theory on the basis of that assumption.

Verse 6. This means that God requires man to be sincere in his thoughts. David had shown that quality when the prophet came to chastise him for his sin.

Verse 7. *Hyssop* was used as an instrument to sprinkle the blood of animals in the sacrifices under the Mosaic system (Num. 19: 18). It is used here in a figurative sense. (See comments at v. 2.) Strictly speaking, nothing can be "whiter" than something else. The expression *whiter than snow* is figurative and means to emphasize the state of purity in one whom God has cleansed.

Verse 8. David's bones had not been literally broken. He was so overwhelmed by the greatness of his conviction that he used the expression for comparison.

Verse 9. David would not even try to minimize his transgressions which he considered were very grievous. But he asked that God in his mercy would overlook them and *blot out* or forgive him his guilt.

Verse 10. The outward and physical acts of David's sins had been ended and he had bitterly mourned in repentance over them. The inner man was next considered in relation to God. *Create . . . clean heart* meant to help him have a heart that would be clean of any desire to repeat such a sin as he had committed.

Verse 11. David was an inspired man and such an honor would not be fitting in one who was guilty of such grievous sins as he had committed unless he received cleansing from the guilt. In that view he made this earnest plea to God for divine mercy.

Verse 12. *Restore* means to reinstate him in the spiritual favor of the Lord.

Verse 13. A man who is under the guilt of transgressions himself is in no position to exhort others. David wished to be cleared of the guilt hanging over him so that he could contact others who were out of the way.

Verse 14. David had been guilty of violating the moral code. He also had been guilty of bloodshed and asked to be forgiven all guilt.

Verse 15. *Open thou my lips* means for God to suffer him to speak the words that would be appropriate under the circumstances.

Verse 16. This verse and the following are related to v. 15. Material sacrifices would not atone for the terrible sin that David had committed. Could such things be sufficient to "balance the account" in God's sight, David would gladly have provided a myriad of the best animals. He knew that God could not be "bought off" in that way.

Verse 17. Instead of offering animal sacrifices to atone for such a sinful circumstance, David named the kind that God would desire and accept. It was a *broken spirit* and a *contrite heart*. That means that the whole being of the guilty one should be brought to the foot of the throne of God, and be prostrated in humble and sincere reverence to the God of all mercy.

Verse 18. This is an exhortation addressed to himself. David means that he should accompany the confession of v. 17 with practical acts of service to Zion.

Verse 19. *Then* means that after showing his faith (penitence) by his works, he could consistently resume the animal sacrifices on the altar in Jerusalem.

PSALMS 52

Verse 1. The preceding psalm was devoted to David's personal sin and he did not spare himself from severe condemnation. He can very consistently address his remarks now to other sinners. They had been boastful of their wrongdoings while David repented of his in bitterness. The constancy of the goodness of God should cause the workers of iniquity to become ashamed of themselves.

Verse 2. A razor can be so sharp that it would cut a gash unnoticed by the victim for the moment. The fact is used to compare the deceitfulness of a wicked tongue.

Verse 3. It would be had enough were a man to put evil and good on a par with each other in one's estimation. It is much worse when he prefers the evil. See ch. 3:2 for explanation of *Selah*.

Verse 4. A tongue does not literally love immoral things. This means that a man who is deceitful loves to use his tongue to speak *devouring* or destructive words.

Verse 5. *Destroy* is used in the light of *devouring* in the preceding verse. Just as surely as a deceitful man would wish to injure an innocent victim, so God will bring that wicked man to utter ruin in the final outcome.

Verse 6. When the righteous people see the fate of a wicked man they will *fear* or respect the judgments of God. They will *laugh at* or belittle the wicked man who is receiving his just deserts.

Verse 7. David here described the man against whom he had been writing in this psalm. The wicked man's conduct was that of one who refused to let God lead him, but trusted in his own riches and other resources.

Verse 8. The olive tree was the principal or only source of artificial light in ancient times. The comparison David made was in that he was enlightened by being a true servant of God. Such service was rendered in the house of the Lord and it entitled him to the mercy of God for which he so often prayed.

Verse 9. David gave the Lord due credit for the favors he had received. *Wait on thy name* means to rely on the good name of God in the midst of the trials of life.

PSALMS 53

Verse 1. *Fool* is from NABAL and Strong defines it, "stupid; wicked (especially impious)." Young defines it, "Empty person, fool." It is the same word used as a proper noun in the case of the husband of Abigail in 1 Sam. 25: 25. That good woman commented on the appropriateness of the word as a name for her wicked and foolish husband. We should be able to see a logical reason for saying it is a fitting name for the kind of person being considered. He made the rash declaration that *there is no God*. It was not merely a denial of the existence of a supreme Being, which would have been foolish enough. This man affirmed something, and before one is prepared to make such a declaration he must be in possession of all the information that pertains to the subject. Unless this man had seen every inch of space in the universe he had no right to make the affirmation he did. We know that no man has seen all of the space, and he does not know but there could be a God in some place which he has not seen. Hence the statement, *there is no God*, is a rash one and no one but a fool would make it. The rest of the verse is a comment on the general character and conduct of a man who would be so rash as to make the declaration at the beginning of the verse. The plural pronoun *they* is used to mean that all persons are in a common class of evil workers who are guilty of this atheism.

Verse 2. *Looked down . . . to see if*, etc., is accommodative language. God knows all things at all times and does not have to make any investigation to find out. But the style of inspiration is to speak to man about the actions of God as if he were also a man. (See Rom. 6: 19.) The present verse means that God would classify all of the men, such as those who would be so rash as to deny the existence of a Supreme Being. In that class it will be seen that not a one would speak with understanding.

Verse 3. Belief in the existence of God is the strongest of motives for a righteous life. By that token we should not be surprised to see the atheists as a class of unrighteous men. These comments are the explanation of the present verse.

Verse 4. The line of thought becomes more specific. The evildoers whom David was considering especially were the persecutors of God's people. *Eat up my people* is a figure of speech, referring to the vicious treatment the unbelievers imposed on the people of the Lord.

Verse 5. Let not the reader be confused about the use of the personal pronouns. This is poetic language and is not bound by the strict rules of whether the pronouns are 1st, 2nd or 3rd person. The verse means that workers of iniquity were fearful when there should have been nothing to be afraid of had they been righteous persons. But since they were determined to injure the servants of righteousness, God had *scattered the bones*, which means the Lord had utterly defeated their purposes.

Verse 6. A general rescue of Israel from all opposition of their enemies is the primary sense of this verse. But in addition to that, the psalmist made a prediction (unconsciously perhaps to him) of the return of the nation from the great captivity, which was fulfilled in the books of Ezra and Nehemiah.

PSALMS 54

Verse 1. The name of God is worthy and his strength is infinite. With the two attributes of his Being he would be able to save to the uttermost.

Verse 2. *Hear* and *give ear* are similar expressions. They mean to grant unto David the relief he was desiring.

Verse 3. *Strangers* were those outside of David's group of friends. His *soul* or life was what they were seeking to destroy. *Not set God* means they did not respect God, therefore they would not respect his servant.

Verse 4. David believed God was his helper. One way of helping him was to strengthen his friends in their support of him. See comments at ch. 3: 2 for *Selah*.

Verse 5. *Reward evil* meant to put some form of punisment upon David's enemies. *Cut them off* denoted that the enemies would be prevented from carrying out their plots against David. *In thy truth* meant that God's dealing with the wicked enemies would be according to truth, that is, it would be the true way of dealing with them.

Verse 6. It is not enough merely to speak praises to God for his favors. David proposed to make an offering that would cost him something. The motive that was expressed in this verse for sacrificing to God was reverence for his *good name*.

Verse 7. God not only desired to save David from his enemies, but he was able to fulfill that desire through his mighty power.

PSALMS 55

Verse 1. *Prayer* and *supplication* differ chiefly in degree of intensity. The latter is a very earnest form of the former.

Verse 2. *Make a noise* means to be greatly agitated, not merely to produce a loud sound. The point was that David's troubles were so grievous that he was constrained to express himself with emphasis.

Verse 3. David's earnestness of voice in complaining of his afflictions was caused by a like voice of his enemies. They opposed him both in word and action.

Verse 4. *Terrors of death* is a strong expression of the intense feelings of David caused by his trials. He was not actually expecting death at the hands of his enemies, but the anxiety that was crowding up upon his heart was such as to suggest the extremity of death or the approach to it.

Verse 5. These feelings pertained to David's fleshly nature. His inner self had not given way to doubt as to the continued support from God.

Verse 6. This verse was another expression coming from the natural reaction of David to the heavy oppression from his enemies. It was but according to human nature longing for relief that he thought of the advantages of a bird when being pursued.

Verse 7. A lonely hiding in some far away wilderness would be preferable to the constant irritation that his enemies were causing David.

Verse 8. *Windy storm* is a figure of speech, referring to the tempestuous attacks upon David because of his service to God.

Verse 9. *Divide their tongues* meant to weaken the force of their stormy tirades against David. Those tirades had caused violence to occur in the city, destroying peace.

Verse 10. The agitation from the enemies of David was ceaseless or *day and night*.

Verse 11. *Deceit* and *guile* are practically the same, and refers to the underhanded methods that were used by the enemies of David.

Verses 12, 13. *It was not an enemy.* That is, it was not one who admitted he was an enemy although in reality he was one. It would be expected that an enemy would seek to injure his victim and such treatment would not cause much surprise. But for such treatment to come from a professed friend would be peculiarly painful.

Verse 14. This verse describes the close association that had been between David and some of the persons who were now acting the part of his enemies.

Verse 15. *Hell* is from a word that has various meanings. One of them is in reference to a state of forgetfulness. David had often prayed for the destruction of his enemies. In this verse he prayed for their complete overthrow. He gave a just reason for this wish; the existence of wickedness in their dwellings.

Verse 16. No earthly help would be effective against the workers of iniquity. David therefore put his trust in God and called upon him for security.

Verse 17. The frequency of David's prayers makes up the subject of this verse. A familiar church hymn is based on this thought, and it was also the practice of Daniel, both before and after the wicked edict signed by the king. (Dan. 6:10.)

Verse 18. A man might overcome his antagonist in battle and yet be in a terrible condition afterward. But David had been given victory with peace. *Many with me* means that many foes had contended with David.

Verse 19. The sense of this verse is as if it stated the reason why the wicked men did not change their ways; it was because they did not fear God.

Verse 20. *He* applies to the evil characters described in the preceding verse. These men were even covenant breakers, and had raised their hands against the very ones who would have been at peace with them.

Verse 21. The wicked character is still the antecedent of the pronoun. The verse describes a hypocrite who uses favorable words to hide the evil intentions that are in the heart. By thus misleading the victim he could be held within the grasp of the foe until the opportune time for striking.

Verse 22. This verse is identical in thought with 1 Pe. 5:7. No human being is able to bear the burdens of life without divine help. The original for *moved* would justify a stronger rendering, such as "to fall." That is better, for a person might be somewhat moved by the opposition of his enemies but yet not be cast down.

Verse 23. But God will cause the wicked men of the earth to be cast down and finally brought to complete ruin.

PSALMS 56

Verse 1. The reader has doubtless observed that David's conflicts with his enemies make up by far the greater portion of the book of Psalms. I know of no special reason for his troubles except his vigorous activities in behalf of the Israelite nation. There were many heathen nations in the land and surrounding territories and they were envious of the success that David was having. He was a successful warrior, yet he relied chiefly on the help of God for victory, hence such prayers as this verse.

Verse 2. The enemies of David outnumbered him, but when God is concerned in an issue numbers do not count; therefore, David called upon the *Most High* for help.

Verse 3. This verse means that David would fear his enemies were it not for his abiding trust in God.

Verse 4. David praised God for the surety of his Word. With the assurance that he had from this divine source, David was encouraged to defy all the powers of the flesh.

Verse 5. *Wrest my words* means David's enemies perverted his statements and gave to them a distorted meaning. That is the kind of tactics that dishonest foes often use. By a misuse of what a man says, his words can be made to have a meaning far different from what he intended.

Verse 6. This whole verse has a simple meaning; David's enemies grouped together to spy on him. When they saw what they thought was the right time they would make an attack on his *soul* or life.

Verse 7. The prayers of David were that his enemies be prevented from "getting away" with their iniquity.

God's *anger* in casting them down would be in the nature of righteous indignation and not in that of petty outbreak of temper.

Verse 8. *Tellest* is from CHAPHAR and defined, "A primitive root; properly to score with a mark as a tally or record, i.e. (by implication) to inscribe, and also to enumerate; intensively, to recount, i.e. celebrate."—Strong. The original for *wanderings* is defined by Strong by the one word, "exile," which refers to the many attempts by his enemies to isolate him by their floods of persecutions. Putting tears in a bottle would indicate they were to be preserved to be considered as a keepsake, in remembrance of some loved one who had shed them. The whole verse means that God notices and remembers the trials and sacrifices his servants experience for His sake.

Verse 9. The mere prayer of David to God would not cause his enemies to turn back or retreat. But such a prayer would bring forth the deliverance from God and that would compel the foes to halt.

Verse 10. The outstanding thought in this verse is the motive for David's praise for the Lord. It was because of his Word, and that had always been a prominent thought with the psalmist, as can be seen in his writings.

Verse 11. Two thoughts are set as opposites of each other. They are trust in God on one side and fear of man on the other.

Verse 12. *Thy vows* means the vows or pledges David had made to God. *Are upon me* means he was not intending to disregard them.

Verse 13. This verse is a recognition of past deliverance from serious evil. On that basis David believed God would again preserve him so that he could continue to serve him among those in the land of the living. In spite of the threatenings from mankind, David was willing and eager to portray his devotion to God in sight of the foes.

PSALMS 57

Verse 1. The bodily parts of God are like those of a human being and not a dumb creature. The comparison to *wings*, therefore, is figurative, and means that as the wings of a bird would provide a shelter, so the Lord would protect David in his trials.

Verse 2. The *cry* was an earnest prayer to God for help. God is the one who *performeth* whatever is done to protect the righteous from their enemies.

Verse 3. *Send from heaven* signifies the source from which all true help must come. The *mercy* that God will send forth will be according to *his truth*. See comments at ch. 3: 2 for meaning of *Selah*.

Verse 4. *Lions* are devouring beasts and fire is a tormenting, destructive element. *Spears, arrows* and *swords* are instruments of death. All of these things are used to compare the character of David's enemies.

Verse 5. As a comparison, David exalts God above the *heavens*. The word is plural and refers to the 1st and 2nd heavens. That means the regions of the air and the planets. Then the psalmist adds the earth in his comparison which makes it complete for the material universe. It would have been inappropriate to name the 3rd heaven, for that is where God dwells as a spiritual Being.

Verse 6. A net is a device of a general nature. It can be spread out in some expected path of the victim, and can be hidden from his view. Another means of capturing a victim is a pit, dug in the route to be traveled so that he will not see it until it is too late. It often occurs that the evil designer has laid his plot so long before that he has forgotten about it, and then he will become the victim of his own plot. In every place where *Selah* is used, the reader should see the comments at ch. 3: 2 whether I mention it or not.

Verse 7. *Fixed* means prepared or settled. It denotes that David was ready for whatever might be in store for him in the divine providence. It is a thought similar to the one in 1 Pe. 4: 1.

Verse 8. David was summoning his various resources to express praise for God.

Verse 9. David was inclined to praise God from personal sentiments. He also was not ashamed for others besides his own people to know of his devotion to God; he would praise him among the *nations* which means the heathen. It recalls our minds to the teaching of Jesus in Mark 8: 38.

Verse 10. *Heavens* and *clouds* are used as things for comparing the greatness of God's mercy. That is, the mercy of the Lord is not only extensive but it is of a high and holy or worthy kind.

Verse 11. The actual position of God cannot be changed by any man. *Be thou exalted* means that David was desirous of seeing God thus exalted.

PSALMS 58

Verse 1. The pronoun *ye* refers to the people who had shown so much unrighteousness. The question form of language here is really a criticism of their pretense to being good when their conduct did not agree with it.

Verse 2. *Weigh* means they would deal out their violence as a merchant would weigh out his goods to the people.

Verse 3. Advocates of "inherited sin" try to find their doctrine in this verse. When a statement is made that cannot be interpreted literally, some figurative or accommodative sense must be given to it. We know that a newborn infant cannot speak at all, therefore he could not *speak lies*. The word *estranged* also proves the writer was not using his language literally. This word means to turn aside or forsake the way. We know that an infant cannot perform anything of that nature. The verse, therefore, means that the tendency of human beings is to follow the fleshly desires, and that they manifest that tendency early in life. We all believe that doctrine, but it has no resemblance to that of the "inherited-sin" variety.

Verses 4, 5. Certain beasts and serpents can be charmed or held spellbound and thus rendered harmless. There are others that will not listen or pay any attention to any attempts at fascination. The latter is used to compare the enemies of righteousness. They will viciously attack those whose lives are better than theirs, then turn a deaf ear to the protests of the victims.

Verse 6. All of the expressions in this verse are used figuratively. The desire of David was that God would deal roughly with his adversaries.

Verse 7. *Continually* has no word in the original and is really against the thought of the writer. The idea is of something that makes a show of activity for a while, then ceases. A stream that runs continually does not vanish and hence would not compare with the fate that David wished for these wicked enemies. *He* and *his* refer to God and *them* refers to the enemies. David prayed that God would destroy them as with arrows.

Verse 8. All of these verses express the attitude of David toward his enemies. He is signifying his feelings by a number of comparisons. Strong defines the original for *melteth* by, "disappearance." The appearance of a snail is trivial and short-lived. *Untimely birth* refers to the case where the prematurity of the child caused its death so that it could never see the light of day.

Verse 9. The speed with which the wrath of God was to work against the wicked foes is the thought in this verse. *Thorns* refers to the fuel used to build a fire under the vessel. The foes were to feel the wrath of God in less time than it takes for the pots to feel the heat. The foes will be taken away *both living* (taken alive) by the whirlwind of God's wrath.

Verse 10. The first half of this verse is literal. It is right to rejoice whenever God brings vengeance on wicked men. The last half means the righteous will see the wicked foes brought to the feet of their would-be victims.

Verse 11. The righteous will be able to realize the justice of God against wicked men. Such a sight will be all the *reward* that the servants of the Lord will receive and should be all they would desire.

PSALMS 59

Verses 1, 2. David was not afraid of righteous men. A good man is not in any danger from other good men. That is why we have so many expressions from him asking for deliverance from evil characters.

Verse 3. The *soul* of man as the inner being cannot be injured by human beings (Luke 12: 4, 5). The word is used here meaning the life of David. He declared he was not guilty of any sin that would justify the enmity of the oppressors.

Verse 4. The enemies *prepared* or plotted against David through no fault of his. Had he been guilty of any act of wrong-doing he would not feel justified in calling on God for help as he did so many times with complete satisfaction.

Verse 5. To *visit* the heathen means to bring upon them some severe judgment. God's mercy was never promised to those who were impenitent. It was proper, therefore, for David to make the prayer of this verse. See comments at ch. 3: 2 for *Selah*.

Verse 6. The enemies are compared to dogs or "evening wolves." The comparison is to show their wild and greedy character.

Verse 7. The envious, cutting words that lying foes were uttering against David were compared to swords. When a man raves about his victim, he expects someone to hear him, else his *belching* would not accomplish anything. The idea is that he thinks the intended victim will not hear it. Only those will hear (he thinks) who might be influenced against the one who is the target for his shafts of spite.

Verse 8. There is One who hears all that is said and who will confound the plans designed by the wicked against righteous men.

Verse 9. David's faith in his God caused him to look his afflictions in the face. He believed God had the strength to defend his righteous servants.

Verse 10. *Prevent* has a meaning opposite of what it has today. It means literally "to go before" for the purpose of guidance. It therefore means that the mercy of God would help David in his conflicts with the foes.

Verse 11. To *slay* the foes would soon put them out of remembrance. David preferred to have them live, but be scattered and defeated which would enable them to realize their shame and thus be punished more extensively.

Verse 12. No actual bodily harm was coming to David from his enemies. But they were uttering vicious words against him and that irritated him.

Verse 13. To *consume* does not mean to destroy literally, for that would contradict v. 11. David wished God to come against his foes with such unmerciful vengeance that all their plans would be destroyed.

Verse 14. Not having been literally destroyed, but only scattered, the enemies would return to the attack, hoping to accomplish their purpose. (V. 6.) David would relish seeing them do so provided they failed in their intent.

Verse 15. This verse shows the motive indicated by my comments on the previous one. David would find much satisfaction in seeing the disappointment of the "dogs."

Verse 16. The *mercy* of which David would sing was that which he expected on the basis of his service to God. The particular form of the mercy was that which defended him against the persecutions at the hands of his enemies.

Verse 17. *God of my mercy* is significant in that no mercy could be expected from earthly sources. Instead, man was causing the conditions that called for God's mercy.

PSALMS 60

Verse 1. David was speaking for the nation as a whole. The people often provoked the Lord by their sins and received the judgments of God as a punishment.

Verse 2. Not the earth literally was made to tremble, but the people who live on it. They were made to feel the force of God's wrath.

Verse 3. *Hard things* and *wine of astonishment* are figurative phrases referring to the chastisements of God upon his wayward people.

Verse 4. A *banner* is from a word that is defined by Strong as a token. It means that people who fear God are "winners" in the contest against sin and God gives them the "blue ribbon" or token as a first prize reward.

Verse 5. David loved his people and prayed for them. Save with the *right hand* means that the salvation that is provided by the hand of God will be righteous.

Verse 6. *In his holiness* means that the sayings of God are holy in form and thought. The preceding verse was favorable for God's people and the same thought is continued in this. *Divide Shechem* means to divide or deal to Shechem, and *mete out* or deal out to Succoth means to give blessings of God to that place.

Verse 7. The places named belonged to God, hence it was fitting that He deal to them the favors previously mentioned. *Judah is my lawgiver* is a prophecy although the italicized word is in the present tense. The law in the days of David was given and administered through the tribe of Levi. But the time was to come when the law of God would come through Judah (Gen. 49:10; Heb. 7:11-14). So this is another of the many places where an inspired writer interrupted his story to make a prediction that was apparently unrelated to the general trend of his thought.

Verse 8. A *washpot* is an article for very humble use, and a place where one would *cast his shoe* would not be very dignified. God considered *Moab* and *Edom* in that light. In the last clause of the verse the word *Philistia* refers to the land of the *Philistines*.

Because in the marginal rendering is "over" and the lexicon agrees with it. The idea is that God was challenging the Philistines to interfere with his dealings with the two peoples, *Moab* and *Edom*. Of course the challenge was made in irony.

Verses 9, 10. David wrote as one who was to share in the triumph over the city of the Edomites. He asked who was to make such a victory sure. He then answered his own question in the words *will not thou, O God?*

Verses 11, 12. God can help one out of trouble, but it would be in vain to look for assistance from man.

PSALMS 61

Verse 1. A *cry* is an earnest form of *prayer*.

Verse 2. *From the end of the earth* indicated that David would call upon God from the farthest extent of his difficulties. *Rock* is from an original that Strong defines as a "refuge." A place of safety that was above the area of David's trials was that to which he prayed God to lead him.

Verse 3. *Shelter* has the same force of meaning as *rock* in the preceding verse. In material warfare a *tower* is constructed for two purposes: One is that of a defensive fort, the other is to give opportunity as a "look-out" post to observe the enemy.

Verse 4. There was a literal *tabernacle* but David used the term to indicate the sanctuary of God from a spiritual standpoint. He would maintain an unbroken relationship with God. *Wings* was also used figuratively to mean the overshadowing protection of Jehovah for those under his care.

Verse 5. His *vows* refers to the professions that had been made of service to the Lord. *Hast heard* means that God approved of them and rewarded David for them. The *heritage* means he rewarded David in the same way he had others who feared the Lord.

Verse 6. God did not wish his people to have a king and suffered them to have one over divine protest. However, after letting them be formed into a kingdom he promised to bless the king if he would remember his God in all his ruling.

Verse 7. *For ever* means "during the age." In this connection it means the king would retain his throne as long as he lived. *Mercy and truth* denotes that the mercy of God will be in harmony with the truth.

Verse 8. A part of the *vows* of David was a promise to praise God daily. In doing that he would be fulfilling his religious obligation to God.

PSALMS 62

Verse 1. *Waiteth* means that David calmly relied upon God for salvation, or protection against the activities of his enemies.

Verse 2. Not be *greatly* moved indicates that David did not expect to escape entirely from the oppression of his foes. But it would not be so extensive that he would be overwhelmed or entirely defeated.

Verse 3. This verse was addressed to the enemies of David. He gave them a warning that defeat was in store for them. *Be slain* did not mean that they would be literally killed. It denoted the complete overthrow of their plots. Their prospects for continuance was compared to a *bowing* (sagging) *wall* and a *tottering fence*.

Verse 4. *They only consult* means they pretended to counsel with a good man in order to obtain instruction. But their real motive was to get "inside" information that would give them an undue advantage.

Verse 5. This verse was addressed by the psalmist to himself. *Wait upon God* meant to rely upon God for deliverance from the foe.

Verse 6. This is practically the same as v. 2.

Verse 7. God was his glory in that David would glorify no other Being. *Rock, strength* and *refuge* have already been commented upon in recent chapters.

Verse 8. Man's trust in God should not be variable. He should rely upon God's help *at all times*.

Verse 9. *Low degree* and *high degree* refer to the professed ranks of the men. But whatever their stations in life, if they are *laid in the balance*, which means to be put to the test of real merit, their pretensions will be exposed.

Verse 10. The first clause is addressed to men using the wrong means for gain. Even if they should apparently succeed, the success would not justify their vain boasts. If riches should come to a man from righteous sources, yet it would be foolish to become attached to them. The mere obtaining of wealth is not wrong. The means of getting it and the attitude towards it or use made of it is what counts. Paul taught this lesson in 1 Tim. 6: 10, 17.

Verse 11. *Once* and *twice* are used in a general sense. It means that God had spoken so clearly on the subject that no room for doubt was left. It was evident that the Lord is the source of all true strength.

Verse 12. The strength of God is not used without mercy. Due consideration is always shown to those who recognize the power of the Lord and who strive to be worthy objects of its benefits.

PSALMS 63

Verse 1. The name *God* is used twice and is from two different originals. The first refers to a supreme Being as a ruler; the second has the special significance of a powerful One. David was not actually in want of the necessary things of life. He used such conditions to compare the feeling he had for the need of divine help.

Verse 2. This verse names the things he longed for in the preceding one. It would not be a new experience, for he had seen them in the sanctuary. He wished for a repetition or continuance of the same.

Verse 3. Lovingkindness really is equivalent to life. The comparison means that life without this kindness of God would not be worth living.

Verse 4. *While I live* did not imply that David would be unconscious after the death of the body. It means he would praise God all the days of his life. *Lift up hands* is a gesture of respect for God.

Verse 5. *Marrow and fatness* are materials very desirable for the temporal body. David meant the spiritual blessings of God were as refreshing to his soul as these literal things were to the body.

Verse 6. The spiritual provisions of God gave David "food for thought" even when in the night watches. He made practically the same remark in ch. 1: 2.

Verse 7. *Shadow of wings* is figurative, comparing the shelter afforded by the Lord to that of a large bird. As a birdling would find comfort under the wings of its mother, so David found a feeling of security with his Lord.

Verse 8. *Soul* is used to include the whole being of David. The word is often so used in the Bible. (Gen. 12: 13; Ex. 12: 15; Lev. 4: 2; Ac. 27: 37; 1 Pe. 3: 20.)

Verse 9. *Soul* is used in the same sense as in the preceding verse. *Go into the lower parts*, etc., is figurative, meaning they will go down in shameful defeat.

Verse 10. David's enemies were to be overthrown in battle. *Portion for foxes* was said to denote the humiliating destruction awaiting the foes.

Verse 11. David was king in Jerusalem when he wrote this psalm. His success over his enemies was to be accomplished through the help of God. Also all others would succeed who had God as the backing for their undertaking.

PSALMS 64

Verses 1, 2. *Secret counsel* of the wicked enemies of David was what he dreaded most. It is not so difficult to meet soldiers who come out like men into the open and fight manfully. But a cowardly plotter is hard to meet, hence the psalmist implored the help of God in his difficulties. An *insurrection* is an unlawful, disorderly uprising against society and lawful government.

Verse 3. As a man would *whet* his sword in preparation for a conflict. so these enemies of David prepared to speak slanderous words against him. It is necessary to bend a bow in order to cast an arrow. Likewise the foes of David drew their tongues into a tension to discharge the arrows of bitter words.

Verse 4. *Shoot in secret* is like the bushwhacker in carnal warfare. This phrase was used concerning the same actions described in the preceding verse.

Verse 5. David continues his description of secret foes. *Laying snares privily* means they were plotting secretly against David intending to injure him at a time when he would not be suspecting it.

Verse 6. *Search out iniquities* means they were trying to find something on which to accuse David of sin. The inward thought of the enemies is that they wish very much to find something of which to complain.

Verse 7. The *arrow* that God will shoot will be his darts of wrath against the workers of unrighteousness. They will be wounded by having their pride brought down.

Verse 8. The lies of the enemies will be exposed. When that is done they will be shown to be the ones who are really guilty of the evils they charged against David. When people realize the wickedness of David's foes they will *flee away* or evade them in fear.

Verse 9. *Men shall fear* means they will respect God for his wonderful works of righteousness. *Wisely consider* denotes they will take a wise and just view of the actions of God.

Verse 10. A righteous man will always be glad when he sees the good work of God. It will cause him to have increased faith in the power and wisdom of divine providence.

PSALMS 65

Verse 1. *Praise waiteth* has the idea of being held in waiting or reserve for God. *The vow* refers to the obligations that faithful servants of God had agreed to perform. A man will gladly discharge his duties to One whom he considers to be worthy of praise.

Verse 2. *All flesh* is used to include mankind in general. That would mean the high and low, the rich and poor, the learned and unlearned.

Verse 3. The *iniquities* were those of David's enemies. They were making his life miserable with their persecutions. David looked upon his afflictions as a means of keeping him humble, and in that way *purge* or cleanse him from his transgressions.

Verse 4. It was to be understood that God chooses only those who are righteous. That explains why David pronounced a blessing on the man that was God's choice. *Dwell in thy courts* is a figurative reference to the intimate privileges of those whom the Lord loves. The *goodness* or advantages of that intimacy would be fully satisfactory to all who love the Lord.

Verse 5. *Terrible things* means the acts of the Lord that should be feared or reverenced. The reason they should be so considered is their *righteousness*. *Art the confidence* means God is the one in whom all people of the earth should have confidence.

Verse 6. It is the power of God that controls the parts of the earth. He caused the mountains to be formed as they are and to be maintained through the centuries.

Verse 7. The Lord's power over the sea was demonstrated in the case of Jonah (Jon. 1), and in the time of Christ (Matt. 8: 23-27).

Verse 8. *Afraid at thy tokens* denotes that the people were impressed by the tokens of God's power. *Outgoings* refers to the sources of the daily appearances of daylight and darkness. God so regulates them that the people of the earth rejoice.

Verse 9. *Visitest* means to bestow something on the earth. *River of God* is a figurative reference to the moisture needed for the production of the earth's crops. That is provided by the Lord and hence the figure of speech used here.

Verse 10. This verse is practically the same in meaning as the preceding one. It refers to the provisions of life that are produced by the earth; these good things all come from God. The same thought is given us in James 1: 17.

Verse 11. *Paths drop fatness* indicates that wherever God moves there are blessings to be had for mankind.

Verse 12. Whether the broad stretches of the wilderness are considered, or the little hills of the homeland, the providence of God gives the necessary seasons.

Verse 13. The pastures receive the rain from God which enables them to produce grass for the flocks. The valleys are the smaller areas and are used for the growing of grain. This is made possible by the watering mentioned in v. 10. *Shout* and *sing* are not used in a literal sense. The good things of life produced by the hills and valleys cause the people to shout and sing for joy. This transition from inanimate to animate things is a form of speech sometimes used in the Bible to give a picture of the goodness of God. See Acts 14: 17 where the heart is said to be filled both with food and gladness; one literal and the other mental.

PSALMS 66

Verses 1, 2. I do not find any original words for the first half of verse one. But the general thought of the paragraph will justify their use. The idea is that men should express their gratitude for the goodness of God by mirthful sounds.

Verse 3. *Terrible* is from the same Hebrew word as "reverend" in ps. 111: 9. It has various shades of meaning including respect and dread. The connection here shows it to have the latter meaning. The enemies dread the power of God and *submit* unto him. The marginal reading says "yield feigned obedience" and the lexicon agrees with it. The enemies do not sincerely worship God but pretend to be in subjection in order to escape his terrible judgments against the children of disobedience.

Verse 4. The *worship* that all the earth (the people) shall give to God will be by way of adoration for and acknowledgment of the great works in the universe. The passage does not mean to predict universal salvation, for that would contradict too many positive statements of scripture that teach otherwise.

Verse 5. *Come and see* is a phrase used to call attention. It is not necessary to *come* to any particular place, literally, in order to see evidences of God's works.

Verse 6. The subject matter of this verse confirms my comments in the preceding one. The miraculous crossing of the Red Sea had taken place hundreds of years before, yet the people were told to *come and see* it. The meaning is they were to consider it.

Verse 7. The rule of God over the nations is one of power in the sense of strength. The majority of mankind do not permit God to rule their lives in the matter of their moral conduct. But the time will come when all rebellious ones will be brought to judgment. In view of the final judgment of God the disobedient ones are warned not to exalt themselves. See comments at ch. 3: 2 for explanation of *Selah*.

Verse 8. Human beings can *bless* God only by acknowledging him as the source of all blessings. This is the truth that justifies the first clause of the familiar Doxology which says: "Praise God, from whom all blessings flow." The same thought is set forth in James 1: 17 regarding the only source of good things.

Verse 9. *Soul* and *life* have about the same meaning as a rule. When they are used in connection with each other as in this verse the first means the vitality of a man and the second is the continuance of that vitality.

Verse 10. Proving and trying was accomplished through the afflictions God suffered to come upon David. *Silver is tried* by putting it through fire to separate the dross from the metal. The process was used to compare the experience of exposure to trial at the hands of the enemies.

Verse 11. This verse is still dealing with the subject of tests brought upon the people of God. It is not difficult to maintain a profession as long as there is no opposition. The real test comes when one is called upon to endure great suffering and danger for the sake of his friends.

Verse 12. *Fire* and *water* is a reference to a practice resorted to as a test. A person accused of some crime was required to submit to the test to prove his guilt or innocence. He would be thrown into a body of water and if he floated it indicated his guilt. Even a thing like a sea would spew up the guilty one. Or, it he were forced to run through some fire it would not harm him unless he was guilty. Occasionally a sympathetic friend would offer to go through the test as a substitute for him. That gave the origin of the saying "go through fire and water" for another. My authority for this paragraph is in Webster's Collegiate Dictionary, article *ordeal;* and Schaff-Herzog Encyclopaedia, article *ordeal.* In the case of David and his brethren it was used figuratively. They stood the test because it says *thou broughtest them out.*

Verses 13, 14. There were certain sacrifices that were required by the congregation, and others demanded of individuals. Besides these, a devoted Jew was encouraged to vow to make sacrifices when his circumstances suggested them. David had promised some of such offerings in the midst of his afflictions. God had given him deliverance and now his gratitude prompted the statements of this paragraph.

Verse 15. The sacrifices under the Mosaic system might be classified as the major and minor ones. *Fatlings* were the larger and *rams* were the smaller sacrifices. Also, *bullocks* were the larger and *goats* were the smaller. The thought is that David wished to go the full extent of sacrificial devotions.

Verse 16. *Soul* is used to include the entire person of David. He meant he was desirous of telling others of what God had done for him.

Verse 17. The *mouth* and *tongue* are both used when addressing the Lord. This form of speech was used to please the sense of variety in emphasis.

Verse 18. To *regard iniquity* means to be favorable toward it. God will not hear the prayer of one who is in that frame of mind.

Verse 19. On the basis of the foregoing truth David was not guilty for God had heard and granted his prayer.

Verse 20. God was *blessed* in that he was acknowledged to be the source of David's blessings. They were manifested in the form of mercy in the time of his trouble.

PSALMS 67

Verse 1. David personally was the greatest sufferer from the opposition of the enemies, but the nation as a whole often was a victim. The prayers, therefore, were in the plural form for David was very mindful of his brethren. There is a noted example of this fact recorded in 2 Sam. 24: 17.

Verse 2. God's special favor upon the children of Israel would be an evidence to the other nations of the world of His goodness.

Verse 3. *Let the people* is a mild form of the more emphatic thought, calling on the people of the world to praise God.

Verse 4. The *nations* that were not directly of God should be pleased to see the goodness he manifests for his people. After all, even the heathen are under the control of God (Dan. 4: 17; 5: 21), and it should be agreeable to them when they observe the kind of Being who holds their very existence in his hands.

Verse 5. *Let the people* is explained at v. 3.

Verse 6. Ingratitude sometimes brings the judgments of God upon the world. In the days of special providence the earth would refuse to produce the necessities of life. (2 Sam. 21: 1.) But if the people will give God the praise due him they will be assured of the blessings of the earth.

Verse 7. All people will *fear* or respect God when they see the great benefits that he gives them through means of the earth.

PSALMS 68

Verse 1. Military victory over his enemies was a thing for which David often prayed. The Jewish nation was secular as well as religious. It is proper for temporal governments to fight for their defense (John 18: 36), hence it was right for David to express himself as he did in this verse and in many other passages.

Verse 2. The brevity of *smoke* and *wax* was used to compare the fate that David wished for his enemies; they were to disappear without delay.

Verse 3. The righteous people have reason to rejoice when wicked persons are overthrown. If their complete destruction is necessary for the good of others, then it would be right to wish for it to be accomplished through the power of the Lord.

Verse 4. *Rideth upon the heavens* indicates that God is above all things in the universe. *Jah* is a short form of Jehovah and means the "self-Existent or Eternal." Having never had a beginning he is logically the ruler of everything in creation.

Verse 5. God's care for all unfortunate persons is as good as that of a father or a husband. The Lord executes his watchful care for the needy from his holy habitation beyond the skies.

Verse 6. *Solitary* is from YACHYD and "lonely" is a leading word in Strong's definition. In the King James version it has been translated by darling 2 times, desolate 1, only 6, only child 1, only son 1, solitary 1. The word primarily has reference to what is commonly called an orphan. *Families* is from BAYITH and Strong's definition is, "a house (in the greatest variety of applications, especially family)." In the King James version it has been translated by family 5 times, home 25, house 1790, household 52. The idea is that God intended the family home as the proper place in which to care for orphans. The same thought is indicated in 1 Tim. 5: 10. The rest of the verse of this paragraph has to do with the subject of liberty. There are no harder *chains* than those of sin. God will deliver all from them who will obey him.

Verses 7, 8. In this paragraph we have an interesting use of the word *Selah*. The comments at ch. 3: 2 show the word to mean a pause for reflection. It is very fitting to pause in the midst of this passage and meditate on the mighty power of God. It was manifested at Sinai and at many other places.

Verse 9. By sending rain God did *confirm* the promise made in Gen. 8: 22.

Verse 10. *Dwelt therein* means the congregation lived within the blessings which God provided by rain for the country of his people.

Verse 11. This verse states a fact that occurred in more than one instance. God could have inspired all men by his word at the same time had he so desired. Instead, he has always committed his law to certain men and then expected great numbers of others to repeat it among the people of the earth.

Verse 12. Persons of contrasting power are mentioned in order to show God's working is not always according to logical rule. A king might not be able to escape being chased, while the female citizens at home would reap the benefit from his defeat.

Verse 13. *Pots* and *dove wings* are used figuratively to compare the conditions of God's faithful servants while in their afflictions and after they have been rescued.

Verse 14. The antecedent of the first *it* is *inheritance* in v. 9. *White* is not in the original and has no meaning as used here. *Salmon* was a hill near Shechem. Snow falling on the hill would be scattered about. That was used to compare the commotion of kings who had opposed God's people.

Verse 15. *The hill of God* meant the spiritual prominence of God's institution. It was compared to a literal hill in the land of Bashan.

Verse 16. *High hills* was a figurative reference to the high esteem the foes of David had of themselves. He indirectly criticized them for their self-exaltation and warned them in view of the spiritual hill of God in which they should be interested.

Verse 17. *Chariots* were instruments of war and when used figuratively refer to the power of God over his enemies. They would be handled by the angels who are the servants of Heaven. The vast number mentioned is for the purpose of emphasis. *Sinai* is named because it was the place where God's law was given after Moses, the first lawgiver, had ascended to its peak.

Verse 18. After such a reference to Sinai and the important things that issued from it, it was logical to pass from that to the second Moses and tell of the things he did. The Psalmist may not have personally understood why he was inspired to write this verse (1 Pe. 1: 10-12). However, it is a prophecy of the ascension of Christ, after which he too caused an outpouring of power from God. It is quoted in Eph. 4: 8 and spoken of as being a saying of old time.

Verse 19. The Lord is the giver of all blessings and in acknowledging the fact we *bless the Lord*. God not only supplies us with the things needful for the body, but he is the means of our salvation.

Verse 20. *Our God* is an expression occurring often in the Bible. There were so many false gods advocated by the heathen nations that it was significant for the servants of the true one to designate him by the possessive pronoun. God is the one who has power to give life to the dead.

Verse 21. The *head* and *hairy scalp* indicate the most vital part of a man. The reference to it is to show the complete defeat of the enemies of God.

Verse 22. *Bashan* was one of the heathen districts and was occupied by strong people. To rescue his people from such a hold would show God's great power. Likewise would it be shone were he to save them from the sea.

Verse 23. *Thy foot* means the foot of God's people. Victory over the enemy is the subject of the verse. That was indicated by the dipping of the foot in the blood of the enemy. The humiliating degree of the defeat to be imposed on the enemy was indicated by the prediction that the dogs of the Israelites would lick the blood of the enemy slain. This kind of comparison was made in the case of Ahab. (1 Ki. 21: 19.)

Verse 24. *They* refers to the enemy before whom the wonderful *goings* or acts of God had been displayed.

Verse 25. David was a great man for musical instruments; used especially in service to God. He represented the victory as being celebrated with the music.

Verse 26. God is the *fountain* of all good, whether material or immaterial. The children of Israel had come from that *fountain*, hence they were told to bless God.

Verse 27. Both large (Judah) and small (Benjamin) groups with their *rulers* or leaders had come from God. The same was true of other tribes so they should praise God.

Verse 28. What *strength* these groups had was by the decree of God. David prayed for continuance of that favor to the nation.

Verse 29. The temple was the headquarters of the Lord's kingdom. The recognition of that government was to be done by the kings of the earth. It would be indicated by their *presents*. See the meaning of that in comments at Gen. 32: 13.

Verse 30. The reference to dumb creatures was to show the low estimate David had of his enemies. He prayed for God to rebuke them so completely that they would pay the customary tribute or "present," which they would do with *pieces of silver*.

Verse 31. This verse means that notable persons in Egypt and Ethiopia would soon acknowledge the supremacy of God.

Verse 32 This was rather in the nature of a command or demand. The kingdoms of the earth were called upon to recognize God. See comments at ch. 3: 2 for *Selah*.

Verse 33. *Rideth upon*, etc., was to indicate the over-all jurisdiction of God. In view of that authority the nations were directed, in the preceding verse, to give due praise unto the God of Israel.

Verse 34. The *strength* of God is greater than that possessed by any other being. That strength was contributed to the oversight of Israel. *Clouds* had reference to the regions of creation, and God's strength was manifested therein.

Verse 35. *Terrible* is from YARE and means that God is worthy to be respected for his might. He is able to give *strength* and *power* unto his people. These words have practically the same meaning and are used together for emphasis.

PSALMS 69

Verse 1. *Waters* in symbolic language means afflictions. *Soul* as used here refers to the whole being. David means he is "flooded" with afflictions.

Verse 2. This is along the same line as the preceding verse. *Mire* and *waters* are used figuratively. *No standing* means it is all mire with no solid footing.

Verse 3. These strong expressions are descriptive of the intense feeling David had because of his many persecutions. He had not lost faith in the Lord, but the flesh is weak and often gives way to sighing and lamentation.

Verse 4. *More than the hairs* is a figure of speech used for emphasis. It is something like Gen. 13: 16; 22: 17. David never did resent any punishment that was due him, but these people were hating him *without a cause*. Although he had been falsely accused of fraud, he gave to his accusers the property they claimed. In other words, rather than cause unnecessary friction he was willing to suffer himself to be defrauded as Paul taught in 1 Cor. 6: 7.

Verse 5. This was an admission of the general weakness of the human being. There was no specific sin of which he was guilty at that time. However, we should note the statement that a man's sins are not hid from God.

Verse 6. To *wait on* God means to rely on him and to expect divine help. David was being shamefully treated by the enemies of righteousness. He was concerned lest the condition might embarrass those who were *waiting* on God and possibly cause them to be hindered in their devotion. The prayer was in behalf of those persons, that they would not let David's afflictions affect them. It was a thought similar to that expressed by Paul in 2 Tim. 1: 8.

Verse 7. David set an example of the courage he desired others to manifest. He had endured the reproaches of the enemies because of his love for God.

Verses 8, 9. Again the inspired mind saw a fitting place to make a prediction of an experience that was to come upon the illustrious descendant of David. Unknown to him (perhaps) he passed from his own experiences to those of Christ, and the prediction is cited in John 2: 16 and Rom. 15: 3.

Verse 10. This means that his enemies *reproached* or made fun of David when they saw him grieving over his persecutions.

Verse 11. *Sackcloth* is a coarse fabric of which gunny sacks are made. It was worn in ancient times when the person was undergoing a period of grief or anxiety. When the enemies saw it they spoke in *proverbs* about it. That is, they made him the target for their jeers and tried to humiliate him.

Verse 12. This verse names persons of two opposite ranks. Those who sat in the gate were representative men because that was the point for diplomatic conversations. Of course it is understood that *drunkards* were of the very inferior rank. Both of these classes showed disrespect for David in his afflictions or persecutions.

Verse 13. These persecutions did not discourage David from his devotions to God. He continued to make his prayer to the Lord. *In an acceptable time* was said in about the same sense as we mean when we say. "If it be thy will." *Truth of thy salvation* indicates that the salvation coming from God is according to truth.

Verse 14. *Mire* and *water*, as in previous verses, are used figuratively referring to David's many trials at the hands of his enemies.

Verse 15. This verse is more along the same line as the others mentioned. Let it be noted that David did not ask to escape all difficulty. He prayed only to be saved from being overwhelmed and completely defeated as his enemies intended.

Verses 16, 17. David believed that God was always just in his dealings. But he also believed that God was merciful and it was on that basis that he could expect relief from his persecutions.

Verse 18. David did not mean his *soul* from the standpoint of spiritual danger. He used the word as applying to his present existence; his life had been threatened.

Verse 19. David would not presume to offer information to God. But rather, the form of speech was his way of acknowledging the complete wisdom of the Lord.

Verse 20. The intensity of David's persecutions was being more definitely described. The mind of inspiration was getting ready to pass again to a prediction concerning the great Descendant of David.

Verse 21. This and several following verses are in reference to the persecutions of Christ and also the fate called for upon his persecutors. This present prediction was fulfilled while Jesus was on the cross. See Matt. 27: 34; Mark 15: 23; Luke 23: 36; John 19: 29 for the record of fulfillment of this noted prophecy.

Verses 22, 23. The Jews rejected Jesus and plotted his death. As a result they were destined to be rejected by the Lord. We do not have to guess at the application of this prophecy, for Paul cites it in connection with his remarks about the Jewish nation and the shortcomings charged against it. (Rom. 11: 9, 10.)

Verse 24. This verse is in the form of a prayer, but it is a prediction of the judgment of God upon that wicked nation for its disrespect of the divine law.

Verse 25. The nation as a whole was considered guilty of the death of Christ. However, the agent in the wicked deed was Judas. This prediction also is clearly interpreted in the New Testament. In Acts 1: 20. Peter quoted it when he was preparing to find a man to take the place of Judas as an apostle. The plural form of the pronoun need not confuse us. Judas was the actor for the nation and it was appropriate to speak of the tragedy in that manner.

Verse 26. It was God's will that Jesus be smitten (Isa. 53: 4), but that did not justify the motives of those who fulfilled that part of the Lord's plan. God gave his Son over into the hands of wicked men, then *they persecuted* him with a bitter hatred.

Verse 27. The original for *iniquity* is defined by Strong as, "perversity, i.e. (moral) evil." In the King James version it has been translated by punishment (or iniquity) as well as by just iniquity. Hence this verse is a prayer for God to add the punishment of iniquity to the wicked Jews for their practice of iniquity. The last clause of the verse means for God not to favor them with a reward of righteousness.

Verse 28. This verse practically means for the wicked Jews to be forgotten and left out of the record. That would cut them off from all sharing with the righteous.

Verse 29. *Poor and sorrowful* is a phrase with mixed meaning. The first word is not literal, for David had much of this world's goods. He was poor in that he was "depressed," which is the leading word in Strong's definition of the original. That would give to the last word of the phrase a literal meaning.

Verse 30. Songs and other poetical compositions were a prominent manner with David in expressing his sentiments. *Magnify him* meant to recognize the greatness of God.

Verse 31. Animal sacrifices were required by the law and were pleasing to God. However, they were material things and in comparison did not equal spiritual praise.

Verse 32. The *humble* would include those too poor to present a costly sacrifice like a bullock. But when they saw that God was pleased with such services as sincere praise, which was something that the poorest could offer, then they were made glad. *Heart shall live* means they would have the heart to seek God when they saw that what they had to offer was pleasing to him.

Verse 33. *Despiseth* means to belittle or think lightly of another. If the *poor* are in the prison or other distress the Lord will consider their case nevertheless.

Verse 34. Inanimate things like the *earth* and *sea* cannot actually praise God. The thought is that God should be praised because of these works of creation.

Verse 35. *Zion* was the capital of *Judah* and God's interest in them was such that he would defend them against all enemies.

Verse 36. This verse is a prediction that the land of Judah would be possessed by future generations. But that was on condition that they *love his name*.

PSALMS 70

Verse 1. *Make haste* is only an earnest plea for divine help.

Verse 2. *Seek after my soul* and *desire my hurt* mean the same thing The personal injury of David in this life is what he means by such references to his *soul*.

Verse 3. *Aha, aha,* is an expression of ridicule, indicating joy at another's misfortunes. *Be turned back* means for the foes to be stopped in their hateful work.

Verse 4. David was as considerate of the righteous as he was of the wicked. That is, he not only prayed for the defeat of the wicked, but prayed God to cause the righteous people to rejoice. God's greatness cannot be increased by man. *Let God be magnified* means for people to recognize his magnitude by proper words of praise; also by a life consistent with His great love.

Verse 5. *Poor and needy* is explained at ch. 69: 29, and *make haste* is commented upon at the first verse of the present chapter.

PSALMS 71

Verse 1. *Confusion is from* BUWSH and Strong defines it, "to pale, i.e. pale, i.e. by implication to be ashamed; also (by implication) to be disappointed or delayed." David was never much worried at the prospect of physical discomfort. What he dreaded most was the humiliation of being gloated over by his wicked enemies.

Verse 2. *Deliver . . . righteousness* indicates that God would not rescue a man from a difficulty unless he was in the right.

Verse 3. *Habitation* is used figuratively, meaning a secure haven of safety. *Commandment* is from a word that means "appoint" also. The thought is that God had appointed that righteous persons should be delivered from wicked enemies.

Verse 4. All *cruel* men are *unrighteous*, but not all unrighteous men are cruel. David was being persecuted by men who had both characteristics. But either trait would render a man wicked in the sight of God.

Verse 5. There is very little difference between *hope* and *trust*. The first refers specifically to a strong cord to which a man might cling; the second means a place of refuge; both denote a condition of assurance. David had enjoyed this support *from his youth*. That is, from the time he was old enough to think and be responsible. He did not believe the doctrine of inherited sin.

Verse 6. This verse does not contradict the preceding one. An infant is in no danger on account of sin, but he could be liable to physical harm. God had cared for him and also his mother before she had given birth to the son.

Verse 7. It is hard for the world to understand the courage that is manifested by a true servant of God. David's explanation of it was the fact that he relied upon God for strength. A similar circumstance arose with the apostles. (Acts 4: 13.)

Verse 8. *Praise* and *honor* go hand in hand. The greatest honor any man can have is to be an admirer of God. David, therefore, would praise him all the day long.

Verse 9. This verse is merely another earnest plea for help against the enemy. *Age* has no original as a seperate word. It is drived from the word for old. And that word is used in a comparative sense, for David was not "aged" as we commonly use that term, being only 70 when he died. (2 Sam. 5: 4.) The meaning of the prayer is that he wished God to be with him to the end of his life.

Verse 10. *Take counsel together* is the significant item in the case. A man may not have much difficulty in combatting a single foe, but a confederation of them acting in secret increases the hardship. The secret nature of the conspiracy is indicated by the words *lay wait*.

Verse 11. God allows his servants to be subject to trials to test their faith. Such a situation is often mistaken by the enemy for indifference on the part of the Lord. They will declare that the servant of God has been cast off, and they will seek to take advantage of it in the hopes of overcoming that servant.

Verse 12. Because of the condition described in the preceding verse, David called upon God to help him.

Verse 13. *Confounded* and *consumed* are strong terms meaning to be completely defeated. Reference to the *soul* was in regard to the general personal life of David.

Verse 14. David's constant trust in the Lord was his greatest quality. During his darkest periods of distress he always turned to God for relief.

Verse 15. *Know not the numbers* was used in the same sense as we say "too numerous to mention." It referred to the manifold instances of God's righteous favors.

Verse 16. David's reliance on the strength of God has a parallel thought in Eph. 6: 10. The latter part of this verse means David would not claim any merit for his own righteousness; only for the Lord's.

Verse 17. *From my youth* is explained at v. 5. *Hitherto* means he had been speaking of the works of God from the time he was old enough to be a responsible thinker.

Verse 18. *Old and greyheaded* is comparative; see comments at v. 9. The central thought of this verse is that, by the help of God David wished to display to all the world the great works of the Creator.

Verse 19. God is not only great with creative power, but all his dealings with man are righteous. David always took delight in praising the Lord for his righteousness.

Verse 20. God showed David these great troubles in that he allowed him to be exposed to them as a test of his faith. *Depths of the earth* refers to the depression that was caused by the afflictions mentioned above.

Verse 21. True *greatness* consists in being in the favor of God. Jesus taught this truth in Matt. 20: 25-29. David took comfort in the assurance that the Lord would recognize his humble devotion to duty.

Verse 22. Mention of the *psaltery* and *harp* reminds us of one of David's specialties which was instrumental music. God had placed his approval on this service as indicated in 2 chron. 5: 13, 14.

Verse 23. *Soul* was not used in distinction from the outer man, but was used to refer to the whole living being, just as it is used in 1 Pe. 3: 20. David meant that God had saved him from death at the hands of his enemies. For this redemption he would rejoice and praise the Lord.

Verse 24. The lips might be properly used in singing the praises of God with more attention to the musical quality than to the thought. Such was the leading idea in the preceding verse. In the present one the tongue was to be used for the purpose of language in describing the righteousness of God. To be *confounded* means to be defeated and shamed in the attempts to injure the servant of the Lord.

PSALMS 72

Verse 1. David was king in Jerusalem and he expected his son to reign in his place. Such officials are called upon to render important decisions or *judgments*. That was the reason he prayed for God to give him his divine judgments.

Verse 2. If the favors mentioned in the preceding verse were granted, the good work of this one would be accomplished.

Verse 3. *Mountains* and *little hills* were used figuratively to denote the extent of the good results that would follow if the preceding conditions were brought about. This extent was indicated by the larger and smaller things in the land.

Verse 4. *Judge the poor* means God would render the proper decisions (through the king) concerning the poor. That class often was slighted because of the humble station they occupied in life due to their financial circumstances.

Verse 5. *They* (the poor) would fear or reverence the Lord because of his goodness to them. No man will live as long as the *sun and moon* exists. The thought is that as long as these heavenly bodies lasted there would be grateful people to respect God. Incidentally we here learn that the production of human generations on earth will end simultaneously with that of the *sun and moon.*

Verse 6. It should be understood that the tribute being referred to in these verses applies specifically to the king. But that is because he had been enabled to do all these good deeds by the help of God. Therefore it can justly be said that both God and his king are the antecedents of the pronouns. The favors from God through the services of the king are here figuratively compared to showers upon the grass.

Verse 7. Consult the comments at v. 5.

Verse 8. God will favor the righteous king by giving him widespread dominion.

Verse 9. People will be encouraged to come from obscure places to serve such a king. On the other hand, those who persist in opposing him shall *lick the dust* which is a figure denoting their humiliating defeat.

Verse 10. *Tarshish, Sheba* and *Seba* were towns having kings ruling in them. *Shall offer gifts* means these kings will be induced to offer the usual tokens of recognition. See Gen. 32: 13 and 1 Sam. 10: 27 for comments on this subject.

Verse 11. This has the same meaning as the preceding verse except that it is general in designating who would bring the gifts.

Verse 12. God will not help a man on the mere fact that he is *poor* and *needy,* for those conditions do not prove that he is worthy. The connection shows that David was considering those who had been imposed upon because they were *poor* and therefore were in *need* of help, it being understood that they were worthy characters.

Verses 13, 14. *Precious . . . blood,* etc., shows that *save the souls* does not have reference to the spiritual lot of these people. It pertains to their bodily safety in this world, which had been imposed upon by deceit.

Verse 15. *Given gold of Sheba* is figurative, meaning the good favor that will come to the worthy man who has been oppressed by the wicked.

Verse 16. Corn usually is produced in the valleys, or at best on the side of the mountains or hills only. But the abundance of the crop will be such that it will reach to the tops of them. *Shake like Lebanon* was said to compare the abundance of the products. Lebanon was covered with a luxurious growth that indicated the fertility and prosperity of the country as being very great.

Verse 17. The God who had given the king strength to go forth in service is the subject of the passages in general. His name was not to cease when the sun failed, but man's life on earth will fail then. Hence the comparison to the endurance of the sun was made in view of the extent of man's opportunity to extol the name of God, which will be as long as there are men on earth to extol it.

Verse 18. God is the source of all great things. Whatever man is capable of doing was made possible by the Lord's power, therefore it was said that he *only* did it.

Verse 19. To bless the name of God means to ascribe all blessings to Him. *Amen and Amen* is a phrase meant for emphatic approval of what had been written.

Verse 20. This should not be regarded as David's last prayers to God for we will read more of them. He did not do all of his writing at one "sitting." This verse means he had come to the close of that particular group of devotions. When a congregation pronounces the "benediction" it does not mean it is the last service it will have.

PSALMS 73

Verse 1. Both parts of this verse should be considered. In proportion to their cleanness of heart God was ready to bless Israel.

Verse 2. This refers to some time in the life of David when the trials were almost too much for his endurance; he almost "gave in."

Verse 3. David had seen the success of the wicked and it staggered him.

Verse 4. *Bands* is from an original that means "pain," and *death* is from MAVETH and one word in Strong's definition is "pestilence." So the meaning of the verse is that the wicked are "lucky" even in their difficulties. They have enough *strength* to feel firm and do not seem to care for that which others would consider terrible.

Verse 5. This verse is different in its wording but takes the same comments as did the preceding one.

Verse 6. The success of the wicked makes them proud, and in their pride they feel as secure as if they were protected by a chain. The *violence* that would stop a righteous man seems to have been only a protection for these wicked people.

Verse 7. These wicked men were so successful in their wickedness that their eyes could see nothing of interest but their own importance. Their wicked prosperity even exceeded their fondest *heart's wish*.

Verse 8. Such wicked men would speak viciously concerning their own evil conduct against the righteous. They were *lofty* or self-important when they should have been brought low in penitence because of their cruel wickedness.

Verse 9. These wicked men not only practiced iniquity, but talked rebelliously against even the works of creation.

Verse 10. This verse is still speaking of the success of the unrighteous. It implies that people are influenced to go after these evil persons because of their wealth.

Verse 11. *How doth God know* means, "what does God care about what is going on?" They consider that success can be had without any dependence on God.

Verse 12. *Prosper in the world* is a key to the whole matter. These wicked men are prosperous, but it is in the things of the world. It is a foolish way to pass their sojourn on the earth, for after this life the great success will be turned into a dismal failure. Let us here consider the great question of Jesus in Mark 8: 36.

Verse 13. David did not teach that it was useless for a man to be righteous as it concerned the Lord. He meant that all the righteousness that he could practice would be unavailable as far as his enemies were concerned.

Verse 14. Another construction of this verse would be to say that every morning the chastening began and continued all through the day.

Verse 15. *Thy children* means the people of God in general. The chastisement upon David, though brought about by the agency of foes, was from God. Were David to complain too much about his trials, it would be offensive to the people who might think he should bear his burdens with more patience.

Verse 16. At times it was hard for David to understand what it was all about.

Verse 17. The uncertainty indicated in the previous verse was solved by the action recorded in this. By consulting the Lord in his holy temple David learned *their end;* that is, he learned that the agents of these tests would get their dues.

Verse 18. *Them* refers to the agents mentioned above. They were also brought to punishment because of the motive prompting their persecution of David.

Verse 19. We have many times learned that God used certain evil characters as his chastening rod for his children. But when those characters took much pleasure in the movement God would punish them. (Isa. 10: 5-19.)

Verse 20. When the evil agents are brought to their own punishment they will be aroused as from a pleasant daydream. They will realize that their pleasure at oppressing God's people was short-lived and that their day of reckoning had come.

Verses 21, 22. After seeing the whole transaction through and the purpose of it, David felt rather ashamed for his impatience.

Verse 23. God did not penalize David because of his anxiety, he continued to hold him under divine protection.

Verse 24. *Counsel* means wisdom and instruction. By that David was guided while in the activities of this life. Since he was willing to take such guidance he expected finally to be received in the Glory World. This is another passage that shows that people in Old Testament times believed in aonther life after death in this world.

Verse 25. A familiar song, "Pass Me Not O Gentle Saviour," includes this verse in its wording. When *heaven* is used in contrast with *earth* it means the 3rd heaven, the place where God dwells personally.

Verse 26. David meant that both his outer and inner beings would fail were it not for the help of God.

Verse 27. *They* means the wicked persons and *thee* means God. Being *far* from the Lord was indicated by the kind of life they were following. *Go a whoring* means to go lusting after other gods and other unlawful things.

Verse 28. *Draw near* and *trust in* God are put in the same connection. It explains why some people will not seek to be near the Lord; it is because they do not trust in him. One motive David had in trusting in God was that he might *declare his works*. This implies that an unbeliever is not authorized to be a proclaimer of the Word.

PSALMS 74

Verse 1. The statements of this verse should not be taken in the literal sense. They were only an earnest plea for God to grant relief from the heavy distress into which the enemies had thrust David and his people.

Verse 2. The *congregation* had been purchased from Egypt by the death of the firstborn. (Ex. 15: 16; Num. 3: 12, 13.) God *dwelt in Zion* in that the capital of his kingdom and the headquarters of the national worship were there.

Verse 3. *Life up thy feet* meant for God to take his steps toward the place of Israel's desolations. These were not against the temporal interests of the people only, but the *sanctuary* or holy place of worship was being descecrated.

Verse 4. *Ensigns* and *signs* are from the same word and is defined "signal." The verse means the enemy planted his post in the midst of the people of God. Of course they did so unlawfully and for the purpose of overwhelming the people with violence.

Verses 5, 6. The enemies were using violence against the institutions of God. Their actions were compared to those of men attacking the trees in the forest.

Verse 7. This language may be considered in the light of both history and prophecy. Historically it meant the mistreatment the enemies were according the buildings of the people. And it was an omen of what was finally to come upon the temple in the Babylonian Captivity that took place many years later.

Verse 8. In a poetical composition, such as the psalms, we should make allowances for strong statements as an accommodative description of something very striking. The language of this verse is justified by the terrible havoc caused by the foes.

Verse 9. This verse means there were no signs left of the former greatness of the nation. The literal force of this language should be understood in the light of comments on the preceding verse.

Verses 10, 11. This is just another one of David's anxious prayers for God's help.

Verse 12. David "got hold of himself" and recalled that God had done great things in the past for the universe and the people of the earth.

Verse 13. For a few verses the Psalmist recounted some of the mighty works of God. He went back to the crossing of the Red Sea. *Dragons* is from TANNIYM, and Strong defines it. "a marine or land monster, i.e. sea-serpent or jackal." It is also rendered by whale in the A.V. According to Ex. 15: 8 the waters were congealed or frozen just before the Israelites crossed over. In the rush and crash of converting the water into two separate walls of ice, some of these whales were caught in the movement and had their heads broken.

Verse 14. The flesh of the leviathan would not be the most desirable of food. Yet it might not be too bad for people *inhabiting the wilderness* where one could not be very exacting in his diet. But the main point of David was the fact that this animal, usually too strong to be captured by man (Job 41:1), was overcome by the Lord and thrown over for the use of the natives nearby.

Verse 15. The preceding verse referred to the crossing over the Red Sea. This one occurred at the crossing of the Jordan. By stopping the flow of the river it was equivalent to having cleaved or demolished the fountain supplying the flood (Jordan).

Verse 16. God has complete jurisdiction over day and night. The reader should note that *light* and *sun* are mentioned separately and that light is named first. That agrees with Genesis 1: 3, 14 which shows there was light 3 days before there was any sun. But it does not agree with the "scientists" who say that all light originated with the sun through its vibratory action on the so-called ether.

Verse 17. *Set all the borders* means that God had made the arrangements that have been followed by the earth.

Since God has made *summer and winter* it is plain to see why he could make the prediction of Gen. 8: 22.

Verse 18. Again David was worried about the activities of the enemy. The thing that concerned him especially was their attitude toward God. He put his personal interests secondary to those of the Lord.

Verse 19. *Turtledove* was a sort of "pet name" for the Israelite nation. David was pleading in behalf of the people of God, especially of that portion of them who were poor. It was that condition that encouraged the enemies to oppress them.

Verse 20. God had made more than one *covenant* concerning the people. But the present subject of interest was the treatment being accorded the descendants of Abraham. We therefore would conclude that David meant the one in the first half of Gen. 12: 3. *Dark places* indicates the secret conspiracies of enemies against Israel.

Verse 21. If God should suffer the oppression to continue without relief they would be ashamed or confused. On the other hand, if they were strengthened to overcome their enemy it would cause them to praise the Lord.

Verse 22. *Plead thine own cause* was said in connection with the state of affairs in the nation. That was similar in thought with an expression in ch. 23: 3 where it says that God would lead his servant aright for his own name's sake. By defending the nation against the enemies the foolish man would be stopped in his reproaches.

Verse 23. *Forget not* meant not to let the enemy "get by" with his vile reproaches against the people of God.

PSALMS 75

Verse 1. The existence (not the mere name) of God is the subject of this verse. And the evidence which David cites to prove it is the wonderful works of creation.

Verse 2. *Congregation* sometimes means the citizens of the nation in a general sense, whether in assembly or scattered about in their homes. Just as we would speak about a congregation today, meaning the members of the church wherever they might be located in their homes. David meant the congregation when it had assembled for a hearing. At such time he promised he would render righteous judgment.

Verse 3. This verse gives a hint of why such an assembly would be formed. It would be because of the confused and disordered condition of the earth's inhabitants. When that occasion should occur David promised to *bear up the pillars* by giving good judgments.

Verses 4, 5. In passing his judgments David admonished men to put away their foolishness. *Lift not up the horn* meant for them not to try showing off their authority.

Verse 6. *South* is rendered "desert" in the margin of many Bibles and Strong's lexicon does the same. Hence only two directions are really mentioned by the writer. The point is that it is vain to rely on any earthly sources for support.

Verse 7. Instead of relying on the human resources, it should be considered that all things are in the hands of God to regulate as he sees fit.

Verse 8. *Cup* and *wine* are figurative references to the wrath of God against sin. However, the various portions of the contents are used to compare the different fates of the good and the evil persons. The good will be permitted to drink off the red (clear) wine at the top. The dregs or settlings at the bottom of the cup will be all that the wicked will get. The only way they can obtain any wine will be to wring or squeeze out the liquid in the dregs.

Verse 9. David regarded the dealings from God as just and for that reason he would sing praises to him for ever.

Verse 10. With the help of God David proposed to act against the wicked. *Horns* means power and David would destroy that of the unrighteous.

PSALMS 76

Verse 1. Judah was the largest of the 12 tribes, and the capital of the Israelite nation was in that tribe. For that reason David declared that God was known or recognized in Judah. The national worship was centered at that headquarters and that was where people had to go to see the divine exhibitions of power and knowledge.

Verse 2. *Salem* was a short form of Jerusalem (Gen. 14: 18), and *Zion* was that particular spot in the city where the king had his headquarters.

Verse 3. Victory over a foe was the outstanding desire of David, and he used a great many different expressions to indicate it. A bow would be useless without an arrow, hence it was said that God would *brake the arrows* and other articles of warfare. See the comments at ch. 3: 2 for the meaning of *Selah*.

Verse 4. Here is another indication of the militant mind of David. Among the things he appreciated was the capturing of those who were arrayed against him. He compared such a result to a mountain covered with creatures destined to become victims.

Verse 5. *Stouthearted* were those who thought they were very brave in conflict. They had become a "prey" to the strength of God and had been put to sleep or rendered unable to move a hand further in combat with the Lord's forces.

Verse 6. *Horse and chariot* again refers to war action. *Into a dead sleep* denotes they had been put completely out of action in battle.

Verse 7. *To be feared* meant that all enemies should fear and respect the might of God. Not one of them would be able to withstand the wrath of God when it was displayed.

Verses 8, 9. God is situated in heaven and from there he issued his judgments. These judgments were directed against his foes. When that was done the earth (its people) feared or trembled and was put out of action. But the *meek* or humble ones were rewarded with the good things of the earth.

Verse 10. The wrath of Pharaoh was suffered to be displayed far enough to give God the opportunity for overcoming it. When that had been accomplished then Pharaoh and his host were overthrown and thus proved that *the remainder of wrath shalt thou restrain*. This is the thought that is intended to be expressed in Ex. 9: 16.

Verse 11. *Vow and pay* meant for them to recognize the duty of sacrificing to God and then of fulfilling the promise to do so. *Bring presents* refers to an ancient practice between various ranks of persons and is explained at Gen. 23: 13 and 1 Sam. 10: 27.

Verse 12. *Spirit of princes* means the spirit of pride that urged the princes to array themselves against God. The kings who do exalt themselves against the Lord will be made to feel his terror against unrighteousness.

PSALMS 77

Verse 1. A person usually cries with his voice, but the expression means that David used his voice in a strong cry for mercy. God heard and granted the prayer.

Verse 2. The general life of David was one of devotion to God. In view of that it was consistent for him to call upon Him when in trouble. *My sore* is rendered "my hand" in the margin which is correct. The statement of David meant he held out his hand in supplication all night because of his sore trials.

Verse 3. Remembering God did not cause David to be troubled. When he was troubled and his spirit was overwhelmed, then he remembered God and prayed unto him.

Verse 4. David was so troubled at times that it kept him from sleeping. His distress was so depressing that he was unable to express himself.

Verse 5. David was a normal human being even though an inspired man when writing or speaking for God. He had his hours of personal sorrow in which he expressed himself from the standpoint of an uninspired man. (See comments at Job 38: 3.) While in one of these moods he got to thinking of the past.

Verse 6. In one of the scenes of the past he recalled that he was able to sing in the night, whereas now he was so sad that he could not even speak.

Verses 7-9. As David contrasted his present state of distress with the joyous ones of the past, he became fearful that the Lord was deserting him. It seemed that God had discarded his former mercies and was displaying his anger instead. With such a scene before the eyes of his memory David again felt indisposed to speak but plunged into a state of meditation which was indicated by the oft-repeated term *Selah*. See the comments at ch. 3: 2 in connection with this paragraph.

Verse 10. The moments of meditation resulted in the realization that David was a human being and had been lamenting over the things that affected his infirmities, but not necessarily his spiritual interests. He then roused himself and recalled other years when the *right hand* of God was beneath him. When things are said to be done by the right hand of God it means that whatever is done by the hand of God is right; even though it might not always appear so in the eyes of man.

Verse 11. David not only recalled his own personal favors from God, but also the great works in general that had been done.

Verse 12. It is not enough merely to recall the works of God to the mind as incidents; David strengthened the memory by *meditation.* (Ch. 1: 2.) He did not stop with that, but talked about it so that others might be encouraged.

Verse 13. The *sanctuary* does not refer to any certain place or structure. It is from GODESH and Strong's definition is, "a sacred place or thing; rarely abstractly [meaning a specific name], sanctity." So whatever and wherever the Lord provided for the holy or religious activities of his people, that was where they should come to get the full knowledge of the Lord.

Verse 14. There were many professed gods among the nations which gave occasion for frequent contrasts between the various ones. David exalted the true God on the merits of his wonderful deeds. He *declared* his strength by something more convincing than mere words. He performed things that could be seen by the public and which showed to the eyes and ears of the witnesses that the God of Israel was great.

Verse 15. David again went back to the historic scenes pertaining to Israel's enslavement in Egypt and the redemption therefrom. Jacob and Joseph were given specific mention for significant reasons. Jacob was the father of the nation of Israel, and Joseph was the one among his sons who went to Egypt first and paved the way for the whole family to come. After that God redeemed them all by his *arm.*

Verse 16. This verse refers to the scenes at and in the Red Sea. The waters were not literally *afraid* or *troubled.* It means that fear was caused by them.

Verses 17-20. The closing verse of this paragraph shows that David was still writing about the deliverance of Israel from Egypt by way of the Red Sea. We therefore should take many of the references to the weather conditions in a figurative or general sense. There is nothing in the history of Ex. 14 and 15 that indicates any literal rainfall at that time. The actual event was the opening and closing of the Sea. That mighty deed induced the Psalmist to paint a picture in general of God's control of all the elements of the universe.

PSALMS 78

General remarks. This is a marvelous psalm and is so full of important subject matter that we shall need to study it carefully lest we overlook some of its teaching. Before taking up the several verses, I shall quote a statement of Dr. Marion McH. Hull, whose remarks I fully endorse, as follows: "This psalm is historic, didactic [instructive], and prophetic. It is a marvelous commentary on the Old Testament. It is a great revelation of the stubborn and unbelieving human heart, and also a great revelation of the patience, grace, love, justice, and divine wisdom of God." The truth in the above quotation will be manifest as we study the verses in their order.

Verse 1. David was going to recount many of the events in the history of the nation under him. *Give ear* was a call for attention to what he was about to say. *Law* was used in an extended sense, including any teaching that would be given, whether in the form of commandments or history, intended for their information and admonition.

Verse 2. *Parable* is from a word that may mean a pithy saying; not necessarily a comparison. *Dark sayings of old* means the important expressions about past events.

Verse 3. Most of the things David intended to write about had occurred many years before and had become a matter of record. But the voice of history has to be repeated many times to impress mankind with its importance.

Verse 4. See the comments on the previous verse. The former generations were the direct objects of the *praises of the Lord* whenever their conduct justified them. But when it was otherwise, then they were made to feel the strength of God in punishing them for their sins. David believed that the children of those ancient fathers should be informed about the past for their own admonition. (1 Cor. 10: 11.)

Verse 5. This whole verse refers to the law of Moses. *Jacob* and *Israel* mean the same people, the latter being a special name for the former (Gen. 32: 28). The law was given to the people who were called by these names. And it was intended that this law should be *made known* to the children yet to be born. That was the reason David called upon these children to give attention to him.

Verse 6. The children of one generation were to tell the story to the next generation, etc., and thus it was to be continued down through the years.

Verse 7. The object of all this repetition was that people would learn to hope in God. It was continued thus over into New Testament times. (1 Cor. 10: 11.)

Verse 8. The coming generations were expected to profit by the mistakes of their fathers. The main lesson to be learned was the folly of being stubborn.

Verse 9. *Ephraim* did not refer to the northern kingdom because the place in history of which David was writing was many years before. But the tribe of Ephraim was one outstanding group of the descendants of Jacob and the writer merely cited it as a typical example of the rebellion of which he was writing.

Verse 10. A covenant is a contract between two or more parties. If either fails to do his part the covenant will be broken. The children of Israel failed in their part and thus were guilty as truce breakers.

Verse 11. They did not forget in the sense of having a lapse of memory. They failed to respect the memory of those wondrous works.

Verse 12. The *marvelous things* in Egypt were the 10 plagues miraculously brought upon the Egyptians. *Zoan* was a city in Egypt near which many acts of Moses took place.

Verse 13. *Stand as an heap* refers to the walls of ice in the Sea. (Ex. 15: 8.)

Verse 14. This verse is a direct reference to that unusual cloud that God used between the Egyptians and Israelites described in Ex. 13: 21.

Verses 15, 16. This miraculous supply of water is recorded in Ex. 17.

Verses 17, 18. *Meat* as used here means food in general. There was nothing wrong in the mere desire for food; the sin was in the manner of the request and the false accusations they made at the time. (See Ex. 16: 2, 3.)

Verse 19. They questioned the Lord's ability to set a table in the wilderness. It seems they had forgotten the mighty works performed for them in the land of their bondage. By such behaviour they showed their lack of faith.

Verse 20. The children of Israel seemed bent on complaining in spite of many evidences of God's goodness. They admitted the provision for drinking water, then specified a charge that the Lord could not produce bread and meat.

Verse 21. The *fire* mentioned here refers to the anger of the Lord at the rebellious cries of his people right while enjoying the many divine blessings.

Verse 22. *Believed not* is an outstanding charge against the Israelites in connection with their complaints. Paul took that view of the case in Heb. 3: 19.

Verses 23, 24. The unbelief of the Israelites persisted in spite of the evident goodness of the Lord. *Clouds* and *doors* are figurative references to food and drink.

Verse 25. *Angel* is from ABBIR and Strong defines it, "mighty (spoken of God)." Young defines it, "mighty." In the A.V. it has been translated by bull 4 times, chiefest 1, mighty 3, mighty one 1, strong 2, strong one 1, valiant 2. Thus the word has reference to the persons supposed to need it and not directly to its composition. To use a popular expression it could be said to have been a "breakfast of champions."

Verse 26. We would not question God's power to bring about a result without using any apparent means, but he frequently employs some agency for his purposes. In the case at hand he saw fit to use a strong wind, something which ordinarily would have no effect in producing a living creature.

Verse 27. *He rained* is a figurative way of saying he sent an abundance. The *feathered fowls* meant the quails recorded in Ex. 16: 13.

Verse 28. This account may be seen in Num. 11: 31, 32.

Verses 29-31. This feature of the case is recorded in Num. 11: 33.

Verses 32, 33. Regardless of the blessings received, the Israelites sinned by complaining and had to be punished severely. *Vanity* means brief or empty. Because of the sins of the people, God shortened their years and consumed them in the wilderness.

Verses 34, 35. Sometimes the Israelites were brought to their senses by their punishments and would appeal to God for mercy. They were always treated with divine compassion, many times far beyond the claims of strict justice.

Verse 36. *Flattered* and *lied* are used in the same sense as they should be. There is a great difference between true praise and flattery. The former is a statement about another that is based on some merit that is recognized. The latter is a superfluous use of adjectives intended only to "bribe" another into granting some favor not rightely coming to the flatterer. We know that God was never misled by the flattery, but he suffered them to have "another chance' for the benefit of others. (1 Cor. 10: 11.)

Verse 37. David gave the explananation for their resort to flattery. It was because *their heart was not right*. Such can truly be said of all persons who attempt to accomplish some purpose with another by using flattery.

Verse 38. Were it not for the mercy of God, his justice would cut off the human race when men reached the years of knowledge. But while the divine wrath was displayed for the benefit of the wayward people, God did not completely destroy them; *did not stir up all his wrath*.

Verse 39. The frailty of the fleshly life is considered in James 4: 14. In view of this fact God made many allowances which a strict accounting would not have suffered.

Verse 40. When man is *provoked* and *grieved* he has an unpleasant feeling. We cannot think of God in Heaven as experiencing any discomfort as we think of such an experience. But let it always be remembered that in speaking to man it was necessary for God to use man's language (Rom. 6: 19). These terms when applied to God mean that in his infinite knowledge and survey of all things he is disposed to regard certain actions of man as exceedingly provoking and grievous.

Verse 41. *Limited* is from TAVAH and means literally to "draw a circle around." It is impossible literally to do such a thing to God, hence we must seek an accommodative meaning in the present case. When men refuse to accept the full benefits offered to them by the Lord it has the effect of limiting or cutting short those blessings. A case in point is that of Christ in Mark 6: 5.

Verse 42. Here is the old weakness, failing to remember. Just one serious glance back to their deliverance from Egypt should have melted their heart of stone and caused them to bow in humble penitential prayers to God.

Verse 43. This is commented upon at v. 12.

Verse 44. The pronoun *their* refers to the Egyptians and the *rivers* were the Nile and other streams of the country. (Ex. 7: 17-20.)

Verses 45-48. This paragraph is given in the history of Ex. 8 and 9 and commented upon in its proper place in volume 1 of the Commentary.

Verse 49. *Anger, wrath* and *indignation* are various names for the attitude of God against the rebellion of man. *Evil angels* were not angels who did something wrong. *Evil* means the different afflictions sent on the Egyptians, and the angels were the agents of God for such work.

Verse 50. *Made a way* means that God did not merely express his anger by words. He found ways and means for making the Egyptians feel it.

Verse 51. This is a brief but complete statement of what is recorded in Ex. 12. The inferior nations came from *Ham* (Gen. 9: 25; 10: 6), among whom were the Egyptians.

Verse 52. David contrasted the treatment accorded the Egyptians with that of the Israelites. One group was the people of the Lord and the other was their enemies. We might justly designate one as a flock of sheep and the other as a pack of wolves.

Verse 53. *They feared not* applied to them after God had given them assurance by the agency of Moses. (Ex. 14: 13, 14) This was just at the time of the crossing through the Red Sea, for the overthrow of the enemies is mentioned in direct connection.

Verse 54. The *sanctuary* was the tabernacle that Moses built and the *mountain* was Sinai. It was not *purchased* in the sense of a business deal. One word in Strong's definition of the original is "procure." God procured the mountain with his *right hand*, which means he made a right use of his hand (or power) to get the mountain into the possession of his people whom he had redeemed from Egypt.

Verse 55. *Cast out the heathen* refers to the conquest of Canaan under the leadership of Joshua. The history is in the book that bears his name.

Verse 56. The Israelites failed to appreciate the goodness of God. *Kept not his testimonies* means they did not obey the commandments of the law. For explanation of *provoke* see my comments at v. 40.

Verse 57. *Turned back* denotes that they let their minds go back to the days of their disobedient fathers and imitated their evil deeds. A *deceitful bow* is one that does not shoot in the direction that is indicated by its position; also, one that snaps and breaks just at the time it was expected to send forth the arrow.

Verse 58. See my comments on *high places* at 1 Ki. 3: 2 in volume 2 of this Commentary. *Graven images* were idols carved out of metal or stone to be worshiped.

Verse 59. *When God heard* does not mean that he has to be informed about what is going on. The phrase was used as if it said, "since God heard or knew."

Verse 60. *Shiloh* was the location of the tabernacle in the days of Eli. (1 Sam. 4: 4.) When the Israelites made the wrong use of the ark, God forsook the whole institution so it was never again as important as it had been.

Verse 61. *Captivity* here refers to the capture of the ark recorded in 1 Sam. 4: 11. In the 21st verse of that chapter the dying wife of Phinehas declared that the "glory" had departed when the ark was taken.

Verse 62. The Philistines were the people who captured the ark from Israel. They were suffered also to make a great slaughter among them.

Verse 63. *The fire* of battle destroyed the young men so that the maidens were deprived of marrying them.

Verse 64. *Widows made no lamentation* seems like a strange statement. The explanation is in the sudden or unexpected instance of the death of their priestly husbands. The women were not present at the event and hence had no occasion to lament then.

Verses 65, 66. God will not always suffer his people to be mistreated by the enemy. He finally came to the rescue and delivered them. *Smote ... hinder parts* indicates the enemies were on the run and were smitten as they fled.

Verse 67. *Joseph* and *Ephraim* are used in the same sense since the one was the son of the other. The kingdom had not been divided when David lived, but he was a prophet and wrote of future events as if they had taken place.

Verses 68, 69. *Zion* was the most important spot in Jerusalem. The city was in the possession of the tribe of Judah, hence that was the chosen religious headquarters.

Verse 70. *David* as an inspired writer spoke of David as a young man engaged in caring for sheep.

Verse 71. The young shepherd was called away from the work of caring for the literal flocks. The new work was to feed or tend the spiritual and national flock. That flock was the children of Israel, the name derived from their founder Jacob.

Verse 72. *Integrity of his heart* means his heart was entirely devoted to the welfare of his people. His *skilfulness* was made sure by the guidance of Him who had already declared him to be a man "after his own heart" (1 Sam. 13: 14).

PSALMS 79

Verse 1. The *heathen* were the idolaters that were continually opposing Israel. Many of the remarks of David could have been said at various times in the history. He wrote both as a prophet and historian. The strange people of the surrounding nations were envious of Jerusalem and used every opportunity for injuring the holy city.

Verse 2. Those who were slain in battle were not even given decent burial. Their bodies were left to become food for wild beasts and birds.

Verse 3. Bloodshed was so great that it was compared to the flowing water as an illustration of emphasis.

Verse 4. The defeat and injustice inflicted upon the nation of Israel should have caused witnesses to sympathize with them. Instead, they ridiculed them and treated them with contempt, holding them up to scorn.

Verse 5. This verse is one of David's earnest prayers for divine help. God had declared that he was jealous (Ex. 20: 5), which meant he would not tolerate any sharing of his people's affections with another interest. The nation had not yet gone off after idolatry, but it had been negligent to some extent in duty to the Lord. David did not protest the chastisement but was pleading that it might be eased up.

Verse 6. While David did not deny the guilt of his people, he still believed that the other nations were much worse. He prayed that God would put the weight of his wrath on them who had not so much as recognized his name.

Verse 7. It was bad enough for the nations to commit idolatry. But they went further and damaged the land of the true people of God.

Verse 8. The plea of David did not deny the guilt of the former generations. He asked that they be now passed by and that the mercy of God *prevent* (assist or go before) them in the time of distress.

Verse 9. Again David did not deny any guilt but pleaded for mercy. He based his prayer on the *glory* and for the sake of the Lord's *name*. For the argument with reference to the name of the Lord see the comments at ch. 23: 3.

Verse 10. David always dreaded to be put to shame by the heathen. If the children of Israel should be punished very extensively, these enemies might laugh and say their God had failed them. In view of that motive the Psalmist called for a demonstration of God's power in the sight of his injured people.

Verse 11. Some of the Jews had been unjustly subjugated to the power of the enemy which made them virtual prisoners. David's prayer was that God would hear the cry of these oppressed ones. Some of them were being held under condemnation of death and the plea of the Psalmist was for their rescue.

Verse 12. The word *neighbors* was not used in the sense of persons in a friendly relation. It meant those who were living near the Israelites and who took advantage of the opportunity to insult the people of God. *Sevenfold* is figurative, meaning for God to deal out a complete revenge upon these *neighbors*.

Verse 13. *Sheep of thy pasture* is an endearing term as well as one that implies a state of dependence. Sheep are loveable creatures, and also are such that must be provided with food and protection by their master. They are appreciative when kindness is shown to them. Accordingly, the Lord's sheep would gladly show their love for their master to the generations around them.

PSALMS 80

Verse 1. Having referred to the Israelites as sheep in the preceding chapter, David here termed the Lord as a shepherd. Joseph was not the head of the nation, but he was the son who first lived in Egypt and through whose means the whole family settled there. It was fitting, therefore, that he be referred to in this affectionate way. He is thus mentioned in other parts of the Bible. Besides the one in the present verse, he is referred to in Ex. 1: 8; Ps. 78: 67; 8: 1; Amos 6: 6; Ob. 18. *Between the cherubims* had reference to the objects on the mercy seat where the high priest met with the Lord on the great day of atonement. (Ex. 25: 18-22.)

Verse 2. Ephraim and Manasseh were sons of Joseph, who was considered in the preceding verse. This is not a repetition of that statement, for he alone was named there. In this place the next generation is considered and thus the writer names 3 of the separate tribes. The whole idea is that David wished for God to give full recognition to the nation from every standpoint.

Verse 3. *Face to shine* is a figurative signal of the favorable countenance of God. It would indicate that the trials to which the Lord had subjected his people would be discountinued or at least be made lighter.

Verse 4. This is one of the supplicating petitions that David often presented to God. *God of hosts* means he is at the head of vast numbers of warriors and other servants who were ready to do the will of their Commander.

Verse 5. God will see that his people are supplied with food, but they must eat it in connection with hardships when the Lord sees fit to chastise them in that way.

Verse 6. The *neighbors* or surrounding nations looked upon the hardships being endured by the Israelites and regarded them as conflicts among themselves. They would naturally be elated over seeing what they thought was internal trouble and would laugh.

Verse 7. This is a practical repetition of v. 3.

Verse 8. This is a parable between the Israelites people and a vine. If a man purchased a vine it would be useless to him unless he planted it. In order to have a place for the vine he would first have to clear his ground of other plants. And so the Lord cleared the ground (land of Palestine) of objectionable plants (the heathen), then placed his own plant (the Israelite nation) in a position to grow.

Verse 9. The parable is continued as a vine would require. There was enough room to plant the vine when the children of Israel crossed over into Palestine. But it was necessary to have more space, hence David says *thou preparedst room*. This was done by the work of Joshua in overthrowing the 31 kings. (Josh. 12: 24.)

Verse 10. As a thrifty vine would spread until it covered the hillside, so the nation of Israel grew until it occupied the whole land.

Verse 11. The extent to which the vine reached is specified in this verse. The *sea* was the Mediterranean and the *river* was the Jordan.

Verse 12. David continued his remarks in the language of the parable. Vineyards were enclosed by hedges for protection (Matt. 21: 33; Mark 12: 1). To break down the hedge would be to expose the vineyard to the ravages of the enemy. The Psalmist was using this to compare the exposure of Israel to the oppression of the heathen which God did for the purpose of chastisement.

Verse 13. These wild beasts were used to compare the heathen nations about the country whose savagery had been felt by the Israelites.

Verse 14. Again David did not deny the justice of the punishment. He only pleaded for mercy by asking God to *visit this vine*. That meant to bestow some relief on the people of the Lord by pushing the enemy back.

Verse 15. *Right hand planted* means it was *right* for the nation to be established by the *hand* of God. Since the Lord had made the vine strong *for himself*, he surely would be inclined to come to its rescue.

Verse 16. The strong terms used referred to the vicious treatment that the heathen had imposed on the nation. David recognized it as a punishment from God, for he lays it to *the rebuke of thy countenance*.

Verse 17. I have explained that the *right hand* of God means that the things done by the *hand* of God are *right*. On that basis a man who is favorable toward God's right hand would be a good man. Such a man might expect that God would give him his hand in the way of support for his life of righteousness.

Verse 18. David promised not to forsake the Lord if he would give him his hand for guidance. *Quicken us* meant to encourage and enliven them by his favors, thus inducing them to call upon the name of the Lord.

Verse 19. This verse is practically the same in thought as vs. 3, 7.

PSALMS 81

Verse 1. A *joyful noise* means an expression that is more than a mere sound. It must have that which indicates an intelligent appreciation of the goodness of God. This idea is also indicated by the fact of the *noise* of singing. Something more than sound is required when one sings; especially when it is used for the purpose of praise.

Verse 2. The *psalm* would be the literary composition that expressed praise to God. And this was to be accompanied by the musical instruments named here.

Verse 3. The religious months were ushered in by the new moon. (1 Sam. 20: 5, 6, 24, 27.) At such times the devout Jews blew a trumpet. (Lev. 23: 24.) This service was to be attended to regularly, *in the time appointed*, regardless of any special favors that might have been received. But there was reason to engage in those exercises with special fervor because of the benefits they had received. Not least of those benefits was the miraculous deliverance from Egyptian bondage.

Verse 4. The references that show this *statute* and *law* were cited above.

Verse 5. The pronouns *he* and *I* refer to God. *Joseph* is used in the same sense as I explained it at ch. 80: 1. One word in Strong's definition of the original for *understood* is "recognition." The verse means that God looked into the situation in Egypt and heard language that he refused to recognize or approve. That language consisted in such as was used against Joseph (the Israelites) in commanding them to labor in rigorous toil and bondage.

Verse 6. This verse is a direct historic statement referring to the work that was done through Moses and Aaron. The *pots* were baskets or other vessels used in carrying heavy loads of material for the work of their severe labor in making brick, etc.

Verse 7. *Thou* (Israel) calledst in trouble and *I* (the Lord) delivered thee. This deliverance was done through Moses and Aaron. *Secret place of thunder* refers to the Lord as the source of thunder and all other wonders. He it was who responded to the cry of Israel. In spite of the merciful help from God the Israelites soon forgot and had to be *proved* or tested. That was done in the case of shortage of drinking water as recorded in Ex. 17. See comments at ch. 3: 2 for *Selah*.

Verse 8. The basis on which God would logically exhort Israel to hear him was the fact that they were *his people*. He would *testify* to them, which is from a word the means to repeat something that had been said before.

Verse 9. The repetition referred to in the preceding verse was the commandment against idolatry. This was first spoken to them at Sinai (Ex. 19 and 20).

Verse 10. The children of Israel were indebted to God for their deliverance from Egyptian bondage. Gratitude should have prompted them to hear what their deliverer had to say. The *mouth* is the inlet for material food and the word was used figuratively to compare the inlet for spiritual food. *Open thy mouth wide* meant for them to open their hearts to the full reception of the truth.

Verse 11. *Would none of me* was a brief way of saying that Israel would not receive any of the Lord's instructions regarding their conduct of life.

Verse 12. God never used physical force to get a man to live right as far as his personal life was concerned. The only means he ever used was teaching, and if he would not accept it to regulate his life thereby he was left to himself. After that the full responsibility for the results would be at the feet of the disobedient person.

Verses 13, 14. God never asks man to do more than the human part. Had the Israelites done what they could against the heathen nations, God would have completed the work by driving the enemy entirely out of the land.

Verse 15. *Submitted* is translated "yielded feigned obedience" in the margin of some Bibles and the lexicon of Strong agrees with it. The heathen would pretend to be convinced by the terror of God's dealing with them, but *their time* (of feeling the wrath of God) would go on unendingly regardless of their hypocritical *submission*.

Verse 16. There is a "switch" made in the pronouns; *them* now refers to the Israelites. Had they hearkened to the words of God he would have given them the best of blessings. *Rock* is from TSUR and according to the Standard Bible Dictionary the word is "used for that which is hard, barren, and unfruitful." The phrase *honey out of the rock* means that God is able to produce the choicest food from even a barren source. Such wonderful care would the Lord have taken of his people had they been faithful and proved themselves worthy of such attention from Him.

PSALMS 82

Verse 1. *Standeth* means to be stationed or established. One part of Strong's definition of the original for *judgeth* is "to govern." The clause means that God's power and right to govern is above that of all other rulers.

Verse 2. David was speaking for God and to the rulers among the Israelites. They were accused of rendering unjust decisions, and of being swayed by the personal influence of wicked men because of some special advantages offered to them.

Verse 3. A poor man may be wrong; but it is also wrong to accuse a poor man falsely and to take advantage of his dependent circumstances.

Verse 4. This language shows that David was not pleading for these men merely because they were poor. *Deliver* implies a condition of oppression and the plea was for their deliverance from it. It was also indicated that their state of oppression had been thrust upon them while they were *needy*.

Verse 5. *They* still meant the leading men in the nation of Israel. In their blind thirst for power over others they were shutting themselves off from the knowledge of God's great works. We should not forget, however, that, while the first application of these exhortations was to the leaders, the nation as a whole was guilty for suffering things to go on as they were going. Hence the passage as a whole should be applied to all the Jews.

Verse 6. This verse was cited by Jesus in John 10: 34 in his controversy with the Jews. *Ye are gods* is explained by the second clause of the verse. Every member of a family wears the name of that family. If a family name is Smith then everyone in that family is a Smith. The family name of which David was writing was God; therefore each Jew was a God, seeing he was one of the *children of the Most High.* God is the family name of the Trinity: God the Father, God the Son and God the Holy Spirit. That is why Jesus is called "God" in Acts 20: 28.

Verse 7. Their being members of a divine family would not save them from human punishment if they conducted themselves like wicked men.

Verse 8. God has rightful control over all things and nations. Therefore David pleaded with him to judge the earth; that is, bring some judgment or punishment upon all unrighteous persons of the earth.

PSALMS 83

Verse 1. The three parts of this verse make up another of David's many supplications to God. He was concerned over the activities of the enemies about him.

Verse 2. *Thine enemies* indicates that David regarded the opposition from the foes as being in reality against God, although the contact was made directly against David usually. God and David and the people over whom he was king were united in purpose. Because of this relationship, any action directed against either of the parties to the unit was considered to be against the others.

Verse 3. *Crafty counsel* means they had consulted together for the purpose of devising some underhanded plot against the Lord's work. *Hidden ones* means God's protected ones; those in His divine and special care.

Verse 4. The enmity that usually manifested itself in those days was from the heathen nations around the land of Israel. They were envious of the success of the people of God and wished, chiefly, to overthrow their national forces.

Verse 5. Individual planning against a righteous cause is always wrong. That kind of evil is much worse when done by a group of persons confederated for the purpose. These confederates had come together in secret meetings and were united in their plots.

Verse 6. *Tabernacles* are places for housing groups of people for various purposes. When used figuratively the word means the groups of the *Edomites,* who descended from Edom (Esau). The *Ishmaelites* came from the son of Abraham and Hagar. The *Moabites* were descendants of one of the sons of Lot. The Hagarenes were people who descended from the same source as the Ishmaelites, but were a specific group of such descendants who took the name of their ancestor Hagar.

Verse 7. These were all groups of the heathen nations that were arrayed against David and the people of the Israelite nation.

Verse 8. *Assur* was another form for the *Assyrians,* and they were *joined with them.* That means that these people had *holpen* (helped) the other nations against Israel. See the comments at ch. 3: 2 for explanation of *Selah.*

Verse 9. The Midianites withstood Israel on their journey to Palestine (Num. 31), and God helped the Israelites. *Sisera* and *Jabin* shared a like fate (Judges 4).

Verse 10. *Became as dung* means they were debased to the state of refuse. But refuse serves a good purpose for the benefit of the earth, and these nations were made to serve for some benefit to the people of God.

Verse 11. The men named were leaders of some heathen nations living in Palestine in the time of the judges. The account of Gideon's victory over them may be seen in the book of Judges, chapters 7 and 8.

Verse 12. The men named in the preceding verse were boastful and thought they would do great harm to the Israelites. Their threats of victory, however, were turned into defeat. David thought back over the history of those times and prayed that a like defeat might come to his enemies who were opposing his service to God.

Verse 13. *Wheel* is from CALGAL and Strong's definition says: "A whirlwind; also dust (as whirled)." The thought of David was that God would whirl or fling the enemies away as so much dust. His other comparison was that God would blow them out of the way as *stubble* or any straw is driven before wind because of its lightness.

Verse 14. Other comparisons were made to the effect that fire has upon material. The wrath of God would be the fire and the enemies the wood to be consumed.

Verse 15. We generally think of *persecute* as meaning unjust rough treatment; the original word does not necessarily mean that. Strong defines it, "To run after (usually with hostile intent)," but nothing is said about its being done unjustly. An officer would have the right to chase a man who was wanted for misbehaviour. David regarded his enemies as wicked people and prayed God to pursue them with just vengeance.

Verse 16. The motive that David expressed for wishing shame on the enemies was a good one; that they might be led to seek the name of God.

Verse 17. To be *confounded* means to be disappointed and defeated. The motive David had for this wish was similar to the one expressed in the preceding verse, and it will be stated in the following verse.

Verse 18. The motive to which reference was made was that men might learn about the true God. They were to know that he alone had right to the name JEHOVAH which means, "(the) self-Existent or Eternal." The nations of the world had their heathen gods, but many of them had been made by the hands of the worshipers. The God whom the Israelites worshiped existed independent of all external forces.

PSALMS 84

Verse 1. *Amiable* means loving or pleasant. There was but one national tabernacle when David wrote his psalms, while the word here is plural. The thought is that it is always pleasant to be in the house of the Lord.

Verse 2. This verse practically repeats the thought of the preceding one, but it is expressed as an earnest wish for those tabernacles. It is like the sentiment which David wrote in Ps. 122: 1.

Verse 3. The reference to the *sparrow* and *swallow* is figurative and shows the interest God has for the most humble creature. See the teaching of Jesus in Matt. 10: 29.

Verse 4. Verse 1 stated that the tabernacles of the Lord were pleasant. In harmony with that fact the present verse would declare it to be a *blessed* (happy) thing to dwell in the house of the Lord. Such a situation would induce the ones therein to praise Him who was the builder of that house and who gave it the blessings contained.

Verse 5. *Strength in thee* is the same thought that Paul expressed in Eph. 6: 10. The last word of the verse has no word in the original. The first part of the verse would justify the pronoun "thee," with the understanding that it means God.

Verse 6. *Baca* is defined by Strong by "weeping." It is uncertain whether this was a literal valley. I shall quote the explanation given in the Standard Bible Dictionary: "Valley of Weeping RV. But there is no trace of a real valley bearing the name. May refer to a group of balsam trees which because such trees exude (shed) beads of gum resembling tears was called Valley of Weeping. In any case in Ps. 84, the phrase figuratively but plainly points to the typical experience of sorrow turned into joy." Article, Baca. I believe this comment is correct and endorse it as my own.

Verse 7. The antecedent of *they* will be found in vs. 4-6. *From strength to strength* means they get stronger as they go. That fact is accounted for by their devotion to God in Zion, the headquarters of the religious life of the nation.

Verses 8, 9. This is one more of David's earnest prayers for divine help. *God of hosts* denotes that all true protection is in Him. Kings or other officials only are literally anointed. Figuratively it means those whom God has chosen as his own.

Verse 10. David describes his preference for spiritual things by using contrasts. One is between being a doorkeeper and an occupant. He would prefer the former if it were in the house of his God, rather than being an occupant in an institution of wickedness. The second contrast will explain what is meant by the first. It means that David regarded one day in the house of God as being worth more than a thousand days in the tents of wickedness.

Verse 11. A *sun* gives light and warmth, and a *shield* is a means of protection. *Grace* and *glory* means that the favor which God bestows will be right and therefore will be truly glorious. It is significant that only *good* things are assured. Man often asks for things that would not be for his own interests; God will not bestow such things upon any man. Another thing to observe is that even the *good* things will be given only to *them that walk uprightly*.

Verse 12. Again we see that the Lord is over the *hosts* which means a company of soldiers or other forceful persons. It would be logical, therefore, that the man who trusted in such a Being would be *blessed* or *happy*.

PSALMS 85

Verse 1. *Captivity* does not always mean a literal imprisonment, but also applies to any state of distress. David was an inspired writer and could deal with the national captivity which was then hundreds of years in the future. But his remarks were equally true of past conditions of the country in which God redeemed the land from the oppression of the enemies, such as the experiences recorded in the book of Judges.

Verses 2, 3. We may rightly think of this paragraph in a general way, because God is always ready to pardon his servants when they comply with his terms of pardon. It we make specific application to the national captivity and return therefrom it will call for the same conclusion. The particular *iniquity* of which the nation of Israel was guilty was idolatry. After they had spent 70 years in the land of their captors they were completely cured of idolatry, and of course the Lord then had *forgiven the iniquity*. This interesting subject will be given thorough attention in the study of the prophecies, some of which will appear in the present volume of the Commentary.

Verse 4. *Turn us* means to reverse the condition of distress that the enemies had brought upon the nation. God's *anger* was manifested by using the enemy as an agent for the correction of His people.

Verse 5. David once more was pleading for mercy. He did not deny their being deserving of chastisement, but pleaded for relief from it.

Verse 6. *Revive us again* means to enliven them by the encouragement of divine forgiveness; this would result in the rejoicing of the people of Israel.

Verse 7. The prayer for *salvation* did not mean that David and his people were in an unsaved condition in regard to their soul. It had reference to being saved or rescued from their national enemies; the people who wished them harm.

Verse 8. *God* and *Lord* have some distinction in their meaning. The first is from EL and means "a strong Being." The second is from YEHOVAH and is defined by the lexicon of Strong as follows: "(the) self-Existent or eternal," and was the Jewish national name of God. David was thinking of Him not only as a Deity of strength, but as the God over the nation of Israel. *Saints* and *people* referred to the same persons; but the first meant they were righteous, the second meant they constituted a people in the sense of a nation. They had been favored of God and the Psalmist exhorted them not to repeat the mistakes they had made before and which had been condemned of God.

Verse 9. The blessings of God are offered upon conditions. It is here connected with fear or reverence for Him, and it will bring glory to the land of Israel.

Verse 10. This verse brings out the same thought expressed in the preceding one, and in a very specific form by pairing the condition and its results in two phases. *Mercy* and *truth* form one pair, *righteousness* and *peace* form the other. The first word in each pair is the condition on which the second will be granted. The reference to *peace* suggests the teaching in James 3: 17.

Verse 11. *Earth* and *heaven* are parts of the material universe, representing opposite ends of it. The thought is that the good things of God will be distributed generally for those who obey the Lord, who is the maker of all good things.

Verse 12. The stipulation was again made that what the Lord gives is *good*. The good things of this life are what the Psalmist had in mind, for he specified the *increase* of the *land*.

Verse 13. If man's righteousness is displayed *before him* (God), then he shall *set* or establish man in the steps of righteousness. (ch. 37: 23; 119: 133.)

PSALMS 86

Verse 1. *Bow down* means for God to open his ear toward the prayer of David. *Poor and needy* referred to his condition of sorrow and distress.

Verse 2. *Soul* is used in the sense of a living and breathing person. *Preserve* and *save* are used in the same sense, meaning to rescue and protect from the encroachments of the enemy. *Holy* means that David was one of God's own servants and by reason of that fact was entitled to divine care.

Verse 3. *Mercy* was asked for in regard to his persecutions. When David *cried* for mercy it meant he prayed earnestly for the favor of God.

Verse 4. *Soul* refers to the whole being as used here. By reducing the persecutions against his body, David would be able to have contentment of mind.

Verse 5. A devoted servant of the Lord is always ready to acknowledge his human weakness. A request for pardon does not always imply some specific sin has been committed. Jesus taught his disciples to ask for pardon on a general principle (Matt. 6: 12), and David was praying from that standpoint.

Verse 6. See the comments on v. 1 and apply them here.

Verse 7. *Day of trouble* again referred to the distress caused by David's enemies.

Verse 8. David contrasted both the personality and works of the true and the false *gods*. The *gods* were the objects of worship that were held sacred by the heathen.

Verse 9. The prediction here made was fulfilled in both the temporal and religious sense. The alien nations were to recognize that of Israel; the whole world, also, was to hear the Gospel and furnish men and women to accept it. (Gen. 12: 3; Isa. 11: 9; Matt. 28: 19; Rom. 10: 18; Col. 1: 23.)

Verse 10. The original word for *God* has a more general application than the one for *Lord*. It embraces all personages that are worshiped or obeyed. It is also defined as a term of comparison between persons and offices of dignity. With all these ideas in mind, David rejected all beings in the universe in favor of the God whom he served. That is, he rejected all others but the one and declared that he was *God alone*.

Verse 11. In this verse David connects *teaching* with *walking*, which is what he also teaches in ch. 37: 23; 119: 133. No man can know the proper way to walk before God without divine instruction.

Verse 12. The names *Lord* and *God* may be used interchangeably for the Supreme Being without any injustice to either. However, there is a distinction in the definition of the originals. With a few exceptions the first is from YEHOVAH and it occurs several thousand times in the Old Testament. Strong's definition of it is, "(the) self-Existent or Eternal; Jehovah, Jewish national name of God." The second is from ELOHIM and Strong defines it, "gods in the ordinary sense; but specifically used (in the plural thus, especially with the article) of the supreme God; occasionally applied by way of deference to magistrates; and sometimes as a superlative." I believe it will be well also to quote from Smith's Bible Dictionary on this most important subject, as follows: "God (good). Throughout the Hebrew Scriptures two chief names are used for the one true divine Being—ELOHIM, commonly translated *God* in our version, and *JEHOVAH*, translated *Lord*. Elohim is the plural of Eloah (in Arabic *Allah*); it is often used in the short form *EL* (a word signifying *strength*), as the EL SHADDAI, *God Almighty*, the name by which God was specially known to the patriarchs. Gen. 17: 1; 28: 3; Ex. 6: 3. The etymology [origin] is uncertain, but it is generally agreed that the primary idea is that of *strength, power of effect*, and that it properly describes God in that character in which he is exhibited to all men in his works, as the creator, sustainer and supreme governor of the world. The plural form of Elohim has given rise to much discussion. The fanciful idea that it referred to the *trinity of persons* in the Godhead hardly finds now a supporter among scholars. It is either what grammarians call *the plural of majesty*, or it denotes the *fullness* of divine strength, the *sum of the powers* displayed by God. Jehovah denotes specifically the one true God, whose people the Jews were, and who made them the guardians of his truth. The name is never applied to a false god, nor to any other being except one, the ANGEL-JEHOVAH, who is thereby marked as one with God, and who appears again in the New Covenant as 'God manifested in the flesh'."

Verse 13. *Hell* is from an original that is used in various senses in the Old Testament; one is that of a state of great depression or forgetfulness. The enemies of David would have forced him into such a state had it not been for the mercy of God. Soul is used with reference to David's general being and earthly life.

Verse 14. Pride may be manifested in various ways, and one of them is to be envious of another's success. David's enemies could not bear to see him in such favor with God, so they formed their *assemblies* (conspiracy meetings) in the hopes of ruining his *soul* or life. The last clause of the verse means the enemy acted in disregard of the Lord as if he did not take notice of what was done to his servants.

Verse 15. *Compassion, gracious, longsuffering* and *mercy* are all so much alike in meaning that it is not necessary to define them separately. The general meaning is that God is very considerate of those who are unjustly oppressed. The Psalmist used the four words for the purpose of emphasis.

Verse 16. *Turn me* denotes a reversal of David's condition of distress. He humbly refers to his mother as the handmaid of God, and for her sake asks for God's favor.

Verse 17. David did not need any special *token* to produce his own faith. He asked for it that his enemies might be forced to see that in opposing David they were opposing God. He wanted his foes to see that God had *holpen* (helped) his servant David against his enemies.

PSALMS 87

Verse 1. *His* refers to the Lord who was named in the last verse of the preceding chapter. *Holy mountains* is figurative, meaning that the Lord has founded his institutions on a high plane, far above the characteristics of the world.

Verse 2. This is another use of contrasts similar to that in ch. 84: 10. The words contrasted are *gates* and *dwellings*, and *Zion* and *Jacob*. Gates would ordinarily be inferior to dwellings, and Jacob (the people in general) would be inferior to Zion which is the capital of the nation. David means that the Lord prefers the capital of the nation above the nation aside from the capital. That is appropriate, for a nation without the right kind of capital would be weak.

Verse 3. *Things* is not in the original as a separate word. *Glorious* is from KABED, and Strong defines it, "numerous, rich, honorable; to make weighty." *City of God* refers to Zion, the capital of the nation, and headquarters of the religious activities of God's people. The verse means that many and important things may, and have been said of that wonderful city of God. See comments at ch. 3: 2 for *Selah*.

Verse 4. The preceding verse said that important things had been said or *spoken* of Zion, which referred to the capital city of God. Among them was the fact that even outside territories were benefited by that city; that is, by the good influences radiating from it. Some of those places are named in the verse. *Rahab* (a poetical name for Egypt), and Babylon were to be mentioned as places that had been benefited by Zion. God would mention it to *them that know* God. *Philistia* or Philistines (from which came the name "Palestine" for the country in general), Tyre and Ethiopia were all benefited by Zion. *Man* is not in the original and is not useful to the sense of the verse. The clause means that *this* trio of places (just mentioned) was *born* or received good effects *there* (Zion).

Verse 5. To be *born* in Zion does not mean that the men had their bodily birth there. The idea is that they received their opportunity for accomplishing things from that source. Zion was to be *established* or made secure by the *highest*, meaning God.

Verse 6. When the Lord makes his list *(writeth up)* of men whom he will recognize, he will include those who had been connected with Zion.

Verse 7. *Singers* and *players* were different persons yet both were to be reckoned in the number. No one man has all of the talents or does all of the service to God. *Springs* means sources of good things. David declared that Zion was the source of all his favors.

PSALMS 88

Verse 1. See the comments at ch. 86: 12 for *Lord God*. *Salvation* is used here to embrace every benefit that

David had ever received from God or expected ever to receive. His immediate concern, however, was salvation from the persecutions of his personal enemies who were daily seeking to rob him of his peace of mind.

Verse 2. *Come before thee* means for his prayer to be admitted into the recognition of God. *Incline thine ear* means about the same as to be "open unto their prayer" as expressed in 1 Pe. 3: 12.

Verse 3. *Soul* and *life* are used in the same sense, meaning David's earthly existence. His enemies were so bitter against him that his life was in danger.

Verse 4. *Pit* is used figuratively, referring to a condition of forgetfulness. By continual oppression of David, the enemies were threatening to reduce his *strength*.

Verse 5. *Free* means he was left alone and forsaken as a man would be were he in his grave. God does not actually forget anything as we commonly use that word. *Rememberest no more* is used as meaning that God does not have any dealings with the body while it is in the grave. The last clause of the verse means the same as the thought expressed in connection with *rememberest*.

Verse 6. David did not charge God with directly dealing with him in the manner described. He knew that it was only in the sense of testing him by suffering his enemies to oppress him. This was indicated by a figurative use of the words *pit, darkness* and *deeps*.

Verse 7. The *waves* were the surges of *wrath* that God suffered to come over David. It was such a solemn period of meditation that he called for the use of the punctuation term *Selah*. See ch. 3: 2 for the explanation of the word.

Verse 8. In times of trouble one's professed friends sometimes desert him. It happened that way to David when he was tormented by his persecutors. His friends held him at a distance so that he could not *come forth* into their company as before.

Verse 9. This verse is a pitiable picture of David's state of mind through his afflictions. He spent much of his time in supplications.

Verse 10. The implied answer to these questions is "no." See the comments on v. 5 which shows that if God is going to do something for a man it will be before his body dies and is placed in its grave where nothing will be done in this age.

Verse 11. This verse calls for the same answer as the preceding one.

Verse 12. *Dark* and *forgetfulness* refer to the state of death. David knows that he cannot be helped against his enemies after he has passed from this life.

Verse 13. One meaning of the original for *prevent* is "to precede." David meant that in the morning he would offer a prayer to precede the favors he expected to get from God through the day.

Verse 14. This is another of David's plaintive appeals to God. *My soul* referred to his life in general. His distress was so great that he felt as if he had been cast off from the face of the Lord.

Verse 15. *Thy terrors* referred to the terrible afflictions that God suffered the enemies to impose upon David. They were so bitter that he was distracted at times.

Verse 16. Again David was using strong language to express the bitterness of his experiences. *Cut me off* means he was undone and cast down in despair.

Verse 17. Water is often used figuratively to compare the volume of afflictions overflowing one. Those imposed upon David were like a continuous flood.

Verse 18. See comments at v. 8 for the explanation of this.

PSALMS 89

Verse 1. The wording of many of the psalms of David was based on his condition of mind. The condition of his mind was caused largely by whatever experiences he was having or considering. The preceding chapter was based on his experiences of distress. The present one is devoted to the pleasant experiences of the Psalmist, and to consideration of the goodness and greatness of God.

Verse 2. *Faithfulness* when applied to God means he is true to his promises. *Established . . . heavens* means the Lord carries out his word to the highest extent.

Verse 3. David speaks for the Lord by using the first personal pronoun *I*. He had chosen David for a special purpose and had made him a sworn covenant.

Verse 4. This verse promised a fleshly favor that would have been fulfilled had the seed of David been faithful. The throne in Jerusalem would have been maintained until the end of the Jewish age, since "age-lasting" is the meaning of *for ever*. It was fulfilled spiritually because Christ was the seed of David and his kingdom is to be everlasting according to the prophecy in Dan. 2: 44.

Verse 5. David now writes of God in the second person. *The heavens* shall praise the Lord in the same sense as was said in ch. 19: 1. *Thy faithfulness* refers to God's promises which he has always kept and always will.

Verse 6. There is only one word in the Old Testament for heaven, whether the 1st, 2nd or 3rd one is meant. However, no man anywhere can be compared to God, hence the word here can be applied to the three heavens. This verse is the basis of part of a familiar church hymn which says: "Whom have I on earth beside Thee? Whom in heaven but Thee?" The implied answer to the questions is in this passage.

Verse 7. *Feared is from* ARATS which Strong defines by, "to awe or dread." *Reverenced* is from the noted YARE which Strong defines by, "to fear; morally to revere." Since both words are used in the same sentence, the distinction between them should be observed. The first means that men should be afraid to do wrong and thus bring down upon them the wrath of God. The second means that God should be respected for his great goodness to the children of men.

Verse 8. *Hosts* means an army or other group of strong men. See the comments at ch. 86: 12 for the distinctive meaning of *Lord God*.

Verse 9. God's power over the sea was demonstrated when he brought the children of Israel safely through it. See cases in Ex. 14 and Jonah 1.

Verse 10. *Rahab* is a poetical name of Egypt. The verse refers to the victory which God gave the Israelites over Egypt in the time of Moses and Aaron.

Verse 11. *The heavens* are the 1st and 2nd heavens in the material universe. God created them and can justly claim them as his own. *World* is from TEBEL and defined as follows: "the earth (as moist and therefore inhabited); by extension the globe; by implication its inhabitants."— Strong. The verse as a whole embraces the same idea as expressed in Gen. 1: 1, referring to the various parts of the universe.

Verse 12. Coming to consideration of the material earth, David specifies its divisions north and south, also some of its mountains; Tabor and Hermon. *Shall rejoice* means that rejoicing will be caused by the blessings brought through these creations.

Verse 13. *Arm* figuratively means strength, and *hand* means the art of using that strength. *High is thy right hand* means that things done by the hand of God are right and also that they are high in their classification.

Verse 14. *Justice* is defined in the lexicon as "the right," and *judgment* is defined as "a verdict." *Habitation* is from an original that is defined "a fixture, i.e. a basis." The whole clause, therefore, means that the throne of God is a fixed place where right verdicts are rendered. *Mercy AND truth* is a phrase that is very significant. God never extends mercy to a person unless it can be in accordance with truth.

Verse 15. *Blessed* or happy are they who *know* or who accept the *joyful sound*. It means the sound coming from the source described in the preceding verse. To *walk . . . the light* means about the same as the teaching in 1 John 1: 7.

Verse 16. To rejoice in the name of the Lord means to have joy because of what that name brings to one who may wear it. True exaltation comes through a righteous life. It was in view of that principle that Jesus said what he did in Matt. 23: 12.

Verse 17. This means that righteous people glory in the strength that comes from the Lord. Paul said he gloried in the cross of Christ. (Gal. 6: 14.) When *horn* is used figuratively it means power or influence. All true power must come from God.

Verse 18. There is perfect safety in the Lord. This is because he is our king and hence can reign for the benefit of the subjects of the kingdom.

Verse 19. The following verse will show that *holy one* in this verse is David. *Spakest in vision* means the Lord revealed something to David, which also means that he was inspired to write a part of the Bible. *Mighty* refers to the power and courage that David showed after he was chosen from among the people to be a king over them.

Verse 20. All men taking an office as ruler were anointed with olive oil. However, the Lord anointed David figuratively by bestowing on him the divine blessing.

Verse 21. The first clause of the verse means that David would be established or made secure with the hand of the Lord. The second clause means practically the same as the first, only that the Lord's *arm* instead of his *hand* is used as the support.

Verse 22. This verse was an assurance that David's enemies would not be suffered to *exact* or take toll from him.

Verse 23. The foes of David would be considered as the foes of God. Because of this they were to be overthrown in the presence of David.

Verse 24. The *faithfulness* of God means his actions of keeping his promises. *Horn* means power of influence. Through the name of the Lord this power would be exalted for David and he would become great among the nations.

Verse 25. *Set his hand* denotes that David's power was to be assured; that it would extend to the (Mediterranean) *sea* and the (Euphrates) *river*. This was practically the same promise that was made to Abram (Gen. 15: 18), and which was actually fulfilled in David's son (1 Ki. 4: 21).

Verse 26. *He* refers to David who was to receive the promise of power mentioned in the preceding verse. *Cry* is not a call of distress or disturbed state of mind as it often means. It is from an original that means to accost or address someone by name. In the present verse it means that David will be encouraged to address the Lord by the endearing name *father* and the respectful name *God*, recognizing him as the rock or basis of his salvation.

Verse 27. *Firstborn* is used in a complimentary sense, meaning that God would place David in the highest rank of importance. That would be in accordance with the estimate he had of him before he was made king. (1 Sam. 13: 14.)

Verse 28. Saul had done so wickedly when he was king that the mercy of God was denied him finally. David was a righteous king and was rewarded for it with God's mercy and the loving favor of the Lord followed him through his reign.

Verse 29. *His seed* had reference to Christ who was often called the seed of David. (2 Sam. 7: 12; Isa. 11: 1; Jer. 23: 5, 6.) The throne or kingdom of that seed was to be an everlasting one. (Dan. 2: 44.)

Verses 30-32. The favors of God are promised on conditions. The children or descendants of David, whether fleshly or spiritual, must follow in the righteous steps of their noted ancestor to enjoy the blessings of God. If they do not, they are to feel the *rod* of correction from the same God whom David served.

Verse 33. Will not *utterly* take implies that some degree of severity would be felt by David, but the lovingkindness of the Lord would not all be taken from him. *Faithfulness* means the keeping of one's promise.

Verse 34. A *covenant* is a contract or agreement between two or more parties. But if one party to a covenant break his word it breaks the covenant. God will never fail to make his word good, but man often breaks his word and that releases God from his agreement. But as for God, he will never fail in his part nor change his word.

Verse 35. An oath is an agreement or other statement that is backed up by the dignity and authority of some being greater than the one making the oath. There is no greater Being than God, therefore he must back up his oath by the greatness of his own personality. That quality is his holiness and it means that the promises of God are as sure as is the fact of his holiness.

Verse 36. This verse is the same in meaning as v. 29.

Verse 37. *Moon* and *heaven* are referred to for the same purpose as in ch. 19: 1. See the comments at ch. 3: 2 for the meaning of *Selah*.

Verse 38. In a partial degree this verse had been fulfilled when David wrote it. But as a prophecy it was to be fulfilled by the national captivity recorded in 2 Ki. 17 and 25. God was wroth with his people because of their idolatry.

Verse 39. This is to be understood practically in the same sense as the preceding verse. *Made void* means that God declared that his covenant was void or of no effect. The cause of it was the failure of the servant to keep his part of it. See the comments at v. 34 on this point of the subject of keeping a covenant.

Verse 40. *Hedges* refers to the fortifications by which Jerusalem was protected. Because of the sins of the nation God was to suffer the enemy to break through the fortifications and take the city that was the capital of the nation.

Verse 41. *Spoil him* means the wealth of the nation was to be taken by the enemy. See the fulfillment of this in 2 Ki. 24: 13.

Verse 42. It was right to bring the hand of Israel's enemies against him because of his sins. This is the meaning of *right hand* as used here.

Verse 43. The unfavorable experiences described in this and several other verses were brought upon the Israelites because of their disobedience. God granted the enemy to have success against the arms of His nation.

Verse 44. The throne of the king in Jerusalem was to be overturned. The prediction was fulfilled in 2 Ki. 25.

Verse 45. The days of man's youth should be his most vigorous ones. But the people of God's nation were met with reverses and felt the hand of divine correction.

Verse 46. David now changed his subject and began his appeal for mercy. He does not complain that his people had been unduly chastised, but pleads for a lessening of it.

Verse 47. David realized the frailty of human life and cited that as a basis for his prayer to God. The same thought is given us in James 4: 14.

Verse 48. Not only is the life of man short at best, but no man can escape death when the time comes. Such a thought should cause us to pause and reflect, hence David used the term *Selah* which is explained at ch. 3: 2.

Verse 49. David never did seriously question the constant goodness of God. This verse is merely a plaintive appeal for the divine help in the times of distress. *In thy truth* indicates that he did not doubt the genuineness of God's promises, for if they were made in truth they would not fail.

Verse 50. *Reproach of thy servants* means that the enemies aimed their reproaches at the servants or people of God. And those darts of reproach were especially directed against the bosom of David because of his position of prominence.

Verse 51. *Wherewith* means that by the mentioned reproaches the enemy's darts had affected the kingdom, seeing that David had been anointed king over it.

Verse 52. *Blessed be the Lord* means that he was to be adored and praised. This adoration was due Him for all of his goodness. *Amen and amen* is a phrase with no added meaning to what the word would have if used only once. It was repeated for the sake of emphasis and denoted a firm approval of what had been said. The definition of the word in both the original and in the English is, "so be it."

PSALMS 90

General remarks. A considerable number of "authorities" say that this psalm was composed by Moses and was included in the collection of David's writings. They do not seem to be very positive about it. Even as substantial a work as the Schaff-Herzog Encyclopedia is willing only to say that it "is ascribed to Moses, and may be his." I offer these remarks in fairness to the readers who may take them for what they are worth. But regardless of whether David or Moses wrote this chapter, it was written by an inspired man and I shall comment on it as such and will notice the many and great truths therein which are of interest to all or should be.

Verse 1. The original for *dwelling place* is defined "a retreat." The idea is of a place where one can be always safe and comfortable against the storms of life. *Lord* is from ADONAI and Strong's definition is, "The Lord (used as a proper name of God only)." Since *God* means the "supreme Being" and has always existed, he would have been a safe retreat *in all generations*.

Verse 2. The existence of the Creator prior to the work of creation is the thought in the beginning of this verse. The writer does not stop with that, but declares the divine existence to have been *from everlasting to everlasting*. Materialists and other critics of the Biblical doctrine of endless punishment make light of the idea that *everlasting* could mean endless. They ask how there could be two of them if one of them is endless. In this they expose their own shortsightedness as well as their ignorance of the subject in general. If the existence of God is endless (everlasting), it follows that His existence would be endless in both directions, or, *from* everlasting (past) *to* everlasting (future. The original for God in this place means strength or might. The sum of meaning of this verse is, therefore, that God has always existed and always will. That he is a Being of might and hence was able to create the mountains and everything that pertains to the earth.

Verse 3. *Destruction* is from a word that means "to be crushed" in spirit; to be made contrite or penitent for one's sins. That is why the rest of the verse shows that God calls for the penitent one to *return* to Him.

Verse 4. God has always existed and always will. What we call "time" is only the measurement of part of that endless duration, measured by the movements of the heavenly bodies. Were it not for those movements we would not know any difference between a "day" and a "year." Since God is not limited by these movements, what we call a thousand years does not mean any more to God than what we call a day. That is the reason Peter said what he did in 2 Pe. 3: 8.

Verse 5. The frailty and comparative shortness of man's life is the general subject of this psalm. Of course, said frailty is made evident by the statements on the boundless might and existence of the Lord and God of all creation. The pronoun *them* refers to man. There are three illustrations in this verse to show the weakness and brevity of man's existence on the earth. He is as helpless as a feather would be in the path of a flood. His life is like a sleep that soon comes to an end, and his stay here is as temporary as the grass of the field.

Verse 6. This verse continues the thought in the preceding one. As grass is permitted to live only through a day, figuratively speaking, so man's life on the earth soon closes. This thought is expressed also in James 1: 10.

Verse 7. These remarks are not directed against any particular person nor concerning any specific conduct of man. They are in consideration of the general situation of mankind since the sin of our first parents. The *anger* and *wrath* of God was provoked by the first sin which was induced by Satan. Because of that event, man was cast out of the garden and doomed to be *consumed* and *troubled* by the ills of creation.

Verse 8. This verse means that none of man's actions are hidden from the Lord. Even the thoughts of the heart are seen by Him. (Heb. 4: 13.)

Verse 9. The fleeting shortness of human life is still the main subject. The *wrath* of God refers to the first sin and the attitude that was declared by the Lord against man over it. As a result of that circumstance, the human family passes through the days of its existence as something that is being spent. *Tale that is told.* The first word is the only one that is in the original. It is from HEGEH and Strong defines it, "a muttering." In other words, our life is as transient as a momentary musing or meditation that ends with a sigh. I will quote from Edward Gibbon, author of the famous *Decline and Fall of the Roman Empire*. He was a skeptic as to the Bible, but was a master of English and a truthful writer as a historian and commentator on human life. He so forcefully agrees with the inspired writer as to the shortness of this life that I wish the reader to have his statement which is as follows: "A being of the nature of man, endowed with the same faculties, but with a longer measure of existence, would cast down a smile of pity and contempt on the crimes and follies of human ambition, so eager, in a narrow span, to grasp at a precarious and short-lived enjoyment. It is thus that the experience of history exalts and enlarges the horizon of our intellectual view. In a composition of some days, in a perusal of some hours, six hundred years have rolled away, and the duration of a life or reign is contracted to a fleeting moment; the grave is ever beside the throne; the success of a criminal is almost instantly followed by the loss of his prize; and our immortal reason survives and disdains the sixty phantoms of kings who have passed before our eyes, and faintly dwell on our remembrance. The observation that, in every age and climate, ambition has prevailed with the same commanding energy, may abate the surprise of a philosopher; but while he condemns the vanity, he may search the motive, of this universal desire to obtain and hold the sceptre of dominion." Chapter 48. I trust my reader will exercise the patience to study this quotation carefully until he has grasped the meaning of its statements. The question with me is how a man who could make such an observation on the facts and then write so majestically about them, could turn away from the Sacred Text and live and die as a skeptic.

Verse 10. All of the things which David says of man's experiences pertain to his life as a human. They do not even consider, much less contradict the truths that refer to his spiritual life. The Psalmist was a great believer in God and said much about his joy and happiness in the divine service. But the frailty and uncertainty of everything that is not connected with a life for God is what is being considered generally in this and other verses. David did not make the statement here as a decree of God on the length of human life. It was rather an observation as to the rule, and the facts of history will bear out the statement of the verse.

Verse 11. This verse means that man generally underestimates the full effect of God's anger against sin. Only in proportion as men *fear* or respect God will they recognize and fully acknowledge the divine wrath.

Verse 12. *Number our days* means to place the proper value on our time; if we do we will not idle it away. We will apply ourselves to those studies and activities that will make us wise and useful in matters that are profitable to all.

Verse 13. This is another of the earnest supplications for divine mercy. Again we observe that no complaint is made as to the justice of the correction that has been placed on God's people. The request is for it to be lessened through mercy.

Verse 14. This is another plea for mercy and for it to come *early* or speedily.

Verse 15. This means a request for relief that is according to the distress that had been suffered. In other words, to counteract the days of affliction with a like number of happy days.

Verse 16. The writer wished the Lord to bring about the work of relief requested. He also wished it to be made so evident that not only the present generation, but the following ones could realize its existence and be led to appreciate it.

Verse 17. One definition of the original for *beauty* is "agreeableness or delight." The prayer is that God would remove the distress of chastisement and give his servants an agreeable experience instead. It should be understood that *the work of our hands* means the righteous works to be performed under the mercy of God. The request is that all such works would be *established* or accepted by Him.

PSALMS 91

Verse 1. For the authorship of this chapter see "general remarks' at beginning of ch. 90. *Secret place* means a place of refuge or safety. He that is content to dwell in the protection of God will *abide* or always have the benefit of it. It will be like a *shadow* or relief from the heat of distress.

Verse 2. The idea of divine refuge is still the leading one of the writer. He regarded God as the true source of protection and therefore he would trust in Him.

Verse 3. A *fowler* is a trapper who sets a trap or snare for his victims. When used figuratively it refers to men who seek to overcome the innocent by underhanded methods. God will keep his righteous servants and help them to avoid the snares if they will heed the divine instructions. *Noisome pestilence* means the unpleasant and harmful conditions that the enemy might seek to create for the servants of God.

Verse 4. A comparison is made to a parent bird that protects its young under the shelter of its wings. The structure of the wing will furnish a protection like an armor, and the feathers will furnish warmth and nestling comfort. *Shield* and *buckler* are articles of protection against attack from an enemy. God will give perfect protection to all who accept His truth and mold their lives thereby.

Verse 5. The antecedent of *thou* is the person described by *he that dwelleth*, etc., in v. 1. The verse means that actual danger (*arrow*) or the fear of it (*terror*) will never affect the one who puts his trust in the Lord.

Verse 6. This verse is similar in thought to the preceding one. *Pestilence* or disease sometimes attacks one in the night, and speedy destruction may come to him in the day. But neither will defeat the one who relies on the help of God.

Verse 7. This verse denotes the safety of those who put their trust in the Lord. Great numbers of the enemy will not count as any more dangerous than would a few to those who have God with them. Paul taught this same idea in Rom. 8: 31.

Verse 8. Those who trust in God will see the *reward* or fate of the wicked, that it will be a just and awful punishment.

Verse 9. *Thou* means the person to whom the writer is addressing his assurances. Such a person who makes God his dwelling place will share the same protection as the writer of this verse, and will find shelter in the same refuge.

Verses 10. This verse is practically the same in thought as many of the other verses of the chapter. It refers to the complete security of all who trust in God.

Verses 11, 12. A promise in the form of a prophecy can be so worded as to have more than one application. The general theme of the several verses of this chapter is the security to be had in the Lord. That is true of all men in general, but this paragraph has been given specific application to Christ in Matt. 4: 6 and Luke 4: 10. It is true that Satan is the one who made the application, but Christ did not take any exception to the reference that Satan made to it. Attempts have been made to show that Satan added to the passage. But he did not add any words that would have altered its meaning, neither did Jesus accuse him of it. The perversion of which Satan was guilty was his misapplication of the passage. The proviso on which the protection was given required that the subject be one who is true to God. But a person who would tempt Him would not be true and therefore could not claim the promise.

Verse 13. The *lion* and *adder* are used figuratively to compare the extent of deliverance that God will give those who trust in him. The *dragon* means some kind of dangerous monster like a sea-serpent.

Verse 14. The several pronouns in this verse should be properly connected or confusion will result. *He*, *his* and *him* means the man who loves God; *me*, *my* and *I* refer to God. *Set him on high* means that God will give true exaltation to those who do right. It is the same thought that is expressed in James 4: 10.

Verse 15. The same connections should be made of the pronouns in this verse as were made in the preceding one. God promised to hear the call of his righteous servant. He will honor the servant by delivering him from his troubles.

Verse 16. No specific span of life is guaranteed to the man of God. It is an assurance of being preserved so that his days would be extended. The *salvation* that was promised to the devoted servant referred to his rescue from the hand of his enemy.

PSALMS 92

Verse 1. Good deeds do not always consist in outward actions that make a show. The Psalmist classes the giving of thanks unto the Lord among good deeds; also the singing of His praises is included in good deeds. After all, if a person is sincerely disposed to remember the goodness of God he is likely to serve him in practical matters.

Verse 2. Another good deed is to display the lovingkindness of God. *Morning* and *night* represents the beginning and ending of a day. The force of the verse is to promise a continual devotion to the Lord for his goodness.

Verse 3. *An instrument of ten strings.* All of these words are from ASOR which Strong defines, "ten; by abbreviation ten strings, and so a decachord." The phrase means to make a chord of ten sounds. The *psaltery* was a stringed instrument especially designed for use in accompaniment with the human voice. The *harp* was an instrument of ten strings and the expression evidently was intended as a repetition of the beginning of the verse for the sake of emphasis. All of this is easily understood when we recall that David was a specialist in the making and using of musical instruments.

Verse 4. David had said (ch. 19: 1) that the heavens declare the glory of God. By that same token the works of God would gladden the heart of mankind.

Verse 5. The works of God are as great as his thoughts. Isa. 55: 8, 9 declares the thoughts of God are as high as the heavens, and the present verse states that they are deep. We thus have the two extremes, height and depth, to compare the greatness of God's mind and contrast it with that of man.

Verse 6. *Brutish* means dull or stupid, and a *fool* has about the same meaning. Such an individual will not be impressed by the greatness of God's works.

Verse 7. This verse denotes the deception in the strength of the wicked people of the earth. It is like grass that springs forth in the morning dew, but wilts as soon as the sun strikes it. This idea also is set forth in James 1: 11. The show or display of the unrighteous people will not endure when the final test is made.

Verse 8. Many persons can be and have been in high position at certain times of special advantage. The great contrast between all other beings and the Lord is that He is high *for evermore*.

Verse 9. It is significant to observe how the Psalmist describes the *enemies* of the Lord who consist in the workers of iniquity. The description and motive for it is praiseworthy; that it is not merely because men happen to be unlikable to God that he considers them his enemies, but it is because they are unrighteous in life.

Verse 10. When *horn* is used figuratively it means power and authority. David was a faithful servant of the Lord and therefore could expect to have divine support. Oil was literally poured on the heads of those who were being placed in a position of dignity. It came to be used figuratively of those who were to be honored with any unusual blessings that brought them overwhelming joy and gladness.

Verse 11. David lived in an age of warfare and had to fight his enemies with the weapons of bodily conflict. For this reason he frequently referred to the subject with earnestness, and prayed for the success of his arms. Moreover, he expected to have such prayers granted and rejoiced greatly over the same.

Verse 12. The *palm tree* was one of the most important of trees in Palestine. It furnished food and material for various other uses. It lived and grew for a century in many instances and was hence a tree with many uses. The *cedar* also had many uses, and one of its chief characteristics was its being evergreen. Both of these trees are used to compare a true servant of God in his responsibility to his Creator.

Verse 13. The comparison to trees is continued in this verse. *House of God* is a phrase referring to the service to Him in general. Those who are *planted* or established in that service will flourish as do the trees described above.

Verse 14. In the service of God there is no such thing as "old age" in the sense of infirmity. The older (in literal years) one becomes in that service the stronger he becomes and the more able he will be in producing fruit unto the Lord.

Verse 15. *To show* is a phrase that means the Psalmist had made the foregoing statements for the purpose of showing the uprightness of the Lord. Because of that great quality the Lord would become the *rock* or foundation of all of David's hopes.

PSALMS 93

Verse 1. *Lord* is from a word that is defined "self-Existent." Such a Being would certainly have the right to reign. To be *clothed with majesty* means to be dignified and great in every good sense. It would also be expected that such an One would be strong and able to *establish* or make firm the whole world.

Verse 2. The Lord has existed always and hence his throne has been established *of old*. That means that He has been in authority and control *from everlasting;* that his reign never had any beginning.

Verse 3. This verse may be taken both literally and figuratively. The mighty oceans are subject to the control of God. It is true also that *floods* of distress have frequently swelled up to threaten the servants of the Lord.

Verse 4. This verse should be considered in the light of the preceding one. It declares that God's supremacy over all imposing objects and conditions is evident, whether the seas of the earth or the billows of afflictions rolling up to threaten the security of the righteous.

Verse 5. The *testimonies* are the declarations of the Lord that have been tried and have stood the test. *Becometh* is from NAAH and Strong defines it, "to be at home." The thought is that holiness is fitting and perfectly at home in the house of the

Lord. This is very significant, for it would be out of place to see a profession of holiness in a place not belonging to the Lord. It would be like "a jewel of gold in a swine's snout." (Prov. 11: 22.)

PSALMS 94

Verse 1. *Vengeance* usually has a harsh sound for our ears and we might be inclined to wonder why it would be attributed to God. The impression is due largely to abuse of the word. The term primarily means "Punishment inflicted in return for an injury or an offense."—Webster. Improper or spiteful treatment of one who is even guilty of wrong would be wrong also, but that is not required by the meaning of the word. And furthermore, even the proper form or degree of vengeance must be administered by one having authority for doing so. The Psalmist here declares that God is the one to whom such right belongs. Paul taught the same thing in Rom. 12: 19. The Psalmist in our verse is calling upon God to show his vengeance upon the wicked enemy.

Verse 2. In the preceding verse David set forth the right of God to bring vengeance on those who deserved it. In this he calls upon Him to use that authority against the *proud*. The original for this last word means not only that the persons are vain of themselves, but also are impudent over it toward others.

Verse 3. This is another of David's earnest prayers for the Lord's judgments upon his enemies. And again we should observe that he does not imply any injustice from the Lord in suffering some affliction to come, but desired it not to continue long.

Verse 4. The boastful sayings of the enemies seemed to worry the Psalmist more than any considerations as to his personal discomfort.

Verse 5. David was concerned for the people of the nation rather than for himself. This spirit of unselfishness was an outstanding quality of this great man. See a demonstration of it in 2 Sam. 24: 17.

Verse 6. It is noteworthy that David's complaints against the evildoers did not consist in mere general assertions. Had that been the case it would have given the impression that his motive was only a personal dislike for them. Instead, he specified their acts of violence against the innocent and helpless people.

Verse 7. These wicked people were so foolish as to think they could hide from God. Such a thought has ever been a common one with man. It was first demonstrated by Adam and Eve when they thought they could hide from God behind the trees. (Gen. 3: 9.)

Verse 8. *Brutish* is from BAAR and Strong defines it, "a primitive root; to kindle, i.e. consume (by fire or by eating)." David compares the enemies of his people to the ravenous beasts because of their oppressive and destructive conduct.

Verse 9. This verse goes back to v. 7 which showed the foolish notion that man could hide from God. The very ears and eyes by which the evildoers were practicing their wickedness were made by the God whom they thought to evade. If He could give to man such organs he certainly could limit their use and not be misled by them.

Verse 10. The same form of reasoning is contained in this verse as was used above. It had been frequently shown that God could punish the heathen, and therefore he surely would bring severe judgment on those who afflicted the righteous.

Verse 11. *Vanity* means foolish and unavailing schemes of man. The Lord thoroughly understands it all and will bring it to nought.

Verse 12. Afflictions are sent frequently for the purpose of correction. That is the meaning of *chasteneth*, and Paul taught the same in 1 Cor. 11: 32. Not all treatment for disease is pleasant to the patient, but a man would be very unwise who refused the treatment because of its unpleasantness. Another thought in this verse is that chastisement is not always of a physical nature. It consists also in the exhortations and admonitions in the law regarding duty and punishment for neglect of it.

Verse 13. If the innocent victim will endure and profit by his chastisement, he will then be given divine relief. His enemy will finally be cast down into the *pit*, which means a condition of forgetfulness and disgrace.

Verse 14. When the Lord punishes his people it is for their good and not that he intends to cast them off. The people are *his inheritance* which means they belong to Him. He certainly will not bring afflictions on them in the sense of forsaking them.

Verse 15. *Judgment* here means that a merciful decision will be rendered by the Lord for the righteous. When that is done it will have a good effect on other people who are upright in heart. When they see the outcome of the Lord's plan of instructions, they will be inclined to *follow it* or profit thereby.

Verse 16. Here is another characteristic attitude of the Psalmist. In his distress over the activities of evildoers he longs for the fellowship of others in his efforts at curbing them.

Verse 17. *Almost* is rendered "quickly" in the margin of some Bibles and the lexicon agrees with it. The thought is that without the help of God, man would be unable to accomplish anything in the midst of uncertainties that surround him.

Verse 18. In times of danger and uncertainty, the Lord's help assures to his servants the support that could come from no other source.

Verse 19. Amid the many things that occupy the mind of God's servants, there is one thought that stands out above others, and that is of the comforts that the true servants may expect from Him.

Verse 20. This verse is in question form but is positive in thought. It means that iniquity and righteousness have no fellowship with each other.

Verse 21. The antecedent of *they* is the group that *frameth mischief* in the preceding verse. A single act of wrong is bad enough, but conspiracy in sin is worse. The ones whom David was considering were doing that kind of evil actions.

Verse 22. The first clause of this verse is literal; the second is figurative. God is a virtual *rock* of *refuge* for a righteous man.

Verse 23. The Psalmist went back to the enemies again. *He* means God who will bring upon *them*, the enemies, the fruit of their own iniquity. Evil workers may seem to prosper for a time, but finally will be brought to feel the folly of their deeds.

PSALMS 95

Verse 1. *Joyful noise* is one of David's expressions for singing lively praises to God for his great goodness to the children of men. *Rock of our salvation* means that the Lord is the foundation for all help that would bring salvation to mankind.

Verse 2. Man is always actually in the presence of the Lord. The thought is that they would make a formal action before the face of the Lord to express thanks.

Verse 3. The terms *Lord* and *God* are used in one sentence which recognizes the distinction between them. The first means the self-Existent Being and the second designates him as a Being worthy to rule with authority.

Verse 4. *Deep places* and *strength of the hills* are figures to express the scope of the knowledge and power of the Lord.

Verse 5. God made the sea and land and they are rightfully his.

Verse 6. In view of the facts mentioned in the preceding verse, the Psalmist bids his people kneel and worship the Maker of all things.

Verse 7. The relationship between "people" and "God" would explain why David had called upon the former to kneel before the latter. *Sheep of his hand* denotes that the people were in the hand of God who cares for them as a shepherd cares for his flock. In view of these important facts the people are exhorted to hear the voice of the great Shepherd and follow him faithfully wherever he leads.

Verses 8-10. These verses are grouped in one paragraph because they pertain to the same thought, and because they are quoted in the New Testament as a single passage. (Heb. 3: 7-11.) It has reference to the time of 40 years when the children of Israel were going through the wilderness. Through all that period the Lord was provoked by the stubborn behaviour of the nation. It was especially the leaders of the congregation who incited the others to rebel. *Not known my ways* means they had not recognized the right ways of life as directed by the Lord. They preferred to have their own way and were continually raising the banner of revolt.

Verse 11. The most specific act of rebellion is recorded in Num. 14: 1-4 where they made the rash statement that they wished to die in the wilderness. That provoked the Lord so greatly that he decreed the death of those leaders in the wilderness, the thing they foolishly requested to happen. *Not enter into MY rest.* This introduces a very interesting subject, that of the 3 rests of God. The matter is treated in Hebrews 3 and 4 where the language clearly shows that 3 different "rests" are considered and each of them is called "my rest." They refer respectively to the 7th day of the week, the national rest in Canaan and the final rest in Heaven. Each of them is called "my rest" because God originated them.

PSALMS 96

Verse 1. *New song* does not necessarily mean that the composition is new. But the people were to sing it anew with fresh vigor.

Verse 2. We may bless the name of the Lord by acknowledging the happiness that comes through the holy name. The simple mention of the name of God is enough to fill a true servant with delight. We may *show forth* the salvation that comes from the Lord by declaring it in words and by producing its fruit in our lives.

Verse 3. The *heathen* means the foreign nations with whom the people of God would come into contact. They should not be ashamed to speak forth the praises for their God as being far above all other objects of worship. And it is not enough merely to assert that the God of Israel is greater than all, but the proof should be called to the attention of all. That would consist in the *wonders* of the universe that were the work of His hands. (Ch. 19: 1.)

Verse 4. We should keep in mind that the word *Lord* means the self-Existent One who never had any beginning. The fact explains why he is *greatly to be praised*. His name came to be used as the Jewish national name for their object of worship, hence David declared that he is to be *feared* (reverenced) above all other gods.

Verse 5. *Idol* is from ELIYE which Strong defines, "good for nothing, by analogy, vain or vanity." In the King James version it has been rendered by idol, no value, and thing of nought. Even the planets and other things of the universe, which were worshiped by the heathen, were "vain" as far as creative power was concerned. On the other hand the God of David was the Creator of those very things.

Verse 6. *Before* is used in the sense of being near and it means that *honor* and *majesty* are to be seen wherever the Lord's presence is known. By the same token the qualities of *strength* and *beauty* are to be found in the holy institution or sanctuary.

Verse 7. Man cannot actually contribute strength to the Lord. But he can give his acknowledgment that strength and glory belong to Him. The Psalmist bids all *kindreds* or groups of people to make such acknowledgment.

Verse 8. Actions speak louder than words. It is not enough to speak of the devotion due to the Lord. The proper way to exhibit that feeling for the Lord is to contribute something of value to the divine service.

Verse 9. *Beauty* is defined in Strong's lexicon as "decoration," and *holiness* is defined as "sanctity." The thought is that sanctity or righteous conduct is a genuine ornament. The Psalmist would have his people worship the Lord under such an attitude. All people of the earth are told to *fear* or respect the Lord of the Israelites.

Verse 10. The *heathen* were the foreign nations surrounding the land of the Israelites. They were to be made to understand that the Lord, not the dumb idols, must be recognized as king and ruler of the world. And it was to be affirmed that the rule of this great Being would be righteous, hence the whole world was assured of the firmness of all things because they were to be supported by the divine foundation.

Verse 11. All of the things named in this verse are inanimate and hence cannot exhibit the emotions mentioned. But intelligent creatures everywhere can and should feel the sentiments because of all that the Lord has done in heaven and earth.

Verse 12. The comments on the preceding verse will apply to this.

Verse 13. The rejoicing should be in the presence of the Lord since he is the creator of all things named. *He cometh* means the judgment of the Lord will come upon the earth. That judgment will consist in righteous punishment upon the world of wicked people, and all of His decrees will be according to truth.

PSALMS 97

Verse 1. Either joy or grief may be brought to a people through the king, depending on his manner of rule. From that great truth the Psalmist formed the concise but clear phrases in the first part of this verse. *Isles* is used in its general sense, "a habitable spot." The clause means that wherever the inhabitants of the earth live they have reason to rejoice for the righteous rule of the Lord.

Verse 2. *Clouds and darkness* often impress us as something depressing. The idea is that even such conditions are subject to His control. *Habitation* is from a word that means a fixture or basis. The statement denotes that the throne of the Lord is established on a foundation of righteousness and judgment.

Verse 3. The *fire* refers to the consuming force of God's wrath against wicked men.

Verse 4. Fire and lightning are similar in nature, yet they were used in two senses. The first was used in the preceding verse as a consuming force, and in this verse the second word was used as an agent of illumination. The truth of this enlightenment made the earth's people to see the majesty of God and to fear or have respect for the dignity of that truth.

Verse 5. Of course the melting of the hills is figurative. The people living in the hills were prostrated by the august demonstrations of God's power.

Verse 6. See the comments at ch. 19: 1.

Verse 7. To be confounded means to be confused and defeated. Such an end was wished upon the worshipers of idols. All *graven images* were *idols* but not all idols were graven images. These last were things carved out of stone or other materials and worshiped as gods. Idols would be anything, whether man-made or natural, that were worshiped as gods. *Worship him* means to worship the Lord.

Verse 8. *Zion* was a prominent part of Jerusalem where David had his headquarters. It came to be called the "City of David," and finally was referred to generally as meaning the institution of the Lord. *Daughters of Judah* means the people of Judah or of the kingdom of which the capital was Zion.

Verse 9. Physical and spiritual exaltation was the subject in the mind of the Psalmist. God is above the earth as to rank or order of existence, and above the idol gods as to spiritual importance.

Verse 10. It is impossible to love and hate the same thing. Likewise it is impossible to love two things that are opposite in their character. Jesus taught this in Matthew 6: 24. On the basis of this truth, David calls upon those who profess to love the Lord to prove it by manifesting hate for evil. God will preserve the *souls* of the saints, but they may be subjected to affliction as to their bodies. Yet if they are faithful through it all they will finally be delivered.

Verse 11. *Sown* means to be spread abroad. The statement means that the righteous will be provided with light or guidance. This instruction will bring them gladness because they are upright in heart.

Verse 12. The first 4 words in this verse are identical with some in Phil. 3: 1. There is no rejoicing promised to any who are not in the Lord and who are not thankful to Him. Any apparent cause of rejoicing out of the Lord is a deception and will bring the persons misled thereby to the brink of disappointment.

PSALMS 98

Verse 1. *New song* is explained by the comments on Ch. 96: 1. *Right hand* and *holy arm* means that the things done by the Lord are right and holy, deserving praise.

Verse 2. *Salvation* is used in a general sense and includes the many favors that had been bestowed on the nation of Israel. Those benefits had been so evident that the heathen or surrounding nations had observed them.

Verse 3. God never forgets anything in the sense we commonly use the word. *Remembered* means that God considered his past favorable treatment of the house of Israel and decreed to continue the same. That treatment of his people was so evident that the people of the earth had been made to recognize and acknowledge it.

Verse 4. *Noise* in the first instance is not in the original, so the sentence means for them to make expressions of joy for all the goodness of God. In the second sentence the word means "to break out in joyful sound." —Strong. The people were bidden also to sing their praises unto the Lord.

Verse 5. David made and used many kinds of musical instruments. He sometimes used them alone and at other times he used them to accompany a song of praise to God. In this verse he called for the latter use of the harp in service to the Lord.

Verse 6. In this verse the Psalmist means two more of his instruments and bids his people use them in praise to the Lord. An added motive for praising the Lord is indicated by the mention of him as King.

Verse 7. The roaring of the sea should be heard as the voice of praise to the Lord. He made the sea and the world and is entitled to all praise for all such wonderful works that exhibit his creative power.

Verse 8. *Floods* and *hills* are inanimate objects; but their importance should cause universal gratitude in the minds of all intelligent creatures.

Verse 9. *Before the Lord* connects this verse with the preceding one on the subject of gratitude for the works of creation. The present verse adds the thought that the Lord *cometh* (when occasion requires) to judge the earth. His judgment will be righteous, for it will be with *equity* which means with fairness. It has always been true that God is no respecter of persons. (Acts 10: 34.)

PSALMS 99

Verse 1. *Tremble* means to respect the Lord and fear to do that which would violate His reign. *Between the cherubims* is a reference to the objects on the mercy seat in the tabernacle. The high priest appeared at that place on one day of the year to communicate with God on behalf of the congregation. (Ex. 25: 17-22.) *Earth be moved* means practically the same as *tremble* in the first part of the verse.

Verse 2. To be *great in Zion* indicates that the greatness refers to the Lord's position of authority. Zion was the headquarters of the kingdom and the seat of government. That position explains how the Lord was *high above all the people*.

Verse 3. We might be somewhat confused at the idea of the Lord's name being both *terrible* and *holy*. It will be of interest to know that the first is from the same original as "reverend" in ch. 111: 9. The word occurs about 300 times in the Hebrew Bible and has a wide range of meaning. In the present verse it means the name of the Lord is worthy to be respected because it is holy.

Verse 4. Kings sometimes use their strength for evil purposes, but the Lord is a king who delights in righteous judgment. *Equity* means fairness, and the Lord executes his authority in such a way that every man receives his own share. *Jacob* is used to denote the nation of Israel who descended through that great patriarch.

Verse 5. Man cannot actually promote the Lord. The statement means to recognize the exaltation of Him and praise him because of it. God is in Heaven and man is on the earth, which is said to be the footstool of God. (Isa. 66: 1; Matt. 5: 35.) It means that while man is on the earth he should worship the Lord in humility.

Verse 6. David cited three special servants of God; Moses was the lawgiver, Aaron was high priest and Samuel was the first national prophet. All of these great persons worshiped God in humility and were favored by Him. Certainly, then, all other persons should "prostrate fall" at the foot of the throne.

Verse 7. This verse refers to the events at Sinai when God came down in a cloud and revealed his word to Moses and Aaron. They showed their respect for that word by faithfully observing its ordinances.

Verse 8. The connection shows that David was referring to the idolatry committed at Sinai. God caused 3000 Israelites to be slain on account of their *inventions* (the golden calf), but he then blessed the nation.

Verse 9. *Exalt* is explained at v. 5. *Holy hill* means Zion where the headquarters were located materially. In its spiritual sense it means the institution of God through which divine worship was offered.

PSALMS 100

Verse 1. *Noise* is not in the original but *joyful* is. The clause means to express joy unto the Lord for all his acts of kindness to the children of men. *All ye lands* means all the people of the earth, for they had all been benefited by the Lord's favors.

Verse 2. We should not offer service to the Lord in the spirit of necessity, or just because we think we have to. It is true that we must serve Him if we expect the reward, but it should be considered a happy privilege to render service to Him who has made us and caused us to be what we are. These remarks apply to man's general relationship to God. The second clause of the verse refers especially to his conduct when in the religious attitude.

At that time it is appropriate to honor the Lord in song, that being a part of the exercises performed in public worship.

Verse 3. The distinctive meanings of *Lord* and *God* should be observed in the first clause. For the critical information on the subject see my comments at ch. 86: 12. David uses the distinction between the words as a basis of an exhortation. The thought is that the One who always existed is the one who only has the right to be the object of worship. Such a thought should have prevented the Israelites from worshiping the heathen gods. Furthermore, the Creator of our being certainly is entitled to all of our devotions. *Sheep of his pasture* signifies that God is able to nourish us. But that is not all; for if we are the sheep of *His* pasture, we have no right nor need to feed in any other pasture.

Verse 4. A gate is an entrance to a city and a court is an enclosure for the vicinity of a king or other dignified person. If a human being is permitted to enter into a city of the King of Heaven, and to go even as far as into the final enclosure of his palace. then thanksgiving and praise should be forthcoming.

Verse 5. Many good men are merciful at times, but the mercy of the Lord continues. The truth of the Lord will stand the test of all time. That truth does not change, but will bless the generation that exists now and will be alive through the time of the generations yet to come and continue its blessed effects on all who accept it.

PSALMS 101

Verse 1. *Judgment* is used here in its fundamental sense of justice. The word means a decree or verdict that is according to the facts in the case, and whether the sentence is supposed to be favorable or not. But in such cases where the strict justice would require an unfavorable sentence, the mercy of God would modify it. That is why the Psalmist would sing of both. For the blended attributes of God the song of praise was to be offered as an expression of sincere gratitude.

Verse 2. The preceding verses showed that God tempers justice with mercy. However, there must be some indications of worthiness before the mercy will be extended. The Psalmist recognized that principle and promised to behave himself accordingly, which would constitute a perfect way. On the condition of his devotion David appealed to God for divine assistance and direction in the chosen course.

Verse 3. The promise of this verse refers especially to the sin of idolatry. David hated that evil and pledged himself not to place any idol before him as an object to be worshiped or adored in any sense.

Verse 4. *Froward* means perverse or stubborn and David declared he would not have such a heart. He also determined not to *know* or recognize a wicked person.

Verse 5. Slander is always wrong, but it is worse when done *privily*, which means to do done "behind one's back." If any such man came under the knowledge of David he was to be cut off. There is not much difference between the meaning of *high* and *proud*. The second refers to the condition of the heart, and the first shows how that condition affects the outward attitude. David gave his word that he would not tolerate such a man to be in his presence.

Verse 6. To *be upon* means to look with favor upon the faithful, and see that they have opportunity for dwelling in the land under the protection of the king. But the Psalmist would not accept service from those whose way of life was not right.

Verse 7. *Deceit* is one form of a lie and David would not harbor such a character. With all of the fault to be found with the Psalmist for his sin with another man's wife, he was truthful when confronted with the facts. He was a lover of truth and could not endure the sight of an untruthful man.

Verse 8. *Early* has no word in the original in this verse. *Destroy* is from a word that is defined by Strong, "to extirpate." *The city of the Lord* means the capital city and David proposed to defend it by destroying all of the wicked enemies.

PSALMS 102

Verse 1. This verse is an example of the supplication form of prayer. The simple word "prayer" means merely an address or request offered to God. A supplication is a request in more urgent and earnest terms.

Verse 2. This verse is similar to the preceding one except that it specifies the subject of the supplication. The Psalmist is worried over the trouble that his enemies were causing him. He appeals to the Lord in earnest tones to assist him.

Verse 3. Of course we will understand this verse to be figurative. David used the strong language to illustrate the great distress his enemies had forced upon him.

Verse 4. This means that he did not have the heart to face the situation without the help of the Lord. It had even taken his appetite which is what he meant by he words *forget to eat my bread* in the close of the verse.

Verse 5. This is another highly figurative passage, referring to David's miserable experiences. But the thought will be grasped more readily by transposing the two clauses of the verse. The idea is that on account of the condition of his skin and bones, his voice gave way to groaning.

Verses 6, 7. These fowls are somewhat "on their own" and isolated. They are liable to meet up with some hostile creatures, so that their hours have to be taken up in being constantly and nervously on the alert.

Verse 8. To *reproach* means to speak evil with the intent to slander one. To be *mad* is to rave about another. David's enemies were so determined to slander him that they gave way to rage, and declared with an oath that they would oppose him.

Verse 9. Ashes were used in ancient times to indicate distress or great humiliation. David uses the word figuratively by saying he had to eat them. Partaking of drink was a desirable act in itself, but the opposition of his enemies caused the Psalmist to weep while partaking of the blessing.

Verse 10. David attributed his unpleasant experiences to the Lord; that is, he believed the Lord suffered the enemies to oppose him as a test of his faith. He never found fault with the Lord for such treatment, but frequently lamented over it and entreated that the afflictions might be lifted or lessened.

Verse 11. This verse is a figurative description of David's trials. *Declineth* is from NATAH and Strong defines it, "to stretch or spread out." The idea is that as the lengthening of a shadow indicates the approach of the day's end, so David compared it to his own declining day of life under the oppression of his enemies. He made a like comparison to the withering grass that yielded to the depressing effect of heat.

Verse 12. The endurance of the Lord encouraged David to look for mercy in his afflictions, for He ever remembers his faithful servants.

Verse 13. *Zion* was said in reference to the nation because that spot was the headquarters. It is interesting to note that David usually associated his own interests with those of his people and country. He expressed the hope that God would *arise* or "show himself" on behalf of the nation because the need for it had come.

Verse 14. *Stones* and *dust* were materials of the capital city. The citizens of the city had sincere love for the great city of God; so much so that even the dust falling from its stones was dear to them.

Verse 15. *The heathen* were the foreign nations that surrounded Israel. They were to *fear* the name of the Lord, which means they would see the mighty works performed under that holy name and would be led to respect it.

Verse 16. *Build up* means to defend and strengthen. David believed that the Lord would do that for Zion and that it would thus be an exhibition of His glory.

Verse 17. *Despise* means to belittle or ignore. God will not ignore the prayer of the *destitute* or needy, but will attend to their requirements in his own way of wisdom.

Verse 18. The reference from this verse correctly cites Rom. 15: 4. The things God did to his ancient people were first for their own benefit. Then he caused an account of them to be *written for the generation to come* for the purpose expressed by the apostle Paul. The motive stated by the apostle, that we might have hope, is similar in thought to the one in the present verse, that people would be led to praise God.

Verse 19. *Sanctuary* means any holy place or where some holy person occupies his place. The religious institution on earth is one such place, but this verse refers to the one in Heaven, hence the phrase *height of his sanctuary*.

Verse 20. This verse gives the purpose of the preceding one. God does not actually have to *look* in order to obtain information. The language simply means that God concerned himself on behalf of his servants, and gave a merciful ear to their groaning. He further determined to give relief by delivering his afflicted ones from oppression.

Verse 21. Not only does the Lord wish to take the side of his mistreated servants, but will also see that His name is recognized in Zion, the particular spot in Jerusalem that was the headquarters of the holy nation.

Verse 22. The objectives mentioned in the two preceding verses will be attained when the present verse is carried out. It is only when people recognize the Lord's authority and respect his kingdom, that he will extend his favors to them.

Verse 23. David again took up the subject of his personal afflictions. *Shortened* is from a word that Strong says has both a literal and figurative meaning. Figuratively it would mean to cut off some of the enjoyment of his days. That was done by suffering his enemies to oppose him for the purpose of testing his faith.

Verse 24. God had no beginning and will have no ending in his existence. He therefore is prepared to extend the life of his servants according to his judgment and mercy. The Psalmist expressed another of his earnest pleas to God for his favor.

Verses 25-28. I have grouped these verses into one paragraph because they are thus grouped in Heb. 1: 10-12. The connection in that place shows that Christ is the one spoken of. The present verse is a prophecy of Christ and the Psalmist made it as an inspired prophet. But while he may not have intended it as a change in subject, it at first appears so to us. Upon close consideration we will see a connection in thought. The writer had just mentioned the endless existence of God; that time would not bring any changes in Him. It was an appropriate place to speak of another person whose work would outlive the existence of material things. That person was Christ and his work would be the great institution of his kingdom that was to stand forever. (Dan. 2: 44.)

PSALMS 103

Verse 1. When *bless* is used towards the Lord it means to praise and adore Him as the source of all blessings. In the language of the familiar Doxology: "Praise God, from whom all blessings flow." *Soul* as used here means the entire living being which is why the Psalmist added the specification in the second clause of the verse.

Verse 2. The close of the preceding verse stipulated the entirety of man's being should bless the Lord. This verse indicates the reason for such praise to the Lord, that it is on account of the benefits received. *Forget not* means not to be inattentive to, not merely that the facts have "slipped the memory." When man fails to give proper consideration to the goodness of God it is as bad as if he had entirely forgotten it.

Verse 3. The emphasis in this verse should be on the pronoun *who* and not on the word *all*. Other passages teach that forgiveness for sin is offered on certain conditions, and that disease is healed only when the Lord's will calls for it. But the thought of the Psalmist is that when these favors are bestowed upon man, the Lord should receive *all* the credit and praise for it.

Verse 4. One way to redeem a thing is to prevent the condition threatened. Those who are faithful to God will be protected from the destruction intended by the enemies. To *crown* means to bestow abundantly the good things considered. The faithful servants of God will thus be given the kindness that springs from divine love, and the mercy that is prompted by His *tender* or mild regard for his children.

Verse 5. The Lord does not always give us what we may think we should have. But he will give us that which actually *satisfieth*, which means to leave no real want of *good things*. These good things of life are what will sustain our existence. No man will actually be made or be kept young. However, if the Lord sustains him he will be kept comparatively young and strong. *Like the eagle's* is a comparison drawn from the enduring strength of that mighty bird. Funk and Wagnalls' Bible Dictionary says that the eagle is used as a figure of various traits. Strength is one quality mentioned and Isa. 40: 31 would justify the figure.

Verse 6. *Judgment* refers to the relief due those who are oppressed unjustly. It will be done according to the Lord's righteousness.

Verse 7. *Ways* is from a Hebrew word that means "a course of life or mode of action," and *acts* is from one that means "an exploit of God." The verse means that God used Moses to teach the people how they should live, and he performed his own great deeds in the sight of the children of Israel for their example and information.

Verse 8. *Merciful* means to be less exacting with another than his conduct demands. *Gracious* indicates the disposition to be pleasantly considerate toward one who is supposed to be lower in rank or deserts. A person might let his debtor off with less than he deserved, yet do so with a haughty attitude. God is both merciful and gracious, combining the two very desirable traits. *Plenteous* in mercy denotes that God does not merely show his debtors some reduction in his just demands, but the reduction he grants them is great which would amount to a great sacrifice when measured by justice.

Verse 9. The two clauses of this verse have practically the same meaning, but the second one should be considered first. Since God does not keep (cherish or hold to as with a grudge) his anger forever, he therefore will not be always chastising his servants. He corrects his children for their good and is prompted thereto by his love.

Verse 10. The simple force of this verse is that God does not deal with mankind to the extent that his wrongs deserve. If it were not for the mercy of the Lord, no man could exist for a single moment.

Verse 11. Here we have some material things to measure the immaterial. The height of the heaven or sky above the earth is taken to compare the greatness of God's mercy. But it must not be overlooked that such mercy is promised only toward *them that fear him*, which means to them who show Him the proper respect.

Verse 12. This is similar to the preceding verse in the nature of its illustration. That verse compared the height or greatness of God's mercy; this one shows the completeness of divine forgiveness. When God "forgives" he also "forgets."

Verse 13. An explanation is given why God is so complete in his favors. The comparison is made to the relationship of parent and child; but again the proviso should not be overlooked. The abundant mercies of the Lord are for *them that fear him*.

Verse 14. *Frame* is from a word that is defined "form," specifically the human form or body. God realizes that man's body is of the *dust* which is another word for "earth." As man's body is of that origin it is inclined to uncertainty in conduct and God takes that into consideration in his dealings with human beings.

Verse 15. The connection shows the remarks in this and the following verse apply to the earthly part of man. His body came from the ground, the place that also supports vegetation. Hence his existence in the flesh is subject to the same conditions that cause the plants to flourish and take on the appearance of strength.

Verse 16. This does not mean that the passing of the wind removes man, but that his fleshly existence is as uncertain and comparatively short-lived as the passing of a breeze. Its *place shall not know it* means that man will not again be seen in the place where he once lived on the earth. (See comments at Job 7: 9, 10.)

Verse 17. *From everlasting to everlasting* means without beginning or end. But mercy is a favor shown to man, and he *did* have a beginning. The statement means that the quality of love and pity and mercy is a fixed attribute of God and hence it always existed. But the application of it came only after there was a man who needed the favor. And again we should note that it is limited to *them that fear him*. There never was and never will be a time or place when God would not do right. *Righteousness* is used in reference to the benefits that it brings to generation after generation.

Verse 18. The favor mentioned in the close of the preceding verse is here based on condition that they *keep his covenant*. The additional thought is given that they remember his commandments in a particular way; that they do them.

Verse 19. *Heavens* is plural and is used as a form of emphasis. It indicates that God's throne is high, and for that reason his kingdom is over all other kingdoms.

Verse 20. See the comments at V. 1 on *bless*. *Excel in strength* refers to the various ranks of the angels. We are not told how or why some angels are above others, we are only made to know that they are. The term archangel (1 Th. 4: 16) indicates a distinction in the rank and importance of some, and Jude 6 does the same. Our verse calls upon these greatest of the angels to *bless the Lord. Do his commandments*, etc. The Bible does not inform us just what laws are placed over the angels, but this passage clearly shows that they are under law. And that further agrees with the fact that angels are capable of sinning. (2 Pe. 2: 4.)

Verse 21. This verse is a general call for all classes of the Lord's creatures to bless him. A motive is suggested in the phrase *do his pleasure*. This means they do things that please Him and do so for that purpose.

Verse 22. The call is made still more general and bids the works of creation all to express praise. This is not a new thought with the Psalmist, it is the same as expressed at Ch. 19: 1. The chapter closes with the same words with which it began, *bless the Lord*, O my soul; see the comments at that place.

PSALMS 104

Verse 1. This verse starts with the same expression as Ch. 103: 1, and I request the reader to see my comments at that place. *Honour* has special reference to grandeur of appearance, and *majesty* refers especially to dignity.

Verse 2. To be covered with anything means to be completely surrounded by it. When light is used figuratively it means that which is good, pure and truthful. The Lord is thus equipped and hence he is properly possessed of power. This power gave him the ability to hold up the heavens or parts of the universe as easily as if they were so many curtains in the hands of a human being.

Verse 3. The clauses of this verse are figurative, and are intended to show the ease with which God manages the parts of His creation. The deep waters, the soaring clouds and the boisterous winds would baffle the limited power of man. But the great One who brought them into existence controls all with infinite might.

Verse 4. Happily the apostle Paul comments on this verse in Heb. 1: 7. And verses 13, 14 of that chapter as well as the general connection, shows the passage has direct reference to the intelligent beings who live in Heaven with God. The Psalmist meant to show some more of the power or authority of God in that he had such control over these angels. For instance, he was able to use them as spirits (1 Ki. 22: 19-24), or to make a flaming fire out of them (Ex. 3: 2). However, even in thus controlling these celestial creatures, God was bestowing a great honor upon them, which was the point the writer of Hebrews was making.

Verse 5. We do not think of the earth as having a foundation in the ordinary sense of that word. The verse has the idea that the existence of the earth is well founded as it is sustained by the almighty power of its Creator.

Verse 6. God's knowledge and control of the works of creation is the theme running through several verses. The mighty ocean as it envelops the earth presents as easy a task in the Lord's hands as the handling of a garment would be in the grasp of a man. See a similar thought in the comments at V. 2. *The waters stood*, etc, refers to the flood in the days of Noah. At that time they were said to have been 15 cubits above the mountains. (Gen. 7: 20.)

Verse 7. *At thy rebuke they fled* refers to the fact recorded in Gen. 8: 1, etc.

Verse 8. This refers to the further abatement of the waters of the flood. After the bulk of the water had been driven away by the wind (similar to Gen. 1: 6, 7), the rest of it sought its original places in the valleys which God *had founded for them*.

Verse 9. *Set a bound* is the same as Gen. 8: 22.

Verse 10. The residue of the flood waters was to serve the needs of living creatures. In order to do so it was necessary to have springs and running streams.

Verse 11. Man needed the services of the beasts and that made it necessary to sustain these dumb creatures with the water.

Verse 12. The fowls were to furnish food for man, also be used in sacrifice to God. It was thus needful that they likewise be supplied with water.

Verse 13. *From his chambers* is a figure of speech, referring to the great bounty and storehouse of God, "from whom all blessings flow."

Verse 14. This verse is more specific and includes much the same list of good things as was mentioned in Gen. 8: 22 regarding the continuance of the seasons.

Verse 15. The products that are named in this verse are necessary for the use of man. Those products, however, could not have been provided naturally after the destructive volume of the flood came upon the earth had the Lord not been able and willing to take control of the situation and turn everything to good account.

Verse 16. This verse considers some items of vegetation that are greater than the herbs of the field. These serve mankind in various ways; fruit, building material, beauty and shade all come from the wonderful plant that towers above all other plants.

Verse 17. Not only do the trees serve man directly in the manner mentioned in the preceding verse, but they make shelter for birds which also serve man.

Verse 18. The Psalmist somewhat departs from the conditions in and after the flood. He is concerned with the great works of God as they have always been from the creation. The perfect adaptation of the various parts of creation to the different kinds of living creatures is the thought in this verse. For instance, the wild goats are "at home" while scrambling over the hills, while the coney, being a small and less rugged animal, would prefer finding its home in the clefts of the rocks.

Verse 19. One shade of meaning of the original for *appointed* is "to use." The thought is that the moon was depended upon to set the dates for certain seasons. For an example, the months of the Jewish calendar were started by the moon as it came "new." (1 Sam. 20: 24-27.) The argument of David is that God has such control of the moon that he could rely on it to signal the season of period called the month. The feasts and other rituals of the Jewish worship were to be at regular intervals, and if they were to be regulated as to date by the moon, then the changes of that body would have to be reliable. The appearances of the sun also would need to be according to God's wish.

Verse 20. In strictness of speech, darkness does not have to be "made." It is a negative condition and is merely the absence of light. In the passage we are considering the Psalmist is discussing God's power to manage the things of the universe, including the "going down" of the sun. That condition was necessary in order to bring the rest in sleep for the comfort and welfare of living creatures.

Vese 21. The darkness is seen to be an advantage to some of the beasts which God created. The lions find the night time the best for their necessity and they unconsciously *roar* the praises of the Maker of all things.

Verse 22. After the lions have captured their prey under cover of darkness, they may confidently use the light of the sun to deposit it in their dens.

Verse 23. This verse was written before the days of "24-hour" programs in the industrial world. The Lord designed the day as the time for work, and the darkness of night as best adapted for sleep and rest. That is why we have such expressions as are in John 9: 4; 11: 9; 12: 35. I realize that Jesus was using the words figuratively, but all figures of speech are based on some literal fact.

Verse 24. This verse is a fitting summing up of the great works of the Lord. Having specified some of them, the Psalmist concludes with this general statement regarding the products of the land and their several uses.

Verse 25. Passing from the wonders of the dry land, David takes up the vast realm of the seas that occupies most of the surface of the globe. *Creeping* is from an original with more general meaning than we are accustomed to give to it. The word merely means to move, and refers to all living things that go from place to place on their own power. That would include the fish as well as mammals that live in the ocean.

Verse 26. The ocean is so formed that man can travel on its bosom, while in its vastness underneath, the *leviathan* (some kind of large water animal) can *play* (be perfectly at home) and move about at will.

Verse 27. *These* as a pronoun refers to the leviathans mentioned in the preceding verse. They are powerful creatures, yet they must *wait upon* God, or depend on him.

Verse 28. *Openest thine hand* is understood to refer to the handiwork of God in providing for the needs of these living things.

Verse 29. This verse is to show the dependence of even the sea monsters upon God. When (or if) He hides his face, these creatures are troubled because of their helplessness. Should this desertion continue it would result in the death of them, and they would return to the source from which they were formed. (Gen. 3: 19.)

Verse 30. This verse is very general, because all things were created by the power and through the spirit of God.

To *renew* means to enliven and keep alive the things belonging to the face of the earth. In other words, God started the existence of all things, and he it is who keeps them in existence.

Verse 31. When God had finished his creative work he declared it was "very good" (Gen. 1: 31). He has never changed his estimate of the great works. That is why David here says the glory of the Lord shall *endure for ever*. The additional thought is given to strengthen the one just expressed in that the Lord shall rejoice in his works.

Verse 32. *Trembleth* and *smoke* are figures of speech, meaning the complete dependence of all the earth upon God.

Verse 33. The greatness of the works and goodness of God caused David to sing praises. This vow was made in view of the many excellencies of which he had been writing.

Verse 34. Not only would the Psalmist audibly sing the praises of God, but he would meditate upon them when alone. This was according to what he wrote in ch. 1: 2.

Verse 35. The *sinners* in this particlar connection would be those who do not appreciate the wonderful works of God. David considered them as unworthy to live in the enjoyment of the blessings of the Lord.

PSALMS 105

Verse. 1. This verse has two separate thoughts. Man should thank God for his favors, then show his appreciation for such deeds of benefit by making them known among the people. Jesus taught the same lesson in Matt. 5: 16. But in that case the matters were to be made known before the world by the lives of those benefited by the favors.

Verse 2. The singing and talking that David called for was not to be mere words. There was a subject that was to be the basis for all the expressions and that was the wondrous works of God, manifested for the benefit of the creatures of His care.

Verse 3. Another instance is seen in this verse where the motive was to be the background of the action. A desire to glory in the name of God was urging the persons to *seek the Lord*. When such was the motive for the action, the Psalmist wished for them a heart filled with sincere rejoicing.

Verse 4. This means to seek the strength that comes from the Lord. No man can actually see the face of God and live (Ex. 33: 20), but the word is used in the sense of favor. Seek to be in favor with God by doing that which will please him.

Verse 5. The wonderful doings of God are not confined to the acts of material creation. His judgments also are marvelous, which means his dealings with the conduct of human beings. When the Lord passes judgment upon the activities of man, whether favorable or unfavorable, they are marvelous in wisdom and fairness.

Verse 6. The *seed of Abraham* and the *children of Jacob* refer to the same people. When God called upon Abraham to leave his native land he obeyed and received the title of servant. When Jacob begat the 12 sons and they became numerous enough to compose a nation, then God chose them to become a nation as his peculiar possession.

Verse 7. See the comments at ch. 86: 12 for explanation of *Lord* and *God*. *Judgments* are the verdicts or decisions of God, and they affect the conduct of all mankind.

Verse 8. God never forgets as we commonly use that word. The statement here means that he had respect unto his covenant and always kept his word with the children of men. We might inquire why speak of "keeping" a word that He had *commanded?* It is because the promises of God were made on condition of obedience to the commandments.

Verses 9, 10. These verses should be grouped into one paragraph because of the unity of thought. When fairly considered, the passage throws much light on the subject of the length of the sojourn in Egypt. For detailed discussion of the matter see my comments at 1 Chr. 16: 16, 17 in Volume 2 of this Commentary.

Verse 11. Since Abraham was the first one called, he was the one to whom the promise was made as to the possession of the land. The pronoun *your* is directly addressed by David to the people of his day. He is telling them that the land of Canaan is theirs by lot by right of inheritance, since they were descended from Abraham.

Verse 12. In the beginning of their living in Canaan they were few in number. Even as late as the time of Jacob and they were about to enter the country of Egypt, they numbered only 70 souls according to the account in Gen. 46: 27.

Verses 13-15. This paragraph is a reference to some facts that are clearly set out in the following passages: Gen. 12: 11-20; 20: 1-16; 26: 6-11.

Verse 16. *Called for a famine* shows that the famine in Egypt was a miraculous one. There could not be a natural famine in that country because the annual overflow of the Nile insured the moisture needed for the crops. That was why a mirculous famine had to be *called for* when the Lord had use for one in his plans.

Verse 17. The simple facts of the history are recorded in the book of Genesis and would not need to be repeated in all of their details. However, some observations may profitably be made. *Sent a MAN* is significant as a contrast with the divine agency of the famine. God wished to employ a human agency in conjunction with His own work.

Verse 18. The original history of this verse is in Gen. 39: 20 and 40: 3. Those passages indicate that these *fetters* of *iron* were not allowed to remain on Joseph. He was given charge of the other prisoners which could scarcely be of any avail if he were hampered with the metallic shackles.

Verse 19. *His word came* refers to the interpreting of Pharaoh's dream. When he was wanted for that purpose he was released from prison and never went back to it. The last clause of the verse means that it was in accordance with the word of the Lord for Joseph's faith to be tested. That test went with him through those years that had been forgotten by the butler. (Gen. 40 and 41.)

Verse 20. This was King Pharaoh who had some dreams that troubled him. Having been informed of Joseph's former work of interpreting dreams, the king sent for him that he might obtain a like service. That plan would make it necessary to remove the prison sentence from Joseph hence the verse says he *let him go free.*

Verse 21. Joseph was given the management of the crops for distribution among the people during the famine predicted by the dreams of Pharaoh.

Verse 22. *Bind his princes* does not refer to any literal bonds that Joseph was to fasten on Pharaoh's princes for he never did anything of that kind. It means that Joseph was given authority over the people of Egypt. "Only in the throne will I be greater than thou" (Gen. 41: 40), was the sense in which Joseph was to *bind* the princes.

Verse 23. *Israel* and *Jacob* are the same, the two names being used to make the identification easier. *Land of Ham* was Egypt according to Ps. 78: 51. That was because the inferior nations came from Ham (Gen. 9: 25; 10: 6, 7), and the Egyptians were of the lower grade of nations when compared with descendents of Shem and Japheth.

Verse 24. The history of this verse is in Ex. 1: 7. The Israelites increased in spite of, not by the help of, the Egyptians.

Verse 25. He (God) turned their (the Egyptians') heart to hate his (God's) people. This hatred was prompted by envy and fear. They could not bear to see the Israelites so prosperous; also they feared they might become strong enough to rise up in rebellion. *Dealt subtilly* means they were treacherous and dishonest in their treatment of Israel.

Verse 26. Moses was sent to be the leader for the people in their escape from the land of Egypt. Aaron was sent to work with Moses and to be his spokesman.

Verse 27. *They* means Moses and Aaron. They worked together in performing the miracles that were to convince the Israelites first, then to bring about their enforced freedom.

Verse 28. *Rebelled not* is rendered "would not heed" in Moffatt's translation, and the context justifies that wording. We know the Egyptians would not submit to God's demands even at the plague of darkness.

Verse 29. This verse refers to one of the plagues sent on the Egyptians when they refused to let the children of Israel go. The history of it is in Ex. 7: 17-21.

Verse 30. This was the 2nd plague upon Pharaoh and his people. See Ex. 8: 5-7 for the original account to which this verse applies.

Verse 31. Since all of this history is so completely given in the book of Exodus, the query might arise why the Psalmist took up so much space repeating it. No specific statement can be cited in the Bible as an answer.

We know, however, that many hundreds of years had gone by since those things occurred. In repeating them in such detail, David showed not only that the account of the transactions in Egypt was preserved down to his time, but that he believed it to be true, and that the Lord was worthy to be praised for the great work. The original account of this verse is in Ex. 8.

Verse 32. This was a regular thunderstorm with lightning. The marvelous phase of the case was the fact that it came at a specified time, and in Egypt where even an ordinary rain would have been regarded as wonderful.

Verse 33. *Brake the trees* means the foliage and fruit was stripped off the trees, not the body of the tree being broken down. In Ex. 9: 25 the trees were said to be broken, but in Ch. 10: 15 of that book it says that the locusts ate the fruit of the trees "which the hail had left."

Verses 34, 35. This paragraph is practically explained in the preceding one.

Verse 36. The firstborn of the Egyptians were the ones smitten. This distinction is made to prevent confusion over the pronouns later on in the chapter.

Verse 37. The pronouns in this verse refer to the children of Israel. The *silver and gold* was given them by the Egyptians, and the account is in Ex. 11: 2, 3; 12: 35, 36.

Verse 38. *Egypt was glad when they departed.* This clause will be better understood and appreciated if the student will read Ex. 12: 31-33 and the entire connection. The readiness of Pharaoh to let the Israelites go was not from conviction that he was wrong and they were right. It was purely a selfish move on his part and was prompted by his desire to get rid of a troublesome element that he could not manage.

Verse 39. The account now passes from the original encampment of the Israelites and is describing some scenes in the march. The description of this unusual cloud is in Ex. 13: 21, 22; 14: 19, 24, which I request the student to read again.

Verse 40 The scene changes again, and the children of Israel are across the Red Sea and journeying in the wilderness. Their tendency toward murmuring was evident very often. They complained that they lacked food and God gave it to them by miracle. The history of this verse is in Ex. 16 where the reader may see the goodness of God.

Verse 41. The next complaint was because of a shortage of water to drink. In Ex. 17 is an account of the provision which the Lord made for them on this subject.

Verses 42-45. These closing verses of the chapter are in the nature of a general summing up, hence I have grouped them into one paragraph. The Lord *remembered* means he had respect for the promise he had made to Abraham. That promise included all of the good things already done for the Israelites, as have been detailed in this chapter, and also the ones to come as indicated in this paragraph.

PSALMS 106

Verse 1. There is nothing new in this verse in addition to the oft-repeated call for praise to God. However, we can never be reminded too many times that the Lord is worthy to be praised. Let us note also that David's call for praise was not a mere expression of sentiment without some practical motive for it. In this verse the reason given is the mercy of the Lord that *endureth for ever.*

Verse 2. We are sure David means that no one can *fully* utter or describe the mighty acts of the Lord. It is practically the same idea in the second clause.

Verse 3. This means that they are blessed who show their good judgment by always doing that which is according to the Lord's law of righteousness.

Verse 4. The Psalmist did not ask for any "favoritism" from the Lord. He wished only the same favors that the people of the nation received.

Verse 5. *See the good of thy chosen* meant he asked to see the good things being bestowed upon God's chosen people. It is virtually the same thought that was expressed in the preceding verse and the comments offered at that place.

Verse 6. The Psalmist was consistent in classing himself with the people in general. He had asked only for the kind of favors that the people received. Now he places himself on a level with them regarding the mistakes of life.

Verse 7. A glance at the history in the book of Exodus will tell us why David wrote this verse. *Understood not* means the fathers did not consider all the wonderful works of God. They seemed to "take them for granted," and thus they underestimated their importance. This lack of appreciation led them to act foolishly and provoke the Lord who was being so good to them in spite of their indifference.

Verse 8. Their disobedience did not cause God to desert them. His own name was at stake and he took care of them, thus showing to the nations near them that He was more powerful than all their gods to which they gave such frantic devotion.

Verse 9. When an inanimate object like a sea is *rebuked* it means that it was taken charge of by One who was able to control it. This rebuke was in the form of a "strong east wind," and the original account of it is given in Ex. 14: 21.

Verse 10. This verse is a brief reference to the thing accomplished by the act in opening the Red Sea for the Israelites, then closing it upon the Egyptians.

Verse 11. This language is very definite. Sometimes a statement may be made about the fate of a group. If the thing said to be done affected the group as a whole, the language will be worded in a general way even if some individual exceptions existed. But in this case we are to understand there were no exceptions. *Not one of them* was permitted to escape. Ex. 14: 6 states that Pharaoh took his people "with him." So we know that the king of Egypt perished in the Red Sea together with his people.

Verse 12. The pronouns *they* stand for the Israelites. They believed his words *then;* which means just as they got across the Red Sea. *Sang his praise* refers to the "song of deliverance" which is recorded in Exodus 15.

Verse 13. Scarcely had they reached the east shore of the sea when they forgot the wonderful works of God. They murmured because of the unsavory taste of the water. *Waited not for his counsel* means they "jumped to the conclusion" that they were to suffer for want of drinking water, without waiting to seek counsel or instruction from God.

Verse 14. Even after this emergency was met, the people continued to complain and call for further things of life that they claimed they needed to preserve themselves.

Verse 15. God gave the Israelites the quail for flesh because of their murmuring. *Sent leanness* refers to the sickness that came upon them even while they were eating the food. See the account of this in Num. 11: 31-33.

Verse 16. This verse takes us down to the time when Korah and his confederates rebelled against Moses and Aaron on account of their authority. (Num. 16: 1.)

Verse 17. This fact is recorded in Num. 16: 30-34.

Verse 18. Following up the history as it was in the making, this verse will refer to Num. 16: 35 which records the miraculous fire that destroyed these princes.

Verse 19. Horeb and Sinai are the same general location. The first is the place as a whole and the second is the peak; but the two words are used interchangeably in the Bible. It was there that the children of Israel made the idol in the form of a calf. It is here called a *molten image* which means it was cast. Ex. 32: 4 agrees with this only it gives an additional item. The calf was first molten or cast "in the rough," then it was shaped more perfectly with the engraving tool.

Verse 20. *Changed* is from MUWR which Strong defines, "a primitive root; to alter; by implication to barter, to dispose of." The glory of God cannot actually be changed or altered. The statement means that the Israelites gave up their glorying and praise for God and gave it to the idol which they had made with their own hands.

Verse 21. *They forgat* does not mean their memory failed them. It had been only a few months since they had seen those great works of God and the mind of a human being does not forget that soon. The word means they dismissed the subject from their minds and turned their attention elsewhere, to something immediately before their eyes.

Verse 22. The Psalmist does not specify the works themselves, but does designate where they were done. The land of Ham was Egypt (see Ch. 105: 23), and the other place named was the body of water that brought salvation to the children of Israel while it brought destruction to their enemies.

Verse 23. After the Israelites had made the golden calf, the Lord was so provoked that he threatened to destroy the nation and start a new one by Moses. But the man Moses acted as mediator and God turned from his wrath. (Ex. 32: 11-13.)

Verse 24. *Despise* means to belittle or refuse to consider. The Israelites closed their eyes of faith against the attractions of the promised land and became impatient on account of some unpleasant conditions connected with obtaining it.

Verse 25. The original word for *murmur* is defined in the lexicon, "to grumble, i. e. to rebel." In 1 Cor. 10: 10 Paul refers to the same subject and Thayer defines the word, "to discontentedly complain." It means a situation where the complainant is dissatisfied, but is not able to specify any valid reason for his discontent.

Verse 26. This verse is a specific reference to the death of the men of war after the return of the 12 spies. (Num. 14.)

Verse 27. This verse refers to the captivity of all the nations of Israel. The history of that tragic event is in 2 Ki. 24 and 25.

Verse 28. The preceding verse covered a wide range of time and events that reached hundreds of years beyond the ones in the wilderness. This one comes back to some details of the misconduct of the nation that led up to the events of the other verse. Baal-peor was one of the forms of heathen worship. Its chief characteristic was the mixing up with immoral conduct in the name of religion. *Sacrifices of the dead* means the religious feasts which the heathen held in honor of their idol gods. As they were sacrificial feasts (those in which eating was done in the name of religion), they would naturally consider their eating as an act of worship toward their gods. There is a good description of these "dead" gods in Ps. 115: 4-8.

Verse 29. *Inventions* is from a word that simply means a work or action. The verse means that God was provoked by the idolatrous actions of his people. *The plague* refers to the various afflictions that were imposed on the nation from time to time, but the specific one in the mind of the Psalmist was the slaying of thousands of Israelites after the affair with Balaam recorded in Num. 25.

Verse 30. The Mosaic system was a combination of religious and civil government. It therefore included both spiritual and physical punishments. When the people fell into the sin of idolatry and its attendant immorality, Phinehas rose up in defence of the purity of the congregation and slew a notable actor and his partner on sight. That execution appeased the wrath of God and he stopped the plague.

Verse 31. It is always right to oppose evil by whatever means the law provides for the purpose. The law had prescribed death as punishment for idolaters (Deut. 17: 2-5), and this man was carrying out the requirements of the law in killing these people. That was why the good citizens counted his act a righteous one.

Verse 32. There was more than one occasion when the people caused a disturbance in connection with water. The circumstances in the present case indicate the one reported in Num. 20. *For their sakes* means on their account or because of them.

Verse 33. *Spake unadvisedly* means he spoke unwisely or rashly. This is the only sin that the scriptures specify against Moses in this noted case. For extended comments on the subject see those at Num. 20: 9-12 in Volume 1 of this Commentary.

Verses 34-36. This paragraph is on the one subject of the mixing up with the heathen. The reader may see a detailed account of the subject in Judges 1 and 2.

Verse 37. The Hebrew word for *devils* that is used here occurs only twice in the Bible; the other place being in Deut. 32: 17. This verse is concerned with the human sacrifices to idolatrous worship. For further comments and numerous citations on the subject see comments at 2 Ki. 16: 3 in the Commentary.

Verse 38. Shedding of *innocent blood* is the slaying of innocent persons. When a man is slain who is worthy of death it is not the shedding of innocent blood. The children of these idolaters were not guilty of any wrong, therefore it was the shedding of innocent blood to slay them in sacrifice to idols.

Verse 39. *Went a whoring* means they went lusting for the practices of false worship. Their *inventions* means their conduct that sprang from their own hearts.

Verse 40. It requires something unusual to cause one to reject his own possessions or people. The Israelites were the personal possession of God, descended through his devoted servant Abraham, yet they were cast off when they followed after idols.

Verses 41-45. It would serve no practical purpose to separate the verses of this paragraph. They all refer to the history recorded in the book of Judges. Since that epoch has been carefully commented upon in its proper place in the Commentary, I shall not take up space to repeat it here but will ask the reader to consult it in that place.

Verse 46. This verse is a prophecy although in the past tense. It was fulfilled when the Israelites were in the captivity. (See Ezra 1: 1-4; Neh. 2: 1-8.)

Verses 47, 48. This paragraph also is prophecy, and pertains to the return of the Jewish nation from Babylonian captivity. For a detailed account of that great event the reader should examine the books of Ezra and Nehemiah.

PSALMS 107

Verse 1. The short or momentary extension of mercy does not require so much of a condescension, but the mercy of the Lord endures *forever*. That does not mean that nothing can terminate it. Unless a person complies with the terms of God's mercy he will not receive it at all. But as long as those conditions are met, the Lord never fails in his mercy toward the unforunate.

Verse 2. The Psalmist is a little more specific in his call for praise. The very fact that a man has been redeemed is proof of the mercy of God. No one will be redeemed on the ground of his own merit; it will be through the mercy of God.

Verse 3. Most of my comments on the preceding verse had in view the general fact of God's mercy and its agency in bringing redemption to man. However, the Psalmist had in mind especially the rescuing of the nation from their enemy nations. Such favors took place in so many instances and under such a variety of circumstances that we will need to be careful in the application of the separate verses of this chapter. Even in the present verse the four points of the compass are named, which shows the writer was taking in a wide scope of history.

Verse 4. This verse could have been said of the children of Abraham's descendants on more than one occasion, hence I will not try to specify anything here.

Verse 5. For the evidence of history as an explanation of this verse, one needs only to remember the quail and manna, the smitten rock and the water at Meribah.

Verse 6. *They cried* includes the frequent murmurings at their misfortunes. In even such cases, the Lord heard his people and provided the things needed for comfort.

Verse 7. Both *city* and *habitation* are from words with wide range of meaning. The outstanding thought is of a place that is settled and permanent, contrasting with the wandering life they had in the wilderness. The passages that illustrate the above thought are too numerous to cite here; let the student read Lev. 25: 18; 26: 5 for two.

Verse 8. No writer in the Bible had more to say about praise and thanksgiving to God than David. It is interesting to note, also, that he always had a strong motive for the praise. It was not merely a meaningless expression of sentiment.

Verse 9. *Soul* is used for the whole human being. We should get the thought that both spiritual and temporal blessings all come from God. (James 1: 17.)

Verse 10. God punished his people very severely for their departures from his law. When they had been chastised sufficiently, their darkness and threat of death was lifted and they were given another opportunity to show their faith in God.

Verse 11. This refers to the corrective treatment described in the preceding verse, and states the reasons why it was inflicted; the people rebelled against the words of God. *Contemned* means they disrespected the *counsel* of the Lord.

Verse 12. *Labor* is used figuratively and refers to the hard time the Israelies suffered for their disobedience. *Fell down* denotes their defeat because of having deserted the Lord. When He decides to punish his servants, there is no one who can hinder.

Verse 13. The mercy of the Lord is again mentioned as being extended to the people when they cried unto Him out of their distress.

Verse 14. *Brake their bands* is figurative and refers to the hardships that had been allowed to come on the Israelites. After suffering them to be brought very low in affliction, the Lord came to their rescue and released them from their troubles.

Verse 15. The quality of *goodness* could be negative only. That is, a person might be considered good just because he had done nothing bad. But that was not David's description of the Lord, for he not only is free from doing wrong, but performs wonderful works for the benefit of man.

Verse 16. *Gates of brass* and *bars of iron* refer to the hardness of the enemies of God and his people. Such obstacles are nothing in the hands of the Almighty.

Verse 17. This verse teaches that men may bring affliction or other evil conditions on themselves. One who thus works transgression and iniquity is a fool.

Verse 18. By such an evil manner of life as described in the preceding verse, these foolish men developed a depraved or deranged appetite. They became so abnormal that they loathed all kinds of food. They had carried on after that manner so long they had been brought *unto the gates of death*.

Verse 19. Some men never call upon God unless they are in trouble. Strict justice would say that all such people should be ignored. But God is merciful as well as just, and when a soul in trouble appeals to Him sincerely he is never turned down.

Verse 20. There are conditions that need curing that are spiritual and not physical. The Lord's means of healing all such is his word.

Verse 21. This is the same as v. 15.

Verse 22. Animal and other material sacrifices were good and were required under the law. But the immaterial kind also is required and the same agrees with the teaching of the New Testament. (Heb. 13: 16.)

Verses 23, 24. The Psalmist has said much in general about the wonderful works of God. He gets a little more specific in this paragraph and calls attention to scenes on the large bodies of water as they were known in that day.

Verse 25. Men were astonished because Christ could calm the sea. David was impressed with the Lord's power to cause the stormy condition of it in the first place.

Verse 26. *They* has direct relation to the men who go to sea to deal in merchandising. But the movements described here are those of the waves caused by the storms. The ships are tossed up and down on the bosom of the deep, and the men in them are frightened; *their soul is melted*.

Verse 27. This is a further description of the state of fear into which the men in the ships are thrown because of the raging sea. A fair instance of this state of fear is recorded in Jonah 1: 5 on the occasion of the run-away prophet, whose presence in the ship provoked the Lord to bring on the storm that threatened to wreck the vessel.

Verses 28, 29. Again we see that man is disposed to appeal to God when in trouble. The voice of divine power is able to calm the raging of the waters, and rescue the human creatures from the threatened destruction.

Verse 30. The men in the storm rejoice because they are saved from what seemed to be certain death. In too many instances, though, they stop with their personal rejoicing when they should think more reverently on Him whose mercy gave them their escape. That is why the Psalmist so frequently gave the statement in the verses below.

Verse 31. This statement is commented upon at v. 15.

Verse 32. Personal or private praise for God is right and pleasing to Him. Yet men should be willing to express themselves for that feeling before others. Jesus taught that idea in Matt. 10: 32, 33.

Verse 33. Many of the statements in this and some following verses have a general meaning or may be said to be true either as history or prophecy. God's absolute control of all the parts of the earth is the basic thought in the mind of the Psalmist. Considering the first clause of this verse as prophecy, I will make a quotation from ancient history to show a noted instance of its fulfillment. "Alexander, designing to fix the seat of his empire at Babylon, projecting the bringing back the Euphrates into its natural and former channel, had actually set his men to work. But the Almighty, who watched over the fulfilling of his prophecy, defeated this enterprise by the death of Alexander, which happened soon after. It is easy to comprehend how, after this, Babylon being neglected to such a degree as we have seen, its river was converted into an inaccessible pool . . . By means of all these changes, Babylon became an utter desert, and all the country around fell into the same state of desolation and horror; so that the ablest geographers at this day (A.D. 1729) cannot determine the place where it stood."—Rollin's History, Vol. 1, pp. 558-560.

Verse 34. A noted instance of this kind of performance was in the destruction of Sodom and the other cities of the plain, recorded in Gen. 13: 10; 19: 24, 25.

Verse 35. I do not know whether the Psalmist had any specific event in mind when he wrote this. We have plenty of evidence in the Bible that God can reverse any condition of the earth and the seasons that he wishes.

Verse 36. The purpose in bringing about the conditions mentioned in the preceding verse was to supply the needs of the hungry people. *City for habitation* meant to prepare a substantial place for them to live.

Verse 37. Although the ground was cursed after the sin of Adam, the normal condition since is the production of crops upon the labor of man with the soil. However, certain times have been when special judgments were placed upon the fields because of the misdeeds of the people. When God's wrath had been satisfied, he then permitted the earth to resume its service for man and *yield fruits of increase.*

Verse 38. The preceding verse has to do with the blessings of the land. This one pertains to the increase of livestock. When the people do that which is right, God will *not suffer their cattle to decrease.*

Verse 39. This verse returns to the thought of God's corrective measures when people depart from the right way. He sometimes accomplishes it through the agency of enemy nations and suffers them to bring *oppression* and *affliction* on his own seed.

Verse 40. The different social classes among God's people were sometimes set in array against each other. When that was the case the *princes* were generally wrong and God would deal with them with contempt, and cause them to *wander in the wilderness* in order to bring them to a better state of humiliation and dependence.

Verse 41. Just as God would humble the prince who exalted himself and went wrong, so He would exalt the poor and meek persons who had been unjustly treated.

Verse 42. Righteous individuals will approve the actions of the Lord as described in the preceding two verses; but workers of iniquity will be forced to *stop her mouth.*

Verse 43. Here is a definition of a wise man; it is the one who *observes these things.* It shows that he understands or appreciates the lovingkindness of the Lord.

PSALMS 108

Verse 1. *Fixed* is from a Hebrew word that means to be prepared or ready. David meant he was prepared to praise the Lord and give him all of the glory due Him.

Verse 2. *Awake* as an intransitive verb means to be aroused to some action of importance. The Psalmist was calling on people to be interested in the praises of God. There is nothing unusual in suggesting the psaltery and harp, for he was known to be a specialist in using such instruments in connection with religious worship.

Verse 3. Private praise was not all that David proposed to offer to the Lord. The *people* of the *nations* were to be witnesses of his praise. (See comments at 107: 32.)

Verse 4. The *heavens* or the *clouds* are inanimate things and are not subjects for the mercy of God. The exalted status that they represent in the universe was used to compare the greatness of divine mercy towards living beings.

Verse 5. The preceding verse affirmed the fact of the exaltation of God's mercy. In this verse the Psalmist endorses such exaltation by bidding the Author of the quality to be himself exalted.

Verse 6. *Thy beloved* means the people of God. Since the divine mercy is so high and great, David felt free to ask its Author to extend some of it to the people who had ever been the objects of divine love.

Verse 7. The first person pronoun *I* refers to God, and he was declaring his claims to certain territories and groups of people, and what he intended to do with them. He would *divide* or reduce Shechem and Succoth.

Verse 8. *Gilead* was a district east of the Jordan and was a very noted territory. It was logical for God to claim it, not only on the ground that "the earth is the Lord's and the fulness thereof," but his people had taken it over in the march from Egypt to Canaan. *Manasseh* and *Ephraim* are mentioned in this way because they were the sons of Joseph and each formed a complete tribe. (Gen. 48: 5.) *Judah is my lawgiver* was said in prospect, for the Old Testament law came through Moses who was of the tribe of Levi. But Judah was the tribe through whom Christ was to come, who was to give the final law of Heaven to the world. (Gen. 49: 10; Heb. 7: 12-14.)

Verse 9. This verse is the same as Ch. 60: 8, and the reader is requested to see my comments at that place.

Verse 10. David was thinking about the mighty support that would be needed to help him encounter his many obstacles. To invade a strong territory (Edom was a powerful enemy) would be an instance of great deeds. The Psalmist was enquiring as to who could enable him to accomplish such an exploit.

Verse 11. David turned in hope toward God, although he was the one who had *cast us off* in the sense of the bitter chastisements. But God has been merciful and the Psalmist expects to be led into victory at last.

Verse 12. The main thought in this verse is the contrast between the help from God and that from man. The former is great while the other is vain.

Verse 13. This is practically the same in thought as the preceding verse. *Valiantly* means forcefully, and David meant that the people could manifest force if they relied on the Lord. This is the same thought Paul expressed in Eph. 6: 10.

PSALMS 109

Verse 1. The word *peace* as used here means to be silent. The Psalmist is begging God to say or do something about the wicked conduct of the enemy.

Verse 2. Mere opposition would not baffle a brave man like David. What he dreaded was the effect of deceitful words spoken against him. It is difficult to make a proper defence against a foe who attacks from ambush.

Verse 3. David was never the kind of man who would deny any act of which he was guilty. Therefore we can appreciate his complaint at being opposed *without a cause.*

Verse 4. Too much favor shown to some men will make them enemies of their benefactors. It has been said that a sure way to lose a man's friendship is to loan him some money. It does not always work that way but often does. Instead of plotting some form of vengeance against the ingratitude of those whom he had favored, David said he would pray for them. That reminds us of the teaching of Christ in Matt. 5: 44.

Verse 5. Ingratitude is a grievous fault and is severely condemned in the Bible in places too numerous to mention here. But it is still worse when a person shows that spirit by doing something evil against the one who has favored him.

Verse 6. *Satan* is spelled with a capital but the lexicon does not justify it. We are sure that David would not wish even the wickedest of men to be presided over by the archenemy of souls. Strong's definition of the original word is, "an opponent." The Psalmist meant that some human adversary should be on hands to oppose those who had rewarded evil for good.

Verse 7. This verse means to wish for the conviction of the enemy whenever he was brought to trial. *Let his prayer become sin* has a clear explanation in Prov. 28: 9, which I request the reader to see. David meant that the prayer of such people as he had been describing should be regarded as an abomination.

Verse 8. We should not be confused by the similarity of language in different passages. This verse sounds somewhat like that which Peter cited in Acts 1: 20, but that case is the one in Ps. 69: 25. The present verse merely means to condemn a character such as the writer has been describing. Such a person is not worthy to retain his *office*, which means any charge or responsibility he may have been exercising.

Verse 9. The gist of this short verse is to wish for the death of the man.

Verse 10. These wishes seem cruel, but they were in line with other harsh measures that David sometimes used against those who opposed the Lord's people.

Verse 11. An *extortioner* is a man who forces another to pay an unreasonable sum in payment of a debt or in the purchase of some necessity of life. *Spoil his labor* means to rob him of the fruits of his labor.

Verse 12. I would make the same comment on this verse as I did on v. 10.

Verse 13. It has always been a natural desire to have children. It is also usual to hope for a continuation of one's children (posterity) through the coming years. The severe wish, therefore, that David expresses in this verse is in line with some others already commented upon above.

Verse 14. As a help in studying this strange verse, let the reader see my comments at Ex. 20: 4-6 in the first volume of this Commentary. Not all of the remarks in that place will apply here, but they will throw some light on the subject. This verse does not mean to put any physical penalties on the present generation that had been imposed on their forefathers. However, since this generation was as wicked as the previous ones, they were to be punished with the unpleasant memory of their ancestors and the punishments that God inflicted upon them for their personal wickedness.

Verse 15. At first sight this verse might seem to contradict the preceding one. *Memory* is from ZEKER and Strong defines it, "a memento, abstractly, recollection; by implication, commemoration." The idea is that the people were not to be remembered as far as granting them any public memorials.

Verse 16. The reason for the foregoing severe wishes is stated here. The men had been cruel toward the poor and needy.

Verse 17. The Psalmist never advocated returning evil for good, but he did call for evil or unpleasant treatment to come upon the workers of evil as a punishment.

Verse 18. *Clothed himself* is figurative, meaning the wicked man enclosed and surrounded himself with his wickedness as if it were a garment. *Bowels* is from a word that is defined "the center" in the lexicon, and *bones* is from one that means the substance of the body as a whole. If water was to saturate the inner body and oil was made to penetrate the whole body, it would be a very undesirable condition. It describes the lot that David was wishing on this wicked man.

Verse 19. The antecedent of *it* is "cursing" in vs. 17, 18, which signifies a state of disgrace or humiliation. The thought in the present verse is that the wicked man who delighted in disgracing others should himself be disgraced. As a garment is used to cover a man and a girdle to bind him, so the Psalmist wished the wicked man to be enclosed and bound by the same kind of disgrace he had been imposing on others.

Verse 20. *From the Lord* is a phrase that shows David was not planning any personal vengeance against his enemies. His idea was that all just punishment should come from the Lord. Paul taught the same thing in Rom. 12: 19 and he also cited Deut. 32: 35.

Verse 21. *Do thou for me* means for God to act on behalf of David. This was in keeping with the sentiments expressed in the preceding verses.

Verse 22. *Poor and needy* referred to his condition of affliction brought on by his enemies. He was in prosperous circumstances as far as temporal things were concerned.

Verse 23. These figures of speech again refer to the helpless situation surrounding the Psalmist. It was the result of hatred from his envious foes.

Verse 24. This weakness may have been literal and physical. However, it was not from lack of food or other necessities at hand. David often resorted to deep devotions when great distress and worry surrounded him. At such times he engaged in prolonged fasting (see 2 Sam. 12: 21, 22) which would cause the weakness he mentioned.

Verse 25. When his enemies saw the wretched condition of David's body, they took much satisfaction from it. They pretended to think it was some just punishment placed upon him for his sins and they reproached him for it.

Verses 26, 27. The finest sentiment in this paragraph is the motive the Psalmist expresses for asking the Lord to help him. It is that the people might know that He was the one doing the work. David was longing for relief from his troubles, but he wanted the Lord to have the glory for it.

Verse 28. *Curse* and *bless* are opposite terms as used in this place. The first means to wish evil and the second to wish good. *Ashamed* and *rejoice* also are used as opposite ideas. If the good wishes of the Lord were brought to pass it would confuse (make ashamed) the enemy, but would cause the Psalmist to rejoice.

Verse 29. The thought in this verse is the same as that in the preceding one. The writer expresses it in figures as he did in v. 18, those of articles of clothing.

Verse 30. Again we see the distinction of making one's praise for God public; David would let it be known *among the multitude.*

Verse 31. *At the right hand* is a figure of speech. It means that the hand of the Lord will do the right thing on behalf of the poor, that they might be protected from the intended destruction at the hands of their enemies.

PSALMS 110

Verse 1. This verse is quoted at Matt. 22: 44; Mark 12: 36; Luke 20: 42; Acts 2: 34. The New Testament passages furnish the information that identify the persons in the verse. *The Lord* is the God of Heaven and *my Lord* is Christ. The whole verse is the direct speech of David, making a prophecy (although past tense in form) of the ascension and crowning of Jesus as King of kings and Lord of lords. *Until* looks to the same period mentioned in Heb. 10: 12, 13, and is practically the same thought expressed by Peter in Acts 3: 21.

Verse 2. *The Lord* is the same person so termed in the preceding verse, and the pronoun *thy* refers to Christ. The thought is that God would empower his Son to become a successful ruler. The reign was to issue from Zion which was that part of Jerusalem that was headquarters for the kingdom of Christ.

Verse 3. One word in the lexicon definition for *willing* is "spontaneity." The force of the word lies chiefly in its contrast with the Mosaic system which included infants in its membership. Such members had no will in the matter but were enrolled in the list as soon as they were circumcised. In the system of Christ a person must be old enough to accept the service of his own choice before he can become a part of the institution. It is the same thought indicated in Heb. 8: 10, 11 which was cited from Jer. 31: 31-34. The added thought would be logical, therefore, that such persons would be expected to be *willing* to obey a ruler whom they had voluntarily accepted over them. *Day of thy power* means the Christian Dispensation. The material appointments of the tabernacle and temple service were designed "for glory and for beauty" (Ex. 28: 2). That was a type of the spiritual service that was to be rendered under Christ, and a service that is rendered willingly would indeed constitute the *beauties of holiness.* Dew appears in the morning and soon disappears as a general thing. As a contrast, the vigor and strength and freshness of the reign of Christ will continue throughout the "day" of the Dispensation; will continue as it was *from the womb of the morning*, or from the time the reign started. (Dan. 2: 44.)

Verse 4. The same identity of persons and pronouns should be observed here as in the preceding verses. God assured his Son that he was to be a priest, and confirmed the promise with an oath. *Will not repent* means that God will not change his mind. In v. 3 a contrast was shown between the priesthood of Christ and the Levitical priesthood. In the present verse another contrast is revealed. That is, the priesthood of Christ was to differ from that of the Levites in the same way that the Levitical priesthood differed from that of Melchisedek. I shall note only one of the types here, and will reserve the more detailed discussion of the subject for its proper place in the book of Hebrews. The family history of Melchisedek was purposely left out of the divine record. The apparent lack of any genealogy for Melchisedek was to be a type of the actual lack of it in the case of Christ. (Isa. 53: 8; Acts 8: 33.)

Verse 5. *The Lord* in this place is Christ, for he is the one who is at the right hand of God. *Strike through kings* refers to the authority of Christ over all other rulers, bringing them either into obedience to his law, or shaming them by his condemnation of them for their rebellion against his divine rule.

Verse 6. This is a highly figurative passage and means the triumph of Christ over all enemies of righteousness. *Judge among the heathen* has special reference to the universal domain of the Christian Dispensation. It was to include all nations, not the Jews only. The same thought is signified by the phrase *many countries.*

Verse 7. When a commander is engaged in a successful campaign into the territory of an enemy, he does not wish to take "time out" to return to headquarters for provisions. If he is being successful in his invasion, he will find drinking water right in the path of the march. Such an exploit will not only supply the army with the physical necessity of the body, but will strengthen the moral by the encouraging prospect, so that all parties will *lift up the head* in the spirit of a conqueror.

PSALMS 111

Verse 1. Wholehearted service is the only kind that will be accepted by the Lord. This was taught by the Saviour of the world when he was on the earth. (Matt. 22: 37.) David was aware of this principle and declared that he would praise the Lord with his whole heart. *Assembly* referred to any gathering of good men, and the *congregation* had more specific reference to the nation as a whole when gathered officially.

Verse 2. The primary meaning of the original for *pleasure* is desire, and a man whose desire is to follow the works of the Lord will seek after them. Jesus taught that if a man would seek he should find. Anything that is worth having is worth seeking after with a sincere and earnest devotion of heart.

Verse 3. *Honorable* and *glorious* mean practically the same thing. When a distinction is to be made, the former refers to the actual character and the latter to the appearance. Everything pertaining to God is enduring, and the righteousness that is prompted by Him will endure throughout the ages.

Verse 4. The material creation of God is not the most important of his works, but the spiritual favors toward the children of men are the great works that the Psalmist was praising. His *compassion* refers to the state of his mind and his *graciousness* denotes the Lord's dealing with his creatures based on that compassion.

Verse 5. This verse is somewhat general and refers to the goodness of God, whether manifested in the form of temporal, or spiritual favors. He has promised such to all who fear or respect him, and he never forgets or breaks his promises.

Verse 6. *Heritage of the heathen* means the lands that had been held in possession by the alien nations. God made a covenant to give these things to his people, and it was fulfilled in proportion as the people complied with the conditions or terms.

Verse 7. *Verity* means truthfulness and *judgment* means fairness; the works of God are according to both of these qualities. This not only applies to his actual dealings with the children of men, but also to the commandments regarding their conduct.

Verse 8. If anything is established it becomes mature, and the passing of the ages will not overthrow it. The works of God are established on truth and uprightness.

Verse 9. *Sent redemption* could be understood as both history and prophecy. God redeemed his ancient people in Egypt from their bondage and brought them out from under their oppression, and this was history at the time David wrote. Then as prophecy it would first apply to the return from Babylonian captivity, and next it was fulfilled when God sent his Son to offer redemption to all the world. The word *reverend* has been greatly misunderstood by many students of the Bible. We should be careful not to let one extreme drive us to another. The popular use of this word is wrong and indicates a tendency toward pride and the desire for personal distinction. I am as much opposed to such usuage of the word as anyone can be. But I am also opposed to the extravagant language that has been the stock in trade argument (?) that is made with reference to the word, which is generally stated as follows: "The word reverend is used only once in the Bible, and then it is applied to God." This is a misleading assertion, for the word is a translation of the Hebrew word YARE, which occures several hundred times in Bible. It has been redered by such words as fear, terrible and dreadful. The inspired writers have used the word with reference to some of the worst of characters. The thought intended by the Psalmist is that God is holy and deserves to be respected.

Verse 10. *Fear* is from a Hebrew word that has practically the same meaning as the one for "reverend" in the preceding verse. Its principal idea is to have the proper respect for any character who is good, and to have a feeling of dread or terror for one who is evil. If we respect the Lord we will wish to learn about him, which is the reason David says it is the beginning of wisdom. People who obey the commandments of God thereby show they have good judgment or good understanding. Praise that is prompted by the spirit of flattery is fickle and often changes over night. On the contrary, the praise of God is genuine and lasting.

PSALMS 112

Verse 1. *Praise ye the Lord* is abbreviated to the simple word "Hallelujah" in the margins of some Bibles and the religious dictionaries agree with it. A number of the Psalms begin with it and probably it was not an integral part of the text originally, but was a sort of heading or introduction to the chapter. The man who fears or respects the Lord will be blessed or happy. Such a man will logically take delight in the commandments of the Lord, and such a life can result only in happiness.

Verse 2. *His seed* refers to the posterity of the man described in the foregoing verse. It is here termed also the *generation of the upright*.

Verse 3. There is no practical difference between *wealth* and *riches;* they are used for emphasis. God does not offer material gain as an inducement for men to live right, but a righteous man has the prospect of such blessings as a result of right living. This lesson was taught by Jesus in Matt. 6: 33. The righteousness practiced by a man who fears God will be lasting because it is based on the truth.

Verse 4. As light will penetrate the darkness, so the influence of an upright man is enlightening to those about him. For explanation of *gracious* and *compassion* see my comments at Ch. 111: 4.

Verse 5. Some men may be *good* and yet not be able to lend unto others through lack of business management. The Psalmist explains the kind of good man he is considering in the close of the verse. It is the one who uses *discretion* or judgment in the management of his business affairs, always acting with fairness and due consideration.

Verse 6. Apply the comments at v. 3 as explanation of this verse.

Verse 7. *Heart is fixed* means his heart is settled in the Lord through an abiding faith. Such a person needs have no fear of *evil tidings*, for even death cannot sever him from the favor of God and the reward of a righteous life.

Verse 8. *Established* in this verse has the same force of meaning as *fixed* in the preceding verse. The reference to his enemies has the same bearing as the mention of *evil tidings* in the other verse.

Verse 9. This verse is still considering the righteous man, and makes a specific mention of part of his righteous conduct. It consists in helping the poor by the blessings that he had himself received from the Lord. The results of such a life will *endure for ever*. The original for *horn* has a various definition in the lexicon, but its simple meaning is "power." When used figuratively it indicates great strength and influence. The Psalmist specifies that when such qualities are possessed by a righteous man, the exaltation following will be an honorable one.

Verse 10. Wicked men are *grieved* or envious at the good standing of righteous men. To *melt away* means to decrease or diminish. The wicked desire prompted by envy will not endure the test of time.

PSALMS 113

Verse 1. For comments on the first clause see those at Ch. 112: 1. The servants of the Lord are those who have such respect for Him that they will wish to obey his law. It is further appropriate that such people will praise the Lord.

Verse 2. To be *blessed* means literally to be happy. It would not make good sense to say that the name of the Lord is happy. It is good usage, however, to say that the name of the Lord brings happiness to men. Such happiness will endure always.

Verse 3. In other words, all of man's waking hours should be filled with praise for the goodness of the Lord.

Verse 4. *High above all nations* means His power or authority is supreme. His glory is logically above the heavens because he was the creator of them all.

Verse 5. *Dwelleth on high* denotes the exalted position of His dwelling. For the distinctive meaning of *Lord* and *God* see the comments at Ch. 86: 12.

Verse 6. The pronoun *who* refers to the person who will observe the things of creation, and give God the credit for such works. True humility will prompt a man to make such an observation, while pride will cause him to ignore all such evidences of divine power; even denying the existence of a Supreme Being.

Verse 7. When *dust* and *dunghill* are used figuratively, they refer to the humiliating situation of many poor people. It has special application when that situation has been imposed upon them by the more fortunate ones.

Verse 8. True merit is often hidden from view by the opposition of jealous enemies. God recognizes it, however, and will reward the humble and worthy persons with proper exaltation. Jesus taught this lesson in Matt. 23: 12 and many other places.

Verse 9. This does not mean that a barren woman would not have a house in which to live. The leading thought will be recognized by considering the verse as a whole. When God acts with compassion on behalf of a childless wife, it turns her into a happy housekeeper with children. The case of Hannah is a noted instance of it, recorded in 1 Samuel 1.

PSALMS 114

Verse 1. *Israel* and *house of Jacob* are the same since the event recorded in Gen. 32: 28. *Strange* means foreign or alien; the Egyptian language was foreign to Israel.

Verse 2. The pronoun *his* applies to the Lord, who was named at the close of the preceding verse. One meaning of *sanctuary* is "sacred thing." Judah was the most numerous of the 12 tribes and Israel stood as a name for all of the tribes. The whole congregation, therefore, was a sacred possession of God.

Verse 3. This verse is a figurative reference to the opening of the Red Sea for the Israelites in escaping from Egypt, and the crossing of the Jordan under Joshua.

Verse 4. Since we know that the mountains did not literally move we must look for the thought implied. The mountains and hills and valleys and all the parts of the land were made to serve the needs of God's people when they reached the promised land.

Verses 5, 6. David addressed these inanimate objects in the spirit of fable. Of course they could not speak, and the language was a challenge to the unbeliever to explain the wonderful control of these things in nature. The only way it could be explained would be to acknowledge the existence of the God of all creation.

Verse 7. The language of this verse was used in the same figurative manner as the preceding paragraph. However, instead of asking a challenging question, the Psalmist put it in the form of a command. *Tremble* means to be filled with awe and respect.

Verse 8. God brought water out of the rock to quench the thirst of the congregation. *Standing water* is figurative, meaning there was an abundance of it. See the accounts of this kind of performance in Ex. 17: 6 and Num. 20: 10, 11.

PSALMS 115

Verse 1. How different this is from the attitude of Moses and Aaron at the rock, referred to in the last verse of the preceding chapter. They took the glory for the deed performed on behalf of the congregation and were punished for the same.

Verse 2. The word *heathen* in the Old Testament is from GOI in every place, and the first definition in Strong's lexicon is, "a foreign nation." It has also been rendered by Gentiles, nation, and people, in the King James version. The word would not have to mean idolaters, although about all of the "foreign nations" at the time David wrote had gone into the worship of false gods. The word in this and the following verses is used in the sense of idolaters. Since many of them worshiped the imaginary gods, it explains why they asked *where is now their* (Israel's) *God?*

Verse 3. In the preceding verse the pronoun for God is in the 3rd person because the writer was quoting the heathen. In this verse it is the 1st person *(our)* because the Psalmist is speaking for himself and his people. *In the heavens* is the answer to the question of the heathen in the last clause of the preceding verse.

Verses 4-8. It would have weakened the argument not to include all of these verses in one paragraph. It should be noted that 7 of the most important members of the human body are named in the description of the idols. The heathen people had drifted into gross ignorance of the true God, yet they had retained the impression that He was a being with body and parts similar in form to those of man. The fact that the writer is the one who has named them here proves that this idea is correct. We observe that David makes no criticism of the items, except that the man-made gods which have them cannot make any use of them. *They that make them are like unto them.* This statement involves more thought than at first might be realized. No person can make anything that could have any more ability than the maker of it. So the fundamental thought is, since man cannot perform the functions named in any supernatural degree, neither can he make a god that can.

Verse 9. The "switch" from the 2nd to the 3rd person should not confuse us. The Psalmist is admonishing Israel to trust in the Lord, not in the dumb idols he had just described. Then, as a basis for such an admonition he states that this Lord is their (everybody's) help and shield, making a general application of the fact.

Verse 10. *House of Aaron* means the same as "Israel" in the preceding verse, and the same comments should apply here that were made at that place.

Verse 11. This verse is like the two foregoing ones except that it is more general as to the persons addressed.

Verse 12. *House of Israel* means the whole nation, and the *house of Aaron* refers specifically to that portion of the nation that composed the priesthood. That function belonged exclusively to Aaron and his descendants. (Ex. 28: 1; 2 Chr. 26: 18.)

Verse 13. *Small* and *great* refer to what might have been the personal advantages and disadvantages of the men involved. God does not show partiality in the bestowal of his favors. The apostle Peter said that God is no respecter of persons. (Acts 10: 34.)

Verse 14. *Increase* is from a word with a very general meaning. The outstanding thought is that God will continue to bless the person who is righteous.

Verse 15. The importance of a blessing would depend on the quality of the one bestowing it. The blessing of which David was writing comes from the Maker of heaven and earth, therefore it will be all the more important.

Verse 16. *Heaven* and *heavens* refer to the firmament where the birds fly, and the expanse in which the planets exist. Actually, all creation is the Lord's, so the expression here has a special significance. It is a contrast with the last clause of the verse which declares the earth is given to the children of men, or is intended as the temporal dwelling place of man. This is not very favorable to the notion that the moon and other heavenly bodies were intended to be inhabited.

Verse 17. This verse and others like it are relied upon by the advocates of materialism. They are the people who teach that man is wholly mortal and all there is of him dies at the same time. This verse claims only that the dead praise not the Lord. We all believe that, for when the spirit leaves the body it results in the death of the body, and then, of course, the body cannot praise the Lord.

Verse 18. To *bless the Lord* means to acknowledge Him as the source of all blessings. *Praise the Lord* is from a Hebrew term sometimes rendered "Hallelujah."

PSALMS 116

Verse 1. The Lord heard the voice of David in that he granted his requests. For such a favor the Psalmist was led to love Him.

Verse 2. One favor encourages a man to ask for and expect another. *Inclined his ear* means the Lord lent a favorable ear to the prayer of David. For this reason he would continue to call upon God throughout life.

Verse 3. Since the word for *hell* has several phases of meaning, the thought here is that David's sorrows and pains were of the severest degree.

Verse 4. In the darkest hours of his distress, the Psalmist always called upon the Lord. *Deliver my soul* meant to rescue his entire being from the threatened injuries that were about to come from the hand of his enemies.

Verse 5. There is only a technical difference between *gracious* and *merciful*. The first has reference to the attitude of God's mind, and the second denotes the dealing with man as a result of that attitude. And then we would understand that the whole program would be *righteous* since it was from the Lord.

Verse 6. *Simple* is from PATHAIY and Strong defines it, "silly (i.e. seducible)." *Preserveth* is from SHAMAR, which Strong defines as follows: "properly to hedge about (as with thorns), i.e. guard; generally to protect, attend to, etc." David cited himself as an example of the Lord's protection, which indicates that he regarded the word with a more liberal meaning than is generally attached to the word "silly." The main thought is that God will not suffer the unsuspecting and innocent characters to be taken advantage of by the better informed ones.

Verse 7. *Return unto thy rest* means about the same as bidding one's self to "take it easy," or to feel reassured. The basis for such a feeling is the bountiful dealing that the Lord had shown.

Verse 8. This verse is largely general and figurative, although some of the favors indicated had literally been bestowed upon David.

Verse 9. This verse is an indirect expression of David's to the effect that he would not be destroyed by his enemies. He fully expected to survive all attempts to destroy him and take him from the association of living beings.

Verse 10. In other words, the Psalmist was not merely desiring the things of which he had been speaking. Or, using a familiar proverb that "the wish was father of the thought," David was more settled than that in his conclusion. He believed the things he had named, and that was the reason he had been outspoken on the subject.

Verse 11. *Haste* is from a Hebrew word that includes the meaning of fear or distraction. In his distracted state of mind over the many afflictions imposed upon him, David had felt that about everybody was unreliable.

Verse 12. The goodness of God is so great that no human service can repay it. However, we are assured that it is not expected of man to match the Lord in any respect. All that is required is that we show our appreciation by a life of faithful service.

Verse 13. *Cup of salvation* is a figure of speech, meaning the gracious provision that God has made for the salvation of the world. But all of this provision will be of no avail unless it is received wholeheartedly. That is why David said he would *take the cup*, which denoted a willingness to accept it on the terms attached.

Verse 14. The cup of salvation is offered to man on certain conditions. Among them, in the days of the Mosaic system, were the ceremonies pertaining to the religious activities, and David lived under that system. That is why he stated he would pay his vows, for he had just agreed to take the cup of salvation, and he knew that he would be required to do his part.

Verse 15. The word for *precious* is defined in the lexicon as "valuable," and it also is used in the sense of being weighty and important. The death of a righteous man would seem to be a matter to be deplored, not thought of as something valuable. The thought is derived from what such a death indicates. It is somewhat like the passage in Acts 5: 41 where the rejoicing was over their being "worthy" to suffer for Christ. On that principle the Psalmist regarded it as meaning so much for a man to die because of his devotion to a righteous life.

Verse 16. The leading thought in this verse is in the line of humility. David acknowledged himself to be a servant of God, and also placed his mother in that class by designating her as the handmaid of the Lord. The last clause of the verse refers generally to the many "tight places" from which the Lord had delivered him.

Verse 17. *Sacrifice of Thanksgiving* is similar in thought to Heb. 13: 15.

Verse 18. This is a repetition of verse 14.

Verse 19. Again the Psalmist is willing for the public to witness his devotions to God. The pronoun *thee* refers to the courts of the Lord's house. *Praise ye the Lord* is from a word that is sometimes rendered "Hallelujah."

PSALMS 117

Verse 1. While this is the shortest chapter in the Bible, it contains some of the most significant truths. Paul quoted the first verse in Rom. 15: 11 where he was discussing the universal love of God. The Jews were thus not the only people whom God loved and was willing to accept, but *all ye nations* were invited to join in His praise. Logically, then, if all people are invited to engage in the praise service to the Lord, they may expect to receive his spiritual favor.

Verse 2. Mercy and kindness are practically the same, and the two words are used for the sake of emphasis. God not only extends the favor toward his people, but does so in large measure; it is *great* toward them. Another important item in this situation is the quality of truth out of which all favors spring. It is also noted that this truth is not short-lived; it *endureth for ever*. The chapter closes with the familiar expression that means "Hallelujah."

PSALMS 118

Verse 1. Appreciative servants of God will thank him for the simple fact of his goodness. That appreciation will be increased upon considering that the good attitude of the Lord is everlasting, thus holding out encouragement for the endless future.

Verses 2, 3. The goodness of God will be a fact whether anyone ever acknowledges it or not. But *Israel* (the congregation in general), and the *house of Aaron* (the priestly family in particular), are called upon to express their appreciation of the fact.

Verse 4. This verse is still more general than the preceding two. Anyone in any station of life who professes to fear God is asked to make acknowledgement of it.

Verse 5. *Large place* means a place of liberty, so that one would not be hampered by the conditions. That from which David had been relieved was a condition of distress. The Lord heard when the Psalmist prayed for deliverance and granted his petition.

Verse 6. *On my side* is worded "for me" in the marginal rendering which is correct. It is the same thought that Paul expressed in Rom. 8:31.

Verse 7. This verse contains the same thought as the preceding one, except that it is more specific. The other merely said that God was for David; this shows to what extent he was for him namely, he helped him in his time of need.

Verses 8, 9. Whether one considers man in general, or the special classes such as princes, it is better to trust in the Lord than in them.

Verse 10. Various peoples had opposed David and envied him because of his exalted position. *Destroy them* is rendered "cut them off" in the margin of the Bible, and the Lexicon agrees with it. The meaning is that he would cut short the attempts of his enemies to destroy him.

Verse 11. *They* means the same evil people referred to in the preceding verse. To *compass* means to surround for the purpose of capturing someone. These enemies of David thought to take such an advantage of him, but he expected to *destroy* (cut short) *them*.

Verse 12. The comparison is not especially to the bee as an individual insect, but rather to the fact that bees swarm in great numbers. But regardless of their great number, the enemies of David were to be *destroyed* (cut off or cut short).

Verse 13. *Thou* refers to the enemy who had been persecuting David. The wicked intention of the foe had been cut short by the Lord.

Verse 14. *Strength* and *song* is a fine combination. Because David was strengthened by the Lord, he would praise Him in song. The importance of that strength was indicated by the fact that it brought salvation to David.

Verse 15. *Tabernacles* is used in the sense of assemblies or groups. Such groups who are righteous only have the right to rejoice in salvation. Paul taught a like principle in Phil. 3:1. *Right hand of the Lord* means that whatever is done by the hand of the Lord is right.

Verse 16. *Right hand* is explained in the preceding verse.

Verse 17. David's enemies would wish him to die. Their expectations were to be disappointed, for David was assured of continuing in life, and of being permitted to declare the works of God to the generations to come.

Verse 18. David believed that the opposition of his enemies was an instrument in God's hands to test his faith. He was aware that it would not go far enough to slay him.

Verse 19. *Gates of righteousness* is a figure of speech, meaning the ways of right doing. It is similar in thought to the expression "door of opportunity." The direct meaning of David was that as the Lord showed him the good and the right way, he would gladly walk therein all the days of his life.

Verse 20. The Psalmist identifies the *gates of righteousness* of the preceding verse by the words *gates of the Lord* in this verse. He furthermore declares that the righteous will enter thereat.

Verse 21. David was ever ready to give God the praise for all blessings. *Become my salvation* here has special reference to his escape from the hands of his enemies.

Verse 22, 23. I have put these verses into one paragraph because it requires both to complete the quotation of Jesus in Matt. 21: 42 and Mark 12: 10. Since our Saviour made the application to himself we know we are correct in considering this passage as a prophecy of Christ and his work on earth. It had special application to the action of the Jewish people in rejecting Christ, whom God afterward exalted to be the head piece in the great edifice of salvation, the church. *This is the Lord's doing* means that it would be the Lord of Heaven who would reverse the work of the Jews and exalt him whom they had tried to debase. No wonder that it was such a marvelous thing in their eyes, for they were completely baffled in their wicked designs.

Verse 24. *Day* is from YOM, and a part of Strong's definition is, "figuratively a space of time defined by an associated term." In the King James version it has been rendered by day, time, age, season, space, year, and many others. Thus we need not just think of a 24-hour period, but of an age or epoch. The context shows the Psalmist was making a prediction of the Christian Dispensation, which was ushered into being by the exaltation of this head stone over all things to the church. *Made* is from a Hebrew word that has been rendered by such English words as accomplish, appoint, bring forth, fashion, grant and prepare. Hence the verse means that God ordained the day or age or period of Christ's reign, and all of us should rejoice in it.

Verse 25. Having interrupted his line for a prophecy concerning his illustrious Descendant, the Psalmist resumes where he had stopped. The *prosperity* he requested was not the temporal kind for he already had that in abundance. He meant for the Lord to prosper him in his conflicts with the foes of righteousness.

Verse 26. The first clause is a general statement that could have been said in any age of the world. It has no specific application as to when or by whom the coming would be done. *You* refers to anyone who had qualified under the terms of the first clause. The blessing upon all such was to proceed from the house of the Lord.

Verse 27. For the peculiar meanings of *God* and *Lord* see the comments at Ch. 86: 12. When anything is bound it is secure. As a figure, indicating the steadfastness of his devotions to God, the Psalmist bids the sacrifices to be fastened to the altar with cords.

Verse 28. Again see the meaning of *God* at Ch. 86: 12.

Verse 29. This verse is a summing up of the words of adoration with which the chapter abounded. God's goodness is worthy to be praised because it includes mercy, and the mercy is the kind that never faileth.

PSALMS 119

General remarks. The main subject of this long chapter is the Word of God. With exception of 3, 37, 90, 121, 122 and 132, each verse of the psalm makes direct mention of that Word under one of the following terms: law, testimonies, precepts, statutes, commandments, word, judgments and ordinances. The chapter is divided into 22 sections of 8 verses each, and the word that stands as a heading of each section is one of the letters of the Hebrew alphabet, thus giving us the spelling in English letters of the complete Hebrew alphabet. I shall make brief comments on the several verses.

Verse 1. *Blessed* is from a Hebrew word that Strong defines as "happy." We should include the idea of the future in the definition. Most of the happiness of the righteous is in the future, although they will be happy now over the prospect of what is in store for them. God's word is designated by *law* in this verse, and the blessing or happiness is upon those who walk according to that law. Those who do so are regarded as *undefiled* in God's sight.

Verse 2. To keep the *testimonies* means to observe the requirements contained therein. They are called by this name because they have been tested and proved true.

Verse 3. The pronoun *his* refers to the Lord in the first verse. *His ways* means the manner of life that is expected of the servants of God.

Verse 4. *Precepts* is used 21 times in this chapter and I will quote the definition in Strong's lexicon for the original. "properly, appointed, i.e. a mandate (of God; plural only, collectively for the law)." The leading idea is of a rule of action that has been fixed by some authority that is specific in form but general in its application. To keep them, therefore, means to observe diligently the specific rule of action.

Verse 5. *Statutes* is another term for the Word of God and it is used 22 times in this chapter. Its meaning is practically the same as that of precepts, so I will not repeat the definition. See the comments on "precepts" in verse 4.

Verse 6. To be ashamed means to be confused and defeated. Such a state will be avoided by having respect unto the *commandments*. This is another term for the Word of God, and carries the idea of an order or positive requirement.

Verse 7. *Judgments* is used as one of the terms for the Word of God because it means a verdict or decision. God has always used the proper judgment in forming his Word for the guidance of mankind. When a man is brought to realize this fact he will do the upright thing by giving the Lord due praise for it.

Verse 8. For *statutes* see the comments at v. 5. David did not believe that even a keeper of them could entirely avoid all testing afflictions; he asked only that he be not *utterly* forsaken.

Verse 9. God's word is designated by a Hebrew term that is here rendered by the simple English one, which is *word*. It is used 38 times in this chapter and indicates that God said or spoke the document intended as a rule of action, rather than merely influencing that action of man by bodily contact or power over him. God has always proposed to lead man into righteous living by appealing to his intelligence; by saying something to him. In this verse the Psalmist is thinking especially of the young man who should cleanse his way by hearing what God says to him.

Verse 10. Wholeheartedness is the main thought in this verse. A halfhearted profession will cause one to wander from the *commandments*.

Verse 11. It will do very little good to depend upon a manual turning to the Word of God if we do not retain it in the heart. That is why David hid it there that he might always be fortified against sin. It is the same thought that is sugggested in 1 Peter 3:15, in which one has the Lord dwelling in him through the Truth.

Verse 12. *Bless* in this place is from a word that means to praise and adore. Such adoration would logically prompt one to desire a knowledge of His *statutes*.

Verse 13. The *judgments* are defined at V. 7. David had such faith in them that he wished to repeat them for the instruction of others.

Verse 14. There will not be any additional term introduced for the Word of God until verse 91. I therefore request the reader to recognize the particular term in each verse, which will be italicized, and see its definition at the proper place near the beginning of the chapter. Paul bade Christians to rejoice in the Lord (Phil. 3:1), and David said he would rejoice in the Lord's *testimonies*.

Verse 15. Both parts of this verse are related to the same thought. If one meditates on the *precepts* of the Lord, it will cause him to show respect to the ways of life that are expected of the servants of the Lord.

Verse 16. We have the interesting circumstances of seeing two of the terms used in this verse. It is logical that if one takes delight in the sacred *statutes*, he will not forget the divine *word* coming from the same source.

Verse 17. The highest motive for wanting to live is expressed in this verse. It is that the Psalmist would have opportunity to keep the *word*.

Verse 18. This meant for God to help David see the beautiful things revealed in the *law*. The thought for general consideration is that if people would earnestly search the Sacred Volume they would be surprised at the *wondrous things* found therein.

Verse 19. A stranger is a foreigner within the meaning of the word here, as the words of a familiar song, "I'm but a stranger here, Heaven is my home," indicates. Such a person would feel the need of the holy *commandments*.

Verse 20. *My soul breaketh* means he was overwhelmed with desire for God's *judgments*.

Verse 21. A proud man is one who feels above the *commandments* of God. Such a man will be cursed and rebuked by the Author of those commandments.

Verse 22. David seldom asked for a favor from God without including some condition on which he expected it. The removal of reproach and contempt was to be as a reward for his keeping the divine *testimonies*.

Verse 23. The original for princes is defined, "a head person (of any rank or class)." Hence it does not always mean officials, but leading characters in a community. Such persons often feel important and are disposed to persecute good men like David. But the Psalmist met the situation by meditating in the holy *statutes*.

Verse 24. The Psalmist said in the first chapter that the happy man was the one who delighted in the law of the Lord. He now says that he delights in the *testimonies*, and also that he takes counsel or instruction from them.

Verse 25. *Cleaveth unto the dust* is a figure of speech, meaning the low condition to which the enemies of David were trying to bring him. But he asked to be quickened or enlivened by the *word*.

Verse 26. *Declared my ways* means he had professed or declared how he wanted to conduct himself. As a guide in such a life, David wished to be taught the divine *statutes*.

Verse 27. The first clause of this verse is like the preceding verse in thought, only the Psalmist uses the term *precepts* that he wished to understand. After having understood them, he proposed to talk about them to others.

Verse 28. Soul is used for the whole being. *Melteth* signifies a state of depression or discouragement. But David never quite gave up hope. When things looked very dark and trying he always turned to the *word* for help.

Verse 29. There had been so much falsehood devised against David by his enemies that he prayed for the removal of all such activities. Granting him the *law* does not imply that God would deny anyone the benefit of it. The Psalmist meant he craved the help of that law in combatting those who were devising falsehoods against him.

Verse 30. In this verse the Psalmist considers the *way of truth* as the equivalent of walking after the *judgments* of the Lord.

Verse 31. A mere profession of interest in a thing, or an occasional use of it, will not avail very much, hence David said he stuck or clung to the divine *testimonies*. On that condition he felt free to pray for help in avoiding an experience of shame.

Verse 32. To *run the way* means to travel it eagerly, referring to the way pointed out in the *commandments*. Enlarging the heart has about the same thought as opening up an avenue of opportunity. Paul wrote along the same line of thought in 2 Cor. 6: 11.

Verse 33. This verse is another prayer for instruction. David craved to know the *statutes* of the Lord, and promised to keep them always.

Verse 34. A man might have a great deal of understanding of some kind and still not be on the right course. David desired that which the Lord would give him, which would come through the divine *law*. He promised to give it wholehearted observance, for he realized that knowing the law alone would not suffice. Jesus brought out that same great lesson in John 13: 17.

Verse 35. In the 23rd Psalm it was declared that God would lead his sheep in the paths of righteousness for his name's sake. The same thought is suggested by the path of the Lord's *commandments*. With such a motive anyone would take delight in traveling over such a pathway.

Verse 36. A man's heart cannot be inclined in two directions at the same time. (Matt. 6: 24.) David places the way of God's *testimonies* as leading in one direction, and the way of covetousness as leading in the opposite direction.

Verse 37. A thing of vanity is something that is useless even though it may have a showy appearance. To quicken means to enliven, and the Psalmist wished to be active in the way of life ordained by the Lord.

Verse 38. The original for stablish means to "rise." The Psalmist means for God to cause his *word* to rise or have a standing before him, since he was devoted to the attitude of fear or reverence for Him.

Verse 39. The reproach that David feared was a threat from his enemies. He believed that God could divert the course of that reproach with his *judgments*.

Verse 40. To long after the *precepts* is similar to taking delight in them. (Ch. 1: 2.) To quicken means to enliven, and such a quickening would be in righteousness.

Verse 41. Salvation does not come to mankind on the ground of merit, but through the mercy of God. This truth is an outstanding one that is taught in the holy *word*.

Verse 42. By trusting in the *word* the Psalmist would be prepared to answer his enemies. We should compare this with the teaching in 1 Pe. 3: 15.

Verse 43. No one who loves God would think he would deprive a man of the privilege of speaking the *word*. This was just David's way of expressing his desire and determination to continue speaking it. One of his motives was his confidence in the *judgments* of God as revealed in the divine revelation.

Verse 44. *For ever and ever* is an emphatic form of saying it would continue to the end of life. David pledged himself to keep the *law* that long.

Verse 45. *Liberty* means to have plenty of room or opportunity to walk. That can be said of one who seeks to find the Lord's *precepts*.

Verse 46. The Psalmist has frequently expressed the sentiments of this verse. His confidence in the *testimonies* of God was so great that he wished others to know about them, neither was he ashamed to speak about them even in the hearing of great men. Jesus taught the same idea in Mark 8: 38.

Verse 47. It is not enough merely to tolerate the *commandments* of God, but a true servant will delight in them. Of course we would expect to find delight in anything we love or have set our affection upon.

Verse 48. Here is another verse that uses two of the terms under consideration, *commandments* and *statutes*. To lift up the hands means to do something about it, not merely make the profession of being interested in the great instrument of right living.

Verse 49. David uses the word "remember" in the sense of a petition only, not that he thinks God ever forgets. The prayer is made because of his hope in the *word*.

Verse 50. It is comparatively easy to bear affliction if one has a reliable basis of support. David was quickened or enlivened by the *word* of God.

Verse 51. Pride is often a symptom of envy at another's good fortune. As a solace the proud man may pretend to belittle the greatness of the other person and he will deride or ridicule him. All of such treatment, however, could not induce David to give up the *law* of God, for he believed that in it there was true greatness.

Verse 52. The record of the Lord's dealings with man was known to David. In that record he observed the form of divine *judgments* and took comfort from it.

Verse 53. Wickedness does not always consist in outright acts of violence. Instead, it is an act of wickedness to forsake the *law* of God. When men do that it may cause the friends of righteousness to be filled with horror.

Verse 54. Pilgrimage means that David regarded himself as only a stranger here on the earth. While passing his days on the earth he composed songs and had them used to reflect the *statutes* of the Lord.

Verse 55. To remember the name of the Lord in the night is similar to the thought in ch. 1: 2. After a man would pass a meditative night over the name of the Lord, he would be likely to pass the next day keeping the *law* in his actions.

Verse 56. *This* refers to the situation described in the preceding verse. David attributes such a state to his keeping the *precepts* of the Lord.

Verse 57. Portion means allotment or share. The most valuable possession one can have, in David's estimation, is that which comes from the Lord. That was the reason he had kept the *words* of the Lord.

Verse 58. In his appeals for the favor of God the Psalmist had been wholehearted. Paul taught practically the same idea when he said for Christians to come boldly unto the throne of grace (Heb. 4: 16). That same mercy of which Paul wrote was expected by the Psalmist because it was according to the *word* which offered that mercy.

Verse 59. *Thought on my ways* means the same as "walk circumspectly" (Eph. 5: 15). When David did this he realized the need for being guided by the *testimonies*.

Verse 60. To make haste does not have reference to speed in action, but to a readiness of mind. It prompted the Psalmist to keep the *commandments*.

Verse 61. Bands means companies, and the thing of which David was complaining was the forming of conspiracy by his enemies. Those who are wicked enough to plot against a righteous man would not likely care anything about the principles of the *law* of God. The meaning of the clause is that even the persecutions of his enemies could not distract the attention of David from the *law*.

Verse 62. A righteous man will not be awakened from midnight sleep by any disturbances of conscience. But other conditions might disturb his sleep, and at such times he will find comfort in going to the Lord and thanking him for his righteous *judgments;* for the benefits he was deriving from them.

Verse 63. David's choice of associates were those who reverenced the Lord, and that meant those whose reverence was proved by their keeping His *precepts.*

Verse 64. The Psalmist believed that all of the blessings enjoyed by the people of the earth were indications of God's mercy. He wished to return the proper conduct in appreciation for those mercies, and for guidance wanted to know the *statutes.*

Verse 65. Not only was the dealing of God well toward David, but it was in harmony with the general principles taught in the *word.*

Verse 66. A man might have knowledge but not possess good judgment in applying it. David prayed for the Lord to give him both, seeing he already had faith in the *commandments* and the correctness of their requirements.

Verse 67. *Went astray* does not especially refer to actions that were considered as sinful although it could include that meaning. It is true that David did sin and had to be corrected by afflictions. But the statement is also one of a great priciple regarding the discipline necessary to hold a man in the line of duty. The Psalmist was always an honest and humble servant of God, and realized that his afflictions had influenced him in keeping the *word* in connection with his daily walk.

Verse 68. There is a familiar saying that a man ought to "practice what he preaches." We should not expect God to do that exactly since he is divine and man is human. However, David says that God not only teaches his *statutes,* but does good things himself.

Verse 69. *Forged* is from TAPHAL which Strong defines, "a primitive root; properly to stick on as a patch; figuratively, to impute falsely." The thought is that David's enemies had besmirched him with lies. The mistreatment, however, did not prevent him from keeping the Lord's *precepts.*

Verse 70. The pronoun *their* stands for the "proud" in the preceding verse. *Fat* is from TAPHASH and Strong's definition is, "to be thick; figuratively to be stupid." *Grease* is from a word that refers to the richest part of any animal. That being the part without muscles, it would be inactive and a fitting illustration of a man who is stupid or inactive as to any great usefulness. In contrast with such a character, David was actively delightful in God's *law* so that he meditated thereon day and night.

Verse 71. This verse takes the same comments as v. 67 except it uses the term *statutes* in referring to the same subject that is under consideration in this chapter.

Verse 72. The Psalmist was a possessor of great wealth, yet he did not value it as he did the *law* of God. He expressed the same sentiment in ch. 19: 10.

Verse 73. This verse is logical in its reasoning. Since God made and fashioned man, he certainly knows what is best for his manner of life. Consequently, David craved an understanding of the Lord's *commandments.*

Verse 74. David's respect for the *word* caused him also to respect those who feared its Author. He intended to show that respect in such desirable measure when they met the Psalmist that it would make them glad.

Verse 75. The main thought in this verse is the justice of the afflictions that had been suffered to come upon David. Since they were beneficial to him, their infliction proved that God was doing the part of a faithful Friend when he suffered them to come. Consideration for all these truths caused him to affirm that the *judgments* of God are right.

Verse 76. When one is tortured with fears of what the enemy might be plotting, he is hungry for the comfort that is genuine. That comfort that would come from the merciful kindness of God would certainly bring the support that could come from no other source. David had reason to expect this relief because it had been promised in the *word* which did not contain any false promises.

Verse 77. This verse is much after the same thought as the preceding one. *Tender* is not in the original as a separate word. *Mercies* is from RACHAM, which is defined by Strong by the simple word "compassion." The motive for requesting this favor from God was David's delight in the law of God, the subject of his meditations.

Verse 78. A proud man is not one who is ashamed. David means for him to be brought to shame as a punishment for his wicked pride. These enemies had dealt perversely or stubbornly with David without a cause. And again he looked for support and solace by meditating on the *precepts* of the Lord.

Verse 79. For comments on the first part of this verse see those at v. 74. To know the Lord's *testimonies* in an available sense means to fear *Him*.

Verse 80. To be sound means to be established in the *precepts* of God. In that condition the Psalmist felt that he would not be ashamed or confused.

Verse 81. David's whole being was hungering and thirsting for the salvation that comes from God. To that end he relied on the *word* for instruction.

Verse 82. This is some more figurative language, denoting the earnestness of the Psalmist in his desire for the *word* of the Lord. His particular desire was for comfort in his afflictions and persecutions at the hands of his enemies.

Verse 83. Bottles were made of skins of animals, and when new were moist and pliable and strong. (Matt. 9: 17.) But when old or if subjected to smoke or fumes they would become shriveled and weak. David compared himself in the midst of afflictions to a bottle in the midst of smoke or fumes Nevertheless, he remembered the *statutes* of the Lord and took courage.

Verse 84. The Psalmist means in his questioning, how many more days of persecution must he suffer? He believed that relief would come whenever God saw fit to apply his law or execute his *judgment* against the enemies.

Verse 85. Pride is often manifested by a rebellious spirit against those who are righteous. *Digged a pit* means they plotted to bring about the downfall of David, and the reason they had such wicked desires was because they were not keeping the *law*.

Verse 86. *Faithful* is rendered "faithfulness" in the margin which expresses the thought correctly. The meaning is that obedience to the *commandments* will cause a man to be a true servant of God. The pronoun *they* stands for the personal enemies of David, so he prayed for the Lord to help him.

Verse 87. *They* again refers to David's enemies who had almost brought him to the brink of ruin. But he clung to the *precepts* of the Lord and thus won the victory.

Verse 88. To quicken means to enliven or cheer up another, and the lovingkindness of the Lord will have that effect on a man. With such an incentive, David felt assured that he would keep and observe the *testimony* that had been spoken by the Lord.

Verse 89. *Settled* is from NATSAB, and the following is the definition: "A primitive root; to station, in various applications (literal or figurative)." —Strong. The verse means that God's *Word* is stationed or established in heaven for ever. If it were possible for infidels to destroy every copy of the Bible that is on the earth, that would not get rid of it. The Sacred Text is reposited in the eternal vault to which no enemy will ever have access. However, I am not in the least uneasy that the copies of the *Word* will all be destroyed. Many attempts have been made to do so but all have failed. At the present time the Bible is placed at the top of the list of "best sellers" by those who are unbiased, and whose chief motive is one of statistical accuracy and not one prompted by any partisan religious interests.

Verse 90. Faithfulness is used in the sense of keeping one's word. God made the earth for man's temporal abode and has promised to preserve it as long as it is needed. At the time David wrote the earth was at least 3000 years old and had been keeping up its daily and annual revolutions with the accuracy of a perfect timepiece.

Verse 91. This verse introduces the one additional term referred to earlier in the chapter, which is *ordinances*. It is from MISPHAT and Strong defines it, "properly a verdict (favorable or unfavorable) pronounced judicially, especially a sentence or formal decree (human or divine law, individual or collective), including the act, the place, the suit. the crime, and the penalty; abstractly, justice, including a particular right or privilege (statutory or customary), or even a style." This is the only place this Hebrew word is used for *ordinance* in this chapter, but it is a word with such a comprehensive meaning that I have copied the definition in full. *They* is a plural pronoun and refers to the items of God's control over the universe.

Verse 92. There was no physical connection between the *law* and the afflictions of David. But he would have given up in despair and thus perished (figuratively speaking) had he not been encouraged by the moral support of the law.

Verse 93. This verse is similar in thought to the preceding one. The *precepts* of the Lord had quickened or enlivened the morale of the Psalmist.

Verse 94. *Save me* did not have reference to spiritual things especially, but to relief from the afflictions of the enemy. The basis on which David expected the Lord to help him was the relation between them, and the fact he had sought His *precepts*.

Verse 95. *Have waited* means the wicked had been spying and watching to detect something in the life of David for which they could ruin him. He had defeated their expectation by observing the Lord's *testimonies* in his daily life.

Verse 96. This verse is a contrast between the best there is in the world and the *commandments* of God. The first is limited while the second is broad.

Verse 97. A person might occasionally think about a matter in which he does not have any interest, but if he loves a thing he will think about it constantly. That was why David passed whole days meditating on the *law* of the Lord.

Verse 98. The wisest man in the world is the one who knows the *commandments* of God. Moses taught this truth in Deut. 4: 5, 6, and the same principle is set forth in other places in the Bible too numerous to cite here. The pronoun *they* refers to the commandments just mentioned by the Psalmist. In order for them to benefit him, however, they must be ever with him as his constant rule of life.

Verse 99. *Teachers* is from a Hebrew word that is defined "a goad," and is used in reference to those who would insist that David observe his obligations but who do not attend to them in their own lives. They were somewhat like the persons of whom Paul wrote in Rom. 2: 21. David set a better example than was ever demanded by these "teachers," because his manner of life was the result of meditation on the *testimonies*.

Verse 100. This verse is much like the preceding one except the contrast is made wtih the *ancients*. It was thought because a man was old that he would possess superior wisdom. That would be true as a general thing, but even "age and experience" will not contribute as much understanding to a person as comes from keeping the divine *precepts*.

Verse 101. A man cannot travel over the evil ways of the world and at the same time be keeping the requirements of the *word* of the Lord.

Verse 102. A man's faithfulness to the things he has been taught sometimes is affected by his confidence in his teacher. David had clung to the *judgments* of God because he had been taught by Him.

Verse 103. The Psalmist had taught practically this same truth concerning the *words* of God in ch. 19: 10. Please see the comments at that place.

Verse 104. The understanding coming through the *precepts* of God was set forth in vs. 98-100 above. Such knowledge so exposed all false ways that David hated them.

Verse 105. This verse is a very similar saying and full of beautiful thought. When one has to make his way through a pathway that is somewhat obscure, and that is beset with dangerous snares and pitfalls, he feels the need of a light to guide him in his walk. The *word* was that light for David and will be so for all who will accept it.

Verse 106. Oaths were permitted in the Old Testament but not in the New. (Matt. 5: 33-37; James 5: 12.) David had made an oath that he would keep the *judgments* of the Lord. He here affirmed that he would not break it and thus violate Lev. 19: 12.

Verse 107. The Psalmist asked to be quickened, which means to be enlivened or cheered up, by the consolation in the *word*.

Verse 108. Some sacrifices were literal or material, such as the offering of animals or products of the ground. Others consisted in the offerings of praise and thankgiving. Paul set forth this truth in Heb. 13: 15. In reward for such offerings David expected to be taught the *judgments* of the Lord.

Verse 109. The first clause is a figure of speech, somewhat like saying "my heart was in my mouth," meaning that the danger of death was very near. In all such circumstances the Psalmist relied upon the *law* for help.

Verse 110. A snare is a trap that is generally set near a beaten path and not right in it because such a path would be clean of anything with which to hide the trap. But being to one side it could be covered in the hope that the traveler would leave the path through the spirit of adventure or perhaps of thoughtlessness and then be caught. The literal meaning of "err" is to wander to one side. The clauses of this verse are hence logical, for David says he did not *err* (wander) from the Lord's *precepts;* he kept within the strait and narrow way.

Verse 111. *Heritage* is used in the sense of a possession, and the Psalmist considers the *testimonies* as a valuable inheritance that he is holding for ever.

Verse 112. It is not the most natural thing for a human being to prefer the spiritual rules of life. But David acted upon his own heart and inclined or trained it for the performance of the *statutes* of the Lord. This service was not for a brief period only but *unto the end.*

Verse 113. Vain thoughts are those that are useless and not containing anything solid. In contrast with these things David loved the *law of* God.

Verse 114. *Hiding place* and *shield* mean the same and are used figuratively. The Psalmist meant that he hoped to be cared for amid all his trials by the *word.*

Verse 115. *Depart from me* is said as an indirect disowning of evil characters. In contrast with this David said he would keep the *commandments* of God. This teaches that one cannot harbor or endorse evilworkers while keeping the commendments of the Lord. Jesus taught the same thing in Matt. 6: 24.

Verse 116. God will not uphold an unrighteous man and David knew it. He therefore prayed to be upheld according to His *word.* A hope based on such foundation would be permanent and not one of which a person would be ashamed.

Verse 117. This verse has the same thoughts as the preceding one, except that it uses a different term which is *statutes.*

Verse 118. To *err* from the *statutes* means to step aside from them. Those who did so were trodden down by the Lord. Sometimes the truth may be handled in such a manner that the hearer will be deceived. The characters David had in mind, however, were bold and misled their hearers with direct falsehood.

Verse 119. The wicked persons were not made literally to disappear, for they were at that very hour alive and tormenting David. But he was speaking prospectively of the fate of all the wicked. They were destined to be brought to ruin while the Psalmist would survive to enjoy the blessings provided for in the *testimonies* of God.

Verse 120. The testing afflictions that God suffered to come upon David were often very severe. For that reason he trembled, which means he was on the alert in expectation of them. To fear and be afraid of the *judgments* as used here meant that he had respect for them to such an extent that he wished to observe them.

Verse 121. The Psalmist really had been a good ruler and judged his people rightly. On this ground he asked the Lord for protection against his oppressors.

Verse 122. The request in this verse is similar to that of the preceding one. "Proud" is from a word that means to be arrogant or overbearing.

Verse 123. *Eyes fail* means he was looking eagerly, and *salvation* means relief from his oppression. The Psalmist relied upon God's righteous *word* for such relief, and for safe guidance through the storms of life.

Verse 124. David never did ask for absolute freedom from trials; he only asked for them to be sent in mercy. In order to conduct himself properly amid the conflicts before him, he desired to be taught the *statutes* of the Lord.

Verse 125. A powerful king was placing himself in the class of servants. Of course such a person would want to render acceptable service, and to do so he should understand how to observe the Master's *testimonies.*

Verse 126. *It is time,* etc., should not be considered as an impertinent speech of David. His meaning was that an instance of great need had come for God to vindicate his *law,* because the enemies had broken it.

Verse 127. The value here placed on the Lord's *commandments* is the same as in ch. 19: 10; see the comments at that place.

Verse 128. It is right to hate the false ways of evil men even though we should love the deluded travelers in those ways. In harmony with those principles we should consider all the *precepts* of God as being right.

Verse 129. *Wonderful* in this verse means outstanding, and David placed that estimate on the *testimonies* of God. By the same token, the man who would keep them would be made into an outstanding character in God's sight. For this reason the Psalmist resolved to keep them with his soul or whole being.

Verse 130. *The simple* does not mean people who are unintelligent, but those who are uninstructed. The entrance or acceptance of the *word* will bring the light of instruction to all people if they will open their hearts to recieve it.

Verse 131. *Open my mouth* is a figure of speech, meaning that the Psalmist was as hungry for spiritual food as the birdling was for material, when it opens its mouth eagerly to receive the nourishment ready to be dropped into it. The food that David was craving was the *commandments* of the Lord.

Verse 132. "As thou usest" does not imply that God ceased to extend mercy to those who love Him. The marginal rendering is "according to the custom." It has always been the manner of the Lord to show mercy to good men and David was praying for it now.

Verse 133. This verse should always be considered in connection with ch. 37: 23. God does not order the steps of man in any direct manner independent of teaching. Instead, he does it through the directions in the *word*.

Verse 134. David had such a spirit of justice and fairness that he did not expect favors of God unconditionally. He asked for deliverance from oppression of evil men, but promised to keep the Lord's *precepts*.

Verse 135. *Face to shine* means to look with favor. As return for such a mercy David offered to be taught the *statutes* of the Lord.

Verse 136. *Rivers of waters* is a figure of speech, meaning that the Psalmist had not fully used his eyes in keeping with the *law*, and as a result he had been brought to tears of shame. The event of himself and Bathsheba (2 Sam. 11: 2) was a noted instance of misusing his eyes, and the 51st Psalm indicates his anguish and tears over it.

Verse 137. No request is expected in this verse. The Psalmist makes another reference to the excellencies of God's *judgments*.

Verse 138. The same kind of praise is meant in this verse as was given in the preceding one. The term *testimonies* is used and David says they are *righteous* and *faithful*. That means that obedience to them will result in righteousness and faithfulness in the lives of those who observe them.

Verse 139. Strong defines "consumed" as being either literal or figurative; the latter is the meaning in this verse. David had been so active in his zeal for the *words* of God that his enemies had all but destroyed him in their hatred.

Verse 140. The general definition of *pure* is "unmixed." The marginal rendering here is "tried or refined." Both definitions amount to the same thought. If a metal has been put through the refinery until all the dross has been burned out it naturally will be unmixed. That condition is used to illustrate the quality of the *word* of God. There is this exception, however, that God's word was always unmixed.

Verse 141. David means that his enemies regarded him as of little importance. To despise means to belittle another, and the evil men in that day were envious of David's true greatness, so they consoled themselves by making light of him. But such evil treatment could not make him forget the *precepts* of the Lord.

Verse 142. Not only is God everlastingly righteous, but those who obey Him will reap the benefits of right living even to everlasting life. The key to these conclusions is in the truth of the *law* that had been approved by the power of God.

Verse 143. Trouble and anguish may disturb our earthly interests, but that need not hinder our delight in the Lord's *commandments*. In fact, in times of distress is when we should take the greatest delight in such a document.

Verse 144. The reader will please apply the comments at v. 142 to this one. The difference is that the term here is *testimonies*.

Verse 145. This means that David's cry or prayer to God was wholehearted. And being thus wholly devoted to the Lord, the Psalmist would logically keep the *statutes*.

Verse 146. David stated a good motive for wanting to be preserved from his enemies. It would give him opportunity to keep the *testimonies*.

Verse 147. To prevent means to precede. David prevented or arose before dawn to go to God in prayer because of his hope in the *word*.

Verse 148. The same word is used as in the foregoing verse, only this time David preceded the night with his prayer. Also, this time he began meditating in the *word* before the night had come, doubtless to continue into the night according to ch. 1: 2.

Verse 149. The Psalmist's cry was not based on his own merit, but on the Lord's lovingkindness. He wished to be quickened or enlivened by the Lord's *judgment*.

Verse 150. The pronoun *they* refers to David's personal enemies. *Draw nigh* means they were approaching David, and their motive was to do him some mischief. The reason for their evil design was their disconnection from the *law* of God.

Verse 151. The way to be near the Lord is to keep his *commandments*. That is because they are according to truth, and the Lord is the source of all true principles.

Verse 152. *Known of old* means that David had known for many years that the *testimonies* of God had been well founded. Their foundation was so firm that it was destined to stand *for ever*, even after the heavens and earth had passed away.

Verse 153. This verse contains the same request that David has uttered a number of times. The affliction of which he complains is not physical, but refers to the oppression from his enemies. He backs up his prayer by profession of his interest in the *law*, which he will demonstrate by remembering it.

Verse 154. To plead the cause of David meant to take an active interest in it by delivering him from his enemies. To *quicken* meant to enliven or cheer up the *Psalmist*, and it was to be done according to the *word* of the Lord.

Verse 155. *Salvation* in this connection means the spiritual kind, and the wicked did not have it because they were far from the *statutes* of God. There could be no salvation through any other source than what is found in the divine document.

Verse 156. In most of the verses the Psalmist connects his petition for further favors with acknowledgement of those already received. The mercies already received from God were many. Now David asks to be quickened or encouraged according to the *judgments* of the Lord, which are recorded in the Sacred Text.

Verse 157. *Persecutors* and *enemies* would be considered the same, only a different form of opposition. The first might be more personal and violent than the second. But all mistreatment failed to draw the Psalmist away from the holy *testimonies*.

Verse 158. David's unpleasant feelings in this verse were not for personal complaints, but because of the transgressions of those who would not keep the *word*.

Verse 159. The basis for his request was named first by the Psalmist; it was his love for the *precepts*. He then asked to be quickened or cheered up in keeping with the lovingkindness of the Lord.

Verse 160. This verse uses two of the terms for the subject being considered in this long chapter, *word* and *judgments*. The significant assertion is made that covers both the past and future. They were true to begin with, were the truth at the time of their introduction, and will be found to be so to the end of their existence, or until they have fulfilled their divine purpose in the conduct of man on the earth.

Verse 161. *Princes* were not officials but were leading persons of any class. Such might feel as if they were privileged characters and would envy a man like David. Their persecution of such a good man would be without a cause to be sure. In spite of such treatment the Psalmist stood in awe, or had deep reverence for the *word*.

Verse 162. David's estimate of the *word* was that it was of more value than *great spoil*, which means great wealth stored away and then accidently found by another.

Verse 163. The record of David's life will bear out the statement of this verse. In the sad affair with Bathsheba he did not attempt even to modify his guilt but plainly admitted, "I have sinned against the Lord" (2 Sam. 12: 13). This would give force to the other part of the verse, that he loved the *law* of God which was divine truth.

Verse 164. *Seven* as a figurative term denotes completeness and it is used evidently in that way here. It means that David's entire life was filled with praise for the Lord and for his righteous *judgments*.

Verse 165. The word *offended* means to stumble or falter in one's pathway. Those who love the *law* of the Lord will have the peace that "passeth all understanding" (Phil. 4: 7), and they will have no occasion to stumble because such persons will be watching where they go. They will be walking "circumspectly" (watching their steps, Eph. 5: 15), and will thus avoid the snares laid for them by the enemy of souls.

Verse 166. David has made frequent reference to salvation, but it is generally concerning relief from his many persecutions. And even the temporal benefits which he expected from the Lord were to be had on condition of doing the *commandments*.

Verse 167. *Soul* is used for the whole being, because a true servant of God will keep the *testimonies* with his mind and body.

Verse 168. This is another verse that uses two of the terms, *precepts* and *testimonies*. The Psalmist had kept them so that all his ways (manner of life) would be before or in the favorable view of the Lord.

Verse 169. When David speaks of his *cry* he generally means his earnest prayer. To *come near* means for it to be heard and considered by the Lord. The Psalmist realized that he needed understanding, both as a king and also as an individual servant of God, and he wished it to be according to the *word*.

Verse 170. *Supplication* is used in the same sense as "cry" in many of the other verses. And, as always, the Psalmist depended on the *word* as the instrument of God through which he was to obtain all divine favors.

Verse 171. Misdirected praise is not desired by the Lord and David realized it. He therefore wished to be first taught by the *precepts* of God.

Verse 172. Here is another verse with two of the terms, *word* and *commandments*. David's reason for speaking of them was the righteousness of the inspired document.

Verse 173. The same One whose hand could help David was the Author of the *precepts* that he had chosen as his rule of action in life.

Verse 174. *Salvation* would be used in its broadest sense in this place, including relief from personal enemies and salvation for his soul spiritually. The Psalmist was not willing merely to accept this salvation but longed for it. This is like the teaching of Jesus in Matt. 5: 6. In keeping with the statement David says he delighted in the *law* which was the instrument that was to guide him.

Verse 175. The word *soul* is used with reference to the whole being. David's life had been threatened many times by his enemies, and he is praying for the preservation coming from the Lord, and it was to come through means of the divine *judgments*.

Verse 176. *I have gone astray* is just a general admission of his mistakes in life, and not necessarily in reference to any specific sin. He prayed for restoration to the divine favor as a sheep that had been found after having wandered. The noted chapter closes with the promise that David will not forget the Lord's *commandments*.

PSALMS 120

Verse 1. David's distress was always that which came from the persecutions of his enemies, not any bodily affliction. In such times he prayed to God and was heard.

Verse 2. The word *soul* is used for the whole being, for the enemies did not have any effect on David's inner man spiritually. But they used falsehood and deceit in trying to persecute him and making his life as miserable as possible.

Verse 3. This verse is addressed to the foes who were resorting to lies in their enmity against David. It is a question for them to answer as to what they expected to gain by such evil means as they were using against the Psalmist.

Verse 4. In this verse the Psalmist answers the question he asked in the preceding verse. The lying enemy was to receive his just dues from the *mighty;* that is, some force greater than he. Those just dues are figuratively called sharp arrows and coals of juniper. This last word is really a name of several evergreen trees. These great plants contain much rosin which is very inflammable, and referred to here to indicate the intensity of the punishment to come on the evil characters.

Verse 5. *Mesech* and *Kedar* were some barbarous tribes of the ancient times. David was not literally living among them, but he used the names figuratively to designate the wicked people who were continually hounding him with their persecutions.

Verse 6. This verse is more along the same line with the preceding one. However, David does not use any figures but makes the plain charge that he was and has been long tormented with people who do not want to be at peace with him.

Verse 7. The Psalmist never advocated "peace at any price," but his enemies did not want peace at all. They preferred to keep up a state of hostility by all means.

PSALMS 121

Verse 1. Hills and mountains are often used figuratively in the Bible, meaning some prominent place or government. David was using it to mean the government and institution of the Lord. From that holy and exalted situation he expected to get help.

Verse 2. This verse gives the same thought as the preceding one, only it speaks in direct language and names the Lord as the source of all help. The logical thought is that a Being who could make *heaven and earth* could surely help a human creature.

Verse 3. The Psalmist addresses himself in the 2nd person; it is a form of self-assurance. The surety of constant help is due to the fact that the Helper never slumbers on the situation, but is always alert and ready for the needed action.

Verse 4. If the care of one servant would require that God should never slumber, then surely the care of all Israel would require as much. There is not much difference between *slumber* and *sleep*, yet there is a slight distinction if the original words are considered. The first means to allow oneself to fall asleep from lack of interest, the second means to go to sleep from physical drowsiness. The Lord will not fail of his care through either cause.

Verse 5. The Psalmist is still addressing himself in a tone of assurance; he believed the Lord would help him in all of his trials. He then used a figure of speech in the form of a shade which would be a great relief from the scorching heat of the sun.

Verse 6. For the undesirable effect of the sun and the relief therefrom, see comments on the preceding verse. There is no actual harm or discomfort that can come from the moon, so the expression is used to complete the sum of protection that may be had from the Lord. In other words, it is an accommodative form of saying to include all extremes. It is somewhat like saying that God will care for one under all circumstances, whether cold or hot, wet or dry, day or night.

Verse 7. There is nothing specific in this verse, but a general assurance that the Lord will abundantly care for his own.

Verse 8. This verse is also a general assurance of the care exercised by the Lord. However, the Psalmist uses some more figures of speech to express the completeness of that care. *Going out* and *coming in* does not have any technical meaning, but being two opposite terms they denote that the preservation which God provides for his people is thorough in its character and complete in its extent.

PSALMS 122

Verse 1. Some people look upon going to the house of the Lord as a duty only, and they go with a kind of "have-to" feeling. It is d o u b t f u l whether such service is acceptable. It has already been learned (Ch. 110: 3) that the Lord's people were to be a willing people. If Christians are true to their profession they will be glad for the opportunity of meeting in God's assembly.

Verse 2. In the time of David the house of the Lord was in Jerusalem. That gave the occasion of standing within the gates of the city.

Verse 3. *Compact* means to be united and knit together, both literally and figuratively. Jerusalem was the capital of the Israelite government as well as the headquarters of the Mosaic religious system. It was important, then, for the city to be thus strong and able to resist the attacks of the heathen around it.

Verse 4. *The tribes* refers to the 12 tribes of Israel that went up to Jerusalem at the annual feasts. *Unto the testimony* means they went to the place where the tables of the testimony had originally been deposited. (Ex. 25: 16.)

Verse 5. Jerusalem was the capital of the Israelite national government. That means that the thrones (seats) of judgment would be located in that city.

Verse 6. There were many heathen nations not far from Jerusalem that would envy its power among the governments of the world. David called for prayers that the capital of his beloved country might reign in peace over her citizens.

Verse 7. The *walls* were for the protection of the city as a whole, and the *palaces* were for the housing of citizens. The Psalmist prayed for the peace of all.

Verse 8. David became more personal and prayed for the peace of Jerusalem for the sake of his brethren who lived in the city, also for all who were his companions.

Verse 9. Coming back to the religious point of interest, David promised to work for the good of the city. That was because the house of God was located there.

PSALMS 123

Verse 1. The word *heaven* in the Old Testament is always from the same Hebrew word, so the connection must be considered in determining which of the 3 heavens is meant. The word is plural in this verse which shows it is used somewhat figuratively. The idea expressed is that the Lord's dwelling is high and above all other things.

Verse 2. A servant and maid are looking for the reward of their services. But they know they must wait until the proper time to receive it. Likewise, the servant of God will wait until he receives his reward.

Verse 3. *Contempt* means an impudent belittling of another. The enemies of David had so treated him and his brethren that they were filled or "had their fill" of it.

Verse 4. The *soul* here means the person as a whole. *Scorning* and *contempt* have practically the same meaning, and it was manifested by those *at ease*, or those who had been spoiled by too much indulgence in earthly prosperity. There were the ones who were designated as *proud* by the Psalmist. Such a person would show this evil attitude toward a good man like David, because he realized that he was a better person than this proud man and took that way to solace himself for his wounded pride.

PSALMS 124

Verses 1, 2. These 2 verses are grouped because they are practically the same in thought. They state a condition (that of the Lord's being with Israel), on which a certain result had depended, and that will be named in the following verse.

Verse 3. This is what would have happened had the fact of the foregoing paragraph not been true. *Swallowed* is a figure of speech which Strong defines, "to make away with." The protection assured is like that expressed in Rom. 8: 31.

Verse 4. When *waters* or the equivalent is used symbolically (such as streams or floods), it means great volumes of afflictions or persecutions.

Verse 5. *Proud waters* refers to the people who would have overwhelmed God's people with their persecutions. To go over the *soul* refers to the effect of their persecutions in this life, not to the spiritual effect in the world to come.

Verse 6. Since God had extended such merciful protection for his own, this verse blesses or praises Him for it.

Verse 7. David used the occupation of a trapper for an illustration. A fowler is one who sets snares to catch fowl and other objects of prey. David's soul (his present life) had escaped the trap through the watchfulness of the Lord.

Verse 8. The Psalmist drops his figures and uses literal terms. His reasoning is that deliverance had come from the One who was maker of heaven and earth.

PSALMS 125

Verse 1. The logic of this verse is evident. Zion was the headquarters for the Lord's interests on earth and had been protected by His might. To trust in the Lord, then, would bring the same protection as had been given to the holy city.

Verse 2. The physical protection of mountains for a city is used to illustrate the encircling shield of the Lord for his people whom he has chosen.

Verse 3. *Rod* is used in the sense of rule or control. If the wicked had been suffered to control the conduct of God's people, they would have been forced to take part in evil deeds. The Lord prevented these evil persons from having such a control.

Verse 4. *Do good* does not refer to the personal conduct of God for he could not do otherwise. It means to ask God to extend good and desirable favors to those who are entitled to such treatment.

Verse 5. *Crooked ways* means the ways of life followed by those who forsake the pathway of righteousness. They shall be classed at the end with the ones who had never professed a life of goodness. This suggests the awful thought in Matt. 25: 41.

PSALMS 126

Verse 1. This verse is in the past tense in form, and as such had been true of Israel more than once, for the nation had been rescued from the hand of the oppressor. But the passage was also prophetic and was fulfilled when Israel was returned from Babylonian captivity, recorded in the books of Ezra and Nehemiah.

Verse 2. *Laughter* and *singing* are used in about the same sense and neither indicates a feeling of lightness or levity. It refers to the spirit of rejoicing that the nation of the Israelites felt after their release from captivity. The last half of the verse was fulfilled by the attitude of the Persians toward Israel after the overthrow of the Babylonians who had taken the Israelites captive. (Ezra 1: 1-4.)

Verse 3. For comments on this verse see those on verse 1.

Verse 4. This verse is in the form of a request, but it is actually a prophecy of the return of the nation of Israel from the Babylonian captivity.

Verse 5, 6. This entire passage is figurative in its application. The thought is somewhat like the old saying, "A bad beginning may have a good ending." The paragraph sets forth a principle of action that would have many opportunities for practice. For instance, if a man was not willing to plant the seed because it was in the early spring and the unpleasant weather that often comes then, he might not have the privilege of reaping a harvest. But the specific application is to the experiences of the Israelite nation in their captivity and the return. The *tears* and *weeping* came at the time of the captivity, and the reaping of the sheaves occurred upon the return.

PSALMS 127

Verse 1. The gist of this verse is that man is wholly dependent on the Lord for the ability to accomplish the things of which he sometimes wishes to boast.

Verse 2. God provides all that is necessary for man's existence on this earth. It is true that he must cooperate, but it is *vain*, or unnecessary for him to spend both day and night to gain the wealth of the world; that is, the amount of it that is needed for his comfort and well-being. I do not believe the Lord planned the night as a work time, but for the time of rest. Or, in the words of our passage, the night is the time that God *giveth his beloved sleep*. If man were satisfied with the things actually necessary for his happiness in this life, he could do enough in the day time to get the production of the earth going, whether direct or indirect, that would be required for his consumption, and then while he was sleeping the Lord would be still at work with the laws of nature while *his beloved* was thus getting his needful rest in sleep.

Verse 3. Heritage means something received from another. Hence, although children are the offspring of human beings, their presence should be regarded as a gift from the Lord. This is far different from the attitude manifested by many people who regard children in an objectionable light.

Verse 4. *Arrows* are referred to as an illustration of the value of children. The comparison is with the idea of defense or support. If a man is equipped with arrows he has wherewith to defend himself. And if he begets children in the days of his youth and strength, they will be a support for him when he is old.

Verse 5. The illustration is still drawn from the bow and arrow. A quiver is a case for holding arrows. A man with a quiver full of arrows would be well supplied for a conflict; so a man with many children should be equipped for the battles of life. He would not be ashamed nor afraid to meet the enemy at the gate of his city.

PSALMS 128

Verse 1. A man proves he fears the Lord by walking in his ways. That means to walk as the Lord has directed. (See chapter 119: 133.)

Verse 2. An unrighteous man may

be permitted to consume what he produces, but he cannot have much appreciation for it if he leaves the fear of God out of consideration.

Verse 3. In the days of special providence, God rewarded a righteous man frequently with the joys of a happy family. (See Job 42: 15-17.)

Verse 4. This virtually repeats the thought in verse 1.

Verse 5. Zion was a place in Jerusalem where the temple was located. The verse indicates that the promised blessings would issue from the divine headquarters.

Verse 6. The prospect of seeing one's children's children means that he will have a long life. *Peace upon Israel* would be welcomed by a righteous man.

PSALMS 129

Verses 1, 2. *Israel* as a nation is meant, and the passage refers to the frequent oppressions that came upon it beginning in the sojourn in Egypt. *Yet they have not prevailed against me.* In the outcome the nation was saved by the Lord.

Verse 3. This is figurative, drawing the likeness from the action of a plow that agitates the earth. *Long furrows* indicates extensive sieges of persecutions at the hands of the national enemies.

Verse 4. It was wrong for the wicked people to bind God's people with the cords of oppression, therefore the righteous Lord properly severed the cords.

Verse 5. To *be confounded* means to be confused, and to be *turned back* means to be defeated and humiliated.

Verse 6. In times of unusual moisture a scant growth of grass would appear on the housetops, but it would have such a weak bed for rooting that the sun would soon kill it. David used the circumstance to illustrate the lot he wished to come upon the enemies of Zion.

Verse 7. Such a short crop would not fill the hand of the harvester. Neither would the reaper be able to fill his bosom (or body) with food, since he had not gathered sheaves of which to make bread.

Verse 8. These wicked men would not enjoy even the good wishes of the passers by. They would become a class of beings rejected by the Lord and ignored by men.

PSALMS 130

Verse 1. The *depths* referred to the great depression into which David's enemies had plunged him with their persecutions. While in that condition he cried to God.

Verse 2. *Supplications* means the more urgent and earnest prayers. That kind of petition to God usually is offered when personal distress is the motive. However, a servant of God might make a supplication if he felt a deep personal concern for some special friends who were in a situation of distress or were threatened with such.

Verse 3. *Mark* is from SHAMAR and also means "regard." The verse means that if the Lord should take our iniquities seriously, intending to hold all to strict account, then none of us would stand to "get by."

Verse 4. Instead of holding us to strict account of justice, *there is forgiveness* from the Lord. However, this leniency must not be abused, but the favored person should thereby be led to *fear* or respect God for his goodness.

Verse 5. *Wait* and *hope* are used in the same sense here. This first is from a word which Strong defines partly, "to expect," and we know that is also a part of the definition of *hope*, the second word in the verse.

Verse 6. *Waiteth* is not in the original as a separate word. The thought is justified by the previous verse which does have the word in the original text. David means that his longing for the favor of God is more intense than that of man generally in wishing for the morning to come to relieve him from the shadows of night.

Verse 7. All true hope is in the Lord; any other will be disappointing. And what man receives from Him will be on the basis of divine mercy, not human merit.

Verse 8. The redemption coming from God is complete and based on his mercies. Redemption from *all his iniquities* means that all redemption that Israel obtains must come from the Lord and not from any human source.

PSALMS 131

Verse 1. *Haughty* is from GABAHH and Strong defines it, "A primitive root; to soar. i.e. be lofty." It has a meaning opposite of humility. Paul instructed Christians to "be not high minded" (Rom. 12:16), and this sort of humbleness is professed by David in this passage. The latter part of the verse has practically the same meaning, except the Psalmist makes a practical application of the humble feelings he professes to have in the beginning of the verse. If he feels humble as to his ability he will also refrain from meddling in matters above his qualifications.

Verse 2. When a child is being weaned he will need special tenderness from his mother to quiet and calm him. David uses the event as a comparison of his feelings of contentment under the Lord. The general context shows he had been made satisfied by the reassuring goodness of God, and was content, like a trusting child, to wait for whatever further favors and support his divine Parent had in store for him.

Verse 3. The Psalmist had trained himself as an individual to behave after the manner described in the preceding verse; he now exhorts Israel as a whole to do the same.

PSALMS 132

Verse 1. The heading placed at the top of this psalm says it was offered on the occasion of removing the ark. The language of several verses will verify it, as also does the history of the event which may be read in 2 Samuel 6 and 1 Chronicles 13. Considering all the circumstances confronting him at that time we can understand why David would ask the Lord to remember him.

Verse 2. In this verse David makes indefinite reference to his previous vows of devotion to the Lord.

Verse 3. Here the Psalmist starts to specify items in which he had promised to sacrifice his personal pleasure to the interests of the Lord. He would not give priority to his own house and comforts of his own bed.

Verse 4. The comforts referred to at the close of the preceding verse are those of rest and sleep. Such joys are right and David did not belittle their importance. He meant that all such pleasures would be given secondary consideration.

Verse 5. This verse states the thing that was uppermost in the mind of the Psalmist. He wished to build a house for the Lord but was not to have that privilege. But the ark was not even with the tabernacle where it originally belonged. The next best thing that David could do was to bring it to Jerusalem and house it in a tent which he pitched for that purpose. The ark was the most important article in the service, for it had received the tables of the law and in its presence the high priests met and communicated with God. That accounts for the language of this verse.

Verse 6. *Heard of it* means the ark was spoken of at *Ephratah*, which is another form of Bethlehem. The ark had been moved about from place to place and had received some prominence among the people in general.

Verse 7. *Tabernacle* is used in a general sense to mean any place where the presence of God would be represented. Such a place would be in the vicinity of the ark that was soon to be brought into the city by David. *Worship at his footstool* indicates the humble attitude of those who would worship the Lord.

Verse 8. This verse might be called a speech of welcome made by David. It was for the coming of the Lord as represented by the ark that was about to arrive.

Verse 9. The pronoun *thy* refers to the Lord, and the priests were the men who were to administer the religious services under the Mosaic system. *Clothed with righteousness* means that those in charge of the high and holy service of the priesthood should be righteous men. If such a condition could be realized it would cause the saints to *shout for joy* because of the spiritual encouragement it would mean.

Verse 10. The Psalmist presents himself in two different phases; the first as a servant and then as a king. Then the prayer is for God to support him as king remembering his faithfulness as a servant while in his early relations with the Lord.

Verse 11. One peculiar trait of inspiration is to break abruptly into a line of thought with a prophecy. And yet it might not be regarded as so abrupt after all. It can often be seen that some relation will exist between the passages. Here we see David in earnest petition for God's favor in this time of important action in the service of God. His prayer was to be heard for the sake of present-day conditions. Then what could be more appropriate than to give him a prediction whose fulfillment would be honoring to him. Of course we know it was a prediction of Christ who was to be a lineal descendant of David. *I set* might be confusing to us if we did not obserse that "set" is a transitive verb with the object named first. It is as if the clause said, "I will set the fruit of thy body on a throne."

Verse 12. The passage is still looking to the service to be carried on under this offspring of David. *Thy children* refers to the ones who would be produced by this offspring. If they will be faithful the Lord will continually bless them. This blessing is figuratively referred to as a reigning on a throne, not that Christians were to sit on a literal throne in the kingdom of Christ.

Verse 13. Zion was that part of Jerusalem that was the headquarters for the Lord's institution in the time of David. It was likewise to be the starting place for the institution under this noted son of David. (Isa. 2: 3.)

Verse 14. Let the reader not forget that the passage is still a prophecy of Christ and the religious system that was to be set up under Him. The verse represents God as recognizing that system (headquarters at Zion in Jerusalem) as his last and complete regime. That is why it says it was to *rest for ever* there. This is the same prediction in thought that the prophet made in the presence of Nebuchadnezzar. (Dan. 2: 44.)

Verse 15. This verse is a reference to the bountiful spiritual provisions that were to be made under the reign of Christ in a spiritual kingdom.

Verse 16. This refers to all Christians who are elsewhere designated as priests. (1 Pe. 2: 9.) They were to be clothed with salvation in that their service will be entirely religious and done for the salvation of those related thereto. *Saints* is another name for the same people called priests above.

Verse 17. *Horn* in symbolic language means power or authority. Christ was a son of David and was to be given great power (Matt. 28: 18). That is why it is said that David would have a horn to bud or spring forth. *Lamp* is another result that was to come into the world through this offspring of David; he was to be the light of the world and the same great truth is set forth in John 1: 4-9.

Verse 18. This is a prediction of the penalties that will be imposed on those who reject the authority of Christ. Their description and various references to fulfillment are too numerous even to cite in this place.

PSALMS 133

Verse 1. *Pleasant* is from a Hebrew word that means delightful and agreeable. A thing might be good and yet not delightful; or, it might be agreeable and delightful and yet not be a good thing. The Psalmist declares that it is both good and delightful for brethren to dwell together in *unity*. That word is from YACHAD and the following is the definition: "Properly a unit, i.e. (adverbially) unitedly."—Strong. It is the word for "alike" in Job 21: 26. the word is stronger than a mere "agreeing to disagree," so as to present merely the appearance of unity. Such a condition is not acceptable to God. "Can two walk together except they be agreed?" (Amos 3: 3) is a question that has a negitive answer implied. For a group of people merely to meet under the same roof does not constitute unity in the Lord's sight. It can be accomplished only by all parties who are proposing to dwell together to agree on the teaching of God's word as the bond of unity between them.

Verse 2. The comparison is to the sweetness of the olive oil and the great extent to which it was in evidence. The oil was used when Aaron was consecrated for the office of priest (Ex. 29: 7). David means that when brethren dwell together in unity of the Spirit it makes a situation of sweet consecration that is as agreeable to the mind as the olive oil was sweet to the eyes of those present.

Verse 3. *Hermon* is the highest mountain in Palestine and its summit is not attained by man. Yet the dew falls upon it which generally turns into snow and betokens an idea of freshness to the sight of people in the lowlands. The blessing of this snow on the mountains of Palestine, coming from the Lord upon humankind as a benediction of nature, was an illustration in the mind of David of the satisfying effect of the peaceful fellowship of loving brethren.

PSALMS 134

Verse 1. *Servants of the Lord* is indefinite, but 1 Chr. 9: 33 shows that the singers were the ones specifically meant here. None of the services of the set feasts required the presence of the men at night. But the singers often remained in the holy place after the hours of day had passed. The Psalmist is calling upon them to use the songs that would bless or praise the Lord.

Verse 2. The lifting up of the hands was a gesture of both respect and appeal. *Sanctuary* means a holy place when the idea of locality is being considered, and it means holiness when the attitude of the worshipers is the point. Certainly none but holy or righteous men would be invited to engage in a praise service to God. The New Testament teaches the same truth in 1 Tim. 2: 8.

Verse 3. The creation of the heavens and the earth is frequently mentioned in connection with some other favor from God. The reasoning of it is that a Being who can perform such a mighty deed is certainly able to bestow other blessings. But it should not be overlooked here that the blessing was to come *out of Zion*. God had a certain headquarters for his religious system on earth, and only through that means might men expect to receive spiritual benefits from Him.

PSALMS 135

Verse 1. In the Book of Psalms the word "praise" occurs a great many times and generally comes from HALAL or YADAH. These Hebrew words have practically the same definition, meaning to celebrate, respect or worship, and it may be expressed either by some motions of the hands or head, or by the voice in song or words of compliment, or, by all of these combined. Hence, when an order or request is made for men to praise the Lord, and no particular form is suggested, it is left to the actor to choose his own method of praising God. The above explanation of "praise" covers so nearly all of the places where the word is used in the Old Testament, that I suggest the reader mark this verse for future reference when the word is under consideration.

Verse 2. The servants of the Lord had been mentioned in a general way in the preceding verse. In this verse the Psalmist signifies the group of servants he had in mind. He refers especially to the ones who appear in the assemblies of the Lord.

Verse 3. Another motive for praising the Lord is stated here; it is because he is good. And here the manner of praise is suggested, that of singing. (see definition above.) Another motive is offered for praising the Lord, which is the pleasantness of the exercise, so that both man and the Lord have motives in this matter.

Verse 4. *Jacob* and *Israel* refer to the same people in the way the names are used here. They are both named because Israel as a nation and people are so named because they sprang from Jacob who had the name "Israel" applied to him personally. *Peculiar* treasure means the Israelite nation belonged to the Lord and to no one else.

Verse 5. See the comments at ch. 86: 12 for the technical meaning of *Lord*. The gods mentioned in this verse mean the idolatrous objects of worship that were honored by the heathen nations in their religious practices.

Verse 6. The things or places named are parts of what we call the universe, and they were all created by the Lord whom David and his people worshiped. The heathen worshiped the things created instead of the Creator.

Verse 7. *Ends of the earth* is said to indicate that man is not the maker of the vapors or rain since they come where no man is. Lightning is the visible sign of the conditions that bring rain and God is the maker of those conditions. *Treasuries* is a figurative name for the vast storehouse of God's resources in the universe. Out of that storehouse he projects the winds in all of their variety of intensity.

Verse 8. This verse is a simple historical statement of an instance of the Lord's power. The original account is in Ex. 12, and nothing but a miracle could cause such an event to occur. A man might slay a few children in the course of several nights before he would be stopped. But the wonderful feature of this great circumstance is the fact that not in one or a few families was there a death, but one in each house. Neither was it upon whichever member of the household who happened to be available, but upon a certain one, the oldest of the family. Nor was the work spread out over a long period of time, but was accomplished in one night.

Verse 9. The death of the first-born was the last of the 10 plagues sent upon the Egyptians. This verse refers to the 9 that preceded this one.

Verse 10. After the Israelites left Egypt they started for the "promised land" that had been guaranteed to their forefathers. On the way they encountered the heathen nations who disputed their right to march through their territories, and it was necessary to overcome them which they did with the Lord's help.

Verse 11. The conflicts with Sihon and Og are recorded in Numbers 21. The kingdoms of Canaan were conquered by Joshua as recorded in the book bearing his name.

Verse 12. *Heritage* is something inherited from another, either by right of a will or through relationship. God had willed that the land of Canaan should become the possession of the descendents of Abram (Gen. 12: 7; 15: 18), and this verse accounts for the fulfillment of that promise.

Verse 13. The *Lord* had performed such wonderful deeds in the sight of many people that his holy name was spoken with a feeling of awe. Of course such a Being could never be forgotten, which is the reason for mentioning "thy memorial."

Verse 14. One part of the definition for the original of *judge* is, "to judge (as umpire)."—Strong. The word is used in regard to Israel's disputes with the heathen nations. God was the umpire and "decided" in favor of his people. *Repent himself* means the Lord had compassion for his people in view of their afflictions. They were required to fight for their rights, and at times were subjected to rigorous experiences for their chastisements. The Lord then "repented," which means he decreed that their afflictions should be turned into victories over their foes.

Verse 15-18. This paragraph is the same as ch. 115: 4-8 and has been fully commented upon at that place.

Verse 19. *Israel* was the name of the people as a whole, and *house of Aaron* was the particular family in which the priesthood was settled. (Ex. 28: 1; 1 Chr. 23: 13.) The verse is a call for all to bless (or praise) the Lord.

Verse 20. Levi was the tribe from which the house of Aaron sprang. The Levites (other than the house of Aaron) had charge of the congregational activities, except those of the priesthood, and hence were in a rank of importance. They were called upon to bless or praise the Lord for they had been given special attention of honor. A general call was then made for all who feared the Lord to bless or praise him.

Verse 21. *Out of Zion* or in connection with Zion; that was the headquarters of the Lord's institution on earth, and all devotions offered to Him had to be done with due regard for this capital. *Praise ye the Lord* is from a wording meaning "Hallelujah."

PSALMS 136

Verse 1. Giving of thanks is an oral expression of gratitude for favors received. There are two facts mentioned in this verse for which the Psalmist requested that thanks be given to the Lord, one pertaining to his personal character, the other to his treatment of the people. They are the words *good* and *mercy* or at least they indicate the two facts. What is significant about the mercy of the Lord is that it is not just occasional or of brief duration, but it endureth for ever. If at any time the Lord's mercy ceases to be enjoyed by some person, it will not be because that mercy has run out or run its course or worn out. It will be on account of the shortcoming of the person in that he has failed to meet the terms on which divine mercy is offered. This clause about the mercy of the Lord is identical in the last part of each verse of this chapter, hence no further comment will be offered on it.

Verse 2. See the comments at ch. 86: 12 for the detailed explanation of the name *God*. He is the only true object of worship, hence the Psalmist declares him to be above the gods whom the heathen worshiped. There is also something significant in the phrase *God of gods*. It means not only that the true God is greater than all, but he is also in control of all these objects that are falsely called gods.

Verse 3. *Lord of lords* will have about the same significance as "God of gods" in the preceding verse. It will be well also again to see comments at ch. 86: 12.

Verse 4. The key word in this verse is *alone*. It denotes that the Lord is independent of all other beings and does things by his own infinite power.

Verse 5. The thought is not that wisdom was the force by which the heavens were made, but that all of the work of the Lord in forming the heavens was wisely done.

Verse 6. *Above* is from a Hebrew word that has also been rendered "beside" 17 times, and "against" over 100 times. It is the word for "beside" in Num. 24:6, in the words "beside the waters." The verse evidently means that God stretched out the earth by the side of or in connection with the waters, and each maintaining its own proper place in the order of things. This suggests the statements in Gen. 1:9, 10.

Verse 7. The *great lights* is a general reference to the heavenly bodies whose creation is recorded in Gen. 1:14-18.

Verse 8. *To rule* means to regulate or measure the day as to the light. In other words, the daylight was to continue as long as the sun was visible.

Verse 9. The moon and stars were to "rule" the night on the same principle that the sun was to rule the day as explained in the preceding verse.

Verse 10. For comments on this event see those at ch. 135:8.

Verse 11. *Brought out Israel* was accomplished on the night of the first passover, when the Egyptians forced the Israelites to leave in haste. (Ex. 12.)

Verse 12. *Strong hand* would indicate the strength of the Lord, and *stretched out arm* refers to the long reach of that strength.

Verse 13. The *parts* of the Red Sea were the walls of ice on each side of the passage. See Ex. 15:8 and the comments at that place for furher information.

Verse 14. Passing through the midst of the sea would indicate that a miracle was performed. An army could travel around a body of water without requiring anything but human strengh or that which would be required in the ordinary walks of life.

Verse 15. Both Pharaoh AND his army were destroyed in the sea. See my comments on this subject at Ex. 14:4 in volume 1 of this Commentary.

Verse 16. This short verse refers to the 40-year journey through the wilderness and the original history is in the books of Exodus and Numbers.

Verses 17, 18. *Great* and *famous* would mean that the kings were not only great in fact, but that it was generally known among the peoples of the country.

Verse 19, 20. The original record of the overthrow of these kings is Num. 21.

Verse 21. The land taken from the above named kings was in the territory that God had promised to the descendents of Abram (Gen. 15:18), so the children of Israel rightfully obtained it as an inheritance (heritage).

Verse 22. Servants may inherit the property of their master if he so wills it. The passage in Gen. 15:18 shows that such a provision was made for these servants.

Verse 23. By the pronoun *us* David includes himself with the Israelites who inherited the land having been held by those heathen kings. *Low estate* refers to the time when the children of Israel were wanderers in the wilderness and exposed to the hostility of the heathen living along their route.

Verse 24. *Redeemed* has an indefinite application. It first occured to the nation when the Egyptians were forced to let Israel go. And it was done many time afterward, when the heathen people sought to conquer them and hinder their travels.

Verse 25. This is too general to admit of any specific detail. In all the earth, wherever there is a creature that lives on food, the hand of God is the provider of it.

Verse 26. The chapter ends about like it began, with a request for the Lord to be thanked for his goodness to the children of men.

PSALMS 137

General remarks. This chapter is like many prophetic passages in that it is written in the past tense. That, however, is often the prophetic style, and indicates that the prophet is as certain of the future as he is of the past. It is understandable that it would be so if the prophet was inspired as was David. This whole passage gives such a deplorable picture of the state of mind the Israelites were in after being taken to Babylon, that I wish to connect it with a statement of actual history to make the paragraph as a whole a fitting place to cite from the many other sad predictions that will be found in the regular prophetic books. The historical statement referred to is in Ezekiel 37:11. It is true that this book is one of the major prophets, but we should remember that it was all written in Babylon after the nation had been carried off in captivity. That being

Psalms 137: 1-8

the case, some of the things contained in the book are literal history and comprise a fulfillment of an earlier prediction. Such is the case with the verse just cited, and since it is so considered I shall quote verbatim that sad speech of the Jews, in which they actually made the complaints predicted in the chapter we are now studying. "Then he said unto me, Son of man, these bones are the whole house of Israel: behold, they say, Our bones are dried, and our hope is lost: we are cut off for our parts." So this speech of the children of Israel, made while they were actually in the land of Babylon, verfies the predictions of the Psalmist. I shall now consider the several verses separately.

Verse 1. As the term *Babylon* is used here it refers to the territory of which the city of Babylon was the capital. This territory had a number of streams, called rivers by the translators. The Jews were scattered over this territoy after the captivity and doubtless spent much time wandering about, or sitting down on the banks of the streams. There they would meditate dejectedly on their fallen state, with sad remembrance of their beloved capital in the land of their forefathers.

Verse 2. The harp was a stringed instrument of music and had been used much as an accompaniment in song. The crestfallen Jews did not feel like singing or making music in such a situation, and so they hung their harps up on the willows that grew on the banks of the streams. I shall quote a paragraph from history that will shed light upon this verse. "All the flat whereon Babylon stood being by reason of so many rivers and canals running through it, made in many places marshy, especially near the said rivers and canals, this caused it to abound much in willows; and, therefore, it is called, in scripture, *the valley of willows*, (for so the words, Isa. 15: 7, which we translate *the brook of the willows*, ought to be rendered:) and, for the same reason, the Jews (Ps. 137: 1, 2,) are said, when they were by the rivers of Babylon in the land of their captivity, to have hung their harps upon the willows, that is, because of the abundance of them which grew by the river." Prideaux's Connexion, Part 1, Book 2, Year 570.

Verse 3. We are not informed as to the motive that prompted the Babylonians to call for these songs. It could have been curiosity, or genuine desire for an exhibition of foreign devotions, or a mixture of both. These new people had been brought in from a distant country, and doubtless it was known that their trouble was connected with their religion. They saw these harps in the hands of the captives and knew they were used in connection with their religious devotions. It was natural, then, to wish to hear some of them. But the Jews were in no mood for singing or making music, so they hung up their harps and sat down on the river banks, sad, discouraged, and completely broken in spirit, almost dying with homesickness for their native land.

Verse 4. Even had their feelings permitted them to sing at that time, their sense of propriety forbade their doing so. They were in a strange (foreign) land, a land possessed and controlled by heathen, and where the true God was unknown. Under those conditions they could not engage in devotions to God.

Verse 5. *If I forget thee.* We know that no one would actually forget a city as prominent as Jerusalem, in the ordinary sense of the word. The original is defined also as "failing to pay attention to," and that is the meaning here. *Her cunning* is not in the original and has been supplied from the thought in the context. The hand is not an intelligent thing as is the mind and cannot literally forget. Therefore, the statement is a sort of self-imposed curse or wish for some evil to come, such as losing the use of the hand, if ever they forget to give attention to Jerusalem.

Verse 6. This verse is more along the same line as the preceding one. If one's tongue should stick to the roof of his mouth it would render him speechless. But that would not be the worst of it, for then he could not swallow food and soon would perish. In this verse the speaker does not merely vow to remember Jerusalem, but he promises to give the holy city preference over all other joys.

Verse 7. Before closing their sad speech, they turned their revengeful mind toward some of their enemies who had wished for just such a calamity to come. To rase means to wreck a city and the Edomites had longed to see that done to Jerusalem. The Jews now wish for some penalty to be brought upon their foes.

Verse 8. This verse turns against

Babylon, and the Jews may not have known that they were actually uttering a prophecy in the words *who art to be destroyed*, but it was really brought to pass a half century later. The ones here promised happiness over it were the Persians, the people who overthrew the Babylonian Empire.

Verse 9. This wish seems harsh, but such is the way of warfare, especially as it was done in anciet times. (2 Ki. 8: 12.) Children were the possible soldiers of the future. When one nation conquered another, it was considered military foresight not only to destroy the men in arms, but also those who might later rise up armed.

PSALMS 138

Verse 1. *With the whole heart* means his praise would be wholehearted. The word for *gods* sometimes is defined as magistrates. David meant he would not be ashamed to sing praises of the Lord in the hearing of the rulers of the land.

Verse 2. *Holy temple* is a reverential expression for the throne of God, and the Psalmist would conduct his devotions in view of that heavenly shrine. A good name is always to be desired and means much to a man's influence. However, it is possible to have a good name that is not merited. But if a man so conducts himself that his "word is as good as his bond," his influence will certainly be great. Comparatively speaking, then, the Word of God is the greatest attribute that he possesses. If the Lord so regards his Word, how terrible it must be in His eyes if man disregards it.

Verse 3. The Psalmist acknowledges that the Lord heard him when he cried or prayed unto him. *Soul* is from a word that includes a living creature with all that it takes to comprise such a being. His whole person had been strengthened by the Lord in answer to his earnest prayers.

Verse 4. These kings may not render full service to God, since most of them were idolaters. But they will recognize that the sayings of Israel's God were wonderful and worthy of praise.

Verse 5. *Ways* is from a word that is defined by Strong, "mode of action." The kings will sing to express their adoration of the activities of Israel's God. This was because the actions not only were mighty, but shed glory in the sight of all.

Verse 6. God has spanned the great difference between himself and the humble of the earth by His great compassion. *Knoweth afar off* means God takes certain notice of the proud, but will not admit such to be near him as far as it pertains to favor.

Verse 7. The meaning of this verse is a simple statement of David's faith in God.

Verse 8. To *perfect* means to make complete. David knew he was an erring creature of the earth and had many defects. However, he believed that if he proved faithful to the Lord he would give him strength to overcome his weakness, and thus would round out his character of righteousness. All of this would be done, not on the merit of the Psalmist, but on the enduring mercy of the Lord. This faith encouraged David to plead that God would not forsake him since he was a part of His handiwork.

PSALMS 139

Verse 1. The main subject of this chapter is the infinite knowledge and existence of the Lord. This verse is a general statement as to that knowledge in regard to the life of the Psalmist, in all of the conditions surrounding his actions.

Verse 2. *Downsitting* and *uprising* are combined to make a figure of speech. They are opposite terms and hence indicate the completeness of the knowledge of God. *Thought afar off* simply means that not even a single thought of David could be so far away that God could not see it.

Verse 3. *Compassest* literally means to diffuse or winnow or fan. In order to fan out a mass of grain one would need to have complete mastery of it, so the Psalmist means that God is complete Master of the situation.

Verse 4. The serveral verses in this part of the chapter are specifications of the complete knowledge of God. David had said that the Lord knew all about his thoughts. Then he surely would *know altogether* the words of his mouth.

Verse 5. To *beset* means to confine or limit. David means that his entire life was within the knowledge and grasp of the Lord.

Verse 6. The Psalmist has reference to himself merely as a human being aside from his inspiration.

Verse 7. This and several verses following will point out various parts of the universe where God's presence exists always. Generally speaking, since He made all things that exist, it would be foolish to think that a man could find a hiding place from Him in any of the parts of creation. The Psalmist will now specify a number of "nooks and crannies" in which there would be no hiding from God. *Spirit* and *presence* are used for emphasis since the very presence of God would always mean that of his spirit according to the language of Christ in John 4: 24.

Verse 8. *Heaven* and *hell* are named together merely as opposites in location. We know the first refers to the region of the planets, not to the place where God personally lives, for there would be nothing significant in referring to that place and saying *thou art there*. *Hell* is from SHEOL and Strong defines it, "hades or the world of the dead (as if a subterranean retreat) including its accessories and inmates." The Psalmist does not mean that God personally is to be found in that place, but that he had complete oversight of it. How foolish, then, is the thought of suicide and cremation as an attempt to run away from Him.

Verse 9. The vast expanse of the boundless sea is not sufficient to outreach the presence of the Lord who created them in the first place.

Verse 10. *Lead* and *hold* are both used in a favorable sense, meaning the universal ability of God to care for his faithful servants. And by the same token, it would be useless for one to think of fleeing to that region to hide from the Lord.

Verse 11. *Night shall be light* is another figurative phrase, meaning that God can see in the darkness as well as in the light. For this reason it would be in vain to count on the darkness as a shield from the eyes of God.

Verse 12. This is practically the same thought as was expressed in the preceding verse. Certainly the One who could "command the light to shine out of darkness" (2 Cor. 4: 6; Gen. 1: 2, 3) would be able to see through it and detect a man trying to hide.

Verse 13. *Reins* is from a word that signifies the mind or controlling faculty. It means that the Lord had taken possession of the Psalmist and was guiding his thoughts and actions. Not that he was deprived of personal responsibility in his conduct, but all of his faculties had been the work of the Lord. That is why he credits the Lord with all of his possibilities, even back to the time he was in his mother's womb.

Verse 14. *Made* has no original as a separate word. *Fearfully* is from the same Hebrew word as "reverend" in Ps. 111: 9, and I ask the reader to consult my comments at that place. *Wonderfully* is from PALAH and Strong defines it, "to distinguish." The whole clause means that God respected and honored man by creating him a distinct living being, different from all others in the whole universe. For this great reason the Psalmist felt constrained to praise God thereby expressing his appreciation.

Verse 15. *Secret* and *lowest part* are used to denote that which is invisible to or unknown by the human mind. But although unknown to finite beings, God knew all about him and how to give distinction as described in the way of strength (here called *substance*) necessary to meet the purposes of the Creator.

Verse 16. God's foreknowledge is infinite and he has performed his works after his own will. He intended to make man just as he is made, and that his *substance* (strength) would be *unperfect;* that is, that man was to have the frailties of a human creature and not the absolute perfection of a divine one. And after making man in that form and nature, He has made his requirements of that creature accordingly. That is why the Psalmist made the statement in ch. 103: 14.

Verse 17. The thoughts of God were precious to David because he knew that they made all due allowances for the frailties of humanity.

Verse 18. A familiar church song says, "Count your many blessings, name them one by one." According to David that would be almost out of the question. Even some of those blessings came when he was asleep, for he said that when he awoke he realized he was still with God; that is, he had been receiving the favors of God during sleep.

Verse 19. Evil and dangerous association was frowned upon by David. He understood that wicked men were to be overthrown by the Lord, and did not want to be near them when that happened for fear of sharing in the penalty.

Verse 20. Those who defy the name of the Lord are considered as His enemies.

Verse 21. The word *hate* has a harsh sound, yet it is attributed to God in more than one instance. The main question is, what does that hatred lead one to do? We know that God's hatred of anything will not prevent him from doing by that thing (or person) that which is right. On this principle, if a man hates that which God hates, or hates those who hate Him, such hatred will not lead him to do what he should not.

Verse 22. *Perfect* hatred is a hatred that is complete. See comments on the preceding verse on the subject of hatred. *Mine enemies* is a significant phrase. Too many people will include the enemies of the Lord among their friends. That should not be done for it makes such people also the enemies of God. (James 4: 4.)

Verse 23. If a man is honestly trying to do right he will even be eager to have his thoughts exposed. This is the teaching in John 3: 19-21.

Verse 24. The *everlasting way* certainly would be the one the Psalmist mentioned in ch. 23: 3. It is everlasting because those who walk therein even down to the "last mile of the way," will close their journey at the throne of God.

PSALMS 140

Verse 1. Violence may be of different kinds. What David dreaded was the man who was violent with evil, and the Lord was asked to deliver him from such a foe.

Verse 2. We usually think of *imagine* as meaning merely to surmise as to the existence of something of which we are not certain. It is used in this place in the sense of scheme or plan. The object of the planning was to prepare war against David.

Verse 3. *Sharpened* is from SHANAN and Strong defines it, "to point (transitively or intransitively); intensively to pierce." We have all seen the pointed projection of the tongue of a snake as he seemed to be in a threatening mood. It is referred to by David to illustrate the vicious attitude of his enemies toward him. An adder is a poisonous snake that coils in a lurking position ready to spring and inject its venom into its victim. See the comments at ch. 3: 2 for explanation of *Selah*.

Verse 4. *Wicked* and *violent* should be understood the same as "evil" and "violent" in verse 1, and *purposed* will take the same explanation as "imagine" in verse 2.

Verse 5. *Snare, cords, net,* and *gin,* all signify the same thing. It means that David's enemies were secretly plotting against him. The *proud* were those who were haughty and impudent; men who realized that David was far better than they, and that they could make no headway against him unless it would be by underhanded plots.

Verse 6. See comments at ch. 86: 12 for distinctive meanings of Lord and God, since both are used in this verse. A supplication is a very earnest form of prayer.

Verse 7. Again see above reference for *God* and *Lord*. *Strength of salvation* means the strength necessary for salvation is to come from God. *Covered my head* means that David was shielded from fatal results when forced to battle with his enemies.

Verse 8. An unselfish man like David would not begrudge anyone a righteous desire. The connection shows he was asking for the disappointment of the wicked man in his *wicked devices*. The motive, also, that David had was a righteous one. He feared the wicked man would be self-exalted if he were successful in his evil designs.

Verse 9. The head is the part where schemes are formed, and then it is the member of the body that will be shaken in a defiant mood against the intended victim, and finally expressing those formed plots with the lips. The Psalmist prayed that those very lips might feel the sting of the wicked plots.

Verse 10. All of the words used against the foes of David in this verse are used figuratively. The meaning is that very severe treatment should be heaped upon them as punishment for their plots against the Psalmist.

Verse 11. *Be established* means to be successful in his wicked plots. *Evil shall hunt* is a phrase that means David believed the violent man would be overthrown.

Verse 12. As a rule we make a distinction between knowledge and faith. Yet the second word is sometimes used in a sense of emphatic assurance. It is so used in Job 19: 25 and 2 Cor. 5: 1. David's firm confidence in the future assistance of the Lord was based on his knowledge of present and past events.

Verse 13. *Righteous* and *upright* are two words for the same kind of people. They are always thankful for present favors, and have reason to look for the eternal favor of dwelling in the presence of Him whom they have served while in life.

PSALMS 141

Verse 1. *Cry* is another word that means an earnest prayer to God. David very frequently made such petitions to the Lord.

Verse 2. The Psalmist compared his prayers to the literal offerings that were used in the Jewish worship. The same comparison is made in Heb. 13: 15.

Verse 3. This verse is a figurative reference to the function of a group of men stationed at important places. Their duty was to watch and see that nothing unlawful might enter the place, nor that any person therein might unlawfully escape. On that principle David was concerned that no unrighteous words might escape from his mouth. He gave the same thought in literal language in ch. 19: 14.

Verse 4. God will never incline or induce man to do evil. The expression is David's way of asking the Lord to help him avoid the evil. *Let me not eat*, etc. In ancient times the act of eating with another signified an intimate friendship for and endorsement of the persons. That was why we have the statements about *eating* in Luke 15: 2 and 1 Cor. 5: 11.

Verse 5. The best and only comment I will make on this verse is to ask the student to read Proverbs 27: 5, 6.

Verse 6. The foregoing verse closed with a reference to the calamities of certain people. Now the Psalmist expresses sympathy for them in their calamities, some of which was to have their judges mistreated by being handled roughly, which is the idea in the term *stony places*. When that occurs David promises to "speak up" in their behalf with sweet words of comfort.

Verse 7. This verse is a highly figurative description of the near destruction that certain enemies had wrought. It is compared to a body whose members had been cut and slashed, as wood is carved sometimes, and made fit only for burial.

Verse 8. In spite of the sorest of afflictions David maintained his trust in the Lord. *Soul* is used for the whole being, and the Psalmist prayed that he might not be left entirely defeated; he did not ask for complete freedom from trials.

Verse 9. *Snares* and *gins* are names of traps set in a hidden manner. David knew they had been placed to capture him but could not always know where they were. He prayed for the Lord to direct his way so that he could avoid them.

Verse 10. There was nothing wrong in this wish against the enemies of David. It is the very fate that was decreed for the wicked plotter in Prov. 26: 27.

PSALMS 142

Verse 1. I will refer the reader to my comments on ch. 141: 1 as applying here.

Verse 2. God does not have to be "overpersuaded" to obtain a favor from him. However, he desires to have his servants manifest their confidence, which is done by earnest or supplicating petitions to Him.

Verse 3. This verse makes another reference to the traps that were *privily* (privately) laid for David. The dread of them about overcame him, but the Lord was his helper for He knew where all of the snares were located.

Verse 4. The condition of distress was so terrible with the Psalmist that all human help seemed to be gone or unavailing.

Verse 5. When human help fails, the Lord will be the sure refuge for those who make the proper approach unto Him, willing to comply with the divine requirements.

Verse 6. When a man realizes his own weakness he is in a better prospect of seeking help from the Lord. Human power is small at best, but when the troubled soul comes to God in his own appointed way he will be able to win over his afflictions through the divine strength. This reminds us of the statement of Paul in 2 Cor. 12: 10.

Verse 7. The *prison* was the siege of persecutions that David's enemies had cast around him. To deliver him from that situation would be like delivering one out of a prison. And by the same token, the persons with whom he would be surrounded after coming out of his prison would be righteous persons.

PSALMS 143

Verse 1. The two sides of the divine plan, the human and the divine, are indicated in this verse. They are the *faithfulness* of man and the *righteousness* of God. Recognizing both those factors, David offered his supplications to the Lord.

Verse 2. This verse means that no man would stand any chance if God were to deal with him according to strict justice. Only through God's mercy will he be able to stand.

Verse 3. *Soul* and *life* are used in the same sense. The *darkness* refers to the depression that had been thrust upon David by the persecutions of his enemies.

Verse 4. *Spirit* and *heart* are used in the same sense. The persecutions had been so bitter against David that he did not have the heart to face the situation alone.

Verse 5. The pronoun *thy* refers to the Lord. In the distress of mind under which David labored, he thought back to the happiness of other days. The remembrance of the mighty works of the Lord would give strength and courage to bear up under the present trial.

Verse 6. Stretching forth the hands is a gesture of pleading. A *thirsty land* is one lacking moisture, and is illustrative of a condition lacking the elements of complete encouragement. See ch. 3: 2 on the meaning of *Selah*.

Verse 7. *Pit* is from a word that sometimes means forgetfulness. To *hear speedily* means to hear promptly and favorably and grant the favor requested.

Verse 8. The significance of hearing *in the morning* is that it would start out the day under the care of the Lord. It is genuine kindness for the Lord to show a man how he should walk. Without divine guidance he might wander into crooked and dangerous paths and be lost.

Verse 9. The Psalmist thought of God as a place of refuge to which he would flee for protection from the threatening dangers at the hands of his enemies.

Verse 10. David was an inspired man when writing his part of the Bible. But the sacred document had not been completed as yet, and a man in the official position of king and counselor of a great people was confronted with various conditions of life. At such times he needed specific instruction concerning the will of the Lord. That was to be given to him by the spirit of God for his infallible guidance.

Verse 11. To *quicken* means to enliven and encourage. *For thy righteousness' sake* meant it would be righteous for God to deliver David's soul (his whole being) from the troubles thrust upon him by his enemies.

Verse 12. Severe treatment of his enemies would be regarded an act of mercy for David. The motive for such an action was the fact that he was a servant of God.

PSALMS 144

Verse 1. *Blessed be the Lord* denotes that all blessings were to be credited to him. Among those blessings was the instruction on how to wage successful and righteous warfare against such wicked foes as were threatening David.

Verse 2. This verse crowds in a goodly number of good things the Lord meant to David. *My goodness* really meant the goodness bestowed on the Psalmist, and the context indicates that it was the good mercy of God that David had in mind. A *fortress* is a fortified place equipped with the means of shelter and defense.

Verse 3. The language and thought of this verse is similar to that in ch. 8: 4.

Verse 4. The frailty of man was what caused David to marvel at the honors that God had bestowed upon him throughout the whole arrangement of creation.

Verse 5. The Lord's absolute mastery of the *heavens* (regions of the air and planets and the earth (mountains) is the thought in this verse.

Verse 6. Having such control of the universe, David concluded that God could use the elements therein to chastise his enemies. It could be done by using the lightning, having the effect of arrows upon the foes of him and other good men.

Verse 7. *Send thine hand* has about the same meaning as if David has said to the Lord, "lend a helping hand." *Great waters* is a symbol of many afflictions. *Strange children* refers to people outside of the Jewish nation.

Verse 8. One word in the definition of *vanity* in the original is "uselessness." The *strange children* of the preceding verse are the ones who speak these vain or useless words. Most people are right-handed and hence would be always regarded stronger for evil if they used their right hand for that purpose. When it is used figuratively as it is here, it means that outsiders are guilty of great falsehood.

Verse 9. We should ever bear in mind that David was a great musician, and used his instruments much of the time in religious services to accompany his song. Hence he said he would sing a new song to God and use the psaltery and harp. The last word is the name of the musical instruments that had *ten strings*.

Verse 10. The passage gives God the glory for the preservation of himself and other kings. Without the help of God, the most noted of kings would not be able to escape the *hurtful sword*, a common weapon of warfare in those days.

Verse 11. This verse is the same as verses 7, 8, and the reader is asked to see my comments on that portion of this chapter.

Verse 12. The plea for riddance of the evil work of *strange children* was to be beneficial to the youth of Israel.

Verse 13. A garner is a place for storing grain. It is desirous that one's sheep be enabled to reproduce abundantly. All of these benefits would be had if the evil work of the strange children were ridded out of the land.

Verse 14. The first clause of this verse continues to wish for temporal prosperity as a result of being rid of the evil men. The rest of the verse refers to the success of the leaders of the land. *Breaking in* means there would not be any raids by these strange (outside) people. *Going out* denotes that the leaders would be able to maintain their place of authority in peace and not be compelled to sally forth to drive the invaders away. With such a condition there would be no occasion for complaints in the peaceful streets, for all things would be satisfactory.

Verse 15. The general conclusion is that people described above will be a happy people. The specific key to the situation is that God is their Lord. It is very important now that the reader sees the explanation of *God* and *Lord* at ch. 86: 12.

PSALMS 145

Verse 1. To *extol* means to elevate or lift up. It is impossible literally to elevate an infinite God, so the clause signifies the giving to Him a high acknowledgment, and recognize his name as the highest of all names.

Verse 2. The significant idea in this verse is that David would make his praises to God a *daily* practice. Too many professed servants of the Lord wish to give their devotions to God secondary consideration only.

Verse 3. To be unsearchable means it is beyond the full understanding of Man. God is infinite while man is finite, hence no human being can go to the end of the greatness of the Lord with his investigations.

Verse 4. The fact of God's greatness has been so well demonstrated from generation to generation that it has been established like a "continued story."

Verse 5. A king or other person in high places might have *glory* and *majesty* showered upon him by an admiring populace and yet not have attained to it by a life of *honor*. David proposed to ascribe all of these virtues to the Lord.

Verse 6. *Terrible* is from the same word as "reverend" in ch. 111: 9. The performances of God in the presence of man had been so awe-inspiring they were being spoken of by the public. David had the same opinion of God's greatness and used his opportunities to declare the same to others among whom he associated.

Verse 7. *They* means the people in general who were impressed with the goodness of the Creator; they made known their impressions in song.

Verse 8. *Compassion* denotes the feeling of God for humanity, and graciousness his treatment of them because of it. *Slow to anger* is one of the marks or indications of this gracious treatment of human beings.

Verse 9. *Good to all* does not mean that God makes no distinction between the righteous and the wicked, for he does. But there are certain natural blessings that are created for human beings regardless of their personal character. As an instance of this fact we might consider the case of rain and sunshine in Matt. 5: 45.

Verse 10. This verse is a companion to ch. 19: 1. The saints *bless* God by acknowledging Him as the maker of these great things of the universe which are real blessings, because they meet the needs of human creatures.

Verse 11. The praise for God does not stop with the works of creation. The people of God will talk of the *power* or authority of the kingdom that pertains to the spiritual interests of mankind, and the divine wisdom portrayed therein.

Verse 12. Unselfish citizens of the Lord's institutions will not be content to enjoy its benefits alone. Their joy will prompt them to tell others the glad story.

Verse 13. *Kingdom* is a very general word and may refer to the rule of God among men in all ages. It evidently has that force in this verse. The specific kingdom or dispensation in which David lived was intended to be discontinued at a certain event (the coming of Christ). But in all ages of the world the God of Heaven was destined to have a rule among men which would continue as long as man was on the earth.

Verse 14. The good things declared here must be understood in the light of the conditions on which they have been promised. Those who are bowed down and fallen will be helped up if they will reach up and take the hand of the Lord stretched out to them.

Verse 15. The thought of this verse is similar to the preceding one; that is, there is a proviso understood. God will give the good things of life to those who *wait* (took toward) upon Him, which indicates their faith in the divine provision.

Verse 16. It should be understood that David was considering the blessings that God gives through nature and necessary for man's temporal comfort and existence.

Verse 17. In all of God's provisions for the creatures of his care he has done the right thing. For that reason we should be satisfied with his providence.

Verse 18. To call upon the Lord *in truth* means to call in the manner taught in His revelation of truth. That will make it necessary for man to study the Word of God.

Verse 19. The condition for granting the favors of this verse is that the persons seeking them must *fear him*. That does not mean merely to be afraid of the Lord, but they must respect him enough to obey his commandments.

Verse 20. The same kind of condition is connected with the favor of God in this verse as that of the preceding one except here it is worded to *love him*. But that will result in the same obedience for Jesus taught the principle that love is proved by obedience. See the passage in John 14: 23 on the subject of love and obedience.

Verse 21. David personally determined to praise the Lord with his own mouth. He was desirous also that *all flesh* (all beings with human flesh) should praise Him, since no man lives who does not owe his very existence to the goodness of God.

PSALMS 146

Verse 1. The first 4 words are sometimes rendered "Hallelujah." To praise the Lord with the soul means to praise him with one's whole being.

Verse 2. *While I live* is equivalent in thought to "faithful unto death."

Verse 3. Nothing permanent or spiritually helpful can be obtained from man, even though he be a prince or leader among the people.

Verse 4. This verse is considering the earthly part of man which lives by breathing air. When the breath ceases to come into the body it results in the death of the body and it goes back to dust. Some people try to make the last clause of the verse mean that when a man dies no part of him is conscious since at that instant his thoughts perish. It is true that all of the plans or purposes that a man meditated over while in the flesh will come to an end at death. But that does not even touch the subject of his mental condition afterward.

Verse 5. *Jacob* is frequently used in the Bible to mean the nation of Israel, because Jacob was the father of the 12 tribes. The *God of Jacob*, then, would be the God who was worshiped by the nation. Certainly it would be a true source of happiness to lean upon Him for help.

Verse 6. The argument is that a Being who could make the universe could certainly help one of the little creatures of that vast domain. *Keepeth truth* means that God always makes his word good, and that proves that his promises were truthful.

Verse 7. *Judgment for the oppressed* would be to decide their case in their behalf and then *execute* or enforce the decision. The last clause means the Lord will loose the prisoners from their bondage to the state of oppression.

Verse 8. All miraculous deeds of kindness are done by power coming from the Lord. Likewise, all favors of a spiritual and mental nature originate with Him. The motive for the blessings is God's love for the righteous.

Verse 9. The *strangers* is defined in the original as "a guest; by implication a foreigner." God is good to all unforunate people if they are deserving, even though they are not of his own. The same principle is taught by Paul in Gal. 6: 10. *Turneth upside down* means the Lord will upset or defeat the way of the wicked.

Verse 10 This verse should be read in connection with the comments at ch. 145: 13. *Praise ye the Lord* is an exclamation, pronounced "Hallelujah."

PSALMS 147

Verse 1. Shouts and exclamations addressed to the Lord in Bible circumstances were not mere emotional outbursts. They were intelligent expressions regarding some of the virtues of the Lord, and the desirable effects they were having on the servants of God. For instance, the present verse names three of such points; *good, pleasant* and *comely*. These combine to form a strong motive for praising the God of Heaven.

Verse 2. This verse is a prophecy of the return of the children of Israel from Babylonian captivity; the history is in the books of Ezra and Nehemiah.

Verse 3. This verse refers to those who are discouraged over the trials of life.

Verse 4. *Telleth* means to count or enumerate the number of the stars. The statement aims to express the boundless knowledge of God. *Names* is from a word that has the idea of individuality The verse as a whole means that God is so great and his spiritual presence so wide that each individual star is present to his all-seeing eye. (How Foolish, then, for a feeble man to think that he could hide from Him!)

Verse 5. We generally think of the word "infinite" as meaning unlimited, and it does have that force with reference to the goodness or knowledge of God. However, in this passage it is from a Hebrew word that means "indefinite." It signifies that no human being can state the number or size or extent of God's understanding.

Verse 6. The *meek* are those who humble themselves and they are the ones whom God will exalt. Jesus taught the same truth in Luke 14: 11. It is interesting to note that David contrasts the *meek* with the *wicked*.

Verse 7. As a rule when the Psalmist suggests the use of a musical instrument in service to God, it is as an accompaniment for singing.

Verse 8. *Heaven* in this connection refers to the first of the 3 heavens, the region of the atmosphere. The verse is concerned with the operation of God through nature in producing rain. *Grass to grow upon the mountains* suggest the power of God in producing the blessing independent of man, since he does not live there as a rule.

Verse 9. The blessings of providence are for the use of dumb creatures, even though they are not capable of engaging in productive pursuits. (Matt. 6: 26.)

Verse 10. Both the *horse* and *men* are parts of God's great plan of this earth. However, they are instruments only in His hands, not that God could not work alone.

Verse 11. While God does not need the assistance of feeble man, yet He loves the one who has fear or respect for the divine source of his existence.

Verse 12. All praise and other service offered to God must be done through the proper channel. The headquarters of God's system at that time were in *Zion*, and that was a particular part of the city of *Jerusalem*.

Verse 13. Jerusalem is the antecedent of *thy*. It refers to the support the Lord had given to the capital city of his beloved nation.

Verse 14. The same city is meant and the *peace* has special reference to the successful rule of Jerusalem over the enemy. *Finest of the wheat* denotes the temporal blessings which God assured to the citizens of the holy city.

Verse 15. This is still on the control of God over the works of creation. The word of the Lord is sufficient to bring to pass any result that is divinely desired.

Verse 16. This is a comparative description of the work of God in the elements of the weather or seasons.

Verse 17. God controls the rainfall for the crops, and he likewise has complete charge of the winter season with its products.

Verse 18. When the cold temperature of winter has served the Lord's purposes, he brings the thawing forces of the springtime, filling the streams and rills. All of this agrees with the promise made in Gen. 8: 22.

Verse 19. The special covenant that God made was with his own people. Jacob was the father of the 12 sons who composed the nation. That nation was called Israel, one of the names of their common ancestor (Gen. 32: 28).

Verse 20. God has bestowed the blessings of nature on all nations alike, but his statutes of government were given only to Israel. The chapter closes with the familiar words that are sometimes rendered "Hallelujah."

PSALMS 148

Verse 1. A part of Strong's definition of *praise* in the original is "to celebrate." The outstanding idea in the word is to give God the most respectful attention, and to accord him the credit for all the great and good things ever done or that exist. When dumb or inanimate things are called upon to praise God, it means that God deserves praise because of those things. When a call is made for praise to God, and no specific motive is mentioned, the phrase may be translated "Hallelujah." This definition of *praise* will not always be repeated, but attention will be called in the following verses to various creatures who are called upon to praise the Lord, or where things will be named for which he should be praised.

Verse 2. The *angels* were the heavenly messengers or ministers of the Lord; the *hosts* were those who made up the Lord's army.

Verse 3. The sun, moon and stars were made by the Lord and are of great service to man; for that reason He should be praised.

Verse 4. *Heavens of heavens* is a phrase for the sake of emphasis. *Waters above* refers to the event recorded in Gen. 1: 6, 7.

Verse 5. The word of God was sufficient to bring the parts of the universe into physical existence. This is also the teaching in Ps. 33: 6-9 and Heb. 11: 3.

Verse 6. About six thousand years have passed since God brought the universe into being. In all of that time there has never been a variation in the revolutions of the earth around its axis, or of its orbital journeys around the sun, except those miraculously caused by the Creator himself, recorded in Josh. 10: 12-14; 2 Ki. 20: 11.

Verse 7. Let praise come from, or because of, the earth. Even the dragons and others of the creatures in the deeps are evidences of the praiseworthy might of God.

Verse 8. The storms and other "weather conditions" fulfill the word of God by occurring just as He decreed they should.

Verse 9. These are all inanimate things and cannot praise God, yet He should be praised because of them and their benefit to the living creatures of the earth.

Verse 10. This verse lists things that are living but are not intelligent, as man, yet they exist by the power of God and for the benefit and control of the human being (Gen. 1: 26), therefore he should praise the Lord for them.

Verse 11. In several verses the writer mentioned inanimate things for which great praise was due to God. He then named some things that are living but not intellectual, and called for praise on account of them. And in the present verse the Psalmist calls upon the intelligent creatures, the ones who have been benefitted by the works of God, to give praise for the same. Even the greatest persons of the earth; *kings, princes* and *judges,* are bidden to praise the Lord, for they owe their greatness to Him.

Verse 12. No class is exempt from obligation to praise the Lord, and none should desire to be excused from the service if they are appreciative of God's goodness.

Verse 13. *Excellent* is not merely a term of flattery; it describes a state of actual superiority. The name of the Lord is above all other names. There is only one thing in the universe any higher than the name of the Lord (ch. 138: 2).

Verse 14. *Horn* means power and authority. God gave his people a place of power among the nations of the earth because he loved them. This psalm closes with the familiar term, "Hallelujah."

PSALMS 149

Verse 1. This verse is another that starts with the term that means "Hallelujah." There is never any good reason for casting away a song because it is old, but there are always *new* reasons for singing praises to the Lord.

Verse 2. Israel owed his existence to the Lord, whether considered as a man or a nation of men. *Zion* and *king* are appropriately named together because the first refers to the capital of the kingdom.

Verse 3. The *dance* is a noun and named as one item in the praise activities offered to the Lord. There was a musical instrument also used in ancient times called the dance. In some passages of the Bible it is clearly what was meant. The following are places where the musical instrument was meant. Ex. 15: 20; Judges 11: 34. But it is also evident that dancing as an exercise of the body was engaged in by people of ancient times. It was sometimes under approved circumstances, but at others was connected with unlawful practices. But however the subject may be viewed, there is nothing in either Old or New Testament that justifies the modern promiscuous dance, engaged in together by the sexes where bodily contact is maintained in the performance.

Verse 4. According to this verse meekness is an adornment of beauty. We have about the same teaching in 1 Pe. 3: 4. *The Lord taketh pleasure* means he is pleased with the conduct and standing of his people.

Verse 5. One of the most glorious actions is to rejoice in the Lord. In the first psalm David endorsed the man who meditated at night in the law of the Lord. In this verse he suggests that the saints sing aloud while in their beds.

Verse 6. *High places* means those in which the saints exalted the name of God. That age was one in which warfare was used by the people of God. Hence David not only called for religious activities of the saints while in the privacy of their homes, but bade them wield a keen sword when they went forth to fight with the foe.

Verse 7. While God's people took vengeance on the heathen it was counted as His vengeance. This principle is taught in Rom. 12: 19 and 2 Cor. 7: 11.

Verse 8. The kings of the heathen nations fought with God's people. The Psalmist wished that those kings and their associates would be defeated by the people of God and be handcuffed. That would be winning a victory against the vicious enemies of God.

Verse 9. *The judgment written* referred to such instructions as Deut. 7: 1, 2. To have carried out that instruction would have brought honor upon the nation. Their forefathers failed to do so and the nation was brought under great shame (Judges 1).

PSALMS 150

Verse 1. The final chapter of the Book of Psalms is an intensive exhortation to praise the Lord. For a detailed definition of "praise" as a word, see my comments at ch. 135: 1 and 148: 1. Sanctuary means any holy assembling of the people of God. *Firmament* has a figurative and very extensive meaning, referring to the heavenly or exalted character of His power; that it is awe-inspiring and full of dignity.

Verse 2. *Mighty acts.* The second word has no original as a distinct term. The first is from one that means force and power. The clause, then, would include the entire field of God's performances, beginning with his creation of the Son (Rev. 3: 14), and considering all that has been done in the realm of "creation, providence and redemption." For all of these things God deserves wholehearted praise. Many things and persons may have greatness, but *excellent* greatness means that it is superior to all other. The contrast is made between the Lord and other persons having greatness.

Verse 3. The *trumpet* was the same as our cornet and played with the mouth. The *psaltery* and *harp* were stringed instruments and played with the figers. Sometimes a clip was worn on the fingers and at other times the bare fingers were used in playing.

Verse 4. A *timbrel* was a kind of drum. See comments at ch. 149: 3 on *dance. Stringed instruments* is a general name, applying to all of those played with the fingers. *Organs* were any kind of instruments played with the mouth, but having the pipes so perforated that a scale of tones could be produced.

Verse 5. Both of these *cymbals* were sheets of metal and struck together with a loud sound. They were used in rhythmic meter to accompany the music or singing, in about the same manner as drums and symbals are used in modern orchestras and other musical organizations.

Verse 6. I will request the reader again to see my comments on "praise" at ch. 135: 1 and 148: 1. Dumb beasts cannot render intelligent praise to God, any more than can inanimate things, yet all are told by the Psalmist to praise the Lord. Hence, we understand him to mean that we should praise the Lord for all the innumerable things in creation that bring us so much joy and other blessing. The book closes with the words on which we have had frequent comments and that are rendered "Hallelujah."

PROVERBS 1

General remarks. Concerning the authorship of this book, Smith's Bible Dictionary has this to say: "The superscriptions [titles] which are affixed to several portions of the book, in chs. 1: 1; 10: 1; 25: 1, attribute the authorship of those portions to Solomon the son of David, king of Israel. With the exception of the last two chapters, which are distinctly assigned to other authors, it is probable that the statement of the superscriptions is in the main correct, and that the majority of the proverbs contained or collected were by Solomon . . . The Proverbs are frequently quoted or alluded to in the New Testament, and the canonicity [authority] of the book thereby confirmed."—Article, Book of Proverbs. Since it is certain, then, that the authorship of the book belongs to Solomon, it will be well to settle the question of his qualifications and authority for writing the book. The wisdom of Solomon has been a subject of discussion among the friends of the Bible. Some have said that, while it was far above what any other person had, it was not in the form of inspiration; that it was mental talent such as all people have through nature, except that his exceeded others. That will not hold, for Solomon was already a mature man, with all natural endowments possessed and developed, when God gave to him the wisdom we are speaking about. Again, it is claimed that his wisdom pertained to his ability as king and judge of disputes, not to his writings; wrong again. In 1 Kings 4: 32, immediately after mentioning his wisdom. the writer tells us of the songs and proverbs he composed. The conclusion is, then, that Solomon was divinely inspired in all of his writings that have been included in the Bible. The fact of his unrighteous life does not affect his inspiration, any more than Peter's hypocrisy at Antioch (Gal. 2: 11-13) affected his inspiration at Jerusalem (Acts 15: 7-11) or his epistles.

Verse 1. The word *proverbs* is from MASHAL and Strong defines it, "properly a pithy maxim, usually of a metaphorical [figurative] nature; hence a simile [comparison], (as an adage, poem, discourse)." The importance of the author is indicated by telling of his ancestry. He was not only a son of David, but David was a king. And David was not only a king, but was king of Israel.

Verse 2. This verse states the purpose of these proverbs; that it was to know *wisdom* and *instruction*, and to perceive words of *understanding*. The three nouns that are italicized have about the same meaning. Generally speaking, they have the idea of information necessary to wise and proper living, and correction when one gets out of the line of duty. The key to the verse is the word *know*. It is from YADAH, and Strong says it is used in a great variety of senses "including observation, care, recognition." In the King James version it has been rendered acknowledge 5 times, be aware 2, discern 4, consider 7, have respect 1, perceive 18. So the force of the verse is, the proverbs of Solomon were written to the end that the reader would be led to recognize and give attention to the things mentioned. Or, using a popular saying, to "know a good thing when he sees it."

Verse 3. *Perceive* is still a stronger word than *know* in the preceding verse. It means not only to recognize and give some attention to the instruction, but actually to accept it. The four items of the list have much in common in their meaning, yet there is some distinction. I shall state the leading idea in each as drawn from the lexicon. *Wisdom* means to be on the alert; *justice*, to be strictly or technically right; *judgment*, a proper verdict when called upon for a decision; *equity*, to show the spirit of fair play in one's relations with others.

Verse 4. *Subtilty* means the exercise of common sense instead of being *simple*, which means to be easily misled. A man might not be "simple" in the sense of the word here, but if he were young he would need to be given knowledge and *discretion*. This word is from an original that means the ability to think for himself.

Verse 5. A *wise* man is one who will hear so as to increase his *learning*. In other words, the wisest man in the world is the one who realizes he does not know it all. Paul taught this same thing in 1 Cor. 3: 18. The last clause of the verse has practically the same meaning as the first.

Verse 6. This verse, like 3 others above, starts with the word *to*. All of verses 2-6 were written to show the purpose of the proverbs that are mentioned in verse one. Among those purposes this verse gives that of helping the reader to *understand* (distinguish or recognize) what he reads. *Proverb* and *interpretation* have the same definition, and mean a "maxim" or comparison. *Dark* and *sayings* are from the same original and mean "puzzling" sentences. All puzzles are possible of solving if one uses the proper key. So as a final summing up, Solomon wished to produce a group of pithy remarks, short but thorough, in many repetitions yet with some distinctions, so that his friends and fellow citizens would be helped in the field of his (Solomon's) own specialty which was WISDOM. These 6 verses should be regarded as a preface to the whole Book of Proverbs, and kept in mind throughout the entire study of the book.

Verse 7. *Beginning* is from RESHIYTH, and one part of the definition is to be first in rank. It is translated "principal thing" in ch. 4: 7. The thought is that when a man learns to fear and respect the Lord, he has learned the most important of all forms of wisdom. By this token a fool is one who does not fear or respect the Lord because he does not want to receive instruction as to his conduct.

Verse 8. *Son* is from BEN, which occurs several hundred times in the Old Testament. The definition in Strong's lexicon is, "a son (as a builder of the family name), in the widest sense (of literal and figurative relationship, including grandson, subject, nation, quality or condition, etc.)." In view of this definition it can be seen that Solomon used the word with reference to young men generally. Parents are the first teachers of children and their advice is backed by years of experience.

Verse 9. *They* refers to the instructions given a boy by his father and mother. The *ornament* is figurative, of course, and used to indicate the value of a good life.

Verse 10. To *entice* means to induce another by deceptive means. The apparent worth of the thing suggested covers the danger therein from the view of the victim. The advice is for the young man not to be misled by the temptation.

Verse 11. It is wrong to overtake even a guilty person by dishonest methods; how much worse to do so against those who have no evil *cause* justly charged to them.

Verse 12. It is not likely that a gang of outlaws would use this language literally in trying to seduce a young man into wrong-doing. The idea is that their persuasive inducements should be regarded in that light.

Verse 13. The motive of violence for the purpose of robbery is what these *sinners* had in mind. The desire for wealth by any means is the subject of this verse.

Verse 14. This is just another way of suggesting that they all work together in the robbery, then divide the spoil among all equally.

Verse 15. A boy might think he would associate with these sinners without joining with them in their evil deeds. But sooner or later he will find himself doing just as they are doing. Paul taught this great truth in 1 Cor. 15: 33. Another thing to consider, if a boy is found in company with those who are engaged in wrongful practices, he will be looked upon with suspicion if not actually charged together with them. Therefore Solomon's advice to the young man is not to go along with them.

Verse 16. The purpose of the enticers may not be seen at first, but Solomon says their path will lead to the greatest sin. By the time the unsuspecting boy learns what he is mixed up with, it will be too late to retreat.

Verse 17. This verse explains why the evil characters keep their real purposes from those whom they wish to mislead. If a bird sees a trap being set he will not go into it. For the same reason, if the evil designs of these "sinners" were allowed to be known, the young man would understand better than to follow them.

Verse 18. Evil often works its own rebuke. In Ps. 141: 10 David wished for the wicked to fall into their own trap. Such is the meaning of the verse we are considering.

Verse 19. If a man is so greedy for gain that he will attempt getting it by "armed robbery," he is in danger of losing his own life.

Verse 20. *Wisdom* is the subject of this and all the following verses of this chapter. It has already been stated (at v. 6) that wisdom was Solomon's specialty. It was the thing for which he asked God at Gibeon (1 Ki. 3: 5-9), and we should not be surprised if it proves to be the most prominent subject running throughout this book. Solomon represents wisdom as the speaker in the following verses, and practically all of the personal pronouns are impersonations of the subject; and without exception that is true of the pronouns in the first person.

Verse 21. The need for wisdom is present in the gates and all other public places.

Verse 22. *Simple ones* means those who will not try to improve their situation in life by seeking for wisdom. A man who belittles the value of knowledge is a fool.

Verse 23. The reader should not forget that it is *wisdom* that is talking. If men will accept the reproof that wisdom offers them, and turn or change their foolish ways, they will be given further words of truth.

Verse 24. Wisdom had been offered to the people of the world but they had turned the offer down. Wisdom had even pleaded *(stretched out my hand)* with men to receive her, but it had been disregarded as if it amounted to nothing.

Verse 25. *Counsel* means advice in general, and *reproof* means an attempted correction of error. To *set at nought* means to regard it with contempt as if it did not have any merit worthy of being accepted or given any consideration.

Verse 26. All the wisdom in the world will be of no avail after a man has ignored it until he meets up with a calamity. In his fear he may recall the words of wisdom that had been offered him but which he slighted.

Verse 27. Such misfortunes as are named in this verse may come to any person and through no fault of his own. But the ones meant here are those which might have been avoided had the victim listened to the voice of wisdom in time.

Verse 28. This verse describes a great many people who try to escape from the results of their own folly when it is too late. Such persons generally are the quickest to cry for help. Yes, they *seek me early* says the voice of "wisdom," but the seeking is too late to be of any benefit because the fruit is ready to be harvested.

Verse 29. These unfortunate people got into their serious trouble because they hated or disrespected knowledge. The author couples hatred for knowledge with rejection of the fear of the Lord because they work the same result to the guilty ones.

Verse 30. *They would none* means they would not receive any of the counsel of wisdom. They despised (belittled) the reproof that was offered them by wisdom.

Verse 31. A New Testament expression with the same meaning as this verse is in Gal. 6: 7 about sowing and reaping. The people of our own verse were to have a similar experience, and all because they would not accept the counsel of "wisdom." A man falling into the pit he had digged for another is another comparison, except that the ones in this verse may not have involved anyone else in their folly.

Verse 32. *Turning away* means a backsliding or departing from the pathway of right. The *simple* means those who would not consult the advice of wisdom. Their own carelessness will be their ruin in the end. Also, those who ignore wisdom's direction in the obtaining or use of their wealth will perish in their own foolishness.

Verse 33. This verse describes a character just opposite to that of the preceding one. By listening to the voice of wisdom the individual will be secure in life.

PROVERBS 2

Verse 1. See comments at chapter 1: 10 on meaning of *son*. *Receive* and *hide* are used in a good sense, meaning to accept and retain the words and commandments of the wise monarch of Israel, since he spoke them by the help of the Lord.

Verse 2. Not only should the young man retain the words of wisdom, but he should have a favorable attitude toward them. And he should display that attitude by making a practical demonstration of it in his manner of life.

Verse 3. This verse is still stronger than the two preceding ones. The young man does not wait to be offered words of wisdom but calls earnestly for them. That is indicated by the phrase *lifting up his voice*.

Verse 4. This is a comparison, considering knowledge as valuable as the precious metal and other treasures of accepted worth.

Verse 5. The search for wisdom will logically lead to a knowledge of God, which in turn will result in *fear* or respect for the Lord. See the comments at Ps. 86: 12 for the distinctive meanings of *Lord* and *God*.

Verse 6. Solomon at first spoke of the commandments as his (v. 1), now he attributes them to the Lord. So we have his own admission that he wrote by inspiration. See the comments in the first verses of ch. 1 on meanings of *wisdom, knowledge* and *understanding* when used as separate terms.

Verse 7. *He* is a pronoun referring to the Lord. *Layeth up* means the wisdom is provided and always at hand for those who are worthy of it. A *buckler* is one who defends and supports another in his activities.

Verse 8. *Paths* and *way* refer to the life conduct of the *saints* or servants of the Lord. He will watch over and protect his righteous followers in their good walk.

Verse 9. To *understand* means to realize through experience what these virtues amount to. *Righteousness* is the act of doing right; *judgment* is the use of common sense in forming conclusions; and *equity* is the showing of fair play with others.

Verse 10. Wisdom must not merely be heard, but must be permitted to enter the heart or mind; it should be considered as a pleasant thing. We are reminded of the statement of Christ on this subject as recorded in Matt. 5: 6.

Verse 11. *Discretion* and *understanding* means the right use of knowledge gained.

Verse 12. Such use of one's knowledge will assure one against being misled by the *froward* (stubbornly wayward) man.

Verse 13. *Who* refers to the "froward" man of the preceding verse. He is contrary in that he will not remain in the right path but deserts it to wander in paths of sin.

Verse 14. The antecedent of most of the pronouns in these verses is the "evil man" in verse 12. Such a person would not only do the evil but would rejoice in it. And his rejoicing would not stop at his own evil practices, but he would actually take delight in the *frowardness* (stubborn waywardness) of others.

Verse 15. *Crooked* and *froward* mean almost the same; to sway back and forth.

Verse 16. The verse starts with *to*, which goes back to the purposes of the book. See the comments at ch. 1: 2. One of the purposes was to put the young man on his guard against the *strange* woman; one who belongs in another and an evil class. It has special reference to the immoral woman who seeks the patronage of the young man, and who uses flattering words to him to win him over to her association.

Verse 17. The description of this *strange* woman indicates that she had belonged with the people of God. Yet she had placed herself in a *strange* class (another class v. 16) by the corrupt life she formed and the associates she had made by such a life.

Verse 18. *Her house* means a house of bad repute. *Death* and *dead* are used in a moral and spiritual sense. If a young man becomes a patron of an immoral house he separates himself from a life of righteousness. That is when he becomes *dead* since the basic meaning of death is a separation.

Verse 19. No one gets so far into sin that God will not receive him back if he makes the proper amends. But the danger and rule is that a patron of the kind of life described above will continue therein to the end of life.

Verse 20. The purpose of the proverbs is again mentioned. That the young man will associate with good characters instead of with the "strange" woman.

Verse 21. *The upright* being considered at present are those who avoid evil companions and prefer the righteous. Such characters are regarded as *the perfect*, and they have the assurance of prolonged residence in the land.

Verse 22. On the principle of the preceding verse, the patrons of "strange" women and other wicked characters will be rejected and brought to ruin.

PROVERBS 3

Verse 1. See comments at ch. 1: 10 on "son." Since Solomon was an inspired man (see "general remarks"), it follows that the commandments are those of the Lord. For the young man to keep them with his heart means that he will be wholehearted in life.

Verse 2. Those who honor the Lord will observe the proper rules of life. That will lead to better health and hence to a longer life.

Verse 3. *Mercy* and *truth* are named together which is very significant. Mercy that is not in accordance with truth would be wrong. The other parts of the verse are figures of speech. Mercy and truth are the most desirable of all ornaments.

Verse 4. Yes, both God and man will be favorable towards the one who is merciful and truthful. Paul wrote something along that line in Gal. 5: 23, second clause.

Verse 5. Human wisdom is frail compared with that of the Lord; however, one should use his own reasoning faculties in applying the Lord's words of wisdom.

Verse 6. *Acknowledge* is from a word that means to give attention to the Lord for the purpose of learning of Him. By such learning the young man will be directed aright.

Verse 7. This is practically the same in thought as the last clause of v. 5. It is also like the statement of Paul in Rom. 12: 16.

Verse 8. *Navel* is from SHOR and Strong's definition is, "a string (as twisted), i. e. (specifically) the umbilical cord (also figuratively as the center of strength)." *Marrow* is from a word that means moisture. The verse is figurative, and based on the literal importance of the mentioned organs for the health of the human body.

Verse 9. Paul says "we brought nothing into this world" (1 Tim. 6: 7), and also teaches that whatever is in our hands now was received from some one else (1 Cor. 4: 7). The wise man teaches the same truth in this verse. It is our duty, therefore, to use our *substance* (possessions) in a way that will honor the Lord.

Verse 10. If man makes the proper use of the blessings God has given him he has the promise of being prosperous again. This also was taught by Paul in 2 Cor. 9: 6-10.

Verse 11. This is one of the passages that is quoted in the New Testament; it is in Heb. 12: 5, 6. To *despise* means to belittle, and the young man is exhorted not to underestimate the value of chastisement. Whether of a physical or mental nature, it is always beneficial to have all disorders corrected, even if the operation is painful.

Verse 12. A true parent, whether human or divine, who administers proper punishment to a wayward son, thereby shows his real love for the child. Withholding a needed correction is not an indication of love, but of hatred and unconcern.

Verse 13. For several verses the subject will be *wisdom*, and it will be impersonated generally by a feminine pronoun. See the comments on this subject at ch. 1: 20. There are several words that may be found in the Bible that are similar in meaning, such as wisdom, understanding, knowledge and discretion. These are so much alike they can be used interchangeably. However, there is a slight distinction in their meanings, especially if two or more of them are used in one connection. For instance, in the present verse the first word denotes mental ability in general, and the second is the right use of that ability. Solomon says that happiness results from these virtues.

Verse 14. *Merchandise* is from a word defined as "profit from trade." The idea is that if one deals in wisdom as his stock, his profits will be greater than if he was dealing in silver and gold, even though they are very valuable elements.

Verse 15. This verse makes the comparison stronger than the preceding. It places the value above everything else, and even above all other desirable things put together.

Verse 16. *Length of days* will be a result of living according to wisdom. It will also bring true riches because it is coupled with honor. Right and left hand are figures of speech to indicate completeness of benefits obtained by using wisdom.

Verse 17. The ways or manner of life directed by wisdom will be pleasant to one who loves righteousness. He may be even forced to endure some physical discomfort as a result of clinging to the right, but the consciousness that he is right will be a pleasant meditation. On the same principle it will give him a perfect peace.

Verse 18. Using some good things in nature for an illustration, wisdom is even compared with a tree of life. That would mean a tree whose fruit produced a never failing source of joyful existence. But to have these good effects the person must *lay hold* of the source of wisdom, not merely long for it. He must go further yet; he must *retain* the wisdom after he has made the effort to lay hold of it.

Verse 19. Wisdom was not the force by which the Lord *founded* (made and established) the earth. It means that he used wisdom in the work. See comments at v. 13 for explanation of *understanding*. The heavens means the regions where the birds fly, and where the planets are fixed in their firm position.

Verse 20. God's control over the sea

has been demonstrated more than once, so we do not know which instance was meant by this verse. And the dropping of the dew is so common, though wonderful, that a bare mention of it should cause adoration for Him.

Verse 21. The pronoun *them* is mentioned before the antecedent, *wisdom* and *discretion*. The two words will take the same comments as v. 13.

Verse 22. People wore ornaments of pearls or costly stones around their necks. The wise man used it to compare the beauty and attractiveness of wisdom and discretion. *Soul* means the entire being and *life* refers to the force that sustains it.

Verse 23. A man need not stumble if he can know the pathway he is trying to travel. Wisdom and discretion will point out such a mode of travel.

Verse 24. The greatest assurance one can have is that which comes from the consciousness of being right. Such an assurance may be had by accepting the words of wisdom offered by the wise king of Israel. It will prepare the mind to relax at the hour of retirement and enter into peaceful sleep.

Verse 25. With the equipment of wisdom one will always be prepared for emergencies, so that he will not have any dread of some sudden crisis. He will not even have to be in dread of the enemy who is not backed up by this wisdom.

Verse 26. The secret of all this confidence is one's faith in the Lord who knows all about the tricks of wicked men, and will protect the righteous from all pitfalls.

Verse 27. No one is required to contribute to the needs of others if he does not have wherewith to do so. But if a favor is due another and the debtor has the necessity in hand he should contribute it to the need of him who makes the request.

Verse 28. This is practically the same as the preceding verse except that it is more specific. But that makes the individual more entitled to criticism than before. The fact that he promises to perform the favor at a specified time, and at a time only one day in the future, indicates that he already has the means of meeting the obligation.

Verse 29. *Securely* is from BETACH and Strong's definition is, "a place of refuge; abstractly safety, both the fact (security) and the feeling (trust); often (adverbially or without preposition) safely." It is a beautiful thought. The neighbor has rested in a feeling of security by you, having no fear of any harm at your hands. Now then, do not betray that confidence by devising or practicing some evil against him.

Verse 30. It is the claim of national lawmakers that our constitution and acts of legislation are based on principles taught in the Bible. It is right that such is the case. The Mosaic system was a combination of religious and civil law, and it was the only government the Jews had. Since that system ceased as it was, and the Christian Dispensation came in, the Lord does not legislate in civil affairs directly. However, he wishes man to have some civil government and endorses the existence of such (Rom. 13: 1-6). It is a mark of good judgment, therefore, for human legislators to respect the laws of the Old Testament in formulating those for our day. And we should also bear in mind that many individual laws set forth obligations that have to do with both one's duty to God and to man. That was true of the verse cited in this paragraph. The courts of the land recognize this principle of fairness in dealing with a fellow citizen. If a man attempts to bring a suit at law and the courts consider the claim of the plaintiff without foundation they will "throw it out of court."

Verse 31. To envy another is to be grieved because of his success; to begrudge him his good fortune. The idea of this verse is that an oppressor (violent man) really has nothing to be envious of. What a man seems to gain in that way will prove to be vain and worthless when all of the results of such a life are made known.

Verse 32. A *froward* man is one who is wayward and stubborn with it. Such a character is abominable in the sight of the Lord. *His secret* means the Lord will be intimate and friendly with a righteous man.

Verse 33. To *curse another* means either to cause him some undesirable experience or at least to wish it upon him. The Lord can do both, and of course the undesirable experience He would cause to come upon a wicked house would be just.

Verse 34. According to Strong, to *scorn* means to "make mouths at, i. e., to scoff." In this verse it is attributed to both God and man. The word is contrasted with *the lowly* in the same verse, as it applies to man. Hence the meaning of the verse is that if a man is proud and makes light of things and persons who are good, then God will belittle that man and abase him. (Luke 14: 11.)

Verse 35. This is practically the same as the preceding verse as to the proud and humble. It also has the same kind of promise as Jesus made in Matt. 5: 5, and the apostle also taught the same principle in 2 Pe. 3: 13.

PROVERBS 4

Verse 1. This verse is addressed to children in general. Solomon wrote as a father in the general sense also, and as an inspired instructor to his and other sons.

Verse 2. *Doctrine* is another name for teaching. The teaching of Solomon would be good doctrine because he was an inspired man.

Verse 3. The personal experiences of Solomon could have been told without the qualification of inspiration, but the recording of them in the Bible was done by the guidance of that faculty to insure their accuracy.

Verse 4. Solomon had great respect for David's teaching even if he did not always carry it out in his own life.

Verse 5. For distinctions between *wisdom* and *understanding* see the comments at ch. 3: 13. To decline from the words of the wise man meant to hesitate at doing them.

Verse 6. *Forsake* is negative and *love* is positive as it concerns the attitude toward the words of wisdom. It is not enough to say of one that he will not forsake the teaching of wisdom coming from the great man; but he should love it. (Matt. 5: 6.)

Verse 7. See the comments on ch. 3: 13 on the distinctive meaning of these words. While wisdom is the principal thing, yet if it is not used properly the benefits will be far from what they should and could be.

Verse 8. All of these remarks of the wise man have to do with the proper attitude toward wisdom. A mere toleration of a good thing will not suffice. It must be ardently loved and embraced. It is like the interest one should have in partaking of the things that pertain to righteousness. (Matt. 5: 6.)

Verse 9. These ornaments are figurative, and the comparison is made because of the value of wisdom and understanding when attached to a person's character.

Verse 10. There was no literal lengthening of a man's life promised as a reward for his acceptance of the wisdom. See the comments at ch. 3: 2 for explanation.

Verse 11. Solomon was a wise man in all of his teaching although he did not live up to his own words, especially in the latter part of his life.

Verse 12. The pronoun *thou* refers to the *son* of v. 10. The verse points out some of the good results of following the words of wisdom offered him. He will not be *straitened* (hindered) in his daily life. *Runnest* refers to the occasions when he would need to make haste in his conduct. If the young man has been relying on the good instruction offered him by this father in Israel, he will not be in any danger of *stumbling* or making a misstep and falling by the wayside.

Verse 13. No additional information on the subject of wisdom is given in this verse. It is rather an exhortation to heed the instructions already given.

Verse 14. The *path of the wicked* means their manner of life, also the association formed thereby. It is dangerous for a young man to form evil companionships (1 Cor. 15: 33), even if he does not intend to take part in their evil deeds.

Verse 15. In view of the preceding advice the young man should avoid the company of wicked persons as he would a rank poison or a vicious beast.

Verse 16. These wicked persons are so devoted to their life of crime that no day is allowed to close without some evil deed having been done. Should they retire at night and recall that no misdeed had been done that day it would be counted as a day lost. The thought of it would so disturb them that they could not go to sleep.

Verse 17. These evil persons do not relish their meals unless they were procured through fraud or violent robbery.

Verse 18. The life practices of mankind do not come to a standstill as regards good and evil. The first will grow into more and greater goodness, while the second will get worse and worse. Hence this verse says that the *path* (life practice) of the just will get brighter and brighter as the person gets nearer the end, even down to the "last mile of the way."

Verse 19. The experiences of the

wicked are just the opposite of that described in the preceding verse. These men not only stumble, but, being in the dark, they do not even know what it was over which they stumbled.

Verse 20. To *attend* means to listen attentively, not merely give a casual hearing. Incline denotes that he goes further than an attentive hearing. It means he is also favorably impressed with what he hears.

Verse 21. Words are not things that literally can be seen. The idea is to see with the mental vision and to keep looking for the good words of advice from the wise man. The last clause of the verse is a little more direct in its meaning. If a young man keeps looking (mentally) for and at the wise sayings of the teacher, that will result in the storing of the words in the heart from where they will come forth in deeds.

Verse 22. Spiritual life and health is what is meant in this passage. The mention of temporal things such as flesh is figurative, because both the flesh and inner beings were created by the same God, and there is much sameness in the laws governing them in their activities and also in their treatment when out of order.

Verse 23. The *heart* is the innermost part of a person, including his mind and emotions. It is the part that thinks; that has motives; that decides for or against any proposition suggested, whether good of bad. That is why Solomon says that the *issues* (source) of life are from the heart. Jesus taught the same truth in Matt. 12: 34 and 15: 19. David likewise considered the heart in that light in Ps. 19: 14.

Verse 24. *Froward mouth* and *perverse lips* mean the same and are given for the purpose of emphasis. The meaning of frowardness is stubborn waywardness.

Verse 25. The idea is to look ahead and not become interested in the attractions along the side of the road of life. To do so may result in sidestepping and finally a failure to reach the desired goal at the end of life's journey.

Verse 26. Strong gives "to weigh mentally" as a meaning of the original for *ponder*. This is the same thought that Paul set forth in Eph. 5: 15. If a man thinks and looks carefully about his walk in life his *ways* will be *established* or well ordered.

Verse 27. This verse contains the same subject matter as v. 25, with an additional implied reasoning in the last clause. We would think of the word *remove* as an active or positive one. Yet it is really a negative term as it is used here. It is somewhat like a familiar saying, "an ounce of prevention is worth a pound of cure." By keeping in the strait pathway of righteousness the young man will avoid the steps of evil at the side of the road. Hence in that negative manner he will *remove his foot from evil*. It will be a kind of negative righteousness with a positive effect for good.

PROVERBS 5

Verse 1. *Attend* means to give respectful attention. *Bow thine ear* is virtually the same in sense as the first clause with the added idea of condescension or humility.

Verse 2. By taking heed to the teaching of Solomon, the young man will know how to use *discretion* (good judgment) in his conduct. To *keep knowledge* means to keep the use of it in all of life's relations regarding principles of right and wrong.

Verse 3. Solomon had much to say of the *strange* woman. The word literally means one outside of the people of God as a race. By extension it means a woman whose manner of life is different from that of the faithful servants of the Lord, whether she be of the Jew or Gentile stock. Such a woman uses flattering words to lure the young man into her path. *Drops as an honeycomb* refers to the sweetness that flattery seems to possess. For comments on the reference to the honeycomb see those at Ps. 19: 10. Flattery also has a smoothness like oil which makes it agreeable.

Verse 4. *Wormwood* was a plant growing in Palestine and was very bitter, some varieties also being poisonous. It is frequently referred to in a figurative sense in the Bible to symbolize the experiences of sorrow and/or death. The *end* (result or outcome) of following in the path of the "strange woman" is here compared to the bitter plant, and it is compared to the sting of a two-edged sword.

Verse 5. This verse is another wording of the thought in the preceding one. *Hell* is from SHEOL which means either a state of forgetfulness in this world, or of utter ruin in the world to come when the sentence of the great judgment day is pronounced.

Verse 6. The life of the strange

woman is deceitful and changeable. The temptation would be to *ponder* or study over it so as to solve the mystery. That is why the wise man offered his advice to keep the "son" from pondering over it.

Verse 7. Solomon uses the term *children* in the same sense he has that of "son." See the comments at ch. 1: 10 for explanation of this use of the word.

Verse 8. The only safe and wise thing to do is to stay as far away from evil as possible. There can be no good come from the house of a corrupt woman, hence the young man should avoid her as he would the den of a vicious beast.

Verse 9. No good man can actually give his honor to a wicked woman by patronizing her. The thought is that in associating with her he lets her destroy his honor. Moreover, by such a life of dissipation he will shorten his days and in that way he will be giving his *years unto the cruel*.

Verse 10. See one of the several previous paragraphs for the meaning of *strangers*. And see the preceding verse on the meaning of giving what he has to another.

Verse 11. This verse refers to the wasting disease that is contracted by intimacy with an immoral woman. For more detailed comments on this fearful subject, see what is offered in ch. 7: 23.

Verse 12. After this awful condition comes to the young man he will recall the many words of warning that were offered to him. He will admit, then, that he *despised* (belittled) those warning words, and in so doing was counted as having hated them.

Verse 13. Solomon was not the only one who had given words of warning to the young man. All persons who had the proper regard would be alert to warn young men of the pitfalls. Alas that so often they would turn a deaf ear to the warning.

Verse 14. *Evil* is from RAH, which Strong defines, bad or (as noun) evil (natural or moral)." The word could apply in all of its senses to this young man. Here he was, in the midst of the congregation and surrounded with all the inducements for clean living. Yet he ignored all those good influences and wasted his physical and moral strength on corrupt women. That brought upon him the contempt of his people.

Verse 15. This and several following verses offer an exhortation to the young (married) man to be true to his lawful partner in the intimacies of life. The terms are used figuratively but very clearly set forth the thought of the writer. The demands of the flesh have been created by the Lord and are not in themselves sinful. But the Lord has ordained the marriage relation as the lawful means of meeting those demands. What Solomon means is for the man to be true to his wife and live with her only.

Verse 16. In this verse the wise man seeks to warn the "son" not to expose his lawful pleasures to the corrupting influences of others, but keep them to himself and within the proper regulations as regards his moral obligations.

Verse 17. The corrupt woman would profess to enjoy the pleasures that the young man would give her by his association with her. The advice is for him to keep them to himself as far as the strange woman is concerned, and exercise them with his wife.

Verse 18. *Fountain* is from MAQOR and I will quote the part of Strong's definition needed here: "source . . . figuratively, of happiness, wisdom, progeny." From this definition we see that the *fountain* which Solomon had in mind was the man's wife. He was to let her be blessed; that is, be treated with proper respect. The second clause has the same thought in different words. *Wife of thy youth* might suggest the idea that Solomon was writing about a man advanced in years. All of the instructions would be appropriate for such a man but the connection shows he is still addressing his remarks to the "son." It is well known that even young husbands sometimes tire of their wives and cast their eyes upon another (strange) woman. Solomon would remind him that his wife was young like him and he should be satisfied with her.

Verse 19. The comparison is made to some attractive creatures of the animal kingdom that are of the more timid and refined character. *Breasts satisfy thee* refers to some of the intimacies that belong to the relation of husband and wife. It is the same procedure that is meant in the second clause of the Song of Solomon, 2: 6. *Ravished* is from SHAGAH and Strong defines it in part, "by extension (through the idea of intoxication) to reel (figuratively) be enraptured." *Love* is from an original which Strong defines, "to have affection for (sexually or otherwise)." Thus the verse means that a husband should be so much in love with his wife that he will always find his complete sexual thrill and satisfaction with her. In that case he will not even be interested in a "strange" woman enough to look in her direction.

Verse 20. This does not present any new material, but is a challenge to the young man to explain why he would not follow the advice offered to him.

Verse 21. Over and above all reasons stated so far, there is the most important one yet to be considered. The Lord knows all about man's conduct and will bring him to an account in the last great day of judgment.

Verse 22. This verse is a way of saying that a wicked man will likely be caught in the trap that he had set for another.

Verse 23. *Die without instruction* denotes that for lack of instruction he shall die or come to a state of ruin. And his folly or foolishness is so great that he will wander off from the pathway of good judgment and be lost.

PROVERBS 6

Verse 1. *Friend* is from a word defined by Strong, "an associate (more or less close)." Hence it does not necessarily mean one who is a genuine friend in the strongest sense of the word. *Stranger* is still less *close* than this *friend*. Solomon is giving advice about becoming a bondman for these persons.

Verse 2. There is an old saying that "a certain way to lose a friend is to loan him some money." I do not know haw far this should be carried, but I am sure there is much truth in it. Solomon had such a thought in mind when he wrote the words of this verse. *Snared* and *taken* mean that the "son" had placed himself in a snare or trap by agreeing to go on the other fellow's bond.

Verse 3. Before the matter goes on and becomes fixed, he should have the promise released. *Humble thyself* denotes that he should go to his "friend" and beg to be released from a bond that he did not realize at the time; he had "spoken too soon."

Verse 4. He should not wait over a single night, but go while the same date is in the calendar. One thing to be gained by going immediately, the other fellow could not have as much occasion to say he had already arranged his business according to the transaction and that it would have to stand.

Verse 5. When a creature in the class of game is first taken is when it makes its most active struggles to get loose. Sometimes it may not have been caught quite completely, so that if it makes a desperate effort while it still has all its strength it may get loose. Solomon cites this illustration to urge the young man to undo his unwise action while the chances are the best.

Verse 6. A *sluggard* is a person who is inactive through laziness. He will let many opportunities pass by because he does not want to bestir himself. *Go to the ant* means "go and observe the ant and take a lesson from the wisdom of her activities."

Verse 7. That is, she does not have any one immediately at hand to see that she performs her duty in providing for the future.

Verse 8. Smith's Bible Dictionary states that there are two species of ants called "harvesting ants," and that they do lay up food as the verse here states. The wisdom and diligence of these ants are seen in that they work while it is the best time.

Verse 9. The wise man asks a criticizing question and accuses the sluggard of being asleep. This would not be literal sleep in all instances, but his laziness is as bad as it regards his usefulness as literal sleep would be.

Verse 10. This verse is a picture of the sluggard along the same line as the preceding verse. *Folding of the hands* is a physical action and is given as a synonym of *slumber*. That indicates the sleep referred to is the sleep of laziness.

Verse 11. *Come and travelleth* should be considered together in order to get the point. If one travels he does not merely stroll along leisurely and slowly; he makes some speed. So will poverty come to this lazy man very speedily. *An armed man* overpowers his victim who is often overtaken unprepared. Thus a lazy man is not prepared to resist the poverty that comes as a result of his indolence.

Verse 12. The original for *naughty* is a stronger word than is commonly considered. The lexicon defines it, "without profit, worthlessness; by extension, destruction, wickedness." Hence we have another word with practically the same meaning and which the translators have rendered *wicked* in this verse. A *froward mouth* is one that stubbornly speaks contrary to the right way of life.

Verse 13. *Eyes, feet* and *fingers* are named because they are parts of the body that act as the outward fruit of the thoughts. This external manifestation is mentioned first, and the basis of it will be shown in the next verse.

Verse 14. *Frowardness* is stubborn waywardness, and such a sentiment in the heart would lead to such conduct as that described in the preceding verse. As a result of said conduct we would expect to witness discord among the people.

Verse 15. This verse takes the same comments as verse 11.

Verse 16. *Six things ... yea seven*. It will not be well to lay too much stress on *seven*, although when used alone and figuratively it denotes completeness. Also the combination of *six* with it should not be pressed too far. In ch. 30: 18-24 the numbers three and four are used in a somewhat similar figure of speech. So the safest and most reasonable view of it is to think of it about as we use such terms as "two or three; four or five; six or seven," and so on. No doubt Solomon could have named even more than seven things which the Lord hates, but he sets forth enough to give us a complete picture of His attitude toward evil characters.

Verse 17. It has been said that "the eyes are the windows of the soul." Hence *a proud look* would indicate a heart tainted with pride, and that is a principle that is always condemned in the Bible. Truth is the sweetest and most valuable sentiment possible to intelligent creatures. How unspeakably wicked, then, is the opposite one. No wonder the apostle declared that all liars would have their part in the lake of fire. (Rev. 21: 8.) The reader should observe the distinction of *innocent* blood. If an officer of the law or other person acting under the law must execute a convict capitally, he will not be shedding *innocent* blood, but would be shedding *GUILTY* blood. But the verse we are now considering does not condemn that kind of act.

Verse 18. To *devise* means to plan and scheme and premeditate. All sins are condemned by the Lord, but those that are deliberately committed are more severely condemned and the Lord hates them. *Swift* does not refer to speed especially, but to the idea of being always ready and eager to go into mischief.

Verse 19. All false witnesses are liars, but not all liars are false witnesses in the sense of this verse. It refers to a person in connection with the legal affairs of another. If such a person should make some false entry on the docket against another citizen, or, if placed on the stand as a witness would give false testimony, he would come under this verse. *Soweth discord* would require whole discourses and volumes to exhaust its significance. There are so many ways by which it can and is being done that the nature of this work makes it out of the question to go into all detail. I will take space only to say that any handling of even the facts of a case in such a manner that it alienates brethren from each other will provoke the Lord's fury to the uttermost and justly so, for no sin can be any greater.

Verses 20, 21. This same advice is contained in ch. 1: 8, 9 and I request the student to read my comments at that place.

Verse 22. *Goest, sleepest* and *awakest* are used to signify the general activities of the young man. In all of life's relations he will be safeguarded by the instructions which he received from his ancestors if he will observe them.

Verse 23. *Lamp* and *light* are used figuratively, referring to the same thought explained in the preceding verse. *Reproofs of instruction* is a very significant term. Another form of the same thought is, "constructive criticism." To criticize one for the pure sake of finding fault is wrong and will not accomplish a good purpose. But a reproof that is coupled with information as to how the person should perform, will lead him into the right way if anything will.

Verse 24. Evil women was the subject that seems to have been Solomon's chief concern. The history of his life may explain that to us. He had a thousand women connected with him in some form of social relation, and most if not all of them were the wrong kind of characters. In his inspired writings he sought to save other men from the pitfalls of which he had so often been a victim. He especially warned against *flattery* of these women. The lexicon definition of this word is "smoothness," and the idea is of a woman who can choose her words in such a manner that they sound good to the ear. The pleasant sensation caused by such speech causes the young man to overlook the poison that is lurking in the background of the conversation.

Verse 25. The warning in this verse scarcely needs any explanation. It refers to the suggestive flirtations that a pretty but evil woman would make to a young man.

Verse 26. Yes, there are instances without number where men have spent their last dollar on an immoral woman, not even leaving any wherewith to purchase the necessities of life for the faithful wife and innocent children. *Hunt for the precious life* describes the heartlessness of the professionally immoral woman. She has no mercy for a man's legal dependents; she seeks only the patronage of the man in order to get his money, or to gratify her own lust, or both.

Verses 27, 28. A man may try to flatter himself into thinking he is strong enough to indulge in pleasurable conduct that is wrong without being hurt. The reasoning of the wise man is that such is not possible.

Verse 29. It is always wrong to patronize an immoral woman. This verse considers the subject from a special angle. The *neighbor's wife* would not be in the class with the public woman. She may or may not be an immoral woman in her general practice. If she is not, the man who goes in to her must first seduce her, and that would be a violation of several principles. It would be taking advantage of her own weakness to satisfy his unlawful desire which amounts to a form of robbery. And if the woman is inclined to evil so that the association is mutual, then the guilty man violates the rights of his neighbor. In any case, the whole affair is grievously wrong and stains the participants with shame.

Verse 30. Robbery is never right, but the motive that prompts an act will have some bearing on the degree of guilt attached thereto. If a man is actually hungry his act could not be attributed to the spirit of crime. Such a man would not be *despised;* he would not be regarded with contempt as would the wilful thief.

Verse 31. This verse shows that Solomon did not mean to encourage theft in the preceding verse. If a man really thinks he is in serious trouble for want of food and cannot wait to be helped, he would better partake of enough to satisfy his immediate weakness and then leave the rest and get away. If he is found it will indicate that perhaps his motive was not for his present distress, but it was to lay up for later use. In that case he is to be penalized to the limit of his resources.

Verse 32. The wise man is back on one of his familiar subjects. *Lacketh understanding* means the man is not using good sense. Such a person is sacrificing all there is worth having by his violation of chastity.

Verse 33. This *wound* may not refer to the physical result of the sin, but rather to that inflicted upon his character, for it is connected with *dishonor*, and we know that refers to his character or reputation. Not *be wiped away* denotes that such a stain upon one's character will trail him throughout life.

Verse 34. Even if the guilty man should accomplish his purpose for the present, he will be exposed to the jealousy of the woman's husband. He will either satisfy his jealous rage by inflicting some bodily harm on the culprit, or by "shadowing" him all his days with the cloud of scandal that his crime produced.

Verse 35. The pronoun *he* refers to the husband of the woman in v. 32. This verse means that he will be so enraged over the violation of his home that he will not accept any "hush" money.

PROVERBS 7

Verse 1. See the comments at ch. 1: 10 for the meaning of *son*. Laying up the commandments means to store them up in the heart for use in the future.

Verse 2. To *keep* is a stronger word than *laying up* in the preceding verse, denoting the observing of them. The result will be to *live* in a moral and spiritual sense. The *apple* or pupil of the eye is a very valuable possession, and used to compare the great worth of the divine law.

Verse 3. This verse is a figure of speech. If something is attached to the fingers it will always be present for use. It also will not likely be forgotten since it will always be in sight. To write the commandments on the heart is the same idea expressed by David in Ps. 119: 11.

Verse 4. *Sister* and *kinswoman* are used to illustrate the affectionate value of wisdom and the nearness of the relationship that would be desirable.

Verse 5. If such pure and refined principles as these divine commandments are cherished by a young man, it will serve to save him from the corrupt intimacies of the *strange* woman. Mention of this woman again seems to have brought the wise man to a decision to write his masterpiece in description of the typical harlot.

Verse 6. *Casement* is from an original that Strong defines, "a latticed window." Solomon looked out through that opening and saw what he is about to describe. It cannot be determined whether, a certain instance was being considered, or if he meant to describe a typical case as an example. The 9th verse indicates the latter view as I will explain below. But in either case, the description is complete and is written by a man who was inspired, besides being one whose experiences in life were many.

Verse 7. This young man was not unintelligent, but was a thoughtless, inconsiderate person who did not use good sense in his conduct.

Verse 8. This does not mean he was purposely walking toward the woman's house. He had not as yet thought about her that we know, but the writer is giving us that information. He was out on a public street but happened to be on one that lead in that direction of this woman's house.

Verse 9. This verse indicates that Solomon was not writing of any specific instance, for the same man would not be met in the twilight and then late at night on the same date. It shows that such a woman as the wise man was considering would be on the lookout for a victim at all hours of the night. However, it would be at some time after close of the day as the darkened hours would best serve her purpose.

Verse 10. There were some kinds of articles worn by harlots that distinguished them from other women. (Gen. 38: 14.) *Subtil of heart* means she was deceitful and disposed to use misleading statements in a way that would make a false impression.

Verse 11. One of Strong's meanings of the original for *loud* is, "to be in great commotion." The word for *stubborn* is defined by Strong, "to turn away, i. e. (morally) be refractory [rebellious]." The main thought in this verse is, this woman is all in commotion in her desire for indulgence and would rebel at any attempt to restrain her. For that reason she will not be content to spend her time in the privacy of her home. This will be a proper place to remind the reader that not all harlots are in that kind of life for the sake of money. As an illustration exactly in point see the instance in Ezekiel 16: 31-34. Some of them are intent on the gratification of their own lust. And a married harlot would tire of her lawful husband and be restless to get out and watch for a younger man, hence the last clause of this verse.

Verse 12. So she gets out onto the street to hunt for her prey. She takes a lurking position first at one *corner*, then at another. By posting herself at a corner she could look for the traffic on two streets at one time.

Verse 13. To *catch* sometimes indicates that an attempt had already been made to flee. But the word here means to grab or seize quickly for fear the victim might flee. At the same instant when she seized upon the young man she kissed him. That would show him that no violence was intended against him. And the magnetic kiss of a woman, out on the street in the shadows of night, would hold the young man in her grasp as certainly as if she had thrown a chain about him. While in the "spell" of the sudden circumstance, she began her conversation with him. *Impudent face* means she looked at him with a countenance that was firm and set.

Verse 14. The language of this verse indicates the woman professed to be religious. According to Funk and Wagnalls Bible Dictionary harlotry was very prevalent even among the Jews in ancient times. It might have been one of the things that God "winked at" (Acts 17: 30). The purpose of the woman's statement was to show that she was attentive to her obligations to the Lord and was free to turn her attention to personal interests and matters pertaining to her own enjoyment.

Verse 15. Having discharged her duties, she was ready to go in search of a good time with some associate. In her flattering strain she would pretend that she had come out in the hopes of meeting just such a fine young man as this one, and lo, how fortunate that she had found him; just the kind of man she was seeking for.

Verse 16. She began her seductions by describing the luxury of her bed. Such a picture was suggestive of a time of complete abandon and indulgence.

Verse 17. We might wonder why the woman mentioned these dainties in connection with her attempts at seduction. It was because she was acquainted with the effect of perfumes as a stimulant for a man's emotional nerves. A very noted doctor and psychologist, member of the faculty of a modern educational institution, says this on the subject: "A perfumed girl is likely to be a greater mental stimulus for erotic feeling," etc. I quote this to show that the woman in Solomon's case understood the subject of seducing a young man by means of these stimulants.

Verse 18. Having built up her background of alluring suggestions, the woman came directly to the subject and made the proposal that he spend the night with her.

Verse 19. But he might hesitate lest they be surprised by her husband. She had already anticipated that and so she told him that the man was not at home but had gone on a *long journey*, so that he would need have no fears from that source.

Verse 20. But even the term *long time* is somewhat indefinite and the man might return almost any time. Again she was prepared to set his mind at ease on that matter. The man of the house had taken a bag of money which denoted that he intended to be gone a considerable time. Besides all this, the very day of his return had already been determined when he left. It was to be at the time of the next new moon. The original word for *appointed* is KECEH and Strong defines it, "fulness or the full moon, i. e., its festival." That settled it as to the time when the man would return. So "the coast was clear" and everything was set for an uninterrupted season of indulgence.

Verse 21. *Forced* means she overpersuaded him by her flattery and other smooth talk.

Verse 22. The reference to the ox and the fool is to illustrate the complete subjection of this young man to the wiles of the woman.

Verse 23. *Dart strike through his liver* is figurative and refers to the terrible infectious disease that the young man contracted by his contact with this morally and physically corrupt woman. The verse begins with the word *till*, which denotes that the state of unawareness described in the preceding verse continued until the young man realized what had been the result of his union with this vile woman. The *liver* is mentioned not because it is especially affected by the disease, but because it is a large organ of the body and thus figuratively represents much of a man's vitality. There is something remarkable about this subject. We know that the relation of the sexes is a perfectly natural one and should not result in any kind of disease. And we also know that the terrible disease under consideration is a venereal one; that it never would have existed without the union of the sexes. The conclusion is unavoidable, therefore, that it has been brought into the world by the Lord as a penalty for the sin of man in abusing one of the most important functions of the human body.

Verse 24. Having completed his details of the special example, Solomon makes a general appeal for his people to give attention to his words.

Verse 25. *Decline* means to go down, and thus the conduct with a *strange* woman is a downward step morally and physically.

Verse 26. Yes, many strong men have been brought down by the influence of bad women, and Solomon was one of them. (Neh. 13: 6.)

Verse 27. *Hell* is from a word that includes all of the conditions of ruin and forgetfulness that are awaiting men who waste their lives in sinful practices. Among those practices is that of contact with corrupt women.

PROVERBS 8

Verse 1. Solomon now takes up his main specialty which is *wisdom*. I have called attention to other words used in this book that have similar meanings and yet require some distinction. Wisdom, understanding, knowledge, instruction and discretion are all used by Solomon somewhat indiscriminately which shows that they mean practically the same thing. But the first one is used more prominently than the others, and where some other term is not used in connection, it is to be understood as standing for all the principles contained in the others named above. I shall make one more comment as to a distinction, then proceed with the one word as practically including all the others. The distinction is between wisdom and understanding. The second means the proper or common sense use of the first.

Verse 2. Wisdom is the antecedent of various pronouns (she, I, it, her, me, my) in this and following verses. *Standeth in the top* means that the highest places in the country are benefitted by the use of wisdom.

Verse 3. Solomon does not mean that in all of these places men act with wisdom. The idea is that in all such places there is great need for wisdom.

Verse 4. Mankind in general is called upon to listen to wisdom and act accordingly.

Verse 5. *Simple* and *fools* may be intelligent persons but do not listen to the voice of wisdom in their ways of life and hence make many grievous mistakes.

Verse 6. *Excellent things* are those superior to others. Such things will be accomplished or possessed if men will act with wisdom.

Verse 7. It is always wise to speak the truth. It is also a mark of wisdom to practice righteousness, for wickedness is abominable to those who love wisdom.

Verse 8. *Froward* and *perverse* are about the same in meaning and are used for emphasis. It means to be stubbornly wayward, which is just the opposite of wisdom.

Verse 9. The antecedent of *they* is *words* in v. 8. If a man will use his common sense *(understanding)* he will realize that the words of Solomon are plain and clear.

Verse 10. As a contrast, Solomon sets instruction and knowledge above silver and gold in value.

Verse 11. After specifying certain articles that are less valuable than wisdom, the writer makes a sweeping comparison. He places wisdom above anything else that one can desire. That rules out any possible exception, and is in perfect agreement with David's exaltation of the Word of God in Ps. 138: 2, for we must remember that Solomon spoke by the inspiration of God and hence his words are the words of Him.

Verse 12. *Prudence* has the same meaning as discretion. *Witty* has no original as a separate word, but *inventions* is from a word that means "plans." The whole verse means that a man of wisdom will make his plans with discretion.

Verse 13. If a man fears or respects the Lord he will hate evil, for the Lord hates it. A man of wisdom will also hate *arrogancy* (self-exaltation) and other evils.

Verse 14. *Counsel* is the same as good advice. All the other good things named in this verse will be found wherever *I* (wisdom) can be recognized.

Verse 15. The greatest kings and judges in the world are those who act according to wisdom. That is better than proceeding on the basis of "policy" or partiality.

Verse 16. This verse takes the same comments as the preceding one.

Verse 17. As a reminder, let the reader understand that the pronouns stand for *wisdom*. Love is indicated by extending favors. If a man will show his love for wisdom he will obtain favors from her that cannot be had otherwise. The degree of love that one has for wisdom will be indicated by his efforts to find it. If he seeks *early* it means he is actually hungry for it (Matt. 5: 6) and is assured of finding it.

Verse 18. Even material riches will be more likely to come to the man who acts with wisdom. There is no question that spiritual wealth *(riches and righteousness)* will be reaped by the man who uses wisdom in his activities.

Verse 19. As gold is when it comes from the earth, all mixed with the dross—even then it is of some value. It is still more valuable after it has become *fine gold* (gone through the refinery). But the fruit of wisdom is better than gold in whatever form. And the business transactions with the best of silver cannot compare with the dealing that is conducted on the principles of wisdom.

Verse 20. *Lead* is from a word that means to walk or travel. The *way* and *paths* described in this verse correspond with those given in Ps. 1: 1. Wisdom is always to be found in these lanes of travel.

Verse 21. A literal and specific reward of temporal possessions is not guaranteed to those who accept the wisdom offered. But the logical result of using wisdom is to be rewarded with good fortune. It is similar to the assurance in Matt. 6: 33.

Verse 22. Wisdom was one of the traits that the Lord possessed in all of his existence, which was and is and will be, from everlasting to everlasting.

Verse 23. *Everlasting* as applied to God means without beginning or ending. Wisdom has been with Him in all of his being as expressed in the preceding verse. Yes, wisdom was with the Lord *or ever* (before ever) *the earth was*. This quality was used by the Lord in planning the earth and all that pertains to it.

Verses 24, 25. The land and water portions of the earth's surface came *after* the exercise of wisdom. That proves that these things were created by some Being who already possessed the faculty.

Verse 26. The pronoun *he* refers to the Creator. The thought of the verse is that He had wisdom always, and used it when he made the parts of the universe named.

Verse 27. *Heavens* is plural as it should be and means the same as Gen. 2: 1. The region where the birds fly is the first heaven, and that where the planets are is the second. These heavens were formed according to the wisdom of the Lord. *Compass* means a circle and *depth* is defined in the lexicon as the sea. The clause refers to the circular form of the earth. The so-called scientists discovered that the earth is round after five thousand years had rolled by. Had they consulted the Bible they would have learned it long before. It required *wisdom* to devise and execute a circular form for the earth, and then hold the mighty oceans in their place in that shape.

Verse 28. The laws of nature by which the watering of the earth takes place were all ordained by the wisdom of God. The deep sends up vapor by the force of the sun, then it is condensed and formed into clouds that send the rain upon the earth. All of this is by the infinite wisdom of the Creator.

Verse 29. In spite of the surging of the tide that seems to be trying to leap out of bounds, yet in a few hours the billows recede into their proper places. And there are no visible foundations of the earth, yet it is firmly fixed and has never slipped out of its place. All of this is by the wisdom of God.

Verse 30. The pronouns *I* and *him* refer to wisdom and God. *As one brought up*, etc., uses the illustration of a parent and child because of the constant association. So God has never been without wisdom, and all of His works have been done by it.

Verse 31. This verse means that wherever there are inhabitants on the earth, their *rejoicing* and *delights* have been in proportion to their usage of wisdom.

Verse 32. After citing so much that the Lord perfected in connection with wisdom, Solomon sees an appropriate time to let wisdom make another exhortation. She (wisdom) addresses herself to the people as *ye children*, and tells them they will be *blessed* or happy if they will *keep* her *ways*, which means to walk in wisdom's ways.

Verse 33. *Hear instruction* means to accept information from the teacher who is *wisdom* personified by the various pronouns. If they will do so they will also be wise.

Verse 34. *Blessed* or happy is the man who will hear the voice of wisdom. *Gates* and *doors* mark the entrances to cities and houses. They are used here to illustrate the entrance to the place where wisdom may be found. If one is seen *waiting* and *watching* at such places, it indicates that he is indeed eager to obtain it. He will surely obtain his object and it will bring him the happiness promised. It is like the assurance that Jesus gave in his great speech on the mount (Matt. 5: 6).

Verse 35. To find *me* (wisdom) means to find life, for no man can truly be said to be living who rejects wisdom. While the acceptance and use of wisdom will please the Lord and it will bring forth favors from Him.

Verse 36. To reject wisdom is a sin, and the man who does so really does wrong to himself. It will injure his *soul* which means his whole being. Since life and death are opposite, the person who rejects wisdom (the thing that is necessary to life) acts as if he loves death. It would be well to consider Matt. 6: 24.

PROVERBS 9

Verse 1. Wisdom is still the principal subject of the Book of Proverbs. Its importance has been illustrated by a great variety of comparisons. For several verses in this chapter the writer thinks of the abundant provisions that wisdom offers to the children of men. The illustration he uses is that of a spacious and well built house, with arrangements for entertaining all who will come to be guests. But the material articles mentioned should be understood to represent the rich fare of genuine wisdom. In this verse the house has been erected.

When *seven* is used alone and figuratively it means completeness. Hence the house of wisdom is resting on firm support.

Verse 2. A hostess in a large mansion who expects to entertain a great many guests would prepare much meat and drink for her table. The material articles represent the mental and spiritual good things in store for those to be served by *wisdom*.

Verse 3. The illustration further carries out the idea of a generous hostess who even makes preparation just in case she may have some guests. Yea, she goes still further and sends her waitresses *(maidens)* out to solicit guests.

Verse 4. *Simple* means one who is willing to be influenced, and, as used in this place, to be influenced for good. It does not mean that the person is unintelligent. The word for *understanding* is used in the sense of knowledge. These persons are being invited to come to the (mental) feast that this generous hostess, *wisdom*, prepared.

Verse 5. As already explained, this eating and drinking means the receiving of words of wisdom that are being served in the home or house of seven pillars.

Verse 6. *Foolish* is from the same original as *simple* in v. 4, but in this place it is used in the sense of being silly or not using good sense. The invitation is to get away from persons who act in that way and come to the table supplied with the food for understanding and so freely offered to those who will partake.

Verse 7. Let us suppose the invited one should ask, "Why are you inviting me to this feast of wisdom. Do you think I am a person with no intelligence?" The *maiden* would answer, "No, if I thought you were that kind of person I would not think it worth while to invite you for *he that reproveth a scorner getteth to himself shame*. But, while I believe you are intelligent naturally, I hoped you were hungry for something to feed that intelligence, and my hostess has prepared just that and you are invited and even earnestly solicited to come and share the banquet.

Verse 8. This verse will have the same comments as the preceding one.

Verse 9. This verse means virtually the same as the two preceding ones except that it is on the affirmation and favorable side. A man who is inclined to use good sense in his conduct will be glad to be taught and will profit by the same.

Verse 10. See the comments on ch. 1: 7 for explanation of this.

Verse 11. The pronoun *me* stands for wisdom. There is no literal guarantee of long life for those who accept wisdom. The thought is that by wise and sensible living one has the better prospect for long life.

Verse 12. The outstanding point here is individual responsibility. If a man accepts wisdom he will be the first to profit by it. If he rejects it he will likewise be the first to suffer and also will be the chief sufferer from it.

Verse 13. It will be seen below that by a *foolish woman*, Solomon means the immoral one. By *clamorous* he shows her to be restless and all in commotion for some associate with her in sin. *Simple* means she does not realize how silly she is acting.

Verse 14. This woman follows a different plan from the one in ch. 7, for that one went out onto the streets in search for a partner. This one occupies a house on a prominent street *(high places)* of the city, and takes a seat at the door of her house.

Verse 15. *Passengers* means people who were passing by. This woman hails them and solicits their patronage.

Verse 16. This verse is Solomon's way of saying that none but the *simple* (those easily seduced) will listen to the call of such a woman. But she knows that many men throw away their common sense when facing the lure of fleshly pleasure. So she makes some suggestive remarks like those of the next verse.

Verse 17. One prominent trait of the human being is to crave most that which he is supposed not to have. This woman knows about such a trait and uses it for her own wicked plans. Her words here are to the same purpose as those of ch. 7: 19, where the woman informed the young man that they would be alone since the man of the house was gone. The idea here is to get the man passing by to think of the seclusion that will surround them. He may then be led to steal into her house, out of sight of the public and of his own family if he has one, and there indulge himself.

Verse 18. Not literal *dead* men are in the house for that is not her business. But all men who go into such a house, or go in to such a woman, will be tinctured with a stain that will mean their moral and spiritual death. And moreover, they will be smitten with the "dart" mentioned in ch. 7: 23, referring to the terrible disease generally connected with that sort of life. The final result of such a life will be a state of forgetfulness in this world and an existence in hell in the world to come.

PROVERBS 10

Verse 1. We generally think of this entire book now being studied as consisting in proverbs, and the definition of the word justifies that idea. However, the connection will show that it is sometimes used especially to mean a short, direct remark, without any necessary application in the form of personal advice or exhortation to some individual or class of individuals. Again, both forms of wise sayings are somewhat intermixed in Solomon's writings. But as the collection for the book has here been again taken from the shorter form, I will repeat Strong's definition of MASHAL, which is the original word. ". . . in some original sense of superiority in mental action; properly a pithy maxim, usually of a metaphorical [figurative] nature; hence a simile [comparison]." Before going further with the line, I will suggest that not all of the proverbs which are generally grouped in pairs are statements of things that are alike. Instead, it will be found that Solomon gave us a large number of proverbs grouped in pairs, and one of each will be a contrast to the other. Such is this verse in which Solomon contrasts a *wise son* with a *foolish son*. Note that the father is named in one case and the mother in the other. No reason is given, but doubtless it is the mother who worries the more over a wayward son.

Verse 2. Wealth obtained wrongfully will prove to be a detriment in the end and hence a loss. On the other hand, a poor man may be threatened with some form of death, but if he will conduct himself righteously there will be some rescue provided for him.

Verse 3. These two proverbs are certainly contrasts in their most fundamental bearings. A righteous man may suffer poverty, persecution and even physical death. His soul, however, will be sustained by the Lord. *Substance* is from a word that includes a wicked man's actual possessions, and also his life devoted to the efforts in obtaining wealth and other worldly gains that are wrong.

Verse 4. These proverbs are based on the general rule of events. If a man tries to defraud the unfortunate, he will finally be understood and exposed and in being deserted by the people will himself come to want. The diligent righteous man does not take possessions from others but instead will help them to increase.

Verse 5. Please turn to ch. 6: 6 for my comments which also apply to this verse.

Verse 6. *Blessings* means happiness will be on the head of a man whose dealings are right. *Violence* is from a word with a variety of meanings, including wrongful conversation with intent to defraud another. That is why the writer says his mouth is *covered* (meaning filled) with *violence*.

Verse 7. Many of us have heard the phrase "happy memory" applied to some departed person who was loved in his lifetime for his righteous way of living. That is the meaning of the first clause of this verse. *Rot* is from RAQAB and Strong defines it, "A primitive root; to decay (as by worm-eating)." People will always be able to recall the name of a wicked man, but the subject will have the elements of decay in it.

Verse 8. The first clause means practically the same as the 10th verse. *Prating* means to use idle or useless language. Such a fool will come to ruin because his own unwise speech will expose him to the just opposition of reasonable people.

Verse 9. There can be no actual failure for the walk of an upright man because such a person is careful about where and how he walks. He is like the one who observes Eph. 5: 15. *Perverteth* means to step aside from the right way. The man who does so will be recognized in his true light and will be rejected.

Verses 10, 11. The importance of wells in all ages has been fully known. They form a fitting illustration for a righteous man because he will speak the truth. The effect of truth is like a spring of pure water to a thirsty man. The second clause is identical with the last of the 6th verse.

Verse 12. There are some things that we should hate, but the kind of hatred that is wrong is that which is born of the spirit of contention. Such a hatred will not be satisfied until an attempt has been made to start trouble against the hated person. *Covereth sins* does not mean to endorse that which is wrong. It has the idea of making all possible allowance for the mistakes of others.

Verse 13. In this verse the words *understanding* and *wisdom* are used in direct connection which shows there is some distinction. The first means the right use of the second. The man who will not use good sense in the use of his knowledge or wisdom is entitled to some punishment that may possibly bring him to his senses.

Verse 14. In this verse the writer reverses the use of words and means that a man of good sense will retain his knowledge for help in the emergencies of the coming days. By an opposite token the other kind of man will talk in such a way that he may bring down upon himself the enmity of the people.

Verse 15. A strong city is a place of security and it is here compared to the security that wealth gives a man against the attacks of human enemies. We should understand that Solomon is considering the man who makes a righteous use of his wealth. On the principle of the above rule, a poor man is without protection against the others.

Verse 16. There is no particular relation between the two parts of this verse. An unrighteous man may labor and yet be working against his own interests. But the righteous man's activities will have their logical fruit and produce the necessities of life, both temporal and spiritual. A wicked man's labor will tend only to sin.

Verse 17. To *keep instruction* means to observe it, and that will outline the pathway of life to the one who practices it. To *err* means to slip off the right path, and that will happen to the man who refuses to be corrected in his conduct.

Verse 18. It is bad enough to have improper hatred, but it is worse to try covering it over with falsehood. A *slander* is an accusation that originates with a person who is a sneak and tries to injure another "at his back." A man who repeats such an accusation, as well as the one described in the first clause, *is a fool*, which is defined in the lexicon as "stupid or silly."

Verse 19. The connection shows Solomon is considering *words* spoken just for the sake of much speaking, and such words will be filled with tendencies to sin. A wise man will not say a word unless he actually has a subject worth speaking about.

Verse 20. *Choice silver* is that which has been purged of its dross. A just man will reject the dross of evil actions and words, hence what he says will be like the good silver. As a contrast, the heart of a wicked man is like dross and worthless.

Verse 21. Righteous lips will give good spiritual food to others. Fools not only will not impart such life-giving properties, but will themselves die for its lack.

Verse 22. The wonderful thought here is, that when the Lord bestows his blessings he does not mix a "sting" with it. In other words, they are blessings indeed and not merely make-believe ones that leave a person worse off than he was before.

Verse 23. *Sport* means "'laughter" in the lexicon. A fool thinks it is a laughing matter to practice *mischief*. The last word is defined "A plan, especially a bad one." *Understanding* and *wisdom* should again be taken to mean the right use of the knowledge that one has acquired.

Verse 24. A wicked man realizes he is doing wrong and has a "jittery" feeling that he will finally be caught. *The desire of the righteous* means a desire that is right. A man may have a desire for something that would really be harmful to him although his intentions were good. Such a desire would not be right and would not be granted to the well-wisher because it would not be for his good.

Verse 25. The apparent success of a wicked man is likened to a whirlwind. Such a wind will cause quite a commotion and raise a lot of dust, but it is of short duration. The conduct of a righteous man is based on principles that please the Lord, and such a life will be in evidence long after the whirlwind has passed by.

Verse 26. *That send him* means the people who employ a sluggard (lazy person) for some purpose that would be worth while if performed properly. The disappointment will be as painful to the mind of his sponsor as vinegar would be to the organ of the body mentined; as smoke would be to the eyes.

Verse 27. The *fear* of the Lord means the respect for him that one should have. The man who has that will live so that the blessings of the

Lord will be added which will assist him in his existence on the earth. A wicked man, having no regard for the One who gave him his body, will abuse it in "riotous living," and cut short his life.

Verse 28. The righteous will be made glad by having their hope realized. Hope is made up of expectation and desire, yet the first item only is mentioned that will perish. That is significant, for a man's desire is his own mental action, while the disposing of his expectation is in the hand of Providence.

Verse 29. *Way of the Lord* means the way that He wishes man to travel. If man will endeavor to walk therein the Lord will give him the strength necessary for such an upright life. Of course the opposite will be true of the *workers of iniquity*.

Verse 30. This whole verse might well be shortened to mean about the same as Matt. 5: 5 which was cited from Ps. 37: 11 by the Saviour.

Verse 31. According to Solomon, justice requires the use of wisdom as certainly as it does other activities that are right. The *froward* (contrary) tongue will not literally be cut out, but the speech of such will be rejected by the Lord.

Verse 32. The thought is, a righteous man speaks what he knows is acceptable. A wicked man will persist in speaking things that are contrary or according to frowardness.

PROVERBS 11

Verse 1. *Balance* is from MOZEN, which Strong defines, "a pair of scales." They were used by placing the article to be weighed in one side and a stone corresponding in weight with the desired amount of the merchandise in the other. A *false* balance would mean the use of a stone that was either less or more than the supposed requirement of the merchandise, depending on whether the dealer was buying or selling. Since such a transaction would be fraudulent it would be abominable to the Lord. For that reason a just *weight* (stone) would be His delight.

Verse 2. *Pride* is never used in a good sense in the Bible. If a man acts on the motive of pride he will be brought down in the end and hence come to shame. The *lowly* or humble will have the opposite experience. (Luke 14: 11.)

Verse 3. *Integrity* means steadiness or consistency in one's conduct, not changing from side to side, or from doing right today and wrong tomorrow. Such a person will have the right guidance in his manner of life. Those interested in him and who are being influenced by him will know "where to find him" so as not to be thrown into confusion. *Perverseness* is just the opposite of the other because it means the disposition to go off the regular pathway and wander into uncertain ways.

Verse 4. Of course this means riches obtained in a wrongful manner. When the time comes for God's wrath to be poured upon the guilty man, his wealth will avail him nothing. On the contrary, a righteous life will prepare a man against even the last test.

Verse 5. *Perfect* means "entire" according to Strong's lexicon, and that is the meaning of the word most generally. The thought here is that the man is not satisfied to be righteous only in part but in all of his life. That degree of righteousness will assure him of the right way of living. The wicked not only has no dependable basis of conduct, but his unrighteous manner will work its own rebuke and bring him a fall.

Verse 6. A righteous man may have to suffer bitter persecution, even to the extent of death. But in the day of final accounts he will come off a victor. The other class may seem to be winning out for a time, but in the end they will be brought to judgment and caused to suffer the reward of an unrighteous life.

Verse 7. There is no action after death. All opportunity for unrighteous plans must come in this life, for there will be no changes of any kind in the next world.

Verse 8. This does not mean that a good man will escape all unpleasant experiences, but they will not be permanent. *Wicked cometh* denotes that what appeared to be a fatal state of trouble for the righteous will actually be so with the wicked.

Verse 9. A *hypocrite* is one who pretends to be what he knows he is not. That means that he is not only wrong but knows it, and endeavors to make others think he is right. It would be natural, then, for such a person to dislike another whom he knows to be actually good, and will show his envy by spreading falsehoods against him. In spite of such false efforts against a just man, when *knowledge* of the truth is made known he will be delivered from the evil intended by the hypocrite.

Verse 10. *Goeth well* means to be successful and prosperous. The rejoicing of the city would be on account of its benefiting by the good fortune of the righteous. A righteous man will share his good things with others. The shouting at the destruction of the wicked would be caused by the relief that would come by reason of the downfall of the wicked class and their designs, and would consider it "good riddance."

Verse 11. This verse means the same as the preceding one.

Verse 12. *Void of wisdom* denotes an emptiness of wisdom. Such a man will *despise*, which means to speak belittling things about the others. But even if there is some question about the neighbor, it is wise to hold one's tongue until the facts can be known and that the public interest demands that they be made generally known.

Verse 13. A *talebearer* is one who peddles gossip, going about for that purpose. Such a man is so eager to have something to talk about that he will reveal things that should be kept within his own knowledge. He might even betray the intimate confidence that some trusting friend had imparted to him. The faithful spirit is one who respects the confidence that another has shown to him.

Verse 14. On matters where the Lord has legislated the advice or *counsel* of man has no authority. But there are numerous subjects on which no inspired legislation has been given and where man must use his own judgment. It is with reference to such that Solomon is writing here. In a matter depending upon the *counsel* (advice) of man, the greater the number of counselors the better.

Verse 15. For explanation of this verse see my comments at ch. 6: 1-5.

Verse 16. The outstanding point in this verse is the contrast between *gracious* (kindness) and *strong* ("powerful or tyrannical"). The former manifested by a woman will gain for her the honor of the people. The latter when exerted by a man gains only an increase of material gains that will not be of benefit to any other persons.

Verse 17. Perhaps the best comment I can offer on this verse is the saying of Jesus in Matt. 5: 7. If a merciful man will himself be shown mercy, it can be seen why it is said that such a person is good to his own soul. It would be well also to consider James 2: 13 on the subject of mercy and who will receive it at the judgment.

Verse 18. It is not even good policy to practice deceit in wickedness, for such a life cannot produce any desirable result. On the other hand, the one *who soweth righteousness*, which means to sow righteous seed or deeds, will certainly reap the acceptable fruit. This is all in accordance with the great law of cause and effect, and taught in Gal. 6: 7, 8 by the apostle Paul.

Verse 19. Life and death are both terms with literal and figurative meanings. A person can be dead and alive at the same time (1 Tim. 5: 6), so the context must determine which is meant in each case. In the present verse the righteous man may die physically for the sake of his principles, but it will mean his spiritual life afterward. Jesus also taught this same truth in Matt. 10: 39.

Verse 20. *Froward* means to be stubbornly wayward, and those who manifest it are an abomination to the Lord. There is good reason for it because the Lord has pointed out a clear and practical road for the righteous to travel and no one needs to miss it.

Verse 21. *Hand join in hand* is another phrase for monopoly. God has never encouraged combines that obtain great power that can be used to oppress the less fortunate. These monopolies may succeed for a while, but they are destined finally to be brought to justice. When that time comes, the *seed* or people who are righteous will be released from the burdens that had been heaped upon them by the monsters.

Verse 22. The nature or value of a thing is often made apparent by placing it with something else for comparison. A swine is a coarse looking creature, and if a farmer should put a ring of gold in the snout of the animal instead of the ordinary iron one, it would certainly look out of place. The word *fair* is defined in the lexicon as "beautiful." A beautiful woman is God's most attractive creature that pertains to this life. But if such a creature acts and speaks without *discretion* or good sense, it is all the more noticeable in her because of the contrast.

Verse 23. A good man will naturally

desire only that which is good, and that will be pleasing to the Lord if his desires are obtained. A wicked man does not necessarily expect the wrath of God. The clause means that if he realizes his expectation it will logically be something evil and that will bring upon him the wrath of God.

Verse 24. Solomon is not specifying any particular person or thing in this verse, but is stating a rule of cause and effect that has many applications. For instance, the more generous and unselfish a man is with his good things of life, the more he will receive from others in the way of love and respect. The second clause of the verse needs no special comment except to say it is the exact reverse of the first.

Verse 25. Both clauses of this verse are to be explained on the same basis as the first of the preceding verse.

Verse 26. Solomon is not condemning a man for the mere fact of his seeking the best market for his product. But *corn* (any small grain) is a necessity of life and God makes it grow for the nourishment of man and beast. It is wrong, therefore, for the grower to keep the necessities of life off the market when the people are actually needing it for food and are in danger of suffering without it.

Verse 27. Sometimes a man will profess to want to do something beneficial, but will say he cannot see any opportunity. Solomon stipulates that such a would-be benefactor should *diligently* seek for the opportunity. It is just as true that if a man is seeking an opportunity to do mischief he will find it. The sad part of it is that it will fall back upon his own head.

Verse 28. The mere possession of riches is not wrong but it is the trust one puts in them that constitutes the evil. Jesus taught the same thing in Mark 10: 24 and Paul in 1 Tim. 6: 17. *Branch* refers to the foliage on a thrifty tree that spreads out and sheds its shade and encouraging verdure before humanity.

Verse 29. *Wind* used figuratively means something that is noisy but vain. If a man brings trouble into his own family it will result in a loss to all. The *fool* becomes a servant because he is the victim of a man wise enough to manage him.

Verse 30. A tree of life is one from which the necessities of life may be gathered. The deeds of a righteous man will offer just such benefits to the world. The most precious things in the world are human souls, hence a wise man is one who prefers the gathering of such fruit to that of perishing wealth.

Verse 31. The final destiny of both good and evil men is to come after the earth has passed away. But each kind of life will bring certain fruit now as a logical result of that life. That is especially true of the unrighteous. *Wicked* and *sinner* differ only in degree of the wrongful life, the first being more active than the second according to the lexicon definition of the original words.

PROVERBS 12

Verse 1. *Instruction* and *knowledge* are used in a way that requires some distinction. The first is from an original that has special reference to corrective discipline and chastisement. The man who welcomes that shows that he has a sincere desire for knowledge and is willing to make all adjustments necessary for it.

Verse 2. The New Testament teaches that God is no respecter of persons (Acts 10: 34), and the next verse there teaches that he does respect those who fear Him. So the verse of this paragraph tells us that the favor of the Lord is for those only who are good, and that is the way it should be.

Verse 3. The apparent success of a wicked man will not endure. *Be established* and *not be moved* have the same force of meaning. The righteous man is laying a foundation that will hold him up after the wicked man has lost out.

Verse 4. Many of Solomon's comparisons and contrasts are expressed by using literal or material terms, and we must make the application to the ideas in his mind. A crown is an ornament that indicates honorable exaltation. Many a man has been accorded a place of respect for the sake of his virtuous wife. On the contrary, if she is an objectionable woman it may be a hindrance to him. One may hear such remarks as, "He is a good man but I cannot endure his wife."

Verse 5. If a man is righteous in his conduct he will be so in his thoughts. (Ps. 19: 14; Prov. 4: 23; Mark 7: 20-23.) Since the thoughts of a wicked man are wrong, he will likewise give evil *counsels* or advice. But he will present them in such a way that they will not appear in their true light; instead they will cause deceit.

Verse 6. In the preceding verse the counsels (words) of the wicked are said to be deceit. In this verse they are described with more definiteness. The wicked man will speak as if he were a friend when in reality he is seeking opportunity to destroy his hearer. The upright man may try to expose the sham and deliver *them*, meaning the ones who were in danger of the bloodshed threatened by the deceiver.

Verse 7. This means the wicked will have their plans overthrown, while the plans *(house)* of the righteous will endure all tests and will stand.

Verse 8. If a man observes wisdom and acts accordingly, he will be commended by those who see his conduct. A *perverse heart* is one that is stubbornly wayward in its intentions, and of course the man will act accordingly. Such a person will be *despised* or belittled because his worthless kind of life is manifest to all who see it.

Verse 9. To be *despised* means to be thought little of. However, that might be done sometimes unjustly and such is the kind of situation Solomon means in this verse. If a man is belittled and yet is able to have a servant, it shows that others are begrudging him his good fortune. But if a man claims to be honored yet is lacking in the bare necessities of life, it indicates that he is really of small importance.

Verse 10. This is similar to the statement of Moses in Deut. 25: 4 and cited by Paul in 1 Cor. 9: 9. Men who are cruel to their work animals will not receive mercy from God. *Tender mercies . . . cruel* is a figure to show contrast. It means that the least objectionable sentiments of a wicked man are cruel enough.

Verse 11. A man cannot do his work of production while spending his time with idlers. *Void of understanding* means he does not use common sense.

Verse 12. *Desireth* is defined in the lexicon "to delight in." The thought is, the wicked are not objecting to being taken in the net of other evil men. Such a person, however, can never produce anything useful for others. As a contrast, the *root* or source of vitality in righteous men is used to bring forth some fruit that will be beneficial to others and hence will continue to be propagated.

Verse 13. It frequently happens that a wicked man who does a great amount of talking will finally "talk too much," and will thereby expose his wickedness and be caught. *Shall come out* denotes that a just man may have to suffer for a while, but if he maintains his just conduct, "time will tell" that he is right, and he will then be relieved of his trouble because the troublers will be compelled to cease troubling.

Verse 14. A man should guard his words and watch his steps. If he will do these things he will be satisfied with the result.

Verse 15. We are to understand that Solomon is writing of the general matters of life in which human judgment is the guide. The thought in the first clause is true both ways in which it could be spoken. It is true that a fool thinks his way is right. It is true also that the man who follows only the way that his own judgment suggests is a fool. The basis for such a conclusion is the truth of the next clause namely, that it is wise to hearken to counsel. This is the truth set forth in ch. 11: 14.

Verse 16. Righteous indignation is a kind of wrath that is based on some fact, and it may take a little time for it to be realized generally. But a *fool's wrath* has no just reason and it can soon be recognized as such. *Covereth shame* is done by preventing it, and that is accomplished by being "slow to wrath" and thus avoiding any premature statements that would cause shame upon the one making them.

Verse 17. Truth is always in harmony with any other truth, and the man who speaks the truth only will be known as a righteous man. In order for a false witness even to appear to be right, he must so word his speech that it will deceive the hearer.

Verse 18. A sword will pierce with pain but seldom accomplishes any good. But when a man uses wisdom in his speech he will bring moral and spiritual health to those who hear him. This will be true even if the words are pointed and somewhat unpleasant.

Verse 19. *For ever* and *moment* are used for comparison only. However, truth is permanent regardless of the shortness of falsehood.

Verse 20. Falsehood is cowardly, and a wicked man is likewise so, hence his efforts to keep his true motives unknown. That is why he uses deceitful words when he speaks. A counselor of peace means one whose advice tends toward peace, and the outcome of it is joy to those who are exercised thereby.

Verse 21. The just may be mistreated for a while but there will not be any evil that is permanent. It is just the opposite with the wicked, for his apparent success will at last give place to *mischief*, defined in the lexicon, "evil, natural or moral."

Verse 22. The greatest principle in all the world is truth, therefore God hates lying. By the same token He not only favors those who tell the truth, but is delighted in them, which is certainly a great honor bestowed upon a human being.

Verse 23. A *prudent* man means one who is cautious and who is not overly eager to tell what he knows. A fool is so much inclined in the other direction that what he blurts out is soon found to be foolishness.

Verse 24. *Bear rule* is figurative, meaning that a diligent man will be an influential and leading man. The *slothful* or lazy man will constantly be depending on others and will ever be in debt to those who have favored him.

Verse 25. The gist of this verse is that we should be ready to speak a word of encouragement to those who are *stooped* or weighted down with sorrow and worry.

Verse 26. *Neighbor* in this verse is anyone who is benefitted by the excellent life of another. To *seduce* is to mislead, and a wicked man's way of life will do that to others instead of benefitting them as does that of the *excellent* man.

Verse 27. A *slothful* man went to the trouble of hunting the game just because of his personal pleasure in the chase. Then after he has taken it the pleasure is over and he is too lazy to prepare it for use as food. A *diligent* man proves that the game taken is *precious* or of real value by preparing it for his nourishment.

Verse 28. The contrasting clause in this verse is what is implied in the closing words. The entire verse could well be placed beside the teaching of Jesus in Matt. 7: 13, 14 and Luke 13: 24.

PROVERBS 13

Verse 1. Age and experience should be respected by those who are younger. This is the point of the first clause, not merely the physical relation of father and son. This comment is borne out by the last part of the verse, for the *scorner* is named as opposite of *wise man*. A scorner is one who makes light of any advice offered him.

Verse 2. This means that if a man uses good sense in his speech he will succeed in producing the good things of life. Of course the man who *transgresses* this principle will have an unpleasant life and be in want.

Verse 3. The comments on the preceding verse should be applied to this one.

Verse 4. A *sluggard* is a lazy person. Such a man will have only the empty desire for good things because he is too indolent to work for what he wants. Of necessity the *diligent* or active man will have the opposite experience.

Verse 5. Since God hates falsehood a righteous man will hate it also. It is not strong enough merely to say that a wicked man's ways are hateful, but he is *loathsome*. The lexicon defines the original of the word, "A primitive root; to smell bad; figuratively to be offensive morally," and we would expect such a man to bring shame.

Verse 6. Wickedness sometimes makes a bold appearance, but finally it will work the overthrow of those who practice it. Logically, then, the righteous person will close the end of his life with that which is desirable.

Verse 7. The only comment I will offer on this verse is to cite James 2: 5.

Verse 8. If a man is contacted by an armed robber he can save his life by surrendering his riches to the robber. If a man has no money to give to the thief, the only thing he can do is to ignore the threat. If that does not open up a way of escape he has no other recourse and will have to take the consequences.

Verse 9. The *light* of the righteous is his life of good works and it will benefit others. Jesus taught this fact in Matt. 5: 14-16. By logical reasoning from this principle we understand that the influence of *the wicked* will be darkness.

Verse 10. Pride is never used in a good sense in the Bible. It is prompted by an inferiority complex in which the possessor pretends to have a virtue he desires but knows he does not have. Such a man will engage in *contention* which Strong defines as a "quarrel." *Well advised* means those who are informed. Such a man does not feel it necessary to quarrel with his opponent, but will reason with him instead.

Verse 11. *Gotten by vanity* could apply to riches that have been inherited. The one receiving them often does not know the value of a dollar, never having earned one. The rule is that he soon "runs through with it." The man who accumulates wealth by his own efforts "knows how he got it," and will also know how to retain it.

Verse 12. *Sick* means to be weak and impatient with longing, and that is the condition when the thing hoped for is delayed. The more eagerly a thing is waited for the more it will be appreciated when it comes. It is compared to a tree of life because it will seem, as it were, "a life saver."

Verse 13. *Word* and *commandment* are used in the same sense and refer to the Word of God. To *despise* it means to make light of it, and all who do so will be *destroyed* spiritually. To *fear* it means to respect it, and that will bring the spiritual reward.

Verse 14. The *law* or counsel of wise men is a source of moral and spiritual life. If one follows it he will escape the snares that would lead him to ruin.

Verse 15. This is similar in thought to the preceding verse. If a man listens to another who has *good understanding* it will result in his favor. *Way* is from a word that means "a course of life," and *hard* is from one defined "to continue." It is used in a bad sense and has been rendered in the A. V. by hard, rough and others. The clause is a contrast with the first one of the verse. The meaning is that while the pathway pointed out by men of good understanding has some favors interspersed through it to make it easier to follow, that which is being followed by transgressors has no relief in sight or prospect and that is why it is said to be "hard."

Verse 16. The key word in the first clause is *dealeth* which means to advance or do something. A *prudent* or careful man will not do anything until he knows what he is doing. A fool plunges headlong without considering it and soon exposes his rashness.

Verse 17. If a man is sent out on a mission he should deliver it faithfully. Failing to do so will get him into trouble.

Verse 18. There is no disgrace in poverty that cannot be avoided after listening to counsel. But if it is because a man closed his ears to advice it is a shame to him.

Verse 19. An unexpected favor will be appreciated, but one desired and finally realized will be still more so. This is a positive pleasure, and a negative one is set forth in the second clause of the verse. If fools object to departing from evil, by the same token they will take pleasure in clinging to it.

Verse 20. To *walk with wise men* means to associate with them and to follow their counsels. The opposite would be true of those who associate with evil characters. This truth is taught by David in Ps. 1:1 and by Paul in 1 Cor. 15:33.

Verse 21. That which pursues comes afterward and may not be seen for a time. For this reason a wicked man many think there is no danger of his getting into any trouble over his conduct. The time will come, however, when his record "will catch up with him." It will be well to consider the words of Moses in Num. 32:23 where he said to certain men who might try to hide their sins, "be sure your sins will find you out." It is just as true of good as it is of evil, that the reward comes afterward and the righteous man should be patient and hope for it. (Gal. 6:9.)

Verse 22. All rules have some exceptions, but if a man is good he will be considerate of the coming generations and the provision he has made for them will be enjoyed by them after their common ancestor has passed away. Since the sinner's wealth is usually obtained wrongfully, it will be right and just for good people to take possession of it, for they will make the proper use of it.

Verse 23. A poor man can produce much food by *tillage* (land cultivation), but if he does not use judgment afterward he will lose the fruit of his labors.

Verse 24. It is false love that causes a parent to refrain from punishment of a wayward son. Solomon's statement is severe but true, that such a parent really hates his son. This is no arbitrary decision but a logical conclusion. If a man refuses to administer that which will be of benefit to his son he certainly does not love him. To chasten *betimes* means to do so promptly, and that also means to do it at the time it is needed. Frequently a parent will threaten to punish his child "the next time you do it." If a child will deserve punishment in the *future* for something that he has done *now*, then the proper time to punish him is *now*.

Verse 25. *Soul* is used of the whole being, of which the body is the visible part, and that by which material food is administered to sustain life. A righteous man takes this view of the matter as he is enjoying his food. Paul had the same thought in mind in the latter part of Acts 14: 17. A wicked man eats without any appreciation of the good things he is enjoying and will hence neglect to do his part in the further production of the necessities of life and will finally come to want.

PROVERBS 14

Verse 1. *House* is used in the same sense as "household" in ch. 31: 15, 27. To *build* means to work for the welfare of her people. A foolish woman may profess to love her family, but by her lack of judgment she will be a detriment instead of an advantage.

Verse 2. It is his *fear* (respect) for the Lord that causes the man to walk uprightly. *Perverse in his ways* denotes that a man is stubbornly wayward. This is different from the person who is in error because of ignorance or other weakness.

Verse 3. A *rod* is used to chastise an erring person, and a man who is so foolish as to speak proudly will feel the chastening rod of his own foolishness in the end.

Verse 4. A man could save his present supply of corn by not keeping any oxen. However, he would not be able to produce the corn needed in the future. The lesson is that all desirable things require that we put up with some inconvenience.

Verse 5. The simple point in this verse is that faithfulness and truth must always be together; one cannot exist in the absence of the other.

Verse 6. A man may pretend to be wanting information even while he is making light of the person of whom he is inquiring. Such a man would not recognize information when it was expressed in his hearing. The same source of information will benefit the one who *understandeth*, which means he uses good sense in applying the information.

Verse 7. We have learned that it is dangerous to associate with a wicked man because it will threaten our own character. On the same principle it would be better to avoid intimacy with a man who speaks contrary to knowledge. His foolish conversation might react in such a way as to corrupt those who hear him.

Verse 8. The first clause is describing a *prudent* (careful) man. He is one who wants to know what is best before he goes on his way. (Eph. 5: 15.) Not only so, but the right kind of man will not hesitate to seek the information even if he knows it may not all be pleasant. The other kind of person is afraid to face the truth for fear it will condemn him. But he is not fair enough to admit it, so he will try to "cover up," using the *deceit* that our own verse mentions. (John 3: 19 20.)

Verse 9. An intelligent man knows that sin cannot be justified and hence knows better than to try. *Fools* may know enough to recognize sin but are so lacking in good sense they resort to mocking as an "alibi" for their evil deeds. A man who is righteous will gain the favor of God; if he makes a mistake he will make amends to God.

Verse 10. A man knows his own heart and realizes his own worries better than anyone else; for that reason he bears most of the burden alone. It would be only fair that outsiders (strangers) also keep their fingers out of his good things.

Verse 11. Solomon has said so much about the apparent success of wicked men that we might think this verse is a contradiction. The idea is that in the end the wicked will fail. This was taught by Christ in the parable of the houses (Matt. 7: 24).

Verse 12. There is an old saying that "the road to perdition is paved with good intentions." That saying is true, and it is true also that the blocks of honest ignorance help to cover the pavement. Jesus taught that also in Matt. 15: 14.

Verse 13. At the same time that one is outwardly rejoicing he may have some sentiments that are not pleasant. It is reasonable, therefore, to expect such a circumstance to end in *heaviness* or sorrow.

Verse 14. The heart is the place where evil deeds are planned, hence if a man backslides in his heart, his *ways* (outward actions) will be accordingly. The second clause of the verse is the same thought that Paul expressed in Gal. 6: 4. The point is that one man will not be blessed because some other one did his duty. Each man must work out his own salvation and win the crown by his own faithfulness.

Verse 15. *Simple* is from a word which Strong defines, "silly (i. e., seducible)." It means a man who just listens to anything that is said to him "regardless." The *prudent* (careful) man *looketh well to his going.* That is the thought in Eph. 5: 15.

Verse 16. *Feareth* means the wise man respects the admonitions offered him and ceases his wrongful conduct. The *fool* is one who pretends to believe he is right *(is confident)*, but it is because he does not want to leave off his sinful practices.

Verse 17. The mere fact of being angry is not sinful, for Jesus got angry according to Mark 3: 5, and Ps. 7: 11 says God is angry with the wicked every day. But it is what a man does under the influence of anger and also his tendency to anger that determines the right or wrong in any given case. One of the negative qualifications required in elders is that they be "not soon angry" (Titus 1: 7). *Wicked devices* are actions that have been planned and that are wicked.

Verse 18. The *simple* are those who are so silly that they never acquire any useful information, consequently they are always seen to *inherit* (possess) foolishness. The *prudent* are those who are careful and use good judgment in regard to the opportunities opened before them, and as a result they gain knowledge.

Verse 19. *Bow* is from SHACHACH, which Strong defines, "to sink or depress." Evil and wicked men do not voluntarily acknowledge their inferiority to righteous men, but at last the contrast will be made so evident that it will be generally recognized.

Verse 20. The poor man is hated in the sense that he is looked down upon and regarded with slight. By the same token, a rich man will have many friends because they are looking to him for favors that his wealth can provide.

Verse 21. *Despise* is used in the same sense as *hated* in the preceding verse. He that belittles or looks down upon a neighbor because he is poor *sinneth* according to this verse. Having mercy on the poor means to help them obtain the things they need. The man with money who does this will be *happy* in the knowledge of having done right.

Verse 22. To *devise* means to meditate on some plan that is to be carried out, whether one of good or one of evil. To *err* signifies that one has stepped aside from the true path, and Solomon declares that such has been done when a man devises evil. *Mercy and truth . . . to them* means these virtues will be attributed to them.

Verse 23. It is generally necessary to plan one's work in order to accomplish success. However, if a man talks only about his plans he will not make any profit.

Verse 24. If a man is diligent and careful in his plans for acquiring the good things of this world he will be crowned with success. Since the figure of speech in the first clause is *crown*, we should look for its equivalent in this. It might well be worded to say a fool's crown is his own foolishness; not a very shining crown!

Verse 25. A *true witness* is one who produces testimony in favor of a man who was about to be unjustly punished. All that is ever obtained from a man who merely pretends to be a proper witness is lies.

Verse 26. If we *fear* or have reverence for the Lord we will rely on Him for help in times of need. *Strong confidence* is the same as hope, and it will be the lot of those who have the proper respect for the Lord. *Place of refuge* is practically a repetition of the first part of the verse.

Verse 27. Life may sometimes consist in escaping from death. If a man fears the Lord he will eagerly drink from the divine spring of wisdom, and that will teach him how to avoid the traps set for him that would cause his death.

Verse 28. Loyalty to one's government is the main point in this verse.

Verse 29. See the comments on v. 17 for the explanation of this one.

Verse 30. There is some truth in the theory of "mind over matter," which is the thought in this verse. If the heart (mind) is settled and filled with good thoughts it will be beneficial even to one's bodily welfare.

Verse 31. God has great compassion for the poor, and for that reason to mistreat them is to disrespect Him. That honoreth *him* means to honor Him, and a man does that if he has mercy on the poor and contributes to their comfort.

Verse 32. *Driven* away applies to being driven from the favor of God, and a man's wickedness will do that. The hope of the righteous will sustain him even down to the hour of death. David expressed this beautiful thought in Ps. 23: 4.

Verse 33. A man who has *understanding* (uses good judgment) shows that wisdom is a regular principle in his life, although it may not always be recognized by others since they cannot read his heart. On the other hand, a fool's unreasonable conduct is so out of line that its folly is evident to all.

Verse 34. According to Strong the original for *exalteth* may be either literal or figurative. A righteous nation may not always become high literally or from the standpoint of worldly greatness, but in reality it is high in true grandeur.

Verse 35. A servant who acts with good sense will be considered the most valuable in the eyes of his master. And if that master is the king, he can and will bestow upon such a servant his royal favors. The opposite treatment would be accorded a servant whose conduct was shameful.

PROVERBS 15

Verse 1. The original for *soft* is defined by Strong as "tender." An *answer* (reply) in a controversy need not be a compromise in order to be tender. A clean, clear-cut statement may be worded in such a way as to manifest some respect for the feelings of the other party, and at the same time be true to all the facts. Such a reply will often quiet the storm of wrath that was about to arise. *Grievous* means sharp and painful, and such words, even if they are technically true, will arouse more anger than was in evidence at the start of the controversy.

Verse 2. This verse is closely related to the preceding one in thought. It is not enough to possess the bare knowledge of any case, but all parties concerned should use common sense in talking about it, and that is what a wise and careful man will do. A foolish man will speak so discourteously that even what truth he happens to have will be hidden or neutralized by the kind of speech he uses.

Verse 3. The eyes of the Lord are spiritual and hence can be universally present, even while his person is on the throne in Heaven. There is no hiding from God, as Adam and hosts of others have learned. David very completely described the infinite presence of God in Ps. 139: 7-12.

Verse 4. A *wholesome tongue* is one that speaks only the truth, and the truth is always a source of life. *Perverseness* is the disposition to be stubbornly wayward. The man who was wholesome previously, and then becomes perverse, thereby makes a *breach* (break) in his spirit or character.

Verse 5. To *despise* means to belittle or make fun of. A fool does not want to change his ways for the better, therefore he scoffs at his father's words of advice. A *prudent* son is one who is careful and uses his common sense. Such a son will appreciate the counsel of his father and will profit thereby.

Verse 6. A righteous man uses the proper means to obtain the good things of the world and hence will have in his house a collection of them which he can enjoy in peace. The gains that a wicked man makes are a source of trouble to him because he got them by trampling upon the rights of others.

Verse 7. What a man has in his heart benefits others only when it comes out by his lips in the form of wise information. The lips of the foolish cannot disperse words of wisdom because his heart does not contain such thoughts, and it is "out of the abundance of the heart the mouth speaketh." (Matt. 12: 34.)

Verse 8. From a material standpoint a sacrifice is more valuable than a prayer. However, when the first is offered by a wicked man, and the second by a righteous, the latter is more valuable in the sight of the Lord.

Verse 9. *Way* is from DEREK, which Strong defines, "a road (as trodden); figuratively a course of life or mode of action, often adverbially." It is the word for "way" in Isa. 35: 8. In view of this definition it is easy to see why the way of the wicked is an abomination to the Lord. The last of the verse is exactly opposite the first.

Verse 10. *Way* is from ORACH and defined in Strong's lexicon, "a well trodden road (literal or figurative);" The connection shows Solomon uses the word for the road of righteousness which the Lord has laid out on which his people should travel. *Forsaketh* is from AZAB, which Strong defines, "a primitive root; to loosen, i. e., relinquish." It therefore applies especially to one who was in the road of righteousness and then became interested in things on the side and decided to leave (forsake) the path. Such a person, then, would object to any attempts at correcting his backslidings. The original for *grievous* is RAH and has the brief definition "bad" in the lexicon. It is significant, for when a man concludes to go wrong he will regard all objections as bad. But the saddest thought is that such a person will die spiritually.

Verse 11. *Before* means to be open and known as if it were present and in sight. If the Lord can see the fact of hell and future destruction, though invisible now, he certainly can see the hearts of men which are ever present for Him to read.

Verse 12. A scorner is one who mocks and belittles that which he cannot oppose with any facts. He is not fair enough to admit the justice of the reproof, hence tries to weaken its force by scoffing at it. Of course such a person would not voluntarily seek instruction from wise men lest it call upon him to change his foolish ways.

Verse 13. This verse is a statement of facts known to almost everyone. It may be asked why take up space in the Bible with something everyone knows. It is for the implied advice it contains. It should always be our desire to be pleasant in mingling with other people, and to that end we should cultivate a cheerful mind. If we imagine there is nothing about which to be cheerful, just "count your many blessings" and you may be surprised at what the Lord has done for you, and change your mind.

Verse 14. *Understanding* is used in the sense of good judgment or common sense, and the man who uses that will be eager to obtain information. On the contrary, a fool would rather be content with his foolishness than take the trouble to learn something worth knowing, for that would require more mental effort than he wants to make.

Verse 15. The word for *afflicted* is defined "depressed," and refers to the state of mind. That is why the last clause contrasts it with one of a merry heart. See my comments on v. 13 regarding the effect of the feelings on the countenance.

Verse 16. Solomon had experienced most of the things he wrote about, especially those connected with power and riches. The fear or respect for the Lord will lead people to find joy in many things that would seem dull and disappointing to the rich.

Verse 17. Neither of these meals is considered wrong in itself; the subject is their comparative enjoyment in connection with certain social conditions. *Stalled ox* means one that has been kept in a stall to be fattened for slaughter.

Verse 18. The comments I now offer are the ones made on verse 1.

Verse 19. A slothful man is one who is lazy and everything that suggests labor looks objectionable to him; consequently he looks upon it as a hedge of thorns. The *way* of the righteous means the road on which they are expected to travel. That road has been *made plain* by the Lord, and there is nothing that looks like thorns to the man who truly wishes to travel thereon.

Verse 20. This is identical in thought with ch. 13: 1, and the reader is requested to see that place again and make the application to this verse.

Verse 21. A man who does not have wisdom does not know any better than to enjoy folly or things that are foolish. *Understanding* is another word for intelligence, with the added thought of making good use of it. The man who does so will walk uprightly or righteously and thus show he appreciates his opportunities.

Verse 22. *Counsel* means judgment or advice of man where there is no direct revelation from the Lord. See the comments on this subject at ch. 11: 14.

Verse 23. The second clause of this verse explains the first. *In due season* means to say the right thing at the right time. It is on that condition his mouth will bring him joy because of the favorable reaction to the good things he says.

Verse 24. There is a familiar hymn that says: "Plant my feet on higher ground," and that is the sentiment of this verse. If a man is *wise* he will consider that the proper way of life is on "higher ground," that is, above the ways of sinful men.

Verse 25. *House* means a home or household, and *border* means a boundary or territory. The former may be attractive and even imposingly grand to suit the fancy of a proud man. Yet it is not useful for much except to gratify the pride of the owner and the Lord will overthrow it in the end. The *border* of the widow includes her field or means of production, and He will reward her simple life by guarding her possessions.

Verse 26. Thoughts are supposed to exist before words, but the Lord knows them before they are spoken and considers them an abomination when evil. In God's sight there is no difference between a man's thoughts and his words as to guilt or innocence. It is therefore for the sake of euphony (pleasing sound) that Solomon switches from one to the other in wording this verse.

Verse 27. The second clause of this verse modifies the first. To desire gain is not necessarily wrong, but to acquire it by accepting *gifts* (bribes) is wrong, and will bring trouble upon a man's household if he gets his wealth in that way.

Verse 28. This means a righteous man makes a conscientious effort to give a true reply to any proposition made to him. The wicked man will treat it with contempt.

Verse 29. The Lord is in every nook and corner of the universe in the sense of his knowledge, but he is not near those who are wicked in the sense of being favorable toward them. In this sense also the Lord is deaf to the prayers of the wicked, but he heareth those of the righteous. (1 Pe. 3: 12.)

Verse 30. If one's eyes can see good things to be enjoyed it makes the heart rejoice. This is the same thought expressed by Paul in Acts 14: 17. On the same principle, but in a more figurative use of words, news of good things about to be enjoyed will nourish the structure of the body.

Verse 31. A man who will listen to words of reproof, even though they be unpleasant, is a wise person. It will mean life to him because it will lead him to avoid that which might have resulted in a fatal misfortune to him.

Verse 32. A man is only "spiting himself" when he refuses to receive correction. If he acts with *understanding* or good sense it will be for his own benefit.

Verse 33. The wisest instruction one can obtain is that which is prompted by the fear (or respect) of the Lord. *Before honor is humility* was taught by Christ in Matt. 23: 12. True greatness consists in a modest attitude that prefers to favor another. That is the spirit of unselfishness, one of the finest qualities possible.

PROVERBS 16

Verse 1. This verse should be considered in the light of ch. 15: 26 and the comments offered thereon. Solomon is writing of thoughts and words that are right, and all such must come from the Lord or be in harmony with him.

Verse 2. This corresponds with the preceding verse in that it shows why our words and actions should be directed by the Lord in order to be sure of having them right. The wisdom of man unaided by the Lord will be very unreliable.

Verse 3. *Commit* means to let the Lord direct the works of man. The one who does so will logically be thinking along the same line and thus his thoughts will be good.

Verse 4. *Hath made* does not refer to the creation of the things in mind. It means the use or disposition that God will make of them. So the thought is that God has his plans all made, and one of them is to bring all wicked men to the day of their doom. As to who are to be included with *the wicked*, that is left for man himself to determine and it is done by the kind of life he chooses to live.

Verse 5. Pride is never used in a good sense in the Bible but is always condemned. The second clause of the verse concerns the proud man who might rely on others to "hold hands" with him in his unrighteous ways. In spite of his evil confederates he will finally be punished.

Verse 6. *Mercy* and *truth* should always work together. An act of mercy that is not in harmony with the truth will work no good to anyone. But if a man in sin is shown some mercy and at the same time is able to see that truth requires that he cease his practice of iniquity, he will be induced to reform. This whole procedure should be induced by *fear* or reverence for the Lord.

Verse 7. This would not mean that a man's enemies would approve of the righteous ways of the Lord's servant, but through the oversight and ruling of the Lord the enemies would be subdued.

Verse 8. See the comments on ch. 15: 16 which is similar in thought to this verse; the terms used to express it only are different. *Fear of the Lord* in one corresponds with *righteousness* in the other. *Trouble* in one is related to *revenues without right* in the other.

Verse 9. An old saying is, "man proposes but God disposes," and it expresses the thought of this verse pretty well. The first clause refers to the plans that a man makes independent of the Lord, and the second tells that the success or failure of the plans is in the Lord's hands. It is well for us to read James 4: 13-16.

Verse 10. *The king* in this case was Solomon and hence we need not be confused at the statement. When he asked God for wisdom to help him judge the people (1 Ki. 3: 5-12) it was promised him, and we believe God fulfilled the promise; that justifies the declaration of this verse. It should be noted that it was in matters of *judgment* he says he would not err and that was all that God promised him at Gibeon. As to his personal conduct no claim was made here, and his mistakes in life had nothing to do with his wisdom in ruling the nation or in his writings. See my comments on 1 Ki. 3: 12 in Vol. 2 of this COMMENTARY.

Verse 11. See the comments at ch. 11: 1 for an explanation of the *balance*. God demands that people deal honestly with each other. *The bag* was the container of the stones used as weights for the balance.

Verse 12. There was no king in Israel except Solomon; he was speaking of kings in general and the principles on which their rule should be conducted.

Verse 13. Apply the same comments offered on the preceding verse.

Verse 14. *Messengers of death* are those sent to carry out the sentence of the king. If a subject of the king causes the royal wrath to be stirred up he might as well get ready to see the executioners. On the other hand, if a man uses wisdom he will comply with the wishes of the king and thus will quiet his wrath.

Verse 15. After it has been hot and dry, a cloud bringing cooling showers would be refreshing. In like manner, if a citizen *pacifies* the wrath of the king, he will see the refreshing light of his countenance in place of the wrath that was threatened.

Verse 16. Both clauses of this verse mean the same and are given for the sake of emphasis. Gold and silver are material objects and may easily be lost or stolen. *Wisdom* and *understanding* are accomplishments of the mind and no one can steal them.

Verse 17. Regardless of how a man travels he will need some thoroughfare on which to travel. Hence there are the two words used in this verse; *highway* meaning the road and *way* referring to the manner of a man's walking in that road. The verse as a whole describes a righteous traveler through life.

Verse 18. Pride is always held in a bad light in the Bible. *Goeth before destruction* means that pride will lead a man to his ruin. The second clause means exactly the same but is expressed in different words to give it emphasis. The verse also is the same in thought as the teaching of Christ in Luke 14: 11.

Verse 19. *Divide the spoil* is a phrase indicating financial success in a conflict since *spoil* means valuables taken thereby. No one can *divide* or share such property unless he has been a victor. Yet if in the conflict he was confederate with the proud he is destined to feel the wrath of God and will finally lose his gains. But the humble will possess the favor of God which is worth more than gold and diamonds.

Verse 20. The second clause should be Solomon's explanation of the first. If a man trusts the Lord he will use the wisdom He offers in handling the affairs of life.

Verse 21. Again the second part of the verse modifies the first. Lips are sweet, figuratively, that speak words of true learning. And thus will the lips speak that belong to those who are *wise* and *prudent* (carefully thoughtful) in heart, for "out of the abundance of the heart the mouth speaketh." (Matt. 12: 34.)

Verse 22. A *wellspring* is a constant source of water which is necessary to life. It is used to compare the supply of *understanding* that a man may possess if he desires. By the same token, all that a fool gets is more *instruction* in folly or foolishness.

Verse 23. It is out of the heart the mouth speaketh. If a man's heart is wise his mouth will know how to speak that which is according to righteousness.

Verse 24. See the comments on the last part of ch. 15: 30. While the main point of this verse is concerning spiritual benefits, it is true also that the health of the body is affected by the mental condition.

Verse 25. This verse is identical

with ch. 14: 12; see the comments there.

Verse 26. This verse is related in thought to the preceding one. The reason a man allows himself to follow the way that *seemeth right*, is because it promises to gratify the *craving* of his mouth (fleshly desires).

Verse 27. An ungodly man will always be favorable to evil that is offered to him by another, but he will not be satisfied with that. He will busy himself in finding it even if he has to *dig* or probe for it. Yes, he is so eager to have something about which to gossip that his lips seem to be on fire and buring with some tale of scandal he wishes to peddle to the injury of another.

Verse 28. *A froward man* is one who is stubbornly wayward. If the said man is a *whisperer* (gossiper) he will persist until he breaks up the fondest of friendships.

Verse 29. *Violent* and *enticeth* might not seem to agree in meaning, yet it is possible. A man would have motives of violence, but would have to use caution in carrying out his wicked designs. That would make it advisable to use *enticement* or underhanded methods. If he succeeded he would mislead his neighbor to his ruin.

Verse 30. A man like the preceding verse describes may know that his plans are extremely wicked, but he will refuse to see the facts; he *shutteth his eyes* against them. Then he will go on and with his words will proceed with his plans.

Verse 31. Pride sometimes causes men to color their hair in order to hide their age. The mere fact of gray hair is nothing of which to be ashamed; it depends upon what has been the practices while attaining old age. If the practices have been righteous, then a gray head represents many years of usefulness on behalf of others, and a life of devotion to God. In that case it means the near approach to a triumphant ending of the race of life. The gray head will glow with the reflection that is theirs who have served the Lord, even until they have reached "the land of the setting sun."

Verse 32. Anger alone is not sinful, but he that is soon angry is condemned. The man who controls his temper shows more generalship than one who can take a city in war, yet who is a victim of a fiery wrath.

Verse 33. One method of deciding questions was by the lot. Various forms of procedure were used in different ages, but whatever form was used, the outcome would be only a chance unless the Lord saw fit to use it, which he often did. The *lot* was the article on which the candidate or contestant was named. These were put into a shielded vessel here called the *lap*. Someone was blindfolded and caused to draw out one of the lots and the one whose name or number appeared on it was the winner. If the Lord was using this practice on any given occasion he would see that the blindfolded person got the right lot. That is the meaning of, *disposing is of the Lord*.

PROVERBS 17

Verse 1. I can offer no better comments on this verse than those on ch. 15: 17.

Verse 2. A son would normally rank above a servant. However, Solomon was so favorable to wisdom as being the most desirable trait that he used it in his comparison of the servant and the son. If the servant is wise and the son is foolish, the former will be preferred by the father to the latter, even to placing him in a position of rule. The master will go even further than that; he will make the wise servant a sharer with the son in the inheritance of the estate.

Verse 3. Fining pots and furnaces are used to separate the silver and gold from the dross with which they are mixed in their native state in the ground. The intense heat will cause the refuse matter to dissolve and disappear, leaving only the pure metals that have withstood the fire. This is used to illustrate any tests that tend to prove what is good and what is refuse in the lives of men. The Lord is the one who puts man through the refinery of trials and afflictions to determine whether his heart is true to Him. Peter writes about these fiery trials in 1 Pe. 4: 12.

Verse 4. Liars and other wicked people will relish the speech of other falsifiers because it encourages their wicked ways.

Verse 5. For the first part of this verse see my comments on ch. 14: 31. *Unpunished* is rendered "held innocent" in the margin of the Bible and the lexicon agrees with it. If a man takes pleasure in some misfortune coming to a poor man, it raises the suspicion that he may have had some part in causing that misfortune. But since such a person would deserve to be punished, the text of the A.V. is correct also.

Verse 6. The mutual relation between parent and child is the point in this verse. There are people who profess to be followers of the Lord, and yet who regard children as a nuisance. If such persons will seriously consider this verse and other passages on the same subject, they will realize their need of repentance.

Verse 7. *Excellent* is from YETHER and Strong defines it, "an overhanging, i. e. (by implication) an excess, superiority." A fool might learn to pronounce words that were far weightier in meaning than his mind was able to grasp. Such a circumstance would be out of order. Likewise, but in a more serious sense, it would be improper for a prince (a leading man in the community) to be guilty of falsehood.

Verse 8. *Gift* is derived from a word that Strong defines, "A primitive root; to donate, i. e., to bribe." *Precious stone* is used in the sense of a "charm" or luck stone. Its owner thinks that *whithersoever it turneth*, wherever he uses it, he will be prospered. Leaving out the superstitious element, even, we know that a bribe has a tremendous influence on a person who accepts it.

Verse 9. The Lord does not ask us to give encouraging protection to transgression which we know another has committed. The second part of the verse will throw light on the subject. The thing that is condemned is *he that repeateth*. The covering that Solomon had in mind consists in not repeating or peddling the matter through the people.

Verse 10. Physical punishment is the only kind that a fool can understand, and it may take a great amount of it to get him corrected. A man of good sense will recognize the justness of reproof and will feel (mentally) the sting of it.

Verse 11. *Cruel* is derived from a word that is defined, "to act harshly." "Desperate cases require desperate treatment" is a familiar saying, and it illustrates this verse. If a man acts the part of a rebel he will have to be handled roughly.

Verse 12. A maddened bear could destroy a man physically only, while a fool could bring him to moral and spiritual destruction.

Verse 13. In this verse we have two rewards and two motives for them. If a man returns evil to one who has done him good it could be for no other motive than malice. The evil that would then be inflicted upon the malicious person would be done by an authorized man for the purpose of deserved punishment.

Verse 14. *Beginning* is a key word and will account for the comparison. If a man were to open a small sluice in a dike or make a small puncture in a tank of water, it would be only the *beginning* of the saturation; however, the extent of the damage done might be enormous. This is used to illustrate the sad result that might come from the first contentious word, therefore the first word should not be spoken.

Verse 15. This is a very brief but complete statement of the Lord's view of equity or fairness. It gives us the principle of responsibility in our relation to the conduct of others. If a man justifies a wicked person it indicates that he would have done the same thing the wicked man did had he been in his place. On the other hand, if he condemns a good man's conduct it shows that he would *not* have done as the good man did had he been in his place.

Verse 16. *Wherefore* is a Biblical way of asking why? A fool might have plenty of money and pretend he wants to spend it for wisdom or knowledge. Solomon's question is, "how come," or what is the use for such a person to buy information, seeing he does not have the *heart* (mind) to use it after he has it within his possession.

Verse 17. The key to this verse is the phrase *at all times*. A pretender might make a show of love occasionally when he has some "ax to grind," but the love of a true friend is constant. The second part of the verse is directly related to the first. In view of that it might well be worded, "and such a brother (friend) is born to be a helper in times of adversity." No person has been predestinated by the Lord as to the kind of man he will be. The course of human reproduction and nature has been left to the universal laws established in the beginning. Among the many kinds of characters that will be born there will be both those who are going to be good and those who are going to be bad. The idea of Solomon here is that when this certain kind of person was born, an inspired prophet could have said that he was going to be "a friend in deed" to those who are "in need."

Verse 18. *Void of understanding* means he does not have or use common sense. Such a man knows no better than to *strike hands* or go on the bond with the other person. See my comments on this subject at ch. 6: 1-5.

Verse 19. The connection indicates that *transgression* and *strife* are used in a bad sense. A lover of such strife would logically be mixed up with transgression of righteous law. *Gate* is used figuratively to mean a man's personal interests. He should know that if he exalts himself he is only inviting his own downfall. (Luke 14: 11).

Verse 20. There is not much difference between *froward* and *perverse*. The first means to be stubbornly wayward and the second denotes the disposition to step aside from the right path. Either of the evils will bring grief to those who are guilty.

Verse 21. Solomon is not blaming the father of a fool; he is merely offering a comment on the situation. With his multitude of wives no doubt he had such offspring and he had experienced the sorrow coming from such a source.

Verse 22. We should avoid extremes on all subjects, and that of disease and medicine is no exception. Doubtless the mind has a great effect over the body, and many "diseases" are more imaginary than real. Such cases can be healed without the use of literal medication. We need not accept the extreme theories of the "drugless" healers of various creeds and cults.

Verse 23. *Bosom* is used figuratively, meaning confidential or intimate. The verse denotes the taking of a bribe secretly as pay for defeating justice.

Verse 24. *Before him* and *ends of the earth* are the contrasting terms in this verse. A man who uses good sense can recognize the wise thing as if it were right *before* his eyes. The fool is as blind to it as if he and his eyes were as widely separated as the ends of the earth are from each other.

Verse 25. I have practically explained this verse at ch. 10: 1.

Verse 26. *Strike* means to treat harshly, literally or figuratively, according to Strong's lexicon. The idea of the verse is that we should not impose on the just and noble men in trying to get our "rights."

Verse 27. Many times he who knows the most says the least. *Understanding* means good judgment and the man who uses it shows the right spirit.

Verse 28. I know of no more fitting place to quote a familiar saying: "Don't expose your ignorance," than the present verse. If a fool will get credit for wisdom he does not have by remaining quiet, it shows the good sense of not "speaking out of turn."

PROVERBS 18

Verse 1. The context indicates this man's *desire* is to pry into another's business. He thinks he can best do so by pulling off from the group and acting as a spy.

Verse 2. *Discover* is from a Hebrew word that means to expose something shamefully. The verse means a fool is not interested in matters of importance, but acts as if he wanted to strip his heart naked so that others could see how ignorant he is.

Verse 3. *Contempt* is the spirit of disrespect and belittling, and that is what is manifested when the wicked come upon the scene. *Cometh* is implied in the second clause. *Ignominy* means shame, and *reproach* means scorn. The clause therefore is as if it were worded, "with shame comes scorn." A wicked man has nothing to justify his life of shame, so he seeks to counteract his disgrace by scorn or scoffing for those who are good. It is exactly the thought Paul sets forth in 2 Tim. 3: 3, last 6 words.

Verse 4. The importance of saying the right thing at the right time has been one of the outstanding subjects of this book. Moreover, we have frequently been reminded by various passages in the Bible that if a man's speech is according to wisdom his conduct will likely be the same. Hence this verse compares it to pools *(deep waters)* and flowing brooks; constant sources of the life-giving substance. The language shows, however, that Solomon was writing of the man who speaks words of wisdom.

Verse 5. The apostle Peter declared that God is no respecter of persons (Acts 10: 34), and the same truth is taught by Solomon. It is especially wrong to allow our personal regard for one man to influence us against a righteous person.

Verse 6. It is the duty of God's servants to practice the right kind of contending in behalf of the truth

(Jude 3), but the *contention* and *strokes* of a fool are used in the sense of unfriendly attacks upon a man who is righteous.

Verse 7. A fool will not use common sense in his speech, consequently his mouth will get him into trouble sooner or later.

Verse 8. *Talebearer* is from an original that means a secret slanderer. Belly is generally translated "body," and refers to the principal portion of a human being. In other words, a secret slander will inflict a major injury upon a man, because he is unaware of the work of the whisperer until its deadly effect is felt.

Verse 9. A *slothful* man will not produce anything, and a *waster* destroys that which another has produced. *Brother* is used figuratively, meaning the two described men are alike in their principles of life.

Verse 10. Towers were used in times of danger and provided places of protection from the enemy. They are compared to the spiritual support that the name of the Lord offers to those who put their trust in Him.

Verse 11. The key to this verse is the phrase *his own conceit*. The thought is the rich man is so foolish he regards his wealth as his protection. He is not like the man in the preceding verse who trusts in the name of the Lord for shelter.

Verse 12. The *haughty* man corresponds to the proud in ch. 16: 18 and the thought is the same. The last clause is the same in effect as Luke 14: 11.

Verse 13. There is a logical reason for the conclusion in this verse. If a man makes his decision in a case before he has heard all the evidence he will likely decide it wrong. Then when the whole truth has been revealed his decision will be held up to ridicule and he will be brought to shame for his unfair procedure.

Verse 14. For an explanation of the first clause, see my comments at ch. 17: 22. If a man's body is affected it may be benefitted by the strength of his spirit or will power. But if it is his spirit that is hurt it is more serious, for the body has very little ability in healing the inner being.

Verse 15. Both clauses of this verse have virtually the same thought. A man who is already prudent or possessed with good judgment, will want to acquire knowledge which means specific information on various subjects. In other words, a man might be naturally intelligent and have common sense and yet not know anything about certain subjects. But such a man will not be content until he obtains the information.

Verse 16. The main idea in this verse is that gifts will gain for a man the favors that true merit might not bring him. If this *gift* is in the nature of a bribe (which is too often the case), it is a transaction to be condemned.

Verse 17. *Searcheth* is from CHAQAR, which Strong defines, "A primitive root; properly to penetrate; hence to examine intimately." When a man presents "his side" of a controversy he is apt to keep back part of the truth, or present what he does offer in such a way as to make a false impression. If the matter is left just as the one "side" has been pictured it will seem to be right. But the other man penetrates the case and shows up the true state of affairs which may reverse the false impression that was made at first in the minds of the hearers. It is not fair to decide the issues in any controversy until both sides have been heard.

Verse 18. See the comments at ch. 16: 33 for explanation of the *lot*. If the parties to a controversy agree to leave it to the *lot*, the contention will be settled by it and thus it will be caused *to cease*. *Parteth between* means the same as when a person gets between two others who are having trouble. He "parts" them or causes them to stop their conflict; he acts as "peacemaker" between them.

Verse 19. *Offended* means to be driven away from one's brotherly friendship by unjust and harsh treatment. If a man thus mistreats his brother it will be difficult to win him back. The difficulty is compared to the feat of capturing a strong city, or of taking a castle whose doors are fastened with iron bars.

Verse 20. The key words of the verse are *satisfied* and *filled*. They are used in a very unusual sense, meaning to satiate or fill to the point of being gorged. If a man were to complain of feeling too full for comfort, he would be told that it was his own fault, that he was in that condition because of what he had taken through his mouth, and that no one was to be blamed but himself. Solomon is using the condition to illustrate a man's responsibility for too unwise use of his tongue.

Verse 21. The first clause of this verse has the same meaning as the preceding verse but is more direct in the form of language used. What a man says may result either in *death* or *life*, depending on whether his words are wise or not. The second clause is practically the same as the preceding verse in its meaning.

Verse 22. The beneficial results of the marriage relation is the thought in this verse; it agrees with Gen. 2: 18.

Verse 23. In the vast domain of Solomon there were all classes of social conditions, and much of his writing consisted of mere statements of the facts without comment either way. However, the right and wrong features in many cases are so evident that the bare mention of the situation is enough. The observation we should make on this verse is that riches will tempt men to mistreat the poor.

Verse 24. If a man expects to have friends he must be friendly himself, and not *answer roughly* as in the preceding verse. The general connection indicates a friendship that is created by actual deeds of benevolence, and not merely one that is somewhat forced from a sense of fleshly relationship. A *brother* may be more or less near a man because of the relationship, but such friendship is likely to vary or even be broken off. But a friendship that springs from appreciation of practical helpfulness is likely to be more deeply seated and lasting than one based only on blood relationship. That is the kind of *friend* (the one who had been really helped) that *sticketh closer than a brother* (the one who was only his fleshly relation and had that for his motive). In direct connection with this noted but much-misapplied passage the reader should study Prov. 27: 10 and James 2: 15, 16.

PROVERBS 19

Verse 1. Solomon was the richest man in the world, yet he made many statements in favor of the poor. Not that poverty is necessarily a virtue; but the poor as a rule are humble, and if they combine that with *integrity*, which means constancy in the right, they are to be commended above other classes.

Verse 2. *Soul* means the person as a whole, which is in a state of real want if there is not the quality of knowledge. *Hasteth* denotes a man who is rash and does not have care as to where he goes; does not "walk circumspectly" (Eph. 5: 15).

Verse 3. *Perverteth* is a step sidewise, which Solomon says is caused by a man's foolishness. *Fretteth* is from ZAAPH, which Strong defines, "A primitive root; properly to boil up, i. e. (figuratively) to be peevish or angry." When a man goes wrong he frequently tries to show a grudge against someone or something, and blame it thereupon.

Verse 4. The advantage of wealth over poverty, from a worldly standpoint, is the subject of this verse. Solomon has made such statements frequently without special comment in many instances. But he has expressed himself also in other places in such a way as to indicate his disapproval of such use of riches.

Verse 5. There is very little difference between a *false witness* and one who *speaketh lies*. The former is one who is placed on a witness stand and then falsifies.

Verse 6. The advantage of wealth and social prestige is the subject of this verse. The question of whether that advantage is used or abused is not considered, the verse being merely a statement of facts.

Verse 7. *Hate* is used in the sense of belittle or slight. A man's near relatives will often shun him if he is poor regardless of that kinship. And if those who are that closely connected with him stand aloof from him, it may be expected that people who are merely fellow associates will do so. *They are wanting* means the poor man's words will not be able to win back the association of those who have shunned him on account of his needy condition, lest they be called upon to assist him.

Verse 8. *Wisdom* and *understanding* are regarded in the same light, being qualities that will benefit the soul or entire being of man.

Verse 9. *Shall perish* corresponds with *not escape* in v. 5; otherwise the the two verses are identical in wording and meaning.

Verse 10. *Delight* is from TAANUGAH, Strong defines with the one word "luxury." The verse means it is not *seemly* or fitting for a fool to be given luxury; he could not appreciate it. It is still more inappropriate for a servant to be given some authority over a man of distinction and special standing in the community.

Verse 11. In James 1: 19 the advice is given to be "slow to wrath" and that is the teaching here. If a man is discreet he will *defer* (postpone) the exercise of his wrath. The chances are that after he has "cooled off" he will see the *transgression* in a calmer frame of mind and will overlook it.

Verse 12. The same person may show two opposite temperaments, compared here to a lion's roar and the dew. The subject of a king may feel one or the other from him, depending on whether he is pleasing or displeasing to the ruler.

Verse 13. No one should be "proud" of his children or of anything else; but a father would be happy to have a wise son. By the same token, a father would regard a foolish son as a calamity upon him and his family. The second clause is worded more completely in ch. 27: 15 which I request the reader to see. We have all heard the continuous and monotonous drip, drip, drip of the rain off of the eaves, on a long, dark, blustery, dreary, chilly day, and can realize the comparison to a quarrelsome, nagging wife. A man who has a silly son and a nagging wife would have to possess the patience of Job to endure it and keep his own temper sweet.

Verse 14. A man may inherit earthly possessions from his earthly ancestors, and such blessings are not to be regarded as of little worth. But above all such good things, Solomon regarded a prudent (sensible) wife as a favor from the Lord. It was He who designed the form and temperament and other qualities of woman so as to meet completely all of the needs of man.

Verse 15. *Slothfulness* is laziness and that will cause a man to be *idle*. The result of it all is like a continuous slumber. Of course while a man is sleeping he is not producing any substance, and so will finally be brought to hunger.

Verse 16. All of the commandments of God are for man's benefit, hence to keep them means to do what is necessary for his *soul* or whole being. According to the connection *his ways* means the ways of the Lord as set forth in the commandments. To *despise* them means to treat them lightly and fail to obey them.

Verse 17. The key word is *lendeth* because what a person lends he expects to receive back. Thus the writer gives us the wholesome thought that what a man bestows upon the poor is not gone forever. Also, it is not the poor man to whom the benefit was loaned who will repay it, but it is the Lord. This beautiful thought was set forth by Jesus as recorded in Luke 14: 12-14.

Verse 18. To *chasten* means to correct by instruction or bodily punishment or both, depending upon the urgency of the case. See ch. 13: 24; 22: 15; 23: 13, 14; 29: 15. *For his crying* is an erroneous translation and seems to mean the parent should not stop punishing his child just because he is crying. The phrase should be worded, "in view of his threatened ruin." Please read the second half of the verse with the closing words translated as above and you will get the intended meaning.

Verse 19. If a man gets into trouble because of his "uncontrolled temper," it is unwise to try to get him released from his just punishment. If one does, the wrathful man will likely soon give way to his temper again and it will have to be done all over. It is better to let such a man "sweat it out."

Verse 20. *Counsel* has special reference to advice and *instruction* means information on how to apply the advice. The man who observes these words will find in the end that he has acted wisely.

Verse 21. Solomon is contrasting the *counsel* (advice) of the Lord with all the *devices* (schemes or plans) of man. The former is to be preferred because it will stand the test of time and all strains that can be put upon it.

Verse 22. The most desirable thing any man can offer another is kindness. For this reason *a poor man* who is kind is better than one who is wealthy but untruthful.

Verse 23. To *fear* the Lord means to respect him, and he who does so will want to obey him. Such conduct will result in spiritual life that will be satisfactory. No real evil can befall one who serves the Lord, even though he might suffer temporally.

Verse 24. The point in the verse is to give a strong description of a slothful (lazy) man. Such a person would be too indolent even to feed himself. The apparent incorrectness of this statement will be explained by the words *will not* in the verse. They mean he does not feed himself willingly but does it rather than starve.

Verse 25. The thought in this verse is similar to that in ch. 17: 10. A *scorner* is one who shows an overbearing attitude toward the truth. Such a man can be chastised only by bodily punishment. When it is done the *simple* or "silly" persons will be induced to *beware*, which Strong defines as "to be cunning" or inclined to run or dodge. That will be about all the good he will get out of seeing the other man punished. But a man of *understanding*, a man of good sense, will be affected even by a reproof and will gain knowledge as a result of it.

Verse 26. The gist of this verse is that a son who does not have respect for his parents is guilty of shameful conduct.

Verse 27. *My son* is explained by the comments at ch. 1: 10. *To err* means to step aside from the pathway of knowledge.

Verse 28. This witness has no respect for righteous verdicts, hence he will deliver a false testimony. *Devoureth* usually means to destroy, but a wicked man would not want to do that to iniquity. The idea is that he "just eats it" or lives on it.

Verse 29. Fools and scoffers cannot understand any lesson but those delivered with a rod; they must be made to feel since they will not hear.

PROVERBS 20

Verse 1. These articles of drink are inanimate objects and could not be said directly to mock or rage. It means the use of them will cause the consumer to act in that manner. There is no original for *strong* as a separate word, but the translators got the term from Hebrew of *drink*. It is from SHEKAR, which Strong defines, "an intoxicant, i. e., intensely alcoholic liquor." The earliest and most common intoxicating drink in old times was fermented grape juice. But Smith's Bible Dictionary says the Jews later learned of other and stronger drinks, some made of barley and certain herbs. They are the ones meant in the various places in the Bible that mention *strong drink*. It would have a more violent effect on a man than fermented wine, hence the two words *mock* and *rage*.

Verse 2. For the first part of the verse see comments on ch. 19: 12. The man who resists the power of the king is working against himself.

Verse 3. Pride will often goad a fool into persistent meddling. It is no surrender of actual dignity to "calm down" when one sees he is wrong in a controversy.

Verse 4. A *sluggard* is a lazy man and does only what he thinks he has to do. An energetic man does not wait until the cold spring days are gone before he works the ground. Then when harvest time comes he has something to show for his industry.

Verse 5. *Counsel* means the advice a wise man is capable of giving. Such a person does not usually offer it voluntarily, but if another man will approach him with good sense he may *draw out* the advice from him.

Verse 6. This verse is similar to the preceding one. A man who really knows something is generally modest about it and not eager to display his wisdom.

Verse 7. *Integrity* means complete and continuous righteousness. If a man walks in that kind of life his children will be *blessed* or happy. The influence of such a father is sure to benefit his descendants.

Verse 8. We are to understand Solomon is considering the right kind of a king. He scatters evil with his eyes in that he sees it and his good judgment tells him what to do about it to bring about its removal.

Verse 9. Solomon's question in reality is an admission that even the best of men are apt to make mistakes. See 1 Ki. 8: 46 where he makes the same admission directly. In view of such universal weaknesss, it is all the more important that the king be a man of judgment so as to handle the mistakes of his subjects properly.

Verse 10. Among the "evils" a king will have to handle are the unfair dealings between some of his citizens. They may be using the wrong kind of scales in their business transactions and thus be defrauding each other.

Verse 11. "Actions speak louder than words" is a familiar saying that is as true of a child as of an adult. The motives in one's mind will show up as fruit in the outward conduct. This is all true whether it is good or evil that is considered. We do not have the right to judge the heart until we see that which proceeds from it.

Verse 12. The mere fact that the Lord is the maker of man's body is not all there is in this verse. The significant thing is the perfect qualification of the different parts for the work expected of them. Had the ear sometimes been deaf and yet would show reaction to a thing because it was beautiful, then the creation would have been defective. And the success of these organs should convince us that their Maker must have ears and eyes also that can perform their office towards the children of men. In connection with this we would do well to read Ps. 94: 9.

Verse 13. The connection will show that Solomon is writing of the man who sleeps when he should be at work. We are sure this conclusion is correct from the many times he has spoken of the sluggard (lazy man).

Verse 14. *Naught* is from a word that means something bad or worth but little. The verse describes a man who talks down an article at the time of making the deal in order to get it at lower price than it is really worth. Then when he leaves the place with the article he will boast about his "good bargain." Such a transaction is an act of hypocrisy.

Verse 15. *Gold* and *rubies* are not represented as articles of no value, nor even of little value. But as a contrast the possession of lips that speak of knowledge are like jewels that outshine and overvalue all the precious metals or gems in the world.

Verse 16. In ch. 6: 1-5 Solomon lets us know his opinion of a man who will go on a bond for a stranger. In the present verse he has the same opinion, and even expresses it by advising against showing him any mercy. If he is so foolish as to do such a thing, then force him to make it good, even if you have to take his garment as payment on the pledge. The same treatment should be given a man who has become indebted to an immoral woman in consideration for her association with him.

Verse 17. Bread is used as an illustration or figure of speech. If a man relies on deceit for his accomplishments, he may think he is having a success for a time. The after effects, however, will be as objectionable as gravel would be in his mouth.

Verse 18. *Counsel* and *advice* mean about the same, except the first generally is thought of more as a co-operating of minds in forming a plan. It is always better to resort to it before proceeding with any important project, especially one of war.

Verse 19. *Talebearer* is from RAKIYL and Strong defines it, "a scandal-monger (as traveling about)." Solomon does not mean that in peddling his gossip the talebearer necessarily gives away any actual secret facts. It means such a person would have that motive and would make general scandal of any personal matters were he to get the least inkling of them. And in order to get a clue for such purpose he will pretend to be a friend and sympathizer in the hopes that one will confide an intimate matter in him. That is why the verse warns against having anything to do with the *flatterer*.

Verse 20. *Curseth* is from a word that means to make light and show disrespect. *Lamp be put out* is a figure of speech, meaning a son who will thus mistreat his parents will some day be covered with the darkest shame.

Verse 21. If a man inherits great riches he does not know how to handle it as a rule, and as a result such a person will soon "run through" with it. But if one comes into possession of wealth through his own industrious management, he naturally will know how to take care of it.

Verse 22. Personal vengeance is condemned in this verse. If one has been treated wrongfully, the Lord has provided a way in which such a person will get his "just deserts."

Verse 23. A balance is an instrument for weighing merchandise. It is used by placing a stone in one side that weighs the same as the desired article of trade. A false balance would be one in which the balancing point is not in the center, and *diverse* weights means stones of different weights, one to use in buying and the other in selling. Such arrangements are abomination to the Lord because they are dishonest.

Verse 24. The first clause is similar in thought to Ps. 37: 23; 119: 133. Man does not know how he should go, hence the Lord offers to show him.

Verse 25. *Devoureth* is from YALA and Strong's lexicon defines it, "to blurt or utter inconsiderately." *Make enquiry* would be to reconsider. The verse means a man rashly makes a promise to God, then afterward calls it in question and even thinks of breaking his vow.

Verse 26. *Wheels* are parts of vehicles used in warfare or other vigorous activities. A wise king will be hard on wicked men and will drive them away.

Verse 27. When God formed the spirit of man within him (Zech. 12: 1), he lighted the *candle* or lamp by which the human being could seek for information. This search for information concerns the entire *belly* or body and all of its interests.

Verse 28. *Mercy* at the expense of *truth* is wrong, and the king who shows such mercy is endangering his own throne. But if he holds to the truth in all of his dealings with his subjects, his throne will be respected and supported by them.

Verse 29. Another word for *glory* is ornament, and Solomon regarded the strength of a young man as his chief ornament. For the second clause of the verse see ch. 16: 31.

Verse 30. Blueness is the black-and-blue condition that comes after a wound. It is nature's way of scattering the evil effects of the wound. It is the effort of the blood to absorb the congestion by taking it up through the circulation. This healing process of a literal wound is compared to the good effects of chastisement on the *inward* or spiritual parts of the *belly*, that is, the whole being of man.

PROVERBS 21

Verse 1. The Lord has full control of the works of creation. The same is true of the heart of the king. It would have been well had Solomon always recognized that.

Verse 2. It is the natural thing for man to justify his own conduct. If such a standard of right and wrong were admitted, there would be about as many rules of conduct as there are men. For that reason the Lord has "taken over" the right to direct.

Verse 3. *Judgment* means a verdict in a controversy, and *justice* means the verdict will be right and fair to all. Such treatment of one's fellow man is acceptable to God. But it is objectionable to Him for a man to defraud another and then think to make up for it by a material sacrifice or other service to the Lord. See Isa. 1: 10-17; 3: 13-15; Matt. 23: 14 which deals with this same subject.

Verse 4. A *high look* is the product of a *proud heart* on the same principle that deeds are its product (Mark 7: 2-23). This entire verse is on the evil of pride in any of its forms. *Plowing* is derived from a word that means to gleam or glisten, and is used in an unusual application here. The showy appearance of a freshly made furrow is used to compare the pretentious work of a wicked man which is sinful.

Verse 5. Thoughtful activity constitutes diligence, and it will result in useful production. Activity that is rash and not directed by thoughtfulness will be a failure.

Verse 6. Possessions obtained by fraud will prove to be *vanity* or unenduring. To practice such things is like being tossed to and fro, and will finally lead to ruin.

Verse 7. *Destroy* is from a word that means to chew or irritate. If a man obtains goods by robbery he will likely refuse to *do judgment* or make things right with those from whom he has taken the articles. But the retaining of them will not benefit him. Their very presence will irritate him, knowing he has in his possession the things that belong to another and that were obtained dishonestly.

Verse 8. The main purpose of this verse is to show a contrast between a bad man and a good man. One is *froward* or wavering, and his conduct is *strange*, which means it is like a foreigner. The other has a *pure* (unmixed) manner of life which is right.

Verse 9. Houses had flat roofs in olden times, and they were used in various ways, although not the most desirable part of a building. *Wide house* is from an original that means the extent or roominess of society. Solomon means he would rather live alone in a small part of the roof of some building, than to be in society if he had to put up with a *brawling* or quarrelsome woman.

Verse 10. *The soul* or entire being of the wicked has only one desire, and that is to do evil. Such a man is not interested in the welfare of his neighbor.

Verse 11. A scorner is a fool and has to be punished before he will learn his lesson and be wise. The man who is wise or uses good sense needs only to be instructed, and he will receive the knowledge offered him.

Verse 12. *House of the wicked* as a phrase refers to the general conduct and situation of the forces of wickedness. The righteous people might not have the power to prevent such a condition, but they can and will *consider* it, and Strong defines the word to inspect or take close notice of. But God is the great Judge with power to act, and he will do more than inspect the house of wickedness; he will destroy it.

Verse 13. A man who turns a deaf ear to the worthy poor may succeed for a time. However, a condition much worse than temporal needs will overtake him and then it will be too late for him to cry for mercy. See the lesson taught in Matt. 18: 23-35.

Verse 14. This *gift* is a bribe and Solomon merely states the influence of such a gift without making any comment thereon. See my comments on a like passage, ch. 17: 8.

Verse 15. The greatest kind of joy possible in this life is that which comes from doing right. The only reward that is waiting for the workers of iniquity is their own ruin, which is a "reward" that will not have any enjoyment.

Verse 16. *Congregation* is used in the sense of group. If a man strays away from the path of understanding he will get lost amid the group who are dead in sin.

Verse 17. Both *pleasure* (idle pastime), and dissipation, *wine and oil* which means expensive living, will bring a man to want.

Verse 18. *For* is used in the sense of "instead." The evil people of earth will have to pay the ransom for their wrong doing, but the righteous will pay no penalty.

Verse 19. This verse has practically the same thought as verse 9.

Verse 20. Oil and other desirable things of value will be reserved by those who use wisdom with them. A supply may be seen at any time because they will not be wasted.

Verse 21. "Like produces like" is a true human saying, and "whatsoever a man soweth that shall he also reap" is an inspired one. Both sayings express the thought of this verse.

Verse 22. This concerns a city that has been made *mighty* or strong with walls of fortification. A *wise man* will devise some means for *scaling* or climbing the wall and taking the city into his possession or control.

Verse 23. The thought in this verse is similar to that in ch. 16: 32 which see. It is set forth also in James 3: 2. The correctness of this verse is so evident that it scarcely needs any comment. A great many serious troubles have their start in unwise remarks and expressions from evil imaginations.

Verse 24. The leading terms in this verse are the same in thought, therefore their repetition is for the purpose of emphasis. When a man *scorns* or scoffs at a proposition, it is because he has no just grounds for opposing it, but is too proud to admit it, or even to try to make any logical reply.

Verse 25. The chief desire of a *slothful* (lazy) man is to be at ease. As a result he will not provide for his own needs and will finally die of hunger.

Verse 26. The slothful man spends whole days longing for the possessions of others, but is too indolent to work for the like and hence will be brought to shameful want. A righteous man will labor to produce the things he needs for himself, and he will also "have to give to him that needeth." (Eph. 4: 28.)

Verse 27. A wicked man is not invited to participate in sacrificial services even if the articles offered are rightfully his possessions. And his service is especially objectionable if the things proposed for sacrifices have been obtained by fraud.

Verse 28. When it is seen that a witness is going to give false testimony he will be shut off. A witness should repeat truthfully what he has learned. One source of such learning is the things he has heard. *Heareth* is from SHAMA and Strong defines it, "a primitive root; to hear intelligently (often by implication of attention, obedience, etc.)." So a witness who has *heard* in this manner will be accepted and will be permitted to *speak constantly*. That is, his testimony will not be shut off as was that of the *false witness*.

Verse 29. *Directeth* is rendered "considereth" in the margin of the Bible and the lexicon agrees. The verse means a wicked man does not care how he acts or walks. A righteous man will consider his way; will try to "walk circumspectly." (Eph. 5: 15.)

Verse 30. Nothing that man may plan in opposition to the Lord will succeed.

Verse 31. The horse was preeminently the most useful and desirable of all beasts for service in war. However, even the horse and all other equipment would be a failure unless the Lord favored the action.

PROVERBS 22

Verse 1. Riches can fade away or be stolen and leave the owner with nothing. A good name and a friendship based thereon will be out of the reach of a thief, and is not subject to decay.

Verse 2. Since God is no respecter of persons (Acts 10: 34), the rich and poor stand on equal footing in His sight.

Verse 3. A *prudent* man is one who uses precaution in his every activity. He will thus watch his step and so will observe any sign of danger and thus will stop before encountering it. The other kind just goes blindly on and falls into the trap.

Verse 4. The kind of *fear* that counts is respect for the Lord, and such fear is always connected with a meek and humble mind. This attitude tends to attain to the good things mentioned in this verse.

Verse 5. *Froward* means to be stubbornly wayward. In stepping from the right path the traveler will get caught in the wild growth of thorns and in the traps set by the enemy, for such things are usually off of but near the beaten pathway.

Verse 6. Much discussion and speculation has been had over this verse. The English word *should* occurs over 300 times in the A.V. of the Old Testament, but it has no original word in a single instance; it has been wholly supplied by the translators. The word *go* is from PEH, which is defined by Strong, "The mouth (as the means of blowing), whether literally or figuratively (particularly speech); specifically edge, portion or side; adverbially (with prepostion) according to." It has been rendered "according" 22 times in the A.V. So the first clause should read, "Train up a child according to the way." *When he is old* means if he has been constant in the way all of his life until old age, then at that time he will not depart. The Bible does not contradict facts. It is maintained that if a person becomes wayward in old age it proves he has not been properly trained, else he never would have done wrong in the latter years. But 1 Ki. 11: 1, 4 and Ezk. 18: 24 shows us that a man who had been properly trained may turn from the right finally. So the reasonable conclusion is that Solomon was not giving a precept but was stating what takes place as a rule; and the passages just cited show this rule, like many others, may have some exceptions.

Verse 7. This is another passage where Solomon is merely stating some facts and not offering any precept. However, the form of the language and the general teaching elsewhere indicates that he was unfavorable to the conditions named.

Verse 8. *Vanity* is defined "nothingness" in the lexicon of Strong. If a man sows iniquity he will have a harvest that will amount to nothing according to this clause. *Anger* is defined by Strong as an "outburst of passion." *Rod* is used figuratively, meaning the appearance of passion. But it will fail to accomplish the evil purpose of such a performer because the Lord will interfere with his plans.

Verse 9. *Bountiful eye* means to look with compassion on the poor, and with a general purpose of supplying his needs. Such a man will be *blessed* of the Lord and will be appreciated by the one receiving the favors so graciously.

Verse 10. A *scorner* is one who has no just cause for his opposition but is too proud and stubborn to admit it; consequently he shows his evil spirit by making light of what he does not like. The advice of Solomon is to *cast out* or exclude such a person from the association of good people and they can then have peace.

Verse 11. A *pure* heart is one that is unmixed with evil thoughts. Such a man will speak or use *his lips* with *favor*, which means kindness and other favorable sentiments. A person like this will have the friendship of the king.

Verse 12. The Lord can see everything that exists, whether visible or invisible to us. Out of all such matters He will recognize and preserve that which is according to knowledge that is good. By the same token that which is seen with the transgressors will be overthrown.

Verse 13. There is nothing objectionable to one's being afraid of a lion; but only a slothful (lazy) man would use such fear to excuse his inactivity.

Verse 14. *Strange woman* means one outside of the proper association; specifically an immoral woman. (See chapter 7.) *Deep pit* means she uses words that flatter and deceive her victim. The last clause is worded in reversal of the thought. It signifies that a man who will let such a woman deceive him is abhorred of the Lord.

Verse 15. *Rod of correction* may not

always call for a literal rod but it does mean that primarily. Ch. 13: 24; 23: 13, 14; 29: 15 shows that Solomon favored the use of a literal rod when other means of correction failed.

Verse 16. The two actions named in this verse are different in form but will have the same effect. The man who takes away the belongings of the poor will be left in want as a punishment. He who gives to the rich will be wasting his goods on one who does not need them, and such people will not show any appreciation by returning the favor, and hence the foolish man will be brought to want in this case.

Verse 17. *Bow down thine ear* means to listen humbly and attentively. After hearing words of the wise king, then make a hearty application of the knowledge.

Verse 18. The antecedent of *them* is "words" in the preceding verse. If wise words are stored up within a person, they will be fitting expressions for his lips.

Verse 19. The pronoun *thy* refers to the good man indicated in v. 17. The great motive of Solomon was that a man should trust in the Lord. As a help for that purpose he made known to the listening ear the words of wisdom.

Verse 20. The things Solomon wrote were *excellent*, which means they were more valuable than others. *Counsels* constituted words of advice on the right use to be made of the *knowledge gained*.

Verse 21. Solomon wished to make his words so plain that he with a listening ear could understand them. This was for the further purpose that he might *answer* or repeat the words to others. (2 Tim. 2: 2.)

Verse 22. Do not take advantage of a poor man because he is poor and cannot help himself. Many cities were walled and persons wishing to enter had to come to the gate. Among the special purposes of these gates was that of using them as places of public resort. At such places the unfortunate persons would gather, hoping to obtain some favor from the passing throngs. Our verse requests that no oppression should be put on such afflicted individuals.

Verse 23. The Lord has always had compassion for the poor. If any men should take advantage of these poor people at the gate by taking from them what little they have, God will *spoil* or take from them all that they have.

Verse 24. *Friendship* is from a Hebrew word that means association of a more or less permanent nature. If a man shows himself to be given to anger it is unwise to become intimate or enter into any association with him.

Verse 25. This verse states a reason for the advice in the preceding one. Intimacy with a high tempered man is likely to cultivate the same disposition in another. Paul taught this great truth in 1 Cor. 15: 33.

Verse 26. *Strike* is from TAQA and Strong defines it, "to become bondsman (by hand clasping)." The second clause is similar to the first except it is more specific. The "bondsman" may be standing good for any kind of obligation, while the other is making himself responsible for debts only. See my comments at ch. 6: 1-5.

Verse 27. The man for whose debts the surety was furnished may have been thought to be honest, and the obligation was assumed to make it possible for him to close a business transaction. However, he may prove to have been unworthy and the bondsman will be called upon, although his necessary articles of life may be his only assets. Therefore in justice to himself and his family he should refuse to become surety.

Verse 28. Let it be noted that the *landmark* had been set up by the fathers in ancient times, not a recent move on the part of some contentious neighbor as sometimes takes place. It is an established principle even in human law that a boundary that has been in use many years should be regarded as legal.

Verse 29. *Diligent* is from a word that is defined "quick; skilful." *Business* means "work" and *stand* means to have a position or employment. The verse means that a man who is a good workman will have employment with kings, and will not have to work for *mean* (ordinary) men. The moral is that a man should develop himself in some useful trade, then he can obtain desirable employment.

PROVERBS 23

Verse 1. One word in the definition of *consider* is "distinguish." The table of a ruler will have many articles of food and more varieties than any one man can even "sample." Solomon advises his reader to look over what is before him and make some distinction between the dishes. That will be specified more fully later on.

Verse 2. The key word in this verse is *given*, which means "master." The meaning of the whole passage is that the guest should be master of his appetite. If he is, then he is invited to use the eating instrument to put food into his mouth.

Verse 3. This verse designates the distinction mentioned in v. 1. The *dainties* were the delicacies on the table of the ruler. They would be prepared so as to look attractive but would not really be wholesome food. There would be plenty of nourishing dishes on such a table, so that the man who wishes to take the advice of Solomon would have no need to eat of the *dainty* ones.

Verse 4. The word for *labor* is a strong one, meaning, "to gasp; hence to be exhausted, to tire, to toil." So the thought is a man should not wear himself out for the riches of this world, for that would not leave him any strength to acquire the more important things. *Own wisdom* refers to human ideas that are not according to the wisdom of the Lord and that are being offered by the wise king.

Verse 5. This verse is highly figurative, meaning the uncertainty of riches. They may be stolen, or lost, or come to naught by any of a number of other accidents. How foolish it is, then, for a man to exhaust himself striving after them.

Verse 6. Do not accept personal favors from an evil man. If he offers you his dainty food he is only seeking to get you into his grasp for some bad purpose.

Verse 7. *So is he* means the real character of the man is not apparent. When he uses his mouth to invite you to eat of his delicacy, he is only pretending to be hospitable. His heart does not mean it but is plotting to get some undue advantage.

Verse 8. This is another figurative passage. The *sweet* or flattering words of the evil man are mixed with his dainties, so to speak, and swallowed together. When this pretended giver of hospitality accomplishes his wicked purpose, it will be as if his deceitful words had fermented the delicacies and caused them to be vomited.

Verse 9. *Despise* means to belittle or underestimate. A fool will thus treat any words of wisdom offered to him, hence the advice is not to waste any of them on him. Jesus taught the same lesson in Matt. 7: 6.

Verse 10. The first clause is explained at ch. 22: 28. The second means not to enter into these fields for the purpose of taking possession of the products.

Verse 11. God has always been considerate of the unfortunate. If a man seeks to take advantage of them in their helplessness he will feel the hand of the Lord against him and will be made to suffer for his heartless conduct.

Verse 12. *Apply thine heart* denotes that a hearty use will be made of the instruction that has been received, then open the ears to receive more.

Verse 13. *Beatest* is from NAKAH and Strong's definition is as follows: "a primitive root; to strike (lightly or severely, literally or figuratively)." *Die* is from MUWTH, which Strong defines, "a primitive root; to die (literally or figuratively); causatively to kill." We thus see that the beating does not necessarily call for harsh or brutal use of the stick, but only such use as to accomplish the correction needed. The dying refers to the moral and spiritual result of sin. The verse means that if the child is punished with the rod properly he will not come to this moral death. By the same token if he is not punished he will thus die. It is the same thought that is set forth in ch. 19: 18, and the reader is requested to see that place.

Verse 14. *Rod* has the same definition as in the preceding verse, and the teaching of the verse is the same as in that one.

Verse 15. Wisdom was the great specialty of Solomon. It was in perfect keeping with his interests, therefore, to be happy over the wisdom of others.

Verse 16. *Reins* is used in the sense of the mind. Solomon would rejoice not only when a young man had wisdom in his heart, but also if he used wisdom in his speech.

Verse 17. The leading principle of *envy* is to be grieved because of the good fortune of others. But sinners do not possess any real fortune, therefore they have nothing that one should envy. *Fear of the Lord* means respect for him.

Verse 18. *End* means the purpose or reward that is coming to those who fear the Lord. Such persons are assured their expectation will *not be cut off;* will not fail.

Verse 19. The use of *son* is explained at ch. 1: 8. *The way* means the same as the word *way* in ch. 22: 6. A young man will be led aright in his pathway of life if he will follow the words of wisdom offered him by the king of Israel.

Verse 20. The young man is warned against association with drunkards and gluttons.

Verse 21. The two evils named here and in the preceding verse will bring a man to poverty because they are wasteful practices. *Drowsiness* is a state of inactivity that will bring a man to want because he will not be engaged in any productive occupation. That will be true whether his drowsiness is caused by his drinking or is just pure laziness.

Verse 22. A man's relation to his son should give him some jurisdiction over him, and he should therefore heed the advice of his father. While a wife is subject to her husband, when she is old her relation to a son should cause him to respect her.

Verse 23. When a man buys and sells the same article it is in view of making a profit. However, one could not sell the truth at a profit unless he had procured it for less than its value from some person who did not value it very much. But even in that case he should not sell it, for no full price can be placed upon the truth. The same things can truthfully be said of the other valuables mentioned in the verse.

Verse 24. A wise and righteous son or daughter is one of the greatest joys one can have in this life. He who has such should thank God every day, and use his every opportunity for helping such a child in his service to Him.

Verse 25. This verse is based on the truths of the preceding one. It is addressed to the son who is cited to the joy he can bestow upon his parents.

Verse 26. Giving his heart to the wise king means to listen wholeheartedly to his instruction. In addition, he should see that instruction as it is acted out in *my ways*, which means the manner of life carried out by Solomon. It must be understood this applies to the years before he became old and departed from the way himself.

Verse 27. A *strange* woman is one outside of the proper group, and such outside classes would include the immoral woman. *Deep ditch* and *narrow pit* are figures of speech and indicate that falling under the influence of such a wicked character as this *strange* woman is like sinking into a fatal depression.

Verse 28. The evil woman is as watchful after the unsuspecting young man as a wild beast is for his prey. She will appear before him unawares and he will be the victim of the surprise attack unless warned about it beforehand. See the complete description of such a character in the passages and comments at ch. 7: 6-27.

Verse 29. *Woe, sorrow* and *contentions* scarcely need any explanations. *Babblings* means wild and idle talk such as generally is heard from a drunken man.

Verse 30. Wine is a slow intoxicant and hence the reason for *tarrying long* at it. *Mixed* wine means a blending of wine with spices or liquids other than the juice of the grape. By seeking such a drink the imbiber would naturally drink longer of it because of its more enticing flavor, and this prolonged use of it would result in an extended state of intoxication.

Verse 31. When the juice is first pressed from the grape it has a certain amount of pulp in it which will give it a somewhat dark color. As the wine stands this pulp goes down as settlings or "lees" to the bottom of the glass and the liquid becomes a clear red. At the same time it begins to ferment which causes it to *move itself* or sparkle. It is then becoming more intoxicating, and the warning of the verse is not to use it after getting in that condition.

Verse 32. At first this sparkling wine will go down smoothly and seem not to have any harm in it. But in a little while the real effects will show up and its sting, both to the tongue and the general system, will be like that of a serpent.

Verse 33. Many crimes of immorality are committed by drunk men, and their acts are often attributed to their drunken condition.

Verse 34. A ship may be out in the midst of the sea and a storm be raging. At the same time a man is fastened to the top of a mast where he sleeps on as if no commotion was going on because he is so "dead to the world." Such a situation is used to illustrate the irresponsible state of mind in one who is under the influence of drink.

Verse 35. This verse describes a man just coming out of a long "spree." He begins to realize that something has been going on with him when he did not know it. He feels very uncomfortable and will decide to drink some more as a "sobering up" process. That is the meaning of the closing words *I will seek it yet again.*

PROVERBS 24

Verse 1. For comments on this verse see those at ch. 23: 17. Also consult the remarks on Ps. 37: 1.

Verse 2. "Out of the abundance of the heart the mouth speaketh" said Jesus in Matt. 12: 34, and such is the thought in this verse. A wicked man first studies up some evil activity then talks about it to others.

Verse 3. *House* is used in the sense of household or an entire family group. Wisdom is more useful in establishing such than is riches or social advantage.

Verse 4. *Knowledge* is used in the same meaning as *wisdom* in the preceding verse. *Chambers* means apartments and the thought is that they will be supplied with various necessities of life as a result of this knowledge.

Verse 5. *Strength* is not always muscular or physical but often consists in the might of intelligence. It is thus understood that a wise man manifests the kind of strength to be preferred, and such a person will become stronger as he proceeds.

Verse 6. A really wise man is not so full of egotism that he will reject all advice offered him; instead, he will seek the cooperation of wise counselors. This procedure will insure the better preparation for war or other conditions of contest.

Verse 7. The gates of the cities were the meeting places of representative men. At such the wise men of various cities exchanged their counsels. However, a fool would have nothing to say at such times because the subjects discussed would be so much in accordance with wisdom that they would be "over his head."

Verse 8. To *devise* any plan is an activity of the mind and lips only. Yet such a man will be called a mischievous person because all active evil is generally started with the thoughts in the heart.

Verse 9. It is a sin even to think evil because the thoughts of the mind come out in words and deeds (Matt. 12: 34). If this foolish man has no direct opportunity for carrying out his own thoughts, he will scornfully regard the work of others, and that will make him abominable in the eyes of good men.

Verse 10. It does not take much courage to appear firm when all things are favorable. If a man's strength is small he will *faint* or falter when *adversity* comes.

Verses 11, 12. If we see a person about to be drawn into a dangerous condition we should help to rescue him. We must not be like Cain who asked "am I my brother's keeper?" The Lord knows our heart and if we try to excuse our neglect on the ground we knew nothing about it we will not be able to deceive the Lord.

Verse 13. The entire product of honey is good food. The great forerunner of Christ lived on a diet composed partly of honey. But Solomon was not putting himself up as a specialist on diet; he wished to lay a basis for comparison.

Verse 14. Here is the lesson of comparison. One principal method of reasoning is to go from the known to the unknown, or from the literal to the figurative. Any man will know upon trying it that honey is good to the taste and will contribute nourishment to his body. Then if an inspired man compares knowledge to honey he should see the lesson of how important it is to partake of this nourishment for *his soul.* The expectation that is based on knowledge will be well founded and *shall not be cut off.*

Verse 15. This verse is a simple charge upon the wicked man not to lurk about the premises of a righteous man. Such conduct could have no righteous purpose and would subject the doer of it to suspicion in case of any future damage to the property.

Verse 16. *Seven* is used as a symbol of completeness and denotes the endurance of a just man. The mere fact of falling does not condemn one, but it is he who will not bestir himself after falling who will be considered the loser. A just man will not let his mistakes keep him down, but he will get up and "try, try again."

Verse 17. Solomon advised against envying a wicked man when he succeeds in his plans. He now warns against rejoicing when one's enemy fails and we will soon see why.

Verse 18. This verse should be considered in connection with the preceding. It indicates the enemy had fallen through the chastising hand of God, and it is always displeasing to Him when one takes pleasure from the punishment of another, even though it was merited chastisement.

Verse 19. See the comments at v. 1 and also at Ps. 37: 1.

Verse 20. Since an evil man will gain no reward, there is nothing about him to be worried about or envied.

Verse 21. It is significant that fear or respect for the *king* is preceded by fear for the *Lord*. All passages in the Bible that command obedience to anyone are made subject to the will of the Lord. When the requirements made by earthly persons conflict with the divine will, then "we ought to obey God rather than men." (Acts 5: 29.) *Given to change* means they want to change or alter the law of God and they should not be encouraged in such an unrighteous purpose.

Verse 22. *Them both* refers to the ruin that will come to them who disrespect the law *both* of the Lord and the king.

Verse 23. *These things* refers to the second clause of the verse. When called upon to pass judgment in a controversy between persons, the verdict should be based on the facts and not on the personality of either of the men involved.

Verse 24. Because of some personal attachment one might be influenced to take the part of a wicked man. That is what the previous verse was considering. He who does so will be condemned by all good people.

Verse 25. The righteous thing to do is to rebuke a man in wrong regardless of how prominent he may be or how much of a personal friend he may be to the judge.

Verse 26. Strong defines the original word for *kiss* as having both a literal and a figurative meaning. He who does the right thing with his lips in passing judgment will be approved by the good of all people who know of it. In that way they will *kiss* his lips; virtually "throw a kiss" toward his mouth in a gesture of approval.

Verse 27. This verse is certainly good business advice. The field produces a man's living and should receive first and the most attention. The house is not a source of income and hence should be attended to as a secondary consideration.

Verse 28. This does not forbid testifying even against a neighbor if the truth requires it. But it does prohibit so testifying *without cause*.

Verse 29. This verse sets forth the same principle that Paul taught in Rom. 12: 19 and 1 Thess. 5: 15, and Peter taught in 1 Pe. 3: 9. If a neighbor has been guilty of wrong-doing, it is proper to testify on the case in the public interest. However, even such testimony should not be given in the spirit of revenge for personal injury.

Verse 30. Solomon classed a *slothful* (lazy) man with one *void of understanding*. But this does not mean lack of intelligence as it is usually applied, for such a man might not be responsible for his lack of business enterprise. It has the meaning of feeling or concern. A lazy man lacks proper concern for his own interests.

Verse 31. The effect of the slothful man's lack of concern was seen in the unkempt appearance of his field, and the broken down condition of the wall.

Verse 32. Upon seeing the condition of this field, Solomon saw a basis for some warning and instruction for his readers and subjects.

Verses 33, 34. Here is the conclusion mentioned in the preceding paragraph. While a man is idly taking his ease his property loss will overtake him. A traveller is usually prepared to take care of himself, and so is one who is armed, so that whatever they see fit to attack they can take. This is used to illustrate the certainty of the attack of *poverty* and *want* upon a slothful man.

PROVERBS 25

Verse 1. It is not presumed that all of the proverbs of Solomon are recorded in the book bearing his name. 1 Ki. 4: 32 says "he spake three thousand proverbs," and the first word in the lexicon of Strong for "spake" is "to arrange." We know there are not that many proverbs in the book we are studying, hence it is a selection out of the group or arrangement previously made by the wise king. The copying was done under the reign of Hezekiah who was one of the best kings of Judah, and thus we are sure the work was correct and in accordance with the original work of Solomon.

Verse 2. The deepest of secrets are with God which fact is one of his chief evidences of glory. However, the Lord intended that man should learn some of the hidden things of wisdom by *searching* which means to study and investigate. A wise king will therefore do himself great honor by making such investigation.

Verse 3. Among the subjects for the king to study is that of the extremes of height and depth of the heart of kings. It is compared to *heaven* (the sky) and *earth*, the two literal extremes in that part of the creation where kings live.

Verse 4. The *dross* is the useless and coarse matter that comes from the earth in which is mixed the silver. *Come forth* is from one original word and *vessel* is from a word that means "something prepared." *Finer* is the one whose business it is to refine precious metal by separating it from the dross. So the verse means that when the dross has been removed, the workman (the finer) will be rewarded by having something prepared for use.

Verse 5. The above is a true description of a material process, but it is given for the purpose of comparison. Wicked persons about the king are the dross and the throne is the silver. If the evil characters are removed from the place the throne will be recognized as a righteous institution.

Verse 6. It might be unobjectionable for a subject of a king to be in his presence, but he should not intrude voluntarily therein.

Verse 7. The only change that can come to one who is at the top is one of humility, while the man at the bottom has the possibility of being promoted. It is therefore a wise thing for a person to take a position of humility. Even if he is never given a higher place he will not be any worse off, and he might stand the chance of being raised. Jesus set forth this very lesson in Luke 14: 8-10.

Verse 8. This verse means a man should not rush into a controversy before he knows what the question is about and learns some of the facts connected with it.

Verse 9. If you have a difference with a neighbor you should talk to him about it; no one else should be told about it. This also was the teaching on the subject of personal differences and it is recorded in Matt. 18: 15.

Verse 10. If a third party is "let in" on the dispute he cannot know all of the particulars and may form a wrong conclusion and think the blame justly rests on the person approaching him with the matter. If that is the case he will condemn the said person before others and he will receive a bad name which is the meaning of *infamy*.

Verse 11. Of course this verse is highly figurative, for the writer is not speaking of literal fruit. Yet we can understand how unattractive it would be to see a fruit beautifully colored and then placed in a field of some drab shade. On that principle a man might have a correct thought in a controversy, then damage its effects by speaking "out of turn." To avoid such a result he should observe the advice set forth in verses 8-10 above.

Verse 12. An ornament of gold will add pleasant attractiveness to the person of one who knows how to wear it, while a decoration of lead would be detracting. Likewise a proper word of reproof spoken to an appreciative ear and at the right moment will result in his moral improvement and attractiveness.

Verse 13. Snowfall in harvest time seems unlikely yet it is understandable how it could be obtained for the purpose of cooling drinking water. On this subject Smith's Bible Dictionary says: "Snow lies deep in the ravines of the highest ridge of Lebanon until the summer is far advanced, and indeed never wholly disappears; the summit of Hermon also perpetually glistens with frozen snow. From these sources probably the Jews obtained their supplies of ice for the purpose of cooling their beverages in summer." This refreshing effect of the snow is compared with the satisfactory results of a faithful messenger's services on behalf of his master.

Verse 14. A man might make an untruthful boast of some gift he claims to have made or proposes to make, thereby gaining some praise from those who hear him. And a black cloud with wind in a dry season may give hope of relief from the drought, but it "blows over" without leaving any rain to the disappointment of the sufferers. Likewise the prospects held out by false boasts of gifts soon are exposed and leave disappointment in the mind of the victim of deceit.

Verse 15. Patience in bearing with another will often win an argument. *Soft tongue*, etc., is the same thought expressed in the passage and comments at ch. 15: 1.

Verse 16. Honey is a pure food but is very rich and the advice is to eat as much as is sufficient (only). A man should be master of his appetite in this matter as well as at the table of a ruler (ch. 23: 2).

Verse 17. In popular language this verse would mean to depart from a neighbor's house before "wearing out one's welcome. It is better to leave while the host is enjoying his company than to prolong the visit until he will rejoice when he leaves.

Verse 18. A *maul*, a *sword*, and an *arrow* are instruments of torture when used by a cruel hand. They are used as a comparison to the cruelty suffered when a man falsifies against his neighbor.

Verse 19. The disadvantage of a broken tooth or a crippled foot is not realized until one needs to use them. In like manner one's confidence in an unfaithful friend is not known to be misplaced until trouble arises and the need for a friend appears.

Verse 20. Appropriateness may well be considered the subject of this verse. Removing a garment when it is cold will result in a disagreeable reaction upon the body. Nitre is an opposite of vinegar which is an acid. If they are brought into contact with each other it will result in a disturbance. And if a man is depressed with some kind of heaviness he is in no mood to enjoy listening to songs. There are times when a man appreciates being left alone in his meditations.

Verses 21, 22. This paragraph is quoted by Paul in Rom. 12: 20. The slight difference is the last clause in our passage. The Lord will reward the one who does this because he did not usurp His business of taking vengeance of a literal kind. *Coals of fire* is figurative and the meaning is that by such kind treatment an enemy may be led to burn with shame at seeing he was not treated with "evil-for-evil" by the other.

Verse 23. *Away* has no word in the original and has been wholly supplied by the translators. *Driveth* is rendered "bringeth forth" in the margin of the Bible and it has been so rendered in other places in the A. V. That rendering also agrees with the reasoning of the second clause of the verse. The meaning of the verse is that as the north wind causes it to rain, so an angry countenaunce will provoke another to use a *backbiting* (gossiping) tongue.

Verse 24. This statement is explained at ch. 21: 9 which the reader should see.

Verse 25. This is practically the same thought as that in v. 13 of this chapter.

Verse 26. *Down* is not in the original and *falling* is from MOWT, which Strong defines, "to waver." If a spring or fountain is troubled or stirred up it will become corrupted. So if a righteous man wavers at the influences of a wicked man it will corrupt his life. See the teaching of Paul in 1 Cor. 15: 33.

Verse 27. Overeating of honey is discussed at v. 16 and the thought is brought out that by such use of a good thing an undesirable result will follow. It is now used as a comparison in the case of a moral subject. *Search* is from CHEQER, which Strong defines, "examination, enumeration, deliberation." It means a man who thinks too much of his glory (even though he really has it), or "enumerates" it too much, which means he talks about it too much. Such conduct will destroy the glory in the minds of those who see it and become sickened over it.

Verse 28. We have this illustration used before at ch. 16: 32. A man who cannot or will not control his temper lays himself open to the just attacks of the public. That is why he is compared to a city that has lost all of its defenses.

PROVERBS 26

Verse 1. This does not contradict ch. 25: 13. That verse compares the cold of snow, while this means the snow falling in summer; it would seem out of place. It would also be unfitting to be raining when it was the time to be gathering the crop. Both conditions are compared to the unbecoming thing of bestowing honor on a fool.

Verse 2. Every effect must have a cause or it would not occur. The destination reached by the birds would not have been accomplished had they not furnished the cause by their own motions. Likewise, when a curse comes there is a cause for it even if we cannot see or understand what the cause might be.

Verse 3. The point in this and several other verses in the chapter is the appropriateness of using certain things in connection with others. A whip will suggest to a horse what he should do, but an ass requires a bridle for his guidance. It is also proper to use a rod on the fool's back because the only

Proverbs 26: 4-15

language he understands is the kind he can feel with his fleshly faculties.

Verses 4, 5. I have made one paragraph out of these verses because they might seem to be contradictory. The word *according* has no original but has been supplied by the translators. The first verse means not to deal with a fool in as silly a form as he speaks if you are giving your actual view of the matter. In that way you would seem to be as silly as he. The second verse means to use just as stupid a speech in answering him as he used, and in that way you might cause him to see how foolish he was. A little girl once set a good example of this verse. A man asked her if she was a boy or a girl, and she answered "a boy." Upon overhearing it her mother rebukingly asked her what she meant by such an answer. She said: "When you are asked a silly question you should give a silly answer."

Verse 6. The satisfaction derived from the services of a faithful messenger is the subject of ch. 25: 3. The opposite is the point in the present verse, and some severe language is used to illustrate it. If a man were to cut off his own feet he would not be prevented from delivering a proper message any more certainly than in sending it by a fool. It would be as rash as if he should drink something that is violently *damaging* to his personal health.

Verse 7. Appropriateness is again the subject under consideration. *Lame* is derived from a word that means to limp, implying that something is wrong with the legs. The explanation is in the words *are not equal* which comes from the one word DALAL. The definition of Strong is, "to slacken or be feeble." Such legs are not able to render the proper service to their owner. Likewise, a fool is not able to make the proper use of a *parable* which means a pithy maxim.

Verse 8. *Sling* is from MARGEMAH and Strong's definition is, "a stone-heap." *Stone* is derived from an original that means a good building stone. *Bindeth* is from TSARAR and Strong defines it, "a primitive root; to cramp." The first clause of the verse means a man jams a good building stone into a pile of ordinary stones which would make it look out of place. That would be like bestowing some honor on a fool; it would be very much misplaced.

Verse 9. If a drunkard should brandish a weapon in the form of a thorn or bramble brush, he would likely injure himself on account of his irresponsible state of mind. Likewise a *parable* (pithy maxim) would be out of place in the mouth of a fool. His awkward use of it would do more harm than good.

Verse 10. The impropriety of certain conditions is again the thought of the verse. The word *God* is not in the original and does not belong to this passage. *Formed* is from a word that means to cause pain or grief or worry. *Rewardeth* is from CAKAR and Strong defines it, "a primitive root; to hire." The verse properly translated would read, "A great man (one who ought to know better) will cause some worry by hiring fools and transgressors." It is just another statement of fact that came under the observation of Solomon, which he considered as another unwise combination.

Verse 11. This passage is quoted in 2 Pe. 2: 22 and applied to a man deserting a life of righteousness and returning to his former life of sin. That constitutes an inspired comment on this proverb. Solomon classed the circumstances with his many other cases of unequal or inappropriate combinations.

Verse 12. *Conceit* is from AYIN, which Strong defines, "an eye, literally or figuratively." So the clause means a man who is wise in his own eyes; he might not be so considered by others. A fool (silly person) would at least not feel so important and hence might listen to advice, but the other man would scoff at offers of counsel.

Verse 13. There is good reason for fearing to meet a lion when it is known there is one along a pathway. The slothful (lazy) man does not know of it as a fact but uses it as an excuse for his unwillingness to go on an important errand.

Verse 14. In looking for the point in a passage like this we know we must find something that will illustrate a lazy man. A door turns in a certain manner because the hinges force it to do so. A slothful man will turn over in bed even while he is asleep. This is not because he reasons that some motion of the body will be beneficial, but only because the involuntary muscles of his body act regardless of the indolent tendencies of his mind.

Verse 15. This verse is the basis for an old saying descriptive of a very slothful man namely: "He is too lazy to feed himself if he could live without it." Fools and indolent persons were two characters that Solomon seemed especially to abhor.

Verse 16. It is a strange fact that sluggards (lazy men) are often very conceited. It probably is an "alibi" for their unwillingness to study. Why should they go to the trouble of studying when they already know more (as they pretend) than seven men who are able to *render a reason*. The phrase means to return a good reason or conclusion upon some important question that has been raised.

Verse 17. If a man was attacked by a dog he would have reason to defend himself. However, he would not do so by taking him by the ears with his hands. Therefore the man who would do so would only be inviting trouble by molesting a beast that might not have given him any trouble had he attended to his own business. It is compared to a man who intrudes himself into the affairs of another.

Verses 18, 19. A *mad* man means one who is insane and who might scatter the deadly things named as if it did not amount to anything. That would be like a man who would impose deceit on his neighbor and then laugh about it.

Verse 20. *Talebearer* means a gossiper who keeps a disturbance going by spreading the matter. If all such would keep their tongues quiet a trouble would subside just as a fire will die down when the fuel is gone.

Verse 21. The two *coals* are from different originals. The first means char coals and hence they are fuel for the fire. The second means live embers and therefore the kind just ready for more fuel. This is used for the same purpose of illustration as the *talebearer* of the preceding verse.

Verse 22. A *talebearer* is a secret slanderer who goes about and peddles his tales. The most generally-used part of the definition for *belly* is, "the bosom or body of anything." It is used figuratively in this verse. The meaning is that a secret slanderer will cause injuries to the whole reputation of his victim.

Verse 23. The most of Solomon's illustrations are in the nature of contrasts showing especially the folly of inconsistency. In this verse he uses *burning lips* in a favorable sense, but as saying words that are not consistent with the wicked heart beneath the words. A *potsherd* is a piece of pottery that has been broken. The vessel had been used over fire to separate silver from the dross, but even the dross would leave a silvery coating on the pottery, thereby hiding the real ugliness of the coarse pottery. It is used to illustrate the deceptive words on the *burning lips*.

Verse 24. This and some following verses proves the correctness of comments on the preceding verse about the burning lips. *Dissembleth* means to speak insincerely and such a man uses deception in his words. He speaks as if he were a friend when in reality he has hatred in his heart for the man to whom he speaks.

Verse 25. *Speaketh fair* means the same as *dissembleth* in the preceding verse. Solomon warns against such a character so that his reader may be saved from the deception. *Seven abominations* means his heart is completely abominable.

Verse 26. This man's hatred is hidden for the time by his smooth words. However, such a character will finally be exposed before the whole congregation.

Verse 27. This is a statement of a fact that human experiences have proved many times. But while it is primarily that form of speech, Solomon makes it with evident approval. If a man devises some evil plot against another it will be just for him to suffer the consequences of his own wickedness.

Verse 28. *Afflicted* means to be injured. The verse sets forth the idea that hatred is the motive of the man who lies about another. In order to accomplish his purpose he will use flattering words to deceive and lead his victim to his ruin.

PROVERBS 27

Verse 1. The thought is not to make statements of what one proposes to do tomorrow. That is not because the thing intended is wrong, but because no man knows even whether he will be living tomorrow. James was not considering the things expected to be done as evil in themselves when he wrote his advice in ch. 4: 13 of his epistle.

Verse 2. A man naturally might think well of himself, for a perfectly normal interest would cause him to place a favorable construction upon conditions. But he likely would be the only person having the same view or at least it could be that way. So it would be the wise thing to wait until someone else spoke favorably of him and then he would know that at least two people agreed on the case.

Verse 3. *Heavy* and *weighty* may be used in either a good or bad sense depending on the connection. In this place the physical weight of sand and stones is used to make an impression on the reader. The comparison is to the burdensome effect of a fool's wrath. Since he is not a reasonable person he will continually nag his victim with his *wrath* which means senseless rage.

Verse 4. *Wrath* and *anger* in this passage are both used in a bad sense, but they are milder than some other terms spelled the same. *Envy* is used in the same sense as "jealousy" in most places of the Old Testament, and each of them is used as a definition of the other in Strong's lexicon. The leading idea in them both means to be displeased because someone else is being favored. It could be possible for jealousy to be right for it is said that God is jealous. But the connection in this verse shows Solomon is using the word in a bad sense. If a man is displeased over the fortune of a righteous person, he will not stop short of doing him all the damage he can. That is the reason for the second clause of this verse.

Verse 5. There could be no good reason for hiding genuine love for another, hence this means the case of mere pretended affection. Such will do no one any good for it cannot show him any advice concerning the proper conduct. But open *rebuke* which means correction will benefit one by pointing out the right way.

Verse 6. *Faithful* is from AMAN and the first definition of Strong is, "to build up or support." The general connection shows that *wounds* is used to mean some treatment that would be unpleasant. But coming from a friend it would be helpful though painful, even as a medical treatment might be. The best explanation of the second clause is in the case of Judas and Jesus (Matt. 26: 49, 50).

Verse 7. This describes a condition that is very natural and needs no explanation. The use that is made of it is that when people are not eager for spiritual food it is because they do not feel the need of it. The same thought was in the mind of Jesus when he spoke the wonderful words in Matt. 5: 6.

Verse 8. A bird could have a good reason for leaving her nest and would do so deliberately, but to wander means to leave it through the spirit of unrest or with the disposition to rove about. Such is like a man who departs from his proper course.

Verse 9. *Ointment* and *perfume* have very little if any material value, yet they may have a good effect as a result of the pleasing sensations. Likewise, the cold truth of advice or counsel should be of some benefit, but it will be more so if it is delivered in a *hearty* form; if offered in a "heart-to-heart" conversation.

Verse 10. *Friend* is from a word that means a person attached to another by the ties of association and acts of kindness. *Brother* means one attached mainly by fleshly relationship, but perhaps without any or much sentimental feeling which is sometimes the case with blood kindred. Such a relative might object to being disturbed by listening to a tale of woe concerning his *brother's* misfortune. On the other hand, this *friend*, having been previously disposed along the line of personal favors, would give a listening and sympathizing ear to it. See the comments at ch. 18: 24 on this thought.

Verse 11. A son's father or other instructor is held accountable (whether justly or not) for the conduct of that son. Solomon pleads for the young man to act with wisdom and thus cause rejoicing in the heart of the instructor.

Verse 12. A *prudent* man is one who is watchful as regards his pathway. In the language of Paul (Eph. 5: 15) he will "walk circumspectly" which means to watch his step. Such a person will see the danger ahead and will avoid it. The meaning of *simple* is to be easily misled, and that sort of person will go blindly on into the trap or other danger and will not realize it until it is too late.

Verse 13. This is verbatim the same as ch. 20: 16.

Verse 14. *Blessed* is used in the sense of expressing praise or adoration for another. The *loud voice* of praise roared out the first thing in the morning will be considered rather out of place. It will not be any advantage to the *friend* for the people might suspect some improper coalition between the two parties.

Verse 15. For comments on this verse see those at ch. 19: 13.

Verse 16. The translation of the words and the sentence construction of this verse is rather unusual. It should be noted that the preceding verse is the basis of this. The persistence in and the almost unavoidable nuisance of the woman described is the chief thought in both verses. *Hideth* means to check or hold under in the sense of control, and *ointment* means richness or something else of value, either of a material or moral nature. Hence the verse means that if a man tries to check her (the nagging woman of the preceding verse), he is using his good efforts (his ointment) in vain; he might as well try to stop the wind.

Verse 17. The effectiveness of association is the thought of this verse. If evil results from the wrong kind of companionship (1 Cor. 15:33), it is no less true that the right kind will have a good effect.

Verse 18. The first clause is similar in thought to 2 Tim. 2:6. It is all on the principle that the sowing must come before the reaping; labor before rest, and investment before profit. It is likewise expected of a servant that he wait on his master if he expects any reward.

Verse 19. This is practically like v. 17 but with a different illustration. It also adds the suggestion that a man will likely see some of the same qualities in his friend that he offers to him. If a person smiles into a reflector he will behold an image smiling at him.

Verse 20. The evil forces in the universe are never satisfied, neither are the eyes of man. The moral is that it will not stop the demands by merely gratifying them. However, we may have the satisfaction of a clear conscience if we deny to the evil forces what they demand.

Verse 21. Few men can endure praise, but those who can will come out with a stronger character than ever. It will serve as a refining process just as the fining pot separates the dross from the silver and gold.

Verse 22. This is an exceedingly strong illustration to show the stubborness of a fool in his folly, that he will maintain it in spite of all efforts to drive it from him. To *bray* means to pound and a *pestle* is a hard stick or other instrument by which to do the pounding. A *mortar* is a strong vessel into which to place the thing that is to be pounded. If a fool could be thus treated, figuratively, it would leave him still a fool.

Verse 23. The point in this verse is simply some advice toward being watchful over one's possessions. It is not enough to be industrious by way of production, but after the goods have been acquired they should be cared for.

Verse 24. Either material or immaterial possessions are subject to decay, therefore the best care should be taken of them. Furthermore, the most proper enjoyment of them should be had while they are still present.

Verse 25. This verse lists some of the productions of nature. They should be considered under the advice of the preceding verses.

Verse 26. These animals furnish clothing in two forms. The hair or wool could be woven into cloth, or the fleece could be cured and worn as a protection.

Verse 27. The goats furnished food for the body through their milk, while the hair could be shorn off and woven into fabrics to be made into garments.

PROVERBS 28

Verse 1. A sense of guilt causes the fear that results in the flight. It is equivalent to acknowledging some sin before any accusation has been made. It is one of the worst forms of panic, and was one of the evils threatened against the disobedience of the Jews (Lev. 26:17). David wrote about the same subject and ascribed the same state of mind to those who deny the existence of God (Ps. 53:5).

Verse 2. A prince is a leading person without official authority as a general thing. Such men are brought into prominence by the misdoings of a country. But one man of substantial kind of knowledge will insure the state of a nation.

Verse 3. A gentle shower will moisten the soil and produce food, but a flood will waste the land and leave no crop. This is compared to one poor man's oppressing another. The oppressor will obtain nothing by overpowering another man who has nothing to begin with for there will be nothing but poverty to greet him.

Verse 4. There is much important teaching in this verse and certain principles are set forth that are morally in force at all times and under all conditions and kinds of government. No wicked man is likely to respect the law, hence one such person will praise another like him. The second clause shows it is the duty of good men not only to keep the law themselves, but to oppose all who disobey it. In other words, no man is a good citizen who is "neutral" when the law is being violated, for all such characters become lawless themselves in the eyes of lawmakers.

Verse 5. *Judgment* is from MISPHAT and Strong defines it, "a verdict (favorable or unfavorable) pronounced judicially, especially, a sentence or formal decree." *Understand* means to make a distinction between one thing and another that might appear similar if carelessly considered. The verse means an evil man will not make any distinction between various kinds of verdicts. He will class a just verdict with an unjust one because the former condemns his evil ways.

Verse 6. *Better* is used in the sense of being more desirable or satisfactory and not necessarily better morally. The Bible does not teach that poverty is equivalent to virtue and riches to vice. There are many instances of poor men who are wicked, and we have information of rich persons who were righteous. (Matt. 27: 57.) This verse means a poor man who is righteous is to be preferred before a wicked rich man.

Verse 7. True wisdom is manifested by respect for the law because such a life will develop a young man into a good citizen. But he who associates with lawless characters not only lays himself open to legal punishment, but brings disgrace upon his father who desires his children to be useful members of society.

Verse 8. The definition of Strong for the original of *usury* is, "interest on a debt." In modern usage it is said to mean unlawful interest, but the Bible does not make any such distinction. The connection in each case must determine whether a creditor has oppressed his debtor by the exaction of interest. But if it is so determined in any instance the fact cannot be taken from the definition of the word. In our verse the word is followed by *unjust* gain which is stated as different from usury. The conclusion of Solomon is that if a man accumulates wealth by taking advantage of the poor he will not get to keep it. Instead, it will finally come into possession of some person who will use it in helping the poor.

Verse 9. *Abomination* is from TOWE-BAH and Strong defines it, "properly something disgusting, i. e., an abhorrence." It is disgusting to God for a man to pray if his life is generally passed in disregard of the law.

Verse 10. This verse considers a man who lays some plot or snare to wean a righteous person from the strait and narrow path. In some moment of carelessness he will become his own victim. As an encouragement to the better class of people they are promised the possession of good things.

Verse 11. Riches are deceptive according to the teaching of Jesus (Matt. 13: 22). A poor man, not being blinded by such deception, is able to point out the mistakes made by the rich man in trying to obtain and keep this world's goods.

Verse 12. *Hidden* is from CHAPHAS, which Strong defines, "to seek; causatively to conceal oneself or mask." The verse means that when righteous men are in the lead it brings glory and honor to the land and the people all rejoice. But if the leaders are wicked it causes the others to hide or "run to cover."

Verse 13. *Covereth his sins* means to deny the guilt or at least try to keep it from the knowledge of others. The greatest folly in such procedure is in thinking it is more important that man does not see our sins than it is for God not to see them. However, we know the Bible teaches it is impossible to hide from God. Therefore it is the part of wisdom as well as higher principles for a man to confess his wrongs, then show the sincerity of his confession by forsaking his sinful life. If he will do this he will receive the mercy of the Lord.

Verse 14. *Feareth* is used in the sense of respect, and such an attitude toward the Lord will always bring happiness to a man. To harden the heart means to be stubborn against the Lord, and that kind of a man will come to great loss.

Verse 15. The physical danger threatened by the actions of these vicious beasts illustrates the moral and spiritual effects of a wicked man who has rule over the people.

Verse 16. In contrast with the unwise prince is a man who hates covetousness. The meaning of the verse, then, is that a covetous prince will oppress others in his search for wealth because he cannot obtain it by the right treatment of others.

Verse 17. *Violence to the blood* means to be guilty of the blood of an innocent man. *Flee to the pit* is a figure of speech meaning he shall be put out of the way. *Let no man stay him* means no man should protect a man who is guilty of innocent blood.

Verse 18. A part of the definition of *saved* is "to be safe." It is general in its application, applying either to temporal or spiritual things. In reference to business interests if a man follows the rule of justice to all, his affairs will be safe. By the same token if he is *perverse* or stubbornly wavering in his dealings he shall meet with reverses and finally fall.

Verse 19. This is on the principle that there is no profit without investment; no rest without labor, and no harvest without the sowing.

Verse 20. A *faithful* man is one who is true to the rights of others. If he observes this in his search for the good things of life he will succeed. If he is active with only the gaining of wealth in mind, being forgetful of the interests of others, he will be considered unjust and will receive due punishment.

Verse 21. Peter said God is no respecter of persons (Acts 10: 34), and it is therefore Godlike for man not to make any such distinctions. A man who acts upon the consideration of the other man's personality only may be "bought off" by him with a trivial sum, which shows the unsound principles of his conduct in life.

Verse 22. This is practically the same as v. 20 which see.

Verse 23. For comments on this see those at ch. 27: 5, 6.

Verse 24. A destructive man would be regarded with disfavor by everyone. Such is the picture Solomon gives us of a man who thinks lightly of the act of robbing his parents. He is so indifferent and cruel toward them that he will take their possessions from them and then assert that no wrong has been done. Jesus had that kind of a man in mind according to Mark 7: 11, 12.

Verse 25. *Proud* and *trust* are the contrasting words in this verse. The thought is that pride is the cause of a man's distrust in the Lord. Such a character will not be satisfied except by contention with those who do have faith in Him.

Verse 26. This man is the same kind as one who is wise in his own conceit. See the comments at ch. 26: 12.

Verse 27. For the first clause see ch. 19: 17 and the comments thereon. *Hideth his eyes* means one who closes his eyes when in the presence of the poor so as not to see the need which he would know he should relieve.

Verse 28. This verse has exactly the same thoughts as v. 12.

PROVERBS 29

Verse 1. To *harden the neck* is a figurative expression for the act of becoming stubborn against all attempts to correct the erring one. *Without remedy* means there is no hope for a man who will not accept reproof. This serious truth is recorded also in ch. 15: 10 and the same thought is repeated frequently in Solomon's writings.

Verse 2. This verse is a repetition of ch. 28: 12 which was commented upon.

Verse 3. No father will be happy over a foolish son. And no son who is wise will spend his money on evil women.

Verse 4. A wise king will render his verdicts according to justice regardless of all personal interests; in such a manner he will keep his country united and firm. If he accepts *gifts* (bribes) he may appear to be the gainer for a short time, but the people will finally discover his corrupt practices and will revolt.

Verse 5. Flattery is different from just compliments. The former is a favorable comment bestowed on one who may not be worthy of it, and the purpose is to obtain some favor to which the flatterer is not entitled. The latter is a sincere word of encouragement for one who is living a life of genuine endeavor. But it also may happen that a good man will be the object of flattery. When such is the case he is warned that the flatterer is laying a plot to entangle him.

Verse 6. When an evil man does wrong he is not the only one affected; innocent people may be ensnared by it unless they take this warning. A righteous man may well sing and rejoice because he has no reason for being downcast.

Verse 7. The simple meaning of this verse is that a good man will be concerned about the welfare of poor people. A wicked man not only will not give any help to the unfortunate, but will not take the trouble to learn about his condition.

Verse 8. *Scornful men* are those who mock or belittle the danger of invasion against a city. The wise men of the city will use discretion with the enemy and thus persuade him to retreat.

Verse 9. A foolish man will not appreciate anything that is said to him. It is therefore useless to waste any efforts upon him, for neither serious nor jovial speech will change him.

Verse 10. Murderers do not have any respect for the righteous man but will carry out their plot for blood regardless of his character. *Seek his soul* means to seek that which will be for the welfare of his *soul* or whole being.

Verse 11. This means the fool blurts out what is in his mind before considering it. The wise man takes time to meditate before speaking. He observes an old saying that says, "Think twice before you speak."

Verse 12. If a ruler judges his servants by everything that is said he will conclude they are all wicked. Jealous men will lie about the servants because they want the position of honor being enjoyed by them.

Verse 13. *Deceitful* is from a Hebrew word that Strong defines, "to crush." It means the man who oppresses the poor; and both classes are dependent on the Lord.

Verse 14. Righteousness is the firmest foundation for a throne. The king who does the right thing by his poor subjects will have their moral support which is more dependable than great armies or other physical forces.

Verse 15. This verse is like a number of others in this book and I request the reader to consult them with the comments offered. (Ch. 13:24; 19:18; 22:15; 23:13.)

Verse 16. The increase of transgressions keeps pace with that of wicked men. They will flourish for a time but the better class will live to see the wicked fall.

Verse 17. The original for *rest* means settle down in comfort and satisfaction. If the son is corrected he will cease his disorderly conduct.

Verse 18. *Vision* means law or revelation and without it the people would go astray. By that same token they who keep the law shall be happy in the knowledge of having done the right thing toward their government and its rule of conduct.

Verse 19. This verse states a general rule that might have some exceptions. Some servants are obedient to the instructions of their master, while many others need to be corrected with punishment.

Verse 20. *Hasty* is used in the sense of being rash and unthoughtful. Such a man will not give another the time to offer instruction. That is the reason Solomon regards his case more hopeless than that of a fool.

Verse 21. *Delicately bringeth up* are all from PANAQ, which Strong defines, "to enervate," and that means to treat with too much indulgence. *Son* is from MANOWN, which Strong defines, "a continuator, i. e., heir.." The verse means that if a man indulges his servant too much he will spoil him. This will finally encourage him to intrude beyond his proper place in the household, even to the extent of sharing in the estate as if he were a son.

Verse 22. There is no important difference between *angry* and *furious* but they are used for emphasis. The effect of them is also the same in the outcome because when a man *stirs up* strife he transgresses the rights of others.

Verse 23. The best comment I can offer here is that of Jesus in Matt. 23:12.

Verse 24. A man may truly be said to hate himself when he does that which tends to his own destruction. A partnership with a thief makes one a partaker of his evil deeds, and he also must share in the punishment that will justly come upon him. When he hears curses expressed he will not *bewray* (report) it because he wishes to protect his wicked partner and that makes him likewise guilty of the curses expressed.

Verse 25. *Fear* is defined in the original as meaning either anxiety or reverence depending on the connection in which it is used. But in either sense it is unwise to exercise it on behalf of men. On the other hand it is safe always for one to put his trust in the Lord for he will never be disappointed.

Verse 26. The favor of a human ruler may be of little or no benefit, and at best can pertain to temporal things only. The *judgment* or instructive decisions that will be of lasting benefit to every man must come from the Lord.

Verse 27. "Birds of a feather flock together" is a human saying that is true. It is on that basis that opposites in character dislike each other. No man who is righteous can feel favorably toward a wicked one, and it is a compliment to a just man to be hated by one who is wicked.

PROVERBS 30

Verse 1. As to the identity of *Agur* and some other names mentioned in this and the following chapter, I will quote from Smith's Bible Dictionary: "Who was Agur, and who was Jakeh, are questions which have been often asked and never satisfactorily answered. All that can be said of the first is that he was an unknown Hebrew sage, the son of an equally unknown Jakeh, and that he lived after the time of Hezekiah. Lemuel, like Agur, is unknown." All of the translations I have seen include this and the following chapter in the Book of Proverbs and I am inclined to accept the scholarship of the world on this kind of subject. My comments, therefore, will be on the basis that the chapters are divinely approved. This verse sets out that Agur addressed his collection to certain men named in the verse.

Verse 2. *Brutish* means hungry; hungry for knowledge. Agur is complaining because he does not have the understanding of the ordinary man, as he seems to think.

Verse 3. In this verse Agur explains what it is for which he is hungry; it is to have knowledge of *the holy* by which he means that which is sacred. This kind of longing is to be commended, for it is what Jesus blessed in Matt. 5: 6.

Verse 4. This verse is a series of questions that are easily answered if one is willing to acknowledge the truth of the Bible. All things in the universe were made and are kept by the God of Heaven and his Son, and *his son's name* is Jesus. The verse is a glowing tribute to the greatness of the Almighty.

Verse 5. God's words are *pure* which means they are unmixed with any error. By the use of these words all may be preserved if they will put their trust in Him.

Verse 6. If the words of God are pure it will be impossible to add to them without producing a mixture. And such an action would imply that the word of God needed some human wisdom to make it perfect which would not be true. Hence the man who did such a thing would make himself guilty of falsehood.

Verse 7. The word for *require* also means "request," and that is the sense in which it is used. Even that is more in the nature of stating his desire, for the thing he will soon mention would not be in the power of Ithiel and Ucal to grant, to whom this desire is addressed.

Verse 8. In this verse Agur specifies the things referred to in the preceding one. In that place he asked only for "two" things while in this he seems to mention more. But the two means the extreme either of which would be dangerous, namely, *poverty* and *riches*. He also wished to receive only the amount of food rightly coming to him or what he actually needed. This is the same thought Jesus had in mind in the passage of Matt. 6: 11 where the original for "daily" means "necessary."

Verse 9. Agur explains why he made the request of the preceding verse. Extreme poverty might tempt him to steal, and too much prosperity would fill him with pride or independence of feeling and make him deny the Lord.

Verse 10. A servant might actually be guilty of some misdeed, yet it would be better for his own master to discover it. There is something in human nature that prompts one to protect his own. A man might secretly know the accusation against his servant is true, yet he would resent any "outside interference."

Verse 11. *Generation* means offspring and the writer is thinking of a group of sons and daughters that did not measure up to the character rightly expected of it. A number of verses will specify some particulars in which the group failed; one was in showing disrespect for parents.

Verse 12. Self-righteousness was the fault of this group. It was similar to being wise in their own conceit, or feeling there was no need for instruction.

Verse 13. This verse describes one group that was tainted with pride or self-esteem. *Eyelids lifted up* refers to a movement of the eyes that indicated an overbearing attitude toward others.

Verse 14. This language is figurative and refers to the vicious treatment of the helpless at the hands of these greedy persons. This eating is considered in the same sense as certain

Proverbs 30: 15-22

ones who "devoured widows' houses" in Matt. 23: 14.

Verse 15. *Horseleach* is a short form of leech which means a bloodsucking worm. *Daughters* is an indefinite rendering of a word that has a great variety of meanings. The sense here is that this leech has two of its kind that are always demanding more. While that thought was in the mind of the writer he notified the reader that he would tell him of three or four other things that are never satisfied.

Verse 16. The four things referred to are here named. The grave is mentioned because as long as the world stands there will be dead bodies to bury. The barren womb, unlike the mother of several children, will always be lacking in the thing it desires. The earth in time of drought is behind with its mission of producing plants and hence is in a state of unsatisfied desire. The fire is in this class because a flame is only the result of fuel previously supplied, and the crackling of the flames is a notice that unless more fuel is furnished the flames will die down.

Verse 17. There is no doubt that a child who will look with disrespect upon his parents deserves the severest of punishments. However, there is no reason for making a literal application of this verse. The severe language was used to picture the disgrace that would be deserving of one who thus treated his father and mother.

Verse 18. The wording that goes from 3 to 4 is only a peculiarity of the writer. No definite meaning is dependent on it since he does not always use it (v. 24). *Too* is not in the original and the verse means the things about to be mentioned are most wonderful and far beyond the full realization of the mind of the writer. He does not mean they are matters that cannot be explained at all, but they are so great as to deserve the greatest possible interest and admiration of man.

Verse 19. An eagle seems to be supported by nothing because the specific gravity of air as compared with that of the bird is not apparent, and the action of the earth's gravity in conjunction with the action created by a vacuum was not recognized in that day. The next item is the serpent, which by use of its peculiar bodily surface can cling to a rock as if fastened there by some adhesive. The third item is similar to the first in that it seems to defy the law of gravity. The material composing a ship is heavier than water, hence it would sink were it not for the fact that the water is displaced, apparently, by a volume of air that is lighter than water. And the general comment on the three items is that they are wonderful and worthy of the greatest adoration because of Him who designed it all. The same awe-inspiring interest is expressed for the fourth item of this verse. *The way of a man with a maid.* The most popular idea formed about this clause is that it means the final intimacy between the sexes, but that is a great mistake. The last word is from ALMAH, which is used only 7 times in the Hebrew Old Testament. It is never used for a married woman, although the intimacy between a married couple would be just as "wonderful" as any were that the meaning of the writer. *Way* is from DEREK and the part of Strong's definition that applies here is, "a course of life or mode of action," and clearly does not refer to some specific act. All that the writer has in mind, therefore, takes place while the female is a virgin, and before the consummation of the intimacy toward which this "mode of action" was tending. Another way to express it is that it refers to the courtship of an ardent lover in trying to win the affections of the girl of his choice. A very beautiful picture of this may be seen in the long coutrship and waiting time between Jacob and Rachel in Gen. 29. Let the reader consult that place and the comments offered thereon in the first volume of this COMMENTARY.

Verse 20. *Eateth*, etc., is used figuratively, because such indulgence is not connected with an adulterous woman any more than another. The idea is she gratifies herself as casually as if she were partaking of a common meal. A person eats and cleanses his mouth and it is all over with nothing to be concerned about afterward. This illustrates an adulterous woman; not one who has been seduced on an occasion and yielded to the temptation.

Verse 21. The writer gives us some more threes and fours for observation. See the comments at v. 18 on this form of speech.

Verse 22. Men experienced in the doings of public works tell us that a secondary foreman, one selected from the rank and file of employees, is more unreasonable than a regular overseer. It is on this principle that a servant raised to the position of ruler will cause an unsatisfactory state of affairs. The overfed fool is like this servant in that he has been given an unusual treat or favor for which his experience has not fitted him and he thus conducts himself foolishly.

Verse 23. This is somewhat along the same line as the preceding verse. *Odious* means hateful and such a woman would certainly cause much unquietness. The second clause is similar in thought to the preceding verse. For a specific instance of this relationship of maid and mistress see the case of Hagar and Sarah in Gen. 16: 4.

Verse 24. In this verse the writer says nothing about "three" things, which shows it was merely an indifferent form of speech. In the sets of numerals now before us the purpose is to emphasize the success of small things when they use their opportunities according to wisdom.

Verse 25. For comments on this verse see those at ch. 6: 6.

Verse 26. Another name for *coney* is rockbadger. Smith's Bible Dictionary says its habit is to live in groups, "living in the caves and clefts of the rocks." *Feeble* is from two Hebrew words that mean "not powerful." The thought is that in spite of their physical weakness they are rugged in their manner of life and seek the crevices of the rocks for homes.

Verse 27. The point in this verse is one of cooperation. By mutual interest these insects proceed *by bands*, which is rendered "gathered together" in the margin of the Bible. They act on the principle "in union there is strength, in division there is weakness," which is an old and very true saying.

Verse 28. *Spider* is from a word that should have been translated "lizard." The technical meaning of the word is "that which clings to the ground." By its peculiar mode of life the lizard can creep unobserved into the very precincts of palaces.

Verse 29. The sets of threes and fours which follow point out the independence of certain beasts and human creatures.

Verse 30. The lion has been termed the "king of the jungle" because of his strength and activity. The reason man can tame or subdue this wild animal is in the fact of his superior intelligence.

Verse 31. *Greyhound* is from two Hebrew words each of which simply means a swift runner, hence the marginal rendering gives us the horse. Any creature that is so formed that it can make speed and thus elude his pursuers would answer the thought of the writer. For this reason the he goat is included because of his independence in moving about at will. A king is mentioned because he has large forces to back up his authority thereby checking all attempts at rebellion.

Verse 32. This verse is some advice for those who had thought of opposing the forces described in the preceding verses. They are counseled to cease all boasting.

Verse 33. The circumstance of producing butter and blood by certain actions is used for an illustration. It is compared with the production of strife which is accomplished by certain activities also; that of wrath, which is temper in action.

PROVERBS 31

Verse 1. See the comments on v. 1 of the preceding chapter as to the identity and importance of *Lemuel*. The wise advice of a mother to her son would be very appropriate in a document devoted to the "wisest monarch of Israel."

Verse 2. Lemuel's mother had made some vows concerning her son (not recorded for us), and she is now asking him to listen as she speaks. The use of *what* is a peculiar form of speech telling him to heed her words.

Verse 3. The original for *strength* has a wide range of meanings. If a man spends his money on evil women he not only wastes the money, but loses in the strength of his body and his morals. A man owes a duty to his country as well as to himself; therefore he should not conduct himself in such a way as to endanger the throne by encouraging some form of rebellion.

Verse 4. On the difference between *wine* and *strong drink* see the comments at ch. 20: 1. This advice was offered to Lemuel because he was a king. (V. 1.)

Verse 5. Kings need always to be in their best frame of mind because of the responsibility of their position. However, they cannot be thus minded if they indulge in the use of liquors as a beverage.

Verse 6. *Strong drink* is a greater stimulant than *wine* (see comments at ch. 20: 1), hence it is recommended as medicine in emergencies. *Wine* is mild and recommended as a cheering treatment for those who are in deep, bitter distress. This, however, would be different from drinking it just as a gratification for a dissipating habit such as is disapproved for kings in v. 4.

Verse 7. See the comments on the preceding verse.

Verse 8. *Dumb* is figurative and means that those who are about to be deprived of the right to plead their cause would be about as unfortunate as if they were dumb. Someone should speak for them and Lemuel is advised to do so.

Verse 9. Being a king in some sense not made known to us, Lemuel could take an official hand in seeing the *poor and needy* got their just deserts.

Verse 10. *Virtuous* is from a Hebrew word that means to be wise, able, and industrious. *Find* is from MATSA and part of Strong's definition is "to acquire." *Who* is defined also by "whoever" in Strong's lexicon. It is as if the writer said, "Whoever finds or acquires an able and industrious wife has found something worth more than rubies." In Gen. 2: 18 God said it was not good for the man to be alone and that an "help meet" (suitable helper) would be provided for him. That was done, and the present chapter is one of the most excellent passages, describing the kind of companion God intended a woman to be for her husband.

Verse 11. *Need* means "lack" and *spoil* means booty or necessities of life. The verse means that such a wife will save her husband's earnings and not waste them.

Verse 12. Because of her thrifty habits she will be a benefit to her husband as long as she lives, helping him meet the obligations of life.

Verse 13. This woman is not willing merely to work up the materials that are brought to her, she makes diligent search for them.

Verse 14. This means she does not stop at the most convenient sources for the things she needs for her family. If necessary she will go into distant places for them.

Verse 15. We should not think of this woman as a "hard-working, overburdened" person who is used as a slave. The fact that she has *maidens* at her service disproves such a conclusion. She is the beloved wife of a husband who appreciates her ability and has provided her with a situation that enables her to do loving and honorable service to her household, day or night as the occasion demands.

Verse 16. Mention of a *field* might suggest the rugged occupation of a farmer which would seem inappropriate for a wife. This conclusion is not necessary, because one need of a field is to produce flax and wool for the spinning machine. Such would be more in the nature of a garden or truck patch and that is a common sight in the activities of the housewives in many communities.

Verse 17. This woman puts a belt around her waist, not for show or ornament, but to assist her in her work for the family. *Strengtheneth her arms* means "to be alert" according to Strong's definition. It means she sees that her arms are ever ready for the performance of ministrations for her loved ones.

Verse 18. In the wisdom of her transactions in dealing with commodities of life she realizes a profit. Her industrious activities keep her busy even into the night.

Verse 19. *Spindle* and *distaff* are parts of a spinning machine that is used in making yarn from flax and wool to be woven into fabrics for clothing.

Verse 20. This godly woman is unselfish and extends her services of mercy beyond the members of her own household.

Verse 21. The woman being considered in this remarkable chapter bravely faces the unpleasant weather to provide the things necessary for her family. By this industrious manner of life she has warm clothing made for all of her household.

Verse 22. *Tapestry* is not in the original as a separate word. Combined with the two words preceding it the original is MARBAD and the definition in the lexicon is, "a coverlet," which we understand to be a covering for a bed. *Silk* is from SHESHIDY, which Strong defines, "bleached stuff, i. e., white linen." *Purple* is a word referring to the brilliant color of the fabric rather than to the material from which it is woven. The verse means to show a fine taste of this wonderful woman and her interest in trying to please the eye of her husband.

Verse 23. The important cities of ancient times were walled and the entrances into them were through strong gates that were closed at night. All communications with other cities of a diplomatic nature were conducted at these gates. For this reason it was that it was very significant to be known at those places, especially when one was admitted among the group of elders or seniors of the country. Had a man been connected with a family of questionable character he probably would not have been allowed to sit with these elders.

Verse 24. *Fine linen* is from CADIYN, which Strong defines, "from an unused root meaning to envelop; a wrapper, i. e., a shirt." *Girdles* is another name for belts which were worn as accessories of these wrappers. These garments were not for the use of her family especially, for it says she delivered them to the merchant, which means she put them on the market for a price as an income for the support of her children.

Verse 25. *Clothing* is from LEBUSH and Strong's definition is, "a garment, literal or figurative." *Strength* means security and praise, and *honor* means magnificent beauty. The verse means this good woman is adorned with all these qualities.

Verse 26. A woman who can accomplish the things accredited to this one would certainly be a wise person, and when she would speak it would be with wisdom. Her instructions for the guidance of others would be prompted by kindly motives.

Verse 27. *Bread of idleness* would be that produced by another while she was idling her own time away. She did not do this but rather was busy looking after the welfare of her family and producing bread for them by her own hands.

Verse 28. *Her children* would not be restricted to the offspring of her body, but all who became acquainted with her would regard her as having been a great blessing to the world. *Husband praiseth her* means he acknowledges her to have been a true wife and mother who had devoted her days to the welfare of her loved ones.

Verse 29. It is no great honor to be classed above ordinary people. But this woman is made to appear equal to the best; yea, to be above the best. The ones to which reference is made are those who had done *virtuously* which means they had acted with force and strength of character and in a beneficial manner for others.

Verse 30. *Favor* is used in the sense of outward kindness. Such demonstrations are often on the outside only and are deceitful. *Beauty* is derived from a word that means "to be bright" which is the reason it is here used as something vain. "All is not gold that glitters" is an old saying and similar in thought to the clause now being considered. In contrast with these uncertain and deceptive appearances, the writer mentions a woman who fears the Lord. There is something in the life of such a character that speaks for itself and leaves no doubt in the minds of witnesses, and hence they give her the praise due her as credit for her good deeds.

Verse 31. "Honor to whom honor is due" could properly be applied here. *Give her* is a phrase that is not complete without the word "credit" or its equivalent. The call is made to give this woman credit for the good things she has done with her hands. In other words, since "actions speak louder than words," the works which this woman performed while with the people will speak well for her and entitle her to the commendations of those who knew her and many of whom had profited by the things she did. All people coming and going should be told of the righteousness of this wife.

ECCLESIASTES 1

Verse 1. *Preacher* is the title of this book recognized in the text of the King James translation, which is a meaning of the original word for the title commonly placed at the head of the book. The word "preacher" is from GOHELETH and Strong defines it, "a (female) assembler (i. e., lecturer); abstractly preaching." We should not be confused by the word "female" in the definition, for in grammar that form does not always signify the sex of the person being considered. On this point the Schaff-Herzog Encyclopedia says, "though feminine in form, it is masculine in meaning." In order to understand many of the statements in this book we need to remember that Solomon is presenting the folly of living for this life of flesh only. He seems to advocate the claims of certain people whom we term materialists who teach that man is wholly mortal and will not exist after this earth life is over. The motive of such a theory is to gratify oneself in the indulgence of fleshly desire. Why not go on and have a good time, they ask, since all will be ended at death. But let the reader bear in mind that Solomon actually was a believer in another life and expected a day of judgment. But he put out the arguments of the materialists in this way so the reader could realize the falsity of their position. The purpose of the book as a whole is to arouse the reader to a sense of his responsibility to God, and therefore of the importance of living the higher life while here on the earth, getting ready for the perfect life beyond the grave. Relative to the thought just offered, I will quote an excellent statement from the encyclopaedia referred to above: "It will be probably best to consider it a unique exhibition of Hebrew scepticism, subdued and checked by the Hebrew fear of God, and reaping lessons on wisdom from the follies of life." Another thing to be remembered is that Solomon uses his own experiences, both favorable and unfavorable, as a basis for his many words of advice. However, although these were his personal experiences, the record of them and his conclusions and lessons drawn therefrom are made with the same inspiration by which he wrote the Proverbs and by which he gave his people their instructions for religious practices.

Verse 2. In this verse and in all other places of this book the words *vain, vanity* and *vanities* are from HEBEL and Strong's definition is as follows: "Emptiness or vanity; figuratively something transitory and unsatisfactory; often used as an adverb." Since the things of this world are to pass away with it, they are said to be transitory which means they are temporary.

Verse 3. *Profit* is from YITHROWN, Strong defines, "preeminence, gain." Inasmuch as the things of the earth will cease to be when the earth is destroyed (2 Pe. 3: 10), nothing a man labors for will be left afterwards, hence no man can get any more out of life than he puts into it. This means that if a man lives for temporal purposes only, he will have nothing left in the end because all such will be destroyed.

Verse 4. The preceding verse sets forth the idea that the earth is to be destroyed, but in this it abideth *for ever*. The explanation is in the full meaning of the term *for ever*. The literal definition of it is "age-lasting." In any place where the term is authorized at all this definition will be correct. However, the specific extent of the thing or idea to which it is applied must be determined by the nature of that thing itself. In the present verse the writer speaks of the generations of men, that they come and go. In contrast with this, the earth remains after a generation of men has gone and another has come to take its place. In other words, as long as the age lasts in which the generations of men are produced one after another, just that long will the earth abide.

Verse 5. The unchanging routine of things is the subject of this verse and also of a number following.

Verse 6. The passing of the winds from one place to another according to the regular course is independent of man. Even the replacing of one generation by another does not affect these movements of nature.

Verse 7. This verse is a statement that agrees with what is taught in the primary grades of geography. Vapor rises from the sea, it is condensed and falls in the form of rain, and the rain swells the rivers which run back into the sea. The wonderful fact is the continuous flowing of the rivers into the sea *and yet the sea is not full.* This would be unexplainable were it not for the action of evaporation. Incidentally, this is one of the many indications that the Bible is a scientific book, although many people do not realize it or will not admit it.

Verse 8. *Labor* is from a word that is defined "tiresome," and the things of nature are so great that it would be too tiresome for man to describe them fully. After a man's *eye* and *ear* have reached out unto the works of the Creator, there is still much left that has not been seen or heard, and so he is still unsatisfied.

Verse 9. *No new thing* refers to the line of thought carried through verses 4-7. Solomon would not go into the face of known facts and say that no man was learning or could learn anything new. That would contradict his own statement in ch. 7: 29. However, the last word in that passage does not mean that man can bring into existence any material thing for that is the exclusive work of the Creator. What are commonly called "inventions" are discoveries only. God made the earth then told man to subdue it. Every so-called invention is only a discovery of a way to use what God has placed in the earth. The only thing that is new is what man has discovered in the materials of God's creation and the laws He has made to govern them. As to the materials themselves we will note our verse says "there is no new thing under the sun."

Verse 10. I will comment on this verse by supposing that some man answered the question of Solomon as follows: "Yes, I know of someting of which it may be said that it is new and that is the airplane. It was never heard of a few decades ago." With his inspiration Solomon could reply to this by saying, "No, that is not new, except the discoveries man has made. The law of gravitation acting upon a vacuum which holds the plane up was in existence when God said that fowl would fly in the air." The thing that is new only is man's knowledge of these existing laws. Every discovery and use that man makes of the elements in the earth is in fulfillment of the order given him in Gen. 1: 28. God intended that man should enjoy these things and thus advance himself in a scientific study and development of these great blessings. But knowing the danger that might come to the human creature of going too far, the apostle has warned against such abuses in 1 Cor. 7: 31.

Verse 11. The original for *remembrance* means "a memento." The thought is that things in the general routine of this world just go on from day to day and year to year, and nature has nothing by which to mark the actions of man.

Verse 12. See the comments at v. 1 on the meaning of *preacher*. This verse is in the first person and confirms the belief that Solomon is the author of the book.

Verse 13. *This sore travail* is a key to the meaning of this verse. The phrase means "a wearisome task." When God made the earth and put man on it the command was given for the human creature to cover the earth with his kind and to subdue the earth. Thus the task of finding out the many laws of nature was imposed upon him by the One who made him and knew just what would be for his welfare. See comments at v. 9.

Verse 14. See the comments at v. 2 on *vanity. Vexation* is from a Hebrew word that means a constant but unsatisfied seeking after something. The urge for man to be always wanting to go further after knowledge of earthly things has been made a part of his nature by the Lord, and the vexation or strain that it places on him was divinely regarded as necessary for his welfare while living upon the earth.

Verse 15. *Crooked* and *wanting* are used with reference to the things in nature that require some labor and adjustment by man before he can enjoy it fully. Such inconveniences are part of the "sore travail" that God placed upon man which was intended for his good. Hence there is no use to worry over it and try to expect it to be different for it will not. As long as the earth stands these *crooked* and *wanting* conditions will be unavoidable.

Verse 16. *Communed with mine own heart* means Solomon took an inventory of all his blessings; "counted them one by one." The result showed his account to be far to the good, even excelling all of his predecessors in Jerusalem.

Verse 17. Being urged on by his many advantages, Solomon decided to employ them in determining to what extent man could go and had gone in his madness and folly. The conclusion was that which is expressed in v. 14.

Verse 18. All good things may be abused and in most cases they are. The greater the opportunities the more will be the grief and sorrow of those who do not make a wise use of them; the greater the expectations, the greater the disappointment.

ECCLESIASTES 2

Verse 1. The attention of the reader will frequently be called to the remarks made on the first verse of this book concerning the purpose of the book. *Go to now* is a peculiar expression that means, "listen to what I am about to say." Solomon concluded to try out the pleasures of this world and found them disappointing.

Verse 2. *Laughter . . . mad* means that it is foolish to think one can remove the stern realities of the universe by any kind of forced or make-believe joy.

Verse 3. In the words of popular language, Solomon (representing the average man) determined to "see what he could get out of life and have a good time." *Acquainting* means "to proceed or guide." Solomon represents a man trying to find he could indulge in wine and do so with wisdom. He would "go the limit" of folly just to see what a good time he could have. If any man could make a complete success in his seeking for worldly happiness, Solomon should have. He possessed super knowledge by which he could devise various plans. He had great wealth so that the financial subject did not have to be considered, and he was in complete control or authority over the nation so that no one could say him nay. Yet with all of these advantages he finally realized and announced that worldly pleasures were vanity and vexation of spirit.

Verse 4. This verse specifies some of the items referred to above. *Houses* and *vineyards* are what is meant by *great works*. Such activities would tend to make a man great in the eyes of others, and also gratify his own desire for worldly glory.

Verse 5. The original for *orchards* is PARDES and Strong defines it "a park." We may better understand why Solomon wished the use of these parks if we read a few words from ancient history. "Among the Persians, a grand enclosure or preserve, hunting ground, shady and well-watered, in which wild animals were kept for the hunt; it was enclosed by walls and furnished with towers for the hunters."—Xenophon, Cyropedia, 1-3-14. And so it passed into the Hebrew language according to Josephus. Incidentally, I will state that the word "paradise" came from this Persian word PARDES.

Verse 6. We know that all trees are *wood*, but that word here means a forest or grove. The pools were for the storing of water to supply the trees with moisture.

Verse 7. *Maidens* is from SHIPHCHAH, which Strong defines, "a female slave as a member of the household." *Servants* is about the same in meaning as the maidens except that they were male and were used for the coarser work outside of the houses. *Cattle* is defined in the lexicon as "live stock," and it would include horses concerning which Solomon made one of his mistakes. (Deut. 17: 16; 2 Chr. 1: 16.)

Verse 8. *Peculiar treasure* both are from CEQULLAH, which Strong defines, "Participle of an unused root meaning to shut up; wealth (as closely shut up)." The thought is he collected such articles as were expected only to be possessed by kings in the various provinces. Solomon was able to obtain a complete assortment of musical instruments and also to employ vocal musicians to sing with these accompaniments.

Verse 9. We should be careful in our criticism of Solomon about these activities. God had promised that he was to have "riches and honor, so that there shall not be any among the kings like unto thee all thy days" 1 Ki. 3: 13). Our present verse as well as several others in the chapter is a statement in harmony with God's promise. The mistake Solomon made was in letting those things lead him astray. The Lord considered the danger of that and warned him to "walk in my ways, to keep my statutes and my commandments." (1 Ki. 3: 14.)

Verse 10. Solomon meant that he could take to himself anything he saw and wanted. That was because of his wealth and authority. The original for *labor* is defined, "toil, i. e., wearing effort; hence worry, whether of body or mind." We do not think of Solomon as performing bodily labor, but he did worry and concern himself in obtaining all of these things. *My portion* means the reward for his efforts was the enjoyment he got out of the things collected. Let us not overlook the important conclusion that Solomon states in this verse. *This was my portion of all my labor.* All that he got out of his labor and worry in collecting the wealth and other objects was his personal enjoyment or satisfaction.

Verse 11. After coming to the conclusion stated in the last of the preceding paragraph, Solomon expressed himself according to this verse. He repeated his familiar saying that it was all *vanity and vexation of spirit.* (See the comments on this phrase in ch. 1: 14.) *Profit* means "preeminence, gain." The man who spends his energies in these things *under the sun* (earthly things) will finally realize that he is no better or more prominent than others.

Verse 12. Then the author did some meditating over these matters. He compared wisdom and folly and observed that the man who came after the king and "labored" in the same way would not be able to accomplish any more than did his predecessor.

Verse 13. The grand conclusion was that wisdom was to be preferred, even as much as light is preferable to darkness.

Verse 14. The first clause may sound strange or unnecessary. The complete thought is as if it said, "the eyes in the head of a wise man are for the use that a man of wisdom is expected to make of them." This idea is borne out by the next clause that says a fool walks in darkness. Evidently the fool has eyes in his head the same as the wise man, but he does not make the same use of them as does the wise man. *One event . . . them all* means that as far as any permanent profit in the end of life of pleasure is concerned, there is no difference between a wise and a foolish man.

Verse 15. This verse is a continuation in thought of the preceding one. As far as any advantage or profit in the end is concerned, even Solomon would be no better than the foolish ones of earth. He then makes a sort of questioning criticism as to why he had been giving so much attention to the pleasures prompted by his wisdom. He answers his own question as if he said, "O well, it is just some more of the vanity to which the human race is inclined."

Verse 16. This verse may be considered a summing up of the reasoning and conclusions that have been offered in several preceding verses. When the time of death comes there will be no difference between a wise man and a fool.

Verse 17. Upon observing how empty was a life devoted to the passing pleasures of the flesh, Solomon was filled with disgust over it. Again he described it with his familiar phrase, *vanity and vexation of spirit*.

Verse 18. One particular reason for Solomon's attitude was the truth that he had to leave his works to the next generation.

Verse 19. The point that concerned him most was the uncertainty as to the kind of man who would have control over the things left to him. This thought caused him again to apply his term *vanity* which means emptiness or uselessness.

Verse 20. When the full realization of the subject loomed up before him, Solomon was filled with despair.

Verse 21. Regardless of how wisely a man plans his work and accumulates the things of value, yet he must leave it and perhaps a man who "never turned a hand" to accomplish a thing will inherit them. His conclusion was that it was all emptiness.

Verse 22. There is nothing new in this verse, just a general statement of the unprofitableness of this worldly life and its apparent gains.

Verse 23. Even while in the midst of the supposed enjoyment of the things of this life there is much sorrow. And with all his *travail* (hard work) there is grief, because a man will always be worrying whether he is going to accomplish what he intends. This anxiety is often so great that it will prevent him from relaxing at night when he should be finding it a time of rest.

Verse 24. Food and water are blessings given by the hand of God and it is right for a man to enjoy them. And if he will "be therewith content" (1 Tim. 6: 8), he will not always be worrying about what worldly success he is going to have.

Verse 25. If Solomon with all of his advantages was dissatisfied with the accomplishments of this world, the average man should not think he could succeed.

Verse 26. *God giveth* is said in the sense that the things named are made possible to man through the providence of God. All have equal right to the favors of the Lord and if a man uses them as he should he will be acting according to the wisdom given of God. But if he chooses to act the part of a sinner and tries to make a success of hoarding the temporary things of this life, God will not prevent him from trying it. If he does, however, it will prove to be empty or *vanity*.

ECCLESIASTES 3

Verse 1. The key to this and several verses following is in the meaning of *season* and *time*. The idea is that one time or event should not be confused with another. The list of things to be enumerated starts with an arrangement of nature, and that is followed by a number of events and actions that are more or less the doings of man. Since in the first item nature is seen to be systematic and orderly, does not do one thing when it should be doing another, so man should take a lesson and observe the advantage in doing appropriate things at the appropriate time.

Verse 2. In this verse nature has fixed the order of events and man cannot change it. For instance, no man can die before he is born or begotten, and it is impossible to pluck up a plant before it has been started and grown.

Verse 3. The actions of man are introduced into the list referred to above. It should be noted that the writer does not profess to state just how the proper *time* is to be determined, that would have to be done in each case on its own merits. The idea is to do things at the appropriate time, and not try to do one thing when it is not the right occasion for it.

Verse 4. Keeping in mind the general explanation offered above, it should be clear why it would be inappropriate either to *weep* or *laugh* when the two actions were reversed. To do the latter when the former is proper would indicate coldness and frivolity. To reverse it would be the act of a pessimist or calamity howler. *Mourn* and *dance* are used in the same sense as *weep* and *laugh* and take the same comments.

Verse 5. It is true that one must gather stones before he can cast them. However, if he delays gathering the stones until the time he should be using them he will make a failure. When the proper *time* comes for two people to embrace it will be right for them to do so. But they should not go to excess with it and should refrain at the proper *time*, which would be before they had gone to extremes.

Verse 6. One meaning for the original of *lose* is *to destroy* or dispose of. Thus the clause means there would be *times* when it would be necessary to seek for some articles of usefulness. But a man might learn that some things he had acquired were impractical, and it would then be the *time* to *lose* or cast off those things. The second clause of the verse is a repetition in thought of the first.

Verse 7. Every woman will appreciate the first clause. A garment might be in such a condition that it would need only to be sewed up. On the other hand, it could get into a state that could not be repaired without first rending it so as to remove the parts that were beyond repair. The second clause is subject to so many possible instances that I scarcely know to what I should refer. There are times when "silence is golden," but at others it would be negligence to keep still.

Verse 8. If a situation develops where a person is sincerely trying to live right, that will be a *time* when others should show their love. But if instead some man rejects all efforts to lead him aright and he persists in a wicked course of action, then it will be proper for the righteous to show their hatred for such a life. The *time of war* is when a nation is attacked and it would need to engage in a war of defense. By the same token, when the defensive warfare has been fought and won, then it is the *time* to seek for peace.

Verse 9. This is the same as ch. 1: 3 which was commented upon.

Verse 10. *To be exercised* refers to the purpose of God in requiring man to develop the elements of the earth. (See the comments at ch. 1: 13.)

Verse 11. *He* refers to God and *their heart* means the heart of man. God has caused man to be interested in the world of creation to the extent that he will labor and toil to find out all about it. However, the creation is so much greater than the knowledge of man that he never *can find out the work that God maketh from the beginning to the end*. That is, he can never fully find out, yet he has the desire and as a consequence he labors at it until he finally is worn out in the attempt.

Verse 12. This verse takes the same explanation as ch. 2: 24.

Verse 13. The main point in this verse is the thought of the source of our blessings. When we are enjoying our food and other blessings of life we should remember they are *gifts from God*. (James 1: 17.)

Verse 14. The things God does, unlike those done by man, are perfect and cannot be improved upon by human beings. Man therefore should fear the Lord and strive to make the best use of the blessings given to him.

Verse 15. This verse is another form of the statement in ch. 1: 9, 10. Extensive comments were made at that place and the reader is requested to consult them in connection with the present verse.

Verse 16. *Saw under the sun* means Solomon took a look at the conditions in the world. He observed that the courts and other places that should be run according to righteousness, were corrupted with the elements of iniquity.

Verse 17. The wise man would have been in despair over the corrupt condition were it not for his faith in God. He believed that divine judgment would be rendered.

Verse 18. When the time finally comes that God takes a hand in the judgment of men, then the wicked ones will be made to realize they had stooped as low as beasts.

Verse 19. This is one of the favorite passages of the materialists. That term is explained in the comments on ch. 1: 1, and I urge the reader to consult that place now. It is true that the fleshly part of man will have the same ending as the beasts. But before this chapter is finished we will see that Solomon was not a materialist.

Verse 20. The *one place* to which all living beings will go is the grave or the dust. The bodies of both man and beast are made of the ground and will return to it when death comes. But Solomon was writing only of the body in this verse and was not considering the soul. "Dust thou art to dust returnest, was not spoken of the soul," as a poet has truly said

Verse 21. This verse shows plainly that Solomon was writing about the body only of man in the preceding verses. Nothing was said about the spirit or inner life as that was not yet under consideration. That subject is now introduced and will receive careful attention. The two words that are outstanding are *knowledge* and *spirit*, and I shall examine the second one first. It is from RUWACH (otherwise spelled RUACH) and Strong's definition is, "Wind; by resemblance breath, i. e., a sensible (or even violent) exhalation; figuratively life, anger, unsubstantiality; by extension a region of the sky; by resemblance spirit, but only of a rational being (including its expression and functions)." In the King James Translation it has been rendered breath 28 times, spirit 232, wind 90. Its specific meaning is that part of a creature that enables its body to live and think. Of course a beast cannot think as man does yet it lives and knows some things. In that sense it also has a spirit without which it would be dead. The first word is from YADA and Strong's definition is the following: "A primitive root; to know (properly to ascertain by seeing); used in a great variety of senses, figuratively, literally, euphemically [a milder expression substituted for a harsh one but with the same meaning] and inferentially (including observation, care, recognition; and causatively instruction, designation, punishment, etc.)" I have copied the definition entire because of the importance of the word. In view of the requirements of the word with its variety of meanings, also the definition of the word for *spirit*, it is clear why Solomon sets forth that no man can know the spirits of man and beast. However, that need not keep us from accepting the inspired statement of Solomon that at death the spirit of the beast goes down to earth with its body, but the spirit of man goes upward as his body goes back to the earth. That conclusively settles the question of Solomon's belief in the superiority of man over all other beings.

Verse 22. Having given us his actual belief concerning man's preeminence over other living creatures, Solomon again comes back to the use that should be made of things while in this world. *Rejoice* does not mean that man should live for this world only, but that he should experience the rejoicing that comes from realizing all good bodily blessings are from the Lord (James 1: 17). And even the righteous use of these things must be enjoyed in this life if at all, because man shall not *see what shall be after him*.

ECCLESIASTES 4

Verse 1. *Returned* means he came back to what has been the main subject of the book. That is the toil and struggle for satisfaction on the part of most human beings in the temporary things of this world. The thought has been frequently expressed that all such activities are empty and will prove disappointing in the end. This verse points out that even in this world a person may be disappointed because of the struggle to excel in the obtaining and use of earthly favors. If the stronger take advantage of their fellows there is not much that can be done about it.

Verse 2. Since all permanent rest and enjoyment will come only after this life, the dead were *praised* or congratulated. They have passed from the turmoil of earthly things and, if they have lived as they should, they will be in a state "where the wicked cease from troubling and the weary are at rest."

Verse 3. In the preceding verse the dead man is said to be more fortunate than the living, because of the unrest connected with the struggle for the things of the world. In this verse the man who is yet unborn is said to be better than both the others.

Verse 4. The man who engages in *travail* (tiresome labor) and righteous work will be envied by his neighbor. That is because he realizes the desirability of the things acquired by the honest labor, yet he is too indolent to secure them for himself. Such a man will pretend to think little of the accomplishments of the other one and will say they are "sour grapes." And this whole situation is one that will finally prove to be temporary and hence *vanity* or emptiness.

Verse 5. *The fool* as he is considered in this connection is the man who craves temporal indulgences, yet he is too inactive to produce them. Hence he will live up what he has on hands with no replenishments, which is equivalent to consuming his own flesh like a man existing on his blood supply without additional food.

Verse 6. This verse is similar in thought to Paul's statement in 1 Tim. 6: 6. A discontented person will be in such misery that he will not appreciate the blessings that may be all around him.

Verse 7. One word in the lexicon definition for the original for *returned* is "again." Hence this verse simply means that the writer took another viewing of the things *under the sun*, which means those belonging to the earth and thus were temporal.

Verse 8. This verse pictures a person going through life single and alone. A part of his situation may be his own choice and part caused by other conditions. He is not responsible for not having a brother, and also it may or may not be his fault that he has no child, but it certainly is his choice if he is single. Such a man has ignored the instructions in Gen. 2: 24, Matt. 19: 5, Mark 10: 7, and Eph. 5: 31. Such a man might well ask, *for whom do I labor?* He has no wife to share his income and no child to be benefited by his hard labor. No wonder Solomon regarded such a life as *vanity* (emptiness) and *sore travail* or tiresome hard toil.

Verse 9. This verse acknowledges the statement of God recorded in Gen. 2: 18. Experience and observation also will teach us the truth of the passage.

Verse 10. The principle of cooperation is taught in this verse, applying to others besides husbands and wives. Both parties will not likely fall or become ill or otherwise needy at the same time, which will give opportunity for one to help another.

Verse 11. This verse continues the thoughts of the preceding verses, even giving a specific illustration of the subject. The facts are so universally known that further comment is unnecessary.

Verse 12. This is another specification of the principle being considered. If two people are joined by some common relationship, then a third party cannot attack one without meeting the other. All of this agrees with other places in the Bible where provision was made for the stronger or more fortunate to come to the rescue of the other. On this subject I request the reader to consult Gen. 32: 6-8, Neh. 4: 19, 20.

Verse 13. The gist of this verse is that wisdom is better than riches or worldly power and glory.

Verse 14. The case of Joseph (Gen. 41) is one in point related to the thoughts in the preceding verse. He was poor and unjustly imprisoned, yet his wisdom procured for him his freedom and promotion to honor.

Verse 15. In his observation of people and conditions Solomon considered more than one generation. The purpose was to see if it just happened to be an unusual experience of a certain man, or was the common lot of mankind.

Verse 16. No, when he fixed his eyes on any specified person and saw his state, then considered others following him and also those preceding him, he found they all had the same story. It was summed up in the phrase *vanity and vexation of spirit*.

ECCLESIASTES 5

Verse 1. *Keep thy foot* is the same as saying "watch your step," or, be careful what you do and say. This is especially important when entering the house of God. A man who is hearing may be said not to be contributing anything. However, he could be showing more real devotion to God than is being offered by a fool in some useless or even harmful performance in the name of religion. What is more regrettable is that the fool does not realize the evil of his doing, and hence it will increase the iniquity.

Verse 2. *Rash* means to be unduly hasty with the mouth. In other words, do not speak until you understand what should be said. (See James 1: 19.) *Few* is not restricted to the numerical meaning literally. The idea is that man's declarations or assertions should be comparatively brief and modest. The basis for such advice is the vast difference between God and man. One is in Heaven and the other on earth. One is the Creator and the other is the creature.

Verse 3. There is not much relationship between *dream* and *multitude of words;* the idea is that effects have their causes. A burden of business will so weigh on a man's mand that he will see it in his dream. Likewise, an undue number of words will result from the activities of a fool's mind.

Verse 4. Vows were not commanded by the Mosaic law, but they were approved when voluntarily made. The general definition in the lexicon for the original is, "a promise." It generally was a promise to make some kind of a gift in the way of sacrifice or the gift of money. However, it might consist in a promise to perform some special service. *Fools* is from a word that means "stupid or silly," and we inquire why the word is used in the present connection. If a person makes some specific promise to God it is for the purpose of obtaining some favor from Him. Only a stupid person would think he could induce God to give him a favor by making a promise that he never intended to keep.

Verse 5. Since vows were not commanded, it would be better not to make one than to break one. That would constitute truce breaking which is condemned by human and divine law. If a man voluntarily makes a vow he is as much obligated to fulfill it as if it had been commanded by the Lord.

Verse 6. The writer is still thinking about vows and the importance of keeping them when voluntarily made. To break one would be to *cause the flesh* (body) *to sin*. *Angel* is from MALAK and part of Strong's definition is, "prophet, priest or teacher." When a person made a vow it would generally be carried out under the services of some man of God. (Such as that of Hannah in 1 Sam. 1: 11-28.) If Hannah had come before Eli and tried to evade the vow on the ground that she erred in making the vow, she would have violated this verse.

Verse 7. If dreams and words are the wrong kind, such as are described in the preceding verse, then the more they are multiplied the worse it will be. Therefore a man should fear or respect God and he will regulate his speech accordingly.

Verse 8. Oppression and violence such as are here described need not cause one to wonder. This refers especially to the men in official position who selfishly impose injustice upon the poor for personal gain. But they will finally get their just deserts at the hand of Him who is *higher than the highest*. He *regardeth* all that is going on and can bring all to strict account because he is *higher than they* (the unjust officials).

Verse 9. No man has such a right to the things of the earth by reason of his official position that he may take advantage of another. The last clause of the verse is given to show that no one is independent of the necessities of the earth's products.

Verse 10. There is no sin in the mere possession of wealth, but there is in the wrong use of it. It was not money that Paul condemned but the love of it (1 Tim. 6: 10). So it is that he that *loveth* silver will be disappointed in the end because it is *vanity* or something that is empty of any lasting value.

Verse 11. This verse evidently considers a case where a man employs a number of helpers to increase his production. It is expected that he will support the ones who work for him. That is the reason for the reference to *they that eat them*. The closing words are descriptive of a miser who takes pleasure in looking at his coins.

Verse 12. If a man is contented with "the simple life" and craves only the necessities, he will work for them and be grateful for having what his body needs. Having nothing to worry over he will lie down at night and enjoy a normal rest. The rich man is so fearful of losing his wealth that it prevents him from sleep.

Verse 13. The key to the point in this verse is in the last three words. The mere fact of possessing wealth is not wrong. The danger is in placing one's affections on it, and in that case men are keeping the wealth *to their hurt*.

Verse 14. *Perish by evil travail* means that earthly gain is uncertain and it is likely to "slip through the fingers" and be gone. When that occurs the man will have nothing to leave his children for all his hard work.

Verse 15. This verse teaches the same truth that Paul wrote in 1 Tim. 6: 7. Solomon was not criticizing the fate decreed by the Almighty for humanity. His idea was to show why it is foolish for a man to wear himself out gathering the wealth of the world, when he will not be able to take any of it with him.

Verse 16. *Sore* means to be irritated, and Solomon regarded it an irritating matter to work all through life and then not be able to take anything along. *Wind* refers to this life and the writer means that all of a man's toil for earthly things will have nothing left after this life is over.

Verse 17. *Eateth in darkness* means a man does not know when his days on earth will end. In view of that it is very foolish for him to devote his time and strength to the perishing things of this world.

Verse 18. Again we are shown that Solomon did not condemn a man for enjoying the good things of this life. What he lamented was to see those who were so greedy for riches to hoard that they could not appreciate the blessings which God had given them.

Verse 19. There are some men who use good judgment in the things of this life. Such persons will accumulate the riches of this world for the right purpose. And that kind of character will take the proper delight in consuming the food and other necessities of life, at the same time be producing a surplus that can be used for the benefit of others. The gift of God means the man who will pursue the course just described is exercising one of the greatest gifts that God ever extended to man, that of good judgment and an unselfish use of it.

Verse 20. The man described in the preceding verse will not *remember* or think sadly about the shortness of man's days. He has followed the kind of life that pleases God, and the consciousness of that fact will give him joy.

ECCLESIASTES 6

Verse 1. *Evil* is not always used as something morally wrong, but it also includes the idea of being unfortunate or undersirable. Solomon had in mind a condition that was not rare or just occasional, but it was *common* or of general occurrence.

Verse 2. *God hath given* ascribes these blessings to God, and they would be for the benefit of man if he were permitted to consume them upon himself. *God giveth him not power* does not blame Him for the misfortunes of the human race. It only means that the Lord does not perform any special miracle to overcome the misfortune that hinders man from the enjoyment of the blessings. *This is vanity* is another angle of the emptiness of the things of this world. One word in the lexicon definition of *disease* is "anxiety," and it well agrees with the idea Solomon had in mind.

Verse 3. The original for *burial* has been rendered by grave 4 times in the King James Version, sepulchre 5, burying place 1. In Bible times people were much concerned about having proper provisions for the respectful interment of the body after death. (Gen. 24.) Our verse has in mind a man who had a large family and was prosperous in the world, yet made the wrong use of his opportunities. As a result of his unwise course of life he had not even made provision for a desirable place of burial when death came to him. Solomon regarded such a fate as worse than to have been prematurely born and died immediately after birth.

Verse 4. *Vanity* and *darkness* are connected in the description of this man because they have one quality in common which is emptiness or uselessness.

Verse 5. The premature infant never saw the sun, but he also never saw the empty turmoil that was experienced by the man described above. For that reason he will have more rest than the other person, because the spirit of the infant will go to the place "where the wicked cease from troubling and the weary are at rest."

Verse 6. *All go to one* place refers to the death of the body. That will come to all classes of men, the rich as well as the poor. The point is that even if a man could live two thousand years, he will finally come to his death the same as others, and leave all his earthly goods behind. For that reason it is foolish for a man to spend his days toiling aimlessly for the goods that he cannot take with him.

Verse 7. The need and desire for things to satisfy the fleshly body will be present as long as man lives. When it has been satisfied at any specific time the satisfaction is soon gone and the call of the body soon is felt again. The thought is that man should be grateful if he is supplied continuously with these necessities, and not labor with tiresome exertions to accumulate that which he could not consume even after he has produced it. Or, if he really could consume all that he is producing, it would not stop the natural craving, for that *is not filled*.

Verse 8. The gist of this verse is that all classes, the poor and the rich, the foolish and the wise, all are headed for the same destination, the death of the body.

Verse 9. "A bird in the hand is worth two in the bush" is a familiar saying that carries the same thought as this verse. The *sight of the eyes* means the things already in sight. *Wandering* desire means the things longed for but uncertain of obtaining. *This* refers to the wandering mind after uncertain favors, for such activities will wear a person out because of the vexation of spirit.

Verse 10. It would be vain for man to search for something new (see the comments at ch. 1: 9), because everything that is named is possible only by reason of the law of God expressed in Gen. 1: 28. If man should think to bring forth a new article, that would show him trying to be a creator. But such an attempt would be foolish for no man can compete with the Almighty.

Verse 11. The finite knowledge of man makes it in vain for him to explore the entire realm of nature. Hence the more attempts he makes to do so only increases his *vanity* or failure.

Verse 12. No man can know by his own searching what is in the future. He should therefore make the best use possible of the good things of life, and be preparing to meet Him who does know all and who is able to pass final judgment on the actions of all human beings.

ECCLESIASTES 7

Verse 1. The connection between the two clauses of this verse is not apparent, but it is there. A good name is a part of one's character and cannot be stolen or destroyed by accident. Ointment is a material substance and any man with money may obtain it. If a man maintains a good name until death it can never be lost. At the time of one's birth the uncertainties of this life are all yet in the future and the risks are still to be met.

Verse 2. The Lord does not require us to go to extreme on any subject. Feasting is not necessarily wrong, but it is a mistake to pass the time in the pleasures of this life and never think of death. *House of mourning* is a reference to the earthly end of human existence at which time one's friends will mourn over his passing. If the living will take the suggestion of Solomon he will think seriously on these matters.

Verse 3. This verse is about the same in meaning as the preceding one. A sad countenance does not directly cause a heart to be better, but it indicates a better attitude towards the serious affairs of life than does a laughing state of mind.

Verse 4. This verse is practically the same as verse 2.

Verse 5. A foolish song may be more agreeable to the ears, but a wise rebuke will be more beneficial in its effects upon the conduct of the hearer.

Verse 6. There is not much lasting fuel in a bunch of briars, but it will make a great deal of noise for a short time as it burns. Likewise a fool's laughter sounds great but it is soon exhausted and exposed so that its *vanity* may be realized.

Verse 7. It has been said that mankind cannot stand prosperity. *Oppression* is from a word that means extortion or unjust gain. A wise man will become *mad* or foolish if he acquires a large gain, especially if he obtains it unjustly or has not earned it by proper labor. On the same principle a *gift* (bribe) will corrupt a heart that was hitherto inclined to be honest and just to its fellow man.

Verse 8. *Better* is used in the sense of being more desirable. After a thing has been accomplished one can say, "now that the task is done it is a relief." A proud man will be hasty and try to force things to come his way, while a patient man will try to work out some satisfactory solution to a problem.

Verse 9. *Be not hasty* is used in the sense of James 1: 19 that says to be "slow to wrath." The criticism is not on the mere fact of becoming angry, but in the disposition to become angry easily. By the same token, if a man is not easily angered he will likely be one who has control of his temper. Such a man will know better than to cherish his wrath or hold it for a long time. A man who would let his anger *rest in his bosom* is here called a fool.

Verse 10. A complainer will say that his lot is worse than that of others; he also will think that things are getting worse as far as they affect him. The thought of Solomon is that "thy fate is the common fate of all."

Verse 11. The marginal rendering is that wisdom is a good inheritance and the connection will bear out the thought. Material wealth can disappear and leave its owner with nothing to show for it. Wisdom will prove to be of actual profit in many ways to *them that see the sun*, or to them who are on this earth.

Verse 12. The original for *defence* is defined "shade" in the lexicon which means a shelter. *Wisdom* and *money* are both helpful if used properly, but of the two, wisdom is to be preferred; it can procure for one what money cannot.

Verse 13. For an explanation of this verse see the comments at ch. 1: 15. The main thought is that man has no control over the general conditions in the works of creation. The thing that he can and should do is to accept the situation as God designed it, and adjust himself to the conditions as far as possible.

Verse 14. If we are prosperous we should make the best use of it and find righteous joy therein. But there will come times when prosperity will give place to adversity. When that happens, one should know there is a cause for it and hence would do well to take the subject under consideration. The conclusion will be that God knows best and has arranged the "law of averages" so that one extreme will counteract the other. All of this was done in harmony with the great truth that man will not get to keep his possession after the race of life is run.

Verse 15. The reasoning in this verse is similar to that of Job in his controversy with the three "friends." Since the misfortunes of this world do not always come to the wicked, or to them only, the fact of experiencing them does not prove anything as to a man's character. *Days of my vanity* is Solomon's expression for referring to the things pertaining to this life.

Verse 16. Considering the following verse in connection with this, I believe all that is meant is to avoid being an extremist. Even in matters that are right in themselves, one should not go to unwise conclusions or become an extremist in his activities. *Destroy thyself* means to stun or bewilder oneself, which would be done by an unreasonable exertion in any field of endeavor.

Verse 17. We know we should not be wicked at all, therefore the conclusion must be that Solomon was thinking of the wickedness of being an extremist. *Die before thy time* means the extremist will bring upon himself a premature failure in life.

Verse 18. The antecedent of *this* is the advice just offered. *Take hold* means to accept and profit by the advice and thereby show that one fears God.

Verse 19. It is well for us frequently to remember that wisdom was Solomon's "specialty," and that many of his comparisons and contrasts were between it and other desirable things. In this verse the contrast is made to *mighty* men which Strong defines, "a prince or warrier." Even ten soldiers who did not use wisdom would not be as strong a defence as one wise man who might not possess much material might.

Verse 20. The key to this verse is in the last 3 words. The thought is similar to that in 1 John 1: 8 and kindred passages. The best of men are still human and make mistakes. This is the reason why we should not go to extremes in our professions.

Verse 21. "Do not believe everything you hear" is not exactly the thought of this verse, but it is suggestive of the same. If a man "takes everything to heart" too seriously that he hears, he will be continually worked up and imagine seeing indications that even his own servant is against him.

Verse 22. Every man knows that he would not want even his own statements to be taken too seriously or interpreted too literally. Were that done he might stand charged with having said the wrong things about others.

Verse 23. In this verse we have two views of wisdom; that of the worldly wise and that which comes from the higher source. *I will be wise* refers to a man who thinks his worldly wisdom can figure out all things. But when he attempts it he finds that *it was far from him*. (See Rom. 1: 22.)

Verse 24. The things that are *far off* and *exceeding deep* are those beyond the reach of worldly wisdom.

Verse 25. Solomon had inspired wisdom and it was with that he proposed to make the investigations mentioned here.

Verse 26. Having made the investigations referred to in the preceding verse, Solomon experienced some important discoveries. The life of the great man was considerably affected by his contact with women. He learned that a deceitful woman was one of the bitterest foes of man.

Verse 27. Solomon speaks of himself in the third person when he mentions *the preacher* (see comments at ch. 1: 1). The verse is on the same thought as that in v. 25. He used his divine wisdom to find out what was true of people and things. Some things could be accounted for and some could not.

Verse 28. Solomon had a thousand women in his collection who were considered his wives or concubines, hence he used that numeral in his comparison. The women were his undoing (Neh. 13: 26), so he now concludes that he could not account for their actions or influence over him.

Verse 29. The imperfections in mankind are not due to any fault of the Creator, for he made man upright. *Inventions* means schemes or plots and the word refers to the evil contrivances of the human being.

ECCLESIASTES 8

Verse 1. The question form of this verse is a way of expressing a condition or proviso. The verse means that if a man will use wisdom his face will *shine;* that is, it will be radiant with wisdom. However, it will not assume the air of boldness that one might have who is full of self-esteem.

Verse 2. Solomon as king had required his subjects to swear loyalty to God. He now exhorts them to discharge that obligation.

Verse 3. The king would counsel his people to serve God, therefore they should not depart from under his jurisdiction, nor stand for things that are evil. *He* (the king) *doeth whatsoever pleaseth him* (the Lord).

Verse 4. This verse considers the kind of king that rules and speaks in respect for God. Such a king should be honored by his people and not be called in question by asking *what doest thou?* (See Rom. 13: 3, 4.)

Verse 5. The commandments expected to be kept are those given by such a king as described in the preceding paragraph. Keeping such commandments will assure the people against *evil things*, because they are intended for the good of man. (Again see Rom. 13: 4.) The last clause of the verse means a wise man is one who *discerneth* (knows or recognizes) the right time and verdict of the king.

Verse 6. It is natural for a man to be anxious for relief from distress. But he should try to be patient and wait for the time when the king can relieve him.

Verse 7. The knowledge of uninspired man is limited, therefore he should wait for the action of the king who is being guided by the Lord.

Verse 8. *Spirit* is from RUWACH and Strong defines it, "wind; by resemblance breath, i. e., a sensible (or even violent) exhalation; figuratively life, anger, unsubstantiality; by extension a region of the sky; by resemblance spirit, but only a rational being (including its expression and functions)." This word, then, like PNEUMA in the New Testament, may mean the natural wind, or the spirit of man, depending on the connection in which it is used. *Retain* is from KALA, which Strong defines, "a primitive root; to restrict, by act (hold back or in) or word (prohibit)." The meaning of the first half of the verse is that no man has any more control over his spirit than he does over the wind in the realm of nature. Man's helplessness in this matter is compared to the obligation of a soldier in war who is not permitted to have a discharge or release. The grand thought of the verse is that when the time comes to die, no man can prevent his spirit from taking its flight from the body. This solemn truth should be considered especially by those who are *given to wickedness*.

Verse 9. To have the preeminence over others is generally regarded as a favor. But the writer says there are times when such an advantage will be to a man's hurt.

Verse 10. Some men who had the advantage referred to in the preceding verse had misused it in connection with the public place of worship. That proved to be to their *own hurt* in that they were forgotten soon after their death and burial. All of this is another instance of the *vanity* or emptiness of this life.

Verse 11. This verse is a sad comment on the attitude of man toward sin. Of course, undue haste in punishing crime is not to be sanctioned, neither is it well to delay the punishment too long. History records thousands of instances where justice has been defeated by prolonging the trial of the accused. When the guilt of a man has been proved beyond doubt, he should be punished without delay.

Verse 12. The apparent success of a sinner should not encourage others to do wrong. The wicked man will finally receive the reward due to him for his evil deeds, and the one who feared God will likewise receive the favor of the Lord.

Verse 13. The seeming length of the wicked man's life will be seen to be as brief as a shadow when the wrath of God is finally brought to bear upon him.

Verse 14. For explanation of this verse see ch. 7:15 and the comments thereon.

Verse 15. God is no respecter of persons in his providence any more than in his offering of spiritual favors. Therefore, if a man desires to obtain the most possible enjoyment out of the temporal blessings of this world, he should take advantage of them while he may, making the proper use of them in the sight of God.

Verse 16. Solomon again refers to his desire to find out all about the things going on under the sun.

Verse 17. The above desire, however, was not accomplished. All of the wisdom and power of man is unable fully to fathom the depths of God's greatness. Since man is the creature and God is the creator, the right thing to do is to rely on the wisdom of God as he sees fit to reveal the great truths unto his created beings.

ECCLESIASTES 9

Verse 1. Man's utter dependence upon God is the subject of this verse. Even the objects and depths of love and hatred are beyond the grasp of man. He must depend upon the wisdom of God for all that he can ever obtain in any field of endeavor.

Verse 2. Again I will remind the reader that Solomon writes many things from the standpoint of a man of the world, not that he personally held to the view expressed. As far as the advantages of this earth are concerned, they are as apt to come to one kind of person as another. The same may be said of the misfortunes of earthly beings.

Verse 3. The record of an evil man simply shows a life wasted in unrighteous conduct with death as the final outcome.

Verse 4. *Better* is used in the sense of being more desirable. Since man cannot take anything with him, the lowest of creatures that are living are having a better time than the noblest of them after they die. If there were to be no life after this one (which the materialists teach but which Solomon really opposes), then it would be well to adopt the doctrine expressed by Paul in 1 Cor. 15: 32.

Verse 5. For several verses Solomon has been writing about the emptiness of the things of this life. He has stressed the truth that no man can take anything with him when he dies. It is in that sense he here states the dead have no reward. It is even affirmed that the dead *know not anything*. This might seem to teach the doctrine of "soulsleeping" if we overlooked the connection which will be seen in the next verse.

Verse 6. *That is done under the sun* is the key to this and the preceding verse. After a man dies his connection with this world is broken and he "knows not anything" that is going on back on the earth. The rich man in Luke 16 only remembered his wicked brothers as they were while he lived with them.

Verse 7. If a man will make the proper use of the good things of this life his enjoyment of them will please God. But that must be done *now* according to this verse; nothing can be done about it hereafter.

Verse 8. White clothing for the body and olive oil dressing for the head indicated a condition of prosperity and satisfaction. Solomon suggested that a person might properly enjoy these while in this life, since they were things given by the Lord.

Verse 9. *To live joyfully* does not mean to live extravagantly or frivolously. It means to rejoice in the favors that *he* (God) *hath given* to be used *under the sun* or while in this life. *Life of thy vanity* is another way of referring to life on earth, because it is *vanity* or emptiness as far as the next life is concerned.

Verse 10. This is another verse that shows Solomon was not a believer in the doctrine of materialism. He words it in such a way as to indicate to the reader he was not considering the state of the inner man after leaving this world. He was writing about that part that will be *in the grave* which is the body. Therefore, all activities that are to be performed by the body should be done while in this life.

Verse 11. *I returned* means he considered again the things going on under the sun. The gist of the verse is that what appears to entitle a man to success does not always work that way. One man may seem to be a good runner and yet he will be defeated by another. Or one soldier might be classed among the valiant ones then be overcome by an apparent weakling. *Time and chance* means that in this world all people are subject to unforeseen conditions both favorable and unfavorable. The verse is not meant to justify inaction or lack of interest.

The point is that since we cannot always know when or how the opportune time will come, we should always be on the alert so that when it does come we will be prepared to make use of it. (See ch. 11: 6.)

Verse 12. This is practically the same in thought as the preceding verse as to the uncertainty of the future. That is the only point of comparison to the net and snare, not that God deliberately hides the future from man in order to ensnare him to his hurt. But since human beings have intelligence that is above that of fish and fowl, there will be no excuse if they run blindly into the traps.

Verse 13. In his observation of things going on under the sun, Solomon saw some cases where men used the good judgment that God had given them.

Verse 14. The particular instance that was noticed concerned a little city that had a small population. Against this little place there came a king with a strong army. He laid siege to it and all appearances were that the city would have to fall before the superior force.

Verse 15. A man could be poor and not be wise and vice versa, but either quality without the other might fail to meet the emergency. That is, if he were rich but did not use wisdom he would not be able to meet the situation. But wisdom would suggest means of resisting the enemy that wealth alone could not buy. What was so regrettable in this case, was the ingratitude of the citizens of the city. After the poor man had saved them from their enemy they forgot all about his service to the city.

Verse 16. The work of this poor man demonstrated that wisdom is worth more than riches. But that worth was not appreciated for the people *despised* or belittled the wisdom of the poor man and thus rendered themselves unworthy of the favor.

Verse 17. A wise man will quietly offer his counsel without great ado. Such a person is more likely to be heard than is one who seeks to impose his foolish sayings by great noise or commotion.

Verse 18. The first clause is the same in thought as v. 15. *Sinner* is from a word whose main idea is of one who errs in judgment. This fits well with the first part of the verse as a negative. Wisdom or good judgment will plan a way to meet the enemy, while one false move may destroy the whole arrangement.

ECCLESIASTES 10

Verse 1. A large bulk of otherwise sweet ointment can be spoiled by the odor of a few dead insects. The fact is used to illustrate the effect that even a little foolishness can have on the influence of a man who has been generally regarded wise.

Verse 2. *Right* and *left* are used figuratively. The meaning is that a wise man will use his mind (heart) in a right manner.

Verse 3. *Wisdom* means a man's heart or mind. The thought is that when a fool is going round among the people his mind is filled with confusion. He thinks he is wise and all others are fools. "Everyone is out of step but me" is a familiar saying and illustrates the man described in this passage.

Verse 4. We have doubtless all heard the advice, "never try to get smart with an officer," and that is the thought in this verse. *Leave not thy place* means not to "talk back" or "resist an officer." By taking this attitude of respect toward a man in authority a charge may be lightened or even dismissed.

Verse 5. *Evil* is used in the sense of something that is undesirable and unfortunate, not necessarily wrong morally. Solomon is going to mention such a circumstance that is allowed to occur *from the ruler*, which means it takes place right under his eyes.

Verse 6. The *evil* referred to is the inconsistency of granting dignity to something that is worthless, then underestimating something that is really valuable.

Verse 7. The preceding verse makes a general statement of conditions, this verse specifies an instance of them. *Servants* and *princes* are named as representing two opposite ranks of society. However, their state is just reversed in the movements attributed to them. There is no particular criticism of anybody, but the story is told to show the uncertainty of earthly advantages.

Verse 8. This verse teaches the lesson that "evil often works its own rebuke." The connection indicates a pit that was dug as a trap for another person. *Hedge* is from GADER, which Strong defines as "an inclosure." A man intended to destroy a fence or wall another man had built to protect his property. In doing this evil deed the guilty person ran up against a serpent that had been lurking in the wall.

Verse 9. *Removeth stones* refers to the malicious interference with some work of a peaceful citizen. In attempting this evil deed the doer of it will be injured by one of those very stones. *Cleaving wood* is not a wrong act in itself. The connection with several other verses shows the writer was considering one who was intending some wrong use of the wood he was cleaving.

Verse 10. This verse is a statement of common sense as against "main strength and awkwardness." Either means might accomplish the desired result but one could do so with greater ease. If a tool is dull it could be made to cut the material but it would require more bodily force. If a little judgment were used the workman would first sharpen the tool, then it could cut the material easier and better.

Verse 11. The quickness of a serpent enables it to bite before it is charmed. Therefore the *babbler*, which means a master in the use of words, would not be of any advantage in the presence of the vicious creature.

Verse 12. It is pleasant and beneficial to hear the words of a wise man. Those of a fool not only are not acceptable, but such a character will eventually expose his own unworthiness and bring himself to a downfall.

Verse 13. The speech of a fool is worthless to begin with, and it will get worse the longer he talks.

Verse 14. The idea here is the fool has an abundance of words only, but they do not make any sense. No one can tell what he means by what he has said nor what he is likely to say further.

Verse 15. Some people are so foolish and rude in both their words and actions that it makes a person tired to observe them. In as simple a matter as making an errand into a city a fool does not know how to proceed.

Verse 16. There were instances when the king of Israel was a mere child (2 Ki. 11: 21; 14: 21; 21: 1; 22: 1). I do not mean these young kings were evil nor that the land suffered in all of their reigns. I cite them only to show that Solomon was not just guessing or imagining things when he mentioned the subject of young kings. But it would be reasonable to think the country would be at the mercy of the "politicians" when the king was irresponsible, and they would take advantage of the situation to "have a time." That is why it is said that they *eat in the morning*. (See Isa. 5: 11.)

Verse 17. This verse describes a situation that is opposite of that in the preceding one. The original for *nobles* is defined "white or pure." Such kings would reign for the good of the nation, and the leading men would eat for the right purpose.

Verse 18. All buildings are subject to decay as every man knows who has owned a home. If a man is slothful he will not keep his place up but will even let the "roof cave in and the walls tumble down."

Verse 19. All that anyone can get out of a feast is a good time with nothing but the bodily enjoyment, and nothing left to show for the expense. But an exchange of actual legal tender will meet future requirements.

Verse 20. We are sure the latter part of this verse is figurative. "Out of the abundance of the heart the mouth speaketh" (Luke 6: 45). If a man indulges in evil thoughts he is likely to forget some time and "think out loud," especially if he thinks he is alone. But it often happens that someone is in hearing though not in sight, and that will result in his thoughts being broadcast. So a man should not indulge in thoughts that he would not want others to know about.

ECCLESIASTES 11

Verse 1. *Bread* is from LECHEM and Strong's definition is, "food (for man or beast), especially bread, or grain (for making it)." It will help to understand this verse if we consider it in the light of some others, especially v. 4. The point is that one should not be discouraged from doing something desired and needed because of unfavorable appearances. If the land is covered with water at the time when the bread "or grain for making it" should be sowed, do not wait for the water to disappear. Cast the grain out into the water; it will sink into the ground and finally grow.

Verse 2. *Seven* and *eight* are used to signify the idea of being liberal in the bestowal of favors. The future is unknown to man and the opportunities for doing good may be cut off unexpectedly.

Verse 3. This verse is to be considered especially in connection with the last clause of the preceding verse. The laws of nature are fixed so that man should make use of present opportunities for doing good, before some action of nature (which is unseen and unavoidable) cuts off the opportunity. Applying the falling of the tree to the future state of man is not only fanciful, but takes the verse out of connection.

Verse 4. See comments on verse 1 for explanation of this. It is foolish never to do anything until all things are favorable. One might always find some excuse for postponing an action if he is looking and desiring one.

Verse 5. We accept as facts many things we do not understand. The development of an unborn child is as far beyond our knowledge as are the works of God in other departments of the universe. The lesson still is that man should make use of present and known advantages, not waiting to figure out the ways of God as to the future.

Verse 6. This verse is a continuation of the thoughts in the preceding paragraphs. If we see an opportunity for doing a thing we know is right in principle, we should not wait for "a better time" to do it, for we are not sure of any better time.

Verse 7. On the favorable side of the subject, there is the enjoyment of sunlight and it is right to take that view of the condition.

Verse 8. This verse presents the other side of the picture and reminds us that many dark days will come. This is true in the material world, and it is referred to as an illustration of the sunshine and shadow that will come into the life of any man who *lives many years*. Solomon does not mention this in the spirit of a pessimist, but to put man on his guard and prepare his mind to make the best use of the enjoyments that God offers him through the realm of nature.

Verse 9. All parts of the Bible harmonize with each other. Throughout this book Solomon has held out the idea that the good things of this world are temporary. Yet he has encouraged man to enjoy them while he can for soon they will be cut off. A proviso that has always been understood whether expressed or not, is that man should make the proper use of the pleasures of this life. Hence in the present verse the young man is advised to get his enjoyment out of the good things around him while he is young and can appreciate them. However, all the while he is having this enjoyment he should bear in mind that he must answer to God for the kind of use he makes of them.

Verse 10. Improper sentiments of the heart and evil deeds of the flesh should be put away, and instead the young man should make a wise use of his time and surroundings. His youth and ability for making the most of life will soon pass away and in that sense it is *vanity* or tempory.

ECCLESIASTES 12

Verse 1. *Remember* is from ZAKAR and Strong defines it, "A primitive root; properly to mark (so as to recognize), i. e., to remember." In the King James version of the Bible it is rendered "be mindful" 6 times. The word means to give to the Creator that consideration due him. It is in the *days of youth* the man was exhorted to remember his Creator. From this basis we must conclude the following verses are a description of the declining years of life. The passages are highly figurative, so we are required to find some condition in the time of the infirmities of age in our application of the figures. In a general sense, the joys that were possible in youth will be out of reach when a man gets to the period of his decline. When that time comes he will feel so weakened and life will hold so little of interest for him that he will not be disposed to give very serious consideration to spiritual subjects if he had not done so while in his youth. On the other hand, if he had thought of God while "in the days of his youth," and had tempered his joys of life by a proper regard for the Creator, then he will have something to cheer him when the days of decline come. His years of devotion to God will still be in his memory when these last ones come upon him so that it may be said that "his last days sloped gently toward the grave."

Verse 2. The sun, moon and stars in the universe are the means of light, and the eyes are the means of light in the human body. When the eyes become dim with age it is compared to the darkening of the bodies of light in the heavens. In favorable weather the refreshing rain is followed by clear skies and cheerful sunshine. At other times it rains but does not clear off afterwards. So in youth the sorrows disappear after a brief season of weeping, but in old age the grief keeps coming up to becloud the life with sadness and anxiety.

Verse 3. The *keepers* are the hands and the *house* is the body (2 Cor. 5: 1). The hands will tremble and become unreliable as age comes on. *Strong men* or the limbs will become tottering and weak so that their owner cannot walk erectly. The *grinders* or teeth will cease to do full service of mastication because they have become few in number. What few are left to *look out of the windows* or show through the partially opened mouth will be discolored by the decay accompanying old age.

Verse 4. The chewing done by an old person is so imperfect due to the fewness of the teeth that it can scarcely be observed. It is compared to the closing of a door opening onto a street so that the sound inside could not be heard by those on the street. *Rise up at the voice of the bird* could be worded *with the voice*. The word for *bird* is defined to mean a little bird with a weak chirp, and it is used to compare the weak and broken voice of the old man. This thought agrees with what follows, *the daughters of music shall be brought low*, referring to the broken voice in trying to sing.

Verse 5. *Afraid of that which is high* means he will be easily frightened and fears in general will seem to threaten the pathway. When an almond tree is in full bloom its top resembles the pale color of a head that is gray with age. *Grasshopper shall be a burden* refers to the little things that can worry an old person. *Desire shall fail* means that about all interest in life will be gone until the aged one finally "passes away." *Long* is from OLAM and Strong defines it, "Concealed, i. e., the vanishing point; generally time out of mind (past or future), i. e. (practically) eternity; frequently adverbially (especially with prepositional prefix) always." The word really refers to the length of time the man will stay in this home, rather than to the *home* itself. In other words, when a man dies he will never come back to the earth again. There is evidence of hired mourners who were sometimes used in old times. However, since this passage is describing the circumstances of man in general, the reference to mourners is general also and means the state of mind in all who are concerned in the death of the aged person who had lived among them for so long.

Verse 6. *Or ever* means before ever the things about to be mentioned have happened. The entire verse is a poetic description of the time of death, when the soul and body separate because of the dissolving of the ties that have bound them together. The *silver cord* refers to the "brittle thread of life" that is snapped in death. A pitcher is used to procure water, a very important necessity of life. The breaking of this vessel would be like putting an end to life. The same could be said of the wheel that was a part of the machinery used to draw the water at the cistern or water tank.

Verse 7. See the comments at Gen. 2: 7 and 3: 19 in Vol. 1 of this COMMENTARY for the meaning of *dust*. This verse is a direct proof that Solomon did not believe in materialism, which is the doctrine that man is wholly mortal. He believed that some part of man is spiritual and lives on after the death of the body.

Verse 8. *Vanity* of *vanities* is a repetition for the sake of emphasis, describing the utter emptiness of things pertaining to affairs of this life. The *preacher* is a term applied to Solomon and it is explained at the first verse of this book.

Verse 9. *The peacher was wise* is not to be regarded as an immodest boast. Solomon knew he had received his wisdom from God (1 Ki. 3: 12), and it was from that source he had the qualification. With such divine guidance he sought to place the proverbs before his people that they might be instructed in the ways of wisdom.

Verse 10. Solomon wished his teaching not only to be correct, but also to be such as would be delightful to his readers. It is not necessary that all teaching be unpleasant in order to be true.

Verse 11. A *goad* is something to urge one to action, and the words of the wise man were intended to influence the hearers unto proper conduct. *Nails* is used figuratively in the sense of "driving a nail home," or making a word so plain and forceful that it reaches its object in the mind of the hearer. *Given from one shepherd* means that the sayings of one wise man (Solomon) if driven properly will affect the minds and lives of all the assembly.

Verse 12. For the significance of *my son* see the comments at Prov. 1: 8. *By these* denotes the words of wisdom referred to in vs. 10, 11 and offered for the guidance of the youth. Solomon bids the *son* to be admonished by these words and not have his mind all worn out with many books of man's production.

Verse 13. *Hear the conclusion* means to give attention and the writer will sum up all of the truths and principles he has been giving in the book. The sum of it is that if one fears or respects God so that he will keep his commandments, he will be discharging the duty of man to the Lord.

Verse 14. *Judgment* is from an original that has a wide range of meanings. Its central thought is a sentence or verdict, and its application is not restricted to any particular time or place. The force of this verse is that God will decide as to the right or wrong of all things pertaining to the conduct of man. The verse is offered as a concluding exhortation and in conjunction with the preceding admonition to do the commandments of God.

SONG OF SOLOMON 1

General remarks: This book describes conversations and visits between Solomon and his favorite wife, the daughter of Pharaoh. (1 Ki. 3: 1.) These associations could have been supposed or actual or both as far as their nature is concerned. However, the probability is that Solomon really put the words into the mouth of his beloved wife to represent what he believed should at least have been her own sentiments. He might have been somewhat disappointed in her final reaction to his ardent advances, and if that is the case, it will throw some light on his statement about women in Eccl. 7: 28. At any rate, whether Solomon actually had such experiences, or if the "wish was father to the thought," he enlarges on the subject and puts it down in his writing to give the reader a view of the love that should exist between a man and his wife. If the reader will keep this in view he will not be confused as to the propriety of the intimate expressions made between the two parties. As a guide in properly classifying each part of the various conversations between this husband and wife, I suggest the reader mark his Bible as follows: Ch. 1: 1-7 is the wife, and ch. 1: 8-11 is the husband. From now on the initial letter of husband and wife only will be used: ch. 1: 12—3: 11, w; ch. 4: 1-15, h; ch. 4: 16, w; ch. 5: 1, h; ch. 5: 2-8; w; ch. 5: 9, daughters of Jerusalem; ch. 5: 10-16, w; ch. 6: 1, daughters of Jerusalem; ch. 6: 2, 3, w; ch. 6: 4—7: 9, h; ch. 7: 10—8: 14, w.

Verse 1. *Song of songs.* In many works of reference this book is called Canticles, abbreviated Cant. It is from the English word canticles which means "A song or hymn." The wife regards a song about Solomon as a song OF songs, or a song of special importance.

Verse 2. *Kiss* is from NASHAQ and Strong's lexicon says it is a primitive root and that it is identical with another Hebrew word through the idea of "fastening up," and which has been defined, "to catch fire." The word of our verse is defined, "To kiss, literally or figuratively (touch); also (as a mode of attachment), to equip with weapons." In view of the wide meaning of the word, we can appreciate the ardor in the request of the beloved wife. She was not asking merely for an indication of affection of some kind, which could be truly considered as a form of kiss, but she longed for the literal kiss in all of its possible intensity, and that would need to be performed with *his mouth* as it is worded here. Such an act would be an expression of deepest love and would be more exhilarating than wine, because its thrilling effect would not merely move the physical and nervous sensations, but would set into vibration every chord of the affections.

Verse 3. See the comments at Prov. 17: 17 on the subject of perfumes, and its relation to the passionate affections between the sexes.

Verse 4. *Draw me* is an affectionate appeal that any wife would have the moral right to make of her husband. *We will run after thee* has been rendered "let us haste" in another translation. The wife is eager for the company of her mate. *The king hath brought me,* etc. Let it be remembered that many a man in olden times had a plurality of wives. It would be understood that he would not live with any one of them continuously, and this would be especially true of kings. Hence when a husband wished to visit one of his wives he would need to make a call on her at her apartment, or have her go with him to his. (See Gen. 30: 14-16.) This will account for the frequent passages in this book that represent the wife as longing for and even seeking the opportunity for the intimacies with her husband. When these customs of those times (as to plurality of wives), which were suffered (not "permitted"), are considered, we will understand the many passionate scenes in the story to be perfectly proper and right. I earnestly request the reader to keep the comments on this verse in mind and refer to them frequently.

Verse 5. Solomon's favorite wife being an Egyptian (1 Ki. 3: 1) she would naturally have a dark skin. She is represented as taking an attitude of self-pity and pleading that notwithstanding being dark she was beautiful. *Kedar* is from QEDAR and means "dusky," and she compared herself to that, which she claimed was an attractive color, also the curtains in the palaces of Solomon were a beautiful dark color.

Verse 6. The brothers and sisters would naturally be black also since they were Egyptians, yet the wife complains that she was darker than the others. She explains that she was compelled to do the rough work for the family. That exposed her to the sun which caused her to be darker than the others who had only their nationality to blame for their complexion. *My own vineyards have I not kept* is a figure of speech, meaning she was kept so busy slaving for the others she had no time to take care of her own personal interests. We should bear in mind that Solomon was the composer of all this language. He represented his beloved wife as having been mistreated by her family, and he was championing her interests because of his love for her.

Verse 7. A person in love wishes to be near the object of that love. This wife could not always be near him (see v. 4), so she inquires where he will be at the noon hour when she would find him somewhat at leisure and could give her some attention. (Ruth 2: 14.) *Why should I*, etc. This means she was not interested in his flocks but in him, therefore she did not wish to spend the time near any other flocks.

Verse 8. The preceding verses were the first speech of the wife and the husband answered her earnest inquiries with replies equally warm. He began his answer with a compliment and said she was the *fairest among women*.

He did not use the first word with reference to the complexion as we use it, for he had just represented her as being darker than the others of her race. It is from YAPHEH, which Strong defines, "beautiful." He told her she could meet him if she would trace the tracks of the sheep until they reached the tents of the shepherds. Thus a meeting place was arranged for these two lovers.

Verse 9. *Company* is not in the original as a separate word. The original for *horse* is in the feminine gender. The strange comparison is due to the fact that a creature regarded as good enough to be attached to the chariot of Pharaoh must not only be full of life, but be very attractive.

Verse 10. Solomon means her cheeks and neck are as beautiful as if decorated with gold and jewels.

Verse 11. *Borders* is from a word that is defined "a string." Solomon promised to give his wife a strand of gold and silver beads.

Verse 12. The wife now takes up the conversation, but it is not all addressed directly to the husband. Much of it is in a meditative form as if she were talking about him rather than to him. *Table* is from MECIBBOWTH and Strong defines it," a divan." *Sitteth* is not in the original. The verse means that while the king is on his divan she will treat him to the odor of her ointments.

Verse 13. *Bundle of myrrh* is a figure of speech as if she would compare her husband to a packet of the most delightful perfume. And just as a woman would wear such an article on her bosom, so she would reecive her husband's presence all the night long.

Verse 14. This is another comparison made by the wife about her husband, likening him to some object that is pleasant to the sight and has a pleasing odor.

Verse 15. *Fair* does not necessarily refer to the complexion, but is defined in the lexicon with the simple word "beautiful." According to Strong's lexicon, the reference to *doves* is because of "the warmth of their mating." The same author says it is derived from another Hebrew word that means something that is intoxicating. It means she regarded her husband's eyes as being intoxicating to her.

Verse 16. The wife again declares her husband is beautiful and pleasant.

Bed is green means their associations are always agreeable.

Verse 17. *Cedar* and *fir* are woods that are beautiful in texture and have a pleasant odor. The verse is a figure of speech to mean the luxuriousness of their dwelling.

SONG OF SOLOMON 2

Verse 1. We might think of this speech as being vain or boastful were it not really the composition of Solomon. He is putting these words in her mouth because he thinks that about her from his heart.

Verse 2. In the preceding verse the wife is compared to some of the most beautiful flowers. In this the other women are compared to thorns and the husband a lily.

Verse 3. Switching from flowers to trees for her comparisons, she likens her husband to the apple tree, which was one of the most desirable because of its delicious fruit. The contrast between it and the common trees of the forest is like the difference between her husband and other men. Continuing her imagery, she sees herself sitting under the shaded protection of the foliage, and partaking of the fruit which is sweet and delightful in its fragrance.

Verse 4. A true lover would entertain his beloved by taking her to the most desirable places of joy and pleasure. While doing so he should act the part of a true escort by guarding her honor and sense of security. The most assuring symbol of protection in this case was the banner or ensign of love.

Verse 5. Of course we will understand the house of pleasure presided over by Solomon would be one that afforded the enjoyment of tender love scenes between him and his favorite wife. With such a vision before her she becomes very affectionate and longs for the return of his affection. To *stay* means to comfort or support. *Flagons* means some kind of compressed fruit and *apples* were noted for their fragrance. The wife is so overcome with sentimental emotions that she pleads for the stimulation of these products of the fruits which would serve as a tonic to a bewildered nerve system.

Verse 6. This verse pertains to some of the sacred intimacies that are permitted between a husband and wife. The second clause refers to the same thought expressed in Prov. 5: 19, second clause.

Verse 7. *Roes* and *hinds* are graceful creatures but possess no supernatural power by which to enforce an oath. The reference to them in this instance is a friendly but earnest request (almost demand) for the *daughters of Jerusalem* to refrain from disturbing her loved one while he wishes to be resting.

Verse 8. She imagines hearing her husband's voice and seeing him springing over the hills toward her.

Verse 9. Her imagination continues and she fancies seeing her loved one standing by the wall and peering at her through the opening. There could be nothing improper in such conduct, for he is her husband. While he has other wives whom he could legally visit, yet it would be thrilling to detect him taking these liberties with her.

Verse 10. But he did not stop at these informal approaches to her place of retirement. He called for her to come out and go with him.

Verse 11. The weather had changed for the better so nothing should prevent them from taking a stroll together.

Verse 12. Spring time had come as indicated by the appearance of the flowers. *Turtle* is a short form for turtle-dove, a bird of the piegon family. It makes a plaintive sound when it sings, and is suggestive of some sweetly-sad love expression.

Verse 13. This verse is still on the subject of the advanced season, and the conditions such as lovers would appreciate while wandering together.

Verse 14. *Dove* is from the same original used in ch. 1: 15. Strong explains the reference to it "from the warmth of the mating." Having used the dove for her comparison, the wife thinks of her beloved husband as hiding in secluded places such as clefts of rocks or covered angles of the stairs. She wishes for him to come out from his cover that she may see him and hear his voice. By *countenance* she means his form of body and says it is comely or beautiful.

Verse 15. This verse may be considered as a little song which the wife sings chiefly for the ears of her husband. She chooses for her little ditty the subject of the foxes that destroy the tender vines. A vineyard of grapes would be an inviting place to loiter, therefore the plea is for the foxes to be *taken* or seized.

Verse 16. This is another declaration of the mutual love that exists between the two. *Feedeth among the lilies* is only a sentimental expression because she wants to say something sweet about her lover. Lilies are delicate and beautiful flowers, and her associating him with them is a way of showing her tender regard.

Verse 17. *Until the day break* indicates she wishes them to wander like some care-free creatures over the mountains of *Bether*. This was a craggy place in Palestine, and she thinks of her lover as being so sprightly in his love for her that he could successfully meet all obstacles, even as do the fleet and nimble creatures mentioned scamper over the rough places of the country.

SONG OF SOLOMON 3

Verse 1. Men with a plurality of wives did not live with any one of them continuously. That explains the circumstance where a wife would not have her husband with her. *Sought* is from BAQASH and is defined, "a primitive root; to search out (by any method, specifically in worship or prayer; by implication to strive after."—Strong. In the night the wife had a desire for her husband who she realized was not with her.

Verses 2-4. She decided to leave her apartment and go out onto the streets; she might find him out there somewhere. But no, she was disappointed at first and did not see him. Meeting the night watchmen she asked if they had seen him, we are not told what they said to her. She continued her search after leaving the watchmen and lo, she soon came upon him somewhere on the street. Being his wife, and not finding him in the company of any other of his wives, she had a perfect right to act as here described. The wives did not live continuously with their husbands, and many of them had their apartments in their original homes. Hence this wife, having made friendly contact with her husband (who especially loved her above his other wives), had no difficulty in persuading him to spend the remainder of the night with her.

Verse 5. As they were making their way to her apartments, she warned the women of the city not to make any disturbance to inconvenience her husband until morning.

Verse 6. The wife now goes into a meditative form of speech about her husband. (See the comments at ch. 1: 12.) Reference is again made to the relation of perfumes to love. (See the comments at Prov. 7: 17.) In the present instance the wife imagines so much of it having been procured from *the merchant* that the burning thereof produces great pillars of smoke.

Verse 7. In her imagery of the beloved husband she sees him with an honorary guard of 60 men about his bed; that is, about the house containing the king's bed.

Verse 8. Each of these armed men is ready for action if it becomes necessary.

Verse 9. *Bed* is from a word that means a portable litter that is borne on the shoulders of men. This conveyance might contain room for two, although it usually had but one occupant. A rich and powerful king like Solomon would have frequent use for such a piece of service, and he would have it made of the choicest kind of wood, such as the *wood of Lebanon*.

Verse 10. The *pillars* (corner posts) of Solomon's litter or manual sedan were made of silver, and a part of the interior was of gold. *Covering* is defined in the lexicon as "a seat," and it was upholstered with purple fabric, indicative of royalty and splendor. *Paved* means "embroidered" and it was done *with love*, or because of his love for the women whose eyes he wished to please.

Verse 11. With the above equipment king Solomon would be transported through the streets of Jerusalem in his royal attire. The women of the city were bidden by the admiring wife to go forth that they might behold the king as he is being borne along.

SONG OF SOLOMON 4

Verse 1. See the comments at ch. 1: 15 for *doves' eyes*, which will show why Solomon attributes such a charactertistic to his wife. *Fair* means she was beautiful in form and general attractiveness, not necessarily in complexion. There were three kinds of goats in Palestine and one kind had "fine long hair" according to Smith's Bible Dictionary. This accounts for Solomon's comparison of his wife's hair to them.

Verse 2. The teeth of a person otherwise dark in complexion would appear especially white, hence the comparison to sheep just recently washed. *Twins* would suggest the idea of two of a kind, and Solomon compared the two rows of teeth in that way.

Verse 3. The personal charms of this favorite wife are described by comparison to other things that are known to be beautiful. The rosy brilliance of her lips suggested the color of a scarlet thread, and these would also be set off by the contrasting color of her skin. Everything coming from one who is ardently loved would seem to be just about right, thus the speech of this woman was complimented. *Temples* is from a word that means the side of the head in general. *Locks* refers to the veil that women wore over the face. Solomon saw the beautiful cheeks of his wife through her veil and it reminded him of the attractive fruit of the pomegranate tree.

Verse 4. The towers of kings were ornamented with the trophies won in their many conflicts with the enemy. To Solomon the neck of his beloved wife was as beautiful as was such a tower. And why not—had she not gained the complete mastery over the affections of the most powerful king of that day?

Verse 5. The point in the verse is in the similarity of twins. If the breasts of a woman were materially different either in size or form it would be unfortunate.

Verse 6. The husband proposed to take a nightly stroll with his wife. *Mountain of myrrh* is a figure of speech and used with reference to the perfumes. We have seen the significance of incense and other toilet delicacies in connection with the subject of love between the sexes. (Prov. 7: 17.)

Verse 7. This is a highly complimentary statement. Not only is the wife a beautiful woman, but her beauty is spotless.

Verse 8. The king proposed a stroll with his beloved wife. This "lovers' lane" included the serene areas of the noted mountain region, and the rugged districts of the lions' lairs. The intense love would equalize all of the differences.

Verse 9. *Ravished my heart* means she had completely captured his heart. The original for *sister* is of very general meaning and may be used as any term of endearment. *Spouse* is a special word for a perfect wife. *Chain* and *neck* are from the same original and mean a necklace. The second clause means that one glance from her eye, together with the decoration about her neck, had completely overwhelmed him and made him to fall "madly in love" with her.

Verse 10. No additional comments will be offered on this verse since it is a repetition of the same "sweet things" he has said about his favorite wife.

Verse 11. This is similar to the preceding verse. He adds the compliment that her lips are as sweet as honey and as dainty as milk.

Verse 12. Exclusiveness is the central idea in this verse. Solomon considered this lovely woman as belonging to him alone, even as a garden would be if walled about against all intrusion.

Verse 13. Frequent comparisons have been made between love and perfumes. In this verse the comparison is to fruits as well as perfume.

Verse 14. This verse is a generous collection of choice perfumes. Seven are specifically named with a reference to perfumes in general.

Verse 15. Some of the attractions of nature are referred to in this verse for comparison to the beloved one.

Verse 16. In this brief speech the wife recognized the comparison her husband made. She called upon the winds to blow upon her garden and thus stir up the perfumes that he so much liked. Then she would have him come and enjoy it to his full content.

SONG OF SOLOMON 5

Verse 1. The husband heard the call of his wife and accepted her invitation. Notice he called it *my garden* although the wife had made the same claim in her last speech. That is very clear because in the case of a husband and wife who truly love each other, what belongs to one belongs to the other. *Sister* and *spouse* are terms of endearment which were commented upon at ch. 4: 10. Having come into *his* garden upon the invitation of his wife, the husband also partook of the delicacies therein. Not only so, but out of the greatness of heart that often possesses a man in love, especially if that love is returned, he extended the favors of these delicacies to his friends.

Verse 2. The wife will be the speaker in this and several verses following. *Waketh* is from UWR and Strong defines it, "to wake (literally or figuratively)." Hence we need not conclude she actually awoke at first but dreamed she did so. In her dream she heard

Song of Solomon 5: 3-13

her husband at the door of her apartment, calling with pleading tones and endearing words for her to let him come in. She dreamed he complained of his head being wet with the dew of night. This item would indicate that it was all a dream with her. The husband would not have waited outside until the dew of night had saturated his hair. Had he decided to make a conjugal call upon his favorite wife he would have immediately knocked for admission.

Verse 3. In her dream she heard him say he had even made preparation for spending some time with her. He had removed his outer garment and washed his feet since he expected to enter presently into her sleeping room.

Verse 4. Not receiving any prompt response the husband decided to open and enter. He put his hand through an opening of the door in order to unfasten it. When *bowels* is used figuratively it means the sympathy or affections. When the wife in her dream heard his hand reaching for the handle of the door, her whole being was stirred up with yearning for his company.

Verse 5. The wife then actually awoke and the dream had been so vivid that she thought it was all a real happening. She arose to let him in and, while the awakening and rising was real, she was still somewhat under the spell of the dream. She imagined that her handles of the door were covered with the perfumes so often connected with love scenes, a subject which we have frequently had brought to our attention.

Verse 6. So real to her was her dream that she opened the door expecting to see her husband standing before it. But O, he was not there and her *soul failed*, or she almost fainted from the disappointment. *When he spake* is still a part of her dream that was so real that she had not fully recovered from its impression although her body was awake and she was actually standing at her door. She left her room and went out in search for him. She called for him in her frantic wandering over the streets, but of course there was no answer for he was not there.

Verse 7. The night watchmen thought there was something wrong with a woman roaming the streets at night and calling after some man. They contacted her because they were keepers of the peace, and had to use force in subduing her. The city was protected with walls, and when a person with a questionable appearance got near the wall it aroused the suspicion of the guards. In order to obtain a better view of the "intruder" they snatched her veil away from her face.

Verse 8. The wife was so intent in her pursuit for her husband that she exposed her state of mind to the girls whom she chanced to meet on the streets. Thinking they might meet her husband before she did, she asked them to "carry her note" by telling him they had seen his sweetheart who told them she was lovesick for him.

Verse 9. Here the story is interrupted by giving us the reply of the *daughters of Jerusalem* to this lovesick woman. They were not personally concerned with her "heart problems" as yet. They asked her how her lover differed from others to the extent that she would ask them to take part in her pursuit after him.

Verse 10. This and a number of verses following is the wife's answer to the *daughters of Jerusalem*. In v. 9 they asked how he differed from other men and she answered. *White* is used figuratively, and *ruddy* means his face was rosy with the vigor of manhood. The marginal translation says, "standard bearer" for *chiefest*, and Strong's lexicon agrees with it. The verse describes her beloved as a man with a rosy complexion and a dazzling countenance. Her lover was the greatest hero in ten thousand men.

Verse 11. Having been asked to identify her lover, she gave various details of his personality to justify her general description of him in v. 10. His head was like gold in that a crown is frequently made of that beautiful and precious metal. *Bushy* means his hair hung in curls and was of a rich black color.

Verse 12. The comparison to *doves* was explained at ch. 1: 15, applying to the bird in general. *Fitly* is from MILLETH, which Strong defines, "a plump socket (of the eye)." The expression means his eyes are like those of a dove, with the sockets full and embracing, and possessing the purity of having been bathed in milk.

Verse 13. To be sure, many of the comparisons derive their occasion from the desire of one ardent lover to say sweet things about the other. Over and over we have been reminded of the comparison to various perfumes. It was usual, therefore, for her to mention a bed of spices and flowers, also of lilies with their odor of myrrh.

Verse 14. A devoted wife would admire the body of her husband. In her desire for expression of that admiration she would think of such things as gold and gems.

Verse 15. Many important structures were supported upon marble pillars. That indicated strength as well as attractiveness, and this wife saw her husband as an upright man of physical strength and masculine beauty. Another reference was made to the idea of perfume. The cedars of Lebanon were known to give off a very aromatic odor.

Verse 16. *Mouth* is from CHEK and Strong defines it, "properly the palate or inside of the mouth; hence the mouth itself (as the organ of speech, taste and kissing)." The wife meant his kisses were most sweet, and then she summed up her description of her beloved by the general clause that *he is altogether lovely*. By mentioning the *daughters of Jerusalem* at the conclusion of her speech, it was to notify them that the speech was in the form of an answer to their question in verse 9.

SONG OF SOLOMON 6

Verse 1. This verse is the speech of the girls whom the wife met on the streets. At first they were rather disinterested in her search for her beloved and asked for more information. In answer to them she gave the speech we have read in ch. 5: 10-16. After such a glowing description of him they became interested and offered to help in the search for this unusual lover.

Verse 2. This verse was the answer to the second question of the girls. In a speech prompted by love the wife described her husband's whereabouts in the language of flowers and spices, which has been seen to be a favorite comparison with lovers.

Verse 3. With another reference to flowers, the wife asserted the mutual love that existed between herself and her husband.

Verse 4. We will find ourselves lost in this book unless we keep in mind that Solomon was the composer of the entire piece. In his personal love for his Egyptian sweetheart, and with his inspired qualification for descriptive writing, he produced this great love story. It is a picture of the deep affection that should exist between husbands and wives. It is composed in the form of supposed conversations and dealings between him and this beloved wife. In keeping with that plot he takes up the story at the place he met her after the girls helped find her beloved in the garden of flowers. Meeting her there he resumed his praises, but the language is a mixture of direct speech to her as if "making love," and indirect words of description of his wife's qualities, given for the information of everybody. Smith's Bible Dictionary says of Tirzah, "Its reputation for beauty throughout the country must have been widespread," and it is used to compare the beauty of this woman. To be terrible in a good sense means to overawe one with some sense of dignity or other qualification. This woman had more subduing effect upon Solomon than did all of the mighty armies.

Verse 5. In the preceding verse the wife had overawed her husband more than could have been done by an army. In this place it is represented to have been so strong a sentiment that he pleaded for a short break in the spell so that he might get his breath, as it were. See comments at ch. 4: 1 on the comparison to goat's hair.

Verse 6. This is identical with ch. 4: 2.

Verse 7. Continuing the comparison the reader will find this verse explained by the comments at ch. 4:3.

Verse 8. Solomon finally acquired domestic relations with a thousand women (1 Ki. 11: 3), but at present he made specific reference to 140, and to an innumerable group of girls. Sixty of these women were in the exalted rank of queens, which shows that the comparison Solomon was about to make for his favorite wife would be elevating to her.

Verse 9. The reader will please consult the comments at ch. 1: 15 on the significance of doves in connection with love. This verse is the language of one who is truly in love with his wife. Such speech generally consists in comparisons and contrasts. Solomon would not have admitted that his estimate of his favorite wife was the result of selfish favoritism natural for a loving husband, but claimed that the queens and other girls praised her. Another thing, he did not account for his wife's special excellence by the fact that she was from a most desirable family (which often does explain a situation), but she was the choice child in her mother's estimation.

Verse 10. *Fair* means beautiful in general, not with reference to the complexion; *clear* means pure and free from all mixtures. For explanation of "terrible," see the comments on last part of verse 4.

Verse 11. Aside from the sentimental strain running through this whole composition there is nothing special in this verse. A man with the extensive possessions such as were held by Solomon, would frequently look over them by way of inspection.

Verse 12. When used figuratively, chariots indicate a condition of power and honor. *Ammi-nadib* is rendered "my willing people" in the margin, and Smith's Bible Dictionary agrees with it. In the exhilaration of his state of love, Solomon felt that he was a specially-favored man among a willing people.

Verse 13. *Shullamite* is defined in Strong's lexicon, "an epithet [pet name] of Solomon's queen." *Return* is from an original with a very wide and indefinite meaning. As it is used in this place it is an indirect call upon the woman of his choice to favor him with her presence again. The second clause is a meditative form of speech, as if he were talking to himself, but voicing the question he imagined others would ask him upon observing his great interest in this special woman. He answered the imaginary question by making a highly complimentary comparison. *Company* is from MECHOWLAH, which Strong defines "a dance." *Armies* is from MACHANEH and Strong's definition is, "an encampment (of travelers or troops); hence an army, whether literally (of soldiers) or figuratively (of dancers, angels, cattle, locusts, stars; or even the sacred courts)." Solomon meant his favorite wife was to him as glorious, attractive and awe-inspiring as a couple of dancing groups.

SONG OF SOLOMON 7

Verse 1. Solomon continued his descriptive praise for the wife of his choice. His minute itemizing of the various charms of her body proves the truth of Gen. 2: 18. The attractiveness of the female form rounds out the kind of companion needed for the happiness and welfare of the man. By this combination both may live in the enjoyment of each other, and together may fulfill the will of their Creator. The comparisons made for the various parts of her body are chiefly from the standpoint of things that are both beautiful and useful, not necessarily in view of material likeness.

Verse 2. Solomon believed he could do the attractiveness of his wife the greatest honor by comparing it to objects of merit in other parts of creation.

Verse 3. See the comments at ch. 4: 5.

Verse 4. For comments on *tower* see those at ch. 4: 4. The comparison to *fishpools* is rather peculiar. There is nothing in the case that calls for any translation but the simple word *pools*. It is from BEREKAH, and Strong says the word is derived from another that he defines, "a primitive root; to kneel; by implication to bless God." Robert Young defines it in this place by "blessing." So the thought of Solomon is the eyes of his wife are as gracious and pleasing as the clear pools near the gates of the great city of Heshbon. Towers were structures that stood out before others very prominently, and they were usually built attractively. By comparing his wife's nose to one of them, Solomon meant she did not have the deformity of a flat nose, as so many persons of the dark race had.

Verse 5. *Carmel* was a prominent mountain because of the many noteworthy deeds that were done there, and the important persons connected with its history. The hair of an Egyptian would not be purple as to color. The comparison is made to its rich gloss, and to the fact that purple was often used in connection with royalty. *Galleries* is from a Hebrew word that Strong defines, "a ringlet of hair." The last clause means the king was *held* or captivated by the beauty of her hair. No wonder Paul said that a woman's hair is a glory to her (1 Cor. 11: 15), and strange that any woman would voluntarily sacrifice such a glorious ornament to her person given to her by the Creator.

Verse 6. *Fair* does not refer to the complexion but to the form of her body. She was beautiful in body and delightfully pleasant in spirit.

Verse 7. *Stature* literally refers to height. A palm tree is tall and straight and has a beautiful top. *Clusters* is defined in the lexicon, "a bunch of grapes or other fruit." The comparison was made in the last clause to attractiveness in general.

Verse 8. Having used the palm tree for his comparison, Solomon proposed to go up to it and enjoy its beauties and products.

Verse 9. *Roof* and *mouth* are from the same word, and Strong expresses it as the organ of "taste and kissing." Solomon meant the kisses of his wife were as sweet as the best wine. *Asleep* is from a Hebrew word defined "languid" or "sleepy," not necessarily in sleep. *Speak* is from DABAB, which Strong defines, "to move slowly, i.e. glide." Hence Solomon meant his wife's kisses would cause his own lips to respond even though he was almost asleep.

Verse 10. From here to the close of the book it will be the part of the wife. The idea in this verse is that love between her and her husband was mutual.

Verse 11. The wife wanted to have a general stroll with her husband. They would ramble through the field in the day, and when night came they would go into one of the villages to lodge.

Verse 12. The next morning she would propose that they arise early and start out again. This time they would wander into the vineyards, but this "tour of inspection" would be mainly as an opportunity for another motive. She promised to give him her tokens of love while in the cozy nooks of the vineyard.

Verse 13. Among the tokens mentioned above were the *mandrakes* which Moffatt renders "love apples." It is from DUWDAY and Strong defines it in part as it pertains to this place "the mandrake (as aphodisiac [exciting sexual desire])." In connection with this, see the comments at Gen. 30: 14 in Volume 1 of this Commentary. These and *all manner of pleasant fruits* the wife said she had reserved for her beloved.

SONG OF SOLOMON 8

Verse 1. A good woman would not want to be intimate with her fleshly brother. The point in her desire was in the advantage of having her lover always near her, as it would be were he her brother and thus a member of the same household.

Verse 2. Continuing her wishful thinking along the line of family intimacies, she pictured bringing him into the house and treating him to some of her mother's prepared wine and other delectable juices.

Verse 3. This is identical with ch. 2: 6.

Verse 4. And this is the same as ch. 2: 7. I request the reader to consult those two verses in connection with this.

Verse 5. In the preceding verse the daughters of Jerusalem were again brought into this mental drama. Now they call out as if they see this person who had given them the charge just reported, and she is approaching from the wilderness, leaning on the arm of her lover. They did not receive a direct reply to their call, but they heard the voice of her beloved speaking and saying *I raised thee up under the apple tree.* We have seen that the apple was often referred to figuratively in connection with love. *Raised* is from UWR, which is defined, "to awake." Figuratively speaking, the lover awakened his darling with his responsive love tokens, and that symbolized the love apple plant. Her mother brought her forth into this world with just such a lot in store, that of a life of love. We will bear in mind this chapter started with the imagery of the family life, and it was repeated somewhat in this verse.

Verse 6. The wife next went to a more direct and literal use of speech. She urged her love upon her husband and wished to be as securely attached to him as a seal would be. The lexicon definition of *seal* is "a signature-ring." This wife had great cause to be jealous if the case should be regarded in the usual sense. Solomon had a great host of women in his group and this Egyptian queen certainly knew something about it. The description of jealousy that Solomon put into the mouth of his favorite wife pictured it as being the cruelest sentiment of the human mind. It was compared to the grave, and well it might be, for it has sent many a man to an untimely grave.

Verse 7. In the mental drama that we are studying the wife was speaking in this verse. However, Solomon was the author and he was inspired, which makes all of his descriptions and other declarations authentic. True love is more overwhelming than a flood, and more valuable than all of a man's material substance. If it were offered in exchange for one's love, it would be *contemned* which means to be disrespected.

Verse 8. This *little sister* had not reached adult age. The question looked forward to the day when she would be old enough to be sought in marriage.

Verse 9. The older sister (Solomon's wife) answered her own question. If the young sister *be a wall*, which means if she will maintain her purity until the age of marriage is attained, then they will encourage and assist her. The latter part of the verse is a figure of speech for the support promised for the young sister.

Verse 10. The wife had proved herself to be just such a *wall* in that she had maintained her virginity until she became the wife of Solomon.

Verse 11. The wife was aware that Solomon had planted great vineyards, but he had leased them to others and was not immediately in use of them.

Verse 12. She still had her vineyard and Solomon was offered it with all of its products. It might be regarded as a sort of loving dowry.

Verse 13. Solomon possessed many gardens and other spots of luxury. He had many friends who were associated with him and gladly listened to all that he said to them. The wife did not object to such friendship from the companions of her husband, but longed to share in the association, and to hear his loving voice.

Verse 14. Make *haste* is an expression of eagerness for the pleasure of her husband's company. See the comments at ch. 2: 17 on the thought of the roe. Many of the comparisons used by both Solomon and his wife were based on the desirable qualities of living creatures and inanimate objects, qualities they possessed aside from their literal natures. *Mountain of spices* is the oft-repeated figure drawn from the relation of perfumes of all kinds to the subject of love, and it was fitting to close the book with this figure, since the leading line of thought through the entiré piece is love.

ISAIAH 1

General remarks: The Book of Isaiah is the first of the Major Prophets according to the compilation of the King James version of the Bible. Isaiah began to write near the close of the kingdom of Israel (the 10 tribes), and its national sun went down before he finished his vision. The kingdom of Judah (the 2 tribes) had also become very corrupt, and though it was to continue for over a century its final downfall was certain. The prophet was chiefly concerned in the matter of the kingdom of Judah as regards to the (then) near future.

With regard to the future in general, he is often styled "the prince of prophets" and also the "Evangelical Prophet," because he said more about the kingdom of Christ than all the other prophets combined. With few exceptions he is cited in every book of the New Testament; in some of them very frequently. His vision included matter pertaining to the Patriarchal, Jewish and Christian Dispensations, and also reached into the eternal state.

There is but one important difference between a prophet and a historian. The one records a fact before it happens, the other records it afterward. If both are inspired of God they are equally authentic since God understands the future as well as the past (Isa. 46: 10). Because of this truth, a prophet does not use the same style of language as does a historian. Being inspired of God as he writes of the future, he often words it as if it were present or even in the past. With God everything is an absolute NOW as far as its certainty is concerned.

An inspired prophet acts as the instrument of God, not always or even often knowing personally "what it is all about." The work and vision of such a writer may well be illustrated by an adjustable telescope. God holds the instrument and adjusts it as to range, according to the nearness or distance of dates he wishes the prophet to see. The prophet is looking through the telescope, at the same time he is speaking or writing. He does not realize when God lengthens or shortens the range of the instrument but only records what he sees. Occasionally God wishes the prophet to write a few words concerning some fact beyond the main subject on which he is supposed to be writing and so will lengthen the telescope until the prophet can see into the time of the Christian Dispensation; or perhaps he may stretch it out still further at rare intervals so that the prophet can see into the Hereafter. Then after his brief "break" from the main subject, God will return the telescope to the regular range so that the prophet will resume his former subject. And we must remember that while the prophet believes in his God and considers that He is the one who is holding the telescope, yet he does not realize the changes and adjustments. This is why we have so much teaching in the Bible showing the prophets did not always understand the meaning of what they were writing. They often wished to know more about it and would inquire about it, but the information was to be reserved for the teachers and writers of the New Testament times. See the following: Matt. 13:16, 17; Eph. 3:9, 10; 1 Pet. 1:10-12; 2 Pet. 1:20, 21. The reader of this COMMENTARY will be frequently reminded of this note which may be identified as the illustration of the telescope. I earnestly insist that he keep it in mind and consult it each time it is suggested.

Verse 1. *Vision* is from CHAZOWN and Strong defines it, "a sight (mentally), i. e., a dream, revelation, or oracle." Isaiah had this sight when he looked into the telescope described above. *Judah AND Jerusalem* are named in this way because the latter was the capital city of the former. The prophet wrote during the reigns of the kings named, beginning near the end of Uzziah's and closing near the end of Hezekiah's reign. The history of those reigns may be read in 2 Ki. 14th to 20th chapters; 2 Chr. 26th to 32nd.

Verse 2. *Heaven* and *earth* are called upon to hear, which is an accommodative form of a general summons for all intelligent creatures everywhere to listen. The *children* are the Israelites (v. 3) and the nourishing refers to the teaching and care the Lord had given his people. *Rebelled* means their general disobedience, but had special reference to their national idolatry which had become serious.

Verse 3. The dumb beast was given credit for knowing more than God's people. Sometimes ignorance may soften if not excuse one's guilt of failure. In the present case it will not do either because the ignorance was their own fault. It is explained they were ignorant because Israel *doth not consider*. That accounts for the ignorance of many people who pretend to desire understanding but say they cannot. The word of God is plainly revealed, but it must be *considered* or studied like all good literature.

Verse 4. *Sinful nation* indicates the people as a whole had gone wrong. There were some individuals who were righteous and who deplored the conditions, but most of them had followed the wicked rulers and other leaders. *Gone away backward* means they had backslidden from the path of righteousness.

Verse 5. The nation had gone so far in wrong the Lord did not expect any improvement but rather that it would get worse and worse. *Head* and *heart* are practically the same, but when used distinctly the latter means the inner motives and feelings, the former the intelligence that directs them. The verse means that God's people had become completely corrupted with iniquity.

Verse 6. This verse is a practical repetition of the preceding one, carrying out the figure to specific items of the spiritual diseases infecting the nation.

Verse 7. The form of this verse is in the present tense but it is a prophecy, written over a century before the fulfillment. It was written about 760 B. C., and was fulfilled near 600 B. C. For the Biblical account of it read 2 Ki. 24 and 25.

Verse 8. *Daughter of Zion* is a term that occurs many times in the prophecies. The first word means the people of a nation or country as a group, and the last means the capital of that nation. When used together it means the people and its capital which is Zion, the chief spot in Jerusalem. This verse predicts the isolated condition of Jerusalem after the Babylonians had taken away all its chief men and dismantled the city of Jerusalem. *Lodge in a garden of cucumbers* is a shed to shelter the one who must keep guard over the field. If we can imagine the desolate lonesomeness of a place like that in the midst of a field of vines, we can appreciate the illustration.

Verse 9. God is merciful and never does entirely desert his people. He decreed they should go into captivity and be chastised for their sins. That would cut down their number, but there was to be a comparatively small number salvaged from the wreck of the captivity. *Remnant* is from SARIYD, which Strong defines, "a survivor." A *small remnant*, then would mean a few survivors. In Ezra 2:64 the number that survived the long period is given as 42,360. In the days of their national strength they numbered about three million, allowing five to each family (Num. 26:51). Had it not been for the Lord's love for his people the captivity would have destroyed them as completely as the cities of Sodom and Gomorrah had been.

Verse 10. Sodom as a literal city had been destroyed hundreds of years before and thus did not have any rulers when Isaiah lived. The term is therefore used figuratively and means the rulers of the people of Israel had become wicked like the men of Sodom;

that is, as bad as they, though in a different manner. Of course the reference to Gomorrah is in the same sense as that of Sodom. The several verses before us will be commented on in turn, but before so doing I will suggest the reader mark his Bible with a bracket to include verses 10-15. To the verses of the bracket as a whole apply the following note. The leaders of the nation, such as their priests and prophets and elders, were held chiefly responsible for the corruptions of the nation. While they imposed their injustices upon the common people and thus led them into wrong, they themselves were condemned in more severe terms than the people. However, since the people often were willing to be thus influenced, and "loved to have it so," God regarded the whole nation as at fault. Yet his rebukes were generally directed to these leaders and his threat of overthrow of the nation and rejection of its services were based upon these injustices imposed by the leaders upon the people. In trying to evade God's judgments upon them for these injustices, the leaders attempted to combine some things that had been commanded in the law such as instrumental music, sacrifices and the like, with their corrupt practices, that had not been commanded, thinking that God would accept the whole program including their corruptions, because of the things they did that had been once commanded and accepted. But God in various places gave them to understand that because of the general state of corruption in their national conduct, he would reject even their attempts of conduct that would have been otherwise accepted. This will explain the various places where it would seem that they were being condemned for these things which we understand were really a part of their divine law. This note should be read in connection with the present passage and also the following: Isa. 5: 11-13; 58: 2-7; Ezk. 34: 2, 3; Amos 5: 21-27; 6: 1-6; Joel 2: 13; Micah 6: 6-8, and in all other places in the scriptures, especially among the prophecies where this apparent contradiction occurs. There are no actual contradictions in the Bible, what seems to be are explainable by considering all of the facts.

Verse 11. *To what purpose* means, what do you think you will gain by your sacrifices? All of the items mentioned in this verse were commanded under the law, and hence were not the inventions of the people. But even such things had become objectionable as explained above.

Verse 12. *Come to appear* refers to their coming to the temple where the altar for sacrifices was located. *Who hath required* is the same as saying God does not call for sacrifices from those whose general practices are corrupt.

Verse 13. *Oblations* is another name for "sacrifices and offerings." *New moons*, etc., referred to their holy days which also were a part of the Mosaic system. *Cannot away with* means the Lord could not tolerate sacrifices from such a corrupt nation.

Verse 14. The Jewish religious calendar was regulated by the moon and the new moon meant the first of another month. All of these dates were holy days and called for certain religious activities. *Appointed feasts* were the ones which the law specifically required, such as the Passover and Pentecost, called "feast of weeks" in the Old Testament. *Soul hateh* means the same as *cannot away with* in the preceding verse.

Verse 15. *Spread forth your hands* refers to a custom used in connection with prayer (Ex. 9: 29, 33; 1 Ki. 8: 22, 38, 54; Ezra 9: 5; Psa. 143: 6). Because of the corrupted state of the nation God declared he would not see their outstretched hands nor hear their prayers. *Hands full of blood.* Doubtless the leaders of the nation had caused the literal shedding of innocent blood, but other serious offences were referred to as being guilty of blood (Lev. 17: 4; 20: 9, 12). This is the last verse of the bracket suggested above; and before going further I insist the student carefully read again the note at verse 10.

Verse 16. This verse is an exhortation to repentance. The first thing necessary for a genuine reformation is to *cease to do evil*. As long as a man continues to practice his evil deeds he cannot truthfully state that he has repented.

Verse 17. It is not enough that an unrighteous man stop doing things that are wrong. The best that could be said of such would be that it is negative righteousness. In addition to that he is required to *learn to do well*. The two clauses, *cease to do evil, learn to do well*, may truly be called a complete Biblical definition of repentance.

Verse 18. This verse also is an exhortation to repentance, with the added promise of forgiveness and restoration to favor as a reward. The fate of the nation facing unavoidable captivity was threatened many times as we shall see. On the other hand, there are frequent admonitions to reform with assurances of the favor of God. This apparent contradiction is explained at length in a note beginning at bottom of page 174, Vol. 2 of the COMMENTARY. To conserve space it will not be copied here and the student is requested to read it in that place. *Reason together.* The second word is not in the original, so the phrase does not mean that God and man were to be joint participants in some kind of discussion. The first is from YAKACH and the part of Strong's definition that applies here is, "a primitive root; to be right (i. e., correct) . . . to decide, justify or convict." It means for them to listen and God will tell them what to do to get right. (Again remember the note referred to above.) When colors are used figuratively for moral subjects, red means guilt and white means innocence. *They* is a pronoun that grammatically stands for sins, but in the meaning of the passage it is that the sins will be removed, leaving the soul as white as snow.

Verse 19. The service offered to God must be done willingly or it will not be accepted. *Eat the good* means they would receive the good things provided by the Lord.

Verse 20. Continued rebellion would bring the sword of the enemy nation upon the guilty. The nation as a whole was to receive that fate regardless (as explained in the long note), but also the individuals who refused to reform when given the opportunity would likewise share in the calamity. Isaiah was the writer of these words but they were by the mouth of the Lord and were certain of fulfillment.

Verse 21. *Jerusalem* was the city referred to and it was called a *harlot.* This is from ZANAH and I shall quote the entire definition of Strong: "A primitive root [highly fed and therefore wanton—Strong]; to commit adultery (usually of the female and less often of simple fornication, rarely of involuntary ravishment); figuratively to commit idolatry (the Jewish people being regarded as the spouse of Jehovah)." The leading corruption of the Jewish nation was idolatry and that was considered spiritual adultery. The comparison is logical because religious intimacy with another than God is equivalent to fleshly intimacy of a wife with a man other than her husband. *Murderers* is to be understood in the same light as *blood* in verse 15.

Verse 22. The *silver* refers to the righteousness and judgment of the preceding verse. Silver is a solid and wine is a liquid and both are valuable substances. In a figurative speech the prophet represents them as deteriorating. To do so in their own classes as to material form, the silver could only become dross (a waste product from which the silver had originally been separated), and the wine would become some other less concentrated liquid such as water.

Verse 23. A *prince* was "a head person (of any rank or class)" according to Strong's lexicon. It refers to the outstanding men in the Jewish nation, not necessarily to officers. But the people attached a great deal of importance to such persons and in turn were largely influenced by them. They were so greedy for wealth that they accepted *gifts* which means bribes. That is why they are said to be companions of thieves. A man who will either offer a bribe or accept one is as bad as a thief. Such men will take advantage of the unfortunate if someone who has enmity for those unfortunate ones will offer a bribe to corrupt a decision they are asked to make.

Verse 24. *Ease* and *avenge* mean the same as used in this verse. *Adversaries* and *enemies* also mean the same in this passage, applying to the people of Israel. By rebelling against the law they had become enemies of God. The verse means God would take vengeance on them by the great event of the captivity.

Verse 25. *Tin* is from BEDIYE and Strong defines it "alloy (because removed by smelting)." Dross has practically the same meaning, and they both are used to compare the chief corruption of the Jewish nation which was idolatry. The verse is a prediction that the judgment to be brought on the nation (which we shall learn was the Babylonian captivity), would completely cure it of that great iniquity. To show that the prediction was fulfilled I shall quote some statements from authentic histories as follows: "But now Pilate, the procurator of Judea, removed the army from Caesarea to Jerusalem, to take their winter quarters there, in order to abolish the Jewish laws. So he introduced Caesar's effigies [his pictures], which were upon the ensigns, and brought them into the city; whereas our law forbids us the very making of images; on which account the former procurators were wont to make their entry into the city with such ensigns as had not those ornaments. Pilate was the first who brought those images to Jerusalem, and set them up there; which was done without the knowledge of the people, because it was done in the night-time; but as soon as they knew it, they came in multitudes to Caesarea, and interceded with Pilate many days, that he would remove the images; and when he would not grant their requests, because it would tend to the injury of Caesar, while yet they persevered in their request, on the sixth day he ordered his soldiers to have their weapons privately, while he came and sat upon his judgment seat, which seat was so prepared in open place of the city, that it concealed the army that lay ready to oppress them. And when the Jews petitioned him again, he gave a signal to the soldiers to compass them round, and threatened that their punishment should be no less than immediate death unless they would leave off disturbing him, and go their ways home. But they threw themselves upon the ground, and laid their necks bare, and said they would take their death very willingly, rather than the wisdom of their laws should be transgressed; upon which Pilate was deeply affected with their firm resolution to keep their laws inviolable, and presently commanded the images to be carried back from Jerusalem to Caesarea." Josephus, Antiquities, 18-3-1.

"The captivity, though a judgment on the people for their sins of unfaithfulness to the covenant, was in reality an unconscious preparation for the times of the Messiah. Their national loss was turned to gain; not only were they *weaned from their proneness to idolatry* [emphasis mine—E. M. Z.], but their departures from monotheism [the doctrine of one only true God] were, after meeting with Persian types of thought, corrected and reformed.... The return from captivity is thus the third and final stage in the growth of Israel as the covenant people. Monotheism, exceptional in the days of Elijah and the early prophets, was burned into them by the fires of persecution. This highest stage of monotheism was the elevated point of view which they had reached in the third and final stage of their spiritual growth on the return from captivity." J. B. Heard, Lecturer, University of Cambridge, p. 68 in "Bible Helps," International. This lengthy quotation from history will not be repeated for the sake of space, and the student is urged to make note of its location in this volume, and frequent reference will be made to it as the studies in the prophecies of the Old Testament proceed.

Verse 26. *Judges* means men who rule and *counsellors* means those who advise. After the return from the captivity the nation was again permitted to have its priests and teachers according to the law of Moses. For the present I shall make only a general reference to the history of the fulfillment regarding this prediction. Read very carefully the books of Ezra and Nehemiah, which gives the history of the restoration that was effected after the release from the Babylonian captivity.

Verse 27. For the meaning of *Zion* see the comments at verse 8. One part of the lexicon definition of *redeemed* is "to release," and refers to the act of the Persian king Cyrus in giving the Jews their liberty (Ezra 1: 1-4). *Judgment* means "a verdict" according to Strong, and the verdict was that of Cyrus just cited. The importance of this verdict is indicated by the fact that it was made a part of the royal record (Ezra 5: 13, 17; 6: 1-3). *Converts* is from a Hebrew word that means those who return, and applies here to the Jews who returned from captivity. *With righteousness* means it was the right thing to allow the Jews to return from the captivity.

Verse 28. The parts of many books in the Bible are not always strictly in chronological order as to the time of the events. An instance of that is before us now. The preceding verse pertained to the conditions after the captivity, the present one to those before. The *transgressors* and *sinners* were the guilty Jews who were to be *consumed* or *chastised* by the captivity.

Verse 29. The mention of *oaks* is an indirect reference to the idolatrous practices of the heathen which were imitated by the Jews, and became their chief national corruption. On the subject of trees as related to religious matters, Smith's Bible Dictionary has the following to say: "In the religions of the ancient heathen world groves play a prominent part. In the old times altars only were erected to the gods. It was thought wrong to shut up the gods within walls, and hence trees were the first temples; and from the earliest times groves are mentioned in connection with religious worship. Gen. 12: 6, 7; Deut. 11: 30." In view of this we will see many references to oaks, trees and groves in the prophecies, and it will be understood to mean the practices of idolatry. *Ashamed of the oaks* means they will be cured of their idolatry by the captivity. (See the note at verse 25.) The *gardens* of the ancient people contained trees as well as smaller plants, and the reference to them in this verse is for the same purpose as the *oaks*.

Verse 30. The nation had worshiped the oaks in their idolatry and that was to cause their fading and downfall as a nation. The fading of an oak tree, therefore, is used to illustrate the fate of the nation. Their gardens contained trees which they worshiped, therefore their sad end is compared to a garden that had been deprived of the moisture needful for its life.

Verse 31. *Tow* is from NEORETH, which Strong defines, "something shaken out, i. e., tow (as the refuse of flax)." The leaders of the nation had been strong like the good part of flax, but the captivity was to reduce them and make them like the refuse of the plant. *Maker of it* means the works of these once strong men. It was to become *as a spark*, referring to the fires of chastisement in the captivity. *Burn together* means these evil men and their works were both to be consumed by this figurative fire. *None shall quench* refers to the certainty of the captivity. On this last thought the student is urged to read the note at bottom of page 174, Vol. 2 of the COMMENTARY, explanatory of one of the apparent contradictions.

ISAIAH 2

Verse 1. The character of the prophetic books will make it advisable for the student frequently to mark a number of verses as one bracket and label it as a whole by a general subject. The several verses may then be commented on in their turn as their particular subject matter may require. Accordingly the first four verses of this chapter should be bracketed, and the subject to be attached is "the kingdom of Christ." This verse starts much like the first chapter but without giving the dates. See comments at ch. 1: 1 for *Judah and Jerusalem*, also for the matter of dates. It also will be well to read again the illustration of the telescope.

Verse 2. *Last days* is a phrase used in the Bible with various meanings, depending on the connection of the subject matter involved. It sometimes means the last days of the Jewish Dispensation, sometimes the last Dispensation as a whole, and sometimes the last part of the third or Christian Dispensation. In our verse it has the first meaning stated, for it was in the closing days of the Jewish Dispensation that the kingdom of Christ was set up. However, the fact of starting this kingdom put an end to the Jewish Dispensation for religious purposes. *Nations* is from GOI and Strong defines it, "from the same root as GEVAH (in the sense of massing); a foreign nation; hence a Gentile." The prediction means that Gentiles as well as Jews were to have access to this new kingdom. (See Eph. 2: 17.) *Mountain* in figurative and prophetic language means a government. The prediction means the government of Christ was to be established *in the top of the mountains*, or that it would be above all other governments. (See Dan. 2: 44.)

Verse 3. *Many* is from RAB and Strong defines it, "abundant (in quantity, size, age, number, rank, quality)." *People* is from AM and Strong defines it, "a people (as a congregated unit); specifically a tribe (as those of Israel); hence (collectively) troops or attendants; figuratively a flock." If the two italicized words are used as a phrase it means the Gentiles as well as the Jews. Perhaps the first word would seem too strong when used for only two classes (Jews and Gentiles), but note that part of the definition includes "size" as well as numerical amount. Since the two classes would include all the people of the earth, the word *many* (with its meaning of "size") would aptly designate them. Then if the first word in the definition, "abundant" or numerous, would refer to the numerical importance of the prediction, the fulfillment of that prediction may be seen in Acts 2: 41; 4: 4; 5: 14; 6: 1; 8: 6; 12: 24. For explanation of *Zion* and *Jerusalem* see the comments at ch. 1: 8. *The law* and *word of the Lord* are the same here and refer to the Gospel of Christ.

Verse 4. This verse has been erroneously interpreted as a prediction that carnal or literal wars would cease. The mistake is obvious when it is remembered that the subject is still the

Isaiah 2: 5-16

kingdom of Christ and does not concern the temporal affairs of the world. It is true that in proportion as men imbibe the principles of the Gospel they will cease to have the motive for carnal warfare. But such a peace might well be considered as a "by-product" of the Gospel and not its direct purpose. The prediction means the kingdom of Christ was not to be supported by the carnal or material sword as was the kingdom in the Jewish Dispensation.

Verse 5. Dropping the role of a prophet for a brief time, Isaiah exhorts the *house of Jacob* or the Israelite nation to walk in the light of the Lord.

Verse 6. *Thou* stands for the Lord who was mentioned at the close of the preceding verse. The prophet acknowledges the just reason of the Lord for having forsaken the house of Jacob, that they were *replenished from the east*. They had taken too much interest in the heathen of the countries lying east of them. *Soothsayers* were people who practiced magic in a tricking manner to get temporal advantage of the foreigners. This unrighteous business brought an immigration of corrupt people and they in turn corrupted God's people with their evil practices.

Verse 7. The possession of wealth is not necessarily a sin but when it is obtained by means and with the motive as was exhibited by the nation of Israel it does indicate that something is wrong. It was obtained by improper association with the heathen about them and then used in conection with idolatry. Chariots were usually employed for war purposes, but otherwise they were used for pleasure and display. They were useless in either case without horses so that called for the obtaining of those animals in large numbers. That was considered an unfavorable indication, especially when indulged in by the kings. (See Deut. 17: 16.)

Verse 8. Idolatrous worship seems to follow logically when great wealth is obtained. That is especially true when it is obtained unlawfully. It is wrong to worship any kind of idols, but special mention is made of the ones which *their own hands* had made. The main point is that of inconsistency. If a man makes an idol he knows it could not be even as great as he, therefore why worship it?

Verse 9. *Mean man* refers to a man of low degree and *great man* is the opposite. The idea is that all classes were bowing to these dumb idols and the Lord was sorely provoked at them both. *Forgive them not* is on the subject of the determination to punish the Israelite nation regardless of some individuals who were righteous. For the explanation of this apparent contradiction, see the long note beginning at bottom of page 174 in Vol. 2 of this COMMENTARY.

Verse 10. This verse is a figurative warning for the corrupt nation. *Rock* indicates strength, and *dust* is a symbol of dejection or a downcast feeling. The passage means they should humble themselves and seek a reliable refuge from God's wrath.

Verse 11. This verse is another prediction of the captivity and its chastising effect upon the nation. The Lord was to be exalted by the event because he would demonstrate his superiority over all the false gods.

Verse 12. *Day of the Lord* means the period covering the captivity. *Proud, lofty* and *lifted up* refer to the same thing. Whenever a man rejects the authority of God's law he is regarded as being proud (1 Tim. 6: 3, 4).

Verse 13. This is a reference to idolatry and its cure. For the explanation of oaks and other trees in connection with idolatry see the comments at ch. 1: 29. On the subject of the cure from idolatry see the historical quotation at ch. 1: 25.

Verse 14. The *day of the Lord* is still in the mind of the prophet in this and the remaining verses of the chapter. (See comments on the phrase in verse 12.) The period of the captivity was to bring about the results or conditions mentioned in these verses. *Mountains* in figurative language means governments or rulers. The government of the Jews and its rulers were to be brought down.

Verse 15. *Towers* and *fenced walls* refers to the defences of the nation. They were to be overthrown by the enemy. The fulfillment of this prediction may be seen in 2 Ki. 24 and 25, and the long quotation from secular history that will be made at the beginning of the next chapter.

Verse 16. The Israelites had done much traffic over the Mediterranean Sea and thereby enriched themselves by dealing with other nations. All of this would be stopped by the captivity.

Pictures is from SEKIYAH, which Strong defines, "a conspicuous object." Pictures of various kinds were used by the heathen as objects of worship and admiration. The Israelites imitated that practice and that caused the displeasure of God to be poured out against them.

Verse 17. This is practically the same as verse 11.

Verse 18. This and the following three verses should be marked as a bracket and entitled "the cure from idolatry," followed with a rereading of the note at ch. 1: 25. Then observe the comments that are offered on the several verses here. The idols literally were destroyed in many instances, but the principal idea is that the worship of them would be utterly abolished.

Verse 19. *They* refers to the idols of the preceding verse grammatically speaking, but really means the worshipers of those idols, because dumb idols could not have any such a sentiment as fear. *Shake terribly the earth* refers to the time when the nation would be convulsed by the siege and captivity.

Verse 20. A *mole* is defined in the lexicon as "a burrower," a creature that seeks to make a hiding place in the earth. The *bats* were found in the caverns of the East according to Smith's Bible Dictionary. The figurative use that is made of these creatures is to compare the desire of the idol worshipers to consign their idols to the regions of darkness so as never to see them again.

Verse 21. This is a continuation of the thought in the preceding verse. The idol worshipers would be determined to put their idols out from their sight or consideration. Such a result is predicted and was actually fulfilled by the captivity.

Verse 22. This verse is a severe comment on the human being, and a prediction that God would reject him because of his evil doings.

ISAIAH 3

General remarks: The first four verses of this chapter should be marked as a bracket and entitled "Babylonian Captivity." Before going into comments on the several verses a few statements will be made on the subject of captivity. There were two of them in the history of the Jews. The first one occurred in 722 B.C. when the kingdom of Israel or of the ten tribes was taken away by Assyria, and this is known in history as the Assyrian Captivity. The Biblical account of this is in 2 Ki. 17. A little more than a century later (606 B. C.), the kingdom of Judah or of the two tribes was taken away by the Babylonians, and the Biblical account of this is in 2 Ki. 24 and 25. But both captivities were predicted by Isaiah and other prophets, hence some secular history will be quoted to show the fulfillment of the predictions. The following will recite the history of the two captivities:

"The Kingdom of Israel (953 ?-722). —The kingdom of the Ten Tribes maintained its existence for about two hundred years. Many passages of its history are recitals of the struggles between the worship of the national god Yahweh (Jehovah) and the idolatrous service of the gods of the surrounding nations. The cause of Yahweh was boldly espoused by a line of remarkable prophets, among whom Elijah and Elisha in the ninth century, and Amos and Hosea in the eighth, stand preeminent. The little kingdom was at last overwhelmed by the Assyrian power. This happened 722 B.C., when Samaria, as we have already narrated in the history of Assyria, was captured by Sargon, king of Nineveh, and the flower of the people were carried away into captivity beyond the Mesopotamian rivers. The gaps made in the population of Samaria by the deportation of its best inhabitants were filled with other subjects or captives of the Assyrian king. The descendants of these, mingled with the Israelites that were still left in the country, formed the Samaritans of the time of Christ.

The Kingdom of Judah (953 ?-586 B.C.). This little kingdom, torn by internal religious dissensions, and often on the very verge of ruin from Egyptian or Assyrian armies, maintained an independent existence for over three centuries. But upon the extension of the power of Babylon to the west, Jerusalem was forced to acknowledge the suzerainty [authority] of the Babylonian kings. The kingdom at last shared the fate of its northern rival. Nebuchadnezzar, the powerful king of Babylon, in revenge for an uprising of the Jews, besieged and captured Jerusalem and carried away a large part of the people into captivity at Babylon. This event virtually ended the separate political life of the Hebrew race (586 B.C.)" Myers' Ancient History, pp. 78, 79.

Isaiah 3: 1-16

"And such was the end of the nation of the Hebrews, as it hath been delivered down to us, it having twice gone beyond Euphrates; for the people of the ten tribes were carried out of Samaria by the Assyrians in the days of king Hoshea; after which the people of the two tribes that remained after Jerusalem was taken were carried away by Nebuchadnezzar, the king of Babylon and Chaldea. Now as to Shalmanezer, he removed the Israelites out of their country, and placed therein the nations of the Cutheans, who had formerly belonged to the innerparts of Persia and Media, but were then called Samaritans, by taking the name of the country to which they were removed. But the king of Babylon, who brought out the two tribes, placed no other nation in their country, by which means all Judea and Jerusalem, and the temple, continued to be a desert for seventy years; but the entire interval of time which passed from the captivity of the Israelites, (the 10 tribes) to the carrying away of the two tribes proved to be a hundred and thirty years, six months, and ten days." Josephus, Antiquities, Book 10, Chapter 9, Section 7.

Verse 1. *Jerusalem* and *Judah* are both mentioned because the first was the capital of the second. *Stay* and *staff* refers to the support from bread and water. These were to be taken away by the siege preceding the overthrow of the city.

Verse 2. These were the leading citizens of the nation who were to be taken away into captivity. (see 2 Ki. 24: 14.)

Verse 3. This refers especially to the men in official position as well as those who were leaders in trades. The removal of these men would leave the country weakened.

Verse 4. With the most influential men removed from their midst, the weaker ones would naturally come to the front and take charge of things.

Verse 5. It would seem that after the captivity occurred there were some people still left in the country, else they could not be oppressed *one by another*. This was due to the fact that the great captivity that lasted 70 years all told was carried out in three separate movements. This is explained in detail in Vol. 2, p 178 of this Commentary, and the student is requested to read that note.

Verse 6. The distress described in this verse would be explained by the note cited in the preceding verse and the comments in connection therewith.

Verse 7. Men would be invited and even urged to take over the responsibility of caring for the people in distress. But each man would be so distressed himself that he could not bear any of the burden of others.

Verse 8. *Is* ruined and *is* fallen (present tense) refers to events more than a century in the future. For explanation of this see the comments in third paragraph of "general remarks" at Ch. 1 of this book. All this was to be brought upon the nation because it had provoked the Lord by evil practices.

Verse 9. The popular phrase "guilty look" has an illustration in the case of the men of Judah. Their arrogant countenance is compared to that of the Sodomites. The brazenness of those people is forceably set forth in Gen. 19: 4-9. *Rewarded evil unto themselves* means they will bring evil upon themselves by their own doing.

Verse 10. This is another verse where the reader should consult the note at page 174, Vol. 2 of this Commentary.

Verse 11. *Reward of his hands* is explained at v. 9.

Verse 12. See the information given at vs. 4, 5 above.

Verses 13-15. This paragraph is directed especially against the leaders of the nation. They had abused their authority and position over the people and hence were held more heavily responsible for the situation. (See the long note at ch. 1: 10.)

Verse 16. In the greater number of cases the men were the ones reproved for selfishness and extravagant living. However, from here to the end of the chapter that charge will be brought against the women of Jerusalem. Their luxurious and gaudy ornaments, together with their impudent and immodest behaviour, displeased the Lord very sorely. Because of this the prophet was inspired to enumerate to these frivolous women the articles of foolish pride which they had displayed, and to predict the humiliation of having them taken away. I shall comment on these articles in their order, in this and the following verses. *Stretched forth necks* means they held their heads high in a haughty manner. *Wanton eyes* denotes a look of flirtation as if to invite intimate advances. *Mincing* is from TAPHAPH which Strong defines, "to trip (with short steps) coquetishly [flirtatiously]." *Making a tinkling* means to put on anklets for the purpose of sound and ornamentation. This verse describes what would be called "loud" or "fast" women today. The anklets attracted attention to the feet that were tripping gaily in a suggestive manner. Added to this was their high-headed posture set off with alluring glances from their voluptuous eyes.

Verse 17. The Lord was sorely displeased with the practices of these women and warned that he would reduce them to deserved shame. The wording of this verse is largely figurative and means the condition of the women would be reversed. The reduction of a person's pride and the exposure of his corruption was elsewhere compared to the act of uncovering his body to his shame. (see Jer. 13: 22; Nah. 3: 5.)

Verse 18. In this and some verses following the prophet itemizes many of the articles of finery by which the women of Jerusalem had decorated themselves in their desire to attract attention to their persons. The Lord predicted the removal of these things which was to take place through the siege and captivity. *Bravery* is defined "ornament" in the lexicon, and means the ornaments of beauty would be taken away from these women. *Tinkling ornaments* are the same anklets mentioned in v. 16. *Cauls* were ornamental networks for the hair. *Tires* is from SAHARON and Strong defines it, "a round pendant for the neck." It was worn like a locket at the end of a necklace.

Verse 19. *Chains* is from NETIYPHAH and Strong's lexicon defines it, "a pendant for the ears (especially of pearls)." They were the same as eardrops of our time, that is, they were worn for the purpose of ornaments in the ears. *Bracelets* means the same as the word does today. *Mufflers* were long veils that were allowed to flutter as the woman was passing along the way.

Verse 20. *Bonnets* is defined in the lexicon," fancy head-dress." *Ornaments of the legs* are all from one word which Strong defines, "an (ornamental) ankle-chain." *Headbands* is defined in the lexicon. "an (ornamental) girdle (for women)." *Tablets* is from a word of such indefinite meaning that I shall merely say it refers to some particular part of the attire. *Earrings* is from LACHASH, which Strong defines, "concretely an amulet [a gem worn for "good luck"]."

Verse 21. *Rings* has the ordinary meaning, but the ancient ones usually had a "set" with a signet engraved. *Nose jewels* were rings worn in the nose as ornaments.

Verse 22. *Changeable suits of apparel* are all from one original word and it is defined, "a mantle (as easily drawn off)." It means a garment that is easily "changed," that is, easy to put on and take off. *Mantles* were cloaks such as are worn today. *Wimples* were wide cloaks made especially for women. *Crisping pins* were bags for holding pins, something on the order of a woman's purse.

Verse 23. *Glasses* were mirrors with the same meaning the word has today. *Fine linen* was a wrapper made of that material. *Hoods* were pieces of cloth wrapped round the head. *Vails* were spreading wrappers for the head. Not all of the articles named in the preceding verses would have been wrong had the general surrounding been proper. Neither were all of them worn by any one woman, for that would have been almost out of the question. But they were the list of ornamental "make-up" from which the vain minded women drew in their efforts at gaudy attractiveness. God was so displeased with the situation as a whole he decreed to take the entire collection from them.

Verse 24. The object in this group of opposite terms is to indicate the reversed condition that would come upon these worldly minded women, not that all of the things named would literally be used. Most of the words are self-explanatory but I shall comment on a few of them. *A stomacher* is a figured or decorated mantle, and it was to be replaced with a simple girdle or belt made of burlap. *Burning* is defined in the lexicon, "a brand or scar." The beautiful skin of these women was to be marred by defects to such an extent that it would render them unsightly.

Verse 25. Another misfortune that was to befall these women would be the loss of their men. They were to become victims of the war brought on by the besiegers. It is true that the women would feel the loss of the men personally which would be a blow to their vanity, but the city as a whole would share in the humiliating loss.

Verse 26. The gates of the cities were the points of diplomatic activities, but on account of the siege these spots would be draped in mourning and in disgrace.

ISAIAH 4

Verse 1. *That day* refers to the time of the siege and captivity predicted in the foregoing chapter. So many of the men were to have been taken away that it would leave a shortage of men; only one for every seven women. It was considered a reproach for a woman to be a "wallflower" in the national social and domestic life. Since plurality of wives had been tolerated, these women were willing to accept the men, not as "meal tickets," but in order to avoid the reproach of being left single.

Verse 2. The scene moves farther ahead to the end of the captivity and *that day* refers to it. *Branch* means a sprout that is used to start a plant, and it is employed to compare the institution of the Lord that will have been stunted by the 70 years of the captivity, but will be permitted again to grow in its own national soil. *Escaped of Israel* means the "remnant" explained at ch. 1: 9.

Verse 3. *Left in Zion and* remaineth in *Jerusalem* is not confined to the few Jews who might have been left in the home land during the captivity. The idea of the recovery applies to all who were fortunate enough to survive the long trial. Although they had been in the land of Babylon, they were regarded as people of *Zion*, the most important district in *Jerusalem*.

Verse 4. *Washed away the filth* refers to the recovery from the scourge of idolatry. (See the comments and note at ch. 1: 25.)

Verse 5. Reference to the cloud and flame is similar to the protection that the Lord gave Israel as they were leaving Egypt (Ex. 13: 21). God promised that his protection would be over his people after they had returned to their home land.

Verse 6. This is practically the same in thought as the preceding verse. It is expressed in figurative language. As extreme heat would call for a shaded place and a storm would require a shelter, so the Lord would be all this to his people.

ISAIAH 5

Verse 1. The complaint against Israel's ungrateful conduct is expressed in the form of a parable. The grape-growing industry was one of the leading ones in the land of Palestine and hence the Bible has numerous references to it. In the present instance the Israelite nation is compared to a vineyard that was well planted and kept. Hillsides were especially desirable spots for the planting of vineyards, so the prophet represents the favor of God to his people by saying he had selected a *very fruitful hill* as the site for his vineyard.

Verse 2. A vineyard should be fenced as a protection against destructive creatures. Smith's Bible Dictionary says this on the present subject: "The vineyard, which was generally on a hill, Isa. 5: 1; Jer. 31: 5; Amos 9: 13, was surrounded by a wall or hedge in order to keep out the wild boars, Psa. 8: 13, jackals and foxes, Num. 22: 24; Neh. 4: 3; Cant. [Song of Solomon] 2: 15; Ezk. 13: 4, 5; Matt. 2: 33. Within the vineyard was one or more towers of stone in which the vine-dresser lived. Isa. 1: 8; 5: 2; Matt. 21: 33. The vat, which was dug, Matt. 21: 33, or hewn out of the rocky soil, and the press, were a part of the vineyard furniture. Isa. 5: 2." Hence God gave his vineyard every attention necessary for its success. He built the fence and removed the stones (the heathen nations, book of Joshua), planted it with a choice vine (the descendants of Jacob), and built a tower (the tabernacle and temple service). With all these provisions the vineyard should have produced the best of fruit. Instead of genuine grapes the vine brought forth *wild grapes*. These words are from one Hebrew word, BEUSKIYM, which is defined in the lexicon, "poison-berries." The *grapes* which the Israelite nation was expected to produce was the true service to the one and only God. The *wild grapes* or "poison-berries" which it produced was the idolatrous worship.

Verse 3. Jerusalem was the capital city of the nation of Judah. The men of the country are called upon to consider the situation very seriously.

Verse 4. An accusing question was asked of them. They were challenged to name one thing that had been left undone that would have helped them in bearing fruit to the owner of the vineyard. Of course there could be no reply to this that would have been any credit to them. Then another question was asked, and that was why the vineyard had produced this poison fruit when it had been provided with everything needful for bringing forth real grapes. Again there could be no truthful answer that would not have been an admission of gross neglect and ingratitude to the Lord of the vineyard.

Verse 5. *Go to* is an expression to call attention to what is about to be said. If the wall about a vineyard was broken down the beasts would ruin the vines. Thus the prediction was made that Israel would be exposed to the enemy beasts (Babylonians).

Verse 6. These figures of speech refer to the condition that would come to the nation by reason of the siege and captivity.

Verse 7. The prophet wrote the interpretation of the parable. *House of Israel* denotes the race in general, and the *men of Judah* the particular part of it that was involved in the present guilt. The word for *judgment* means a verdict, either favorable or unfavorable. The context shows it means favorable in this case, and the men of Judah should have rendered favorable verdicts for the poor people under them, but instead they imposed upon them. *Cry* is defined in Strong's lexicon as "a shriek." That was what the leaders wrung from the people instead of dealing righteously with them.

Verse 8. The various evils that are described in this chapter were charged against the nation, especially the leaders. This verse means the practice of getting a monopoly of the land by getting possession of all the property possible.

Verse 9. *In mine ears* means the Lord hears and knows everything that his people are doing. It was for that reason their country was to be laid bare.

Verse 10. Ten acres of land and an homer of seed were large compared with a bath and an ephah. The contrasts were drawn to indicate the extremes to which the land would be brought by the invading army.

Verses 11, 12. This paragraph deals with the subject of the mixed activities of the nation. They were wicked in the main, but thought they could "get by" if they would mix some of the things that had been approved by the Lord. The reader is urged to read the note at ch. 1: 10.

Verse 13. People *are* gone is past tense in form but future in thought because it is a prophecy. This is explained in "general remarks" at ch. 1 of this book. The prediction has reference to the captivity (then more than a century in the future). *Have no knowledge* is explained by their lack of attention in ch. 1: 3. *Honorable men* are the ones recorded in 2 Ki. 24: 14 who were carried away into the captivity.

Verse 14. *Hell* is from SHEOL and Strong defines it, "hades or the world of the dead (as if a subterranean retreat), including its accessories and inmates." Robert Young defines it. "the unseen state." In the King James translation the word is rendered grave 31 times, hell 31, pit 3. *Hath enlarged* is another prediction in historic form, referring to the time of the captivity. The pronoun *their* stands for the chief men of the preceding verses. No doubt most of them were destined to die and enter the place in the unseen world where the spirits of wicked men go at death. However, the figurative sense also applies to the case for *their glory* was to fade away and be forgotten.

Verse 15. *Mean* man was the common ordinary fellow, and the *mighty* and *lofty* was the opposite. The verse means the national downfall would affect all classes of men.

Verse 16. When an unrighteous person is given divine chastisement, he does not receive any glory from it, but the Lord does obtain exaltation and glory from it.

Verse 17. The first part of this verse is figurative. It represents the freedom of the country after the nation had been shorn of its violent men. Things were to be so calm that even lambs would feel safe to graze in the pastures. *Strangers* means the invading forces that were to take possession of the things formerly enjoyed by the *fat ones*, meaning the leaders who had grown fat at the expense of the common people.

Verse 18. A *cord* or *cart rope* is a strong implement by wihch anything might be drawn or handled. To use one in drawing or producing iniquity would indicate a very vigorous life of unrighteous practices. The leaders especially had been doing that.

Verse 19. This verse shows the sneering attitude of the corrupt leaders toward the Lord. They are expressing a scoffing challenge for God just to try carrying out the chastisements predicted. They are saying, "let him [the Lord] hurry and perform his threats so we can see how it looks."

Verse 20. No man in his right mind would deliberately say that an evil thing is good. The prophet means they were mixing all kinds of principles and not distinguishing between things that differ. The motives for such conduct might be many, but one would be an effort to evade responsibility for their guilty behaviour.

Verse 21. *Wise in their own eyes* is similar to being "wise in their own conceit," and that was condemned by Paul in Rom. 12: 16. Such a man will not likely listen to instruction because he thinks he knows more than do his teachers.

Verse 22. About the greatest boast these men thought they could make was to be able to keep up with the most extravagant imbibers in drink.

Verse 23. The *reward* means a bribe that was offered to defeat justice and deprive a good man of his rights in connection with a controversy.

Verse 24. This verse is a figurative prediction of the utter defeat that was to come upon these wicked leaders when the invading army was brought against them.

Verse 25. The future degradation of the Israelite nation is still the subject, and this time it is likened to a very low material. The violence to be exerted upon their bodies is compared to something *torn.* That word is rendered "dung" in the margin, and Strong's definition of the original is, "something swept away, i.e. filth." It will help to clarify the illustration to quote Smith's Bible Dictionary on this subject. "The uses of dung were twofold—as manure and as fuel. The manure consisted either of straw steeped in liquid manure, Isa. 25: 10, or the sweepings, Isa. 5: 25, of the streets and roads, which were carefully removed from about the houses, and collected in heaps outside the walls of the towns at fixed spots— hence the dunggate at Jerusalem— and thence removed in due time to the fields." *For all this . . . stretched out still* is a statement that is peculiar to the book of Isaiah. It is to convey the idea of the repeated and continuous display of God's wrath against them.

Verse 26. This and all the rest of the verses in the chapter should be marked into a bracket. It is a prediction of the invasion of the Babylonians, and the Biblical account of it is in 2 Ki. 24: 10-16. An *ensign* is a signal and to *hiss* means to whistle, calling attention to the signal. The idea is that God would call upon some foreigners to come promptly in answer to the signal.

Verse 27. This verse describes the completeness of the equipment with which the Babylonians would come at the Lord's call. They were to be an instrument by which God purposed to chastise his disobedient people.

Verse 28. Warfare was conducted largely with the bow and arrow. It is significant, therefore, to say the arrows of the invading forces would be sharp, and their *bows bent* which would mean they would be drawn ready to thrust the arrows. Horses were used to draw the war chariots. These horses would have such hardened hoofs that they would speed along so fast the wheels would spin like the whirl**wind.**

Verse 29. The fierceness of the Babylonians is likened to the roar of lions, and their eagerness to conquer with savage pressure is compared to the ravenous appetite of those wild beasts. The unavoidable surety of the capture is predicted in the verse.

Verse 30. *Darkness and sorrow* refers to the desolate condition that would be left after the invasion and carrying away into Babylon.

ISAIAH 6

Verse 1. The death of king Uzziah is recorded in 2 Ki. 15: 7 (there called Azariah), and 2 Chr. 26: 23. By consulting those places the reader can get a glimpse of the situation existing at that time, and it was about that time when Isaiah began his writing. (see ch. 1: 1.) *I saw* means that the prophet looked into the vision presented to him which I have illustrated by the telescope in the "General remarks" at the beginning of the book. *Train* means the skirt of a robe and this one filled the temple, which indicated the greatness of the Lord's glory.

Verse 2. *Seraphims* is from SARAPH and Strong defines it, "burning, i.e. (figuratively) poisonous (serpent); specifically a seraph or symbolical creature (from their copper color)." Smith's Bible Dictionary calls them "an order of celestial beings." This vision of Isaiah occurred before the events of Matt. 27: 52, 53 and Eph. 4: 8, therefore these creatures must have been among the heavenly beings that take the general name of angels. Evidently the special name given them here was because of their fiery appearance, since that is the outstanding item in the lexicon definition. The whole scene was set to display the glory of the Lord. The seraphims engaged at this particular scene had each six wings. The suggestions of Smith's Bible Dictionary on the significance of these wings and their use of them, seems reasonable to me and I shall quote them: "With one of which [pair of wings] they covered their faces (a token of humility); with the second they covered their feet (a token of respect); while with the third they flew." These creatures had also some parts of a human being (v. 6).

Verse 3. These heavenly creatures were exclaiming to each other in honor of the Lord. *Earth is full* was indicative of the majestic power of the Lord over the forces of the earth. The prediction was about to be made of the revolutionary events of the captivity. Those events would be in protest against the national corruptions.

Verse 4. Even the parts of the heavenly temple were affected by the tribute of these seraphims to the glory of God. *Filled with the smoke* indicated the fullness of God's glory.

Verse 5. Isaiah was a righteous man and no uncleanness had been charged against him. It was natural, however, for him to have a feeling of pollution when he was so completely surrounded with the iniquities of which his people were guilty. This caused him to accuse himself of being unworthy in the sight of the Lord. For his personal satisfaction, the Lord accepted the complaint as if it were a confession.

Verse 6. The altar near the entrance to the tabernacle and temple had a fire going continuously while in service. That fact was the background for this vision in which the seraphim was seen to get the live coal. It was appropriate for this heavenly being to get this purifying substance from that place, even though the entire procedure was in the form of a vision for the information of the prophet.

Verse 7. The *iniquity* and *sin* is explained at v. 5. The reason for applying the fire to his lips was his complaint of being a man of *unclean lips*, which meant they were unconsecrated or unworthy. He used the term in the same sense as Moses used *uncircumcised lips* in Ex. 6: 30. It was significant also for the lips to be the point of application for the purifying element. The special work for which the Lord wished to use the prophet was that of speaking to the people, both to the ones then living and others who were centuries in the future.

Verse 8. *Send* means to call upon one to go on some errand or to perform an important task. The Lord had a great message to be delivered to his people and called for volunteer service. Isaiah felt ready for the service since he had just been cleansed from his unworthiness by the seraphim, and he offered his services to the Lord. It is interesting to note that both the singular and plural forms of the pronoun for the Lord were used. It is the same "us" that is meant in Gen. 1: 26.

Verse 9. The condition in the nation of Israel at the time of the prophets or soon after, and what they were to be in the time of Christ and the apostles had many similarities. Because of this we will find numerous instances where a prophet will be instructed to write in such a way that his statements would apply to the Jews of both periods. The prophet might not understand the meaning of it and at times would have an inquiring mind on the subject. The illustration of the telescope will help to clarify this subject. The verse of this paragraph is one of the kind of statements just set forth above. The prophecy in this and the following verse was quoted by Jesus in Matt. 13: 14, 15 and by Paul in Acts 28: 26, 27.

Verse 10. *Make the heart* meant the prophet was to make his prediction conform to the truth as to future conditions. It is as if the Lord had said: "The heart of my people are and will be such and such, so then make your prediction accordingly." *Fat* means dull, and *heavy* means to be so disinterested that it would be a burden to listen. *Shut* is to be explained on the same principle as *make*. *Lest* means "for fear that," and the idea was that the people would be so averse to the results of accepting the Lord's will that they will shut out the means of accomplishing such results.

Verse 11. *How long* meant how long would such conditions continue as those the Lord told the prophet to predict. In answering it the Lord shortened the range of the "telescope" so as to make the scene apply only to ancient Israel. The verse means the rebellious behaviour of the people of

Israel was to continue until the calamities mentioned should be brought upon them.

Verse 12. Following the sad conditions predicted in the preceding verse, there was to be a removal of their men away into captivity. *Forsaking in the midst* is the same thought as the prediction of the *lodge* in ch. 1: 8.

Verse 13. We have seen that the great captivity was carried out in three separate movements. (see the note on page 178, volume 2 of this Commentary.) After the second action there were but a few of the people left *(a tenth)*. But even this small amount of the nation was taken over at the third and final action. (see 2 Ki. 24 and 25.) *Teil* and *oak* are two varieties of large trees. Even after the foliage is stripped off of a tree, leaving it with the appearance of being dead, there is still some substance left in the body of the tree. Likewise when the flower of the nation's citizens will have been stripped from it, there was to be left still a little substance of the nation in the form of the poorer citizens. But that was to be taken off through the ravenous appetite of the invading forces.

ISAIAH 7

Verse 1. The Lord's people were involved in dealings with foreign nations throughout their history. But since they had become two kingdoms themselves (see 1 Ki. 12: 16), they were almost continually in hostility with each other. Not only were these kingdoms often engaged in war against each other, but at certain times one of them would form a confederacy with a heathen nation and together they would come against the other kingdom of the Jews. This occurred at the time of the present verse, the confederacy being formed between the kingdom of Syria, just north of Palestine, and the kingdom of Israel (the 10 tribes). They joined their forces and made an unfriendly approach to Jerusalem, the capital of Judah (the 2 tribes). They were not able, however, to accomplish anything but throw the people into a panic of fear. This was in the days of Ahaz, king of Judah, and about twenty years after Isaiah began to write.

Verse 2. *House of David* means the kingdom of Judah or of the two tribes with its capital at Jerusalem. Word came to the people of this capital of the confederacy and unfriendly approach toward their city. *His heart* means the heart of the people, the phrase being so worded because David had been named in direct connection with the people of the kingdom. *Was moved* means their hearts or minds trembled with fear as a tree would quiver in the wind.

Verse 3. The prophets were employed by the Lord for the purpose of immediate instruction, as well as to make short and long-distance predictions. Accordingly, Isaiah was directed to give the king of Judah some information for his consolation. He was to take his son with him and meet with the king at the end of a water course or conduit, a spot near the walls of the city of Jerusalem.

Verse 4. Upon their meeting at the designated spot, Isaiah was to bid the king of Judah not to be afraid of the foes threatening him. The two kings were compared to something very insignificant. *Firebrand* is defined by Strong as a poker used to stir a fire. In the comparison the kings were likened to only the tail ends of such pokers, and they with only enough of the fire in evidence to make a smoke.

Verse 5. These two kings not only had come against Judah, but had *taken evil counsel* against that kingdom. That meant they had consulted together or had conspired to come against Judah. Conspiracy is always considered worse than independent deeds.

Verse 6. This verse reveals the conspiracy that was formed against Judah. The conspirators proposed to break through into the city and overthrow the throne, to be reoccupied by an Ephraimite named Tabeal.

Verse 7. *It* refers to the counsel or conspiracy mentioned in the preceding verse.

Verse 8. The expressions in this and the following verse were to indicate that the forces arrayed against the city were not as important as they might appear. Not all of Syria was there, only the king who represented Damascus. As for Ephraim (representing the 10 tribes), that power was to be broken with in 65 years. The formal captivity took place in less than the stated time, hence the general wording of *within*. This event is recorded in 2 Ki. 17 which the reader should consult.

Verse 9. *Ephraim* was frequently referred to when the kingdom of the 10 tribes was meant. That was because its capital, Samaria, was located in the possession of that tribe (Josh. 16). On this point it will be well to quote Smith's Bible Dictionary: "After the revolt of Jeroboam the history of Ephraim is the history of the kingdom of Israel, since not only did the tribe become a kingdom, but the kingdom embraced little besides the tribe." For the present the only person to be considered was Pekah, Remaliah's son. He was not a strong king (see 2 Ki. 15: 29), and Ahaz was assured that little trouble would come from him. The last sentence of the verse meant that if the king of Judah would not believe the prophet's words, it was an indication that his faith in the Lord's word was weak.

Verse 10. *Lord spake* is to be understood as the speech of Isaiah speaking for God.

Verse 11. Many times the Lord has refused to grant a request for a sign or omen. We do not understand why Ahaz was bidden to call for one, but he was told to ask it in the *depth* or *height*, which meant he could ask for one ever so difficult.

Verse 12. For some reason (also unrevealed to us) Ahaz would not take advantage of the offer. He declared it would be like tempting the Lord, which might have been true had not the inspired prophet given him the privilege of asking. Since that was done, Ahaz's refusal to make the request was regarded by Isaiah as disrespectful to God.

Verse 13. Strong defines the original for *weary*, "to be disgusted." Isaiah told Ahaz (representing the *house of David*) that he not only was disgusting to man but also to the Lord. That was because he had been told to ask for a sign but had refused to do so. His refusal indicated that either he doubted the ability of the inspired prophet to give an omen, or that it would not be of much importance. He should have considered the wisdom of the Lord and that no inspired predictions in whatever form were unimportant. Since the sign intended to be given would be for the benefit of others besides the king of Judah, the Lord decreed to give it in spite of the attitude of this disrespectful king.

Verse 14. This and the two following verses should be marked into a bracket, and the subject noted as a prophecy of Christ (Matt. 1: 23). This prophecy was to be fulfilled many centuries after all the persons then living were dead. However, another prediction was soon to be made that would be fulfilled in the time of that generation. That should help them to believe the truthfulness of this other prediction that was to be fulfilled in the distant future. We shall now consider the verses of the bracket in their order. The significant thought is that the child was to be born of a virgin. A virgin might conceive at her first relation with a man and thus no miracle would be performed. But from that instant she would not be a virgin. Hence, when her child should be born it could not be said that he was born of a virgin. But in the case of this verse, the child was to be both conceived and born of a virgin. *Immanuel* in the Old Testament and Emmanuel in the New both mean "God is with us."

Verse 15. *That he may know* means he will eat this stronger food, such as butter and honey, when he becomes old enough to know right from wrong. Before that he will live on the same kind of food as other infants. Notwithstanding Jesus was the Son of God, while he was in the flesh he was subject to all the laws of nature as pertaining to physical and mental growth as was others. (See Luke 2: 40, 52.)

Verse 16. This verse is where the two predictions were made that were related to each other, though their fulfillments were destined to be hundreds of years apart Such unusual form of language is a part of the prophetic style. It will serve to clarify the thought to make the language read, "Before—yes, long before," etc. But the fulfillment of one of the predictions was to come not so long after the time Isaiah made the prediction, and it pertained to the two kings who were at that very time causing Ahaz to be so worried. The fulfillment of it is recorded in 2 Ki. 16: 9; 17: 6.

Verse 17. The prophet next turned his attention to the fate of Judah and her captivity. He called it *Assyria* because at the time of the writing the land was in control of that people, although destined to be in the hands of the Babylonians at the time Judah was to be invaded and taken away into captivity.

Verse 18. *In that day* means that about the time all these calamities were coming upon his people from the Babylonians, God would bring other people into the land to worry his disobedient nation. *Hiss* means to whistle as if to make a shrill call for the foreigners to come. *Fly* and *bee* are used figuratively, referring to the swarms or hordes of the heathen who were to be called into the service of God to chastise his people. *Assyria* is explained at v. 17.

Verse 19. This invasion was fulfilled as predicted, and the record of it is in 2 Ki. 23: 33-35.

Verse 20. The king of Assyria (Babylon) is figuratively called a razor because that instrument is used to rid a body of some of its parts. *Head, feet* and *beard* were named to indicate the completeness of the predicted invasion. To use a familiar expression, the disobedient people of Judah were to have a "close shave."

Verse 21. The predictions were still on the subject of the Babylonian invasion and the shortages that were to be forced upon the land in punishment for its iniquities. A man who had been the owner of great herds of cattle would be reduced to one cow and two sheep, and would have to be satisfied with that amount of living source.

Verse 22. God did not intend to starve his people to death in their own country, but only that they should suffer many inconveniences. Hence this small number of beasts would supply their owner with sufficient to keep him alive, in conjunction with the honey that was produced wild in the land.

Verse 23. This verse is a description of the reduced state the land would be in as a result of the invasion from the Babylonians. *Silverlings* means the money paid for the vines that grew in abundance. In their place were to come briers and thorns.

Verse 24. The *arrows* and *bows* were to be used by the heathen invaders. That would throw the land into the state of desolation described because not enough men would be left to keep down the thorns and briers.

Verse 25. We must understand this verse in the light of the preceding ones. Men will not be seen working with tools to rid the hills of the briers, but the territory will be neglected and run over by the animals.

ISAIAH 8

Verse 1. The *roll* to be used was in the nature of a board or other hard and flat surface, and the *pen* was an instrument somewhat like a graver's tool. Isaiah was to carve the words on this board which would give it a more permanent form. All of this indicates the great importance of the subject at hand.

Verse 2. *Record* means literally to duplicate what is seen. The witnesses would be able to reproduce what Isaiah engraved on the board, if necessary, since they saw what was done. They could testify to the agreement of their copy with the original.

Verse 3. *Prophetess* is from NEBIYAH, and Strong defines it, "a prophetess or (generally) inspired woman; by implication a poetess; by association a pophet's wife." The connection indicates the last part of the definition applies here. There was nothing miraculous in this relation of the prophet with his wife, unless it was the fact that a child was caused to result from his particular relation, and that it was caused to be a son. After the birth of the son the Lord told the prophet what to call him. But that name had been inscribed on the board and witnessed by the men selected for that purpose. The proper names used in Bible times usually had some special significance. The one which the Lord instructed Isaiah to call his infant son is defined in Strong's lexicon as follows: "hasting (is he [the enemy—Strong] to the) booty, swift (to the) prey." In other words it means the enemy was to be hasty in coming for his prey, and the name was given to this son as an omen of the near approach of the fulfillment of the prediction against Damascus and Samaria.

Verse 4. This verse predicted the invasion of the Assyrians into the territories of Damascus, capital of Syria, and of Samaria, capital of the 10 tribes. The fulfillment of these events is recorded in 2 Ki. 16: 9; 17: 6. That was in 740 B.C. and this son was born in that year. But before the child was old enough to talk this prediction was carried out.

Verse 5. The form of this verse shows the manner in which Isaiah was inspired.

Verse 6. *Shiloath* was a soft-flowing stream near Jerusalem. It is called "Siloam" in the New Testament. The reference to it was figurative and contrasted with another stream that will be considered in the next verse. But for the present verse, the Lord represented his people as preferring the boisterous atmosphere created by the presence of the hostile kings named, to that of the quiet and gentle stream.

Verse 7. Continuing his figurative use of the streams, the Lord said if his people desired something stronger or more vigorous than the quiet waters of Shiloath, he would bring upon them the waters of the *river* which referred to the Euphrates. This mighty river flowed in the country then controlled by the Assyrians. Of course this river was not literally to be run over the land of Judah, but the figure was continued that was introduced in the preceding verse. The people in possession of this river were to be brought up over the land of God's dissatisfied nation, and their channels and banks were to be (figuratively) overflowed.

Verse 8. The language is still in terms of waters and flood. This greater stream was to overflow the land until it would be neck deep. *Immanuel* means "God with us," and is used in this place to indicate the land of God's people which was to be overflowed. *He* and *his* refer to the king of Assyria, who was ruler over the nation that was destined to bring the overflow mentioned above. The first definition of the original for *wings* is "an edge or extremity." The thought is that the king of Assyria would overrun the extreme limits of the land of Judah. The fulfillment of this prediction may be read in 2 Ki. 18: 13-16.

Verse 9. This verse was a warning against the heathen people. The thought was as if it said, "though you associate or conspire together against us, ye shall be broken in pieces by the strength of the God whom you oppose."

Verse 10. This verse has practically the same meaning as the preceding one. The counsel and boastful words of the enemy were not to stand, because God would still be with his people whom he loved. (Rom. 8: 31.)

Verse 11. Isaiah was in the midst of a corrupt people and the Lord gave him an exhortation. One does not literally speak with his hand, but *with a strong hand* means God spoke to the prophet with great force, and warned him not to walk in the way of the people among whom he was compelled to live as a prophet.

Verse 12. If the people suggested that a confederacy be formed, Isaiah was not to agree with them. If they tried to influence him by raising a cry of fear, he was not to give heed to them but trust in the protection of his God.

Verse 13. The only power the prophet was to fear was that of the Lord, and that was the fear caused by his reverence for Him. *Sanctify the Lord* means to pronounce or observe or regard the Lord as being pure and holy.

Verse 14. This and the following four verses should be marked into a bracket and understood as a prophecy relating to Christ and his followers. The second word of this verse is a pronoun standing for Christ. *Sanctuary* means a consecrated place and such was the presence of Christ to be for those who would trust in him. But some would not believe in him and they would stumble at his word; this prediction was cited in 1 Pe. 2: 8. *Both houses of Israel* referred to the two parts of the nation that formed the kingdoms known as Israel and Judah. A *gin* was a net spread out so wide that one could scarcely avoid being entangled with it. A *snare* was a trap set in some hidden place that would catch the unwary. Both contrivances were used to illustrate the lot of those who would be averse to Christ and his teaching.

Verse 15. This verse itemizes the results of being caught in the gin or snare described in the preceding verse.

Verse 16. The pronoun is in the first person and represents Christ as telling what he would do for those who would accept him. He would *bind up* or *seal the law* which means he would guarantee his word on behalf of his disciples, which means those who would become learners and followers of his teaching.

Verse 17. *I* means Christ and the *Lord* means God who was hiding his face from the house of Jacob. (see v. 14.) Christ would *wait upon*, which means he would respect God's attitude toward the rebellious Jews.

Verse 18. This verse is cited by the writer of Heb. 2: 13. The prediction was that Christ was to be given a group of persons who would accept his teaching. *Signs and wonders in Israel* means the effect it would have on the houses of Israel in general to see men and women accepting the teaching of Christ. One instance of its fulfillment is recorded in Matt. 7: 28, 29.

Verse 19. This prophecy of Christ was ended with the preceding verse and God again advised the prophet on his conduct among that corrupt people. Since they were inclined to go after wizards and those with familiar spirits, they would likely try to interest the prophet in them. The last part of the verse means that living people should consult God for information and not appeal to the spirits of the dead.

Verse 20. "But it might be desirable to obtain information that would be beneficial; would that not justify one's consulting these persons for that purpose?" To this imaginary question the Lord answered in the language of the present verse. *The law and the testimony* of God was in their possession and would supply all the information needed. "But suppose these characters would offer some information different from what could be found in the written law?" Then that would be proof that they were a group of deceivers, and described here as having *no light in them*.

Verse 21. This verse describes the lot of those who practice witchcraft or who follow after such who do. They will come to realize their utter failure and unworthiness, and curse the king and God and be generally against everything that is good.

Verse 22. This verse continues the description of the characters who deal in witchcraft, and those who consult them instead of the law.

ISAIAH 9

Verse 1. I earnestly request the reader to make frequent reference to the illustration of the telescope at the beginning of this book. The line of predictions will many times be interrupted in order to let the prophet see far into the future. The telescope was extended in this and several other verses in this chapter, enabling the prophet to see some things that would take place in the time of Christ. *Nevertheless* was an introduction to a contrast between conditions in the country at the time of the invasion by the heathen and what would be in that future time. In the former time the land was dim from lack of receiving the light of God's law. The places named in this verse were in the territory of the kingdom of the 10 tribes, which was the victim of the invading forces. But the prophet saw better things coming for it.

Verse 2. *Have seen* is past in form although referring to the future. This is the prophetic style and it is explained in "general remarks" at the beginning of this book. The *light* meant that which was to be shed by the teaching of Christ. We know this is the interpretation of this prediction for it is so applied in Matt. 4: 12-16.

Verse 3. *Not increased* is rendered "to him increased" in the margin. Both Moffatt's translation and the American Standard Version also render the place by that thought, and the context agrees with it. Certainly, by favoring those districts with the teaching of Jesus it would add to their joy. The increase of their joy was compared to that produced by a good harvest or a victory over a foe and taking the prey.

Verse 4. The sad situation imposed upon these territories by the invading forces was to have been removed. The relief thus afforded was compared to that enjoyed by the Lord's people in the time of the judges, when the Midianites were driven to defeat on behalf of Israel. This event may be read in Judg. 7: 22.

Verse 5. This verse gives a strong description of the conflicts of God's people in the past, in which they had to contend with the enemy amid the shedding of blood. But those enemies were finally subdued and their forces given over to their own destruction, even as fuel is fed to the fire. After such a victorious recovery from their ancient enemies, their lot suggested the propriety of a prediction concerning the redemption from the oppression of sin. Such a redemption was to be accomplished through the means of a most unusual person to be brought into the world. We may here see the reason for the Lord's extending the "telescope" so that the prophet could see and describe that great person which will be the subject of the next two verses.

Verse 6. This and the next verse gives us one of the great predictions of the coming of Christ. Of course all predictions of him are great, but this one contains so many of the characteristics that were peculiar to him. Not only was a child to be born to the race but that child was to be a son. That was one of the most important qualifications expected of a ruler. A yoke is used to compare a government (Matt. 11: 29, 30), and since that instrument was borne upon the shoulder of the creature using it, the government was said here to be *upon his shoulder. Wonderful* is from PELE which Strong defines, "a miracle." That was true of Christ in many respects, but especially was it true with regard to his birth which was accomplished by a virgin, predicted in ch. 7: 14. *Counsellor* is from YAWATS and defined by Strong, "to advise; reflectively to deliberate or resolve." This definition surely belonged to Christ for he was the greatest teacher ever to be on earth. *Mighty God* will not confuse us when we remember that "God" is the family name of the Deity and that Christ was a mighty member of that family. *Father* is from AWB and Strong's definition is "a primitive word; father in a literal and immediate, or figurative and remote application." Certainly the last part of the definition is the sense of the word here for Jesus was not literally a father. But his great and unending care for the children of his own divine Father would entitle him to the name. The original for *prince* is defined, "a head person," and it has been rendered in the King James version by captain, chief, general, master and others. Many such men in temporal life were interested in conflicts for personal advantage. This great person was to be a prince who would offer *peace* to his subjects. This word is from SHALOM and defined by Strong, "safe, i.e. (figuratively) well, happy, friendly; also (abstractly) welfare, i.e. health, prosperity, peace." It can thus be seen that Christ was to give to his subjects that kind of peace that would be for their good, even if they might have to receive it in connection with unpleasant experiences with the world.

Verse 7. The government of this ruler was to have no end, which was also predicted in Dan. 2: 44. He was to sit upon the throne of David in that he was a lineal descendant of that great king of Judah. It was *his kingdom* in the same sense as it was his throne. The throne and kingdom of David was a restricted one in that it admitted only the fleshly members of the nation. But God had promised David that he would have a son or descendant who would be a king over all the people who would accept his yoke (Psa. 132: 10-12). All of these predictions were to be brought to pass through the *zeal of the Lord of hosts*.

Verse 8. The "telescope" was shortened to its normal length and the prophet saw more that pertained to ancient *Jacob* and *Israel*. These two names were used because the first is the head and the second is the people that sprang from that head.

Verse 9. *Ephraim* and *Samaria* are explained in connection with ch. 7: 1-9. Those people were rebellious against the Lord and pretended not to have any fear of the future.

Verse 10. Their boasts were described in figurative language. They spoke as if the threatened overthrow of their kingdom might be like losing a brick structure, but they would be able to replace it with a better one. Or, their present situation might be like a sycamore tree, and though it would be cut down they would replace it with the beautiful cedar, a kind of tree that was prized very highly for its grain.

Verse 11. Against this boastful arrogance God threatened to raise up enemies. The phrase *adversaries of Rezin* has the sense as if it said "adversaries, consisting of Rezin," etc. *Join his enemies* meant that God would bring more than one group of enemies against his people for their stubbornness in resisting the divine law.

Verse 12. This verse names two heathen nations that were to be raised against the Lord's stubborn people; the Syrians on one hand and the Philistines on the other The first is recorded in 2 Ki. 16: 6, and the second is in 2 Chr. 28: 18. See the comments at ch. 5: 25 for explanation of the last sentence.

Verse 13. This verse was given to account for the statement at the close of the preceding verse. God's anger was continued against the people (of Israel) because they turned not unto him (the Lord) who was smiting or chastising them. They were not willing to seek the *Lord of hosts*. The last word means large groups of men, especially an army. This would be true from more than one standpoint. The Lord is able to defeat an army of enemies and thus prove his ability to be a Lord or power over them, and he also has under him a large group of servants who would fight for the right cause.

Verse 14. In the great chastisement that God decreed to bring upon the nation, no exception was to be made of any class, all were to take their share of the national humiliation. (see note at page 174, Vol. 2 of this Commentary.) But at least the better individuals were to be shown some consideration in the illustration by being called the head, while the others were called the tail.

Verse 15. The general classification in the preceding verse is made specific in this, and it shows that character and conduct determined it. Thus the honorable people were put at the head while the lying prophet made up the tail.

Verse 16. The leaders were always held especially to blame, yet the people in general were made to share in the condemnation for following them. Jesus taught this same principle while he was on the earth. (Matt. 15: 14.)

Verse 17. About all rules have some exceptions, and there were some good men in the Jewish nation. But the group as a whole had become corrupt, both old and young. Hence the Lord made this severe decree against them, which was appropriate for the age classes mentioned. Had the young men been righteous, God would have had joy in them because they would have been the strength and defence of the nation. Had the widows and other unfortunates been good, the Lord would have shown them special favor in the nature of mercy. (See ch. 5: 25 for explanation of the last sentence.)

Verse 18. Ordinarily we would count it a favor to have briers and thorns destroyed. The thought in this verse is to show the completeness of God's wrath against the moral and spiritual wild growth in the conduct of the people.

Verse 19. This verse helps to understand the preceding one. The wicked people were the briers that were to be destroyed by the wrath of the Lord.

Verse 20. The pronoun *he* refers to *brother* in the preceding verse. He is represented as *snatching* here and there to find something to eat but failing to find it. The extremes of destitution are pictured as a man eating his own flesh in his hunger.

Verse 21. *Manasseh, Ephraim.* The full meaning would be that in their distress even the various tribes would attack each other, *no man shall spare his brother* (v. 19), and even the two kingdoms will suffer by the treatment accorded each other through the discouraging situation. (See ch. 5: 25 for notes on the last sentence.)

ISAIAH 10

Verse 1. This woe was directed against the leaders of the nation who oppressed the common people. They did it by forcing such decrees upon them that it grieved them.

Verse 2. This verse has practically the same meaning as the preceding one, and as the thoughts in vs. 14-16 in the preceding chapter.

Verse 3. Most of Isaiah's writing was against Judah, but he also paid some attention to Israel (the 10 tribes), whose downfall had just taken place when the prophet began to write this chapter. *Day of visitation* referred to the invasion *from far*, which meant the army of the Assyrians.

Verse 4. *Without me* was a notice that when the invasion came, the Lord would not help them. *Under the prisoners* and *under the slain* was used in the sense of being among the prisoners and the slain persons. In other words, when the invasion comes there will be no chance to escape with their property. They will be brought down in helplessness along with the others of the nation. And even this will not be the end of their chastisement from God, but his anger will be further felt. (See ch. 5: 25.)

Verse 5. God was going to use the Assyrian army to chastise his wayward nation, even as a father would use a rod to punish his disobedient son.

Verse 6. This prediction was fulfilled as recorded in 2 Ki. 18: 14-16. Let not the reader mistake that event for the captivity of Judah. That was a century in the future yet and was to be accomplished through the Babylonians. But the present prediction had to do with a temporary chastisement of Judah at the hands of Assyria.

Verse 7. *He meaneth not so.* The Assyrians had just carried the 10 tribes off into captivity. They were elated over their success and concluded to accomplish the same thing with Judah. The italicized words mean the Assyrians did not attack Judah for the purpose of serving God as an instrument to punish the evil nation. Their motive was the same with which they attacked other nations, and that was for the military and political purpose of overthrowing the nations. But that motive did not prevent God from using the occasion to give his wayward people a severe punishment. Many of the following verses specify some particulars of the boastful motive of the Assyrians, that brought the wrath of God down upon them also, after he had used them for his own purpose. Before going on with that line of verses, I shall quote from authentic history to show the correctness of the statements about Assyria, and the fulfillment of the threats the prophet was inspired to predict against her: "Saracus, who came to the throne towards the end of the 7th century B. C., was the last of the long line of Assyrian kings. For nearly or quite six centuries the Ninevite kings had now lorded it over the East. There was scarcely a state in all Western Asia that during this time had not, in the language of the royal inscriptions 'borne the heavy yoke of their lordship,' scarcely a people that had not suffered their cruel punishments, or tasted the bitterness of enforced exile. But now swift misfortunes were bearing down upon the oppressor from every quarter. Egypt revolted and tore Syria away from the empire; from the mountain defiles on the east issued the armies of the recent-grown empire of the Aryan Medes, led by the renowned Cyaxares; from the southern lowlands, anxious to aid in the overthrow of the hated oppressor, the Babylonians joined the Medes as allies, and together they laid close siege to Nineveh [capital of Assyria]. The city was finally taken and sacked, and dominion passed away forever from the proud capital. Two hundred years later, when Xenophon with his Ten Thousand Greeks, in his memorable retreat passed the spot, the once great city was a crumbling mass of ruins of which he could not even learn the name." MYERS, Ancient History, p. 66.

Verse 8. Assyria claimed that her princes or leading men were as good as kings.

Verse 9. The first four cities named had been taken over by the Assyrian power. Samaria, the capital of the 10 tribes, and Damascus, the capital of Syria, had also been taken over. (See 2 Ki. 16: 9; 17: 6.)

Verse 10. One word in the lexicon definition of the original for *found* is "acquired," and here means the Assyrians had taken over the kingdoms that worshiped idols, referring to the heathen nations. *Images did excel* was said to indicate the power of the Assyrians over the idols of greater strength. And since the idols of Jerusalem and Samaria were of less power, then surely he (the Assyrian) would be able to take them, and his boastful attitude was based on this consideration.

Verse 11. Assyria thought the idols of Samaria were superior to those of Jerusalem, but such a conclusion was purely unfounded in fact, for none of the idols had any actual force except in the imagination of the worshipers. Having overcome the former idols he thought he would have no trouble with the latter.

Verse 12. The four preceding verses were the boast of Assyria concerning her treatment of Judah and Jerusalem, not realizing that God was only using her as an instrument for chastising his own disobedient children. Hence God now declared what he would do after he has finished his work upon his own nation. He said he would punish (cut short) the fruit (plans) of the stout (proud) heart of the king of Assyria. This threat was fulfilled as per the historical quotation at verse 7 above.

Verse 13. In this and the following verse Assyria's boasts are again recounted. About all of the things claimed to have been done were so, but the error was in her boast that it was by *my hand* that the work was accomplished.

Verse 14. Assyria's boast was likened to one's finding a nest with eggs and taking them for his own use. The fowl that deposited the eggs did not so much as move a wing nor even peep in protest. Likewise when Assyria helped herself to the spoils of the nations the owners thereof were not able to make any effective protest.

Verse 15. The unreasonableness of Assyria's boast was compared to that of an ax boasting about the work of skill that it had accomplished. The like comparison was made to various other implements of work.

Verse 16. This verse was a prediction of what God was to bring against Assyria. The things threatened referred to the defeat of Assyria at the hands of her enemies and the fulfillment is recorded in the historical quotation at verse 7.

Verse 17. The pronouns in the verse stand for Israel and Assyria. The *Holy One* of Israel, the Lord, shall be a destructive fire. This fire shall devour the (national or political) thorns and briers of the Assyrian army.

Verse 18. A standardbearer is an outstanding character in an army or nation. *Forest* and *field*, *soul* and *body*, are used figuratively. The meaning is that the Assyrians were to be completely defeated.

Verse 19. This verse was intended as a continuation of the figures of speech on the complete overthrow of Assyria. The number of her military and other important men were to be so reduced that a child could describe them.

Verse 20. *That day* refers to the day when the people of Israel were to be released from captivity. The prediction was fulfilled and the record of it is in the books of Ezra and Nehemiah. *No more stay upon* means that Israel will not depend upon his captor but will depend upon the Lord. This was especially true as regards to idolatry. After the captivity the Jewish nation never committed idolatry. For the historical quotation on this subject see the comments at ch. 1: 25.

Verse 21. The *remnant* was a prediction of the small number of Jews who survived the captivity and returned to their home country. (See Ezra 2: 64.)

Verse 22. The reference to a *remnant* is the same thought that was expressed in the preceding verse. The *consumption* means the effects the captivity would have in decreasing the number of the Jews. Overflow with righteousness means it would be a righteous thing for the chastisement to come upon the nation, even though it did reduce them to a mere remnant.

Verse 23. The *consumption* that was to come would not be a mere chance or accident. The Lord had determined to bring the punishment upon them for their corruption.

Verse 24. Many of the things being threatened in several verses had a general bearing and included the effect of the great 70-year captivity. But the immediate subject was the situation created by the presence and threatening attitude of the Assyrian army. That situation is recorded in 2 Ki. 18, and came after the 10 tribes had been taken off by the Assyrians. Having been so successful they were encouraged to think they could accomplish the same thing with Judah or the 2 tribes. But their success was to be short, and God wished his people not to be unduly alarmed over it.

Verse 25. This verse predicts that it would be but a little while until the *indignation* (of God against his people) would cease. His anger was to cease *in their* (the Assyrians) *destruction*. In other words, when the destruction or overthrow of the Assyrians will have been accomplished, God's anger will be satisfied and it will cease.

Verse 26. A *scourge* means something that will serve as a punishment, and the one predicted here was fulfilled by the hand of the Assyrian army (2 Ki. 19: 35). The Lord was to be the one who would use the lash and thus would force the Assyrians to serve Him. The reference to the slaughter of the Midianites (Judg. 7: 25) was to illustrate the severity of the chastisement God meant to inflict upon the Assyrians. The reference to the *rod upon the sea* (Ex. 14: 26) was to illustrate God's defeat of the Assyrian plans, even as the plans of Egypt were defeated when the rod was stretched out over the sea that was about to hinder the Israelites from escaping.

Verse 27. This verse is still on the specific subject of Assyria's yoke of terror that has been the theme for several verses.

Verse 28. *He* refers to the Assyrian who will be forced to leave the land of Judah and retreat toward his own country. The towns named were places through which the Assyrians would pass in their return, defeated, to their own territory.

Verse 29. These are some more spots in the route of the retreat. As they swept through the various territories they spread fear among the natives, some of whom fled.

Verse 30. The condition of fear continued to be the subject of the prediction. *Gallim*, *Laish* and *Anathoth* were in the path of the retreating army.

Verse 31. This verse names two other places that were to be in the path.

Verse 32. The retreat of the Assyrian army was with reluctance; if it could delay the march out of the country it would do so. *Nob* was an important city in the possession of Benjamin (one tribe of the kingdom of Judah), and the Assyrian army paused there to make a parting "fling" at the nation they were being forced to leave.

Verse 33. *Bough, high ones* and *haughty* refers to the leaders of the Assyrian nation who had been puffed up against God's people. The Lord would finally subject those arrogant people to a humiliating defeat as if the boughs of a tree were lopped off.

Verse 34. The leveling of the things mentioned in this verse is figurative. However, the reference to Lebanon is literal as to the location. That place had been in the possession of the 10 tribes previous to the captivity of Israel, but after the kingdom was taken by the Assyrians the territory was in the control of the victorious nation. Therefore any damage done to it would be a chastisement of Assyria.

ISAIAH 11

Verse 1. Verses 1-10 should be marked into a bracket and labeled "kingdom of Christ." The many important items connected with that subject will be studied as the verses are taken in their order. Jesse was one of the more prominent ancestors of Christ. He was the father of the first righteous king that the Israelites had (Ruth 4: 22; 1 Sam. 13: 14; 16: 1), and he is the ancestor specified in the present imagery because the fate of kingdoms was the immediate subject of the prophecy. The kingdom of the descendants of Jesse was destined to be defeated as far as its earthly importance was concerned. But this great ancestor of that kingdom had a far more important part to play in the great drama of the Lord's scheme of things. The apparent defeat of that kingly line was compared to the cutting down of a tree but where the plant was not killed. The figures of speech used were to illustrate the renewal of the tree in a more glorious form. *Rod* is defined by Strong as "a twig," and *stem* is defined "a stump." *Branch* means "a shoot" that springs up from the roots of the stump that was left after the tree had been cut down. And so, although the tree of Jesse's kingdom was to be overthrown, he was destined to have a "new start in life" by the shoot that would spring up from the same line. Of course we know that shoot was Christ who descended through Jesse and David.

Verse 2. For the specific meaning of *Lord* see the comments at Psa. 86: 12. In this verse it means God the Father, and *him* means his Son Jesus. The Father was to give his Son the spirit that would impart unto him all the qualifications named. There is not much difference between the meaning of the words, yet there may be seen some variation that would serve to emphasize them. For instance, *understanding* would mean he would have a comprehension of a subject, and *wisdom* would mean he would use it properly; *knowledge* refers to the subject of information in general. *Fear of the Lord* denotes the respect this Son would show for his Father.

Verse 3. *Quick* is not in the original as a separate word. It is rendered "smell" in the margin and both the lexicon and other passages in the King James version agree. It is the word for "smell" in Ex. 30: 38; Lev. 26: 31; Psa. 115: 6. The word is also defined as "accept" in the lexicon. The meaning of the passage is that Christ would recognize the quality of understanding when he smelled it and would accept it because of his fear or respect for the Lord. The latter part of the verse means he would not decide matters by the mere outward appearances.

Verse 4. The judgments or decisions concerning the poor were to be righteous, and he would reason with *equity* (fairness) with the humble. The *smiting* and *slaying* was figurative and referred to the force of Christ's words against workers of evil.

Verse 5. *Loins* is from MOTHEN, which Strong defines, "the waist or small of the back," and as a girdle will give support by the being attached around one's waist, so the righteousness of Christ was to be a strong recommendation for him in the eyes of those who would behold him. *Reins* is from CHALATS and is defined, "the loins as the seat of vigor." The clause means that Christ would be strong in his service for humanity because of his own faithful life. (See Heb. 2: 18; 4: 15.)

Verse 6. The reader will certainly understand that none of these dumb beasts will literally have anything to do with the kingdom of Christ. The situation with such creatures was used to illustrate the spiritual peace and safety to be enjoyed by the citizens of that kingdom. It was to be true that the most vicious of human characters would become friendly toward the opposite kind because of their common relation to Christ and their interest in each other. If a child would be able safely to *lead* or herd these beasts that had formerly been dangerous, it would illustrate the civilizing influence of the Gospel upon the hearts and lives of mankind.

Verse 7. This verse uses different creatures for the illustration, but the meaning is the same as that of the preceding verses.

Verse 8. *Asp* and *cockatrice* are varieties of poisonous snakes. The safe and peaceful condition (spiritually) in the kingdom of Christ was illustrated by this harmony between the babes and the poisonous creatures.

Verse 9. *Mountain* in prophetic and figurative language means government, and here referred to the government or kingdom of Christ. *Shall not hurt* has the same meaning as several preceding verses. *Earth shall be full* is a prediction of the final and complete extension of the Gospel throughout the world. This prediction was fulfilled according to Rom. 10: 18; 16: 26; Col. 1: 23.

Verse 10. For explanation of *root of Jesse* see the comments at verse one. *Ensign* is from a word that means a "signal or token," and referred to the Gospel of Christ that was to be the token of good will and salvation offered by this descendant of Jesse. *Gentiles* is from GOI and its fundamental definition is "nations or people." In its application at this place it means the people of the world generally, hence not to one race only as was the system under Moses.

Verse 11. The preceding verse closed the bracket for the kingdom of Christ, and the "telescope" was returned in its range to the more immediate time of the prophet and his vision concerning ancient Israel. This verse predicted the recovery of the "remnant" that will have survived the strain of the captivity. Mention is made of some other countries besides Babylon or Assyria. That is because some straggling Israelites were found in some of these places although the bulk of the nation of the Jews was in the region of Assyria first, then of Babylon.

Verse 12. This verse refers to the same facts as that of the preceding one, and it was fulfilled when the Jews were permitted to return to their own land.

Verse 13. *Ephraim* refers to the 10 tribes (see comments at ch. 7: 2, 9) and *Judah* to the 2 tribes. Formerly these two kingdoms had been at enmity against each other, and also both had been envied by other nations. After the captivity this was changed and the 12 tribes were united as one nation back in Palestine. This great fact was predicted in clear language also in Ezk. 37: 15-22. The familiar doctrine of "the lost 10 tribes" has no foundation in prophecy or history.

Verse 14. After the 12 tribes were again settled in their own land they were to override the heathen nations named in this verse. During the absence of the tribes in their captivity, these foreign people had taken advantage of the situation and helped themselves to the territories before them.

Verse 15. The phraseology of the first clause of this verse is based on the ancient escape of Israel from Egyptain bondage. *Tongue* is from IESHOMAH and the part of Strong's definition that applies here is, "used figuratively (speech, an ingot, a fork of flame, a cove of water)." The last phrase is the meaning used in this verse. The Red Sea was depended upon by the Egyptains to protect them from the loss of their servants, the Israelites. But the Lord *utterly destroyed* that hope by opening up through it a way of escape. And as the Lord overcame the barrier of the sea with the wind (Ex. 14: 21), so he will master the obstruction of the *river* (the Euphrates) that would seem to be an obstacle in the way of Israel's escape from their bondage in Babylon. The feat was accomplished by lowering the stream through the strategy of Cyrus. The historical record of this feat will be found in connection with the comments at ch. 45. 1. *Seven streams* was used because seven in symbolic language means completeness. The Euphrates River was such a mighty stream that it would seem to be a complete barrier against the escape of the captives.

Verse 16. *Assyria* is used in the same sense as was explained at ch. 7: 18. The escape of God's people from this country is compared to their deliverance from Egypt.

ISAIAH 12

Verse 1. This verse is a prophecy with a twofold bearing. Its first application is to the recovery of Israel from the sad condition of the captivity. The "telescope" was then extended to reach into the time and work of Christ.

Verse 2. The *salvation* was also twofold as per the first verse. The first was a national salvation from the state of captivity, and the next referred to the spiritual salvation to be offered to mankind through Christ.

Verse 3. This promise was cited by

Jesus in John 7: 38, and it referred to the living water of truth that He would give to all who would accept it. The result of this living water would be the salvation of all who would drink of it.

Verse 4. It was true that when Jesus gave the truth into the world, many took up the sweet story and told it to others.

Verse 5. *Known in all the world* was a prediction that the Gospel of Christ was to be made known throughout the world. This was accomplished under the commission given to the apostles according to Matt. 28: 26; Mark 16: 15; Rom. 10: 18; Col. 1: 23.

Verse 6. Zion was the most important district in Jerusalem and was the capital of the Jewish kingdom; it in turn became the birthplace of the kingdom of Christ. It was therefore proper that the inhabitants of this place should rejoice with shouting. Their joy would be based on such glorious promises that meant so much to them.

ISAIAH 13

Verse 1. God's ancient people had so many dealings with the heathen nations existing at the same time that the inspired prophets were called upon to write concerning them. Some of their writings were in the form of admonition and others were predictions concerning their fate. An occasional favor was predicted for the few good people who had respected the Lord and his servants, but most of them were threats to bring some punishment for their wickedness and misuse of the people of God. *Burden* is from MASSA and the part of Strong's definition that applies here is, "an utterance, chiefly a doom." Hence the expression means that Babylon will have to bear the burden of the doom that the prophet was about to predict. Some of the predictions against *Babylon* had reference to the kingdom as a whole, and others applied especially to the city which was the capital of that mighty government. However, in any case, the destruction of the city would mean the overthrow of the kingdom. I shall here quote from ancient history a description of the destruction of the city. "Concerning the complete destruction of the city of Babylon, the city ceased to be a royal city, the kings of Persia choosing to reside elsewhere. They delighted more in Shushan, Ecbatana, Persepolis, or any other place, and did themselves destroy a great part of Babylon. . . . The new kings of Persia, who afterwards became masters of Babylon, completed the ruin of it, by building Ctesiphon, which carried away all the remainder of the inhabitants. . . . She was totally forsaken, that nothing of her was left remaining but the walls. And to this condition was she reduced at the time when Pausians wrote his remarks upon Greece. . . . The kings of Persia, finding the place deserted, made a park of it, in which they kept wild beasts for hunting. . . . Instead of citizens, it was now inhabited by wild boars, leopards, bears, deer and wild asses. Babylon was now the retreat of fierce, savage, deadly creatures, that hate the light, and delight in darkness. . . . But it was still too much that the walls of Babylon were still standing. At length, they fell down in several places, and were never repaired. Various accidents destroyed the remainder. The animals, which served for pleasure for the Persian kings, abandoned the place; serpents and scorpions remained, so that it became a dreadful place for persons that should have curiosity to visit, or search after its antiquities. The Euphrates that used to run through the city, having no longer a free channel, took its course another way, so that, in Theodoret's time, there was but a very little stream of water left, which ran across the ruins, and, not meeting with a descent or free passage, necessarily expanded into a marsh. In the time of Alexander the Great the river had left its ordinary channel, by reason of the outlets and canals which Cyrus had made, and of which we already have given an account; these outlets, being all stopped up, had occasioned a great inundation in the country. Alexander, designing to fix the seat of his empire at Babylon, projecting the bringing back the Euphrates into its natural and former channel had actually set his men to work. But the Almighty, who watched over the fulfilling of his prophecy, defeated this enterprise by the death of Alexander, which happend soon after. It is easy to comprehend how, after this, Babylon being neglected to such a degree as we have seen, its river was converted into an inaccessible pool. . . . By means of these changes, Babylon became an utter desert, and all the country around fell into the same state of desolation and horror; so that the ablest geographers at this day (A.D. 1729) cannot determine the place where it stood." Rollin's Ancient History, v. 1, pp. 558-560. Additional information concerning the destruction of the kingdom of Babylon may be found in Myers Ancient History, pp. 93, 275-285.

Verse 2. A *banner* is an ensign indicating the presence or coming of some army or other power. The prediction here was concerning the power of the hosts of the Lord that were to subdue Babylon. *Go into the gates of the nobles* indicated the entrance into the strongholds of the enemy that God's forces would accomplish.

Verse 3. *Sanctified ones* would apply to whomsoever the Lord designated to act for him in the overthrow of Babylon. In the present case it was to consist of the Persians as we have seen in the quotation from the history in v. 1 above.

Verse 4. The subject matter of this verse is the same as the preceding ones. The tumult and disturbance described referred to that of the gathering army outside of Babylon. It is said that *the Lord of hosts* was to do this, because it was by His decree that the Persians were to overthrow the Babylonians.

Verses 5, 6. The rulers and citizens of Babylon were told to *howl* because of the destruction that was to be brought to them. They were informed that it was to come from the Almighty whom we understand to mean the Lord.

Verse 7, 8. This bracket follows close to the predictions of the preceding verses. It was specifically focused upon the final event that marked the overthrow of Babylon, and that was the memorable death of Belshazzar and his thousand lords. The Biblical account of this event is in Dan. 5: 6, 9. But this epoch in the affairs of the nations was so significant as touching the prophecies of the Bible that I shall quote at length from secular history, that my readers who do not have access to the sources may have the information here. This and other lengthy quotations from secular productions will be quoted only once in this Commentary in order to conserve space. The reader is therefore earnestly requested to make careful note of them, and when reference is made to them from time to time, he should take the pains to find them and read, as they will have an important part to play in the comments on the verse or verses under consideration. Following are the quotations referred to above: "When Cyrus had avenged himself on the river Gyndes by distributing it into three hundred and sixty channels, and the second spring began to shine, he then advanced against Babylon. But the Babylonians having taken the field, awaited his coming; and when he had advanced near the city, the Babylonians gave battle and, being defeated, were shut up in the city. But as they had been long aware of the restless spirit of Cyrus, and saw that he attacked all nations alike, they had laid up provisions for many years; and therefore were under no apprehensions about a siege. On the other hand, Cyrus found himself in difficulty, since much time had elapsed, and his affairs were not at all advanced. Whether therefore some one else made the suggestion to him in his perplexity, or whether he himself devised the plan, he had recourse to the following stratagem. He stationed the bulk of his army near the passage of the river [Euphrates] where it enters Babylon, and again having stationed another division beyond the city, where the river makes its exit, he gave orders to his forces to enter the city as soon as they should see the stream fordable. Having then stationed his forces, and given these directions, he himself marched away with the ineffective part of his army; and having come to the lake, Cyrus did the same with respect to the river and lake as the queen of the Babylonians had done. For having diverted the river by means of a canal, into the lake, which was before a swamp, he made the ancient channel fordable by the sinking of the river. When this took place, the Persians who were appointed to that purpose close to the stream of the river, which had now subsided to about the middle of a man's thigh, entered Babylon by this passage. If, however, the Babylonians had been aware of it beforehand, or had known what Cyrus was about, they would not have suffered the Persians to enter the city, but would have utterly destroyed them; for having shut all the little gates that lead down to the river, they would have caught them as in a net; whereas the Persians came upon them by surprise. It is related by the people who inhabited this city, that by reason of its great extent, when they who were at the extremities were taken, those of the

Babylonians who inhabited the center knew nothing of the capture; (for it happened to be a festival) but they were dancing at the time, and enjoying themselves, till they received certain information of the truth; and thus Babylon was taken for the first time."
—HERODOTUS, 1-190.

"When Cyrus got to Babylon he posted his whole army round the city, then rode round the city himself, together with his friends, and with such of his allies as he thought proper. When he had taken a view of the walls he prepared for drawing off the army from before the city; and a certain deserter coming off, told him that they intended to fall on him when he drew off the army. Then Cyrus said: 'Crysantas, let us lay aside these things that are above our force: it is our business, as soon as possible, to dig as broad and as deep a ditch as we can, each part of us measuring out his proportion, that by this means we may want the fewer men to keep watch? So measuring out the ground around the wall, and from the side of the river, leaving a space sufficient for large turrets, he dug round the wall on every side a very great ditch; and they threw up the earth towards themselves. In the first place, he built the turrets on the river, laying their foundation on palm trees, that were no less than a hundred feet in length, for there are those of them that grew even to a greater length than that; the palm trees that are pressed, bent up under the weight as asses do that are used to the pack-saddle. He placed the turrets on these; for this reason, that it might carry the stronger appearance of his preparing to block up the city, and as if he intended that if the river made its way into the ditch it might not carry off the turrets. He raised likewise a great many other turrets on the rampart of earth, that he might have as many places as were proper for his watches. These people were thus employed. But they that were within the walls laughed at this blockade, as being themselves provided with necessaries for above twenty years. Cyrus hearing this, divided his army into twelve parts, as if he intended that each part should serve on the watch one month in the year. And when the Babylonians heard this they laughed yet more than before; thinking with themselves that they were to be watched by the Phrigians, Lydians, Arabians, and Cappadocians, men that were better affected to them than they were to the Persians. The ditches were now finished. And Cyrus, when he heard that they were celebrating a festival in Babylon, in which all the Babylonians drank and reveled the whole night; on that occasion, as soon as it grew dark, took a number of men with him, and opened the ditches into the river. When this was done the water ran off in the night by the ditches, and the passage of the river through the city became passable. When the affair of the river was thus managed, Cyrus gave orders to the Persian commanders of thousands, both foot and horse, to attend him, each with his thousand drawn up two in front, and the rest of the allies to follow in the rear, ranged as they used to be before. They came accordingly. Then he making those that attended his person, both foot and horse, to go down into the dry part of the river, ordered them to try whether the channel of the river was passable. And when they brought him word that it was passable, he then called together the commanders, both foot and horse, and spoke to them in this manner: 'The river, my friends, has yielded us passage into the city; let us boldly enter, and not fear anything within, considering that these people that we are now to march against are the same that we defeated while they had their allies attending them, while they were awake, sober, armed, and in order. But now we march to them at a time that many of them are asleep, many drunk, and all of them in confusion, and when they discover that we are got in, they will then, by means of their consternation, be yet more unfit for service than they are now.' When this was said they marched; and, of course that they met with some they fell on and killed, some fled, and some set up a clamor. They that were with Gobryas joined in the clamor with them, as if they were revelers themselves, and marching on the shortest way that they could, they got round about the place . . . As soon as the noise and clamor began, they that were within perceiving the disturbance, and the king commanding them to examine what the matter was, ran out throwing open the gates. They that were with Gadatas, as soon as they saw the gates loose, broke in, pressing forward on the runways and dealing their blows amongst them, they came up to the king, and found him now in a standing posture, with his sword drawn. They that were with

Gadatas and Gobryas, being many in number, mastered him." XENOPHON, Cyclopedia, Book 7, Chapters 4 and 5. This information may be verified by RAWLINSON, Five Great Monarchies, Vol. 3, pages 70, 72.

Verse 9. Since this entire chapter was written against Babylon, both as a kingdom and in regard to its capital, we should interpret the variuos predictions in that view. Many of the expressions are figurative in form but refer to conditions of desolation and despair that were to result from the attacks by the Persians. The pronoun in the first person in many of the verses means that the Lord used the Persians as instruments in his hands for chastising the Babylonians.

Verse 10. The stars and other heavenly bodies were named with a figurative meaning, referring to the rulers and other men in high places in Babylon who were to be brought down by the invasion of the Persians.

Verse 11. *World* was used of the Babylonian Empire because it was so extensive. God threatened to humble the haughty leaders of that nation.

Verse 12. Man was to be precious in the sense of being scarce in number. That would be on account of the destruction of them by the men under Cyrus.

Verse 13. *Heavens* and *earth* were to be understood in the same sense as *stars* in verse 10, and referred to the prominent persons in the kingdom.

Verse 14. The people who made up the army of Babylon were from various parts of the dominion. Cyrus was to defeat them completely, and as a result those who survive will flee the city and try to escape to their particular districts of residence.

Verse 15. But even those who were living after the fall of the city will not all live to reach their homes. Many of them will be caught by the pursuers and slain.

Verse 16. Some of the survivors will be chased even to their homes where they will be subjected to great indignities. Their families will be disgraced before their eyes; the children being slain and the wives being assaulted.

Verse 17. *Medes* are named here while it is the Persians we have been hearing about all along. The explanation is in the fact that the full title of the kingdom that came against Babylon was Medo-Persia; or, when worded without the hyphen, it was the Medes and Persians. It was a government formed by the two countries which joined each other; the Medes on the north of the Persians. I shall cite a statement in a text book of ancient history: "Medes and Persians are names of people who sought homes on the plateau of Iran. Those who settled in the south were called Persians. Those in the northwest were called Medes. It seems on account of their common origin their names were closely associated. The people were coming into prominence in course of the days of the Later Babylonian Empire."—Myers, Ancient History, pp. 73, 88. The Persians were by far the more important part of the empire, and for that reason were generally named alone; but occasionally a writer named the Medes. But whichever was named, the Medo-Persian Empire was meant. In this verse it is described as a people that would *not regard silver* or gold. That meant they could not be bought off from the siege when the Lord brings them against the Babylonians.

Verse 18. This verse was a prediction of the severity of the forces that will be brought against the city of Babylon.

Verse 19. From this to the end of the chapter the verses should be marked into a bracket. It was a prediction of the complete ruin of the city of Babylon. The history that proves the fulfillment of it is quoted at verse one. The student should carefully read that, then consider the several verses as they are commented upon here. *Chaldees* are named because they were the most outstanding people in the Babylonian Empire. Smith's Bible Dictionary says the following of them: "The Chaldeans were really the learned class; they were priests, magicians or astronomers." Both in history and prophecy, the terms Chaldeans and Babylonians were used to refer to the same empire. Reference to the overthrow of Sodom and Gomorrah was made because the ruin of Babylon was to be as complete and lasting as was that of those cities.

Verse 20. It would be desolate enough if a city ceased to have a single permanent resident. But Babylon was to become so deserted that no Arabian, a people who were only wanderers and usually spent only a short time in any place and that in a tent—not even such a person would ever dare occupy the place.

Verse 21. The creatures named were such as preferred the most lonesome and weird of places. *Doleful creatures* is defined by Strong as "a howler or lonesome wild animal." The houses that once were occupied by the high classes of the Chaldeans shall be full of these weird, lonesome beasts, that will pierce the darkness with their howls. *Owls* is from YAWEN and Strong's definition is, "the ostrich, probably from its answering cry." These other creatures would rend the air with their howls, and then the others would reply with their cry, and thus the lonesomeness of the place would be emphasized by this horrible exchange of the wild beasts. *Satyr* is from SAWER which Strong defines, "shaggy; as noun, a he-goat; by analogy a faun." Smith's Bible Dictionary says: "Satyr, a sylvan deity or demigod of Greek mythology, represented as a monster, part man and part goat. Isa. 13: 21; 34: 14. The Hebrew word signifies 'hairy' or 'rough,' and is frequently applied to 'he-goats.' In the passages cited it probably refers to demons of woods and desert places." *Dance* is from RAQAD and is defined, "to stamp, i.e. to spring about (wildly or for joy)." And so we can get a picture of the situation. These doleful creatures would set up their howling and the wild ostriches would join in with their ansering cries. Such "music" would then cause these hairy goatlike beasts to dance about wildly.

Verse 22. *Wild beasts of the island* must be considered together for they all come from the one word IY, which Strong defines, "a howler (used only in the plural), i.e. any solitary wild creature." The first clause of the verse means practically the same as *doleful creatures* in the preceding verse. The meaning of *dragon* is not definite, but refers to some horrible wild beast, and such were to occupy the spots that were once the pleasant palaces of the Chaldeans. The last clause of the verse was a warning that the fate threatened was not far off in the future. Comparatively speaking that would have been true, even though the literal time was over a hundred years. But in the large scope of time covered by the prophecies concerning the world and its national transactions, a hundred years is a short period.

ISAIAH 14

Verse 1. The close of the preceding chapter predicted the downfall of Babylon. It is an interesting coincidence that the fall of that city also marked the end of the 70-year captivity of the Jews, for when Cyrus took over the territory he found these captives there in bondage under the Babylonian Empire. But God put it into his heart to free the captive people; not only to free them but also to assist them in restoring their own institutions in Jerusalem. Accordingly, he gave orders that his own subjects should assist these former captives in whatever way it was needed. The Biblical account of this is recorded in Ezra 1. The secular information on the event is stated in Smith's Bible Dictionary as follows: "Babylon fell before his [Cyrus'] army, and the ancient dominions of Assyria were added to his empire B.C. 538. The prophet Daniel's home for a time was at his court. Dan. 6: 28. The edict of Cyrus for the rebuilding of the temple, 2 Chr. 36: 22, 23; Ezra 1: 1-4; 3: 7; 4: 3; 5: 13, 17; 6: 3, was in fact the beginning of Judaism; and the great changes by which the nation was transformed into a church are clearly marked."—Article, Cyrus. *Set them in their own land* was fulfilled in Est. 8: 17, when "many of the people of the land became Jews; for the fear of the Jews fell upon them." That means that because of the high standing the Jews then obtained under the support from Cyrus, these people accepted citizenship in the kingdom of Israel.

Verse 2. This verse is merely a detailed account of the fact stated in general terms in the preceding verse. *Shall take them captives* means they would take possession of them for the purpose of making servants of them.

Verse 3. *Rest from thy sorrow* means the relief from the Babylonian captivity. The sorrow did not indicate any special bodily mistreatment, but it was what they felt from being in a heathen land where they were not permitted to serve the true God.

Verse 4. *Proverb* is defined in the margin as a "taunting speech," and the connection agrees with it. The Jews would be able to chide Babylon with her disgrace of being forced to cease her luxurious way of life and oppression of God's people.

Verse 5. Credit for the overthrow of the wicked empire and city was given to the Lord, even though Cyrus was the human agency by which it was done. *Scepter of the rulers* refers to the official signal of royal power that was to be broken through the Lord's decree. That event happened when the last ru'er in Babylon (Belshazzar) was slain as recorded in Daniel 5.

Verse 6. *He* means the Babylonian power and the description of it refers to the harsh treatment that was to be imposed upon those who will fall under its jurisdiction according to the predictions that had been made on the subject. *Persecuted* is derived from a word that means to pursue with intent to inflict a deserved harsh treatment. Certainly the Babylonians deserved very severe punishment for their unjust handling of the unfortunates who fell to them. (see Psa. 137.)

Verse 7. *Whole earth* is accommodative as to extent, and means that when Babylon was put down there was a general feeling of relief. It is a thought similar to that expressed over the conversion of Saul and the easement that came to Christians (Acts 9: 31).

Verse 8. Reference to the trees is figurative, and it is to illustrate the relief that was to be caused by the overthrow of Babylon. A *feller* is one who "cuts down" something. As a ruthless destroyer would cut down the beautiful trees of the forest, so Babylon was pictured as a heartless destroyer of innocent people. But the defeat of that nation was to put a stop to such vandalism.

Verse 9. *Hell* is from SHEOL in the Old Testament and Strong defines it, "hades or the world of the dead (as if a subterranean retreat), including its accessories and inmates." It has also been rendered by grave and pit in the King James version of the Bible. Doubtless the leaders of the wicked nation actually were consigned to the region of Hades, the place of departed wicked souls of men, the place where the rich man went after death. (Luke 16: 22, 23.) But since SHEOL has also a figurative meaning of a state of forgetfulness, it was likewise true that the wicked nation and its men of power were destined to go down never to arise. *Stirreth up the dead* referred to the general rejoicing that would be had by the other nations and kings who had suffered a like experience in downfall. They naturally would rejoice in the calamity of Babylon on the principle that "misery loves company."

Verse 10. This verse is a continuation of the thoughts in the preceding one.

Verse 11. *Grave* is from the same word as *hell* in verse 9, and evidently must take the figurative meaning in the definition since *pomp* is not a material thing. *Noise of viols* is also not something that could be literally transferred to any certain place, hence the word was used here to mean the state of dejection and forgetfulness. As a figurative picture of the lowly state of disgrace to be suffered by Babylon, it was likened to a man's body in the grave, decaying and preyed upon by maggots.

Verse 12. *Lucifer* is from HEYLEL and is defined by Strong, "the morning-star," and he says it is from another word that means "brightness" of a showy character. It was used figuratively in this verse to symbolize the dignity and splendor of the Babylonian monarch. His complete overthrow was likened to the falling of the morning star.

Verse 13. These were some of the boasts of the king of Babylon.

Verse 14. The last word is capitalized by the A. V., but the Babylonian monarch knew nothing of Him. The meaning of his boast was that he would be high above others.

Verse 15. *Hell* and *pit* are both used in the same connection, showing they must be understood in a figurative sense. The second word is from an original that Strong defines, "a pit hole (especially one used as a cistern or prison)." The last word of the definition explains why it was used, for certainly the Babylonian king was made a prisoner by the succeeding government.

Verse 16. *Narrowly look* are together in the original and Strong's definition is, "to peep, i.e. glance sharply at." The meaning is they will take one straight look at the fallen hero, then meditate on his changed situation. They will next begin to make remarks about his former greatness and cruelty.

Verse 17. The first part of this verse refers to the Babylonians in overpowering other nations and making devastation of their cities. The last clause refers to the strangle hold the cruel nation maintained of its victims, especially the Lord's people.

Verse 18. The kings of other unfortunate nations are pictured as having gone down in honorable defeat. They were to lie in their graves and leave behind them the respectful memory of the living.

Verse 19. Using the action of interment as the basis for his imagery, the prophet represented the Babylonian king as being denied burial. *Branch* means a descendant, and the king will be treated as if he were an abominable relative whom his ancestors would deny respectful burial. The remainder of the verse is for the same purpose as the forepart, and is a picture of the dishonorable end of the once great king of Babylon. In the words of a poet, he shall "Doubly dying go down, unwept, unhonored and unsung."

Verse 20. *Thy people* would be the unfortunate subjects of the Babylonian king, who had been cruelly treated by this monster of a ruler. They would be given respectful burial but the guilty king would be denied such honor.

Verse 21. The children of such a wicked ruler might imitate him if permitted, therefore they too will be cut off. That prediction is contained in the words *prepare slaughter*, since predictions were sometimes made in the form of an order.

Verses 22, 23. This is a direct prediction of the downfall and perpetual ruin of Babylon. For the historical fulfillment see the quotation at ch. 13: 1.

Verse 24. The mere prediction uttered by the prophet was emphasized by the Lord. It is significant that as the Lord thought or purposed, so he would act when the time came for the carrying out of the prediction of the inspired prophet.

Verse 25. For *Assyrian* see the comments at ch. 7: 18. *Mountains* in symbolic language means government. God was to use certain governments or kingdoms to crush the Babylonians. *Yoke depart off them* means the yoke of bondage that the Babylonians had been imposing upon God's people would be lifted and they would be made free. The reader should turn to Ezra 1: 1-3 for the Biblical account of the noted release.

Verse 26. *Whole earth* was used in this prophecy because the Babylonian Empire was one of the world empires. *All the nations* were the various smaller kings and their governments that had been taken over by the Babylonian king to form his vast dominion of the (then) civilized world. God's purpose included this accumulation of nations and districts into one absolute system of despotic rule.

Verse 27. This verse is similar to the 24th. It is an emphatic declaration of God to bring his predictions to complete fulfillment.

Verse 28. This prediction was made just prior to the reign of Hezekiah. See 2 Ki. 16: 20 in connection with the present verse.

Verse 29. *Palestina* is from PELESHETH and Strong defines it, "rolling, i.e. migratory; Pelesheth, a region of Syria." We know from the context that the prophet had reference to what we call Palestine, although the lexicon's definition does not seem to carry out that idea. The apparent difficulty is clarified by a statement in Smith's Bible Dictionary which I shall quote: "Palestina and Palestine (land of strangers). These two forms occur in the Authorized Version but four times in all, always in poetical passages; the first in Ex. 15: 14 and Isa. 14: 31; the second, Joel 3: 4. In each case the Hebrew word PALESHETH, a word found, besides the above, only in Psa. 60: 8; 83: 4 and 108: 9, has been rendered by our translators by 'Philistia' or 'Philistines.' Palestine in the Authorized Version really means nothing but Philistia. The original Hebrew word PELESHETH to the Hebrews signified merely the long and broad strip of maritime [near the sea] plain inhabited by their encroaching neighbors; nor does it appear that at first it signified more than that to the Greeks. As lying next the sea, and as being also the high road from Egypt to Phoenicia and the rich regions north of it, the Philistine plain became sooner known to the western world than the country further inland, and was called by them Syria Palestina—Philistine Syria. From thence it was gradually extended to the country further inland, till in the Roman and later Greek authors, both heathen and Christian, it became the usual appelation [title] for the whole country of the Jews, both west and east of Jordan. The word is now so commonly employed in our more familiar language to designate the whole country of Israel that, although biblically a misnomer [misleading name], it has been chosen here as the most convenient heading under which to give a general description of *THE HOLY LAND*, embracing those points which have not been treated under the separate headings of cities or tribes." God was always jealous for his people and was ready to punish any nation that abused them. But he also warned them not to take too much joy from the downfall of their enemies. *Serpent* and *cockatrice* were used as symbols of the various nations with whom Israel had to deal. If she became too jubilant over the destruction of one of her enemies, another would arise to punish her.

Verse 30. The leaders of the nation were chiefly to blame for the corruptions, and the severest warnings were directed against them. On the other hand, the helpless common people were to be spared some of the severest punishment. Such favor was expressed in the phrase to *lie down in safety.*

Verse 31. *From the north.* A glance at the map will show that the lands forming the headquarters of the Babylonian Empire lay east of Palestine. It would seem, therefore, that any statement regarding an invasion by Babylon into Palestine should have described it as coming from the east. The explanation of the apparent difficulty in the sacred text is to be drawn from the peculiar nature of the intervening lands, forming a great inconvenience if not an actual barrier against moving any army directly westward from Babylon. I shall quote from an authentic source of ancient history a statement to confirm the foregoing remarks: "Extending for about two hundred miles from north to south, (that is, from near Mt. Amanus to the hills of Galilee) almost in a direct line, and without further break than an occasional screen of low hills, it furnishes the most convenient line of passage between Asia and Africa, alike for the journeys of merchants and for the march of armies. Along this line passed Thothmes and Rameses, Sargon and Sennacherib, Necho and Nebuchadnezzar, Alexander and his warlike successors, Pompey, Anthony, Kaled, Godfrey of Bouillon; along this must pass every great army which, starting from the general seats of power in Western Asia, seeks conquests in Africa, or which, proceeding from Africa, aims at the acquisition of an Asiatic dominion." Rawlinson's Ancient Monarchies, v. 2, p. 443; Rawlinson's History of Egypt, v. 1, p. 21. From the above considerations the student can understand why the citizens of Palestine would see their enemies coming in upon them from the north of them, and the predictions and other remarks in the inspired writings would be made to conform to that fact. I trust the readers will mark this paragraph for future reference when it is cited. *None shall be alone* means the troops of the invading forces will be joined in close ranks and in solid formation for military service, hence will present a front that the victims will not be able to resist.

Verse 32. The *messengers of the nation* were the representatives who would need to treat with the invading forces. They were instructed to state that although they must suffer invasion for the time, yet the Lord had founded Zion and would finally take care of it. Upon this assurance the people of God were to rest their hopes of the future and not allow themselves to become completely dejected.

ISAIAH 15

Verse 1. For the significance of *burden* see the comments at ch. 13: 1. Also take note of the remarks concerning God's attitude toward the various heathen nations that came in contact with Israel. The Moabites descended from Lot who was a near relative of Abraham, and hence the nation was related to Israel. However, it was always an enemy and the Lord directed the prophet to write some predictions against that people. *Ar* and *Kir* were cities or districts in the land of Moab. *Brought to silence* means to be cut off or brought to ruin. The present tense of the verb is explained in the comments at ch. 1: 1 of this book.

Verse 2. *He* is a pronoun for Moab, and represents the people of that country as weeping over the fallen conditions. The names are of other places in the country that were to feel the hand of misfortune as a punishment for their mistreatment of the people of God. The baldness and cutting of the beard is figurative, and referred to the humiliation that was to be brought upon them.

Verse 3. *Sackcloth* was the same as burlap, a coarse cloth that was used in times of great distress. It may have been literally used at the time of Moab's defeat, or the term could have been used by the prophet as a figurative description of the humility to be felt by the Moabites over their national disgrace.

Verse 4. These names are of other places in the land of Moab that were destined to feel the sting of defeat at the time being predicted by the prophet.

Verse 5. *My heart* referred to the personal feeling the prophet had for the coming misfortunes of Moab. The citizens were to flee from the invaders, going over to *Zoar*, a town just across the Jordan from Moab. The weeping of these fugitives was compared to the sound of distress that a young mother of the cattle would make over the loss of her offspring.

Verse 6. *Nimrim* was a stream in the land of Moab, but the reference to it was figurative. The desolation to be brought upon the land was likened to the effects of drying up the water sources so that vegetation in general would be withered.

Verse 7. Continuing the figurative description of desolation, the people of Moab were pictured fleeing with the products they had saved to find places of moisture.

Verse 8. This verse is a description of the general cry of distress that the Moabites would make when the threatened invasion takes place.

Verse 9. *Dimon* was another stream in the land of Moab. The bloodshed that was to be suffered by the Moabites was described as if the streams of the land would be made red by the slaughter. The original for *lions* sometimes means a literal lion and at other times it means any kind of violence. In either case the citizens of Moab who ascaped the besiegers would be overtaken by some other misfortune.

ISAIAH 16

Verse 1. The subject of the preceding chapter is carried over into this, which is the prediction concerning the people of Moab. They had been described as fleeing in dismay from the invading forces to be brought against them. But though such forces would be some other heathen nations, they would be acting according to the degree of God. He had his headquarters in Jerusalem which is meant here by *mount of the daughter of Zion*. *Send ye the lamb* meant these fleeing Moabites better seek for help from that divine source, and that should be accompanied with a lamb as a tribute of acknowledgement to Judah for the favor so earnestly to be requested.

Verse 2. This verese describes the panicky flight of the Moabites who will arrive at the places named. It is similar to the prediction made in ch. 15: 5, 7.

Verse 3. The first verse warned the fleeing Moabites to send an offering to pacify the Lord. This called upon them to accompany the sacrifice with a plea for mercy. *Take counsel* advised them to act with wisdom and call upon Judah and ask the people to give the outcast Moabites some shelter. The people of Judah were to spread over them the protecting shadow that would be as complete even at noon (or the height of their distress) as the shades of night would hide one out of sight of his foe.

Verse 4. The present contsruction of the first clause looks as if Moab was being addressed, yet we know the connection is against such a conclusion. The statement should read, "Let the outcasts of Moab dwell with thee (Judah). *Covert* means a sheltered place and was used in the same sense as *shadow* in the preceding verse. *Extortioner* is from an original that means "an oppressor," and the last part of the verse is a sort of "wishful thinking" on the part of the Moabites. Isaiah represented them as making these remarks in a form of plea for mercy and shelter. If Judah will grant the favor requested, then when the oppressor has finally been at the end of his ravages, the throne in Zion will stand out as a champion of the rights of afflicted nations.

Verse 5. The foregoing remarks were expressed on the basis of the mercy of the throne of David (Judah) in Zion. Of course we know the Moabites would not be able to form such a conclusion as described here, but the inspired prophet could word it in that way, and record it in his book as a form of prediction against the Moabites.

Verse 6. The prophet continued his denunciations of Moab and this verse is especially severe. *Pride* and *haughtiness* mean practically the same thing, and such a disposition has always been displeasing to God. The attitude of pride may be manifested in various ways. One exhibition of it was shown by the Moabites in the events recorded in Deut. 23: 4 and Num. 22. It is likewise described in 2 Pe. 2: 15, 16.

Verse 7. *Moab howl for Moab* means the Moabites will howl over their own miseries that will be brought upon the land. *Kirhareseth* was a city of some importance in the land of Moab, and it was destined to suffer in the misfortunes coming.

Verse 8. The places named in this verse were in the land of Moab and were to share in the distress predicted of it.

Verse 9. This verse is a group of literal and figurative terms. The places named were literal, but the prophet represented the Lord as shedding tears (through the prophet's eyes) enough to water the vines of the country.

Verse 10. Doubtless many of the things predicted here were literally carried out when the country of Moab was attacked.

Verse 11. When *bowels* is used figuratively it means the affections or emotions. The Lord's feelings against Moab was so tense that it was compared to the vibrations of a harp, which was an instrument of many strings.

Verse 12. When Moab sees the unfortunate conditions thrust upon the land, it will be in vain for him to resort to his religious rites.

Verse 13. *Since that time* meant that many predictions had been made against Moab down through the past years.

Verse 14. *As the years of an hireling* means the period of *three years* was a specific term, meaning that within three years the land of Moab was to suffer some defeat. In other words, the prediction of this verse was more "up to date" than the other.

ISAIAH 17

Verse 1. For the meaning of *burden* see comments at ch. 13: 1. The scene changed and the prophet directed his predictions rather promiscuously. The present verse is a foreshadowing of the misfortunes coming upon Syria. *Damascus* is mentioned because that city was the capital of Syria, a country lying just north of Palestine. The fulfillment of the prediction is recorded in 2 Ki. 16: 9.

Verse 2. There were three places called *Aroer* and it is not certain which one was meant by this verse. But as they were all near the country west of the Jordan, we know it meant that the distress threatened was to come to one of them.

Verse 3. In this one verse the prophet gave warning thrusts against the kingdom of Israel and that of Syria. *Ephraim* meant the former (see comments at ch. 7: 2, 9), and *Damascus* meant Syria since it was the capital city of the country.

Verse 4. This verse is a prediction against the two-tribe kingdom of Judah, signified by naming *Jacob* because he was the founder of the tribes of Israel. The fulfillment of this prediction is recorded in 2 Ki. 24: 14.

Verse 5. When a man reaps his crops he takes the good of the field away. That fact was used to illustrate the event described in the passage cited above. The best of the nation was taken out of the land, leaving the poorest and weakest of citizens.

Verse 6. The likeness of gathering various crops was continued by the prophet. After the general ingathering there is always some grain left in the field, and some grapes left on the vines, and some olives left on the tree. The comparison was made to the "remnant" of which frequent mention has been made (see Comments at ch. 1: 9).

Verse 7. When a man is in trouble he realizes his need of the Lord more than before. This verse is a prediction of the attitude the Jews would have after they had suffered the chastisement of the captivity.

Verse 8. *Not look to the altars* is a prediction of the complete cure from idolatry which the Jews experienced after the captivity. See the quotation of history in connection with ch. 1: 25. *Groves* is explained by the comments at ch. 1: 29.

Verse 9. The unchronological style of the prophecy in the Bible must be borne in mind or the reader will frequently be confused. For instance, the preceding verse predicted the conditions to come after the captivity, while this verse goes back to the time and conditions that caused it. *Strong cities* and *forsaken bough* referred to the desolation in the land to come after the invasion (see ch. 1: 7, 8).

Verses 10, 11. The reason for Israel's grief is stated in this paragraph. God had been forgotten and the real source of strength had been ignored. Though the nation should plant seeds and set out plants that would seem to be unusually thrifty (figuratively speaking), when the time for gathering the crop should come there will be nothing to receive because of the effects of the inroads made by the enemy.

Verses 12-14. God has used heathen nations to punish his own people. However, after getting his service out of them he never permitted them to take pleasure out of the distress of the victims. Especially if they boasted of their success, the Lord brought upon them some evidence of his wrath. This is the subject of these verses which I have grouped into one paragraph.

ISAIAH 18

Verse 1. This chapter is against the land of Ethiopia. *Shadowing* is from an original word that means to flap or flutter, and *wings* is from one that means the extremity of something The clause means to make an ado over the wide extent of territory controlled; it referred to the boastful spirit of the country. The last clause of the verse identifies the country meant by the prophet because the Nile flowed through the land of Ethiopia and the word *rivers* is defined as such a stream.

Verse 2. The Ethiopians would traffic with other countries by means of water transportation over the Nile and thence over the Mediterranean. One of their means for this business was of the *vessels of bulrushes*. Some interesting information concerning them may be obtained from secular history which I shall quote as follows: "A sort of light canoe, formed (we are told) of the papyrus plant, and propelled either by a single paddle or by a punting-pole, furnished the ordinary means of transport from one side of the Nile to the other, and was also used by fisherman in their occupation, and by herdsmen, when it was necessary to save cattle from an excessive inundation. The stem and stern of the vessels were considerably above the water; they must have been flat-bottomed and broad, like punts, or they could have possessed no stability. They are probably the 'vessels of bulrushes' spoken of by Isaiah, which were common to the Egyptians with the Ethiopians."—RAWLINSON, History of Ancient Egypt, Vol. 1, p. 236. *Saying* is not authorized by the original and it is out of place here. There was no quotation about to be made, but God was telling the prophet what to do regarding the haughty people of Ethiopia. *Go* is defined "cause to carry," and the prophet was told to give a swift (urgent and severe) message to the nation about to be further described. One part of the definition for *scattered* is "to sound," and the word for *peeled* is defined, "obstinate, i.e. independent." The phrase meant to describe the nation as boastful, and it is rightly rendered in the margin by "outspread and polished," and that means the nation was showing off its splendor. *Meted out* is from QAVQAV and Strong defines it, "stalwart." *Trodden down* is from MEBUWCAH and Strong's definition of it is, "a trampling." Thus the five words beginning with *meted* means the men of Ethiopia were stalwart or strong and fierce, and they trampled under foot other people in their boastful feeling of self-importance. *Rivers* is from NAHAR and the full definition of Strong is, "a stream (including the sea; especially the Nile, Euphrates, etc.); figuratively prosperity." *Spoiled* is from BAZA which Strong defines, "a primitive root; probably to cleave." The meaning of the clause is that the land through which the Nile flowed had become boastful of its supposed greatness, and had been cruel in its treatment of other countries with which it came into contact.

Verse 3. The attention of people of the world was called to the decree being announced by the prophet. They were charged to hear when *he* (God) gave the signal *(ensign)* of his dealing with the nation described in the preceding verse.

Verse 4. *Take my rest* means the Lord would take up his watch in his dwelling place. God's ability to see all that is going on was described as being as clear and sure as his operations of the things of nature.

Verse 5. The imagery in this verse is drawn from the conditions of various crops. Before the production could have time to mature the vines and branches would be clipped and allowed to fall to the ground.

Verse 6. These fallen products will do the owner no good. They will be left for the wild beasts and fowls to consume. The meaning is that God would cut short the work of the Ethiopians and expose it to the nations around them.

Verse 7. *That time* meant the time when the land of Ethiopia will have been chastised according to the predictions made in this chapter. *Present be brought* referred to the customary tribute that was paid in ancient times by one nation to another, or by one person to another. It was either as an expression of respect, or in the nature of a concession of defeat, to pacify the demands of some victorious contestant. For more comments on this subject see those at Gen. 32: 13 and 1 Sam. 10: 27, in the 1st and 2nd volumes of this Commentary. This *present* will be brought by the people described in this and the 2nd verse. Bringing it to the *place of the name of the Lord of hosts, the mount Zion,* meant it would be a tribute of submission to the national headquarters of God's people which was located at the mentioned spot in Jerusalem.

ISAIAH 19

Verse 1. See comments at ch. 13: 1 for the meaning of *burden.* In prophetic literature we may expect to find much figurative language. The Lord was represented as riding on a swift cloud, which meant he would make a swift and overpowering invasion into Egypt. When anything is done by the directon and decree of the Lord, it is the same as if he did it personally. God often used one nation to punish another, and the present verse, with most of the chapter, is a prediction of the punishment of the Egyptians by the hand of the Assyrians. *Idols be moved* means the plight of Egypt would not be relieved by the gods upon which the country had professed to depend.

Verse 2. It is not uncommon in a case of great military disturbance, for the closest of friends and relatives to be thrown into confusion and become enemies to each other. Jesus made such a prediction against Jerusalem to be fulfilled when the city would be surrounded by the Roman army (Matt. 24: 10; Mark 13: 12).

Verse 3. The people of Egypt will be thrown into a general panic and a spirit of fear and distrust will prevail. In their desparation they will seek for help from their idol gods, but they will not receive any benefit from that source. The first verse shows that the idols themselves were to be alarmed at the presence of the invading army. And neither will such characters as "fortunetellers" be able to give them any information that would be of the least amount of consolation.

Verse 4. It was predicted that a *cruel lord* would rule over the Egyptians. That was fulfilled when the dynasty of Greek sovereigns was placed over the land. Those rulers were known as Ptolemies, and I shall give a citation from ancient history to confirm the prediction: "With the cities of Phoenicia and the fleets of the Mediterranean subject to his control, Alexander [The Great] easily effected the reduction of Egpyt . . Altogether the Ptolemies reigned in Egypt almost exactly three centuries. The rulers who held the throne for the last two hundred years or more, with few exceptions, were a succession of monsters, such as even Rome in her worst days could scarcely equal." MYERS, Ancient History, pages 276, 292.

Verses 5, 6. This prediction was evidently figurative, for history does not record any time when such conditions ever became true literally as described. But the depression that was to come upon the land was aptly compared to the misfortunes named.

Verse 7. *Paper reeds* is from ARAH and the lexicon defines it, "a naked (i.e. level) plot." It means the meadows near the brooks would be dried up and the grass withered.

Verse 8. The creatures in the streams would be diminished so that the fishermen would be disappointed when they tried to carry on their occupation.

Verse 9. A dearth of vegetation would cut off the supply of flax. That would interfere with the weaving trade and thus confuse or confound the weavers.

Verse 10. This is similar to verse 8 in its meaning. *Sluices* is from a word that means "wages," and *fish* in the original may signify any kind of living creatures. The verse means that fishermen or any others who expect to make wages by dealing in such commodities would have their purposes hindered.

Verse 11. *Zoan* was once the headquarters of royalty in Egypt which accounts for the mention of *the princes of Zoan.* I shall quote from Smith's Bible Dictionary on this subject: "This city [Zoan] is mentioned in connection with the plagues in such a manner as to leave no doubt that it is the city spoken of in the narrative in Exodus as that where Pharoah dwelt, Psa. 78: 42, 43, and where Moses wrought his wonders, on the field of Zion, a rich plain extending thirty miles toward the east. Tanis gave its name to the twenty-first and twenty-third dynasties, and hence its mention in Isaiah 19: 11, 13." The prophet chided the princes of this city who had been disposed to boast to Pharaoh of their ancestry as being wise.

Verse 12. What had become of these wise men? If they possessed as much knowledge as they claimed, they should have been able to tell their king something in explanation of what the Lord had threatened against the land.

Verse 13. This is much the same as v. 11, with the added thought that the princes of the city had been deceived.

Isaiah 19: 14-18

As a result of their own deception they had also misled Egypt. This is on the principle set forth by Jesus when he said: "If the blind lead the blind, both shall fall into the ditch" (Matt. 15: 14).

Verse 14. *Mingled a perverse spirit* denotes that God had confused the princes since they were already disposed in the direction of error After having their minds warped it would be expected that they would mislead others. This is somewhat like the prediction that was made concerning the followers of Rome (2 Thess. 2: 11). To *err* means to step aside from a straight path, which is likened to the acts of a drunk man.

Verse 15. *Head or tail*, etc., means the extremes as to classes, and the prediction was that all would be affected by the conditions brought into the country.

Verse 16. Because women are naturally more timid and more easily disturbed, the fact was used by the prophet to illustrate the condition of fear to be created in Egypt. The hand of the Lord was to be manifested by the presence of the forces from the territories used by the Lord as his agents in the case.

Verse 17. The Egyptians will be brought to know that God was the one who decreed the misfortunes of their country, which was for the purpose of punishing it for its corruptions. And it was also known that He was the one who ruled over the land of Judah, hence the terror that would be caused by the very mention of that country. A further reason for this feeling will be seen in some verses following.

Verse 18. After the rule of the Ptolemies (described at v. 4) had been established over Egypt, one of their kings took many of the Jews down to that country (see JOSEPHUS, Antiquities, Book 12, Chapter 1, Section 1).

Doubtless it was largely through the presence of these Jews that the people of Egypt became aware of the importance of the God of Judah. As a result of these influences, the feeling of the Egyptians finally changed to that of respect for the newcomers from the foreign land, and this respect even awakened in them a desire to know more of their sacred literature. *Speak the language of Canaan* was a prediction along the line of the remarks above. In connection with this subject, I believe it will be profitable to copy from Smith's Bible Dictionary the account of a famous Greek version of the Old Testament that was made in Egypt in course of the Ptolemaic dynasty. The title of that work is a part of the quotation which follows which I trust the student will mark for convenient future reference.

"SEPTUAGINT *(the seventy)*. The Septuagint or Greek version of the Old Testament appears at the present day in four principal editions . . . The Jews of Alexandria had probably still less knowledge of Hebrew than their brethren in Palestine; their familiar language was Alexandrian Greek. They had settled in Alexandria in large numbers soon after the time of Alexander, and under the early Ptolemies. They would naturally follow the same practices as the Jews in Palestine; and hence would arise in time an entire Greek version. But the numbers and names of the translators, and the times at which different portions were translated, are all uncertain. The commonly-received story respecting its origin is contained in an extant [existing] letter ascribed to Aristeas, who was an officer at the court of Ptolemy Philadelphus. This letter, which is addressed by Aristeas to his brother Philocrates, gives a glowing account of the origin of the Septuagint; of the embassy and presents sent by King Ptolemy to the high priest at Jerusalem, by the advice of Demetrius Phalereus, his librarian, 50 talents of gold and 70 talents of silver, etc.; the Jewish slaves whom he set free, paying their ransom himself; the letter of the king; the answer of the high priest; the choosing of six interpreters from each of the twelve tribes, and their names; the copy of the law, in letters of gold; the feast prepared for the seventy-two, which continued for seven days; the questions proposed to each of the interpreters in turn, with the answers of each; their lodging by the seashore, and the accomplishment of their work in seventy-two days, by conference and comparison. This is the story which probably gave to the version the title of the Septuagint, and which has been repeated in various forms by the Christian writers. But it is now generally admitted that the letter is spurious, and is probably the fabrication of an Alexandrian Jew shortly before the Christian era. Still there can be no doubt that there was a basis of fact for the fiction; on three ponits of the story there is no material difference of opinion, and they are confirmed by the study of the version itself:—1. The version was made at Alexandria. 2. It was begun in the time of the earlier Ptolemies, about 280 B.C. 3. The law (i.e. the Pentateuch) alone was translated at first. The Septuagint version was highly esteemed by the Hellenistic Jews [Greek-speaking Jews] before the coming of Christ. Wherever, by the conquests of Alexander [The Great] or by colonization, the Greek language prevailed, wherever Jews were settled, and the attention of the neighboring Gentiles was drawn to their wondrous history and law, there was found the Septuagint, which thus became, by divine Providence, the means of spreading widely the knowledge of the one true God, and his promise of a Saviour to come, throughout the nations. To the wide dispersion of this version we may ascribe in great measure that general persuasion which prevailed over the whole East of the near approach of the Redeemer, and led the Magi [the wise men] to recognize the star which proclaimed the birth of the King of the Jews. Not less wide was the influence of the Septuagint in the spread of the gospel. For a long period the Septuagint was the Old Testament of the far larger part of the Christian Church. *Character of the Septuagint.*—The Septuagint is faithful in substance, but not minutely accurate in details. It has been clearly shown by Hody, Frankel and others that the several books were translated by different persons, without any comprehensive revision to harmonize the several parts. Names and words are rendered differently in different books; those of the Pentateuch are the best. The poetical parts are, generally speaking, inferior to the historical, the original abounding with rarer words and expressions. In the major prophets (probably translated nearly 100 years after the Pentateuch) some of the most important prophecies are sadly obsured. Ezekiel and the minor prophets (generally speaking) seem to be rendered better. Supposing the numerous glosses and duplicate renderings, which have evidently crept from the margin into the text, to be removed, and forming a rough estimate of what the Septuagint was in its earliest state, we may perhaps say of it that it is the image of the original seen through a glass not adjusted to the proper focus; the larger features are shown, but the sharpness of definition is lost. The close connection between the Old and New Testament makes the study of the Septuagint most valuable, and indeed indispensable, to the theological student. It was manifestly the chief storehouse from which the apostles drew their proofs and precepts" (pp. 604, 605).

Verse 19. The Lord never sanctioned the building of an altar away from Jerusalem, but this was merely a prediction that something of the kind would be done. An account of it may be read in JOSEPHUS, Antiquities, Book 13, Chapter 3, Section 1.

Verse 20. Despite the fact that this altar was built only by the authority of man, the inspired prophet made a prediction concerning it. To predict a thing does not necessarily mean either to approve or condemn it. There is no mention in this verse of any animal sacrifices being offered on this altar. It became a public signal of the respect that came to be had for God, and resulted in some favorable treatment for the Jews by the Egyptians. That is what was meant by *he shall send them a saviour.*

Verse 21. *Do sacrifice and oblation* does not mean that God authorized animal sacrifices to be offered by the Egyptians. Men sometimes express themselves in gratitude for favors received, or in tribute to the greatness of the God of the earth. And even all this could be done without literally offering animal sacrifices.

Verse 22. This verse is partly a repetition of the predictions made earlier in the chapter as to the changing attitude of the Egyptians toward God and his people. After the country had felt the chastising hand of the Lord, it improved its conduct and in turn enjoyed some of the fortunes that were predicted by the inspired prophet.

Verse 23. This verse predicts a time when the national lines would be somewhat broken up, and there would be more or less a fusion of the races It will be well to cite some secular history in confirmation of this prediction as follows: "Upon the partition of the empire of Alexander [The Great], Ptolemy had received Egypt, with parts of Arabia and Libya. To these he added by conquest Coele-Syria, Phoenicia, Palestine, Cyrene, and Cyprus. Following the usage of the times, he transported a hundred thousand Jews from Jerusalem to Alexandria, attached them to his person and policies by wise and conciliatory measures and thus effected, in such measure as was possible, at this great capital of the Nile, that *fusion of the races* [emphasis by E.M.Z.] of the East and West which was the dream of Alexander." MYERS, Ancient history, p. 291. Information on this point may be found also in JOSEPHUS, Ant. Book 12, ch. 1, Sec. 1.

Verse 24. The three countries named were to form a kind of three-power pact as described in verse 23.

Verse 25. When a nation does what is pleasing to God, he makes a sort of claim over it. This is the meaning of the words *Egypt my people*, and the other possessive terms in the verse. There is nothing new in this passage as to God's connection with temporal governments. (see Dan. 4: 17; Rom. 13: 1-6; 1 Tim. 2: 1, 2.)

ISAIAH 20

Verse 1. This verse sets the date of one of the predictions of Isaiah. I do not mean the exact year or month, but the period in general. We may read about this Tartan in 2 Ki. 18: 17, and can learn there that he moved in the days when the Assyrian Empire was strong and was acting against other nations.

Verse 2. The prediction of the prophet was preceded by some manual performances. On the subject of prophets "acting," see the comments at 1 Ki. 14: 21 in the 2nd volume of this Commentary. The performance was to remove the covering from around his waist and the shoes from his feet. Strong defines the original for *naked* by, "nude, either partially or totally." Since men wore other articles besides this sackcloth about the loins, the definition would apply the restricted meaning in this place.

Verse 3. Isaiah was required to go thus partially nude and with his feet bare for three years. *Sign* means some visible thing that would attract attention, and *wonder* means practically the same thing. It was one of God's methods of impressing mankind with the importance of the message about to be delivered. It would seem to us to be a severe experience required of a righteous prophet in God's behalf, but there were other cases far more disagreeable than this that were imposed upon the prophets of the Lord. But the special reason for this acting on the part of Isaiah will be seen in the prediction about to be made.

Verse 4. Let the reader take careful note of the terms of this prediction, especially those about the exposure of the body. Then read also the following quotation from secular history which shows the fulfillment of the prediction: "Sennacherib now pressed on against Egypt . . . The condition of Egypt at this time was peculiar. . . The second great battle between the Assyrians and Egyptians took place near the place called Altaku, which is no doubt the Eltekeh of the Jews, a small town in the vicinity of Elkron. Again the might of Africa yielded to that of Asia. The Egyptians and Ethiopians were defeated with great slaughter. Many chariots, with their drivers, both Egyptian and Ethiopian, fell into the hands of the conqueror, who also took alive several 'sons' of the principal Egyptian monarch . . . The princes and chiefs who had been concerned in the revolt he took alive and slew, exposing their bodies on stakes round the whole citcuit of the city walls. Great numbers of inferior persons, who were regarded as guilty of rebellion, were sold as slaves." RAWLINSON, Ancient Monarchies, v. 2, pp. 159, 160.

Verse 5. *They* means any who had expected great things of Egypt and Ethiopia. They will be ashamed of them when they see the events predicted in verse 4.

Verse 6. *Isle* is from a Hebrew word that means "a habitable spot." It is used indefinitely of the various places where people had been looking to Egypt and Ethiopia as a place of refuge from the Assyrians. But when they see these very countries subdued themselves by the Assyrians, they will ask each other, *how shall we escape?*

ISAIAH 21

Verse 1. See the comments at ch. 13: 1 for the meaning of *burden*. *Desert* is from an original with a wide range of meaning, having been rendered in the A.V. by such words as "speech," and is defined in the lexicon by "driving." *Sea* is from YAM, and the first definition of Strong is, "from an unused root meaning to roar." The thought of the first sentence in this verse is that the prophet heard a driving roar, referring to the severe message he was about to receive to be delivered against a certain nation. The remainder of the verse is for further description of the message.

Verse 2. The prophet here came

more directly to the subject with his description of this message by calling it a *grievous vision*. He wrote in this and several following verses as if he personally was affected by the heavy news about to be delivered. Some country (to be named later in this chapter) had been guilty of unrighteous dealings with the unfortunate people. They had been *dealing treacherously* and spoiling or defrauding the citizens and God was determined to punish the nation. And, as was so often done before, the punishment was to be inflicted by the hand of another nation, and it is named in this verse. *Elam* was another name for Persia, and *Media* was the same as the Medes. *Go up* is a prophetic style of making a prediction, and in the present case it was a prediction that the Medes and Persians would be the nation used to chastise the nation complained of.

Verse 3. The prophet continued his complaints, as if the severity of the message was still affecting him personally. Doubtless a good man would sincerely be concerned with the interests of others, but in this case the victim was very wicked, hence the passage was meant to depict the feelings said wicked nation should have.

Verse 4. This is more along the same line as the above. *Heart* means the mind and *panted* means to reel or stagger. Let the reader still observe the comments in the preceding verse as to why the prophet took this worrying unto himself.

Verse 5. *Prepare the table* is a predicting of some banqueting that the prophet saw as he was looking through the "telescope," and a notice of that feast is in Dan. 5: 1.

Verse 6. Isaiah explained why he was reporting the things named above. It was because the Lord had told him to *set a watchman*. Although the grammatical form of the sentence puts his watchman in the third person, it really meant Isaiah, because he it was who saw this table or banquet with his prophetic eyes.

Verse 7. This banquet was destined to be broken up soon, for the watchman saw some military forces approaching. This was indicated by the horsemen and chariot.

Verse 8. *Lion* is from ARIY which Strong defines, "in the sense of violence, a lion." The forces that the watchman saw approaching grew in their intensity until it was compared to a lion, that beast being a very fierce and violent creature.

Verse 9. Again the watchman saw chariots drawn by horses and with their drivers with them. Such an array suggested a military attack. The prophetic story was made short by stating the result of this military attack in the words *Babylon is fallen, is fallen* Thus the overthrow of Babylon has been the theme of most of the chapter, and it was to be accomplished by the hand of the Medo-Persian Empire as specified in verse 2. Mention of the destruction of the images was to show that false gods cannot deliver a kingdom from punishment if the true God decrees its defeat.

Verse 10. The rendering in this verse is somewhat indefinite. *Threshing is* from MEDUSHSHAH and Strong defines it, "down-trodden people." *Corn* is from BEN which the same author defines," a son (as a builder of the family name), in the evident sense of literal and figurative relationship, including grandson, subject, nation, quality or condition, etc.)" The meaning of the verse is an address of the prophet to his brethren the Jewish people. He was remembering their many misfortunes that had been predicted, and was describing them as such. He wished them to take note that the foregoing predictions had been delivered to him from the Lord.

Verse 11. For the meaning of *burden* see the comments on ch. 13: 1. The *watchman*, of course, was Isaiah, and *Dumah* is a region in Arabia. That land was occupied by enemies of the Jews. *Night* is from a Hebrew word and Strong gives its figurative meaning as "adversity." The people of Arabia were represented as inquiring about their future as to fortune or misfortune.

Verse 12. The *morning* means the opposite of night, and the people of Arabia were warned that adversity and relief from it would alternate with them in their experiences. *Enquire ye, return*, meant for them to look out for further happenings to their country.

Verse 13. This is a continuation of the predictions against Arabia. The people were represented as in flight from the sword and must take refuge in the forest.

Verse 14. *Tema* was another heathen people, and they were called upon to refresh the refugees with water as they were shut in at the forest.

Verse 15. One heathen nation was often set against another to carry out the decrees of God in punishment for its great wickedness.

Verse 16. *Years of an hireling* means in exactly one year the thing predicted would happen. *Kedar* represented another group of people in Arabia descendent from Ishmael, and they had usually been against God's true people.

Verse 17. *Archers* were men who used the bow and arrow in battle. It was predicted that the war forces of these descendants of Ishmael would be reduced. The prediction was from God and was sure to be fulfilled.

ISAIAH 22

Verse 1. For the significance of *burden* see the comments at ch. 13: 1. *Valley of vision* is a figurative reference to the area around Jerusalem. This chapter is a series of predictions concerning the people of that region, who we understand were the Jews. *Gone up to the housetops* referred to the habits of pleasure in which the Jews were indulging, not realizing the fate awaiting them. It will be useful information about the activities that took place on the roofs of the houses to quote from Smith's Bible Dictionary: "In no point do Oriental domestic habits differ more from European than in the use of the roof. Its flat surface is made useful for various household purposes, as drying corn, hanging up linen, and preparing figs and raisins. The roofs are used as places of *recreation* in the evening, and often as sleeping-places at night"—Article, House.

Verse 2. The first half of this verse refers to the same facts as were indicated in connection with the housetops in the previous verse. *Not slain with the sword* refers to the fact that the country was taken with very little bloodshed.

Verse 3. The people, especially the leading citizens, were taken alive and carried away. (2 Ki. 24: 14.) *Bound by the archers* means they were taken captive by the military might of the enemy nation invading the land.

Verse 4. The prophet "took it to heart" again when he saw the unpleasant events that were to come upon his people, as he did in the preceding chapter.

Verse 5. Much of the language of this verse is figurative, but the thought is directly on the subject of the captivity that concerned the Jewish nation.

Verse 6. *Elam* as a geographical territory was usually considered about the same as Persia. However, while it was the Babylonians (politically) that subdued Israel, the people of Elam or Persia made up a great part of that government. *Quiver, chariots* and *shield* are all military terms. The first refers to the bow and arrow and the second to the vehicles of war. The third is a protective covering, but the men of *Kir* (a place in the territory of Assyria) were going to strip this shield from the victims in the attack, leaving them helpless at the mercy of the foe.

Verse 7. This is a continuation of the prediction that the land of Israel was to be invaded by the war forces from a distant country.

Verse 8. *Discovered the covering* means the same as *uncovered the shield* in v. 6. *House of the forest* refers to the capitol building in Jerusalem (1 Ki. 7: 2; 10: 17), and it was destined to be destroyed at the time of the captivity. (2 Ki. 25: 9.)

Verse 9. The prophet could see the reduced condition that was coming upon the city of Jerusalem. The walls would be attacked until there would be breaks in them. Supplies of water would be threatened so that they would be confined to the lower pools.

Verse 10. In the desperation over the damaged walls, they would *number* or take an inventory of their houses, to see how many of them could be spared for material in repairing the walls and thus strengthen their defence.

Verse 11. As further means of conserving the water supply they would make a tank between the two walls of the city. All of these conditions should cause them to reflect on the case and turn their minds to the Maker of all things. Yet it was predicted that they would not think of Him.

Verse 12 *In that day* means the day of their subjection to the besieging army. God will call upon them to weep over their undone state, indicating their feeling of dejection by wearing sackcloth as was the custom at such times.

Verse 13. Instead of the fruits of penitence that the Lord called for (indicated in the preceding verse), the people will be thoughtless of their shortcomings, and will be passing the time with activities of pleasure. They will be engaged in banqueting and

Isaiah 22: 14-25

high living. They will be acting on the principle that eating and drinking is to be indulged in, when they should be concerned about the awful fate just ahead.

Verse 14. *This iniquity* means the sin of idolatry, which was the national evil for which they were doomed to go into captivity. That experience was decreed for them as the only cure for their idolatry. For the long historical proof that the captivity did cure them of that national disease, see the comments at ch. 1: 25. *Till ye die* referred to their national death (see v. 18) which took place when the nation lost its standing as a government, and was buried (figuratively) in the land of Babylon.

Verse 15 *Shebna* was a man of great importance in Jerusalem, and held at different times some office regarding the finances of the city, as well as part of the work connected with the secretary.

Verse 16. Shebna was found preparing a burying place as if he expected that he and his people would live and die in their home land. I believe this was a figurative picture of the state of mind which the nation as a whole had, even in the face of the many divine predictions that the nation was to fall. The figure drawn from the supposed activities of Shebna was in view of the national grave outside of the native ground of the kingdom of Judah. Babylon was to be the natonal grave, even as it was to be the caldron as per Ezk. 11: 11.

Verse 17. This verse is so literally true to the facts of history that we know the figurative language of the verses connected also means the captivity. The *mighty captivity* is recorded in 2 Ki. 24 and 25. *Will surely cover thee* is the only figurative part of this verse. It was used because a burial requires a covering over.

Verse 18. The nation of the Jews was to be *tossed like a ball* which indicated a rough and not too respectful treatment. The *large* country was Babylon into which the kingdom of Judah was to be cast. *There thou shalt die* referred to the national death that was discussed at verse 14. The *chariots of thy glory* referred to the former greatness of the nation that had been abused and devoted to the worship of idol gods. By such misuse of their opportunities the glory was turned into shame upon the *lord's house*

namely, the house of the true God in Jerusalem.

Verse 19. *Thy station* meant the position of honor which the nation enjoyed in Palestine while it was in control of that great country. *He shall pull thee down* meant the king of Babylon would take the kingdom of Judah out of its realm and cast it down into captivity.

Verse 20. *That day* is a phrase found often in the prophetic writings, and it is not always used with the same definiteness as to dates. Another thing, the Biblical writers are not always strictly chronological in the order of their events. In the present verse the date is over a hundred years before the date of fulfillment of the predictions in the preceding verses. Eliakim lived in the days of Hezekiah as may be learned in 2 Ki. 18, so the expression *that day* referred to the time in general when the affairs of the nation were declining rapdly toward the fall predicted earlier.

Verse 21. *Him* means Eliakim and *thy* means the nation as a whole, but whose priests and rulers had become so corrupt that they were not worthy of having charge of the institutions of God. Eliakim was not to have formal jurisdiction, but was to be a strong moral factor among the people.

Verse 22. *Key* was used figuratively and applied to the work of Eliakim in opening an opportunity for the *house of David* (people of Judah) to reform their manners. *Be a father* was a term of endearment to indicate the hearty interest he would have in his people who had deprived themselves of the favor of the Lord through their iniquities.

Verse 23. *Nail* is from YATHED which Strong defines, "from an unused root meaning to pin through or fast; a peg." Its use is to indicate a secure place to hold possessions of value. *Throne* has a figurative or complimentary meaning since we know that Eliakim was never made king in a literal sense.

Verse 24. Continuing the figure drawn from a nail or peg, the former good qualities of the people were to be hung upon this secure place The *vessels* was a figurative reference to the divine services that had been so grievously corrupted.

Verse 25. *That day* was again used with a general application, yet focusing the "telescope" upon a definite period in that *day*. Even the good work of Eliakim, as well as that of Hezekiah and Josiah and other good men, would not be able to prevent the great calamity of the captivity. So the *nail* was destined to be removed and the things that had been hanging on it were to fall as per the predictions in vs. 14-19. The prophet did the writing of the predictions, but they were bound to come true because *the Lord hath spoken it*, and he is able to carry out all of his plans.

ISAIAH 23

Verse 1. For the meaning of *burden* see the comments on ch. 13: 1. *Ships of Tarshish* referred to the commercial traffic on the water, to be discussed at verse 3. This was to be brought to an end as a chastisement for the wickedness of the city. *Land of Chittim* means the island of Cyprus according to Strong's lexicon. The prediction meant the shipmasters would first learn about the destruction of their business as they touched at this island on a return trip from abroad.

Verse 2. *Of the isle* had reference to the position of the city of Tyre. I shall quote some information from Smith's Bible Dictionary on this subject: "TYRE (a rock), a celebrated commercial city of Phoenicia, on the coast of the Mediterranean Sea. Its Hebrew name, *Tzor*, signifies a rock; which well agrees with the site of *Sur*, the modern town, on a rocky peninsula, formerly an island. There is no doubt that, previous to the siege of the city by Alexander the Great, Tyre was situated on an island; but, according to the tradition of the inhabitants, there was a city on the mainland before there was a city on the island; and the tradition receives some color from the name of Palaetyrus, or Old Tyre, which was borne in Greek times by a city on the continent, thirty stadia to the south." Further information will be cited from a secular work, bearing on the subject at hand: "The Tyrians also offered submission, but refused to allow Alexander to enter the city and sacrifice in the temple of Hercules. Alexander was determined to make an example of the first sign of opposition that did not proceed from Persian officials, and at once began the siege. It lasted seven months, and, though the king, with enormous toil, drove a mole from the mainland to the island, he made little progress till the Persians were mad enough to dismiss the fleet and give him command of the sea through his Cyprian and Phoenician allies. The town was at length forced in July, 332; 8,000 Tyrians were slain, 30,000 inhabitants sold as slaves, and only a few notables . . . were spared. Tyre thus lost its political existence, and the foundation of Alexandria, presently changed the lines of trade, and gave a blow perhaps still more fatal to the Phoenician cities" BRITANNICA, v. 18, p. 809. This is also confirmed in MYERS, Ancient History, p. 275; JOSEPHUS, Antiquities, Book 11, Chapter 8, Section 3, ROLLIN, v. 3, pp. 187-204.

Verse 3. This verse describes the traffic that brought Tyre so much revenue, of which she boasted so loudly but which was to be cut off. *Great waters* means the Mediterannean Sea, and *Sihor* was another name of the Nile. *Mart* means a market. The Nile River enabled Egypt to produce great crops of grain and other foodstuff. The merchants of Tyre, on the other side of the Sea, would send their ships over the *great waters* and trade their manufactured wares to Egypt for her agricultural products. They then took them back to the home city where they were offered for sale to the world. In this way Tyre was a mart or market of nations. But all of this business was to stop at the fulfillment of the predictions of Isaiah.

Verse 4. Zidon was not directly concerned in the foregoing predictions, but was destined to suffer as a result of the commercial ruin of her sister city Tyre. The latter half of the verse will have some light thrown upon it by some statements in Smith's Bible Dictionary in the article *ZIDON*: "All that is known respecting the city is very scanty, amounting to scarcely more than that one of its sources of gain was trade in slaves, in which the inhabitants did not shrink from selling inhabitants of Palestine." It is little wonder, then, that Isaiah made such a prediction as this.

Verse 5. The predictions concerning Egypt and Tyre will all cause a distressed feeling when the report of their fulfillment is heard.

Verse 6. Tarshish and Tyre were related through their trade dealings. The former was situated in the south of Spain. It was natural, therefore, for the misfortunes of Tyre to affect the other city. The apparent command for the inhabitants of the isle (Tyre) to howl, was a prophetic form of prediction that they would howl.

Verse 7. Tyre was reminded of the great antiquity of her commercial sister city. At the same time she was notified that the city would remain away from her (Tyre).

Verse 8. The prophet asked about the source of the predictions against Tyre. Was it some unauthorized or uninspired human being? If that were the case she need not be concerned over the warning even though it seemed to be serious.

Verse 9. The question of the preceding verse was answered in this. It was the Lord of hosts who had his own purpose in view. That was in order to stain or cast down the pride of the city, which would be accomplished by causing her leading men to be held in cotnempt by the people of the world.

Verse 10. *Daughter of Tarshish* is a figurative reference to the citizens of the city. Those citizens were bid to make a tour of inspection through the place, as complete as a river would make that flowed through it. Upon such a tour they would find the city to have *no more strength.*

Verse 11. *He* means the Lord, for it was he who had stretched out his hand over the (Mediterranean) Sea. That fact was to shake the kingdoms that had been depending on the merchandising with Tyre for their means of financial support.

Verse 12. In the study of verse 4 we learned that Zidon was connected with Tyre by common interests of some kind. And at verse 1 it was seen that *Chittim* was the same as Cyprus, and that the mentioned cities were interested in that isle. Zidon was notified in the prophetic style of language that her days of rejoicing and prosperity would be ended. It would not do her any good to look toward the island of Cyprus expecting to find rest from her distress.

Verse 13. This verse is an interruption of the story of Tyre to call attention to some facts about the Chaldeans. The prophet cited the undesirable experiences of that people as an example of the Lord's power to predict the affairs of nations, and also of His ability to bring about such changes as he saw fit. After this brief diversion the prophet resumed his predictions against Tyre.

Verse 14. This is identical with the first part of verse 1, which see.

Verse 15. This prediction did not mean that Tyre was to be entirely destroyed during the 70 years, but only that its glory should be partially eclipsed. This experience was not expected entirely to cure Tyre of her corruptions, but later a more drastic treatment will be given her according to the decree of God.

Verse 16. The prophet represented the situation as if some musician marched around Tyre in a sort of mocking serenade. The musician ironically bid Tyre to resume her own expressions of merriment in an effort to regain her past prestige.

Verse 17. The period of 70 years ended but found Tyre not fully reformed. She *turned to her hire* which means she went back to her old evil practices for gain.

Verse 18. But this time the Lord will take more drastic control of the affairs of the city Her revenues will not be allowed to be laid up for her own use. Instead, they will be *holiness to the Lord,* which is a Biblical way of saying they were to be used for the benefit of the Lord's servants.

ISAIAH 24

Verse 1. After a few chapters against other nations, the prophet again turned his attention to the kingdom of Judah. This chapter will be concerned with the great captivity that occupies so much of this book. *Earth* is from ERETS which Strong defines, "from an unused root probably meaning to be firm; the earth (at large, or partitively [partly] a land)." The last portion of the definition applies to our verse. The part of the earth that was occupied by Judah was so much more important than any other part that the prophet called it *the earth.* Making it empty had direct reference to the captivity in which the land of Judah would be emptied of its inhabitants.

Verse 2. The outstanding thought in this verse is that no partiality was to be shown in the capture and enslavement of the population. The account in 2 Ki. 24 and 25 verifies this prediction.

Verse 3. The prediction in this verse is the same as that in verse one. But I call attention to the significant remark of the prophet as to why the thing predicted was going to take place, that it was because the Lord had spoken the word. He not only has the knowledge of the future, but when he makes a prediction he is able to see that it will be fulfilled just as it was predicted to happen.

Verse 4. *The earth* is used in the same sense as it was in verse one. Because of the desolated condition brought on by the captivity, there shall be mourning and regrets.

Verse 5. The cause of the captivity was in the mind of the prophet when he wrote this verse. The *ordinance* was the law concerning the year of rest for the land that was required by the Lord. That ordinance is recorded in Lev. 25. Let the reader carefully examine that chapter. The outstanding iniquity of the Jewish nation was idolatry, yet in this verse it seems the reason for the captivity was the neglect of the sabbatical year for the land. There is no conflict between the two subjects. When man ceases to give the true God his entire devotion, but becomes interested in other gods, he will likewise lose his respect for God's laws. Consequently, when Israel became interested in false gods he also became concerned in his own selfish interests. This was why he so greedily abused the soil by defrauding it of its deserved rest every seventh year. Such an unlawful practice had been continued until the land had been wronged out of 70 years of rest. The captivity was brought upon the nation in order to give the soil its much deserved rest.

Verse 6. *Few men left* was fulfilled as recorded in 2 Ki. 24: 14. When the king of Babylon made his principal draft upon the citizens of the country it says, "none remained save the poorest sort of the people of the land."

Verse 7. This verse predicted the stoppage of agricultural activities of the land. *Wine mourneth* is an accommodative form of speech, meaning the people would mourn because their industry of the vineyards would be made to cease.

Verse 8. Not only would the productive industries be brought to an end, but their recreations also would stop; they would not be in any frame of mind to engage in them.

Verse 9. The downhearted frame of mind would be such that wine would taste bitter.

Verse 10. A state of general disorder was predicted to come by reason of the besieging forces.

Verse 11. *Crying* is from TSEVACHAH and Strong's definition is, "a screech (of anguish)." The wine will be so bitter (v. 9) that when men drink it they will screech because of the abominable taste it will leave in the mouth.

Verse 12. This is the same prediction as that in verse ten.

Verse 13. This verse predicted the same facts as those of verse six. *Few men left* in that verse corresponds to *gleaning grapes* in this.

Verse 14. *They* does not mean any persons in particular. The prediction pointed to a general recognition of the greatness of the Lord.

Verse 15. Ths verse is practically like the preceding one in that it predicts a general tribute of praise. However, some of the terms have been so indefinitely translated that much confusion might result. I shall examine the two key words in the passage. *Fires* is from UWR and Strong defines it, "flame, hence (in the plural) the East (as being the region of light)." *Sea* is from YAM and the part of Strong's definition that applies here is, "locally, the West." So the verse really is a prediction that God's greatness will be recognized from the East to the West.

Verse 16. The first sentence of this verse is the same in thought as the preceding two verses. But after making these predictions, the prophet came back to the awful conditions of his people that had been the subject of his writing most of the time. *Leanness* means the reduced state his people were to have thrust upon them because of the invasion by the enemy Such an event was to be brought upon the nation because of its own evils, prominent of which was the *treacherous dealing* of men in positions of advantage which they abused for their own gain and enjoyment.

Verse 17. *Fear, pit* and *snare* means the same and refers to the situation that was to come upon the nation when the Babylonians came against the city. *The earth* is explained in the comments at verse 1 of this chapter.

Verse 18. This verse refers to the same event as the several preceding ones. The various phrases were used to show that when the time of the invasion arrived there would be no escape for any class.

Verse 19. See the comments at verse 1 for the significance of *the earth*, that it meant that part of the country occupied by Judah. The prophet was still on the main subject, the Babylonian captivity, which was begun by the siege of Jerusalem, at which time the powers therein were overthrown.

Verse 20. A stunning blow on the body of a man will cause him to stagger and sway as if he were drunk. It was used to compare the effect upon Jerusalem of the blow that would be dealt the city by the Babylonians. *Cottage* is also defined "hammock" in the lexicon in which the meaning as of a swinging couch is seen. Such a back-and-forth movement is like the reeling and staggering of the kingdom of Judah at the attack given it by the besiegers from the country of Babylon.

Verse 21. This verse gives the reason for the events described above. The Lord was going to punish the nation for its iniquities, especially those of the *high ones* or those in the lead among the citizens who were chiefly responsible.

Verse 22. *They* means the leaders especially, but it was to include the people also since they "loved to have it so" (Jer. 5: 31), and hence were partakers in the evils. *Shut up in prison* referred to the land of Babylon which became the national prison for Judah for 70 years. The Biblical account of this captivity is in 2 Ki. 24 and 25, and the secular history that confirms it was quoted at ch. 3: 1. A remarkable feature of this verse is the abrupt change of subject without any apparent break in the story. Immediately after the word *prison* the subject is the return from the captivity. The *many days* means the 70-year period of the captivity after which the Jews were to be permitted to return to their own land. The Biblical account of that bright period is in the books of Ezra and Nehemiah. The secular confirmation of it as cited at ch. 14: 1. *Visited* is from a Hebrew word with a various meaning. It is defined in Strong's lexicon, "a primitive root; to visit (with friendly or hostile intent); by analogy to oversee, muster, charge, care for, miss, deposit, etc." The connection would require the part of the definition that says "with friendly intent," since that was what took place at the end of the 70-year captivity.

Verse 23. *Then* is an adverb of time and refers to the return from captivity which was the subject in the close of the preceding verse. This conclusion is supported by the word *when* which also is connected immediately with the resuming of divine rule in mount *Zion* and in *Jerusalem.* These two names are frequently mentioned in connection with each other because the first was that particular spot in Jerusalem that was the headquarters of the nation. The reference to the moon and sun is figurative and illustrates, by contrast, the brightness of the reign of the Lord after his people will have come back from the captivity and resumed their proper place in Jerusalem.

ISAIAH 25

Verse 1. The prophet was impressed with the greatness of God and was moved to praise his holy name. The direct basis for such an expression was the picture of the events just seen in the "telescope" (see illustration at ch. 1) concerning the captivity and the following return of the Jews to Jerusalem.

Verse 2. *Hast made* is to be understood as a form of inspired prediction. The events described in this verse were about two centuries in the future. For the details of the destruction of Babylon, see the comments and quotations at ch. 13: 1.

Verse 3. *Strong people* and *terrible nation* means the heathen who had held the Lord's people under subjection but were finally induced to release them. In so doing they were led to recognize the glory that was due Him.

Verse 4. During all the terrible years of the captivity, the Lord sustained the righteous ones among his people. See the long note on this point in Vol. 2, page 174 of this Commentary.

Verse 5. The figures in this verse were to illustrate God's mastery of the forces that had oppressed his people. It would be disagreeably hot because of the scorching sun and the dryness of the earth. Then a cloud would be brought over the spot and its shadow would relieve the condition of the heat. Likewise, the heat of the oppression during the captivity was to be relieved by the divine shade from the cloud of God's presence in leading his people out of their bondage, even as the cloud guided them from their bondage in the land of Egypt (Ex. 14: 19, 20).

Verse 6. This and the following verses should be marked into a bracket and entitled, "Introduction of the Gospel." Then consider the verses in their order as they will be commented upon. The "telescope" was extended into the future so the prophet could see the glorious reign of the Lord in the time of Christ. *This mountain* means mount Zion as of ch. 24: 23, the place where the Gospel was to be first proclaimed. The *feast* referred in general to the rich provisions that would be made for the servants of God under the Christian Dispensation. Many of the terms used were figurative and were used to illustrate the purity and richness of the divine blessings. *Wines ON the lees.* The last word means dregs or the settlings that come from wine after it has been pressed from the grape. As long as this refuse matter is mixed through the juice it will not be pure. When the wine is *ON* the lees or dregs—the dregs have settled to the bottom—the wine will then be pure and rich. This fact was used by the prophet to illustrate the purity of the Gospel. *Fat* and *marrow* are both from an original word that Strong defines by "richness."

Verse 7. *This mountain* is the same that is named in the preceding verse. *Face of the covering* has the order of the words reversed and it should read *covering of the face. All people* means the same as *the earth* in ch. 24: 1; that is. it means the people who occupied that territory, namely, the Jews. The *covering* had special reference to the same thing as the *vail* in the last clause. 2 Cor. 3: 13-16 will shed much light on this subject and let us understand that the *vail* means the unbelief in Christ that the Jews had and still have. But both Isaiah and Paul have prophesied that the Jews will someday cast off that vail of unbelief and will acknowledge the salvation that is offered through Christ. (See Rom. 11: 26.)

Verse 8. The unbelief of the Jews is a special subject and is applied to their rejection of Christ as the divine Son of God. However, there is a general state of sin and unbelief in the world. The resurrection of all the dead and the immortality of the righteous beyond was predicted and typified in the Old Testament. That great truth could not be published as a demonstrated fact, however, until Christ actually performed it in Jerusalem, "this mountain," by coming forth to die no more, and bringing a multitude of others from the grave in like manner. This is the force of Matt. 27: 53; Acts 13: 34; 26: 23; Rom. 6: 9; 8: 29; 1 Cor. 15: 20; Eph. 4: 8; Jude 14. With the establishing of the faith in the resurrection, the servants of the Lord will be able to face death with a feeling of victory.

Verse 9. This verse predicted the state of mind and expressions of joy that would be fulfilled at the end of the captivity. The Jews would be so glad for their regained freedom that they would give the credit for it to the Lord.

Verse 10. Moab was only one of the many nations who had opposed God's people, but it was a prominent one and was singled out as an example of the vengeance of God upon his enemies. *Straw is trodden down* refers to the use that was made of manure in ancient times. I shall quote from Smith's Bible Dictionary on this subject: "*DUNG.* The uses of dung were two-fold—as manure and as fuel. The manure consisted either of straw steeped in liquid manure, Isa. 25: 10, or the sweepings, Isa. 5: 25, of the streets and roads, which were carefully removed from about the houses, and collected in heaps outside the walls of the towns at fixed spots— hence the dung-gate at Jerusalem— and thence removed in due course to the fields." This was to illustrate the lowly use which the Lord would make of those who disrespected Him.

Verse 11. The action of a swimmer was described to illustrate the success of the Lord in his movements among his enemies. The very resistance of the water furnishes the swimmer with the means of navigation. Likewise, the opposition of the heathen was to be used by the Lord as an item in his power over the foe. This use of the enemy nation would overthrow his *pride* which was an outstanding characteristic of Moab (ch. 16: 6). As the Moabites enriched themselves by *the spoils of their hands,* so God would use his hands to *swim* among them and recover those ill-gotten gains.

Verse 12. A fortress is a place of defence against war, hence to *bring down* was a signal that the defence was overthrown. Thus the Lord was going to bring defeat to this proud nation who had misused God's people, but it was to be so complete that it was described as being brought down to *the dust.* The walls of protection relied upon by the heathen would be demolished before the mighty power of the army of Heaven, and their materials would lie prostrate in a mass of dust on the ground.

ISAIAH 26

Verse 1. *That day* meant the time of the return from the captivity. The people of God would have much cause for rejoicing over such a great deliverance. *Walls and bulwarks* mean literally the provisions for defence against a foe, and the Lord gave assurance that he would take care of his own.

Verse 2. *Open ye the gates* is a prophetic style of speech, and was a prediction that the gates of the city would be open to admit the Lord's people.

Verse 3. It was appropriate to write as the prophet did in these verses after the nation had been predicted to overcome the captivity. For the mind to *stay* on the Lord means for it to be settled or fixed there and not waver from time to time. Such will be the case if one has abiding trust in the Lord.

Verse 4. This verse continues the thought of trust in the Lord. *Jehovah* is from YEHOVAH which Strong defines "the self-Existent or Eternal; Jehovah, Jewish national name of God." Because they believed Him to be sure they accepted him as their ruler.

Verse 5. The *lofty city* was Babylon that had just been overthrown. (See the comments and long note at ch. 13: 1.)

Verse 6. The *poor* and *needy* had been the victims of the haughty Babylonians, but now they were to be free from the oppressor and were to have their day of triumph. Not that they would actually have any rule over the Babylonians, for that city was down never to rise again. But it was in effect as good as if they did bear rule over it.

Verse 7. The heathen city and her people had won and held their sway over others by force. The progress of the just class was to be supported by an upright life. *Thou most upright* refers to the Lord who will *weigh* ("prepare"—Strong) the path of the just. This is a beautiful thought and means that if a man indicates a desire to walk in a just path, God will provide such a path for him. (Ch. 35: 8; Prov. 4: 18.)

Verse 8. The Lord's judgments are always right, therefore it is well for man to *wait* or rely upon His instructions that he may never go astray.

Verse 9. The prophet Isaiah was a righteous man and personally had the sentiments he describes in this verse. However, he had in mind also the attitude that he believed the people of the nation should have. They had been redeemed from a terrible captivity through the might and goodness of the Lord, and hence should be glad to honor him.

Verse 10. *Let favor be shewed* means though it is shewed, yet the wicked will not appreciate it or improve his conduct. Even though he is surrounded by the goodness of the upright, he will continue his unjust life and disrespect for God.

Verse 11. *They* refers to the wicked of the preceding verse. *Will not see* and *shall see* might seem to be a contradiction. The prophet meant that the wicked would not intend to see, but the Lord was asked to make them see the uplifted hand of divine power. *Fire of thine enemies* means the fire prepared for the enemies of God should be applied to these wicked people. (See Matt. 25: 41.) This punishment will make them be ashamed for the envy they had felt for God's people.

Verse 12. There is logic in the conclusion of the prophet. Since God had brought about all of the works connected with the people, he would certainly be able and willing to give them such peace as only could come from the divine source.

Verse 13. *Other lords* had reference to the rulers in Babylon where the people of Judah had been in captivity for 70 years. But those lords had been dethroned and the servants of the Lord were again free to glory in the divine name.

Verse 14. *They are dead* refers to the "other lords" who had held dominion over the Lord's people. They were literally all dead, but their kingdom also was dead and destined never to live again as a world power.

Verse 15. *The nation* was that of the Jews that was increased. This did not apply literally to their number when they returned from captivity. It really had been decreased until only a "remnant" came back. But it was increased in honor before the eyes of the world. It was also destined to be increased in number as the years passed by. That is what is meant by the reference to *the ends of the earth*.

Verses 16-18. These verses have been put into one paragraph because it is impractical to comment on them separately. The anguish and sorrow that the people of God suffered while in the captivity is likened to the distress and preliminary pains of a woman expecting to go through childbirth. But the situation was even worse than a normal case of labor and birth. All of the pain and desire for completion of the process was there but was not successful, as sometimes is the case when a woman is brought to bed for the expected purpose. She may go through all the agonizing throes of the period and then not be able to bring forth a child. That is what is meant by the words *brought forth wind*. Likewise the Jews in captivity went through all the sorrows and mental pain here described, and yet were not able to bring about any relief. On the subject of these terrible experiences see the comments at Psa. 137.

Verse 19. The preceding paragraph dealt with the conditions in the time of the captivity. This verse predicted the release of the nation from that bondage and likened it to a resurrection from the dead. The death is the same as was predicted in ch. 22: 14, 17, 18. All of the leading words in this verse are figures to illustrate the glorious recovery of the Jewish nation from its political death and burial in the country of Babylon which was referred to as its grave.

Verse 20. This verse was addressed to the Lord's people while they were yet in the land of captivity. It means for them to take courage and patiently wait a little while longer. *The indignation* is defined in the lexicon as God's fury against sin. The Jews were in captivity on account of their sins against God. As soon as that had served the purpose of divine punishment they were to be given their freedom.

Verse 21. *Punish the inhabitants*, etc., applied both to the Jews and the Babylonians. The former were to be sent into Babylon for their sins caused by their idolatry. The latter were to be chastised because of their attitude toward the Jews, even though they were carrying out the decrees of God. *Disclose her blood* means that all iniquity, whether committed by the Jews or the Babylonians, was to be exposed and punished.

ISAIAH 27

Verse 1. The subject still is God's wrath against the Babylonians because of their mistreatment of his people. These people were to be retained in captivity for a while to punish them for their disobedience of the divine laws, but the kingdom that was the instrument in God's hands for that purpose was finally to "pay up" for its hardness of heart against their victims. In a literal sense a leviathan and serpent and dragon are vicious creatures of the sea or land. They were used in this place to compare the wicked and violent character of the Babylonian Empire.

Verse 2. *That day* meant the day when the Jews would be guarded by the Lord even as a husbandman would watch over his vineyard.

Verse 3. Even though the people of God were to be in captivity, He will keep his eye upon them to see that no permanent damage be done them.

Verse 4. One word in the definition for the original of *fury* is "poison." We should attempt to get the meaning of the first clause by the process of elimination. We know from numerous passages that God does have fury against evil. But it will not act as a "poison" within him; that is, it will not be any harmful condition to Him. But he will be a destructive force against his enemies and will be too strong for the enemies of his vineyard to succeed in their attempts to damage it. Even an entanglement of briers and thorns would be unable to hinder the Lord in his battle with the enemy; he would *go through them* as easily as if they were not there.

Verse 5. *Strength* is from an original that is defined, "a fortified place; figuratively a defence." The verse means that if the enemy should *take hold* or attack the fortification of God with the expectation of forcing him to come to terms of peace, he will be disappointed because of the superior might of his would-be victim. Instead, he will be compelled to come to the terms of peace that God will dictate.

Verse 6. *He* means God who is the owner of the vineyard which was composed of the Jewish people. *Take root* is a figurative term and was used as a prediction of the return of the Jews from their captivity in Babylon.

Verse 7. This verse is worded in a very unusual manner, and the pronouns will need to be carefully assigned in order to avoid confusion. The facts referred to pertained to God's punishment of Israel for his sins. For that purpose Babylon was used by the Lord as the instrument to *smite* or punish Israel. But God in turn was going to punish Babylon by smiting him for slaughtering His people. And the punishment that God was going to inflict upon Babylon was going to be more severe than that which he put upon his own people Israel. I shall reword the verse with explanatory words inserted as follows: "Hath he (God) smitten him (Israel) as he (God) smote those (Babylon) that smote him (Israel)? Or is he (Israel) slain according to the slaughter of them (Babylon) that are slain by him (God)?" Of course the answer to the question was "no." This same idea is set forth in Jer. 30: 11.

Verse 8. This verse means the same as the preceding one as it pertains to Isaiah. *Debate* is from RUWB which Strong defines, "a primitive root; properly to toss, i.e. grapple; mostly figuratively to wrangle, i.e., hold a controversy." God was going to have a *measure* of controversy with his people over their departure from the true worship. But he was not going to let it be as rough (a wind) as it might usually be when coming from the East. Such was the meaning of *stayeth his rough wind*, etc.

Verse 9. This refers to the fact that Israel was cured of idolatry by the captivity. The terms used in this verse are related to altars that are used to burn sacrifices to the idols. Those altars were generally made of stones, so those stones were to be turned into chalkstones to render them useless for sustaining fire. And those altars were frequently erected in groves, so accordingly the groves with their images were to be destroyed; *not stand up*. For the historical confirmation of this prediction see the quotation and comments in connection at ch. 1: 25.

Verse 10. While the Jews were in Babylon undergoing their cure for idolatry, their own country was lying in the condition described in this verse. *Defenced city* means Jerusalem that was caused to be *desolate* by the ravages of the Babylonians. It is the same thought expressed by ch. 1: 7, 8. The land was not to be cultivated but would be thrown open for the live stock to browse in at will.

Verse 11. *Boughs* is from an original with a general meaning. Being *withered* referred to the state of vegetation when no intelligent care would be given to the trees or shrubs or vines. There would naturally be dead branches still projecting from the plants since no caretaker was attending to the pruning at the proper time. The only use that will be made of these branches will be to build fires of them by the women living in the land. *He that made them* means the Lord, who will suffer his people to fall into this terrible state of desolation because they persisted in acting as *a people of no understanding*. On this last phrase see the comments at ch. 1: 3.

Verse 12. The "telescope" was lengthened so that the prophet could see into the time when Israel was to be gathered again to their own country. *Beat off* meant to thresh or gather the crops or other materials of usefulness. *River* means the Euphrates, and *stream of Egypt* is the same as "river of Egypt," which was a part of the southern boundary of Palestine. The Babylonian Empire had all of the territory between these two bodies of water under control. This verse was a prediction that God would gather up all of his people wherever they might be scattered throughout that vast territory. The Jewish people as a whole were confined within the immediate scope of Babylonia, but some were scattered in various places, and God proposed to gather them again in their original city of Jerusalem.

Verse 13. It was customary to sound a trumpet when an important event was about to take place (Lev. 25: 9), and that fact was used figuratively by the prophet to announce the release of Israel from captivity so they could return to their own land. *Assyria* is the same as Babylonia and it is explained at ch. 7: 18. For the historical confirmation of the predicted return from the captivity, see ch. 14: 1 and the quotation.

ISAIAH 28

Verse 1. When *Ephraim* is named other than as a single tribe it means the 10-tribe kingdom or the kingdom of Israel as distinguished from the kingdom of Judah. Smith's Bible Dictionary says this on the subject: "After the revolt of Jeroboam the history of Ephraim is the history of the kingdom of Israel, since not only did the tribe become a kingdom, but the kingdom embraced little besides the tribe." When Isaiah began his book the kingdom of Israel was still in existence in Palestine, with its capital at Samaria, but it was soon to be taken into captivity by the Assyrians. Some of the prophet's predictions were against this kingdom of Israel. As in the case of Judah so in that of Israel, the severest complaints were against the leaders of the nation whom the prophet called *drunkards*. That word is from SHIKKOR which Strong defines, "intoxicated, as a state or habit," and he says it is also from another word which he defines, "a primitive root; to become tipsy; in a qualified sense to satiate [gorge] with a stimulating drink or (figuratively) influence." The whole clause means the leaders were filled or gorged with their indulgence in pleasure. Not only had they been doing these unrighteous things but were proud and haughty over it. The prophet warned them that their pride would become like a fading flower.

Verse 2. *Mighty and strong one* referred to the Assyrian Empire that the Lord soon would bring against the kingdom. The event was figuratively described by such terms as *destroying storm*, a *flood*, an *overflowing* and a *casting down*. The Biblical account of the fulfillment of this prediction is in 2 Ki. 17. The secular confirmation was quoted in connection with the comments at ch. 3: 1.

Verse 3. This verse takes the same comments as verse one.

Verse 4. The *fat valley* referred to the extravagant life of the leaders which they had been following for so long. *Hasty fruit* is defined by Strong, "the first-fruits of the crop." The comparison was merely to the greediness with which a person would devour the first piece of fruit that would appear after the winter season. The coming "strong one" (v. 2) would eagerly take possession of these people of God's nation.

Verse 5. The "telescope" was lengthened again until the prophet could see into the general future. His vision was to include the Jews as a whole, but especially the leaders in Jerusalem who had the charge of national worship. A few verses will concern the corruptions of that people down to the time of the captivity which was designated by *that day*. These remarks apply to this and the following verses through verse eight. *Crown of glory* means that the people will see the power and glory of the Lord in evidence when he brings his judgments to bear upon the unrighteous leaders.

Verse 6. God will always give guidance to the leaders of his people if they will accept it. In battle with the enemy at the gate, if the soldier will rely on the divine support he will not be disappointed in the outcome.

Verse 7. The priests and the prophets were outstanding among the leaders of the nation. They were frequently charged with living in ease and luxury (ch. 5: 11, 12; Lev. 10: 9; Amos 6: 6), and this kind of life made them unfitted for the divine service.

Verse 8. These statements would be true literally as the results of drinking and banqueting would prove. And they would likewise illustrate the moral corruption and filthiness of those who were guilty of such practices.

Verse 9. All of the verses from this through 22 should be marked into one bracket with the general subject of "the time of Christ." However, there were so many phases of that great period and so many different characters entering into it, that each verse will need to be considered as it comes, at the same time referring again in some cases to the context as it affects certain verses especially. The present verse pointed to that particular feature of the Gospel instruction that considered the principle of growth. In Heb. 5: 13, 14 it is shown that babes in Christ must grow and finally become able to partake of the strong food. That is what this verse means by being *weaned from the milk and drawn from the breasts*.

Verse 10. The thought of the preceding verse is carried on in this by comparing it to the literal method of composing a document. No writing was ever produced all at one stroke or even a single line. The writer always wrote it a line at a time, but found it necessary to follow each line with another. Likewise, the Lord always gave his revelation of truth to man a little at a time. The writer (or speaker) was always directed to give it to the people in such amounts and measure of thought as they could understand and receive. By receiving it I mean the ability to make a use of it in life, and Jesus taught that idea just before he left the disciples, in John 16: 12.

Verse 11. *Stammering* is from LADAH which Strong defines, "a foreigner." The verse is a prediction of the use of spiritual gifts in the beginning of the Gospel period and refers to the act of speaking with foreign tongues. We are sure this is the meaning of the verse because Paul cites it in direct connection with that in 1 Cor. 14: 21.

Verse 12. *Rest* and *refresh* are given practically the same definition in the lexicon which means a settling down or state of satisfaction. The application is to the consoling effect the word of Christ would have had on the people if they would have received it as intended. But this verse predicts that it would not be accepted, and especially would it be rejected by the Jews to whom it was first offered.

Verse 13. The first part of this verse has the same meaning as verse 10. The last clause might be a little confusing and leave the impression that God gave these lines in order that the people might fall. The meaning will be clear from Paul's wording of the same passage in 1 Cor. 14: 21. After quoting the words about giving the revelation by the use of other tongues he says: "and yet for all that will they not hear." This shows Isaiah meant that even though the people were given these lines of instruction, they would stumble and fall and be snared by their own disobedience.

Verse 14. The rulers of God's people were of the same class that misled them in ancient times, but the prophecy was directed against the ones living in the time of Christ. *Scornful men* were men who would make light or belittle what they did not like. The Jewish leaders in the time of Christ did not like his teaching because he rebuked them for their wicked lives. He warned them that though they rejected his teaching, they would finally feel the force of them through the judgments that God would bring.

Verse 15. The Jews scorned the warnings of Christ and determined to prevent their fulfillment by a most desperate and wicked plot, that of the murder of the one who was giving them these unpleasant warnings. They were so foolish as to think that by killing an inspired prophet his warnings would also be destroyed. We must not think these people themselves called their plans or claims by such terms as *lies* or *falsehoods*. Those are the names by which the prophet Isaiah designated them, but those Jews were so foolish as to think they could accomplish them. I trust the reader will keep these distinctions clearly in mind as he follows my comments on this verse. *Covenant with death* refers to the covenant that was made wih Judas. The purpose of this was that they could cause Jesus to be put to death. By getting Jesus out of the way by death they thought the *scourge*, as they considered his teaching, would be rendered harmless for them. But all of these claims and expectations of theirs were considered as *lies* and *falsehood* by the prophet who was able to see the outcome of the whole case.

Verse 16. The Jews did not realize that in carrying out their wicked designs against Christ they were fulfilling the great prediction that was ever made concerning the welfare of humanity. I call it the greatest because all others rested upon its fulfillment. The death and resurrection of Christ alone could have made any of the other predictions of any value. But regardless of this weighty truth, Judas and the Jews working with him must be charged with the murder of Jesus because of their motives in the transaction. But their wicked purposes in the tragedy did not prevent God from directing it into the fundamental result of laying the foundation for the salvation of the world. *Zion* refers materially to Jerusalem which was the scene of the resurrection of Christ, and spiritually it refers to the Church, because it is in that institution that Christ became the basis for the hope of salvation (Heb. 12: 22, 23; 1 Cor. 3: 11; Eph. 5: 23). A *tried stone* means he was to be put to the test in his life and death. He met the test and withstood it (Heb. 2: 18; 4: 15; 1 Pe. 1: 3). *Not make haste*. The last word is from CHUWSH, which Strong defines, "to be eager with excitement." Those who believe in Christ will be able to feel calm in the assurance that belongs only to the true servants of God.

Verse 17. It was stated in the preceding paragraph that the Jews unintentionally fulfilled an important prediction of God when they caused Christ to be put to death. That is as far as their part went, however, for they had nothing to do with his resurrection. Had they been able to prevent that, or had the resurrection never taken place, their expectations would have been realized to some extent. But the triumphant ascension of Christ from the grave to die no more defeated their wicked designs. It also opened the way for God to proceed with his purposes which include the humiliating defeat and chastisement of the Jews. *Hail* and *waters* are used figuratively, referring to the storm of God's judgment against the wicked schemes of those who had plotted the death of his Son. The *lies* means the same as was explained in verse 15.

Verse 18. The *covenant with death* and *hell* was also explained in verse 15. *Overflowing scourge* means the resurrection of Chist, because that fact overthrew and destroyed all the wicked intentions of the murderers.

Verse 19. The general thought in this verse is the bitter disappointment of the Jews when it was reported that Jesus was alive. The very news of the event filled them with dismay, and they began at once to seek some way of counteracting the effect of the report. Let the reader see the account in Matt. 28: 11-15.

Verse 20. This highly figurative passage means to show the insufficiency of the basis on which the Jews rested their hopes of success. If a person were to prepare a bed and its covering in accordance with ordinary or small requirements, it might be satisfactory at the time. But if the needs should be increased, such as a person's growing in stature and the temperature becoming cooler, then the bed would not be large enough and the covering would not be sufficient. Likewise, as long as the Jews were doing the part that was as supposed to be done, the Lord did not interfere with their operations and the *bed* and *covering* seemed to be sufficient. But when the test of the resurrection came, their expectations were proved to be short of success—the *bed* was too short and the *covering* was too scanty. That was why the Jews had the sensations described in the preceding verse.

Verse 21. The Lord's victory over his foes is likened to that which he had through David (2 Sam. 5: 20) and through Joshua (Josh. 10). Not the same kind of a contest, but as complete in the success over the enemy. The two instances of *strange* are from different originals but they have virtually the same meaning. The central thought is that of something different and wonderful. Bringing Christ from the dead to die no more was something that had never been done before.

Verse 22. The prophet closed this noted prophecy with an admonition to the Jews who were predicted to be defeated in their plot against Christ. *Lest your bands be made strong* being uttered just after the admonition in the beginning of the verse indicated a possible offer of mercy upon the proper proof of penitence. Indeed, the exhortation of Peter to the guilty ones (Acts 2: 36-40), and their following obedience to the command, confirms this conclusion. *Consumption* means consummation or completion. God had revealed to Isaiah that he would complete his decrees as they affected the conduct and the fate of the whole world.

Verse 23. The leading thought from this verse to the close of the chapter could aptly be stated by the word "appropriateness." Some of the prophecies against the Jewish nation were severer than others; also, some were to be fulfilled at one time and others later. Likewise, no chastisement was intended to destroy the people but only to render them more serviceable. The prophet was ready to write an illustration covering the above line of thought and here called for earnest attention. Let the reader keep the foregoing comments in mind as he follows through the succeeding verses.

Verse 24. No plowman spends all the time getting the ground ready for sowing; if he did he would not get to sow. Likewise, God will not always be making predictions and never take the time to bring about their fulfillment.

Verse 25. The illustration continued, showing that after the ground has been prepared, the farmer would put in the seed. *Fitches* and *cummin* are small plants and the seeds were used mostly for flavoring. They were not so important, perhaps, yet were very desirable. Then the heavier crops were planted such as wheat and barley. *Ric* was a variety of wheat, and *place* means "border." This grain seems to have been placed around the body of the field where it would not take space from the main crop.

Verse 26. *Discretion* is the key word in this verse, and it was the rule by which the farmer managed his crops. If God thought enough of his human creature to give him this discretion, he certainly would use it in his own works of prophecy and fulfillment.

Verse 27. "Severe cases require severe treatment" is a saying that is true and illustrates the point in this verse, and also agrees with the comments on "appropriateness" at verse 23. *Fitches* and *cummin* were small plants with light fruit and would not require heavy instruments or rough treatment to separate the grain from the chaff. *Threshing instrument* comes from one word that means a heavy sledge. *Cart wheel* refers to the vehicle as a whole which was a large one with much weight. The statement means that it would not be appropriate to use such instruments to prepare such light crops at the time of preparing them for use. Instead, they were treated with a *staff or rod*, both of which means a stick that a man would use by hand.

Verse 28. The idea of consistent or appropriate progress was further illustrated. Grain that was intended for bread could not always be under the process of threshing, but it should be *bruised* or ground into flour. Were the farmer to continue the threshing even after the separation from the chaff had been effected, it would *break* or "destroy" it so it would not be fit for food, or at least much of it would be lost through unnecessary pulverization. On that principle God would not chastise his people so heavily that they would not be of any use to Him afterwards.

Verse 29. The chapter concludes with a significant declaration that the prophecy came from the Lord, which would guarantee its fulfillment.

ISAIAH 29

Verse 1. The "telescope" was again shortened to be focused upon the Jewish nation at the time just before the captivity. *Ariel* is defined by Strong, "a symbolical name for Jerusalem," and Smith's Bible Dictionary defines it, "a designation given by Isaiah to the city of Jerusalem." Also the wording in the text bears out this definition in that it says, "the city where David dwelt." The last clause means as though it said, "though ye add and kill sacrifices from year to year."

Verse 2. *Yet* is directly connected with the close of the preceding verse. The clause means that in spite of the sacrifices that were killed in Jerusalem, God was determined to *distress Ariel. It shall be unto me as Ariel* means that *it* (the sacrifices) will be rejected as well as the city. It was true that in all of their sojourn in Babylon the Jews were not permitted to offer any sacrifices to God (ch. 1: 10-15; 5: 11, 12; 43: 22-24; Zech. 7: 5, 6). For the Biblical account of the fulfillment of this prophecy as a whole see 2 Ki. 24 and 25. For the extended comments on it see ch. 1: 10.

Verse 3. God was going to bring a foreign army (the Babylonians) against Jerusalem and lay siege to it. A *mount* is a military post and *forts* means an embarkment. These things were to enforce the siege to keep the citizens from escaping.

Verse 4. The language of this verse is mostly figurative. It describes the prostrated and humiliated condition the people would be in when they found themselves so helplessly shut in with no apparent prospects of relief.

Verse 5. A humane parent will feel compassion for his child even while administering a severe punishment. Likewise God shows his love for his people in spite of the severe chastisement he was to bring upon them. In the midst of the prediction that a foreign nation was to be brought against the Jews, the prophet saw the overthrow also of that foreign power. This verse and the following through verse 8 predicts how it will be with the enemies who were to be used by the Lord to punish his people. They were to be reduced and scattered as dust and chaff.

Verse 6. *Thou* means the people of God, and they were to be *visited* with a great deliverance. *Thunder* and the other like terms in this verse means the power by which God would overthrow the enemies of his people.

Verse 7. *Munitions* means the city of Jerusalem in the sense of a fort. The great nations that will bear down so heavily against this city will be so completely defeated that when it is all over the memory of it will "seem like a dream."

Verse 8. The closing thought of the preceding verse is continued through this. All of the experiences stated as taking place while a man is sleeping are merely described to show the completeness of the victory of God's people over the foe. That when it is all over and all traces of the opposition are wiped out(the Babylonian Empire went down never to rise again), the thought of their terrible trials of the past will then seem as unreal as are the things described in connection with this dream. We should not attach any further significance to this curiously interesting verse.

Verse 9. *They* has special reference to the leaders of the nation who were held chiefly responsible for the corruptions. *Stay* and *wonder* has the sense of saying, "pause and you will be amazed when you are told of the condition you are in." Then follows the description of that condition, that *they* were drunken and were staggering. But it was not a material state; it was one pertaining to their spiritual conduct.

Verse 10. Frequently a prophet will give a description of conditions and events that were true both in the time of ancient Israel and of that at the time of Christ. The characteristics of the Jews are such that their conduct has been "true to form" all through the ages. That is why it so often happens that a prophecy will apply both to ancient and later Jewish history. We know the line running through many of the verses of this chapter not only was a description of conditions in the time of the prophet, but was fulfilled in the days of Christ for he quoted it and so applied it (Matt. 15: 8, 9). If there are some statements that must be applied particularly to the time of Christ, it will be noted as they come in order. Otherwise, the meaning of the several expressions will be explained in connection with each verse. *Lord hath poured*, etc. is a Biblical way of saying the Lord gave the people over to the kind of life they were determined to follow. If they were bound to think and do so and so, He would use no force to prevent it. This is the meaning of the many places in the Bible where it might seem that God caused the people to go wrong or to fall into some sinful state. It means he gave them over to such a state because their conduct called for and deserved it. (Ps. 81: 11, 12; Ezk. 20: 24, 25, 39; Acts 7: 42; Rom. 1: 24; 2 Thess. 2: 11, 12.) This is the sense in which God gave people to have their "own way" sometimes.

Verse 11. The senses of the people had become so dulled by their sins that it was compared to a man of learning excusing his inability to read a book on the pretense that it was sealed. But that was an excuse only as the next verse will show.

Verse 12. This man did not say anything about the book being sealed, but that he was not learned. That could not have been the real cause of his trouble, for the one in the preceding verse had the learning yet could not understand the book. The explanation is the dull state of their minds due to their repeated indulgence in and preference for the things that were coarse and worldly.

Verse 13. This is the particular passage that Christ cited in Matt. 15: 9. *Mouth* and *lip* service is merely a profession and comes from one who is not sincerely devoted. *Their fear* refers to their form of service; it was regulated by the teaching of men. This is exactly the thought in Col. 2: 22.

Verse 14. The leaders of the Jewish nation were filled with self-esteem, and it caused them to think their wisdom was exceptional. They were to be so completely overcome in their plans that it would baffle them.

Verse 15. One lexicon definition of *counsel* is "plan." The head men of the Jews thought their plans could be kept hid from the Lord. At least they tried to do so, and because God did not always expose them on the spot they were so foolish as to feel secure in their unrighteousness.

Verse 16. *Turning of things upside down* was Isaiah's way of accusing them of perverseness or contrariness as to God's law. Their responsibility was the same as in the case of a potter and his work. The clay would not take the blame if it was not made into something useful but would leave that up to the potter. Likewise the Jewish leaders could blame none but themselves for the worthlessness of their life's products.

Verse 17. The "telescope" was lengthened and the prophet saw the time of Israel's return from captivity. This was in keeping with God's great love for his people. He determined to punish them with captivity, but he tempered the threat of that prediction with one of the opposite character. Most of the forecasts from here to the close of the chapter were so general in their nature that we can find them fulfilled also in the days of the Gospel. However, the immediate application was to the time when the Jews would recover from their fallen state at the hands of the Babylonians, which had been brought on them through the stubborn blindness of the leaders in Jerusalem.

Verse 18. The *deaf* were the ones who had stopped their ears against the truth, and the *blind* were those who had closed their eyes against the light of God's instructions. Chapter 1: 3 and Jer. 5: 21 should be consulted in connection with this subject.

Verse 19. The *meek* and *poor* had been imposed upon by the selfish leaders, but after the return to their own country these unfortunate citizens will be able to rejoice in their freedom, not only from the captivity among the heathen but from the wicked leaders among their own people who had taken advantage of them in former years.

Verse 20. *Terrible one* and *scorner* is the same one as *scornful*, ch. 28: 14. It refers to the haughty leaders among the Jews who had been largely responsible for all of the misfortunes that befell them. It was true they were to share in the blessings of the release from captivity, but the class described in the preceding verse would get special satisfaction from the release by observing that they were also delivered from the tyranny of those described in this verse.

Verse 21. The wicked leaders is still the subject of this verse. *Make a man an offender for a word* means they caused an innocent man to be convicted unjustly through their false testimony. *Lay a snare for him that reproveth* denotes that they misled the judges by their false testimony. They would *turn aside the just* or defraud him of his rights by quibbling over a trivial point.

Verse 22. *Redeemed Abraham.* The Jews descended from Abraham, and when they were redeemed from captivity it was considered as the Lord's having redeemed the great patriarch. *Shall not now be ashamed* means the feeling of triumph the people would have upon their deliverance from captivity.

Verse 23. When the people shall see the good work of the Lord among them they will rejoice. They will *sanctify* or bless the *Holy One* for his wonderful favors.

Verse 24. The leaders who had erred in their conduct will learn better. They will learn it the "hard way" which will be through the experience of the captivity.

ISAIAH 30

Verse 1. The *rebellious children* is a term of general application for the Jews as a nation. It could be justly so applied because the common people endorsed the teaching of the prophets and the doings of the religious leaders. (Jer. 5: 31.) That is why it was said in this verse that the *children* took counsel but not of the Lord.

Verse 2. The Israelites were always interested in Egypt and frequently showed a desire to go there for assistance or other advantages. *Walk to go down* indicates their walk or practices were inclined toward Egypt. They preferred the advice they thought they could obtain from Pharaoh to that of God.

Verse 3. When they would expect Egypt to give them the support they wanted it would not be realized. This would shame them and throw them into confusion.

Verse 4. *Zoan* and *Hanes* were places in Egypt. The Israelite chieftains were so confident of receiving help from Egypt that they came to these localities to receive it.

Verse 5. Their expectations were to be disappointed and the Egyptians were to prove to be the shame of the Israelites.

Verse 6. See the comments at ch. 13: 1 for the meaning of *burden*. The uselessness of looking to Egypt for anything is still the subject of this verse. *South* is a reference to that country from its direction from Palestine. *Trouble and anguish* was true both as concerned the actual experience of Israel with Egypt in the past, and also in view of the disappointment that was awaiting them upon their approach to that country for help. Reference to the beasts was a description of the wild and rough nature of the country under consideration. The Israelites were represented as carrying whole beast loads of *riches* to Egypt as presents (see the comments at Gen. 32: 13; 1 Sam. 10: 27), to purchase the services of that country. The prophet then commented that those people would be of no profit to Israel.

Verse 7. Even if the Egyptians should try to help Israel, it would be of no avail if the Lord were minded to punish his people. *Strength* is defined in the lexicon as "bluster," and *sit still* means to refrain from any activities. The thought is that all of the show and ado that might seem to be coming from the Egyptians would amount to nothing and the Israelites would have been as well off not to expect anything.

Verse 8. The Lord directed the prophet to write this declaration in a *table* (tablet) as a permanent record for future reference.

Verse 9. God was accusing his own people of being rebellious and given to lies. This accusation was to be written in a book that later generations might know why He had dealt thus with Israel.

Verse 10. *Seers* and *prophets* as used in this verse referred especially to those who not only could see into the future, but who admonished the people concerning their duties. The people did not want to be disturbed in their selfishness by unpleasant rebukes or threats of the future. The descriptive word *deceits* was not what Israel actually called for, but was the prophet's description of the things called for by the disobedient people. See the comments on a like passage in ch. 28: 15, and see also the statement in Jer. 5: 31 regarding the general attitude of the people.

Verse 11. The Jews never demanded directly that the prophets were to turn the Lord against them, but that was what their clamor meant in the view of Isaiah.

Verse 12. The Lord then made a direct charge against his people, that they *despised* (belittled) his word and chose the way of fraud and oppression.

Verse 13. The downfall of the nation was sure to come and it was not far off. The condition was likened to a weakened place in a wall that was liable to fall any time.

Verse 14. This verse is a figurative picture of the breakup of Judah by the siege and captivity that was near at hand. A vessel of pottery was broken so completely to pieces that not a scrap was left large enough to carry a coal of fire or a drink of water. The fulfillment of this prediction is recorded in 2 Ki. 24 and 25.

Verse 15. The last four words of this verse indicate the meaning of the passage. *Returning and rest* denotes a state of trust and satisfaction. Had the people of Israel been content to rely on the Lord instead of turning to Egypt or other heathen nations, they would have been *saved* or preserved from the calamity about to be brought upon them.

Verse 16. The first clause repeats the close of the preceding verse. The people of Israel boasted that they would help themselves by the horses and other means of rapid travel, and they thought to obtain these things from the Egyptians and other heathen nations. So the prophet warned them that they would travel, indeed, by such means or causes and at such a rate of speed, but it would be on account of the cavalry and speed of their pursuers at the time of the invasion of the enemy.

Vese 17. The prediction of the preceding verse was continued in this. These predictions may be found also in Lev. 26: 8 and Deut. 28: 25. The fulfillment may be seen in 2 Ki. 24 and 25. *Left as a beacon* refers to the same state of isolation as was predicted in ch. 1: 8. *Beacon* is from TOREN and Strong's definition is, "a pole (as a mast or flag-staff)." The deserted condition was likened to that of an army that was completely routed until nothing was left but a solitary pole on top of a hill.

Verse 18. The patience and compassion of the Lord is the most wonderful thing that was ever known to man. Whatever chastisement the people deserved, it was always administered in love and for their own good. (See Heb. 12: 5-11; Rev. 3: 19.) *Wait* is from CHAKAH and Strong's definition is, "properly to adhere to; hence to await." The meaning of the verse is that God would give his people the punishment they needed, including the period of the captivity, but would not lose patience with them. He would wait like a loving parent until they had learned their lesson, then receive them back again into his favor. In view of such a kind and indulgent Father the prophet declared all would be *blessed* (happy) who would *wait* (rely) on Him.

Verse 19. In keeping with the spirit of compassion described in the preceding verse, this one predicts the return of the Jews from the Babylonian captivity. The Biblical account of that event is in the books of Ezra and Nehemiah. For the secular account of it see the quotation in connection with ch. 14: 1.

Verse 20. *Bread of adversity* and *water of affliction* is a figurative description of the sorrowful state of mind the people would be in while in the captivity. (See Psa. 137.) *Teachers* is from YARA and Strong's definition as it applies to this verse is, "figuratively to point out (as if by aiming the finger), to teach." *Corner* is from KANAPH and a part of Strong's definition is, "an edge or extremity." The meaning is that even in their distress the Lord (their teacher) will not be far away, but will be using their very sad experience to lead them to a better life. (See verse 22.)

Verse 21. This verse continues the thought at the close of the preceding one.

Verse 22. This verse predicts their

cure from idolatry. For the historical fulfillment of this prediction see the quotation at ch. 1: 25. Not only did Israel turn from the practice of idolatry, but their abhorrence of it was compared to the disposal of a defiled garment.

Verse 23. This passage is a promise that after returning to their own land, the people of Israel would be permitted again to use their farms. The land had been let rest from cultivation for 70 years to recover the years of rest taken from it by the greed of the nation, but after the return it would again be tilled.

Verse 24. What livestock had remained while the citizens were away had to live on the rough and wild vegetation that grew of itself. Afterward the cattle will be fed upon grain and roughage that has been properly harvested and prepared.

Verse 25. The subject still is the triumph of Israel over their foes. The verse is highly figurative in describing the returned prosperity after getting back into their own country. *Great slaughter* and *towers fall* refers to the overthrow of the Babylonians who had been holding the Jews in captivity.

Verse 26. The good fortune of the Israelites continues to be the subject, expressed in symbolic language for comparison. The dark years of bondage in Babylon will give place to the great light of freedom in their own land. *Breach* and *stroke* refers to the broken condition the Jewish nation suffered by being taken out of their own land and their institutions being left in ruins.

Verse 27. After the people of God had been punished sufficiently, he turned his wrath against the nation that had been the instrument for the chastisement. *Cometh from far* shows that God occupies the space even to distant points, yet he can cover the expanse and come to any spot where it is necessary.

Verse 28. The wrath of God against the Babylonians is still the subject of the prophet. Of course it is being described in figurative terms, which is in keeping with most of the expressions in the prophetic writings. *Sift the nations* means to shake them down because of their vanity or national pride.

Verse 29. The subject is again the joyful feeling of the people of God because of their release from the captivity. The exercises described are those in connection with the services to the Lord and they are enjoyable.

Verse 30. In several verses the prophet has been writing on the two subjects, now on that of the wrath of God against the Babylonians and now on the joy of the Jews over their deliverance from the captivity. In this verse it is the arm of the Lord as a heavy power pressing down with indignation upon the foe, all of it being expressed in figures of speech. The Lord's *voice* refers to the mighty predictions that He made against the people who were to bring the captivity upon them of Jerusalem. It was to be done as a chastisement of the Jews for their sins, but the instrument of that service was in turn to feel the mighty hand of God in righteous revenge.

Verse 31. It appears that the term *Assyrians* is used by the prophet from time to time with a various application. While that people was in power under that name they actually persecuted God's people (2 Ki. 17 and 18), and when the Babylonians came into power, the term Assyrians was used sometimes because they all occupied practically the same territory in their turn. Hence it matters little which term we are reading, the final results of God's wrath as predicted were fulfilled.

Verse 32. *Grounded staff* was the rod of God's rule against any who incurred the divine wrath. In the present case it was the destruction of the foe who had been in control of God's people and had held them in captivity. *Tabrets and harps* were instruments of music that were used in connection with any successful triumph over an enemy.

Verse 33. *Tophet* is defined by Strong as follows: "a place of cremation." It referred to a place near Jerusalem where fires were kept burning to destroy the bodies of animals and convicted criminals. But previously the place had been used for the burning of sacrifices, even the living children cast into the fire, to the heathen god Moloch (2 Ki. 23: 10). It is used figuratively in our verse to signify that God would destroy the Babylonian Empire and sacrifice it to His righteous indignation. *The pile thereof is fire and much wood* is figurative, and referred to the same thought expressed in the preceding sentence. No literal fire and wood was to be used, but the figure was based upon the fact that such literal elements were used on the altars in *Tophet* where sacrifices were offered to the heathen god.

ISAIAH 31

Verse 1. The chapter starts with another rebuke of the Jews for their reliance upon Egypt. I request the student to read carefully all of the comments on ch. 30: 2-7. The present verse gives some of the specific items of interest that induced Israel to turn to Egypt. That country had long been noted for its horses, and God's people had been warned on the subject (Deut. 17: 16; 1 Ki. 10: 28). It was bad enough for them to seek help from Egypt, but worse still they did not even seek counsel of the Lord.

Verse 2. *Will not call back* means the Lord would not reverse his predictions against his disobedient people. He was determined to *arise against* them and also against any who would be so rash as to offer them help.

Verse 3. The leading thought in this verse is that human strength is useless when it is arrayed against the Lord. No matter how many or how much are the men and power that are conspiring against God, they will surely fail in the end. (Rom. 8: 41.)

Verse 4. The helpless efforts of human shepherds against the strength and destructiveness of vicious beasts is likened to the opposition by heathens against God.

Verse 5. Birds fly over the heads of men and thus are superior to them in the surety of their movements. This fact is used to compare the independence of God in his defence of his beloved people when they are misused by the nations of the world.

Verse 6. God has decreed to defend his people against the heathen nations even though they (his people) had revolted from their Lord. The prophet gave a general exhortation to all people to turn unto Him from whom Israel had revolted.

Verse 7. God's successful dealing with the foe who had held his people in captivity will free them from that captivity. The purpose of that chastisement was to cure them from the proneness to idolatry. Having accomplished that purpose the instrument of that service was to be overthrown. The present verse was a prediction of that cure, and the historical confirmation of it was quoted at ch. 1: 25.

Verse 8. For comments as to the *Assyrians* see those at ch. 7: 17 and 30: 31. The great Babylonian Empire fell on the night of Belshazzar's feast (Dan. 5: 30, 31). It is true that the sword was used and doubtless many were slain; but that was not the way the city was entered. The walls were not stormed and the defending army subdued by military force of arms. The city was entered by the peaceful strategy and activities of Cyrus. For the historical account of this see the quotation at ch. 13: 7, 8. *Flee from the sword and his young men shall be discomfited* (confused and scattered). On this point I shall quote a part of the historical note referred to above. "When this was said they [the Persians] marched; and, of course that they met with some they fell on and killed, some fled, and some set up a clamor."

Verse 9. This verse continues the line of thought running through the preceding one, which is the complete overthrow of the Babylonian Empire. *Fire* is used in the sense of home fires and signifies one's headquarters or dwelling place. That was said of Zion which was the capital in Jerusalem. The overthrow of Babylon by the Persians was by the decree of God, whose headquarters were in Zion.

ISAIAH 32

Verse 1. It has been often stated, and correctly so, that Isaiah said more about Christ and his church than all the other Old Testament prophets put together. Many times, too, he wrote his predictions just after having dealt with ancient Israel's recovery from the long captivity and restoration to power in their own land. It was appropriate that he do so, for the reign of Christ, like the restoration of Israel, came after a period of spiritual decline. Although this and the following chapter will be leading up to a more direct picture of the Gospel plan of salvation, the prophet will intersperse his writing with frequent denunciations of the Jewish nation. Their leaders especially had been corrupt so frequently that the Lord wished to keep them reminded of the effect it had upon the lot of their national inheritance. He also will make charges against certain heathen people who had shown enmity against those of the Lord. I trust these general remarks will be borne in mind as the study of the text is continued. *A king shall reign in righteousness* evidently refers to Christ. At the time Isaiah wrote this the Jewish nation had already been living under kings for hundreds of years, so that fact would be nothing new. But most of them were unrighteous, and the prediction of the present verse was looking to the future and would mean Christ.

Verse 2. Jesus was both God and man and was therefore a suitable person to provide comfort for others who were men only (Heb. 2: 16-18). The spiritual comfort that was to come to the followers of Christ was compared to a shelter or *covert*, to water for the thirsty and cooling shade in a parched and desert land.

Verse 3. Further benefits under Christ were likened to improved seeing and hearing.

Verse 4. The superior instruction to be had by the citizens of the kingdom of Christ was seen by the prophet. The *rash* means the ones of poor judgment and the *stammerers* are those who have poor speech. All will be benefited by the instruction offered in the spiritual school of Christ which means the church. They will be taught to "speak as the oracles of God."

Verse 5. *Vile* means stupid and impious, and *liberal* means gracious and friendly. *Churl* means stingy and *bountiful* means freehearted. Under the reign of Christ a man will be given credit only for his true character.

Verse 6. This verse shows why such characters as are described in the preceding one will not be given endorsement in the kingdom of Christ. It is because a vile man would speak *villany* (wickedness), and his heart would plan some iniquity in a hypocritical manner. He would deprive the spiritually hungry and thirsty of that which would satisfy them. In Matt. 5: 6 Jesus shows that such desire is for righteousness and the evil characters of this verse would interfere with it.

Verse 7. The *churl* or stingy man will use any means within his reach, whether right or wrong, to gain the possessions of the poor. Such a person will make up a story as a basis for his demand for the other man's money. *Needy speaketh right* means the poor man complains of the treatment he is being accorded by the greedy man, and even when his complaint is just, he is forced to give up his belongings. This kind of mistreatment was a common practice among the people (ch. 5: 8, 23; 58: 3).

Verse 8. A man who is friendly and freehearted will scheme and plan, but not for the purpose of defrauding another. Instead, he will be seeking ways to help some needy person, and as a result he will be backed up or caused to *stand* by the very good provisions he had brought about for others.

Verse 9. *Women* at ease were those who wasted their time and energy with their vanities. See a detailed description of them in the verses at ch. 3: 16-23, and read the comments on the several verses.

Verse 10. These frivolous women were told their days of luxurious living would give way to years of trouble. They were destined to be taken away into captivity along with the men. *Vintage shall fail* means the source of their extravagance would fail.

Verse 11. *Strip you and make you bare* sounds like an order or command. It is the prophetic style of making a prediction that such a thing would take place. Their flashy and extravagant life was to be reversed, and their perfumery and personal make-up would be replaced by opposite conditions. (See ch. 3: 24.)

Verse 12. *Lament for the teats.* The first word is from CAPHAD which Strong defines, "a primitive root; properly to tear the hair and beat the breasts (as Orientals do in grief); generally to lament; by implication to wail." The last word is from SHOD, and Strong's definition is, "in its original sense of contraction; the breast of a woman or animal (as bulging)." The meaning of the verse is that they shall beat their breasts in lamentation over the loss of their fields and vineyards. The fields and vines furnished a source of their luxurious living, and that was to be denied them because they would be in a foreign land. They then could only lament the loss of those things which they had so thoughtlessly misused.

Verse 13. This verse could have a figurative meaning, for *thorns* and *briers* fitly represent a condition of desolation and distress. But it was also fulfilled literally in the years of the captivity. The land was to be given a 70-year rest in order to regain those taken from it by their disregard for the Sabbatical year. (See Lev. 25.)

Verse 14. The forsaken condition of the land during the captivity is the subject of this verse. (See ch. 1: 7.)

Verse 15. After the Jews will have suffered sufficiently to satisfy the Lord's plan of chastisement, the captivity will be ended and they will return to their own land. The verses including this to the end of the chapter should be marked by a bracket and titled "the return from captivity." This favor is described by the prophet as the spirit's being poured upon them from on high. The Biblical account of the fulfillment is in the books of Ezra and Nehemiah. The historical confirmation is at ch. 14: 1.

Verse 16. *Judgment* is used in the sense of justice for the people. It will be a contrast with the state of tyranny the leaders imposed on the common people previously.

Verse 17. *Peace* will be brought about as a result of righteousness in the rulers and hence will be just. *Quietness* and *assurance* mean the same as peace.

Verse 18. *Peaceable habitation* means the Jews will again reside in their own land in peace. The enemy nation will have served the Lord's purpose of chastisement for the disobedient people of Israel, and will not be permitted to enslave them again.

Verse 19. A short diversion to predict the downfall of Babylon is the subject of this verse. That event was necessary to make possible the return of Israel to Palestine.

Verse 20. The waters of peace and prosperity is the figurative reference to the happy condition that will be enjoyed after the nation returns from captivity. The people will again be permitted to follow their agricultural pursuits. The land will have received its deserved rest and its owners may use it for their personal good.

ISAIAH 33

Verse 1. Many of the statements of this verse could truly be applied generally because of the principles involved. However, following close on the line of thought at the close of the preceding verse, the evident reference is to the Babylonians. They had never been wronged by the people of God, yet they had wronged them by taking them away into captivity. Therefore, when the captivity is over—*when thou shalt cease to spoil*—that people in turn shall be spoiled. It will be done through the instrumentality of the Persians but by the decree of God.

Verse 2. This verse predicts the prayerful state of mind the Jews will be in while in the land of their captors. (see Psa. 137.)

Verse 3. *Lifting up of thyself* denotes that God will be the cause of the overthrow of Babylon by the hand of the Persians. The great world empires were composed of many smaller nations, hence the overthrow of the Babylonian Empire would mean that *the nations were scattered* in the sense of the prophet's expression.

Verse 4. The pronouns *your* and *he* refer to the Lord who was to direct the movements of the Persians against the Babylonians. *Caterpillar* and *locust* were species of the same insect. Their widespread ravaging of useful vegetation is used to compare the thorough overthrow of the enemy by the Lord.

Verse 5. The Lord dwells *on high*, that is in Heaven, but Zion or Jerusalem was the earthly headquarters of His dominions. He had endowed that place with *judgment and righteousness*, which assured the citizens of their just consideration.

Verse 6. All justice must be according to wisdom and knowledge, therefore God stabilizes his *times* or period of his reign by such qualities. Such endowment will give to His kingdom the strength of salvation. The fear or respect for the Lord is indeed a great treasure, and such a prize will be for those who are faithful citizens of His.

Verse 7. Let it be remembered the leading thought in these verses is the Lord's wrath against the Babylonians, even though their services were wanted in the chastisement of the wayward Jews. Because of that wrath the motives of the *valiant ones* or messengers, and the *ambassadors* of the enemy shall be disappointed.

Verse 8. It will be well for the student to read very carefully the comments on ch. 32: 1. This will refresh him as to the intermixing by the prophet of the references to the disobedient Jews and the cruel Babylonians. Some of the shortcomings of the Jews are included in this and some following verses.

Verse 9. *The earth* is a figurative

Isaiah 33: 10-21

reference to the land of the Jews. (See at ch. 24: 1 etc.) This is a prophecy of the depression that was to come on the nation because of its sins. *Lebanon* and the other places named were choice spots in Palestine. They were all to be despoiled of their benefits by the invasion of the Babylonians.

Verse 10. This is expressed in the first person because it was the Lord who was to cause the invasion. The foreign nation would be acting (unintentionally) as an agent to bring about the chastisement of a disobedient people.

Verse 11. This refers to the helplessness of the Jews when their land is attacked. It is compared to the disappointment a person would have whose harvest would leave nothing but the straw and chaff. The grain will have been taken by the foe.

Verse 12. *Lime* is from SIYD which Strong defines, "lime (as boiling when slacked)." The boiling of slacking lime and the burning of very combustible fagots is used as a figurative description of the national destruction.

Verse 13. *Far off* and *near* is a warning that all the people should take notice. *Have done* is past tense in grammatical form, but is a prophetical style of predicting something yet to come by the decree of the Lord.

Verse 14. *Sinners in Zion* has special reference to the leaders of the Jewish nation who were chiefly responsible for the corruptions. The *fire* and *burning* means the same as that of verse 12. The leading characters are called hypocrites because they had used their religious rituals as a covering for their wickedness. (See ch. 1: 10; 3: 13-15; 58: 3, 4; Amos 6: 6.) The hypocrites are predicted as asking how they can stand such burning chastisement.

Verse 15. The question of the preceding verse is answered in this. I request the student again to read the long comment at 2 Ki. 22: 17 in Vol. 2 of this Commentary. Note especially the part that sets forth the advantages of those who were religious among the leaders, for that is the meaning of this verse.

Verse 16. The thought of the preceding verse is continued in this. The righteous man shall have a high place in the eyes of the Lord. His refuge with God will be as strong as a fort built of rocks, and his provisions will be an abundance of food and drink. Of course this would be true both literally and spiritually.

Verse 17. Isaiah seldom leaves a prophecy touching the improved condition of ancient Israel after a period of depression, without seeing something pertaining to the time of Christ. Hence the title "Evangelical [of the New Testament] Prophet" that has been generally ascribed to him. He is introducing a few verses now on that subject, and the *king in his beauty* is evidently a reference to Christ.

Verse 18. After the captivity was over, the Jews could muse over their past experiences with great satisfaction. They could ask with exultation about their former tormentors who had been subdued. *Receiver* (of tribute) and *towers* refers to the officers and armaments of those tormentors who were finally defeated. The circumstance also illustrates the spiritual victory of those who will be in the kingdom of Christ.

Verse 19. *Thou shalt not see*, etc., means first that the Jews were not again to be enslaved by such people as the Babylonians. They were described as a fierce people; a people who used a tongue foreign to the Jews. No, they will never again be forced to look at such a despotism as the one that had forced them into bondage, for all world powers were destined to be overthrown never to rise again.

Verse 20. The preceding verse brings the scene down to the time of Christ when the *king* of verse 17 was to take the throne. That kingdom was destined to cause the final end of such institutions as have been under description in the preceding verses. The same fact is predicted in Dan. 2: 44. As a result of this edict of the Lord, his people will no more have to look upon those institutions; instead, they will look upon *Zion the city of solemnities. Tabernacle* and *stakes* and *cords* refers to the temporary nature of the former structure in which the Lord's people worshiped him. It will now be the kingdom of Christ that is destined to "stand forever."

Verse 21. The practices of mankind are often used in the Bible to illustrate either by comparison or contrast, the spiritual benefits and enjoyments under Christ. A *galley with oars* was an ancient form of ship that was propelled by oars that were operated by human strength. The oars were arranged in long rows on the sides of the vessel, and those rows of oars were called *galleys*. In many cases they were worked by prisoners who were penalized or "sentenced to the galleys." The circumstance was used by the prophet to illustrate (by contrast) the freedom enjoyed in "the ship of Zion."

Verses 22, 23. The subject of a seagoing vessel as an illustration of the ship of Zion is still in the eye of the prophet as he looks through the "telescope." *Tacklings* means "inheritance." and *loosed* is defined "to disperse." The meaning is that in the church the good things will be for all, not just for the selfish leaders as they did it in ancient Israel. *Strengthen* is defined "to seize," and *mast* means a "flag-staff" as a signal of defense. The poor had previously been denied their rights and they could not help themselves. *Could not spread the sail* denotes that the common people did not have any voice in the management of the vessel. The last two clauses are less figurative and means the benefits will be fairly distributed. The verse as a whole means that in the reign of Christ will be equal privileges for all, and no discrimination will be made between persons. (See Gal. 3: 28.)

Verse 24. In the kingdom of Christ there need be no spiritual sickness which means a condition of sinfulness. The remedy for such illness is the blood of Christ, applied to all who will comply with the conditions. The true inhabitants of this new spiritual country need not complain, saying *I am sick*, for such a state will have been removed by the healing virtues of the blood of the Son of God. (See 1 John 1: 7.)

ISAIAH 34

Verse 1. Before launching again into the favorite subject of the time of Christ, the "telescope" was shortened to give the prophet a view of the world in general. Various heathen nations had opposed God's institutions all through the years, some of them more viciously than others. The terms used in this chapter will be found to have a figurative application. The political and national "heavens" or skies had been overcast with clouds of confusion, and filled with stars or rulers who were wicked and unmindful of the Maker of all things. Even the Jewish as well as the Patriarchal Dispensation was polluted with religious and moral evil. The Lord then was ready to bring the whole mass of mankind under condemnation, and demand attention to the great "day" (Psa. 118: 24) of the Lord. The various warning predictions uttered in this chapter will be considered as we approach the verses in their order.

Verse 2. The indignation of God against the nations is still the subject. *Hath destroyed* is past tense in form but future in thought because such is the style of prophetic language as a rule.

Verse 3. *Mountains* in symbolic language means governments and other public institutions. They were destined to be *melted* or dissolved by *their blood*. The specific definition of the last word is "bloodshed," sometimes rendered "blood-guiltiness." The leaders of these institutions had been so guilty of crimes against the people that it was finally to be the cause of the overthrow of the institutions themselves.

Verse 4. With the foregoing thoughts before us, we should have no trouble in understanding this verse, and not apply it to "the last great day" as so many public speakers dramatically do. It had reference to the break-up of the national and political "heavens" that was to take place at the coming into power of the reign of Christ. I very earnestly insist that the student read again, very carefully, the comments on verse one above. If a scroll or written document is rolled up it becomes a "closed book" or a thing of the past. These figurative heavens were to be thus rolled up because the power of God would cause them to "fold up" to use a familiar figure of speech. The end of those men and institutions is also illustrated by a leaf or fig that is caused to fall to the ground and be allowed to go to waste.

Verse 5. Special attention will now be given to one of the heathen nations that had opposed the Lord and his people. That was *Idumea* which is another name for the Edomites or the descendants of Esau. *Sword bathed in heaven*. The second word means "to satisfy" or be made ready. The sword of God's wrath was prepared or made ready for use, and the place of such preparation was to be in heaven. The preparation, then, would be complete and it would bring swift vengeance on the wicked people of Edom.

Verse 6. The imagery is changed from warfare to sacrificing and feasting. The Lord's sword is used to take

Isaiah 34: 7-17

rich game for use in the feast, and the blood is shed according to the established law that it should not be eaten. The choicest of the animals are to be slain for the occasion. *Sacrifice in Bozrah* means the sacrifice was to be at the expense of Bozrah which was an important city of Edom.

Verse 7. A *unicorn* is a large, wild bull. *Bullocks* and *bulls* are practically the same except the second is used more figuratively to include strong and outstanding men. Strong's definition of the original is, "chiefest, mighty (one), stout [-hearted], strong (one), valiant." The literal definition cited should be applied because the whole prediction in the passage is one of defeat of the wicked men of the Edomite nation. However, in the figurative view of the event, the prophet saw the whole land saturated with blood of the victims slaughtered for the great sacrifice.

Verse 8. Paul said (Rom. 12: 19) that vengeance belongs to the Lord. In the present verse the Lord's vengeance is prediced to be poured out to recompence for the injustices commited by the leaders in Edom. They had perpetrated those evils against Zion which represented the nation of the Lord.

Verse 9. This verse through verse 15 should be marked as a bracket and regarded as a prediction against the land of Edom. Many of the conditions sound like those made against Babylon (ch. 13: 19-22), but nothing strange should be thought of it. If a territory should be as completely shorn of attention and care as was predicted of these places, the result would be largely as predicted as a natural consequence. That would be especially true if the Lord decreed that the caretaking was never to be resumed. The *pitch* is the same as tar and the *brimstone* is like sulphur. The two elements would be set on fire which would fill the land with sulphurous fumes.

Verse 10. This verse is what makes the prediction permanent. The territory was to be made lie waste and be impassible continually.

Verse 11. The land in general was to lie in the terrible state described above so that human beings would be unable to endure in it. However, there would be certain isolated spots where the doleful creatures such as are mentioned could live and propagate from generation to generation. Hence, even if man could think of avoiding the direct effects of the burning tar and sulphur, he could not endure the presence of these horrible creatures. *Live in confusion* indicates the state of disorder that would come into the territory under the above-described condition. *Stones of emptiness* denotes a field barren of all useful products and scattered over with stones.

Verse 12. This call is used in irony. A great occasion will be going on and the nobles will be invited to attend. But the invitation will be in mockery for they will not be in reach, having been destroyed or banished.

Verse 13. The desolation of the headquarters of the nation of the Edomites will be indicated by the wilderness that will be in evidence.

Verse 14. The doleful site of the place or people will be inhabited by unclean beasts. They will find intimacy with each other and fill the air with their howls. It is characteristic of the owl to prefer the night, hence such unclean creaures will find rest in this abandoned spot.

Verse 15. *Great owl* is a species of the darkness-loving fowl, and a vulture is one that lives on filth. These vile creatures will not be alone when they come to this place, but each will have her mate. A fowl may be able to *make her nest and lay* but the eggs would not hatch unless the female has relations with the *mate*.

Verse 16. *Seek ye out*, etc., means to note what the book of the Lord declares. The declaration is that *no one of these shall fail, none shall want her mate*. The prophet had predicted that the land of Edom was to be occupied by such creatures as are described in the preceding verses. That could be accomplished by the Lord's power in miraculously extending the lives of the originals. Instead of doing it that way, it will be done by seeing that at all times each creature will have a mate, so he can propagate and continue the production of its kind. *My mouth* means the mouth of the Lord, although it was through the services of the prophet that the prediction was made. When anything is uttered either by the Lord direct or by some agency at His direction, it makes that word infallible.

Verse 17. *Cast the lot . . . by line* means the various creatures will be restricted from interfering with each other. Some of them might be inclined even to destroy each other and thus work against the fulfillment of the prediction. This will be prevented by the line that will keep each species in its place. By thus prescribing the state of these unclean creatures they will continue to exist and reproduce in the land. Hence *they will possess it forever, from generation to generation shall they dwell therein,* thereby demonstrating to the whole world the surety of all the Lord's predictions.

ISAIAH 35

Verse 1. This entire chapter is a prophecy of the Christian Dispensation, otherwise called the kingdom of Christ, with its many advantages and obligations. Many of the items are figurative, the prophet using them to illustrate the subject either by comparison or contrast. Other expressions, however, are not figurative, although they are spiritual rather than material in application. This is one of the most noted of Isaiah's chapters and we should give it our best consideration. This verse is one of the figurative ones, comparing the refreshing effect of serving Christ to that of finding a blooming rose in a dreary desert.

Verse 2. The rejoicing with *joy and singing* is a direct reference to some of the exercises engaged in by those in the service of Christ. (Eph. 5: 19; Col. 3: 16; Jas. 5: 13.) *Lebanon* is a noted mountain range in northern Palestine and was famous for its outlook above other ranges. It was also celebrated in poetry and song for the beautiful cedars with their fragrance, and for the texture of the wood. *Carmel* is the name of a mountain not far from the Mediterranean Sea, and its greatest fame was in connection with the contest which Elijah conducted there with the worshipers of Baal (1 Ki. 18). The significance of *Sharon* will be best appreciated by a quotation from Funk and Wagnalls Bible Dictionary: "SHARON, probably from a root meaning 'plain' or 'level country': The undulating [rolling] plain extending from Joppa and Ramleh northward along the Mediterranean coast to Mt. Carmel, about 50 miles long and varying from 6 to 12 miles in breadth. It is unusually fertile (Isa. 65: 10; Song 2: 1). The oak still flourishes in the northern portion as probably in the days of Isaiah (35: 2); the southern portion is richly cultivated. In early spring the luxuriant grass and richly colored flowers render the plain the garden of Palestine." With the description we have of these places it is easy to see why they were used to compare the glories of the kingdom of Christ and the desirability of being members thereof.

Verse 3. This verse is a prediction of the spiritual benefits there were to be received from Christ. In His service the humblest of mankind may be encouraged and given strength not possible for those who depend upon human sources alone. Paul gives us this same thought in 2 Cor. 12: 10; Eph. 6: 10.

Verse 4. *Say to them* is a prophet's form of promising these things to the ones who will accept Christ. *Fearful heart* means those who are unsettled about their prospects. They were to be given the assurances that in Christ they need have no fear.

Verse 5. One outstanding meaning of *opened* is to "observe" or "be aware." Under the reign of Christ men would be led to observe the teachings offered and they would not be blind to the beauties of holiness. To hear in a spiritual sense means to understand and heed what is said. The instructions that were to be offered in the kingdom of Christ would be so clear that the commonest person would be able to grasp it.

Verse 6. The lame (spiritually) would be shown the right of way (see v. 8 below), and would be given strength to walk therein. All of these terms are figurative and yet refer to a direct condition of a spiritual character. Just as a physically dumb man would be miraculously helped were he to be given the power to sing, so the man of the world will be afforded the ability to sing praises to God. A stream of water in a desert would be such a wonderful thing that one whose mouth had become parched through lack of moisture would be enabled to sing for joy by the supply of water.

Verse 7. The use of figures is continued as an effective means of showing the great advantages to be enjoyed in the kingdom of Christ. The illustrations are used in contrast for the good effect of the impression. There are two of the figures in this verse, one dealing with a desert condition and the other with some vile creatures. They were to be made to give way to a condition of life and peace.

Verse 8. *Highway* is from MASHLUL and Strong defines it as follows: "from *SAWLAL*, to mound up (especially a turnpike); figuratively, to exalt; reflex, to oppose (as by a dam): cast up, exalt (self), extol, make plain, raise up." *Way* is from DEREK which Strong defines, "A road (as trodden); figuratively a course of life or mode of action . . . from DAREK, to tread; by implication to walk." The first word means the same as the "narrow way" spoken of by Christ in Matt. 7: 14. The second means the way a man should conduct himself while in this narrow way. *It shall be called* can truly be applied to either separately or to both combined; in either case the idea of holiness is present. Jeremiah (6: 16) had the same subject in mind when he wrote of the *old paths*, applying both to the highway of truth which needs to be sought, and also the manner of one who would "walk therein." Moffatt renders the first part of the verse, "a stainless highroad shall appear, the name, 'The Sacred Way.'" *The unclean* means persons who have not been made free from their sins by obedience to the Gospel. In entering upon this highway of righteousness one must submit to the requirements of the King, and that will cleanse him from his sins and qualify him to travel in the holy pathway. *Shall be for those.* The pronoun stands for the ones already described as having been made free from their spiritual uncleanness. They are specifically called *the redeemed* in the next verse. *Wayfaring* is from a combination of two Hebrew words, one meaning "to walk" and the other "a highway." The word simply means the men who are walking on the *highway* defined at the beginning of this paragraph. A *fool* as used here does not mean an idiot or one who is altogether unintelligent, for such a person would not be in this highway since he is not responsible and hence has no need of being cleansed. It means an ordinary man, one who does not possess any special amount of keen insight. The word *though* is not in the original and is not called for by the context since it adds nothing to the thought. *Err* is from TAWAH and the definition of Strong is, "A primitive root; to vacillate, i.e. reel or stray (literally or figuratively); also causatively of both." The thought is that a man of ordinary intelligence who has entered this highway by obedience to the Gospel, will have no cause for being unsteady or uncertain about how he should walk. The reason for such a conclusion may be seen in a part of the definition quoted of the word *highway* in the beginning of this paragraph. Let the student look again at that place and he will find the words "make plain" in the definition. In attempting to quote this famous passage many people add the words "need not err." The text does not directly contain such an expression, but the sense of the connection would justify its use. But while the above remarks are true, this is a prophecy pertaining to the personal life to be followed in the New Testament period. It will therefore be proper to add a few statements in view of that document. The things necessary to please God are clearly revealed so that no cause exists for being puzzled or confused as to one's duty. However, that does not mean that he can be inattentive and stumble along and expect to keep in the right pathway without giving any serious consideration to the subject. That is why Paul in Eph. 5: 15 instructs Christians to "walk circumspectly," which means to "watch your step" to use a familiar precautionary warning. If a man of ordinary intelligence will use that degree of care that he is able to use, there will be no reason for him to go astray in the manner of his life service for Christ.

Verse 9. Lions and other ravenous beasts are dangerous and otherwise undesirable in the material world. They are used to illustrate (by contrast) the safe and peaceable characters of those who are to travel upon this way of holiness. It is true that such wild creatures as lions will exist near the pathway, lurking near it to grasp any who might be so careless as to step aside from "the good and the right way;" yes, even the worst of all lions, the devil (1 Pe. 5: 8), will be dangerously near, and the travelers on the highroad of truth are warned to be always on their guard, watching their every step lest they slip. But they have the assurance that if they will thus watch and always "walk in the light," no harm can come to them. (Rom. 8: 31; 1 Jn. 1: 7.) *The redeemed* are the ones referred to as "those" in the preceding verse.

Verse 10. *The ransomed* are the ones who will have been redeemed and made ready to travel on the pathway of holiness. *Shall return* denotes those who had been walking in the ways of the world but who left that manner of life and came back to the Lord who had redeemed them with his blood. *Zion* literally speaking was the most important part of Jerusalem, the capital of fleshly Israel. But it was the place from where the Gospel was first preached (Luke 24: 47), and the place at which the church first was spoken of as being in existence (Acts 2: 47). Because of all this the word Zion came to be used as a figurative designation for the church of Christ (Heb. 12: 22, 23). *Songs* would be a part of the exercises of those who were to be travelers on the highway of holiness (Eph. 5: 19; Col. 3: 16; Jas. 5: 13). *Sorrow and sighing shall flee away* does not mean that Christians are to have no unpleasant experiences while in the world for they will. But they will be enabled to find joy even in their troubles and comfort in their griefs (Matt. 5: 4; Jas. 1: 2, 3).

ISAIAH 36

Verse 1. *Now it came to pass.* These words introduce a change in the subject matter of this book where it seems that Isaiah turns historian. However, the works of reference that I have consulted seem a little undecided as to whether Isaiah actually wrote these chapters, or that they were added to his book by those who had charge of compiling the Old Testament. In either case the validity of it would not be affected. Since the passage as a whole is almost verbatim like that in the history proper, I shall refer to my comments on it in the second volume of this Commentary. See the verses from 2 Ki. 18: 13 through 20: 19. That will save much space and will take care of all the chapters in the book of Isaiah through chapter 39. That period of the history covers the time when the Assyrian Empire was threatening the kingdom of Judah, having just successfully taken the 10 tribes off into captivity. It was fitting to insert those chapters at this place, if at all, because it was the interim between the downfall of the 10 tribes and the heavy predictions of the fall of Judah which was to come next against God's people. Thus I again insist that the readers go back to that place in the history and see the chapters with my comments thereon.

ISAIAH 40

Verse 1. We have quite a diversion from the usual procedure since starting in this book. The main thread of thought will now be resumed, and we should expect to find many predictions concerning the captivity of the kingdom of Judah and its return to the home land. Furthermore, there will be frequent instances where the prophet will see into the time of Christ. When the triumph of ancient Israel over her national foes is the subject of the prophet's writing, it might well be expected that he would see some comparison to the grand victory of Christ over all foes in that he was to be able to build his church amid the ruins of all the powers in the world, both religious and political. But for the present verse let us see the attention given to ancient Israel. It promises comfort for the people of God who were destined to go into captivity as a punishment for their sin of idolatry.

Verse 2. *Comfortably* means "to the heart" as if the prophet was told to have a heart to heart talk with the people of God. *Warfare* is a figurative reference to the period spent under Babylonian domination because that event was accomplished by the use of a large army. *Is accomplished* is present tense in grammatical form but is a prophecy then still over a century in the future. But we have already seen that it is according to the prophet's style to speak of future facts in the past tense because with the Lord the future is as well known as the present or past. *Her iniquity is pardoned* means the people of God will have been punished sufficiently for the sin of idolatry. *Double* is from KEPHEL which Strong defines, "a duplicate." Hence it does not mean that God punished his people twice as much as their sins called for. It means the punishment was on a par with or equal to the enormity of the sins. The verse is a prophecy of the return from the Babylonian captivity.

Verse 3. This and some following verses prophesy the work of John the Baptist. (See Matt. 3: 3.) John's work was in preparation for the coming of Christ. The Jews had been the nation of God for fifteen hundred years, and that had been promised to Abraham over six hundred years before the nation was formed at Sinai. In spite of the care the Lord had bestowed upon that people, they had departed from the teaching of the law and had become corrupt in their lives. Now it was necessary for someone to call upon them to make a personal reformation in life and thus form a special group who would be ready in life and character to become the material from which the Messiah could select his first workers. This preparation was to be accomplished through repentance and baptism. (See Matt. 3: 11; Acts 13: 24.) The last part of our verse has reference to this work of reformation.

Verse 4. *Valley* and *mountain* are used figuratively, meaning that all extremes of character were to be adjusted to the requirements of the preaching of John. Those who were low in sin were to be lifted up and their feet be placed on higher ground. Those who were perched upon the mountains of pride and hypocrisy were to be made humble by the teaching proclaimed to them. The other terms of the verse are also figurative and simply mean that all conditions among the Jews were to be made conformed to the teaching of the great Harbinger.

Verse 5. It is reasonable to locate this verse with the work of John, although it is more general in its expressions. But it certainly was true that the work of John caused the glory of the Lord to be exalted. *The mouth of the Lord hath spoken it* means that the preaching of John was by inspiration of God and that would leave no doubt that it would be fulfilled.

Verse 6. The preaching of John was for the special purpose of preparing a people for Christ who was soon to appear among the Jews in Palestine. The definite requirement was that the hearers repent and be baptized for the remission of sins. However, that preaching included many important truths concerning man and his life on this earth. Hence, in the spirit of inquiry, the forerunner of Christ asked for a general subject on which to address those who came out to hear him. He was told to preach of the uncertainty of human existence, and to compare it to the life of grass and other things in the vegetable world. We know this was to have a general application, for Peter quotes it almost verbatim (1 Pe. 1: 24, 25), and applies it to man in general.

Verse 7. The subject is continued as to the uncertainty of human life, also its helplessness when the might of the Lord is turned loose upon it. Such will be the case when the divine law is rejected, for the Lord will cause all the vain purposes of man to wither as surely as the winds of summer heat will blast the growing grass.

Verse 8. In contrast with the fickleness of fleshly existence, the word of God is said to be enduring, even unto the age unending. On this basis the preacher in the wilderness exhorted the people to accept the Lord's word and reform their lives.

Verse 9. See the comments at ch. 35: 10 on the meaning of *Zion*. The *good tidings* that was to come out of Zion was the Gospel and it was preceded by the preaching of John. *Get thee up unto the high mountain* is a prediction that Zion was to become an exalted kingdom, because mountains in symbolic language means governments or kingdoms. Jerusalem was the general city in which Zion was the most prominent spot. *Say unto the cities of Judah* signified that the Jewish nation was called upon to look unto Jerusalem instead of Sinai as the source of the new law. (ch. 2: 3; Luke 24: 47.)

Verse 10. *Lord God will come* is a phrase that may be applied to more than one event, but it here had special reference to the coming of Christ to take over his kingdom (Matt. 16: 28). *His reward is with him* means the reward that Jesus was to receive for his victory over the grave. That contest and his triumph over death and hell won for him the right to become a king over his own kingdom which is the church. This was the subject of the conversation between Christ and Peter in Matt. 16: 18, 19.

Verse 11. Christ was not only to be a king, but also a shepherd over his flock and John was preparing that flock for him (John 1: 11, 12; 10: 1-5). But while the first application of this prediction was to the flock (or fold) that John prearranged for Jesus, it was also true that Jesus was to be shepherd over all people who would become the sheep of his pasture (1 Pe. 5: 4).

Verse 12. Idolatry was the chief sin of the Jewish nation, and it caused its people to disobey the laws of God, prominent among which was the one requiring a rest for the land every 7th year. As a punishment for their sins the people were to go away into captivity and that event is predicted all through this book. In keeping with the subject, the greatness of God's power and knowledge over that of the idol gods is also discussed by the prophet on behalf of the true God. Such is the theme of this and several following verses. *Who hath measured the waters* means who but God could have done such a wonderful work? *Span* is defined, "the spread of the fingers," as if God is so great that just by a motion of his fingers he can decide the limits of the heavens. *Comprehended the dust* means God can account for every grain of dust that it on the earth. *Weigh the mountains* indicates that God knew how to arrange the balancing of the mountains so they would not interfere with the regular rotation of the earth about its axis.

Verse 13. If the Lord had such a wise and powerful control over the whole creation, what human being would be so foolish as to think of being able to direct Him? Man does not even know what is in the mind of the Lord, much less is able to give him any instructions about his wonderful works in the universe.

Verse 14. This verse is a continuation of the idea expressed in the preceding verses. It all is a challenge to the wisdom of man to consider the wisdom of God.

Verse 15. The insignificance of the nations as compared to God is likened to a drop of water in a bucket. The weight of their importance is compared to a grain of dust placed in a balance or "a pair of scales." On the same principle God can lift the *isles*, spots of land containing inhabitants, as if they weighed very little.

Verse 16. For the purpose of comparison a reference is made to the trees of Lebanon as fuel. Though such forestry was regarded as great and important, yet all of its growth would be insufficient to supply the just demands of the Lord. And if all of the animals that roamed the hills of that noted region were sacrificed to the Lord, they would not constitute a service equal to the deserts of the Almighty.

Verse 17. This verse is a general summing up of the comparisons just made in several preceding verses. The conclusion is that the nations of men are as nothing when compared with God, either in power or authority or dignity.

Verse 18. The greatness of God has been the subject of the prophet for a number of verses, describing it in direct contrast with other things that are really of much importance. He now issues the question based on the foregoing comparisons.

Verse 19. Of course no direct answer was expected from the idolatrous people because their own sense would tell them that any attempt to reply would condemn their own inconsistencies. The prophet, therefore, will give his own description of the foolish pretensions of idolaters. One man will make a casting of some kind of metal and then shape it up with an engraving tool. After that another workman will ornament the image with a plating of gold. Then, as if the image might escape or be taken away, another workman will make silver chains to hold it.

Verse 20. God does not require any more from a man than he is able to give. If he is so poor that he cannot furnish an *oblation* (a present), he is excused without doing anything to take the place of the present. But the idolatrous persons are so foolish as to become interested in a god of their own production, since such an image would not be able to make any formal demands. Such an impoverished man will select a durable kind of tree and carve for himself an idol out of the wood. Or perhaps he can secure another workman who will make a metal or stone idol that will be stationary. This is the best that idolatry can do, yet how weak and foolish it is! The inconsistency of turning to an inanimate object like a tree after rejecting the true God is treated at greater length in ch. 44: 13-17.

Verse 21. This verse is a general call to attention. A look at the many evidences in nature would teach these idolaters the folly of their lives. Paul deals with this thought in Rom. 1: 19, 20. None of these works in creation of an inanimate kind have ever been known to reproduce their kind, or to bring into existence any other kind of object, hence their utter weakness should have been apparent to these idolaters.

Verse 22. Verses 19-21 should be considered rather as an inserted passage, or a break into the discussion of the greatness of the true God. Verse 18 called attention to Him by asking some questions regarding possible comparisons, and implying that nothing could truly be compared to such a great Being. Then after the verses on the foolishness of idolatry, the prophet resumes his remarks about the One of whom he had asked the questions in verse 18. He adds emphasis to the questions by stating some facts that specify the boundless might of Jehovah. Combining the inquiry in verse 18 with our present verse, it is as if the prophet had written, "To whom then will ye liken God? I mean he that sitteth on the circle of the earth," etc. *Circle* is from CHUWG which Strong defines, "a circle." It is the word for "compass" in Prov. 8: 27 where we know Soloman was writing about the bosom of the sea. These expressions show that the writers of the Bible understood the earth to be round and they were written hundreds of years before "scientists" thought they had made the discovery. In comparison with such a Being the inhabitants of the earth are as insignificant as grasshoppers. The *heavens* means the sky, and its appearance is that of a curtain or tent. This comparison of the sky to a tent also corresponds with the circular form of the earth.

Verse 23. God has as great a control over the rulers among men as he does over the things of creation. Pharaoh, Balak, Ahab, Jeroboam, Sennacherib, Nebuchadnezzar and many others were made to feel the strong arm of Jehovah against their evil designs.

Verse 24. The great men who exalted themselves in their unrighteous intentions were to be disappointed. Their failure was illustrated by figures of speech drawn from plants in the vegetable world. Such is the application that should be made of the phrases *not be planted, not be sown, not take root.* Wind shall blow upon *them* is like the withering of a weakened plant by the blast of a dry wind.

Verse 25. Once more the Lord challenges his enemies to name something to which they could compare him.

Verse 26. No comparison can be made and the Lord again refers his enemies to the great works of creation. He specifically cites the stars or *host* of heaven and demands of his enemies that they account for them. It was said that Napoleon overheard some critics once ridiculing the idea of there being any God. Interrupting their conversation, Napoleon pointed to the myriads of stars overhead and asked, "Who made all of those?" The silence of humiliation was all the answer the former monarch received to his question. *By number* means that God can account for each star in the universe. Jesus used the word in the same sense when he said that the hairs on a man's head were all numbered (Matt. 10: 30). The last word is from SHEM and Strong defines it, "An appellation [name], as a mark or memorial of individuality." The idea is that God made and continues to recognize each star as completely as if it were the only one.

Verse 27. The greatness of God over all idols has been the subject for several verses. It might be wondered why this verse seems to single out the people of Israel in the criticizing question. It is because they had been so guilty in going off after the heathen nations in the practices of idolatry. That was the reason why the 10 tribes had been given over to the captivity under the Assyrian Empire, and the 2 tribes (kingdom of Judah) was destined to go away under the Babylonian Empire before long. The people of God had become careless and felt secure in their corruptions as if they were not known to the Lord. That is why this verse represents them as saying their *way is hid from the Lord.*

Verse 28. This verse is the prophet's expressions of praise for the greatness of the God of Israel. He reminds the people of what they never should have forgotten, that God is everlasting and that he created all things. *No searching* means that no man is able fully to comprehend the understanding of the Lord, though it is expected that all should learn as much as they can about the divine wisdom.

Verse 29. God is a helper for those who are in need, and will give strength to the weak who are worthy. But he will not bestow such favors on those who do not manifest the proper regard for the blessing. (See Jas. 4: 6.)

Verse 30. Young people naturally are stronger than others and can withstand more trials. However, even they will faint and utterly fall if they do not respect the wisdom and might of God.

Verse 31. *Wait upon the Lord* means to rely upon him and do his bidding. *Renew their strength* means they will increase in the strength of the Lord. *Mount up* means they will be elevated by the Lord with just exaltation. (See Matt. 23: 12.) They *shall run* or exercise themselves in the service of the Lord and will be able to hold out to the end of the race through the assistance coming from the divine source.

ISAIAH 41

Verse 1. The Lord used human agencies to carry out his plans. Sometimes the nations or persons would be a desirable kind in their natural disposition and at others they would be objectionable. It would depend on the nature of the event predicted as to which kind of agency the Lord would choose. However, regardless of the character of the agency employed in any case, the Lord's purpose was always righteous. The outstanding events predicted by Isaiah as pertaining to the Old Testament period were the captivity of the Jews to punish them for their idolatry, and then their release from the captivity and return to their own land. To accomplish these purposes the Lord used various nations; the Assyrians, Babylonians and Persians. In the grand scheme thus formed, some of these nations were used to chastise others for their own unrighteous motives even when they outwardly were performing the will of the Lord. This chapter deals with the events connected with the release of Israel from captivity in Babylon. To accomplish that purpose it was necessary to overthrow the Babylonian Empire, and the agency in God's hands for that work was the Medo-Persian Empire, led by the noted Cyrus. This verse opens up the subject by a call to attention of the people of the earth to the mighty plans of the Almighty. *Islands* is from a Hebrew word that Strong defines, "A habitable spot." It calls upon all people to consider what is about to be accomplished on behalf of the Jewish nation who will have been in bondage under the Babylonians for 70 years. The things about to be predicted will be for the benefit of God's afflicted people. In order to accomplish that, another nation will be given the power to act against the oppressor, and in so doing the people of the Lord will be given a "new birth of freedom," predicted in the words *let the people renew their strength. Let us come near* indicates the spirit of co-operation that will be shown by all parties concerned in the overthrow of the wicked Babylonians, and the release of the oppressed Jews.

Verse 2. For a few verses the prophet speaks for God and centers the attention of mankind upon the One who decreed to bring about the great events soon to come. *The righteous man from the east* means Cyrus, who was destined to lead the forces of Persia against the Babylonians and release the Jews from captivity. The sentences of this whole verse predict the success of Cyrus over the surrounding kings, and his final victory over the mighty empire of the Babylonians.

Verse 3. This is past tense in form as I have previously explained it to be a style of prophetic speech. *He pursued them* means Cyrus pursued the kings and safely overcame them. *Way he had not gone before* denotes his success was in new fields.

Verse 4. Once more the question is asked as to who caused all these things to take place among the heathen kings and nations. Then the answer comes from the Being himself. *First* and *last* is a figurative way of saying that the Lord is all and in all. It is like the declaration made of Christ in Rev. 1: 11.

Verse 5. *Isles* is from EE which Strong defines, "properly a habitable spot (as desirable); dry coast, an island." It means that the inhabitants of all the civilized countries will know about the success of Cyrus and will be *afraid*. That means they will have respect for his work and will give it the deserved attention.

Verse 6. Because of the respect that people will have for Cyrus and his work on behalf of God's nation, they will co-operate and encourage each other in the procedure. See the fulfillment of this prophecy in Ezra 1: 5, 6. That passage shows that the Jews responded to the invitation of Cyrus, and also that the people around them joined in the good work by furnishing animals and materials for the program.

Verse 7. The actions described in this verse took place literally, in all probability, as the work of rebuilding proceeded in Jerusalem after the captivity was ended. But the passage may also be considered as a true picture of the harmonious work of the various forces that responded to the call of Cyrus. The fuller view of the subject will be had by reading the entire books of Ezra and Nehemiah.

Verse 8. This verse gives us the reason why the Lord took such an active interest in the affairs of nations. It was for the sake of his people Israel who had descended from Abraham through Jacob. He punished them for their sins to bring them to repentance, but it was because of his great love for them that he did so.

Verse 9. This verse was true in both general and specific senses. Abraham was called out of Mesopotamia and the

Israelites were taken out of Egypt. Now the prediction was made that they would be taken out from their captivity in Babylon. In all of God's severe chastisements of his people, he kept them near his heart and did not *cast thee away* according to the final declaration of this verse.

Verse 10. Many of the expressions concerning Israel are general and refer to the care that God always had for his people. This verse, however, may truly be understood to have special reference to the release of Israel from captivity and their return to the home land. *Right hand of my righteousness* means that what is done by the hand of the Lord is right.

Verse 11. The events treated of in the prophetic writings are not always chronological as to order and dates of their occurrences. For instance, the preceding verse predicts the return of the Jews from Babylonian captivity, and the present verse predicts the overthrow of Babylon which was to take place before the return of the Jews. However, the manner of presenting these events is logical, for after telling us of the great deliverance of Israel. it was fitting to explain how such a revolutionary happening could take place, that it was through the downfall of Babylon; that is the subject of this and the following verse. The special feature of the subject predicted in this verse is the complete defeat of the Babylonian Empire.

Verse 12. This verse considers the completeness of the ruin of Babylon in that after the empire has been overthrown there will be no trace of its capital remaining. Such is the significance of the words *shalt not find them* and *as a thing of nought.* For the historical confirmation of the prediction see the quotation at ch. 13: 1.

Verse 13. The pronouns *thy* and *thee* refer to Israel and the verse is a promise from the Lord to help them and give them strength to resist their enemies.

Verse 14. *Worm* is used in the sense of the weak and lowly condition of the descendants of Jacob because of their situation in captivity. In spite of their low estate, the Lord will defend them and lift them out of the mire.

Verse 15. *Instrument* is not in the original as a separate word, but the Hebrew word for *threshing* means a sledge or hammer with which grain that is piled on the barn floor could be beaten out for threshing. The figure is used to illustrate the success of God's people over the *mountains* (governments), and they were to have this success by the help of their God.

Verse 16. The figure of a threshing process is still the subject used for illustrative purposes. The power of God's people over others is the thing illustrated.

Verse 17. Previous to the captivity, the rich men and other leaders among the Jewish nation had been taking advantage of the poor and had deprived them of the things necessary for their comfort. All that was to be changed after the return from captivity. When the poor and needy seek for comforts the Lord will supply them.

Verse 18. These contrasting terms in nature are used to make further comparisons of the bountiful provisions that God promised to make for his oppressed people.

Verse 19. There is no historical account of any literal planting of trees as described in this verse. The whole passage is figurative and is intended to give a picture of the good fortune to come to Israel after coming back from exile.

Verse 20. By producing what would seem to have been the impossible, the Lord will prove to the nations his power and superiority of wisdom over all the gods.

Verse 21. This verse is a challenge for all peoples to compete with the power and understanding of the God of Israel.

Verse 22. It would come with poor grace for any god or nation to boast of what it will do in the future if it had nothing great in the past to show. Hence they are here demanded to *show the former things.* All history would put them to shameful silence were they to attempt any such claim.

Verse 23. The challenge continues on the basis of the past. What evidence in the past would prove the power of the heathen gods. The Lord is even willing that the gods of the heathen should perform any evil transaction that would prove their claims upon the fear or respect of man.

Verse 24. The challenging is over and the Lord comes directly to the conclusion that the heathen nations and their gods are nothing. He proposes to show this to be the case by bringing them under shameful defeat. Yea, the gods of the Babylonians were to be overthrown and that event was to take place on the night of Belshazzar's feast at which time they "praised the gods of gold and silver" (Dan. 5: 4).

Verse 25. *I have raised* is the prophet's way of saying "I will have raised." It is a prediction of the rise of Cyrus. As he was actually east of Babylon that direction of the compass is used literally. Then he is said to be from the *north* because the kings and armies from the Mesopotamian region always came into Palestine from the north. (See the note at ch. 14: 31.) The power of Cyrus over the great men of Babylon was to be as sure as that of a workman over clay or building material.

Verse 26. The questions are again in the nature of a challenge to the people of the world to account for the ability to look into the future. The Lord is the only one who has that power, therefore none of the heathen nations were able to resist the decrees announced by the God of Israel.

Verse 27. *Will give to Jerusalem one* is a prophecy of Cyrus. His services were to be used for the benefit of the capital city of the Jews. *Bringeth good tidings* refers to the announcement that Cyrus made concerning the restoration of Jerusalem. This announcement may be read in Ezra 1: 2-4.

Verse 28. The weakness of the nations in the affairs of the future is the thought in this verse. There was no one among them who could show any knowledge of the future or of a choice of person to carry out the Lord's plan concerning Jerusalem.

Verse 29. The prophet makes a final thrust at idolatry. It was the cause of Israel's downfall, but that event was soon to be reversed and the power of the heathen gods will be shown to be vain.

ISAIAH 42

Verse 1. Almost the entire previous chapter was devoted to the calling and work of Cyrus to be the deliverer of Israel from the Babylonian captivity. Much space is yet to be given to the captivity and the return of the Jews to their own land. However, it has been observed that Isaiah often combines his predictions concerning ancient Israel with those of spiritual Israel. Thus we may expect him to intersperse his writings with glimpses of the latter subject. We have such an instance of it in the present verse and it is continued for several more. But to be more specific, perhaps we should regard this passage as bearing on the personal character and work of Christ, who was destined to be the leader of spiritual Israel. We know the present verse had reference to Christ, for it is so applied in Matt. 12: 18-20. The pronoun *my* refers to God and the *servant* means Christ. The *Gentiles* are mentioned because the kingdom of Christ was to be open to Jews and Gentiles alike.

Verse 2. This predicts the mild conduct of Christ. He was not to be a noisy or boisterous speaker, but was to be a modest, retiring person.

Verse 3. A *reed* was the hollow stem of a tender plant. *Bruised* is from a word that means cracked, and *break* means to crush. The gentleness of Jesus was illustrated in this way. He would not be so rough as to crush a reed that was already cracked. *Smoking* is from KEHEH which Strong defines, "feeble, obscure." *Flax* is from PISHTAH and Strong's definition is, "flax; by implication a wick." The clause means that Jesus was to be so undisturbing in his manner of life that even a dimly burning wick would not be snuffed out by his movements near it. *Judgment* is from an original that means a verdict or sentence or conclusion. Jesus was to go about his work quietly and without boisterous pretense, yet his teaching would be firm and his declarations all were to be according to truth.

Verse 4. Jesus was to continue his public teaching unafraid of all of his adversaries. (See all this set forth in Matt. 23.) He would go on in his work until he will have completed the task for which he came into the world. The record of his life shows that he did the very thing that Isaiah here predicted. (John 17: 4.) The *isles* (inhabited spots) were to *wait for* (rely upon) his teaching. (See Mark 12: 37.)

Verse 5. *God* and *Lord* are used in their distinctive senses. (See the comments at Psa. 86: 12.) Both terms apply to the same Being and his great works are mentioned in this verse. The *heavens* means the sky around the earth that has the appearance of a tent spread out. The earth was created to be under the heavens as a dwelling place for certain things coming from it. There is very little difference between the originals for *breath* and *spirit* as used in this place. What little there is may be expressed by saying the first indicates a being that has life, the second that the living being may have an intellect.

Verse 6. *I the Lord* is the Father and *thee* is Christ whom the Lord called, and the call was a righteous one. God promised to hold up his Son so that he could perform the work for which he was to be called. Through Christ the new *covenant* was to be given to the people (Heb. 8: 10). The work of Christ was for the benefit of the Gentiles, not for the Jews only as was the Mosaic covenant.

Verse 7. The terms of this verse are figurative and refer to men who are blind spiritually. The *prison house* is the state of sin in which all people are living until they are turned to Christ. Paul taught that if a man serves a life of sin he is a prisoner to that kind of life (Rom. 6: 16-18).

Verse 8. The importance and significance of the sacred name is shown in detail at Psa. 86: 12. He is jealous of his honor and will not tolerate any competition from other gods. This was taught the Israelites when they received the tables of the covenant at Sinai (Ex. 20: 5). And the same truth is taught by the apostle Paul in Eph. 3: 21. The ancient Israelite nation ignored this teaching and went off after strange gods. As a punishment for this grave error they were destined to spend 70 years in captivity in a foreign land. Likewise, if the professed Israelite of God under the Christian Dispensation disregards the glory of the church, they will suffer for it.

Verse 9. This verse virtually covers the same thought as expressed in the preceding one. The thought is set forth in the words *former things* and *new things*. In other words, the history of the past should have shown the people that the Lord is always displeased when his people try to mix the divine worship with the human. On that basis the prediction was made that future generations would suffer the chastisement of God if they were untrue to Him.

Verse 10. From this verse through 17 the passage may be considered a prediction of the return from the captivity, with some reference to the improved condition that will have come upon the Israelite nation as a result of their period of chastisement. To *sing a new song* means to sing again a song of praise to the Lord for his wonderful blessing in releasing his people from the bondage. All people were to be informed of the gracious deliverance that the Lord will have brought to his oppressed nation.

Verse 11. Various localities are named in order to set forth the general knowledge that will be given of the great blessings bestowed upon the nation that was sent into exile for its sins. *Kedar* was one of the tribes of Arabs who descended from Ishmael. They are singled out here because of their prominence among the enemy nations. This prediction was to remind them that the God of Israel had not forgotten his beloved people, and intended to bring for them a strong revenge for the oppression that the heathen nations had imposed upon them.

Verse 12. *Islands* means the spots or regions that were inhabited. They will be called upon to recognize the greatness of the God of the descendants of Jacob.

Verse 13. This verse is a direct reference to the works of God in overcoming the enemies of his people. Of course it was to be accomplished through the agency of another nation (the Medes and Persians), but it was to be the work of the Lord in reality. God designates himself as *a man of war* because the great deliverance of his people from their bondage will be accomplished through military activities. (See the historical quotation at ch. 13: 7, 8.) *Stir up jealousy* is another reference to the declaration in Ex. 20: 5. It was because of their idolatry that God sent his people into captivity, and then the same jealousy was to stir him up against the idolatrous nation that had been used to chastise the disobedient children.

Verse 14. God had been longsuffering with his own people before he sent them off into exile. Then he was going to be patient with the heathen nations that were to be used as agencies in punishing his disobedient nation. But the time of waiting will be over when the date for the fulfillment of this prophecy comes due. *Will destroy and devour* is a prediction of the complete overthrow of Babylon. The Biblical account of this fulfillment is in Dan. 5. For the historical confirmation see the quotation in connection with the comments on ch. 13: 1.

Verse 15. The reversal of desirable conditions in nature to those undesirable illustrates the calamity that was to come on the heathen country. It had oppressed the people of God, and in turn it was to feel the sting of God's rebuke. The geographical terms of the verse are used figuratively.

Verse 16. The preceding verse was against the Babylonian Empire because it had been the oppressor of Israel. This verse is in favor of the people of God and the terms are also used figuratively. The favor of conducting the blind over a way they had never seen is used to compare the great road to freedom that the Jews had not seen and that appeared to be impossible previously. The *darkness* of their captivity will be penetrated by the *light* of their release from bondage. *Crooked* is from MAAQASH which Strong defines, "a crook (in a road)." Such a road would be unpleasant and difficult to travel, and such is compared to the difficult life the people of God were to experience while in captivity. Their release from that bondage was to remove all such difficulties, and open before them a straight and just pathway of living. This prediction was made for the consolation of the people of the Lord who were destined to go through a long and bitter trial.

Verse 17. The special effect the captivity was to have on the Israelites was to cure them of idolatrous tendencies and practices. It was true that after that experience in their lives they never did again practice the corrupt service. They not only ceased the active practice of it, but were so turned against it that they abhorred it as is predicted in this verse in the words *be ashamed that trust in graven images*. There is a lengthy quotation from history on this subject whch is in connection with comments on ch. 1: 25. This is very interesting as well as important, and I shall insist that the reader take the time and have the patience to read carefully that place.

Verse 18. *Deaf* and *blind* were those among the leaders of the nation who had refused to hear the word of the Lord and who refused to see the folly of their own sins.

Verse 19. The figurative sense of the language is discussed in this verse. The very person whom the Lord had counted on to carry out his will was the one meant. *Perfect* is from SHALAM which Strong defines, "a primitive root; to be safe (in mind, body or estate)." The thought is of one who is self-satisfied that he does not see the dangers that threaten him. That is why this servant is charged with being blind.

Verse 20. This verse brings out more clearly the figurative sense of the blindness charged against the servant of God. He was not literally blind because it says that he was *seeing many things*. The explanation is in the next phrase *observest not*. That word is from SHAMAR and the part of Strong's definition that applies here is, "attend to." In the King James translation of the Bible the word has been rendered by beware, be circumspect, take heed, mark, look narrowly, regard and watch. With the literal and figurative sense of the word in mind, it is easy to understand the several passages in the Bible that speak of people as seeing and yet not seeing. (Psa. 69: 23; 115: 5; 135: 16; Isa. 44: 18; Jer. 5: 21; Ezk. 12: 2; Matt. 13: 13; Mark 4: 12; 8: 18; John 9: 39-41; Acts 28: 26, 27; Rom. 11: 8, 10.) It recalls an old saying that "no one is so blind as the man who will not see." On the same principle this verse also would regard the man as deaf because he refused to hear.

Verse 21. The Lord was not disappointed over his own purposes. The failure of man to do his best was to be expected and such was the meaning of the prediction. The law of the Lord is righteous regardless of whether it is disobeyed or not. When the shortcomings of man are punished, such as inflicting the 70-year captivity, it really does honor to the law and magnifies its authority. Similar principles are taught by Paul in Rom. 3: 3-7 and 2 Cor. 2: 15, 16.

Verse 22. From this verse to the close of the chapter is a prediction of the captivity. *Robbed and spoiled* means the Israelites were made to lose their possessions (2 Kl. 24: 13). *Snared in holes* is a figurative picture of the undone condition the nation was to be in by the attacks of the Babylonians. The whole verse corresponds with the treatment accorded the nation when Jerusalem was attacked.

Verse 23. This verse is a call to attention for the warnings that the Lord intended bringing the punishment on his people in the time to come.

Verse 24. *Jacob* and *Israel* are mentioned in this connection because the latter was the name once given to the father of the 12 tribes, and it in turn came to be a designation for the nation that came from him. The Lord affirms that he it was who was to give Israel over to the robbers (the Babylonians). The reason for it is also given, that it was because of their sins. They refused to walk obediently according to the law of their God. The specific law they violated was that against idolatry, which induced them to disregard the law of rest for the land every 7th year. That law was set forth in much detail in Lev. 25.

Verse 25. *Hath poured* is in the past tense in form but is a prophecy that was yet to be fulfilled. *Fury of his anger* refers to the jealousy the Lord has when his people betray him and turn to other gods. (Ex. 20: 5.) *Strength of battle* was fulfilled when the forces of Babylon came against Jerusalem. (2 Ki. 25.) *Yet he knew not* denotes that the nation of Israel did not realize what it was all about when their city was besieged and finally taken by storm of battle.

ISAIAH 43

Verse 1. The present chapter and the following one will contain some lengthy brackets, generally on the return from the captivity. I suggest that the reader mark his Bible accordingly and make notation of the general subject, then consider the several verses as they are commented on in their order. The first bracket goes from the first verse through 21, and the subject as a whole is the return from captivity. *I have redeemed thee* is prophecy although sounding like history, and it means that God would rescue his people from Babylonian captivity. *Name* is from SHEM and Strong's definition is, "a primitive word . . . an appellation [name], as a mark or memorial of individuality." The idea of the clause is that Israel had a distinctive place in the affections of the Lord and he was going to favor that distinction by calling them His and then bringing them out of their exile.

Verse 2. This verse is a special feature of the general promise for divine support in a time of trial. All of the terms, *water, rivers, fire* and *flames* that Israel will be able to survive, are used in a figurative sense. The force of the passage is to the effect that Israel will be able to survive the test of the captivity and the rough treatment given them by the Babylonians. The promises in the verse have been woven into poetry and song for many years when authors wished to treat of the kindly Providence that attends the people of the Lord. The principles implied in the passage may truly be so used, but it really pertains to the ancient people in captivity.

Verse 3. *Egypt for thy ransom* could justly receive a general application, but it has special reference to the deliverance of Israel from that country in the time of Moses. It was appropriate to mention that fact in this place, because a similar situation was under consideration. The nation had once been in bondage to Egypt for several centuries when God brought them out into their freedom. Now that same nation was to be in captivity for 70 years and the Lord predicted they were to be released. Moreover, in freeing the nation from the grasp of Egypt, that country lost its king and hundreds of its choice men (Ex. 14). Likewise, the deliverance of Israel from Babylon was to be accomplished by the overthrow of that government. *Ethiopia* and *Seba* were districts in Africa and the passage has reference to the service that was received from them on behalf of Israel. (See Psa. 72: 10.)

Verse 4. This is more along the same line as the above. The fact of abandoning the nation to the enemy was not a sign that God ceased to love it. On the other hand, his love was the reason for his doing so and it was for the good of the nation. *Give men for thee* was fulfilled when the leaders of the Babylonian Empire were overthrown and forced to give up their hold on Israel. (Dan. 5.)

Verse 5. This bracket as a whole predicts the recall of the Jews from Babylonian captivity. But it should not be forgotten that God had people scattered over various parts of the world. The account in Jer. 43 may be noticed as an instance of it. Also, when a prophet is in the midst of a passage that started with a specific situation in mnd, he often branches off into a more extended application of the things he started to write about. God always has been attentive to the needs of his people and seen to it that proper measures were taken to meet them. Since *east* and *west* are opposite terms, they are used to express the complete oversight of God for his own.

Verse 6. On the same principle that *east* and *west* were used in the preceding verse, the prophet uses *north* and *south* in this. The idea is to emphasize the thorough watchcare of the Lord over those he claims as his own servants.

Verse 7. The outstanding clause in this verse is, *I have created him for my glory*. The last word is defined in the lexicon as "splendor." This was not a selfish motive on the part of God. If the creation of man may add splendor to the Creator, then man must be a wonderful creature. How regretful it is, that he will often so conduct himself as to lose that splendid character, and become instead a shame upon his Maker. The object of the Lord in making man is the same thought expressed by Paul in Acts 17: 26, 27. Here is another thought for us to consider in this connection. God's purpose to have man as an ornament to the greatness of His own self accounts for the fact that he was made in the image of God. (Gen. 1: 26, 27.) This was not done for any other creature in all the earth.

Verse 8. On the two meanings of seeing and hearing, see the comments and references at ch. 42: 20. The present verse predicts that the people who had been in captivity because they had been blind and deaf spiritually, will have their eyes opened and their ears unstopped as a result of the captivity and its enlightening influences.

Verse 9. This verse is a challenge somewhat like that in ch. 41: 23, and the student will please read that place again, with the comments offered thereon. There was no literal gathering of nations for the purpose suggested here. It is like saying that the combined knowledge of the nations of the world would not be able to explain the great works of God. And neither could they produce any evidence that would justify their opposition to the God of Israel and their rough treatment of that nation.

Verse 10. God's people were his servants and were destined to witness the great events to be brought about by the power of the ruler of the universe. There was no god before the One who made all things that exist, neither will there ever be another. He is the self-existent One who has no beginning and will have no end.

Verse 11. This verse reaffirms the incomparable greatness of the Lord, then adds the quality of being a *saviour*. It is from a word that is defined, "to free or succor." The significance of the quality is in the fact that Israel was to be in captivity, and would need some friend strong enough to rescue them from their peril. The Lord God was to come to their rescue at the proper time and save them from bondage.

Verse 12. God went to the rescue of his people when they were in Egyptian bondage and was successful in delivering them. That was before they had begun to rely on heathen gods. This verse uses that fact as an argument that He is all-powerful and that strange gods are unnecessary.

Verse 13. The Israelites had their book that showed the account of the creation which they professed to believe. That volume sets forth that darkness was everywhere until God said, "Let there be light." Such is the meaning of the words *before the day was, I am he*. Surely, a creator who was in existence before there was any light and who caused the light to come, could be able to resist all enemies including the false gods and the nations that served them. God challengingly asks *who shall let it?* The word *let* is an old rendering of a word that means "hinder."

Verse 14. The prophet now comes directly to the subject on which he has been writing through most of the chapter, which is the deliverance of God's people from their oppressors. The Chaldeans were a special group of leading men in the old times and they finally got control of the Babylonian Empire. Because of that both terms came to be used interchangeably. *Cry is in the ships* is a reference to their navigation on the beautiful stream of the Euphrates. *Brought down* is a prediction of the defeat of their great men of the Chaldean origin. It was accomplished on the night of the famous feast of Belshazzar recorded in Dan. 5: 30.

Verse 15. The surety of the fulfillment of the prediction is indicated by the character of the source from which it was made. This verse is a condensed description of that great Being. *Lord* means self-existent; *Holy One* means he is altogether righteous; *creator of Israel* means He not only was the general source of things, but in a special sense was the originator of the nation addressed; to be *King* means to be the ruler of all. With such an individual back of the promises and predictions they were bound to be fulfilled when the proper time has been reached.

Verse 16. God's power was proved when he opened a way through the Red Sea (Ex. 14), and a passage across the Jordan River (Josh. 3).

Verse 17. *Bringeth forth the chariot and horse.* As a simple statement of fact, this clause may be understood in both a favorable and unfavorable sense. In the former it could be applied where the Lord led the forces of war of a nation to carry out His plan. That took place when the armies of Assyria were used to punish the 10 tribes, and when those of Babylon were brought against Jerusalem. But the connection shows that it is used in this verse in the unfavorable sense. The forces of Babylon were to be led as by an arresting officer, and finally placed in the condition of ruin arranged for them. That was to take place when the Persians would be brought against Babylon. The result of that attack is predicted in the remainder of the verse. Not only was Babylon to be defeated in the attack, but the city was never to be rebuilt. Such is the meaning of *extinct* and *quenched as tow*. The historical fulfillment of this prophecy was quoted in connection with comments at ch. 13: 1.

Verse 18. *Remember ye not* is used as a stirring up of the memory. It is as if it said "Do you not remember the things that have happened?"

Verse 19. The words of this verse are used figuratively but apply to the release of Israel from captivity. That event had never taken place before, hence it would be *a new thing*. A pathway in the wilderness and a river in a desert would not only be a miracle, but would be one to cause much joy. The subject is used to compare the great favor of being freed from the desolation of the Babylonian captivity.

Verse 20. Dumb beasts cannot intentionally give honor to the Lord, but they can be so used that they fulfill the divine predictions, and in that manner they will do honor to God. That specific thing was to take place in Babylon after the Lord takes his people out of it to enjoy the *waters in the wilderness* and *rivers in the desert* (explained in the preceding verse). This prediction is described in detail in ch. 13: 19-22, and the secular history that confirms it is quoted at verse one of that chapter.

Verse 21. In forming the nation of Israel for himself, the Lord was bestowing a greater favor upon them than he was taking upon himself. Therefore they should gladly have done what they could to bring praise unto Him.

Verse 22. From here to the end of the chapter should be included in one bracket and the subject is, "during the captivity." Most of the predictions which we have been studying were either before the event of the captivity, or the return to Palestine afterward. The present passage describes conditions and conduct of Israel while in the land of their captivity. The general theme is that while in that country the Israelites were not even permitted to worship the true God as they should have done in Palestine. Not only so, but they were to be required to participate in idolatrous practices in order that they might get an "overdose," so to speak, of the evil that had been their downfall. Of course these remarks should be understood as applying to the nation as a whole. There were certain individuals who had been true to the Lord who did not have to take part in these heathen services. Among them were Daniel and his three companions (Dan. 3: 12, 18, 27; 6: 10, 23). There is a long note explaining this feature of the subject in connection with 2 Ki. 22: 17 in Vol. 2 of this Commentary. Having seen these comments on the bracket as a whole, the reader will now give attention to those on the verses in their order. *Hast not called upon me, O Jacob* was because the Lord did not permit them to while in captivity. *Hast been weary* means to be tired of something. The Israelites were compelled to act as if they were worn out and not feeling like serving the Lord.

Verse 23. *Small cattle* is rendered "lambs or kids" in the margin which is correct. It indicates a young animal and that was the kind that the law of Moses required of the Jews. But while in the captivity such services were not permitted them. The *sacrifices* would include the larger beasts and other articles of value that the nation offered to God when they were in their own land. Even as small a service as the burning of incense was not acceptable at the time of their stay in Babylon.

Verse 24. *Sweet cane* must be considered as one word and refers to some kind of hollow reed whose fibers were used for making paper. If a Jew wished to present such material for the use of the Lord's scribes, but could not produce it himself, he could buy some with his money and bring it to the headquarters. This service was not possible during the captivity and would not have been acceptable even if it had been possible. The fat (such as the suet) of their cattle always was to be brought to be burned on the altar of the Lord. That was discontinued while in the land of Babylon. *Serve with thy sins* means the only way the Jews served God while in captivity was by continuing in the sins that brought them into their state of bondage, and that consisted of the practices of idolatry. This was predicted so much in detail in an earlier scripture that I think it will be well to quote it, which is as follows: "The Lord shall bring thee and thy king which thou shalt set over thee, unto a nation which neither thou nor thy fathers have known; and there shalt thou serve other gods, wood and stone" (Deut. 28: 36). The Lord really was *wearied* or almost out of patience over their iniquities.

Verse 25. If the Israelites had been dealt with according to strict justice, they would have been utterly rejected; but instead, the Lord promised to forgive and redeem them. However, it was not to be as a reward for their religious activities in Babylon, for such sacrifices never could win the favor of God, even though he had forced them to practice such things. But that was as a corrective punishment upon them and not as an act "for the remission of sins." But this verse explains why the Lord was going to blot out their sins; it was for His own sake, for the honor of his name.

Verse 26. This verse is a challenge for the people to recall any reason if such existed, why the Lord should justify them on the basis of their own merit.

Verse 27. Beginning with the ancestors of their race and coming on down through the lives of their teachers, sin had been committed against the Lord.

Verse 28. *Therefore* is a conclusion that the Lord finally became weary with the oft-repeated and continued transgressions, and hence the bitter experiences they were undergoing in the land of Babylon.

ISAIAH 44

Verse 1. This chapter may be divided into three quite lengthy brackets and each given a general subject. As the case usually is, certain verses in a bracket will have specific applications, yet all bearing some relation to the main topic by which the bracket was designated. It will always be well for the student to keep the main subject in mind while reading the comments on the several verses which will be considered in their order. The first bracket includes this verse through 8, and the subject is the return from Babylonian captivity. The first verse is a call from the Lord for his people to give attention to the word about to be spoken. *Jacob* and *Israel* now apply to the same group. The two names so used go back in history to the time when Jacob had his wrestling match with the angel (Gen. 32: 24-38), at which time he received the name *Israel*. After that the name came to be applied to the nation that descended from Jacob's 12 sons, so that *Jacob* and *Israel* mean the one people.

Verse 2. This verse is an assurance to the people of God that they need not be fearful of the outcome of the captivity. *Jesurun* (like Jeshurun) is from a Hebrew word which Strong defines, "upright; a symbolical name for Israel." Because of its descriptive significance, the word has been used a few times in the Bible to designate the ancient people of God. Since the Lord formed the nation he had a great interest in it and did not intend to let it perish.

Verse 3. These are figurative expressions to compare the help that God was promising to his people who will have been in captivity for 70 years.

Verse 4. Nothing could be more desirable than the results of refreshing moisture, and the subject is used to illustrate the turn of affairs in the Israelite nation.

Verse 5. It is human nature to desire a share in the good things of others. When the lot of Israel turns in their favor, many will want to be classed among that people. There is an outstanding instance of this recorded in Est. 8: 17. This item may be regarded as a side glance of the favorable things that were to happen for Israel when their misfortunes were reversed and they again gained their freedom.

Verse 6. The completeness of the God of Israel is the principal thought in this verse. The title *King* is used because much respect had come to be paid to persons who had it in the affairs of the world. The king of Babylon had taken the Israelites off into captivity and ruled them by his iron power. It was very fitting, therefore, that Israel be reminded of the real King over them. He also called himself their *redeemer* because the subject immediately at hand is the rescue of Israel from the grasp of the heathen power. He also uses the phrase *Lord of hosts*, and the third word is from TSEBAAH. Strong's definition of the word is, "a mass of persons, especially a regiment organized for war (an army)." The Lord has power that is as great as that which can be manifested by all the soldiers in the world. *First* and *last* is a symbol of the entirety of His existence. Such passages as these were especially appropriate because of the central cause of Israel's downfall, and that was their service to the strange gods. They were to have learned the fundamental truth that beside God there is no other, and that all idols are void of any good.

Verse 7. The special feature of God's greatness that is emphasized in this verse is his endless existence. That fact was proved by his ability to appoint *ancient* people and also *things that are coming*. All others are challenged to show a like power.

Verse 8. On the basis of this might of Israel's God, they are given assurance of deliverance from their misfortunes. The declaration of the exclusiveness of the one true God needed to be repeated over and over again, because of the chief weakness of the nation for going after idols.

Verse 9. The subject matter changes and from this verse through 20 the prophet will describe that of idolatry, to show the weakness and foolishness of everything connected with it. Let the reader keep this general subject in mind as he follows the comments on the various verses of this bracket. The first charge the prophet makes against the formers of idols is that they are *vanity*. That word is from TOHUW and Strong defines it, "to lie waste; a desolation (of surface), i.e. desert; figuratively a worthless thing; adverbially in vain." This definition will show us that the charge is correct, for idolatry has nothing to offer mankind but disappointment. *Delectable* means desirable and such things are promised through the services to the true God that cannot be supplied by any idol. *Their own witness* means that the evidence of the uselessness of idols is proved by what can be observed of them, namely: they cannot see and therefore cannot know anything.

Verse 10. This verse is in the form of a derisive question as if it said, "Who would ever think of doing such a foolish thing as making an image that is good for nothing?" *Molten* and *graven* are two ways of making an image. The first means one that is cast and the other means to shape with an engraving tool.

Verse 11. When these men who make idols look at each other and then at their helpless idols, they should be ashamed of the whole situation. They should realize that they are but men themselves and have no superhuman power. Then how could they make any god that would have any more power than they possess themselves? It would seem that they would not have the face to even look at each other.

Verse 12. The work of making these idols is like any other labor of a blacksmith. About all that results from it is the physical exhaustion that comes to the smith, just the same as if he was making an article by which to cultivate the soil. And to think that after he gets the piece made, he will set it up in a corner and bow before it as if it were a god! The whole performance is thus described that all might see how ridiculous the subject of idolatry is.

Verse 13. If a man wanted to build a house in which he or some other human being intended to live, he would be expected to observe the rules and care described in this verse. A structure that is intended to house a human creature should be so built that it would be satisfactory both in appearance and comfort. All of this because man is the most important being under the skies and deserves the best. But here is a workman using the same care in forming an idol which is so inferior to man that it needs to be housed in the same place where its maker lives. A god that is made by the kind of workman that can build a house for an earthly occupant could certainly not have any more power than its maker. So the inconsistency of idolaters is the main point in this verse.

Verse 14. *He strengtheneth* is rendered "taketh courage" in the margin, and the lexicon agrees with it. The thought is that the idolaters count on the use of the trees to make themselves a god that can help them. And yet these are but the plants of the forest that another power caused to exist. Even the ash or other tree that a man might plant must depend upon the rain that the true God causes to fall if it is to be able to live and grow. How foolish, then, to rely on the materials thus produced by the true God, to form man-made gods to worship in opposition to Him!

Verse 15. The weakness of idolatry continues to be the theme of the prophet which he demonstrates by the way its advocates mix it up with other things that are so common. For instance, the same material that is used for fire to warm by and cook man's food, is also used to make a god. *Graven image* means one that is shaped with a carving tool, whether it is metal or wood that is to be carved.

Verse 16. This is practically the same as the preceding verse except that perhaps the prophet tries to show up the inconsistencies of the idolaters a little more by a repetition of the acts in practice among them. Here is this idolater, using part of the same material from which he made his god, to cook his food and warm his body. And yet all the actual benefit he is able to derive from such a source is signified by his common and temporal enjoyment of the comforts of the body. The highest praise he has for this material from which his god is made is, *Aha, I am warm, I have seen the fire.* It is almost juvenile in its sound.

Verse 17. *Residue* means the wood that is left after the meal has been cooked and a warming fire has been made. This wood is then used to form an idol before which the man will fall down and perform acts of worship. He is so foolish as to ask this wooden god of his own manufacture to *deliver* him. This word will be understood better by remembering that the whole passage is a prediction of conditions that will wind up in Babylonian captivity. This idol-worshiping Jew will be so foolish as to call upon his man-made image to get him out of his bondage, and all that when he will know that it was the worship of such dumb idols that got him into his state of bondage.

Verse 18. God does not directly cause any man to do wrong, but he does often abandon a wicked man to his own evil desires, and in such a manner will *shut his eyes.*

Verse 19. This verse gives an explanation of how the eyes were closed as per the preceding verse. *None considereth* accounts for the blindness spoken of and lays the blame for it at the door of the individual himself. After a man has given himself up to such a senseless line of conduct he will become practically blind and deaf to his foolish acts and unreasonable remarks. Hence this idolater forgets all about what he did in cutting down the tree and making an image with part of the wood.

Verse 20. *Feedeth on ashes* is a figurative phrase to show how trivial the interests are of the kind of person being considered. He is completely duped and does not realize that his entire motive in life is false.

Verse 21. The general subject again changes. From this verse to the end of the chapter it will be the return from captivity, with certain predictions of how the event will be made possible. The agency of man and his earthly powers will be seen to be a part of the Lord's great scheme. *Jacob* and *Israel* are directly addressed in this verse because the Lord is concerned in their welfare. Jacob's name was changed to Israel (Gen. 32: 28), and after that the two words were used together as referring to the same nation. The prophecy of the captivity and also the return from it has been the burden of the prophet's writing much of the time, and will continue to be so for much of the remainder of the book.

Verse 22. *Have blotted out* means that the period of the captivity will have satisfied the Lord's anger against the sin of idolatry committed by the nation. After that they were to be released from their bondage and permitted to return to their own land. *As a thick cloud* is a comparison for the completeness of God's mercy toward his people. A thick cloud would hide everything behind it, and the mercy of the Lord was to hide the errors of the nation. *Have redeemed thee* is past tense in form but refers to the rescue of the nation from Babylonian captivity which was to take place at the proper time.

Verse 23. *Heavens, earth, mountains* and *forest* are used figuratively, and it means there should be general rejoicing over the redemption of God's people from the oppression that had been over them for so long.

Verse 24. The Lord frequently identifies himself in addressing the Jewish people and it is done in connection with the things he has accomplished. This is especially appropriate because of the outstanding weakness of the nation. They had forsaken the true God and gone after false ones, those that could do nothing. They could not even move themselves, much less perform any work upon others or in their behalf. God made the heavens and earth unaided by any other being.

Verse 25. The Lord not only can bring to pass his own purposes, but can oppose successfully those of others, which is the meaning of *frustrate*. *Tokens* means signs or omens held out as a prophecy that certain things were going to happen. God knows when these are false signs and exposes them. *Diviners* were people who pretended to foretell the future by some kind of magic or mysterious numbers. *Mad* is from HALAL and one part of Strong's definition is "to rave." When the wicked *diviners* would try to impose on the people, God would expose them which would cause them to rave with shame and disappointment.

Verse 26. God acts in an opposite manner toward the predictions of his own servants and prophets. He not only enables them to see and predict the future, but sees to it that the predictions are fulfilled. The particular event that was in the mind of the Lord, expressed by the prophet, was the restoration of Jerusalem so that God's people could inhabit it again. We should observe that we are still in the bracket that predicts the return from the captivity, and the rebuilding of the capital city would be connected with that affair. The rebuilding of Jerusalem is recorded in the book of Nehemiah.

Verse 27. This verse could truly be said in a general sense because of God's power over these works of creation. However, it has special reference to the overcoming of the Euphrates River which would have been a barrier to the entrance to Babylon had the great military general not used the proper strategy at the time.

Verse 28. This verse comes appropriately in connection with the preceding one since it was Cyrus who was to overcome the obstacle of the great river. He is here called the Lord's *shepherd* because a shepherd exercises a certain care for a flock. And that was truly to be a task placed upon him by the God of Israel. Since the next chapter opens with the same great person, and there are several predictions there concerning him and his work, I will not make further comments on it now.

ISAIAH 45

Verse 1. One meaning of *anointed* is to be consecrated. God selected Cyrus as his agency for accomplishing the overthrow of Babylon and in that sense he consecrated or devoted him to that particular work. It had nothing to do with his personal character, although he was already a good man morally. *Right hand I have holden* means God would give Cyrus success in his work. *Loose the loins of kings* was fulfilled with Belshazzar (Dan. 5: 6). *Open the two leaved gates.* The wall about Babylon had gates or doors, as did the one that was built on the banks of the Euphrates River that ran through the city. In order to get to the king's position it was necessary to get through these gates. The details of that interesting event are quoted at length at ch. 13: 1, 7, 8. In reading that historical quotation I suggest that the student especially observe the part that fulfills the words *and the gates shall not be shut* which are a part of the prediction of the present verse.

Verse 2. *I will go before thee* means that God would be the force in reality that would make the activities of Cyrus successful. *Break in pieces* is figurative and means the gates would not be any hindrance to the entrance of Cyrus and his army into the city. *Gates of brass* are the same gates that are mentioned in the preceding verse, and the history shows they were made of that kind of metal, together with the iron that was used in the structure. It is remarkable to note the detail in which the prophet describes in advance this very important epoch in history. He refers to the very means by which Cyrus was to enter the city, and also gives the name of the man who was to be God's agent in the transaction. It should also be remembered that this noted prophecy was made over a hundred years before it was fulfilled, thus proving the wisdom of the God of heaven who inspired Isaiah to write it.

Verse 3. This verse is a promise that Cyrus would get possession of the treasures that had been hoarded up in Babylon. The motive for making such a prediction in behalf of Cyrus and then fulfilling it upon him, was to prove to him it was the God of Israel whom he was serving in the great movement. Even the detail of putting his personal name down in the inspired prophecy was a link in the chain of divine evidences.

Verse 4. *Surname* is from KANAH and Strong's definitioin is, "a primitive root; to address by an additional name; hence, to eulogize." Thus we understand the statement does not refer to the name Cyrus for that was not an additional name, and it was the one commonly known to belong to him in his own day and that he had received independent of God. The mention of that name was merely a prediction of the inspired prophet which was one of the evidences that God was able to see into the future and enable his servants to foretell it. But God did eulogize and hence *surname* Cyrus in that he called him his *anointed* and said other favorable things about him. *Though thou hast not known me.* Cyrus was a good man morally, but he was a heathen in religion. The above clause means Cyrus unconsciously fulfilled the predictions of the inspired prophet. In other words, he was not called to this work on account of any previous devotion to or knowledge of the true God of Israel.

Verse 5. The language is still addressed to Cyrus and repeats the fundamental principle that there is only one true God. It is not enough to acknowledge the Lord God to be such, but he must be recognized as the only one. That would mean that all other gods are false and without any authority. To *gird* means to bind one's body so as to support it. God did this for Cyrus though he had never previously known Him. (See the comments on this point in the preceding verse.)

Verse 6. *That they may know* is an explanation of one of the reasons God had for using a man who had not previously been his servant. It would prove to the witnesses that Cyrus was not performing his geat deeds in return for some favors that had been shown him before; that it was purely because of some invisible power or influence that was being exerted upon him. And the final conclusion would be that *there is none beside me. Rising of the sun* is a reference to the East which is the opposite of the West. The clause means that people everywhere were to learn the great truths just stated, that the Lord of the Hebrews was the one and only true God.

Verse 7. Darkness is a negative condition and did not require any act to originate it but is the absence of light. (See Gen. 1: 2, 3.) This verse means that God has complete control over all nature, so that if he sees fit to make it dark at any time by suspending the presence of light he can do so. *Evil* is from RAH and in the King James version has also been rendred by adversity, affliction, calamity, distress, misery, grief and others, hence the word does not always mean something sinful. The phrase in our verse means that God is able to cause either peace or the opposite, depending on the deserts of the case. The lesson intended is that God is able to bring the predicted distress upon the Babylonians for which he will use Cyrus as his agent.

Verse 8. All of these figures of speech are used to indicate the universal tokens of God's great power and his boundless love for his creatures. *Bring forth salvation* means to ascribe salvation to God because he hath created all things that exist.

Verse 9. It is foolish for a man to strive with his maker, because it is evident that nothing can be as great as the power that brought it into existence. If a man is bound to compete with anyone, it should be with another person in his rank. That is the thought in the clause about the potsherd which is a piece of pottery. Such a worthless scrap would at least be consistent if it tried to array its strength against another such scrap. But it would be out of order if the clay, from which this piece of pottery had been formed, should criticize the potter and blame him for the broken condition of the scraps. Many a good vessel has been made by a wise potter, and afterward that vessel would be broken through the carelessness of another.

Verse 10. The same argument as the preceding is continued in this verse. The illustration is drawn from a different subject, that of a parent and his child.

Verse 11. A God who is as great as the foregoing facts prove him to be, can foretell and direct the future in the interest of his children. *Ask me of things to come* is a form of speech that means God is able to tell the world what is going to happen. *Command ye me* is the same thought as the italicized words above. It is as if it said, "command or appoint or call upon me, and I will show that I am able to tell of the future and my control over it."

Verse 12. The Lord again refers to the things that have already been done as evidence of his might. Such a Being can certainly do other things that are great, which the prophet has been predicting all through this passage that were to be done.

Verse 13. *I have raised* is in the past tense as to form but refers to a fact yet to be accomplished. *Him* means Cyrus who was to be brought up to the work planned by the Lord on behalf of the Jews who will have been in Babylonian captivity. *Righteousness* does not refer directly to the personal character or life of Cyrus although he was a good man morally. It means the work God designed for him to do would be right. That work was to cause the release of the Jews from the captivity, then help them get their city of Jerusalem built. The record of this rebuilding and restoration is in the books of Ezra and Nehemiah. *Not for price nor reward.* Cyrus did not receive any money from God's people for the work he did for them; instead, he contributed money and other material for the great occasion (Ezra 1: 4).

Verse 14. *Labor of Egypt* means the products of that country, because it never failed to produce since it had the benefit of the Nile for irrigation. Ethiopa was just south of Egypt and gained much by trading with other people. This verse predicts that Palestine was to receive some of these desirable things by having them brought over by the producers themselves. *Chains* literally means a bond or fetter, but the meaning of it here is that persons from these places were to come to Jerusalem with the attitude of those in chains. It will all be done because those heathen people will be convinced that the God of the Jews is the true source of power. The fulfillment of this verse is recorded in Est. 8: 17.

Verse 15. *Hidest thyself* is an acknowledgment that the God of Israel is a mystery to the foolish inhabitants of the earth. His power to overthrow human governments is beyond all calculations, and that power was to be manifested by saving Israel.

Verse 16. This is the same prediction that has been made a number of times, of the cure from idolatry that would result from the captivity. The historical fulfillment of this prophecy may be seen in connection with ch. 1: 25.

Verse 17. This means that Israel will be saved nationally from captivity and restored to her native land. *Everlasting* means age-lasting, and Israel was never again to suffer punishment for the sin of idolatry.

Verse 18. *Formed* and *made* the earth means God originated the material of which the earth is made and also put it into its shape. *Vain* is from TOHUW which Strong defines, "from an unused root meaning to lie waste; a desolation (of surface), i.e. desert." This clause gives the information that God not only created the earth, but he designed it to have a surface that would not be like a waste plain or desert. We have information that other planets were so made, hence the fact that the earth was not and the further fact that the prophet saw fit to tell his readers of it signifies that something of importance was in the mind of the Lord. That important matter is the subject of the next clause which reads *he formed it to be inhabited.* That was never said concerning any other planet which should be regarded as a very significant truth. It is not necessary to go too far in speculation on the subject introduced here, but the impression is strong that no other planet besides the earth was intended by the Creator to be inhabited. Had such been His intention he certainly would have formed them in such a way that they also could "be inhabited." But because the Lord did intend for the earth to be so used he not only gave it a form as we have it, but made the surface of it different from a waste plain, so man could live on it.

Verse 19. A Being who can produce

so great a work as the earth as just described, does not have to use trickery or mysterious means in dealing with the creatures who are to live upon its surface. Hence, when he invited Jacob to seek Him it was not in vain, but was with the understanding that he would not be disappointed if he sought the Lord with a sincere mind. All of the Lord's declarations are true and no one will be left in confusion who honestly tries to receive him.

Verse 20. This verse is a general call to attention for all who will have escaped from bondage in the nations, to realize that idolatry is foolish and contrary to all knowledge. These dumb idols *cannot save*, and the past enslavement of which they have been the victims ought to teach them that truth.

Verse 21. These people are advised to consult with each other on the great subject, considering it in the light of their own experience. Their long suffering as captives in a strange land should be a lesson to them. They should ask each other who was the One to foretell the very facts that they have just been feeling in their own experience. The conclusion they will be impelled to arrive at will be that the one and only true God is the source of all such knowledge. He is a just God and the only one who can save them from their enemies.

Verse 22. God's great deeds both in creatinon and in his dealings with the nations of men proves that he can give such favors as are beyond all other gods. These facts would justify the general invitation of this verse for all to look to Him for help.

Verse 23. *Sworn by myself* was necessary because there is no greater power or authority in existence by whom to swear. *In righteousness* means the word issued by the mouth of the Lord is right because it will be shown to be the truth. The immediate subject of the passage is God's dealings with his ancient people and the heathen nations associated with them. His great success in all of the predictions and fulfillments seemed to suggest the idea of making some more extensive declarations concerning the distant future in regard to man in general. Hence follows the solemn announcement that the whole human creation will some day bow in acknowledgment of the authority of God. We know this is what the prophet meant by the prediction for Paul quotes the passage and so applies it in Rom. 14: 11.

Verse 24. The future success of God's plans, assured by what he has accomplished through the past ages, should bring all intelligent creatures to their knees. They should all be constrained to acknowledge Him as the truly strong and righteous ruler of the universe. Those who will make such concessions willingly will be blessed for them, but willingly or otherwise, all must finally make the confession.

Verse 25. *Seed of Israel* or the descendants of Jacob are especially mentioned because at the time of the prophet's writing they were the objects of the Lord's immediate attention.

ISAIAH 46

Verses 1, 2. This bracket is a prediction against Babylon that will have held the Jews in captivity for 70 years. *Bel* was the Baal of the Babylonians, and the overthrow of that nation would be a blow to their god. *Boweth down* means the god of that heathen nation would be prostrated before the power of an invading force. While Baal was their chief invisible god, the Babylonians had many smaller images they worshiped. But all these were to be of no avail when Cyrus makes his attack upon the city. Instead, the golden images of their boasted gods, helpless to save not only their city but even themselves, will be hauled away as loot on beasts and in wagons.

Verse 3, 4. This bracket predicts the return of the Jews from Babylonian captivity to their own land. The Biblical account of the fulfillment is in the books of Ezra and Nehemiah. The historical account was quoted with the comments at ch. 14 of this book. The *remnant* refers to the 42 thousand Jews who survived the years of the captivity. (See Ezra 2: 64.) The word *borne* and others on the subject of nativity and birth are used figuratively. The relationship between God and the Jewish nation was as close as that of a parent and offspring. That closeness was not to cease when the offspring grew to maturity. Even when they become gray with age the Heavenly Father promised to care for them with all the tenderness of a loving parent.

Verse 5. This and the following two verses are a description of idols to show how weak and useless they are. The bracket begins with the previous challenge for the worshipers of idols to find anyone to whom they could liken their own true God.

Verse 6. *Lavish gold out of the* [money] *bag* indicates that men bargained for their images in the same way they would purchase any necessity of life. *Hire a goldsmith* just as they would if they wanted to have a pin made to hold their clothing. And such a commercial article was that before which they would fall down and worship!

Verse 7. And this object of worship was so helpless that it had to be carried and put in its place as if it were a piece of furniture. Even some toys of children can keep on moving after being given a start. But after this idol god has been moved it will not proceed after the owner lets go of it; *from his place shall he not remove.* A weak mortal being may not be able to move bodily, yet will be able to indicate some other form of life and intelligence. This manufactured god, however, can make no response when its worshipers cry unto it. Of course such an object could not be able to *save* its owner *out of trouble.*

Verse 8. After the preceding shameful but just description of the idol god, the prophet attempts to get its servants to come to their senses. They are asked to search their memories in favor of the true God against whom they have been transgressors.

Verse 9. We should not be confused over the frequent repetitions of statements like this verse. The nation of Israel had been guilty of idolatry for so many years. And of all people in the world, they were the less excusable in view of their many experiences that proved beyond all doubt that their God was the true one. Hence the many passages that call attention to the past, such as the present verse.

Verse 10. This is more specific than the preceding verse as to the greatness of the true God over all others. *Declaring the end from the beginning* is a fundamental declaration and is not restricted to any one subject. *Beginning* and *end* are the two extreme poles of any force or activity. *Declaring* is from NAGAD and the leading part of Strong's definition is, "specifically to expose, predict, explain, praise." It thus does not mean to predetermine or foreordain. There are some things that God has foreordained, but the passage just cited does not require that definition. Its purpose is to express God's complete knowledge of all events that are going to take place, no matter how far they are in the future. *Counsel* means "plan" and *pleasure* means "desire." Since God is able to see into the future that enables him to know what would be best for all concerned and to plan for the same. So it is declared that whatever He plans for the future will be brought to pass regardless of all enemies.

Verse 11. *Ravenous bird* sounds harsher than the original thought intended. The definition in Strong's lexicon is, "a hawk or other bird of prey." It was used with reference to Cyrus, and the illustration was proper for he certainly did prey upon the other heathen kings who resisted him. It would be especially proper for him to take over the resisting birds (heathen kings) since the God of Israel desired to have him perform that work. Cyrus was *from the east* because Persia was in that direction from Babylon, and he was *from a far country* because it was a great distance from Palestine. In this case God not only saw into the future but planned a part of it. But he could not have done so did he not have the ability to see ahead and thus know what would be for the best.

Verses 12, 13. The work of Cyrus that was predicted in the preceding verse was to overthrow Babylon. That event would set Israel free and permit the nation to return to Jerusalem. That logically is the subject of the present paragraph. *Stouthearted* means the strong men of the Jewish nation who had been chief in leading the people into sin. Their punishment will have been complete when Cyrus is called into action, and the righteous purposes of God for restoring his people to their own country will then take place, which is recorded as history in the books of Ezra and Nehemiah.

ISAIAH 47

Verse 1. The predictions in this chapter are not all made in the order of their fulfillments. The first five verses are a bracket on the downfall of Babylon. The historical fulfillment is quoted with the comments at ch. 13: 1. *Sit in the dust* is a figurative prediction of the humiliation to be thrust upon Babylon by Cyrus. Strong defines the word for *virgin* as meaning "sometimes a city or state," and it is so used here to refer to the Babylonian city and Empire. *There is no throne* predicts that the Babylonian Empire will never again have any rule over others. *Daughter of the Chaldeans* means the city that the Chaldeans had possessed and ruled.

Verse 2. The humiliation to be thrust upon Babylon is still the subject of the prophet. The Chaldeans were a proud race and the figurative language is to indicate a woman who is above doing any humble bodily exercises. But the service described in this passage is a prediction of the debased situation that would be brought upon the proud city by the successful attack of Cyrus. Not only was this proud "woman" to be forced into servile work, but her finery of attire and exclusive arranging of her hair and other articles of supposed refinement were to be taken from her. Millstones were used for grinding grain into meal or flour, and only the lowest of slaves were usually employed to do that work by turning the stones round and round by means of a beam attached to the top stone in the form of a large lever. *Uncover thy locks* is rendered "remove thy veil" in the Revised Version and also in Moffatt's translation. It doubtless refers to the veil of the hair which modest women used as a covering in ancient times (1 Cor. 14: 15). *Make bare the leg* indicates that the long train worn by ladies of rank was to be discarded to make possible the manual labor they were to be forced into. *Pass over the river* was required of slaves in securing water for the domestic use of their masters. This service would require them either to discard their long train (trailing robes) or else gather it up so they could wade the streams; that action would expose the leg.

Verse 3. When the proud city of Babylon was thus brought down the condition was *seen* by the world. *Not meet thee as a man* means God would not permit any man to argue with him or to make any kind of interference with the divine plans against Babylon.

Verse 4. The Lord of Hosts is called *redeemer* because he would rescue Israel from the Babylonian captivity.

Verse 5. *Silent* and *darkness* refer to the national "black out" that would be put into effect over the Chaldean city by the attack of Cyrus. After that event the city was never again to be called the *lady of kingdoms.* This phrase means a city or state or both (see comments at v. 1), and it is a prediction that Babylon was never again to be a capital city nor ever be inhabited. (see the historical fulfillment of this quoted at ch. 13: 1.)

Verse 6. This verse jumps back in point of time and makes a prediction of the captivity. One part of Strong's definition of the original for *polluted* is "to dissolve." God decreed to dissolve his nation and give it over into the hand of Babylon. The pronoun *thine* refers to that kingdom because it was the subject of the preceding verse. *Didst show them no mercy* is a prediction of Babylon's treatment of the Israelites during the captivity. The people of God deserved some severe punishment for their iniquities, yet the nation that was to accomplish that purpose was to feel the hand of God in revenge for it because of its motive in the affair. That was why the destruction was threatened against it as per the preceding verse.

Verse 7. This boastful attitude of Babylon is well illustrated by the words of the king of the city as recorded in Dan. 4: 30-32.

Verse 8. *Dwellest carelessly* means that Babylon was enjoying a corrupt and luxurious life, unmindful of whether it was right or wrong or of what might be the outcome of it. *Not sit as a widow* is figurative and means that Babylon would not become "a desolate place." *Loss of children* denotes the loss of citizens of the great city, and Babylon boasted that she would never suffer such a loss.

Verse 9. The prophet predicted that both evils would come upon the city. It was to have its citizens taken off and the place become desolate and waste continually.

Verse 10. This verse continues the accusations against the Babylonians for their boastful attitude. *Trusted IN thy wickedness* means Babylon felt secure even while continuing in her wickedness. This view of the phrase is indicated by the following one, *none seeth me.* Because the Lord is not visible it is common for the wicked people of the earth to fall into a feeling of security. Such a state of mind will cause them to be *perverted* (turned aside) from the right way. But the wicked city of Babylon was soon to realize that all her movements and even the evil thoughts in the minds of her rulers were to be exposed and punished.

Verse 11. From this verse to the close of the chapter is a bracket of predictions of the overthrow of the city of Babylon which was the capital of the government. There is a long historical quotation on this event in connection with ch. 13: 7, 8 of this book. I urge the reader to find that place and have it before him as he follows the comments on the present verses. Especially should he note the outstanding expressions in connection with the italicized words of our bracket. *Not know from whence it ariseth* was fulfilled when it said, "Had the Babylonians known what Cyrus was about." *Desolation; suddenly,* came in one night and thus was not a long-drawn-out affair. (See Dan. 5: 30.)

Verse 12. *Stand* predicts that Babylon will rely on her so-called wise men to explain the crisis and point out some way of escape (Dan. 5: 7).

Verse 13. *Wearied* is from LAWAH and Strong defines it, "a primitive root; to tire; (figuratively) to be (or make) disgusted." The clause predicts that Babylon will become tired and disgusted with these special wise men because of their failure. Yet the challenge is made for her to go ahead and call for them. *Astrologers* were those who pretended to foretell events by the appearance of the heavens. *Stargazers* were those who claimed to make predictions by looking at the stars. *Monthly prognosticators* were men who professed to give predictions based on the beginning dates of the months, and that was because the new moon was observed at the beginning of the month. In a derisive way the prophet calls upon Babylon to call for all these mysterious servants who had claimed to have superhuman knowledge. This very call was made by the king of Babylon as recorded in Dan. 5: 7.

Verse 14. The words on the subject of *fire* are used figuratively, referring to the complete failure of these so-called wise men of Babylon. They were not to be able to do themselves any good or to help the king out of his difficulties.

Verse 15. *Wander to his quarter* predicts that when the king calls for these men to help him, they will be unable to do so. Realizing this they will retire from their monarch and shall go in confusion to their personal homes.

ISAIAH 48

Verse 1. The reader should be cautioned to "keep his bearings" as to the dates of the things which he is studying. Many times it sounds as if the language should be regarded in the same way as history, and that he is being told of conditions and events being such at the time of the writing. According to actual dates the prophet Isaiah was through his writing a hundred years before the Babylonian captivity as will be seen by reading the first verse of the book. Hence, when the language seems to be history from its tense form, it may be a prophetic statement. However, where the Lord accuses the nation of its idolatry and other sins, it can be and often is referring to conditions in general. Such is true of a great portion of this chapter although it will contain some predictions which will be noted as they appear. *Jacob* and *Israel* refer to the same people because the latter was an additional name given to Jacob when he had his wrestling test with the angel (Gen. 32: 28). *Waters* is figurative and is used in the sense of fountains or fountainhead or sources. The phrase *waters of Judah* means that Judah was the source from which the nation sprang. It was right to swear by the name of God if done with due respect. But the nation through its leaders had made a mere form of their services in that they were done insincerely.

Verse 2. They made much ado of their relation to the holy city (Jerusalem) because it was the capital of the kingdom. *Stay themselves* means they professed to depend on the God of Israel. That was the proper profession to make but they refused to follow the counsel of the One on whom they claimed to rely.

Verse 3. Their profession of trust in the wisdom of God should have been sincere. They had plenty of evidence that He was entitled to such trust since he had made far-reaching statements that had all been proved to be true by the test of time. *Suddenly* means instantly, *and they came to pass.* God did not make his predictions in the nature of a continuous speech, "stalling for time" as it were, so that the things being predicted would have time to begin showing themselves even while the predictions were being made.

Any human being might do that kind of "prophesying." God uttered his predictions in short time and a long while before they were to come to pass. History then recorded the occurrences of the events just as they had been predicted. All of that proved His infinite foreknowledge and should have caused the house of Israel to be warned when God told them what was coming upon them at last.

Verse 4. Iron and brass being metals are used figuratively to illustrate the stiff, unyielding. stubborn disposition of the Israelites in spite of God's many attempts to bring them to respect him and his laws for their guidance.

Verse 5. This verse opens with about the same thought as that in verse 3, which see. The added argument here is concerning the claim that might have been made for the idol. Had the remarks been made on the events while they were taking place, even though they were true and significant and had the appearance of having come from a source of great intelligence, the idolaters might have attributed the statements to their gods. That is, they would have insisted that the prophet obtained his information from the idol notwithstanding it was made of dead material of the earth.

Verse 6. Instead of dealing only with current events, the prophets of God have made predictions of events that were far in the future. Many of these seemed unreasonable or impossible of becoming facts, yet history proved them to have been true and thus were inspired by a wisdom that was not human or by such a dead thing as a man-made god, derived from the metal of the earth or the tree of the forest.

Verse 7. The proofs of God's exclusive wisdom were drawn from facts that were new as to date and yet which had been foretold many years before. This would prevent the idol worshipers from laying claim to a knowledge of them previously.

Verse 8. This verse sums up one line of argument for the divine source of the prophet's writing. The predictions were made long before the present generation even lived, yet were being fulfilled right before their eyes. All of this precaution was taken by the Lord because he knew his people would *deal treacherously*, which means in an underhanded manner. *Called a transgressor from the womb* means the nation had a lifelong reputation for disobedience of the law of God.

Verse 9. This verse has to do with the mercy of God in his dealings with his wayward people. However, that mercy was to be extended toward them more on behalf of his own good name than because of their deserts. This is why their future captivity (which is about to be predicted) was not going to be fatal to them as a nation.

Verse 10. *Have refined* is past tense which we have learned is a common form of speech with inspired prophets. The prediction in this verse is of the Babylonian captivity which was to come a hundred years in the future. *Refined* means to be purified by fire so as to separate the good metal from the dross. *Not with silver* means not for the purpose of obtaining literal silver. In other words, the refining process that was to come upon Israel was for a far more important purpose than that of purifying silver. *Furnace of affliction* is a figurative prediction of the Babylonian captivity. That experience was designed to purify the nation of Israel by separating it from the dross of idolatry. It accomplished that purpose as proved by the historical quotation made in connection with the comments at ch. 1: 25.

Verse 11. It will be well to have the complete definition in Strong's lexicon for the original of *sake*. The Hebrew word is MAHAN and the definition is, "properly heed, i.e. purpose; used only adverbially, on account of (as a motive or an aim), teleologically [referring to motive] in order that." *Polluted* is from CHALAL, and the part of Strong's definition that applies here is, "to break one's word." The verse as a whole means that God will not utterly forsake his people. He has promised many times to be their shield and preserver. And so in order to make his word good and maintain the honor of his name, he will come to the rescue of Israel as soon as she has suffered the punishment necessary to bring her to repentance.

Vere 12. *Jacob* and *Israel* have been explained as referring to the same people. The pronouns for God are used without naming Him otherwise. That indicates the greatness of the One who is the *first* and the *last* which means he is without beginning or end but has always been in existence and always will be.

Verse 13. *My hand* and *my right*

hand have the same application. The meaning is that God has made and controls the things of the universe with his own hand; also that such use of his power is right.

Verse 14. The first part of this verse is another call to attention addressed to everybody in general. The Lord then challenges them to point out any person who had been able to see into the future and predict the things that were going to take place. No one would be prepared to make such a declaration, much less have anything to do with the transactions among the nations. God's reason for what he did in connection with Jacob (v. 12) was that he *hath loved him*. Hence the Lord predicted that he would do what pleased him concerning the nation that was to be used as an instrument in chastising the wayward children of Jacob. That nation is designated by both Babylon and Chaldeans. The latter were a special race of ancient people who finally came into power in Babylon. After that time the two names were used to denote the same government, especially if only one was used in a single passage. When used as they are in this verse the Chaldeans mean the people of that particular name of which the city of Babylon was the capital. This government was to be used to punish the Jewish nation, after that service the Chaldeans themselves were to be severely treated, and the latter part of the verse is a reference to that event. The historical fulfillment of it was quoted in the comments at ch. 13: 1.

Verse 15. *Have called him* means the call of Cyrus although his name is not mentioned here. But we know that is the meaning of the statement since it was Cyrus whom God called to overthrow Babylon and set the Jews free. *He shall make his way prosperous* means that Cyrus will prosper in his work against Babylon. Of course we understand it would be because he will have been *called* to the work by the Lord.

Verse 16. God declares his word has been "above board" so that no one can complain of having been put at a disadvantage. The prophet is writing the words of God by the guidance of the spirit of God so that was bound to be true.

Verse 17. Isaiah further repeats the words that the Lord was giving him. Again the people of Israel are reminded that the Lord is their redeemer which had special reference to their release from the captivity. *Teacheth thee to profit* means that Israel would always prosper if she would heed the teaching of this Redeemer.

Verse 18. This verse is a pathetic reflection on the past stubborn actions of the Jewish people. Instead of profiting by the kind and wise counsels of their God, they had gone off after idols and false devotions. *Peace as a river* is an illustration of the continuous, agreeable and abundant flowing of the blessings that come from the throne of God to those who will avail themselves thereof.

Verse 19. When the nation of Israel was compelled to live 70 years in captivity it reduced its number until only a remnant survived (Ezra 2: 64). The present verse means that just the reverse of that would have existed had they been true to the Lord.

Verse 20. Notwithstanding the disobedience of his people, God continued to love them and promised to deliver them out of their afflictions. This verse and the following refers to the return from the captivity. *Go ye forth of Babylon* is the prophet's style of speech, predicting that Israel would go out of the Babylonian captivity. This prediction was made almost 200 years before it was fulfilled. The Biblical account of the deliverance is recorded in the books of Ezra and Nehemiah. The historical account was quoted in connection with ch. 14: 1. They were to be in a state of joy over their freedom when they went, which is evident from the account in the books just named. Although Cyrus was the man who was to have charge of the great event, they were told to attribute their release to the Lord.

Verse 21. *Led them through the deserts* was fulfilled in Ezra 8: 15-32. The remainder of the verse is figurative and refers to the providential care that God was to give his people as they made their journey from Babylon to Palestine.

Verse 22. There is no special time or place for the application of this verse. It is a declaration of truth that is always in force. It does not mean that the wicked man will never think he is doing well and that he is free from care. In fact, such a person is apt to conclude that all is well with him since he does not see any evidence of God's displeasure. (See Ecclesiastes 8: 11.) But the time will come when he will realize that his feeling of security was but "the calm before the storm," and he will then feel the wrath of God upon him.

ISAIAH 49

Verse 1. Some of the prophecies have a two-fold application due to the subject matter involved. That is because so many of the things that happened to ancient Israel and at that time to others, were like those of spiritual Israel or at the time of that dispensation. These remarks will be found to be true of much of this chapter, and the language is in the first person as to grammatical form in many of the verses. *Isles* is from a word that is defined "a habitable spot." The sentence is a call for the inhabitants of the earth to listen. The speaker is either Cyrus or Christ or both, because each was named before he was born (ch. 45: 1-4; Matt. 1: 21). The words *from far* would have a special meaning in the case of Christ because he was to be preached to the Gentiles who were considered the people "far off" (Eph. 2: 13).

Verse 2. The general thought in this verse is the support which God promised to give Cyrus in his work against the Babylonians, and the backing he would furnish for Jesus in his service of truth for the whole world.

Verse 3. The language of this verse would seem to be applied more directly to Israel instead of either Cyrus or Jesus. But it was because both of these persons were to act for God on behalf of fleshly or spiritual Israel.

Verse 4. The prophet is now more especially concerned for the fate of the people of Israel who were to be punished for their sins. They are represented as lamenting the vanity of their actions. Yet they had not lost all hope for they expressed confidence in the judgment of their God. That constituted a prediction that their affairs would yet "take a turn for the better." Such was to be the case at least and the next verse will be more directly on that subject.

Verse 5. *Formed thee from the womb* denotes that they owed their existence to the Lord. *Bring Jacob again to him* is a prediction of the return from captivity. *Though Israel be not gathered* refers to the time just before the release from bondage in Babylon. Even while the nation of Israel was *not gathered;* while still in captivity, it was glorious in the eyes of the Lord, which was the reason he was determined to bring them unto him in Jerusalem again.

Verse 6. The first half of this verse refers to Cyrus who was to *raise up the tribes of Jacob* and restore them to their own land of Palestine. The last part is a prediction of the service of Christ in bringing salvation to all the nations of the earth. This is signified by the mention of the Gentiles who had not been included in the provisions made under the Jewish system.

Verse 7. This verse is a prediction of Christ. *His Holy One* means that the Lord is the holy one of Christ, and this Lord is making a favorable prophecy of what will happen to Christ in spite of the unfavorable things that some will do. *Man despiseth* means that Christ was to be belittled by men, which is abundantly proved in the accounts of the Gospel. *The nation abhorreth.* Even his own nation, the Jews, denied Jesus and had him put to death. *Servant of rulers* predicts the respect that Christ was to show for constituted government, and it was fulfilled in one instance as recorded in Matt. 17: 26, 27. *Kings . . . princes shall worship* predicts that the greatest of persons would finally become admirers of Christ. All of these things were to be done because of the faithful watch and care that God would have over his beloved Son.

Verse 8. Paul cites this verse in 2 Cor. 6: 2 where we know he is writing about the grace of God for salvation of man through Christ. *Give thee for a covenant* was promised through Abraham when God said to him: "And in thy seed shall all nations of the earth be blessed" (Gen. 22: 18). *To establish the earth* means to offer the support of salvation to the people of the earth. *Inherit the desolate heritages* applies first to the return of the Jews to their own land, and second to the spiritual benefits to be offered the world through Christ.

Verse 9. The first clause of this verse was fulfilled the first time when Cyrus told the Jews to go free out of Babylon. It was fulfilled the second time when Christ offered spiritual freedom to all who were prisoners under the bondage of sin. The remainder of the verse pertains to Christ and his service of salvation for humanity.

Verse 10. Spiritual favors are often illustrated figuratively. They are contrasted to things that are undesirable, and likened to those that are desirable. The absence of any ungratified hunger and thirst and scorching heat would all be a great favor. Such a condition is likened to the spiritual comforts that Christ was to provide for mankind. *Spring of water* suggests the refreshing influences that the Gospel was to have upon those who would accept the same upon the Lord's own conditions.

Verse 11. *Mountains a way* and *highways exalted* corresponds with the preparatory work that John the Baptist was to do for Christ (Luke 3: 5).

Verse 12. The blessings of Christ were to be offered to the people of the world, not to the Jews only as was the case under Moses. *Sinim* is defined in Strong's lexicon, "plural of an otherwise unknown name; Sinim, a distant Oriental [eastern] region." The word is used as a specific instance of the far-reaching provisions through Christ.

Verse 13. This verse is a bid for rejoicing over the redemption of the Jews from captivity. *Heavens* and *earth* are two extremes or ends of the universe and the expressions denote that a general state of rejoicing would be experienced when the enemy was overthrown and the people of God released. *Mountains* is used figuratively and signifies that men and governments would have cause for rejoicing at the fortunate turn of affairs of the Jews who had been under such depression.

Verse 14. Zion is used in this place to mean the Jews in captivity. They were in a discouraged frame of mind and many of them despaired of ever having any relief. This is the same thing that is set forth in Ezk. 37: 1-11 and Psa. 137.

Verse 15. As an argument of reassurance the Lord reminds his people of the close tie that binds a human parent and child together. It is not expected that such a father or mother could be unmindful of his offspring. Much less would the divine Father forget the people whom he had begotten in the time of great pressure and opposition in Egypt and the wilderness.

Verse 16. It is considered a great and reassuring favor for the Lord to "hold us, as it were, in the hollow of his hand." He makes it more precious than that by promising to have them *graven* upon the palms of his hands. That would make it permanent so that it would be out of the question for the Lord ever to forget them. *Walls* is from a Hebrew word which Strong defines, "a wall of protection." The significance of the phrase is that God is always concerned about the protection of his people which is generally associated with the use of walls.

Verse 17. *Shall make haste* means the delivery of the Jews from their captivity will be prompt when the time comes. *Shall go forth of thee* denotes the withdrawal of the forces that had been oppressing Israel.

Verse 18. This verse is a prediction of the interest that will be shown toward the Jews by the other nations; an instance of it is recorded in Est. 8: 16. *Clothe thee with them* was fulfilled when the citizens of Persia furnished materials for the use of the Jews in restoring the state of their capital city (Ezra 1: 4).

Verse 19. *Waste and desolate places* refers to the land of Palestine. While the Jews were in captivity their country was neglected and somewhat overrun by the heathen nations, all of which was to be changed after the return. *Shall be too narrow* means the population of the rightful citizens shall increase until they will have to spread out and occupy more territory. *They that swallow thee* refers to the heathen invaders, and they were to be forced to vacate the land and leave it in possession of its true owners after they got back from the land of captivity.

Verse 20. In Ezra 2: 64 is a statement of the remnant that survived the captivity. Such a decrease of their number is what is meant here by the words *hast lost the other*. They were to be replaced in such numbers that request will be made for more room as a place in which to dwell.

Verse 21. Here the prophet blends his predictions of the ancient with spiritual Israel. The former will be surprised to see so great a replenishing of her people after the desolation of the past years. The increase will be so unexpectedly great that the inquiry will be made as to how it came about. This question was another time for the "telescope" (see the illustration in "General Remarks" at the beginning of Isaiah) to be extended until the prophet could see into the time of Christ. He considered the improved situation of ancient Israel an apt type of the increase of God's spiritual children under Christ which is the subject of the next two verses.

Verse 22. Under the Mosaic system only the Jews were considered God's children, but under Christ the Gentiles were to be included. The *standard* or signal of authority under Christ will be raised among them and they will be invited to come into close relationship with the Lord. The language in the close of the verse is what is called accommodative and refers to the joyous activities of those who had for years been excluded from the Jewish Dispensation. (see the fulfillment in Acts 11: 18.)

Verse 23. This is a continuation of the same prediction that was given in the preceding verse. It is a figurative picture of how the various classes of mankind, the high and the low, will accept the Gospel and become worshipers of God in fellowship with the humblest of His children. (See Acts 17: 4, 12.)

Verse 24. The "telescope" is again returned to its former position and the prophet sees the events at the end of the Babylonian captivity. The prediction is made in the form of a question, but the force of the thought will be understood by adding "yes" at the end of the verse. *Lawful captives* is rendered "the captivity of the just" in the margin, and the R. V. as well as the lexicon will sustain it. The meaning is that the captivity of the Jews was just, because the Lord decreed it to take place. In view of that, it would seem wonderful if such a captivity could be reversed.

Verse 25. The Lord assures his people that *the mighty* (meaning the Babylonian) will be forced to give up the captives whom God had permitted them to take. *I will contend* refers to the attack that Cyrus would make upon Babylon under the instructions of the Lord. (See the historical quotation at ch. 13: 1, 7, 8.)

Verse 26. *Feed them with their own flesh* is a figurative way of saying the Babylonians would be given an "overdose of their own medicine." They had oppressed the Jews and taken undue joy from the unfortunate experiences that they had suffered while in captivity. That period will be past, however, when this prediction is fulfilled, and the Babylonians will themselves feel the sting of God's jealousy for his people. *Drunken* is from SHAKAR, and Strong defines it, "in a qualified sense, to satiate [act the glutton]." The clause means they will be fed their own blood (figuratively, of course) until it will make them as sick as if they had drunk too much sweet wine. The statement has no connection with the ordinary subject of intoxication. One meaning of the original for *flesh* is "person." The statement means that all persons will be made to realize that the God of Jacob is the mighty Redeemer of the people who had been oppressed through the years of the captivity.

ISAIAH 50

Verse 1. The relation between God and ancient Israel has been compared to various others. Sometimes it is a husbandman and vineyard; sometimes to master and servant; at other times it is husband to wife; at others it is parent and child, and the last two are used in this verse. First, the subject of divorcement is considered and the Lord is calling for the wife to show her bill of divorce. This is based on a law of Moses (Deut. 24: 1) that provided a husband with the right to divorce his wife if he was not satisfied with her. As the bill would show the cause of the husband's complaint, if she had been guilty of gross misconduct it would be natural for her to hesitate at producing the writing. Some commentators think this passage means to deny that the wife had any legal paper, and that the aggrieved husband had only *put away* his wife. I believe it means the husband actually divorced her, because the word *put* is from the same word as "send" and "sendeth" in Deut. 24: 1, 3, 4, where we know the husband divorced his wife. And so the bill of divorce that God gave to Israel showed that she was divorced or put away *for her transgressions*. Those sins consisted in her idolatry which was the same as adultery and would certainly arouse the jealousy of God who was the husband (Ex. 20: 5). Using the illustration of parent and child, a provision of the law allowed an unfortunate father to sell his child to pay off a debt (Ex. 21: 7; 2 Ki. 4: 1). In this case the parent was not under necessity to sell his child, but the child had made his own transaction and sold himself. Such a deed was also permitted under the law (Lev. 25: 47, 48), but it was to be done in cases where a man was actually under the stress of poverty. In the case of Israel the excuse of poverty could not be made because the parent (God) was making abundant provisions for his children. Notwithstanding all this, the aggrieved husband was willing to take his wayward wife back also to redeem his unappreciative children from the hand of their creditors. In the figurative setup of our verse, Zion or Jerusalem is the mother (and wife) and the Israelites are the children.

Verse 2. There is so much blending of the subject matter for the Old and New Testament times that it is difficult in some places to determine which is meant. It appears evident in this verse that God is calling for some one to serve him in bringing about his plan for the people. God also asks why no one responded, and then suggests that some doubt must have been felt as to the power of the Lord. In opposition to such a thought the people are reminded again of the great works of the past.

Verse 3. God's complete control over the elements is the subject of this verse, and that fact should have silenced all resistance to the authority of divine law.

Verse 4. The pronoun *me* is used somewhat indefinitely, and could apply first to the servant who should have *answered* as per verse 2. Had he done so, God would have given him all necessary qualifications to act on behalf of the needy. In its second application the statements were true of Christ although the prophet seems to have his mind mostly on conditions at the time of Israel's corruptions.

Verse 5. This verse has specific reference to Christ because all of the remarks were true of him. *Was not rebellious* should remind us of Heb. 10: 7.

Verse 6. This verse predicts first the turning of Israel over to the captivity. It also portrays the treatment Christ suffered at the hands of his tormentors. He willingly submitted to their insults and inhuman treatment. *Hid not my face from shame and spitting* was fulfilled in Matt. 26: 67; 27: 30; Mark 14: 65.

Verse 7. God promised to help his people Israel after they suffered a while in captivity. He also upheld Jesus in all of his work among his enemies on earth. *Like a flint* means Jesus was unflinching in his devotion to his Father midst all persecution.

Verse 8. God was *near* when ancient Israel needed someone to defend the nation against the Babylonians, and for that reason the members were encouraged to *stand* together. All of this was especially true in the case of Christ. It is no contradiction that he was put to death after having been shamefully mistreated; that was necessary for the great plan of God in saving the world. But though Christ had to descend into death, he was not forsaken of his Father but was given power to come forth alive.

Verse 9. Those who would condemn Christ are the antecedent of *they*, and their defeat is likened to the destruction of garments by age and moth.

Verse 10. This is a call for all who fear the Lord to heed the voice of his servant. That would have been useful advice for the people of Israel to listen to the warnings through the prophet. It was also of much importance to obey the words of Christ. *Walketh in darkness* means those who are groping in sin without seeking the divine instructions for right living.

Verse 11. This verse refers to those who are in darkness but will not come to the light of divine truth. They prefer to furnish their own light by building a fire (self-righteousness) and walking therein. All such persons will come to nought by the vengeance of God, and *shall lie down in sorrow*.

ISAIAH 51

Verse 1. This chapter as a whole is a prediction of the return from Babylonian captivity, with an occasional insertion of other specific subject matter and some remarks of a general nature. *Hearken . . . ye that seek the Lord* is addressed to the Jews. It does not mean to acknowledge them as being righteous, for they were to be in bondage because of their iniquities. The clause sets out the idea that if they are willing to seek the Lord they will hearken to him in order to obtain much needed instruction.

Verse 2. This is another passage where the Lord reminds the Jews of the might of their God. It is backed up by what he did for their father Abraham. *Called him alone* denotes that Abraham was without any son when he was called, yet he was made to increase in the number of his descendants and was blessed abundantly in other ways. The argument is that if God could call an old and childless man and make him the ancestor of

Isaiah 51: 3-15

many people, then certainly He will be able to take care of those descendants even though they are enslaved for a time by a strong nation.

Verse 3. The first clause is a specific prediction of the release from captivity, Zion being the capital of the home land of the Jews. *Waste places* refers to the neglect of their land while they were away in Babylon. The verse concludes with a figurative description of the restored condition of the land of Palestine to come about after its people get back into it as its rightful inhabitants.

Verse 4. The word of the Lord was to be obeyed by Cyrus and it would cause the release of the people from their captivity. *Make my judgment to rest* means that God's decree would be established and it would bring *light* or instruction to the nation that had been for so many years in the darkness of bondage in a strange land.

Verses 5, 6. This verse is symbolical and refers to the revolution that was to come upon Babylon. It would be accomplished by dethroning her kings and demoting other leading men. It is compared to the idea of removing both the heavens and the earth. It is also likened to the decay of a garment through old age. It does not mean exactly that such things were literally to take place in the universe. The thought is as if it said "even though all these things were to happen, yet *my salvation shall be forever*." It is another way of declaring that the overthrow of Babylon was sure to occur.

Verse 7. This verse has the same meaning as verse 4, which see. It is an assurance that Israel will be able to overcome the reproaches of the enemy nation.

Verse 8. A garment that is eaten with insects would be weak and useless thereafter; likewise the Babylonian government was to be rendered useless to themselves after Cyrus got through with it. *My salvation* refers to the redemption of God's people from captivity. That is, the first application is to that event, and also the generations of mankind to follow will realize that it was a righteous act of the Lord.

Verse 9. We know that God does not have to be reminded of his own strength although the language here might seem to have that meaning. It is the prophet's way of demanding the attention of humanity (generation to generation, v. 8) to the fact. And as proof of it, the actual achievements of the Lord in the past are cited. Among those are the ones over *Rahab* and the *dragon*. The first word is defined by Strong, "an epithet of Egypt." The second word is defined. "a marine [water] or land monster, i.e. sea-serpent or jackal." It is in reference to the Nile River because the Egyptians worshiped the stream with all its living creatures. By overcoming Egypt with the 10 plagues God showed his superior power over that country and all its gods.

Verses 10, 11. This verse has specific reference to the joy that was to be experienced by the Jews when they come to Jerusalem after the captivity. The Biblical account of the event is recorded in the books of Ezra and Nehemiah. The historical report may be read in connection with comments at Isa. 14: 1.

Verse 12. With the Lord to comfort Israel the heathen nation should not have been permitted to cause much fear. Human creatures certainly ought not have as much consideration as the Lord who has made all beings and things.

Verse 13. *Lord thy maker* is a very significant phrase. A being who can create a living creature after His own image is surely great enough to care for him. The enemy nation that was to hold the Jews in captivity would have to rely on the strength of its walls that are made of earthly material. Yet those very materials were made by the same God who made mankind. Such a Creator could certainly see that the inferior materials of his handiwork would be overcome if necessary to release the superior works. The conclusion is that Israel should not be frightened at the threatening attitude of the nation holding them in captivity.

Verse 14. *Hasteneth* is from an original that Strong defines, "to hurry, promptly." The thought is that when the time comes the Jews will go promptly from the land of their captivity, *the pit* being a figurative reference to **Babylon.**

Verse 15. *Divided the sea* refers to the opening of the Red Sea for passage of the Israelites (Ex. 14). That was done to allow them to escape from bondage in the land of Egypt. It is referred to here as an argument in support of the prediction that the same people would be released from the Babylonian captivity.

Verse 16. *Put my words in thy mouth* means the Lord brought his knowledge near his people to show them that the divine care was over them. *Heavens* and the associated terms are figurative, referring to the national forms of life among the Israelites. God proposed to establish his people again in their own land and recognize the inhabitants of Zion, capital of the country, as His people.

Verse 17. From here to the close of verse 21 is a bracket that predicts the experiences and conditions of Israel in captivity. *Hast drunk* is past tense in form but is a prophesy of what was to take place when the Jews were taken into the land of Babylon. For many years a common figure of speech for the bitter experience of life was to refer to it as "drinking the bitter cup," or some such like expression. (See Psa. 11: 6; 73: 10; 75: 8; Zech. 12: 2; Matt. 20: 23; 26: 39.) God's punishment of his people for their sins is referred to as the act of drinking from a cup filled with the wine of divine wrath. The dregs are the settlings in the bottom of the cup. The experiences of the Jews were to be so bitter that they were illustrated by the act of draining the cup down to the very dregs. But they were not to be allowed to stop there; they must squeeze the dregs to get a little more of the wine of God's wrath that is being held therein.

Verse 18. The people of Israel had yielded to the influence of their priests and prophets who led them off into the worship of idols. But when the misfortune of the captivity came upon them, there was not a man of their number who was able to lead them out of their trouble; all were punished together.

Verse 19. These severe terms predicted in a general way the undone condition the nation was to suffer at the hands of the Babylonians. *By whom shall I comfort thee* indicates that no relief would be found for Israel in the distress of the captivity until the Lord was ready to take a hand and put an end to their bondage.

Verse 20. The prostrated condition of the Jews in Babylon was the design of God to punish them for their disobedience. The figurative language in this verse is a prediction of that situation.

Verse 21. *Drunken but not with wine* is another figure of speech referring to the state of being overcome by the distress of the captivity. However, the Lord never forgot his people and now calls upon them to hear what he has to say for consolation.

Verse 22. The literal fact that is predicted in this verse is the overthrow of Babylon. It is described with the same figure of a *cup* that was used in connection with the people of Israel in verse 17. The cup of *trembling* (defined "reeling") was to be taken out of the hand of Israel which means she was no more to be afflicted by the bitterness of a national captivity.

Verse 23. With all of the same meaning of the figure, the Babylonians were to be handed the *cup* and forced to drink of it. Not because God did not want them to afflict his people, but because they took too much personal delight in oppressing the unfortunate captives. For the Biblical account of this downfall of Babylon see the books of Ezra and Nehemiah. For the historical account see quotation at ch. 13: 1.

ISAIAH 52

Verse 1. This chapter is a mixture of two subjects, the release of the Jews from captivity and the era of the Gospel. The direct application of this verse is the former of the mentioned subjects. *Awake, awake* means to rouse the people of God that they may receive the good news of their predicted deliverance from their oppressor and their return to the beloved Jerusalem. *There shall no more come,* etc., means the people of God would never again be taken away into captivity. In its spiritual application it denotes that when the church is set up in Jerusalem it will be occupied by clean and circumcised (consecrated) people.

Verse 2. *Dust* in symbolic language means humiliation and oppression. *Shake thyself* means the Jews were to cast off the dust of their shame and then *sit down* in peace and honor. The captivity was to be lifted from them and they were to be again a free nation.

Verse 3. In regular business transactions if an article is sold or pawned for a certain sum, it may be redeemed by paying the amount of the pawn. In the case of the Israelites they *sold* or pawned themselves without having received anything from their creditors (the Babylonians). In like manner they were to be reclaimed without the consideration of a ransom price. This would be appropriate since there will be a change of "creditor" and Cyrus would have nothing invested in those people. It was to be a free discharge from the condition of slavery and thus Cyrus was to receive no ransom money for the ones whom he found in bondage in the country that he captured.

Verse 4. This verse is a brief reference to some previous oppressions the Lord's people had suffered at the hands of the heathen. The instance of the Egyptian case began in Gen. 46: 7 and the Assyrian invasion is recorded in 2 Ki. 17: 6. It is true that both of these events had been decreed by the Lord, yet the oppressors were destined to feel the divine wrath because of the attitude toward the captives. The second instance, however, embraced the ten tribes only who had gone off with Jeroboam and formed the northern kingdom known thereafter as the Kingdom of Israel.

Verse 5. At the time of this writing the prophet had in view the two tribes who had remained with the lawful headquarters in Jerusalem and were known as the Kingdom of Judah. This kingdom was also destined to go into captivity and this verse is going forward to the period of its captivity and describing the character of the Babylonians who were to have their hold on God's people. This heathen nation not only was mistreating the Jews but was blaspheming the name of their God.

Verse 6. In revenge for their mistreatment of the captives and for their disrespect for the name of their God, the Babylonians were to be brought under and the victory turned to the benefit of the unfortunate people.

Verse 7. At the favorable turn of affairs for ancient Israel, the "telescope" was extended so the prophet could see another and more important release for the people of the world. The era of the Gospel was destined to offer freedom for a world of people who were in the bondage of sin. We know this verse was a prediction of the Gospel period for Paul so applies it in Rom. 10: 15. *Feet* is from REGEL which Strong defines, "a foot (as used in walking); by implication, a step." The clause means that the footsteps or manner of life that leads a man to preach the Gospel will be regarded as beautiful or pleasant to the Lord.

Verse 8. In ancient times the cities had men stationed on the walls for the approach of either friend or foe. This verse refers to the arrangement to illustrate the joy at seeing the exiled citizens returning. *See eye to eye* means the watchmen will all see together because the return will be so complete and show evidence of God's presence.

Verse 9. This is a prediction in the form of history that the Lord's people will be comforted and relieved of their oppression brought on by the captivity. *Waste places in Jerusalem* refers to the fact that the country was neglected while the inhabitants were in exile in a heathen land.

Verse 10. *Made bare* denotes that the nations were to see the strength of God's arm in the rescuing of his people from their bondage. It was true that the change from Babylonian to Persian rule was so revolutionary that all nations knew about it.

Verse 11. *Depart ye* is another form of prediction that the Jews would leave the heathen city of Babylon. That was an idolatrous country and the Jews had been required to participate in their practices while in the control of the idolaters. That was a decree of God and was to cure them of their tendency toward the evil religion. But the cure will have been effected when the period of release comes and when they go they will leave all of their idolatry behind them.

Verse 12. *Not go out with haste* is a contrast of their departure from Egypt (Ex. 12: 11). At that time they were urged to leave the country and were so rushed about it that they did not have time to let their bread become leavened. It was not to be that way when they left Babylon although there was not to be any undue delay. But their leaving would be in perfect order and free from all fear or panic. God was to be their *rereward* or general guard to insure their safe journey.

Verse 13. Again the "telescope" was extended and the prophet could see into the time of Christ. He saw this *servant* of God exalted before the eyes of the people.

Verse 14. Many people were stunned or *astonied* (astonished) at the works of Jesus to see that such an unpretentious person could accomplish the things that he did. (See Matt. 7: 28; 13: 54; Mark 10: 26; Matt. 9: 8.)

Verse 15. The people who are referred to in the preceding verse were few when compared with the number who were destined to see the wonderful power of Jesus as it would be manifested through his Gospel. The original for *sprinkle* is rendered by the word "startle" in the A.R.V., and the connection would justify it. The word *astonied* in the preceding verse and *sprinkle* in this have the same force. They have the idea of causing surprise or astonishment at the demonstrations of the wonderful works of Jesus. We are also to catch the thought that *many nations* had reference to the truth that Gentiles as well as Jews would be called to service under Christ.

ISAIAH 53

Verse 1. This entire chapter is a prediction concerning Christ and others connected with him in his great work on earth for the introduction of the Gospel. We will not be confused by the present and past tense of many phrases since that feature of inspired prophecy has been explained frequently. This verse is quoted in two places in the New Testament which makes it plain as to the application. The first place is John 12: 38 and is used in connection with the personal teaching of Christ. The other citation is in Rom. 10: 16 and is applied to the preaching of the apostles of Christ. Therefore we know the verse is a prediction in question form that the majority of people were going to reject the truth when it was preached. *Arm of the Lord* has reference to his power, and most of the people failed to see or realize that power because they would not hear the truth that portrayed it to them.

Verse 2. *He* (Christ) *shall grow up before him* (God). *Tender plant* is from YOWNEQ which Strong defines, "a sucker; hence a twig (of a tree felled and sprouting)." *Root* means he was to grow up as from a root of a tree in dry ground. Jesus came from the stock of Israel which was in a rather decaying condition at the time. That is why his appearance in the world is compared to the sucker and sprout as above. *No form nor comeliness* should not be interpreted carelessly. We know that any living creatures would have some shape. But the entire description in the last half of the verse means that nothing in the form or personal appearance of Jesus would attract the attention of mankind. We do not have to conclude that he was unusually homely, neither do we have the right to picture him as a very handsome man as many artists do.

Verse 3. To *despise* means to belittle or treat with contempt and that was the way men treated Christ. No doubt part of the reason was his humble, unpretentious appearance and surroundings. (As an instance of it see the statement of Nathanael in John 1: 46.) *Man of sorrows and acquainted with grief.* In the lexicon the leading words of this clause have both a literal and figurative definition. Since Jesus had a body that was both human and divine, it is reasonable to conclude that both senses of the words applied to his experiences. In one instance we may be sure the literal sense was meant (John 4: 6). That text says that Jesus was wearied with his journey and sat down on the well. Thayer defines the word for *wearied*, "to grow weary, tired, exhausted." If our Lord could become tired in body from physical exercise, it is logical that he could experience other afflictions of the flesh. And it would also be true that he could know what it is to be sorrowful and concerned in a situation of grief and disappointment. His actions and words at the grave of Lazarus (John 11: 33-35) prove the above conclusion to be correct and also demonstrate the language in Heb. 4: 15. But while Jesus never resorted to his supernatural power as a personal help in his own afflictions, yet his superior knowledge enabled him to understand all the more thoroughly those of others; hence the phrase *acquainted with grief*. *We hid* refers to no particular persons but to mankind in general. The thought is that Jesus was so humble and unattractive from the popular standpoint that men turned their faces from him as if they were ashamed to countenance him. *Esteemed him not* means that Jesus was belittled by humanity and yet *we* were not concerned about it.

Verse 4. The prophet writing by inspiration declares that Jesus would bear the griefs and sorrows of others. But hardhearted men *esteemed* or considered the afflictions of Jesus were a stroke of chastisement from God. Such is the meaning of the closing part of this verse.

Verse 5. The inspired prophet corrects the wrong thinking of *we* as to why Jesus was afflicted. It was not because of any transgressions of his (he had none) but it was because of ours. On the same principle as the above Jesus was bruised because of the iniquities of others, the very ones who had belittled him. *Chastisement of our peace* means the chastisement that man should have suffered in order to satisfy the Father and be at peace with him. But that chastisement would have been so severe that it would have been impossible for man to endure it, hence Jesus took the blows instead. *By his stripes we are healed* has the same idea of substitution by the innocent on behalf of the guilty that the other illustrations of the verse have. But this one is peculiarly interesting because it supposes a transfer of conditions from one person to another that could be accomplished only by miracles. *Stripes* is from CHABURAH which Strong defines, "properly bound (with stripes), i.e. a weal (or black-and-blue mark itself)." It is the word for "blueness" in Prov. 20: 30 where it says, "The *blueness* of a wound cleanseth away evil." The black-and-blue or blueness of a wound indicates that the blood is circulating and that will finally wash away the infection. Our passage represents man as suffering from deserved wounds that are not being cured. Jesus then suffered himself to be wounded and have the benefits of his circulation (blueness of the wound) transferred to the otherwise incurable wounds of sinful man.

Verse 6. The pronoun *we* has a more definite application than it did in earlier verses of this chapter. It has specific reference to the apostles who deserted the Lord before they realized that he had risen from the dead (John 21: 3). "I go a fishing" in this passage fulfills *turned every one to his own way* in our verse in Isaiah. *Like sheep* is said because of the disposition of that animal to become panicky and flee if its master is taken from it (see Matt. 26: 31). *Hath laid on him* sets forth a situation where all of the persons in a group engaged in a task desert but one, and he is compelled to perform the task alone.

Verse 7. *Opened not his mouth* in protest or complaint is the meaning. We should not think of Jesus as one who would be sullen when being mistreated, for he did speak when asked questions and when general interests called for it (see Matt. 27: 11; Luke 22: 70). But when it was a matter of mistreatment and false accusation *he opened not his mouth* (see Matt. 26: 63). *Sheep before her shearers is dumb*. The last word is from ALAM and Strong defines it "a primitive root; to tie fast; hence (of the mouth) to be tongue-tied." If the reader has ever watched a sheep being sheared and observed the look of dejection in its face, he can appreciate the illustration here. But we must not think of that attitude of Jesus as being from any sense of shame on his part. He was bowed down over the awful condition of mankind through sin that made it necessary for him to be put to shame on their behalf.

Verse 8. *Taken from prison and judgment*. *Prison* is from OTSER and Strong defines it "constraint." This clause is rendered in Acts 8: 33, "In his humiliation his judgment was taken away." The meaning of the passage is that Jesus did not have a fair hearing but by constraint and unjust verdict he was condemned to die. *Generation* is used in the sense of age or period of time and *declare* is defined by Thayer in Acts 8: 33, "set forth, recount, relate in full . . . describe." The passage means that it would be difficult if not impossible to describe fully the people of the age in which Christ lived. As a specification of the wickedness of that generation the prophet states that they cut the Lord off from the land of the living. However, they would not have been able to carry out their wicked design against Christ had it not been the will of God for it to happen. But the tragic event was necessary for the salvation of man which is the significance of the words, *for the transgressions of my people was he stricken.*

Verse 9. *Grave with the wicked and with the rich*. In these few words are predictions of two separate and opposite kinds of events. The enemies of Jesus classed him with the vile criminals by crucifying him between two thieves. It was a special disgrace to be executed by crucifixion and such victims were even denied honorable burial. By treating Jesus as they did the expectation was that he would receive the same kind of burial (if any) as the thieves. It was in view of that situation that the prophet saw him making his grave *with the wicked*. But a rich and righteous man by the name of Joseph, (Matt. 27: 57-60) had doubtless feared just such an event and wished to prevent it. He possessed a tomb near the place of crucifixion which had never been used by anybody. Having obtained possession of the body of Jesus from the governor, Joseph laid it away in his own burial place. This is what the prophet saw when he wrote that Jesus made his grave *with the rich.* Because is rendered "although" by the A.S.V., by Moffatt and some others, and Strong's lexicon does not disagree with it. The sense of the passage also would call for such a rendering. Hence the clause means Jesus recieved the mentioned dishonor by the wicked men *although he had done no violence;* they had executed an innocent man.

Verse 10. *Pleased the Lord to bruise him.* God did not find personal pleasure in the suffering of Christ, but it was his will that he suffer so that man might be saved. *Soul* in the Old Testament is from NEPHESH and its primary meaning is "a breathing creature." The clause means that Christ was put to death (ceased breathing) as an offering for the sins of the world. After God saw his seed (Christ) go through the sacrificial offering he took the case in hand and rescued him again from death. By doing this the Lord *prolonged his days* and declared to the world that his Son should never die again (Rom. 6: 9).

Verse 11. *He* (God) *shall see the travail* (worry) *of his* (Christ's) *soul.* On the cross Jesus made the heart-rending cry, "My God, my God, why hast thou forsaken me?" This was a complete experience of suffering and was all that God required; he *was satisfied. By his knowledge* means the knowledge of the Gospel which Christ was to offer to the world; all who would accept and obey it would be justified or be forgiven of their iniquities. Not that the actions of man can atone for his sins, but by obedience he can obtain the benefit of the sacrifice of Christ because it was for that purpose that he was to *bear their iniquities.*

Verse 12. *Divide with the great* and *spoil with the strong* is an illustration drawn from the practices of war. An ordinary person could overcome a weak foe and get his belongings. But the power of Christ was to be seen in that he would overcome the great and strong foes and take from them their *spoils* or possessions. *Poured out his soul* has the same meaning as travail *of his soul* in the preceding verse. *Numbered with the transgressors* was fulfilled when Jesus was crucified between the thieves (Mark 15: 27, 28). *Bare the sins of many* is the same as *bear their iniquities* in the preceding verse. Jesus *made intercession for the transgressors* when he said, "Father, forgive them; for they know not what they do" (Luke 23: 34). That dying statement of Christ was verified by Paul in 1 Cor. 2: 8.

ISAIAH 54

Verse 1. Almost every time some favorable turn comes for ancient Israel the prophet will see something concerning spiritual Israel. A great part of this chapter will deal with the good fortune of the Jews in being restored to their own land and to the favor of their God from whom they were alienated on account of their iniquities. But for a few verses the writer will be dealing with the subject referred to in the first sentence. We do not have to be in any doubt as to the application of this verse for Paul has made the application in Gal. 4: 27. We understand that the subject of that book is the advantages of Christians, whether Jews or Gentiles, under Christ. Those advantages are contrasted with the ones of the Jews under Moses. In the progress of his argument the apostle quoted our verse of the present paragraphs. Of course the terms are largely figurative, using the relation of husband and wife for the illustration. Sarah, the barren woman, became finally the mother of many nations. Likewise the church of Christ, composed of both Jews and Gentiles, will bear to God a far greater number of children than all of ancient Israel amounted to.

Verse 2. The thought of the preceding verse is continued in this. It pertains to the extension of favor to all nations of the world and not to the Jews only. That would make it necessary to *enlarge the place of thy tent* so as to make room for the increase of spiritual inhabitants that would be gathered in from the whole earth.

Verse 3. This has the same thought as the foregoing only it is more specific and names the Gentiles as people who were to be benefited by the plan under Christ.

Verse 4. Having "taken time out" from the general subject to give us a glimpse into the time of Christ, the prophet resumes his prediction of the recovery of ancient Israel from captivity. That period is compared to a separation of a wife from her husband in which she would be virtually a widow. She was to be taken back and her former unfaithfulness not held against her.

Verse 5. This wife had the greatest of all husbands for he was her Maker. He not only was great enough to make or bring into being an institution to serve as his wife, but he is Lord of hosts which means he has control over the vast throngs of living creatures elsewhere in the universe. This husband did not merely say pleasant words to his wife to win her back, but took active interest in the matter of getting her out of her difficulties; he became her *Redeemer*. And so great and evident will be that transaction that he will be recognized as the *God of the whole earth*.

Verse 6. Husband and wife relationship is still the subject, to illustrate that between God and Israel. The wife had been put away in her unfaithfulness and left to grieve for her husband. But the wronged husband will be willing to receive back his wife.

Verse 7. *Small moment* actually will be 70 years so the phrase is figurative or comparative. Israel had been God's people for many centuries so the period of captivity will seem short in comparison. *With great mercies gather* was fulfilled as recorded in the books of Ezra and Nehemiah. I believe I should keep the reader reminded as to the date in history for the location of our study. Try to bear in mind that Isaiah completed his writing at least a century before the Babylonian captivity started. Thus it will be understood that all or most of his statements are predictions, though they are past tense in their grammatical form.

Verse 8. This is the same prediction as the preceding verses, referring to the captivity and release therefrom.

Verse 9. The question has been raised as to whether the promise of this verse was contradicted by the destruction of Jerusalem by the Romans. It will not be so considered when the comparison is observed which the Lord made. He referred to the covenant with Noah and then declared that the promise to Israel would be as sure. But the oath to Noah did not say the earth would never again be destroyed; only it was not to be destroyed again by a flood. On the same principle, Israel as a nation intact was never to be taken away again into captivity and it never was. But her downfall through decay (see comments on *root* in ch. 53: 2) would be another matter.

Verse 10. The sense of the language is, "though the mountains shall depart," etc. God's promises to mankind are always reliable.

Verse 11. *Tossed with tempest* is a figurative phrase, likening the experiences of Israel in captivity to a vessel on the sea that is shoved about by the waves and storms, without the help of propeller or rudder. The vessel was finally to be rescued from the raging sea (captivity in Babylon) and towed into the harbor of her own shore. The imagery now changes from that of a wandering vessel to a structure that had been torn down but was to be rebuilt. In reality the prediction is virtually literal for it refers to the rebuilding of the city and buildings at Jerusalem that was to take place after the captivity. The materials named should be regarded rather as figurative, but the fact of rebuilding the structures was to be literal.

Verse 12. This verse has the same meaning as the preceding one with reference to the materials used in the rebuilding carried on in Jersusalem after the captivity.

Verse 13. *All shall be taught* was fulfilled as set forth in Neh. 8: 1-9. It is true that God expected to offer mankind in general the opportunity for learning more about divine truth. That was to be brought to its greatest state of perfection through the era of righteousness that Christ would establish. But this prediction was actually fulfilled as recorded in the passage referred to above.

Verse 14. *In righteousness be established* means that it would be a righteous thing for Israel again to be established in their own land. *Be far from oppression* means they would be entirely released from the oppression of the captivity, and would need have no more fear of a like experience.

Verse 15. The antecedent of *they* is any people who would think to come against Israel after the captivity has been over and the servants of God have been resettled in their own land. *Not by me*. Previously it was the Lord who had caused the nations to come against his people to chastise them. But after the return from captivity that will not be done any more. If such an attempt is made against the land of the Jews it will not be caused by the Lord. *Fall for thy sake* has reference to the protection that God will give for the *sake* of his love toward his people. The attempts thus made against them will fail through the overruling influence of the Lord.

Verse 16. There is a significant argument in this verse. In forming any attack upon another body of people it would be necessary to have weapons made of metal. But the man who knows how to make those weapons obtained that ability from his Creator. Certainly such a smith would not have any more knowledge or ability for making the weapons than has the One who gave such talents to him. And if God can enable one man to form such tools he certainly can enable another to make weapons to oppose them.

Verse 17. On the basis of the truths set forth in the preceding verse, the people of God are given the assurance of this verse. If any man uses his God-given talent to form weapons of war intended to be used against the Lord's people, then surely He will enable his own servants to resist such force with like force. There might be occasions when the enemy will attempt such an action and for a time will seem to prosper, but all such attempts will finally be overcome. A noted instance of just such an attempt is recorded in history. A wicked man named Epiphanes started an armed attack on the institutions of the Jews and appeared to be successful until a valiant group of God's people took up arms and put down the invader. I shall quote some history for the information of the reader which is as follows: "Mattathias and Judas Maccabaeus supported the distressed nation [of Israel], and the almost universally abandoned religion, with so small a number of forces, that we can consider the success which the Almighty gave their arms no otherwise than a miracle. The troops grew more numerous by degrees, and afterwards formed a very considerable body." ROLLIN, Vol. 4, page 242. "At this time Judas Maccabaeus, with some others that accompanied him, fled into the wilderness, and there lived in great hardship, subsisting themselves upon herbs, and what else the mountains and woods could afford them, till they gained an opportunity of taking up arms for themselves and their country as will be hereafter related." PRIDEAUX, year 168. "These measures [of Epiphanes] induced an open revolt, whose leader was the priest and patriot Mattathias. His bold deed of the public murder of a royal official was the sign for the beginning of the revolt. Fleeing to the mountains, he, with the co-operation of his five heroic sons, organized war on a small scale. He died 166 B.C." SCHAFF-HERZOG, Article, Maccabees. We thus have a well authenticated account in history of an arming against God's people that was brought to defeat. Of course the tongue that rose against the Jews was likewise put to shame. Epiphanes used some vile language against the Jews, but he was finally subdued and his career ended in his own disgrace. There will be more predictions and history concerning this wicked man to be considered when we come to the study of the book of Daniel. But for the present it is sufficient to observe the complete fulfilling of this part of Isaiah's interesting book of prophecy.

ISAIAH 55

Verse 1. The leading thought running through this entire chapter is a prediction of the benefits to be had under Christ in the centuries to come. See the comments on Ch. 54: 1 with regard to the occasions when the prophet goes from ancient or fleshly Israel to spiritual Israel. That chapter deals mostly with the improved conditions that would come to fleshly Israel after being brought from the captivity. But all of this book was written a century or more before the captivity even began. Hence the exhortations to repentance in this chapter were made to the people of Israel right at the time when it had been declared by the Lord that nothing could be done to help matters; that the nation had to go into captivity. The apparent contradiction is explained in the long note written at 2 Ki. 22: 17 in Vol. 2 of this COMMENTARY. However, the prophet has the subject of spiritual benefits in general before him, especially as they will be offered to mankind under Christ. It will be from that viewpoint the several verses will be commented upon in their order. *Ho* is an interjection to secure close attention. *Waters* is figurative and refers to the spiritual blessings to be obtained from the Lord. It is one of the most common figures in the whole Bible because literal water fills so great a place in the needs of living beings. *Wine* and *milk* also are used figuratively for the same purpose as *waters*, applying to the provisions of spiritual life under God's favors. *Without price* does not mean that a man will not be required to contribute anything for the benefits of salvation. It means that no material possessions of man could purchase salvation, but it will be possible to obtain it through the favor of Christ for those who obey him.

Verse 2. The contrast between spiritual and material food is the main idea in this verse. Men will devote their time and energies to obtain the temporal things of life, when those things are to be destroyed as soon as this world is brought to an end (1 Cor. 6: 12, 13). If they would devote themselves to the service of Christ, they would receive that kind of meat and drink that would never fail but would sustain them unto the life eternal after earthly things have ceased to be.

Verse 3. *Mercies* is from a word that means "kindness," and the expression means that Christ was to bestow the kindness that had been given to David, and promised through him to the world. (See Psa. 89: 1, 28.) Christ was a lineal descendant of David and many things that are said of Christ are spoken of as from his noted ancestor.

Verse 4. It seems that both David and Christ are in the mind of the prophet, or, that what is said could be regarded as applying to either of them. That is not strange because the Bible frequently refers to the two great persons in a common relationship. David was the first king in the blood line of Christ, and he was the ancestor of Christ on both sides of his parentage. But in a more direct and personal sense God decreed to give Christ *for a witness to the people*, and he also was to be their commander. This was fulfilled after he conquered the grave and appeared alive to his apostles whom he had chosen before death. He then declared that all power (command) was given to him in heaven and in earth (Matt. 28: 18).

Verse 5. This verse is a prediction of the call of the Gentiles under the reign of Christ. Under the Mosaic system Christ *knew not* the Gentiles and they *knew not* him. *He hath glorified thee* means God hath glorified his Son Jesus to have all this honor and power. This was testified to in those very words in Acts 3: 13.

Verse 6. This verse says *while he may be found* and Jesus said *he that seeketh findeth* (Matt. 7: 8). We do not believe the Bible contradicts itself, but that all apparent difficulties of that kind may have a satisfactory explanation. The word *found* is from MATSA and Strong defines it, "to attain or acquire." The Lord has always made his promises of favor conditional. If a man ignores the opportunities of obtaining the favor of God until his circumstances make it impossible to comply with the conditions, then it will be too late for him to "attain or acquire" the Lord's blessings. The word *near* is to be understood in the same sence as *found*. But it should be observed that in order to obtain the Lord even under the proper conditions it is necessary for man to *seek* and *call*. God has done all that he will or that needs to be done for human salvation until man makes the next move.

Verse 7. Forsake means to let go of, not merely ease up in the practice of that which is evil. Not only must all outward actions be abandoned but unrighteous thoughts must be forsaken. There is abundant reason for this as many passages in both the Old and New Testaments teach. (See Psa. 19: 14; Pr. 15: 26; Matt. 15: 19; Acts 8: 22; Phil. 4: 8.) But even all of this reformation in the individual sinner is not enough to obtain the favor of God. He was the one who got away from God by his sins and he is the one who must come back. *Have mercy upon him*, not hand over to him what strict justice would allow, for it is the mercy of God that makes it possible for man to hope for salvation. *Our God* is significant in view of the many false gods that were worshiped in those days. The sinner must not turn to the gods of the Egyptians or Babylonians or Canaanites, but to the God of Israel; to *our God*. *Abundantly pardon* means full and unreserved for all the sins. God does not give his pardon for sins in degrees or installments. If a sinner has not complied fully with the divine terms of pardon God will not forgive at all.

Verses 8, 9. I believe these two verses should be in one bracket to get the clearest understanding of the very important subject. *Thoughts* is rendered "plans" in some versions. The lexicon gives "intentions" as part of the definition of the original Hebrew. But either rendering will leave the meaning of the passage the same. We just learned that a man's outward actions are affected by his thoughts, so either of the words meets the point the Lord was making. The difference between the thoughts of God and man is compared to that between heaven and earth. If the thoughts of God are that much higher than those of man, then if those thoughts had been put in language correspondingly high when addressed to earthly beings, no man could have understood what was being said. That is why Paul said he spoke after the manner of men. It was because of the infirmity of the flesh; that is, because fleshly man is too far inferior to God to comprehend any but human speech (Rom. 6: 19).

Verse 10. This verse refers to the regularity and success of the processes of nature as regards temporal results. It is an argument to show that God's plans always work as he expects as far as he has to do with them.

Verse 11. Having laid the foundation for the argument on the success of the Lord's plans in nature, the same principle is affirmed to hold good in the effects of the word that is sent forth from his mouth. This verse has been misused by many well-meaning persons. The passage is made to mean that in every case where the word of God is preached it is bound to result in obedience of those who hear it. That conclusion cannot be drawn from this verse for it makes no such declaration. It only affirms that it will accomplish what the Lord expects it to accomplish. A clear passage for this purpose is in 2 Cor. 2: 15, 16 whch I request the student to read carefully. That passage from the apostle Paul teaches that God's word has a twofold object in view; to save the obedient and to condemn the disobedient. It is bound to do one or the other, and whichever it does it will bring about the result indicated by our present verse.

Verse 12. When fleshly Israel went out of captivity there was general rejoicing or a feeling of congratulation. But in a more important sense, when men accept Christ and are released from their captivity in sin, there is great happiness for all concerned. Mountains, hills and trees are used figuratively because they represent the principal parts of a country.

Verse 13. The figurative line of thought is continued in this verse. It shows the improved condition of all who will accept the provisions of mercy that Christ has to offer to the world. Thorns and briars are unsightly and destructive. A fir tree is useful as well as pleasant to the sight, and a myrtle tree is especially adapted to the use of ornamentation. These terms are the prophet's way of picturing some of the good results for men who will accept the word of Christ.

ISAIAH 56

Verse 1. Isaiah did all of his writing more than a century before the Babylonian captivity started. But the people were told many times that after that period was over they would be permitted to return to their home land. In the meantime they were exhorted to make personal amends and correct their individual errors. And, as usual, the exhortations and promises were of such a character that they would apply to people and circumstances in the time of Christ. These remarks are offered as comments on this verse, also to apply in general to many following verses.

Verse 2. Mention of the sabbath does not prevent this exhortation from applying to men in the time of Christ. At the time the prophet was writing it the law of Moses was in force and the violation of the sabbath law was a prevailing iniquity. But the same principle holds good concerning the law of Christ. The man who will keep His commandments will be *blessed* as surely as did the one who kept the sabbath under Moses.

Verse 3. Figurative language is based on some literal fact for its form of speech even though the application is different. Under the Mosaic system a *stranger* (foreigner) or eunuch was not admitted to the advantages of the system. It will not be so under Christ, but all ranks of mankind will have the same privileges of the Gospel.

Verse 4. *Eunuchs* and *sabbaths* are again used figuratively, the point being that under Christ all grades and classes of men will be invited to serve alike.

Verse 5. If these men will serve Christ faithfully they will receive blessings that will far outshine those that had been denied eunuchs under the Mosaic system.

Verse 6. Doubtless the prophet has the call of the Gentiles especially in mind in these verses. We know they were considered strangers in the time of the Mosaic law according to the language of Paul in Eph. 2: 12, 19. These were to be admitted to the privileges and expected to obey the commandments of Christ the same as the Jews.

Verse 7. *Mountains* in symbolic language means governments and institutions of power. This verse is a prediction that the Gentiles were to be invited to come into the government or kingdom of Christ. There will not be any literal sacrifices in that service, but using the terms of the old system for the figures, the prediction is that the nations will be accepted in their spiritual offerings to Christ. *Mine house shall be called an house of prayer* was quoted by Christ in Matt. 21: 13, and that was while the Mosaic system was in force. This might seem to conflict with the idea that the passage we are studying is a prediction of the Gospel epoch. But such is not the case for there are some truths or principles that are always valid. Jesus knew it was taught that the house of God (meaning the temple in Jerusalem) was to be used in a respectful manner from its beginning; he therefore knew that the Jews were violating that divine purpose. But that did not prevent the prophet from predicting a time when the Lord's house would be a house of prayer *for all people.* The last three words are the key to the passage, and identifty it as a prediction of the call of the Gentiles. Of course when the time comes for fulfillment of this particular part of the prophecy, the *house* of the Lord will be the church that was started in Jerusalem, the same city in which the Jews had their material house of God.

Verse 8. In this one short verse will be found predictions of two separate operations of the Lord that were to be hundreds of years apart. The first is the return of the people of Israel from captivity. This is the literal meaning of *gathereth the outcasts of Israel. Gather others to him* refers to the admission of the Gentiles into the kingdom of Christ with the same privileges as those enjoyed by the Jews.

Verse 9. This verse is highly figurative and refers to the use God was going to make of the heathen kings in chastising the corrupt leaders of his nation. These heathen men (such as the Babylonians) were the *beasts of the field.*

Verse 10. All through the study we have seen that God was chiefly moved with wrath against the leaders of his nation. They had abused their position of power to mislead the common people and cause them to commit iniquity like the idolatrous people about them. The Lord had often warned of what he would do to his nation as punishment for its corruptions. He had told them through the prophets that at last the heathen forces would be brought against Jerusalem, and that they would take it under control. But these selfish leaders refused to be admonished by the warnings and continued in their unlawful way of life. In this situation they were compared to *watchmen* who were blind to the threatening conditions, and to *dumb dogs* that failed to bark at the approach of the wolves that were coming to attack the flock.

Verse 11. The comparison is continued in this verse. The leaders are likened to watch dogs that are so greedy that they are interested only in satisfying their ravenous appetite of watching out for the appearance of an enemy. They are also compared to shepherds who are as selfish as their watch dogs and who are always looking after the interests of *their own way,* seeking always for their own gain.

Verse 12. This verse repeats what these selfish leaders would be saying among themselves regarding their extravagant way of living. They proposed to procure wine and other luxuries and consume them in their own selfish manners. *Tomorrow shall be as this day* portrays a very corrupt thought. It is always bad to practice the things that are connected with fleshly extravagance, but it makes it worse when such a life is deliberately planned for the future as these wicked leaders did. Their conduct was bound to be corrupt when the expressed intentions were already headed that way.

ISAIAH 57

Verse 1. The subject of the preceding chapter is continued over into this. The selfish leaders took advantage of the people under them and caused many of them to perish. *No man layeth it to heart* refers to the cruelty of these leading men among the priests and prophets who had become corrupted by their own selfish purposes. That cruelty will be described in more detail in the study of the next chapter.

Verse 2. When a righteous man perishes through the cruelty of the wicked, he is not the loser in the end. By being taken away in his upright life he thereby misses the evil and trouble that is awaiting the wicked who are left in the land of the living and who had been responsible for the tragic end of the innocent one's life.

Verse 3. *Draw near* is a call to attention for the wicked characters in the nation who have been abusing the helpless common men and women. These persons were the descendants of the vilest of creatures and were imitating their ancestors.

Verse 4. These wicked men intended their oppressions to affect the unfortunate ones subject to them only. The question asked them by the prophet implies that God was the actual target for their misdoings and He would finally bring them to justice.

Verse 5. This verse describes some of the worst of the idolaters among the people of Israel. Some of them even offered their children in sacrifice to the idols, and the altars were built in valleys and under clifts of rocks.

Verse 6. These idolaters would gather the stones that were worn smooth by the current of the *stream.* These were not permanent rivers or it would have been very difficult if not impossible to obtain the stones. Strong defines the original word to mean a winter torrent. In that way the stones would become smooth by the wearing of the water during the wet season, then dry up at other times so that men could descend into the bed of the stream and get the stones. With these the idolaters would erect their altars and on them make offerings to the false gods. *Should I receive comfort in these?* This clause means the same as if it said: "Do you think I will put up with such conduct and not punish you for it?"

Verse 7. *Bed* is from MISHKAB, which Strong defines, "a bed (figuratively a bier); abstractly, sleep; by euphemism [substitution of a milder word] carnal intercourse." Throughout the Bible the sin of idolatry is likened to unfaithfulness in the marriage relation. The *bed* here then means this altar for the service of idolatry which would be compared to adultery against the marriage bed. The Jews chose many of the mountains as places for their idols, and altars were erected in front of them.

Verse 8. Unfaithfulness in marriage is still the illustration. (See the comments on the preceding verse.) When a Jew who was in love with the idols of the heathen people would see one of the images it would stir him into the service connected with it. Such a fact is illustrated by a woman who is inclined toward immoral practices. She will prepare her own bed for the use of her lovers wherever she can find a suitable place. *Where thou sawest it* is rendered "thou providest room" in the margin and the ASV agrees with it. *Sawest* is from CHAZAH and Strong's definition is, "A primitive root; to gaze at; mentally to perceive, contemplate (with pleasure); specifically to have a vision of." The passage means that the unfaithful wife was even picturing in her mind the vision of her bed to be occupied jointly with her by one who was not her husband. Such conduct actually takes place frequently in the social world, but it is used in this place to compare the religious unfaithfulness of the nation of Israel that is considered as the wife of the Lord.

Verse 9. This unfaithful wife even planned to entice the king. To make herself the more alluring to him she used *ointment* and *perfumes* on her body. We might wonder why these bodily dainties are mentioned in this connection, but it is because of the effect they have in stimulating the emotional nerves of a man. A very noted doctor and psychologist, member of the faculty of a modern educational institution, says this on the subject: "A perfumed girl is likely to be a greater mental stimulus for the erotic feelings," etc. Again let us remember the prophet is using these strong emotions and actions in the literal world to illustrate the zeal with which the unfaitful Israelites went after idols.

Verse 10. Israel wore herself out with her extreme activities on behalf of the idols yet would not give up and admit it was all hopeless. After a slight pause she would feel somewhat revived and then would renew her idolatrous practices. *Wast not grieved* means she was not worried in conscience over her unfaithfulness to God.

Verse 11. An unfaithful wife often makes up excuses or "explanations" for her conduct, but such tales generally prove to be lies. God asks his unfaithful wife whom she fears. She cannot claim it is her rightful husband seeing she *had not remembered* nor regarded him. The statement is then made that the wife had thus mistreated her patient husband just because he had not been making any complaint; he had *held his peace.* Such is the weakness of humanity, that if he is suffered to go on unpunished in his sin, he will take advantage of it to sin all the more. (See Ecclesiastes 8: 11.) And so this unfaithful wife went on and on in her unrighteous life without any pain of conscience for the sake of her true husband whom she had wronged.

Verse 12. One word in Strong's definition of the original for *declare* is "expose," and another is "explain." The verse means God would expose the pretended righteousness of these unfaithful people of his. Even the things they did that should have been according to divine law were done for the wrong purpose and hence were rejected.

Verse 13. *Companies* refers to the group of idols they had been worshiping. When times of distress came upon the idolatrous Jews they would wish for help from God. But they were told to cry unto their idols for help which was an appropriate suggestion. If the idols were good enough to be worshiped in times of prosperity, they should be the proper source of help in times of adversity. But the prophet gave them to understand that their idols would do them no good. *Wind shall carry them all away* is a figurative way of showing how light and useless the idols were. On the other hand, the man who trusts the Lord has the assurance of favor from God.

Verse 14. *Cast ye up* is a prediction of the return from captivity and the restoration of the country. *Take up the stumblingblock* means practically the same as the first of the verse. The Babylonians had interrupted the progress of the nation of Israel, but at the end of their period of control they were to be removed and no more be a hindrance to the people of God.

Verse 15. This verse states the truths and general principles on which God always deals with man, whether his ancient people or with man in any age. The dignity of the Creator contrasted with the weakness and dependency of man is set forth in the passage. But it should be noted while studying the verse that man's helpless condition is no hindrance to his receiving the attention and favor of God if he is of the proper frame of mind. Let us consider the leading terms of this unusual verse. *Inhabiteth* is from SHAKAN and Strong defines it, "a primitive root . . . to reside or permanently stay." *Eternity* is from AD and the leading word in Strong's definition is "duration," without any specification as to whether it may be long or short. The word has practically the same meaning as the word "time." The popular notion is that the Bible considers the duration before the judgment day as "time" and after that it is "eternity." But it makes no such distinction and as far as the Bible is concerned "time" simply means duration, and consequently there has always been duration and always will be. Therefore it is not correct to speak of the "end of time," because "time" as a distinction from "eternity" will never end. To sum up this particular part of the subject, time had no beginning and will have no end. The phrase of our verse means that God permanently occupies duration. That is another way of saying that He never had a beginning and will have no end. Certainly, then, such a Being has the right to expect the proper respect from man who is the creature of the endless Creator. *Dwell* is from the same word as *inhabiteth*, so the verse means that while God inhabits or occupies all duration, yet he will admit certain ones to come and dwell with him, the ones to be described yet in this verse. *Contrite* and *humble* mean practically the same thing in the original, which is to be crushed or bowed down. If a man comes to realize his unworthiness and the greatness of his sins, and is completely humiliated by it, he is then in a state of mind to be received favorably by the Lord.

Verse 16. This verse teaches that God does not go to extremes. He will contend or accuse as long as it is necessary, but he will not hold out in his wrath indefinitely. The reason for thus limiting the divine wrath is that the *spirit should fail*.

Verse 17. The cause is stated for bringing chastisement upon the Lord's people which was the *iniquity of his covetousness*. This was especially true of the leaders who oppressed the poor in order to enrich their own possessions. (See the comments at ch. 58: 3). *I hid me* is a prediction of the period of the captivity when God turned his face against his disobedient nation. This bitter punishment was necessary because they went on *frowardly*, which means in a contrary and backsliding manner.

Verse 18. This verse describes the principles on which God deals generally with man. He has *seen* and thus knows all about his ways or manner of life and is always ready to rescue him whenever he complies with the terms. In a special manner, however, this is a prediction of Israel concerning the national sin of idolatry. God beheld all of that distressing history and decreed to punish the nation with the captivity. The prediction further promises that God *will heal him*. This cure from idolatry was accomplished by the bondage in Babylon, and the fulfillment of it has been verified by the history as per the quotation in connection with ch. 1: 25.

Verse 19. The particular *fruit of the lips* referred to here is the word *peace*. *I create* means that the lips of man cannot truthfully speak of peace except as God authorizes them so to speak. *Far off* and *near* has a general sense of meaning all the grades and classes of man. Its special sense is the prediction that the favors of the Lord were to be offered to the Gentiles as well as the Jews. (See Eph. 2: 17.)

Verse 20. When the sea is calm its waters are clear and pure. When it is stirred up it throws out various kinds of waste matter. This is used to illustrate the fruits of a wicked life that is agitated by the turmoil and strife of worldliness.

Verse 21. This verse should be considered in connection with verse 19. God does not authorize the lips of a wicked man to speak of peace, therefore we have the statement here that such a character can have no peace.

ISAIAH 58

Verse 1. The date of this writing is at least a century before the Babylonian captivity and thus was while the nation was in the midst of the corrupt practices complained of. God is instructing the prophet to preach against the people in severe terms. *Cry aloud* is from original words that literally mean to speak out with a strong voice against the evil doers. *Spare not* means not to be restrained in his denunciations against that guilty people so they will realize the greatness of their transgressions against the God who had been so gracious toward them.

Verse 2. This verse will be the better understood by remembering it is a description of the religious activities of the Jews as they appeared outwardly or as they wanted them to appear. A companion passage is in Jer. 3: 10 where the Lord said that Judah had turned to him "feignedly" which means in pretense. From this verse through verse 7 should form a bracket and the subject as a whole is the outward, insincere practices of the nation and particularly those of the leaders. The reader should consult the note that was given in connection with comments at ch. 1: 10.

Verse 3. The previous verse showed God speaking and describing the religious activities of Israel which they were doing insincerely. This verse shows the people doing the talking and giving an account of their doings. They are complaining that the Lord does not recognize them in their practices. But they are told why it is that the Lord does not accept them in what they are pretending to be a true devotion. Fasting was not generally commanded under the Mosaic system but it was permitted and when properly performed was blessed. But these people were pretending to be going through a period of fasting and *afflicting their souls.* The last phrase means to be having a time of great humility and sorrow for their unworthiness. Such conduct would have been appropriate for people who had so often been guilty of wrong-doing. This was especially true of the leaders who had been so cruel toward their poor and unfortunate subjects. When a man is going through a season of sincere penitence he is all the more kindly toward his fellowman, but these leaders were not doing that way. While they were pretending to be penalizing themselves for their past luxurious living, they were being cruel and hardhearted against their unfortunate brethren. At the very time they were pretending to be feeling depressed for their sins they were enjoying themselves and *finding pleasure. Exact* is from MAGAS and Strong defines it, "To drive (an animal, a workman, a debtor, an army) by implication to tax, harass, tyrannize." *Labors* is from ATSEB, which Strong defines, "A (hired) workman," so the meaning of the sentence is clear. At the very time these leaders were pretending to be having a period of humbleness and softheartedness, they were overworking their hired laborers and using harsh measures to collect from their brethren who were indebted to them. Of course the Lord would not recognize the pretended sacrifices of these leaders when he knew they were only done as a cloak for their unrighteous dealings against their poor brethren. In connection with these remarks I request the student to read Ezk. 34: 2, 3; Amos 6: 1-6.

Verse 4. Actual fasting will cause a man to feel some bodily discomfort. This feeling will be endured uncomplainingly if it is done sincerely. On the other hand, if it is merely for a cloak, it will render him ill-tempered and he may "take his spite out" on some innocent "bystander." It was having just that effect on these wicked leaders which is the meaning of *fast for strife* and *smite with the fist.* As long as they conducted their fast as they were doing then, their voice would not be *heard on high* or be heard by the Lord of heaven and earth.

Verse 5. The Lord asks in an accusing manner if it is a day or time for them to be putting on such a fast as they were doing. One that consisted only in an outward show of punishment or restrictions on their body as to the enjoyments of life.

Verse 6. If a man appears to be going through restrictions against his own body but at the same time makes others "pay for it," he will receive no credit from the Lord. This was no time for them to be depending upon the outward ritualistic performances, when their unfortunate brethren were undergoing such restrictions forcibly to the advantage of these hypocritical leaders. At such a time the appropriate kind of *fast* would be such as now will be described. First to cease their own practices of *wickedness*, then to lighten the burdens of their brethren that were so heavy.

Verse 7. If they not only abstained from bread for themselves, but dealt it out to the hungry who had been going through an enforced fast, then their practice would show evidence of being sincere. The rest of the verse is along the same line of thought. We may see a similar teaching in James 2: 15, 16.

Verse 8. *Then* means that if they would perform the kind of "fast" as the two preceding verses describe they would obtain the favor of God. Their influence would be compared to the morning light that betokens a day of joy and gladness for the oppressed. They would then receive the glory of the Lord as their reroward or general guard, as that obsolete word signifies.

Verse 9. This verse describes the opposite of what is set forth in the preceding ones. Instead of the frown of disapproval from the Lord, he would hear and answer the call of his servants. Instead of increasing the hardships of their subjects they would take the yoke of servitude away. *Speaking vanity* means to say things that are not true and that will come to nought. The reason their speech was considered in this light is that it was influenced by their devotion to idols.

Verse 10. For the comments appropriate to this verse see those on vs. 6, 7 above.

Verse 11. These terms are all used to describe the prosperous state that will come to the man who will conduct himself in a way pleasing to God. Most of the words are used figuratively because they pertain to the blessings generally that the Lord promises to bestow upon men and women who conduct themselves righteously.

Verse 12. This verse could have a literal as well as spiritual application. It was true that after the return from the captivity the nation of Israel was permitted to rebuild its city and other places of the country that had been destroyed.

Verse 13. *Turn away from the sabbath* is explained by the words that will soon follow; *doing thy pleasure on my holy day*. It means that if they will cease using the sabbath as a day for their own pleasure, but will delight in it as the holy day of the Lord, then they will be doing that which is right.

Verse 14. If the people will do as the preceding verse outlines, then they will be delighted in what they will receive of the Lord. *Heritage of Jacob* means the good things the Lord had promised to Jacob and the people descending from him.

ISAIAH 59

Verse 1. At the time the prophet was writing this the people of Israel were actually enjoying many of the good things of life and hence were really in possession of the fortunes that their position in the world made possible. But we should remember that Isaiah was writing of some things that were to take place a century or more in the future. At that time the nation will be in captivity and it will seem that the Lord's hand had failed. But this verse declares that the hand of the Lord had not become short or reduced, neither had his ear lost its ability to hear.

Verse 2. This verse explains the preceding one. The people will be without the help of their God but it will be their own fault. Their own iniquities will have caused the separation between them and Him. (See ch. 50: 1.)

Verse 3. The leaders of the nation were the ones especially meant in this accusation. (See comments on ch. 58: 3.) They were using their position of authority and other advantages to benefit their own interests. In carrying out this wicked practice they abused the common people and sometimes even caused them to lose their lives. When called upon to explain their acts they built up excuses and resorted to lies.

Verse 4. The outstanding men in the Jewish nation were guilty of these iniquities. They had about lost all regard for God's truth, and when an unfortunate brother was crying for help from oppression he was ignored.

Verse 5. This verse is figurative and describes the schemes and dark plots that were formed against the victims. A *cockatrice* is a poisonous snake and it is used to illustrate the deadly effect these wicked leaders were having upon the common people. A *spider* will entangle its victim in its web and render it helpless. This is also used for comparison purposes and is applied to the unfair treatment these corrupt leaders heaped upon the people under them. *Their eggs* means the eggs of the cockatrice but applies to the plots of the leaders; all who "fall" for such will be destroyed.

Verse 6. *Webs shall not become garments* means the schemes that are concocted by these corrupt men will not cover their wickedness any more than a web would hide a person's body. *Violence* may be either physical or otherwise. The priests and prophets had become so covetous and thirsty for power and special privilege that they wronged the people out of their rightful possessions. To cover up this crookedness they perverted the scripture to make it support their evil practices.

Verse 7. *Run to evil* indicates a tendency toward evil and *haste to shed innocent blood* means they are so eager to shed blood that they will not investigate first. It is well to take note of the phrase *innocent blood*. Not all deaths are alike, and if a man is slain as a punishment for murder that would be the shedding of *guilty* blood. Such execution was commanded by the Lord in Gen. 9: 6 and has never been repealed.

Verse 8. Peace based on principles of right is what these corrupt men did not know; that is, they would not recognize it. They were so bent on carrying out their own interests that all rights of others were trampled upon. *No judgment in their goings* denotes the utter disregard these people would show for the rights of others. A *crooked path* is hard to follow and by laying out such a road for their subjects to travel they would hope to get them confused. Such a condition would give an opportunity for preying upon the victims and robbing them of their goods and other rights.

Verse 9. Up to this verse the prophet has been speaking on God's part directly to the Jews and thus was using the second person. Now he speaks in the first person and makes the people of his nation complain and hence acknowledge their own iniquities and the just consequences. For a number of verses this grammatical form of person will be used. *Therefore* introduces conclusions to be drawn from the truths stated in the preceding verses. Among the sad results of their corrupt doings is their inability to get any justice done even when they might have had a just complaint had they been worthy. Of course many of the expressions are to be understood figuratively, the point to be observed being the contrast between the terms used. *Light* and *obscurity* are opposite terms and so are *brightness* and *darkness*. The illustrations are intended to show the disappointing results of living in such a manner as to lose the favor and other assistance from God.

Verse 10. *Grope* means to search by feeling and such an act would be necessary either because the light had been shut off or the person was blind. Both effects had come upon these people because of their departures from God. If one had been deprived of his eyesight he would be as helpless at noon as at midnight. Their life had become as desolate as if they had died.

Verse 11. To *roar* means to complain so heavily that it is like the voice of *bears*, at the same time it has the note of despair that is compared to the sound of *doves*. *Judgment* and *salvation* are used in the same sense as "judgment" and "justice" in verse 9.

Verse 12. This verse is a confession by the people of Israel. The significant words *before thee* means that the Lord knows all about what they had been doing. *Sins testify* denotes a self-accusing conscience and an acknowledgement that all the charges that are being made against them by the Lord through his prophet are true. *Transgressions are with us* is a candid admission that none but themselves could be blamed for their undone conditions. *We know them* signifies that they could not plead ignorance as an explanation for their past record of wrong-doing.

Verse 13. This is a continuation of the acknowledgment in the preceding verse. It is significant to observe that *lying against the Lord* and *departing away from our God* are named together as if they mean the same. That is true, for when a man forsakes the way which the Lord has pointed out for him to travel he thereby implies that the Lord's way is wrong which would be a falsehood against Him.

Verse 14. *Backward* and *far off* are terms used for the purpose of emphasis meaning that these favors had come to be out of reach of them. *Street* is from a word whose outstanding meaning is any place of much room. The point in the figure of speech is that truth had been let down publicly and then abandoned. *Equity* means fairness which was a quality that was not welcomed by these corrupt leaders.

Verse 15. *Maketh himself a prey* means that the man who dared try to do right would only expose himself to the anger of the mob of evil doers. All of this wicked practice was seen by the Lord and hence he decreed some punishment should come to them.

Verse 16. The pronoun *he* refers to the Lord whose name was used in the close of the preceding verse. In that place it expressly says that the Lord *saw* the corrupt condition of his people and was displeased. The subject is not changed in this verse except to make the situation look still darker. *No man . . . no intercessor* means the Lord saw there was no one in the nation upon whom he could depend. We understand all these remarks could be applied spiritually to the necessity for some one besides mere man to bring salvation to the world. But the direct sense of the verse is that God would have to take over the whole case and work out some plan that would result in the national salvation of his people. That plan will include first the captivity of the nation and that to be followed by the overthrow of the enemy and return of Israel to her native land. *Righteousness sustained him* indicates the above plan for the sake of the nation of Israel will be the right one.

Verse 17. These military or protective terms are used figuratively and still apply to the righteousness of the Lord's plan on behalf of his people Israel.

Verse 18. From this verse to the close of the chapter is a bracket dealing with the overthrow of the Babylonians by the Persians. That event was to end the captivity and permit Israel to return to Jerusalem. Babylon took too much personal satisfaction out of the chastisement of Israel and that displeased the Lord. *Fury to his adversaries* is a prediction of the severe experience that Babylon was destined to suffer for her harsh treatment of the Jews. The historical fulfillment of this prophecy may be seen in connection with the comments on ch. 13: 1.

Verse 19. *West* and *rising of the sun* are opposite terms and are used to indicate the general recognition that will be given to the revolutionary change from Babylonian to Persian domination of the world. *Come in like a flood* refers to the sudden and complete overthrow of Babylon which will be seen in the historical quotation referred to above. *Lift up a standard against him* refers to the Persian forces that God would bring against the Babylonians.

Verse 20. The *Redeemer* refers to the Lord who was to overrule the oppression caused by the Babylonians. That would release Israel so she could again return to Zion or Jerusalem which was the capital of the nation.

Verse 21. The prediction of the overthrow of Babylon and restoration of Israel was to be regarded as a covenant between the Lord and his people. But the covenant was not to be limited to the mere deliverance from the captivity. God promised to give his people divine instruction that would be continued through the present generation and handed on down to their descendants.

ISAIAH 60

General remarks. It should be observed on this chapter that the prophet often speaks of Israel and the church as if they were one, or that the one was a continuation of the other. Hence, some things he says will apply to either or both. Sometimes they apply to both in the same sense, while at other times they apply in a literal sense to one and in a figurative or spiritual sense to the other. I shall insist that the reader carefully study this note, and also make frequent reference to it as he follows through the comments on the various verses in their order.

Verse 1. This verse logically follows the subject matter in the closing verses of the preceding chapter. After the Babylonian Empire was overcome, its successor, the Medo-Persian Empire, was friendly toward the people of Israel and gave them permission to return to their native land, which is the event predicted in this verse.

Verse 2. The thought here is as if it said *though the darkness shall cover the earth,* etc., yet the Lord will be strong enough to lift his people out of it and let his light brighten their national life.

Verse 3. *Gentiles* is from a word that is sometimes rendered "nations" and "peoples," and it was true that many foreign people showed a favorable attitude toward Israel after the captivity. (See the books of Ezra and Nehemiah.) However, that was always the case to some extent at certain times. But the prophet evidently got a view of the time of Christ in this verse and in a number of verses following. Under the system that Christ gave to the world all the Gentiles were admitted to its benefits and privileges. The form of language indicates the prediction was made as a favor or honor bestowed upon Israel since we have such terms as *thy light* and *thy rising*. But that is all very consistent because Christ came through the Jewish nation.

Verse 4. This verse evidently is a prediction of the call of the Gentiles. The words *from far* would especially suggest such an interpretation in view of a like expression in Eph. 2: 13, 17. *Nursed at thy side* is a figure of speech to indicate the affectionate relationship that was to come between the Jews and Gentiles under Christ.

Verse 5. *Flow together* has the same significance as the expression just commented upon in the preceding verse. *Sea* and such like terms in symbolic language has reference to multitudes of people. *Forces of the Gentiles* is a direct prediction that Christ would give a system of religion to the world that would admit the Gentiles on the same footing as that extended to the Jews.

Verse 6. *Camels and dromedaries* are used figuratively because such animals were a means of travel commonly used in ancient times. The nations are predicted to be going to Zion to recognize and enjoy the benefits offered, and their usual mode of travel would naturally be considered in the figures. *Midian* and *Sheba* were among the nations of the Gentiles and they are represented as bringing of their possessions to contribute to the support of Israel. Their motive in bringing this wealth is signified by the words *shew forth the praises of the Lord*.

Verse 7. *Kedar* and *Nebaioth* were tribes of the descendants of Ishmael, and are named among the Gentiles as those who would come to the support and enjoyment of Israel. *Come up with acceptance* is a prediction of the invitation for the Gentiles to be partakers of the blessings through Christ or spiritual Israel. (See Acts 11: 18; Eph. 2: 13, 17.)

Verse 8. Flying clouds and doves are illustrative of the gathering of human beings toward the great provisions made by Christ. However, the subject matter is such that we may also think of the return of good fortune for fleshly Israel after the captivity. It is well that we not lose sight of that phase of the text, for it will be still more evident in other verses.

Verse 9. *Isles* is from an original that means the inhabited spots, and *wait* means to rely upon the Lord of Israel. *Ships of Tarshish* is a figurative reference to the same facts already predicted a number of times, the contributions of the nations to the institution of the Lord. This may be applied either to ancient Israel in a temporal sense or to spiritual Israel under the system given by Christ.

Verse 10. The prophet now comes more specifically to the case of ancient Israel as far as the unfavorable experiences are concerned. He is writing of the captivity that was to be brought upon them a little over a century later. *In my wrath I smote thee* is specifically a prediction of the event of the captivity and its cause is stated to be the wrath of God. But Ex. 20: 5 will indicate to us the basis of that wrath which is the divine jealousy over the idol gods that Israel had been serving. And in the same sentence the favor of God also is predicted which was fulfilled by the return from captivity after being released by the Persians.

Verse 11. This verse may properly be applied to both modern and ancient Israel. It was true that the gates of Jerusalem were thrown open freely after the return from exile in Babylon, but the more significant fulfillment was to consist in the extended provision in favor of the world in general. The rest of the verse has direct reference to the call of the Gentiles. *Forces of the Gentiles* means that these people would bring their wealth and activities to the support of the cause of truth that the Jewish nation would offer to the world through Christ.

Verse 12. To a great extent this verse was true of the worldly nations that Israel of old had to deal with. But it was to be more emphatically true spiritually, for Christ was to come into the world through the Jewish race and he would call upon all mankind to hear him. It is here predicted that any nation that would not respond favorably would be *utterly wasted*. The same prediction was made by Moses and the noted passage is in Deut. 18: 18-20 which the student should carefully read.

Verse 13. This entire verse is one of figures used to illustrate the grandeur to be brought to Israel by the Lord, and again the prediction may be applied to both fleshly and spiritual Israel. *Glory of Lebanon* as a general phrase is followed by some specifications concerning the region. So many references are made in the Bible to Lebanon that I believe it will be well to make a quotation from Funk and Wagnalls Standard Dictionary of the Bible as follows: "Lebanon is from LABHEN 'to be white,' because of its appearance when the snow covers its summits, as it does for the greater part of the year, though according to some it was the whiteness of its cliffs that gave L. its name. . . . The whole mass [the two ranges] abuts on the Mediterranean to the W. and slopes down into the plateau of Syria to the E. The average height of the range is not far from 6,000 feet, rising, however, at the highest point (Mt. Hermon) to 9,166 feet. The general structure of Lebanon is rugged and irregular, except for the main direction of the chain of summits, and abounds in precipitous [steep] cliffs and hollows, which make it difficult for the traveler, and at the same time an easy hiding-place for the fugitive. . . . In other particulars the Lebanon is noted for its height, which makes it a place of outlook (Song 4: 8), for its streams (Song 4: 15), its snowy summits (Jer. 18: 14), its fragrance (Song 4: 11; Hos. 14: 7), probably the odor of its cedar forests; these are also mentioned on their own account (Judg. 9: 15; Isa. 2: 13, etc.) and poetically called 'the flower of Lebanon' (Nah. 1: 4), 'the glory of Lebanon' (Isa. 35: 2; 60: 13). The 'violence done to Lebanon' is evidently the cutting down of these stately forests (Hab. 2: 17). Besides the cedars, however, large pines, firs, oaks, and cypress groves are to be found on the range; while the almond, the mulberry, the fig, the olive, the walnut, the apricot, the pear, the pomegranate, the pistachio, and the grapevine also flourish." In view of the prominence given to Lebanon in the Bible, both as to its literal value and also as a basis for political and spiritual comparisons, I trust the reader will carefully note this quotation and be prepared to make frequent reference to it when the occasion presents itself. One such occasion is the present verse where the prophet is using it for the purpose of comparison as stated at the beginning of comments on the verse.

Verse 14. The prophet wrote his book over a hundred years before the captivity began, and the release from that bondage came after the 70-year period had passed. Hence most if not all of the generation who performed the action of capturing the Jews were dead when the time of release came. That is why we have the reference to *the sons also of them that afflicted thee.* It is true these descendants of the enemy nation were brought to yield to the people of Israel when their return to power came about. The latter part of the verse was especially fulfilled as recorded in the books of Ezra and Nehemiah concerning the work of restoration in Jerusalem.

Verse 15. *Forsaken and hated* refers to the period of the captivity. God did not hate his people but he did forsake them as a chastisement for their unfaithfulness to him, and they were hated by the Babylonians who treated them very harshly. While the Jews were in Babylon their home land lay untilled and desolate. As a result the caravans and other travelers avoided that territory as they were passing through the country. All this was to be reversed after the captivity so that the people of the world would consider it a pleasure to travel that way on their journeys.

Verse 16. *Suck the milk* means they will partake of the wealth of the Gentiles. This is just another form of the same prediction that we have previously studied, and it was to be fulfilled first when the nation came into "diplomatic" relations with Israel. It was to have its spiritual fulfillment when the Gentiles were admitted to the benefits and obligations of the Gospel. (See Acts 11: 18; Eph. 2: 13, 17.)

Verse 17. These figures of speech have a special application to ancient Israel. They are used because of the contrast between the terms that are named in pairs. The first of each pair refers to the former unpleasant situation through which Israel passed, and the second that which came to them after the captivity. Brass is less desirable than gold, iron less than silver, wood less than brass, and stones less than iron. The last clause of the verse is especially for the consolation of the common people of Israel. They had been mistreated by the leaders of the nation even before the captivity. After the return there was to be a change of treatment and the officers would rule peaceably. Instead of the cruel exactors (see comments on ch. 58: 3, their creditors would deal righteously with them. (See an instance of this in Neh. 5: 1-12.)

Verse 18. Israel was to be a happy nation after being restored to her native land, and nothing like a national captivity was ever to occur again. However, the vision of the prophet has so much of the institution of Christ in it that a mixed application of the predictions need be no surprise to us. *Salvation* is therefore a prediction that has special reference to the spiritual benefits the world was to be offered through the dispensation of religion under Christ.

Verse 19. The sun and moon are great blessings for man in the material world, and the remarks here made about them should not be thought of as a belittling of them. On the other hand, even the form of contrast presented is a compliment for the wonderful benefits these works of creation are to the world. The illustration is somewhat like the ones in verse 17 in that the contrasts pertain to the degree and not to the quality of the things being considered. In other words, the things spoken of are both desirable but one is more so than the other. Man needs the light of the sun and moon but he needs spiritual light much more. The Lord was to furnish that light through the spiritual system to be introduced into the world through Christ.

Verse 20. As great as the blessing of sunlight is, yet it has to be withdrawn at the close of the day. In the great arrangement of the spiritual system through Christ there will be no suspension of that light. Citizens of the new nation under the Lord may have unbroken light. *Days of mourning* is a figure used in reference to the past misfortunes of ancient Israel but is meant to apply to the same benefits that Jesus had in mind in Matt. 5: 4.

Verse 21. *People shall be righteous* is one of the contrasts between citizenship in the nation of fleshly Israel and that in the kingdom of Christ. A fleshly birth and circumcision at the age of eight days made a person a full citizen in the ancient kingdom. In that to come under Christ a person must become righteous or spiritually changed before he can even become a citizen therein. (See John 3: 3, 5; Heb. 8: 10.) *Inherit the land for ever* is an allusion to the break that was to come in the residence of Israel in Palestine, but its significance is in reference to the permanence of spiritual blessings to come unto the citizens of the kingdom of Christ. *Branch of my planting* evidently has direct reference to the church of Christ and to him as its founder. That such is the meaning of the term is evident from the wording of Isa. 4: 2; 11: 1; Jer. 23: 5; 33: 15; Zech. 3: 8; 6: 12.

Verse 22. These are more figures in the form of contrast as to degree. *A little one* would not be expected to have much power when measured from a literal standpoint, but under Christ the smallest servant may become a mighty force for good. Paul gives the secret of this kind of strength where he exhorts Christians to be "strong in the Lord" as soldiers of the cross. (See Eph. 6: 10.)

ISAIAH 61

Verse 1. The first three verses of this chapter should be marked as a bracket and labeled as a prophecy of Christ. We are left with no doubt as to the application for Jesus as interprets it in Luke 4: 16-21. With this general comment on the bracket, let us consider more particularly the items in the various verses. The *Lord God* is the Father and *me* is a pronoun for Christ. *Spirit is upon me* means that Christ spoke as the Spirit of God directed him. He had been born of a human mother but his inspiration was from the divine source which made his teaching infallible. *Anointed* is from a word that the lexicon defines "to consecrate." The figure is based on the fact that when a man was set apart to be a king or to some other important office he was anointed by having oil poured on his head. This figurative sense is the meaning of the words, "hath anointed thee with the oil of gladness above thy fellows" (Heb. 1: 9). The special work for which Christ was anointed was to *preach good tidings* which means the good news of the kingdom. The *meek* are those who are humble enough to be taught, for the others will spurn the simplicity of the Gospel from them. That is why Jesus said, "Blessed are the meek for they shall inherit the earth" (Matt. 5: 5). *Bind brokenhearted* corresponds to the promises of Jesus that they who mourn shall be comforted (Matt. 5: 4). *Liberty to captives* is a prediction that men in the service of sin would be offered their freedom (Rom. 6: 16-18). Opening the prison is a repetition of the preceding clause and takes the same comments.

Verse 2. *Acceptable* means delightful, and the original for *year* is defined "a year (as a revolution of time)." The clause means that Christ would announce an epoch in the process of time in which people would be delighted with the favors offered to them by the Lord. *Day* is used also as an indefinite period of time coinciding with the year of the preceding clause. While men will be delighted with the favors offered to those who accept the glad tidings of Christ, those who reject them will be warned of the vengeance of God against them. *Comfort all who mourn* has been explained in the preceding verse which the reader will please see.

Verse 3. The first half of this verse is made up of contrasting figures as have been used a number of times. *Beauty* is from PEER, which Strong defines, "an embellishment, i. e., fancy head-dress." *Ashes* were spread on the head in times of distress according to a custom in ancient times. The statement means that the ashes of mourning will be replaced by the beautiful garments of righteousness provided by Christ. *Praise* and *heaviness* are used as contrasts for the same purpose as the figures in the preceding clause. Continuing the use of figures for the benefits under Christ, his servants are likened to trees whose fruit is righteous. The reason for such successful fruitage is given in that these trees were the *planting of the Lord*. Some further reasoning on the subject is offered to show the motive of the Lord in doing the kind of planting referred to, and that is *that he might be glorified*. A fruit grower who was particular about his reputation in that industry would be careful what kind of trees he set out. Another thing a careful grower would do is to be on the lookout for strange trees or plants that were not authorized to be put in his ground, and if any should be found they would be destroyed. (Matt. 15: 13.)

Verse 4. The "telescope" is shortened again and the prophet sees the improved conditions in Palestine after the captivity. The country was to be renewed by having the buildings rebuilt and the land put into cultivation again.

Verse 5. This is a prediction of the friendliness that was to be shown to Israel by the surrounding nations. The fulfillment in part may be seen in the books of Ezra and Nehemiah as the Biblical history on the subject.

Verse 6. Again the prophet has his vision extended and he sees into the conditions of the world under the Gospel dispensation or system of religion under Christ. *Ministers* does not have any official meaning, but means those who serve or attend upon the Lord and it applies to all persons who will have accepted Christ. *Eat the riches of the Gentiles* is the familiar prediction that under Christ the Gentiles and Jews were to be on equal footing as to the rights and privileges in service to the Lord.

Verse 7. *For your shame* means in place of the shame that the nation had been through in the captivity, and it was to have double that amount of honor bestowed upon it afterward. This was fulfilled literally when the Persians and other people showed so much attention to the work of reconstruction of the country. It was to be fulfilled spiritually when the Gentiles responded to the call of the Gospel.

Verse 8. This verse is directed against the leaders of the Jews because of their inconsistent practices through the years. They would impose on the poor by withholding from them their just dues, and by cruel exactions in cases of financial obligations. They would then seek to make up for it to the Lord by pretended religious devotions. (See ch. 58: 3.) That is why the Lord declared he hated burnt offerings when the articles to be used had been stolen. But God does *love judgment* which means he desires his people to deal justly with each other. But the captivity was to work a reformation among these offenders and when they get back into their own land again the Lord would bless their nation abundantly. And while on that line of thought the prophet saw this same nation being honored by giving to the world a spiritual religion based on the *everlasting covenant* that is referred to also in Heb. 8: 8-12.

Verse 9. *Seed shall be known among the Gentiles* is the same prediction of the call of the Gentiles that has been repeated so frequently. The quality of the spiritual stock to be produced through Christ and his church will be such that it will be generally recognized. A specific instance of such a fact is recorded in Acts 4: 13.

Verse 10. The pronoun *I* represents Israel responding to the favorable prediction just uttered of the good fortune to come to her. It was to cause great rejoicing both temporally and spiritually. *Garments of salvation* are the robes of righteousness that the people of God were destined to wear in the new dispensation under Christ. The decking and adorning predicted are to be spiritual such as named in 1 Pe. 3: 3. 4.

Verse 11. There can be no effect without a cause which is shown when a plant springs forth in a garden. And the same God who rules in the kingdom of nature will also be the cause for the great spiritual blessings to spring forth in the world. The universal extent of the spiritual growth which was to include the call of the Gentiles is indicated by the closing words *before all nations.*

ISAIAH 62

Verses 1, 2. The pronoun *I* stands for the prophet Isaiah who is making it emphatic that he will not hold his peace. The subject of what he sees in his vision is so important that he is determined to continue predicting the progress of the coming events until he reaches the climax of the favors to be poured out upon the ones intended in the blessings of God. The recipient of these blessings is here called *Zion* and *Jerusalem.* The first is an outstanding hill in Jerusalem that was the site of many noted events. It was also thought of as the capital of the nation and sometimes was called the "city of David." Because of its prominence both geographically and politically the word was often used for the city of Jerusalem as a whole. When the word *Zion* is used figuratively it refers to God's people both fleshly and spiritually. For the latter meaning see Heb. 12: 22. Since Zion was the capital of ancient Israel geographically, and also since it was the place where Jesus died (that is Jerusalem) to establish the new or spiritual Israel, Zion or Sion came to be a figurative name for the people of God in the institution of spiritual Israel. The church was founded by Christ who came into the world as a Jew and thus as a production from the people whose capital was Zion. This explains why so many of the good things said of the church and its members are attributed to Zion, and hence the prophet here declares it is for *Zion's sake* that he is about to make this noted prediction. In the language of grammar we should say that *Zion* and *Jerusalem* form the antecedent of the following pronouns in the paragraph: *Thereof, thy and thou.* Therefore, whatever is said of any of these pronouns is to be applied to Zion if considered of fleshly Israel, or the church as a prediction of spiritual Israel. The *new name* was therefore promised to Zion and was to be fulfilled when spiritual Zion came into being. The word *new* is derived from an original that is defined, "to be new; causatively to rebuild." *Name* is from SHEM and Strong defines it, "A primitive word; and appelation [name or title], as a mark or memorial of individuality; by implication honor, authority, character." The sense of this famous passage is thus very clear, that the people represented by Zion would some day take on an entirely different character that would give them a new name, one by which they had never been known before. The wording of the comments on this clause is so well done in Pocket Bible Handbook (by Halley), that I shall give the reader the benefit of it. "Up to the coming of Christ, God's people were known as 'Jews' or 'Hebrews.' After that, they were called 'Christians.'" This comment agrees with the other part of the prediction in that it was to be fulfilled at the same time that "the Gentiles shall see thy righteousness," which we know was to be after Christ called these nations to become a part of his people.

Verse 3. *Crown* and *diadem* are two names for practically the same thing. It sometimes means a symbol of authority, at others it is an adornment of the head as a reward for faithful and dignified service. When it is bestowed by a person of high rank it signifies all the more glory and honor. Certainly, then, if such an ornament is bestowed by the Lord it indicates the greatest of honors possible and proper for human beings. Such an honor is here predicted in favor of the Lord's people who will be called by the new name of Christians (Acts 11: 26; 26: 28; 1 Pe. 4: 16).

Verse 4. This verse should have an application to both ancient and modern Israel. The application to ancient Israel is literal and refers to the period of the captivity through which she will have passed when the prediction becomes due for fulfillment. The land of Palestine was actually forsaken during the 70 years for the Lord had turned his people over to a foreign nation as a chastisement for their sins. This fact resulted in a desolate condition because the land was not cultivated through that period. The people of Israel were previously likened unto a wife and God was her husband, but this wife was guilty of unfaithfulness and her husband became displeased with her and "put her away" (ch. 50: 1). When the unfaithful wife reformed, her husband, though deeply wronged and grieved, again took delight in her and took her back into the marriage relationship again. *Hebzibah* is from CHEPHTSIY and Strong's definition is, "My delight (is) in her." *Beulah* is from BAWAL, which Strong defines, "A primitive root; to be master; hence to marry." In view of the particular meaning of these words I have made the comments in the verse as per above.

Verse 5. *Sons* is a strained translation here and throws the composition somewhat into confusion. The outstanding thought in the original word is "founder or builder." In keeping with the figure of the marriage relation introduced in the preceding verse it is God (here erroneously rendered *sons*) who will remarry Israel, who is the antecedent of *thee*. The whole verse is parallel in thought with the preceding verse. After taking back his penitent wife with the same feeling of admiration a young man would have for his virgin bride he gives her a beautiful wedding dowry. That gift is in the form of a prediction that they (this husband and wife) would some day give to the world a most wonderful kind of offspring, which we should understand will be the same people with the new name of verse two.

Verse 6. *Watchmen* is from a word that refers to sentinels who were used in ancient times by walled cities. It was the duty of these men to be always on the watch for any approach of either friend or foe. In the case of the former the idea was to be expecting the arrival of someone with news of interest for the city. An instance of this may be found in 2 Sam. 18: 24-27 where David was depending on his watchman on the wall to announce the coming of some person with news of the battle that was being waged against his wayward son Absalom. The word is used figuratively in our verse and primarily has reference to the inspired prophets who were on the watch for approaching events. By the eye of inspiration they could look into the future and see the things that were to come to pass regarding their country and people. *Never hold their peace* signifies that these inspired prophets will be constantly alert and ready to report what they see in the future. In a spiritual but more general sense the Lord has also some men on the walls of Zion today who are to be ready to detect and announce all information that will be of interest to the church. *Make mention*. Others besides the inspired prophets were expected to be interested in the welfare of their nation and add their words of admonition to those of the prophets, that the people might be exhorted to keep respectful remembrance of their own true God and his goodness to them.

Verse 7. *Give him no rest* denotes the constancy of these *watchmen* in their service on behalf of *Him* who is the one over the people and concerning whose activities these prophets were speaking. *Till he establish* has practically the same thought and is a declaration that God will finally bring to pass all the events he has inspired his sentinels to announce.

Verse 8. *Right hand* and *arm of strength* are figurative expressions, meaning the Lord had put his whole being behind the predictions on behalf of his people. *No more given thy corn*, etc., is a promise that Israel would not again be turned over to her enemies to be despoiled of her possessions. Regardless of what other misfortunes awaited the people of God, there was never to be another captivity in which the nation would be taken possession of as a whole by another nation brought against them.

Verse 9. Instead of producing the fruits of their labor for the benefit of others, God's people would be permitted to enjoy them as their rightful privilege. They not only would consume these good things but would recognize the source from where they had come and would praise Him. *Drink it in the courts* means they would not have to slip out their provisions and partake of them in secret for fear of the enemy. Instead, they will be free to engage in all of their activities under the very protection of their Lord's institutions.

Verse 10. Once more the "telescope" is extended into the next dispensation and the prophet sees the great favor of God to be given his people. The form of language pertains to the literal rebuilding and restoration of the land of Palestine after the captivity. But the important application of the prophecy is to the work that was to be accomplished in the time of Christ. We shall have this statement verified before getting through with the chapter. *Lift up a standard* means the prophet was to raise a flag or banner in token of the universal provision the Lord would some day make for the *people*, which includes a promise to the Gentiles as well as the Jews.

Verse 11. *Daughter of Zion* means the people of Jerusalem who were destined to have a great blessing bestowed upon them. *Thy salvation cometh* is a prophecy of Christ beyond any doubt for it is so applied in Zech. 9: 9 and Matt. 21: 5. *Reward is with him* is a prediction that Jesus will have the power to reward all those who serve him in truth. In other words, he will not have to leave the rewarding of his workers to another, but will be given the authority to manage that feature of his system himself, which he indicated by his statement to his apostles recorded in Matt. 28: 18.

Verse 12. *They shall call them* indicates that the world will recognize such qualities in the followers of Christ. *Sought out, a city not forsaken* was fulfilled for fleshly Israel when Jerusalem was restored after the captivity. But while the wording of it is based on that literal event, its spiritual fulfillment was to be when Christ would have built his church. That word is from EKKLESIA and Thayer's first definition of it is, "Properly a gathering of citizens called out from their homes into some public place." This would constitute the people of Christ as a *sought out* or "called out" group which would fulfill this prediction.

ISAIAH 63

Verse 1. The grape industry was a leading one in Palestine and hence many illustrations have been drawn from it in the Bible. These illustrations are sometimes based on the industry as a whole, or they may be made by reference to the juice of the grape, depending on the particular point the writer has in mind. Also, the juice is used both favorably and unfavorably in the illustration, this depending likewise on the purpose of the comparison. Since wine is a nourishment and serves as a tonic to the physical system, it is used favorably in comparison with the blood of such a body because blood is the life of that body both human and beast (Gen. 9: 4; Lev. 17: 14.) And since pure wine is red it is referred to in cases of wrath (both human and divine and both righteous and otherwise) because when the individual in the case is stirred up his blood (which is red) is in an agitated condition. A few places in the scriptures to show that wine is referred to as wrath are Jer. 25: 15; 51: 7; Rev. 14: 10; 16: 19. With the foregoing information in mind we should understand why a reference might be made to a place or other subject because of the color of wine, there being no other relationship between the thing referred to and the point being made by the writer. Such an instance is now at hand in the present verse and two following it. The passage as a whole (first three verses of the chapter) is a prediction of Christ who was to come into the world and shed his blood for the redemption of man from his sins. Thus the only reason for mentioning *Edom* is that the word means "red" and *Bozrah* was the capital of that country. The prophet makes his prediction in the form of a supposed scene coming up before him. He sees a man coming from a distant place which, on account of the meaning of the names of it causes him to "see red." He asks who it is and receives the answer from the person himself: *I that speak in righteousness, mighty to save*, and we understand it to be the voice of Christ.

Verse 2. The imaginary conversation continues between the prophet and the person coming *from Edom*. Having been told that he was righteous and able to save, it might seem strange that such a person would have the appearance which the prophet sees. He asks that righteous saviour why his garments looked as if he had been treading in the *winevat* (winepress) and the next verse will explain it to him. That the reader may better understand and appreciate this wonderful subject as it is treated here and in other parts of the Bible, I shall make some quotations from works of reference as follows: "The gathered grapes were thrown into the press, consisting of a shallow vat, also excavated in the rock (Joel 3: 13). The grapes were then crushed by treading; and the treaders sung and shouted (Isa. 16: 10) while the red blood of the grapes flowed around them, and stained their skin and garments (Isa. 63: 1-3; Jer. 25: 30; 48: 33; Lam. 1: 15; Rev. 19: 13-15). From the upper vat the juice of the crushed grapes trickled down into the lower vat." Schaff-Herzog Encyclopaedia, article Wine. "Every vineyard had its wine-press, a stone tub or vat in which, with shouts of joy the grapes were trodden ... If the soil was rocky, the press was hewn out in the rock. Connected with it, but on a lower level, was a receiving-vat into which the must (unfermented grape juice) flowed to be clarified. From this it was drawn off into jars (Jer. 48: 11), or skins (Job 32: 19)." Funk and Wagnalls Dictionary, page 938. "The wine-presses of the Jews consisted of two receptacles or vats placed at different elevations, in the upper one of which the grapes were trodden, while the lower one received the expressed juice. The two vats are mentioned together only in Joel 3: 13: 'The press is full: the fats overflow'—the upper vat being full of fruit, the lower one overflowing with the must. The two vats were usually hewn out of the solid rock. Isa. 5: 2, margin; Matt. 21: 33. Ancient wine-presses, so constructed, are still to be seen in Palestine." Smith's Bible Dictionary, article Winepress.

Verse 3. In the preceding verse the prophet asked the person approaching why his garments had the appearance of having been worn by one who had been treading in the winefat. The answer shows that a very good reason existed for their appearing just that way for indeed he had been doing such a work; not only so, but he had been doing that alone. If a person would get his garments stained in that work when assisted by others, how much more so if deserted by all the others and he would need to tread round and round until the grapes were completely crushed. This feature of the picture is a prediction that Christ alone would be able to furnish the blood required for the salvation of mankind. But while it was necessary that Christ be the sole person who could give the blood that would save those who applied it, the attitude of others in letting him suffer alone is none the less to be condemned. The apostles all forsook Christ in his darkest hours which was also predicted in Isa. 53: 6 and fulfilled in Matt. 26: 56. Passing from the favorable to the unfavorable phase of the subject the lone treader thinks of the evil characters in the world whose sinful life made it necessary for him to tread out the grapes, and in this view of the case he is doing it as a demonstration of wrath against evil doers. Hence, this performance of Jesus will at once serve two purposes. Those who partake of this wine with the right motive will be cleansed by it and made fit for service in the kingdom of Christ now, and for eternal joy hereafter. Those who reject the benefits offered through this wine (blood of Christ) will find it to be a signal of the fury of the Lord against all who thus rebel. Instead of merely having his garments stained with the blood of the grape that would have cleansed these sinners, the Son of God will crush them by his divine vengeance so that their guilty blood upon his garments will be a token that he has attacked and crushed them in his holy wrath.

Verse 4. The first part of this verse corresponds with the last part of the preceding verse. For those who refuse the offered mercy of Christ, nothing is awaiting but the *day of vengeance* which Christ himself will use as his judgment day. This same declaration is made by Paul in Acts 17: 31. The last part of the verse is a prediction of the Gospel dispensation which is here called *the year of my redeemed.*

Verse 5. The solitary work of Christ in saving the world is still the subject of this verse. There was no man on whom the Lord could call to bring about the plan of salvation, so he went alone through the ordeal even to dying the shameful death on the cross. *Mine own arm brought salvation to me* does not mean the salvation was for the sake of himself because Christ was never lost. It means it brought to him the means of saving the world for whom he died.

Verse 6. This verse is largely figurative but based on the subject of wine and the activities connected therewith. As it was necessary to tread upon grapes to extract the blood (juice) therefrom, so Christ will tread upon the impenitent sinners who refuse to be cleansed by his blood. When a person is drunk literally on wine it overcomes him and makes him subject to another. Likewise, the people who persist in their rebellion against Christ will be *drunk* on the wine of his divine wrath. This will dispossess them of their strength and subject them to the will of another.

Verse 7. The prophet being a part of *us* now speaks what he regards as the proper attitude for his people to take toward the Lord. The verse is made up of items concerning the goodness of God toward the nation, even when it was disobedient and unappreciative in its conduct. Isaiah and a small number of other people of Israel always remained faithful and protested the backslidings of the nation.

Verse 8. For a few verses the prophet will be concerned with ancient Israel, recounting the many favors of God upon them even though they were so often guilty of unfaithfulness. The Lord's goodness to the Israelites though unworthy is accounted for by the words *they are my people. Children that will not lie* appears to disagree with the general accusations that are so frequently found against the nation, but it is well to consider the context in order to see the point. God is always ready to give his people "the benefit of the doubt" and does not throw them overboard until there is no hope of their reformation. On this principle he deals with them as if they were faithful children at heart, and that at last they will prove obedient to the divine law. It is somewhat like the thought advanced from the psychological standpoint that if a man is "placed on his honor" he is often influenced thereby to make an effort to merit the confidence. God thus deals with his servants because of his great love for them. However, if longsuffering and repeated warnings prove in vain the Lord will at last turn from them. That is why he had the prophet sound the call for reformation of life that is in ch. 55: 6, 7.

Verse 9. *In all their affliction he was afflicted* expresses the feeling that God has for his people when they are in trouble. The same is said of the love of Christ for his people in the dispensation of spiritual Israel (Heb. 4: 15). God often sends his angels to carry out his purposes. The instances on record are too numerous to note in this place, but I shall make a few references (Gen. 16: 7; 24: 7; Ex. 3: 2; Dan. 3: 28; 6: 22; Acts 5: 19; Heb. 1: 14, 14). In the present verse God worked directly on behalf of his people and let his presence (in spirit) be the angel for the service of love to them. It was this fatherly care that was always over the people even though they were so often guilty of ingratitude.

Verse 10. The comments on verse 8 should be read in connection with this. *Turned to be their enemy* should not be considered in the light of a foe who is personally bitter, for God is not disposed in that manner. One word in the lexicon definition of the original is milder which is "adversary." We can understand it to be one who is opposed to another but still leaving the cause for the opposition and the method of expressing it an open question. A child might resist all efforts to administer treatment for some terrible disease. It could even be necessary for the parent to use force to the extent of beating the back of the child; yet that would not mean the parent had ceased to love his child. Such treatment would really be for the good of the offspring according to the idea set forth in Heb. 12: 6-12.

Verse 11. The history of Israel is one filled with rebellion and forgetfulness of God's kindness. Back as far as the time of Moses when they had not been more than a few months out of bondage, they became impatient just because their leader was called from their sight a short while to receive the law. They forgot the 10 plagues and other indications of divine power manifested while yet in the land of Egypt.

Verse 12. And if the scenes in Egypt were too overwhelming for them to have a distinct remembrance of them, they surely should have remembered seeing the Red Sea parting and standing like two walls of ice with no apparent cause but an east wind.

Verse 13. Had the whole matter stopped with the opening of the sea they might have assumed that what they saw was more imaginary than real and that no benefit could have come to them by the circumstance. But when God *led them through the deep* there could be no doubt of the real facts in the case. They were at the very time referred to in verse 11 on the opposite side of the sea and a safe distance from their old enemy. This fact should have stood out in their minds and caused them to be ashamed at the mere thought of complaining. *As an horse in the wilderness.* An animal lost in the wilderness would likely go in the opposite direction from the correct one if not guided by some higher intelligence. Likewise, even after the Red Sea was divided until a tunnel appeared before them, none but the divine Being would have conducted them safely through that strange and uninviting passage.

Verse 14. God is the maker of all things that exist and their welfare is according to the laws established for their regulation. When a beast finds a quiet place between the hills and lies down to rest it is according to the arrangement of God. He is still more concerned about the comfort of his people and will always do that which will be to their advantage. *Make a glorious name.* When a people like Israel is brought up against other nations more numerous and powerful than they, no human help would get them out of their difficulty. The fact of their successful encounter with such foes would go to the praise of their God and thus give him a glorious name.

Verse 15. The prophet is making a fervent appeal to God for mercy on behalf of his people. *Bowels* and *mercies* are used in the same sense and refer to the affections of the Lord. *Toward me* is said because the prophet "takes it to heart" when the nation is in trouble. He does not excuse the shortcomings of the nation but implores the Lord to have compassion on the people.

Verse 16. One of the prominent practices of the Jews was to boast of their relation to Abraham (Matt. 3: 9) and to count on that to justify them before God. But this verse represents them as overlooking that supposed advantage and relying on the love of God for his created beings regardless of their earthly blood line. They are even so confident of the favor of God that they believe they would receive it even though Abraham still lived and would disown them. That idea is correct for if God cares for the people of his creation he will take care of them regardless of the attitude of any earthly ancestor. If this verse is carried over into a spiritual application we will find it to be true there also. In Gal. 3: 29 Paul states that Christians are Abraham's seed, but it is not through the blood line of that patriarch. Instead, it is because of their spiritual relation to Abraham through Christ who descended from the patriarch, the man who was called out from his home and people to become the ancestor of a special race. And in that sense it could truly be said that Abraham (as to race or blood) would *be ignorant* of Christians. It is true that the blood flowing in the veins of Jewish Christians had been received from Abraham, but the Galatian brethren were not Jewish in blood and hence Abraham would have no connection with them in blood any more than would other generations long gone by.

Verse 17. God does not directly cause a man to do that which is evil nor make him to err. But he does leave a man to his own unrighteous ways whenever that is necessary to teach him a lesson. It was in that sense that God *made them to err* from his ways. On the same principle they were left to harden their hearts so that they did not fear God as they should. But now they realize their mistake and are begging the Lord to return his mercy to the tribes for the sake of his servants. This form of speech truly represents the state of mind that the people of Israel will yet possess (Psa. 137) and the prophet makes the prediction by putting these words in the mouths of his people. It also is a prediction that God will return to the nation and bring an end to the captivity that had been suffered as a national chastisement.

Verse 18. This verse looks forward to the time when the captivity will come upon the nation. Israel is represented as complaining at that time because she had possessed the holy land *but a little while*. No doubt it will seem that way to them for when men have been dispossessed of a great blessing they often feel as if the time of enjoying it was short. To add to the sadness of the situation, the cherished and holy institutions were to be trodden down and possessed by the adversaries.

Verse 19. *We are thine* is said in protest against losing their country, especially when it was to be possessed by a people that had never been subject to the Lord's rule. They will be a people who had never worn the name of God, and yet were destined to take possession of the land belonging to his people. This was the thought that grieved the prophet and he expressed it on behalf of the nation as sharing it.

ISAIAH 64

Verse 1. The penitential attitude of Israel is continued as we start the study of this chapter. *Rend the heavens* is a phrase of emphasis to indicate the tension in the minds of the people, or at least to show what the prophet thinks should be their condition of mind. *Mountain flow down* is figurative and means the overwhelming effect of God's power over those who have disregarded his law. And since *mountains* in symbolic language means the governments of the earth, this phrase is a demand for and prediction of the subjection of the governments to the power of the God of Israel.

Verse 2. The prophet would have the power of the Lord so intense that it could be compared with the heat of a melting pot. The material that he would have thrown into this melting pot was the enemy nations who were destined to afflict God's people in about a century later. The captivity was necessary for the correction of the Israelite nation, yet that would not justify the personal satisfaction that the heathen took from their part in the plan. *Nations may tremble* is a prediction of the effect that would be experienced by the various nations when they see the overthrow of the particular one that had oppressed God's people. But in addition to the above thoughts we should not lose sight of the fact that Isaiah saw much in the happenings to fleshly Israel that was to be accomplished in the days of spiritual Israel though not in a material or literal sense. When the Gospel was preached to "all nations" as the apostolic commission required, the people of those nations, Jew and Gentile *trembled* in the sense of respecting the great truths and many individuals accepted them.

Verse 3. *Terrible things* means things that could either frighten in the common use of that word, or fill the mind with respect. It doubtless had the first meaning when applied to the heathen nations connected with the oppression of fleshly Israel as indicated in Dan. 5: 6. It was to have the second meaning when the Lord set up the spiritual reign of Christ under the administration of the Gospel. *Mountains* in symbolic language means governments and any public institutions. It is true that the church was instrumental in bringing into the world the great truths of human freedom of conscience and thus paved the way for the downfall of world-wide monarchies. (See Dan. 2: 44.) In this sense the *mountains flowed down* according to Isaiah's prediction.

Verse 4. This is the only place in the Old Testament where this passage occurs. If it is referred to in the New Testament we will be certain as to the correct application. Well, that has been done with regard to this verse in 1 Cor. 2: 9 where Paul was writing on the subject of the work of the apostles through the power of the Spirit. This passage means that man is not able by his natural senses to discover the spiritual things that God has in store for those who *wait for* (rely upon) him. That would make it necessary for some supernatural means to be used to impart the information. The next verse (1 Cor. 2: 10) gives the explanation by saying it had been revealed to "us" (the apostles) by the Spirit.

Verse 5. *Him* stands for the one who waits for or relies on the Lord mentioned in the close of the preceding verse. *Meetest* means to be favorable and God will be so toward the *him* just described. *Worketh righteousness* is a phrase with a similar thought to much of the New Testament teaching. It is not enough to profess a belief in God's system of righteousness, but it must be put into practice or worked out. (See Acts 10: 35; 1 Cor. 15: 58; Gal. 5: 6; Jas. 1: 25.) *Remember thee* does not mean merely that a man have a good memory so that he can repeat the scriptures one verse after another. The passage requires that he remember the Lord in *thy ways*. The last word is from DEREK which Strong defines, "a road (as trodden); figuratively a course of life or mode of action, often adverbially." In direct connection with this clause is the phrase *worketh righteousness*, and that shows the prophet means the individual is expected to remember the ways of the Lord by doing the things that make up those ways. The next clause of the verse is a confession of wrong doing which caused the Lord to be wroth; the people had sinned against Him. They acknowledged that it could have been avoided had they shown the proper respect for the divine law. They admitted that in *those (thy ways)* is *continuance*, which means that the favor of God will be unfailing upon those who walk in the ways of the Lord. *Shall be saved* is true both as to their national life, and also in regard to the spiritual welfare of all mankind.

Verse 6. This verse is a continuation of the confession which the prophet makes on behalf of the nation, and the figure of speech used is one of the strongest that could be set forth. A person's manner of life has always been compared to a garment to cover his body. It is still so used in this verse except to compare the life to the most corrupt of garments. The word *filthy* is from AYD and Strong's definition is, "From an unused root meaning to set a period; the menstrual flux; by implication, soiling." So the soiled condition of a woman's clothing at the time indicated is used to illustrate the corrupt religious garments that Israel had been wearing, and she is represented also as making acknowledgment to the disgraceful fact. Their sinful life is also likened to a faded and wilted leaf that had become so light and worthless that the wind pulled it from the tree and blew it away.

Verse 7. The nation as a whole became so corrupt that God turned from it and let the enemy nation take it over. *None that calleth* represents the leading men of the nation. They had oppressed the common people and influenced them into a life of corruption like that of the heathen about them. Now as a chastisement for their sins they were to be turned over to the power of that very kind of people to continue their idolatrous practices right in the land of the heathen whose ways they had been following. *Hast consumed us* is past tense in grammatical form but it is a prediction of the national downfall that was to come upon them a century later.

Verse 8. This is a sincere acknowledgment in form, but it really is an inspired prediction of what was destined to be their frame of mind after the effects of the captivity will have come before them (Psa. 137). Just as the potter has the right to use the clay as he sees fit, so God has authority over the people whom he has created, to do with them as his divine wisdom will dictate.

Verse 9. This is another prediction in the form of a plea for mercy and pardon. Those very favors were destined to be granted to the people after they have suffered in a strange land. The greatest of all reasons for the Lord's mercy is indicated in the words *we are all thy people*.

Verses 10, 11. While the form of speech here as in so many other places is the present tense, the paragraph is a prediction of the literal facts that were destined to take place over a hundred years in the future. When the Babylonians invaded Palestine they concentrated their principal efforts on Jerusalem and finally burned it. They also removed the inhabitants out of the land into the land of Babylon. This state of affairs resulted in the desolation of the country in general. The Biblical account of this terrible event is in 2 Ki. 24 and 25. The historical account of it was quoted in connection with the comments at ch. 3: 1.

Verse 12. The comments on verses 8 and 9 will be applicable on this as to the state of mind of the Jews and the prophetic characteristics in them as the prophet was using the situation. The frame of mind that the Jews exhibited in Babylon was one of great remorse and acknowledgment of unworthiness. The prophet makes a prediction of that condition by wording their complaints according to this verse.

ISAIAH 65

Verse 1. The "telescope" is again extended and the prophet sees into the time when the Gentiles were to be taken into the same relationship with the Lord as the Jews. We know this is the meaning of this verse because Paul so applies it in Rom. 10: 20. *Am sought* and *asked not* is the prophet's way of expressing the change that was to come into the position and activities of the Gentiles. They had not asked for the Lord by way of the Mosaic system because no invitation had ever been offered them to do so. But this was changed in Acts 10 where they were even told to make inquiry for information that would bring them into covenant (saving) relationship with Christ. These people finally *found* the Lord who had not even been searching for him for the reason just stated. The Gentile nation had not been given the privilege of even wearing the name of the Lord. The point the prophet is making is that the Gentiles with comparatively small opportunities had become happy servants of the Lord at the first opening and had been appreciative of the favors granted them.

Verse 2. In contrast with the preceding circumstance, the Jews who were God's people had been unmindful of the many privileges they could have enjoyed. And this, too, in spite of the fact that the Lord was continually pleading with them to show some appreciation for the offered favors by accepting them on the terms stipulated. Isaiah calls them a *rebellious people* and indicates the cause for their rebellion, which is that they walked *after their own thoughts*. This sets forth a principle of action that is always the same in its results. If a man is determined to walk according to his own thoughts and desires he is bound to disregard the law of the Lord for the two principles of conduct do not agree. This great truth is abundantly taught in the New Testament. (See Matt. 6: 24; Rom. 6: 16; 7: 15-25.)

Verse 3. This verse has special reference to the idolatrous practices of the Jewish people. In Ex. 20: 5 God said that he was a jealous God and it was said in connection with the commandment against making any gods to worship besides the true God. This corruption was what continually provoked the Lord. There is no hiding from God at any time or in any sense, so that all is done is as naked and open before him as if he were present in person. But the phrase *to my face* indicates the boldness of these idolaters and their utter disregard for the Lord. Smith's Bible Dictionary says, "The retirement of gardens rendered them favorite places for devotion," which accounts for the reference to them in this verse. In these gardens the idolatrous Jews would build altars of brick on which to burn incense to their heathen gods and thus commit the abominable treason against the God of Israel who had directed where and in what manner incense should be burned in religious devotions.

Verse 4. *Which remain among the graves* has reference to the people called "necromancers" which means people who pretend to seek information from the dead. They were loitering around the graves for that purpose. Moses wrote against such impostors in Deut. 18: 11 and warned his brethren to have nothing to do with such characters. The practice was a form of witchcraft which was a thing God always hated. Such people would also be inclined to pass their time in the solitude of the mountains in order to meditate on the corrupt notions of idolatry. On the same principle that even the ordinary eating of swine's flesh for food was abominable to God in the Old Testament times, so would an idolater regard it pleasing to his god if one not only partook of it for the common use, but would eat it as a part of his religious devotions to the idol. *Broth* is rendered "pieces" in the marginal translation and the lexicon practically agrees with it. *Abominable* is from PIGGUL, which Strong defines, "From an unused root meaning to stink; properly fetid, i. e. (figuratively) unclean (ceremonially)." The clause means these people were so eager to please their heathen gods that they devised all possible schemes to get as low as they could in their devotions. They would gather pieces of spoiled scraps of meat and other articles that were supposed to be materials for food. They would dump these vile scraps into their vessels and thicken their soup with them and then eat the mixture as a religious feast to their gods.

Verse 5. It would be bad enough if these vile persons pretended to be as worthy as the average man which would be far from the truth. But these filthy perverters of righteousness claimed to be better than other men. They not only boasted of being better in their own character, but they demanded to be disconnected from the society of others, hence their impudent order to others was to *stand by thyself, come not near to me*. These people were like the Pharisees in Matt. 9: 11 and the one in Luke 18: 11, 12. *Smoke* is from a word that also means "anger," and *nose* is also sometimes used figuratively. The clause means these corrupt idolaters irritated the Lord to the point of anger even as a vile smoke would irritate the nostrils of an innocent bystander. "Where there is smoke there is fire" is an old and true saying, and it might be asked why the presence of fire was mentioned when it had already been indicated by the words regarding smoke just commented upon. The significant point in the last expression is in the words *all the day*. The continuous existence of the evil is the special phase of the subject meant by the words *underscored*.

Verse 6. *Written before me* has about the same force as the words *to my face* in verse 3. A truth does not have to be literally written before the Lord for him to know about it, but the attitude of these evil doers was so brazen that it was equivalent to a direct account that would be inscribed in bold letters right in the face of Jehovah. *I will not keep silence* is a prediction that sure and strong judgment was to be meted out against these sinners. *Into their bosom* means the recompense or punishment was to be brought home to them in the most intimate degree, so that it would strike at the very base of their emotions. (See the fulfillment as indicated by Psa. 137 and Ezk. 37: 11.)

Verse 7. This verse does not add much new thought as to the nature or completeness of the chastisement to be meted out to the guilty nation. The other thought to which I invite the attention of the reader is the mention of the *iniquities of your fathers* in connection with *your iniquities*. At the time when the Israelite nation was to be taken into captivity by the Babylonians the land had been defrauded out of 70 years of rest (Lev. 26: 33-35). However, this delinquency against the land could not have been all committed by the generation living at the time of the captivity. It had been going on for hundreds of years until the "accumulated vacation" due the land amounted to 70 years. That is why this verse connects the iniquities of the fathers with those of the people to whom the prophet was writing.

Verse 8. The compassion of God is very great and always asserts itself on behalf of humanity in spite of their many shortcomings. For a number of verses the sins of the people has been the subject, and the nation was destined to be sorely punished in a foreign land. Now the subject changes and this and the two following verses form a bracket that predicts the rescue of

God's people from the captivity before it is entirely consumed. That fact is predicted in a beautiful figure or comparison whose outstanding idea is that of preserving something because of a hidden value that is in it. The figure is drawn from a cluster of grapes that has not been pulled from the vine. The blessing of wine is recognized to be in the grapes and for that reason the plant should be preserved. So the nation of Israel was compared to a cluster of grapes which still has a value in it and hence it was to be preserved from destruction in the captivity. Incidentally we have some information on another subject. The juice of the grape is called *wine* even before it is extracted from the fruit, which disproves the theory that the word "wine" always means the fermented juice of grapes and never called by such a term while sweet.

Verse 9. This verse is a direct prediction of the release of a part of the nation from the bondage in Babylon. *Bring forth a seed* has special reference to the remnant of the nation that remained after the period of the captivity was completed. The fulfillment of this is recorded in Ezra 2: 64. *Inheriter of my mountains* would literally mean the repossession of the land of Palestine with its hills and valleys. Also, since *mountains* symbolically means government, the prediction was looking to the return of Israel to power in their own land. This is also fulfilled in the books of Ezra and Nehemiah.

Verse 10. This verse aplies to the same event as is predicted in the preceding verses, and refers especially to some of the material blessings to be enjoyed after the return. *Sharon* is a broad, rich tract of land which lies between the mountains of the central part of the holy land and the Mediterranean Sea. During the captivity it was left desolate but was to be used again for the flocks. The valley of Achor was another spot in Palestine that had been left unused for 70 years, but it was to be restored to usefulness after the captivity was over.

Verse 11. The foregoing bracket of favorable predictions will now be dropped and the prophet will again take up the Lord's complaints against his people. They are accused of forgetting the holy mountain which means the institution with headquarters in Jerusalem. *Troop* is from a word that means about the same as the familiar expression "good luck." The idea is that because of the great number of persons interested in the system of idolatry it would bring a stroke of good fortune to join in the movement by spreading tables everywhere on which to have the idolatrous feasts.

Verse 12. *Number you to the sword* is a prediction of the sword of the enemy that would defeat them and decrease their number. The reason for this severe chastisement was their utter disrespect for God. They would not even show the courtesy of answering the call of the Lord. Their evil conduct was not merely an oversight or done unthoughtedly, but they *did choose* to walk therein, which means their course of action was taken deliberately.

Verses 13, 14. The "telescope" is again extended and the prophet sees the conditions that will happen in the time of Christ and his system of righteousness. It is appropriate to bring up this subject here for it will be the same rebellious Jews to deal with in those years that the Lord was suffering in the days before the captivity. And still remembering Abraham, Isaac and Jacob, and the nation that came down from them, the Lord was minded to give them the first opportunity when the new and final dispensation was to be launched in the world. This truth is specifically taught in Acts 13: 46, where the apostle Paul was preaching the Gospel to an audience made up mostly of Jews. Accordingly, the Gospel was not even offered to the Gentiles for over three years after it was first given to the Jews. And even after the Gentiles were brought into the same privileges with the Jews, in some cases a special effort was made first to get the Jews into the work. (See Acts 13: 46 again.) Finally, the Jews as a whole rejected the Gospel and became its bitter enemies. After that the Lord instructed his teachers to warn this same old stubborn people of the divine wrath against them, and to show the world the Lord's pleasure at the willingness of the Gentiles to accept the law of Christ and become humble servants under his law. The above facts and truths are predicted in the present paragraph. Let us notice the particular items in this interesting prophecy. The *eating* and *drinking* is figurative and refers to the spiritual blessings that will be enjoyed by those who accept the Gospel. Foreseeing the attitude of the Jews and Gentiles as described in this paragraph the Lord declares *my servants* (the Gentile Christians) *shall eat,* but *ye* (the Jews) shall be hungry. The same contrast is made between the two peoples as to the Gospel blessings of drinking and rejoicing. All the good things mentioned in this paragraph that are to be given to the world through the Gospel will come to the Gentiles because of their obedience, but will be denied the Jews as a whole because of their disobedience. It was fitting that the prophet be inspired to make this prediction right at the time that the same Jewish people were so disobedient that the captivity was being predicted against them.

Verse 15. In this short verse the prophet spans many centuries of time and makes predictions concerning both fleshly and spiritual Israel. Also, he makes predictions that apply to fleshly Israel in both the Old and New Testament times. The word *curse* is from SHEBUWAH and Strong defines it, "properly something sworn, i. e., an oath." Moffatt renders the place: "Shall use the name you leave in uttering a curse." In other words, the Jews had been the ones who had exclusive right to the name of God in their oaths or vows. But they were to lose that privilege and the Gentiles would be given the right to the name. But the Gentiles would not be restricted to the name that had been permitted in olden times, for they were to be called by *another name.* This is the same name that is predicted in ch. 62: 2 which I request the reader to see. Following a practice that frequently is used by the writers in the Bible, this short verse is injected with a prediction of another great event besides the relation of the Jews and Gentiles towards the Gospel, and it is pertaining to the captivity. *Shall slay thee* refers to that event which means they shall die nationally, by reason of the captivity, which is the same subject that is predicted in ch. 22: 14. Between the word *thee* and the next word there is a jump in time of many centuries even though there seems to be one continuous thought. But the prophet goes from the captivity in Bablyon to the new name of Christian that was to be given to God's people. While this procedure in writing might impress us as being a disconnected one, it is not so uncommon in the style of the prophet. And in such an instance as the present one we can see a logical basis for it. Fleshly Israel furnished the first recruits for the institution of spiritual Israel for over three years. It almost seemed as if they alone were considered in the development of the Lord's plan. It was therefore an orderly method of writing to mention the advantages to be received under Christ as being favors that were bestowed on fleshly Israel.

Verse 16. The first application of this verse is to fleshly Israel at the time of their release from Babylon, and the next is to spiritual Israel at the time of Christ. *Blesseth himself* means to pray for blessings and he will do so by calling on the name of God and not the idols if applied to fleshly Israel, and to God and Christ if to spiritual Israel. *Sweareth* is from SHABA, which Strong defines, " a primitive root; but used only as a denominative of SHIBAH ["seven"]; to seven oneself, i. e., swear (as if by repeating a declaration seven times)." The idea is that by repeating a declaration seven times in the ears of God it would demonstrate the sincerity of the one who did so and show his confidence in expecting the divine blessing. This view of the word makes the application of the prediction proper to both fleshly and spiritual Israel, for while the Jews were permitted to swear in the ordinary sense of the word, Christians are forbidden to do so (Matt. 5: 33-37; James 5: 12). *The former trouble* has special reference to the captivity in Babylon as a punishment for their iniquities. *Hid from mine eyes* means God will be so pleased with the national reformation after the period of the exile that he will not longer look upon the past and hold it against his people.

Verse 17. From this to the close of the chapter the verses should be marked as a bracket and given the general title of "kingdom of Christ," then note the comments verse by verse as they are offered in their order. These verses are highly figurative, but all figures of speech must have some literal facts or truths for a basis or there will be no meaning in the figures. And in the use of figures the writer does not stop to give us the explanation, so we must discover that from the information available and that is actually appropriate. The present temporal dwelling place of man is the *earth* with the *heavens* (air and the region of the planets) surrounding it. Spiritually, then, heavens and earth would be the spiritual world, which is the church connected with the new or Christian Dispensation. This is what Paul means in 2 Cor. 5: 17, and is what Isaiah means in this verse. *Forever . . . not come into mind* denotes that after the new creation has been brought into the world, the former (Jewish law) will be no longer in force and no one will have the right to live by it any more. This is the teaching of Paul in Rom. 10: 4 and Gal. 5: 1-4 which should be read carefully.

Verse 18. Jerusalem was the capital of the nation of Israel although its law had come from Mt. Sinai. The kingdom of Christ was not to have any particular city for its headquarters for the government would be local or congregational in form. But the law that was to govern it was sent forth from Jerusalem, and in a spiritual sense that city has been the mother of the people of Christ. The blessings of the citizens of the new creation will be so great that rejoicing is predicted. *Her people a joy* indicates that the presence of the people of the new creation will be a cause of joy in the world because of their benefits to life in general.

Verse 19. Not only will the people of the new creation be a cause of rejoicing to the world, but God will also take pleasure in them. The greatest reason for such joy will be the fact that they will be those who are created in his only and beloved Son. (2 Cor. 5: 17.) *Voice of weeping no more be heard* does not mean that all natural expressions of grief will be banished. Such a conclusion would contradict Rom. 12: 15; 1 Cor. 12: 26 and kindred passages that teach Christians to expect some experiences of grief. But it is more in the nature of Matt. 5: 4, which means that in the kingdom and service of Christ there will be a true source of consolation. There is no genuine occasion of rejoicing out of the Lord which is taught in Isa. 57: 21; Phil. 3: 1.

Verse 20. Let us remember that we are studying a highly figurative description of life in the spiritual realm of Christ. There was to be no such a condition of inability as is true in the physical world as infants, or men who have become old through some infirmity before their actual years would have rendered them infirm. We should picture a country where the long life of its inhabitants is such that even when disease or accident would cause the death of a little child, a reference to dates would show that he is a hundred years old. In such a country if a sinner cannot live more than a hundred years it will be on account of some curse of God upon him.

Verse 21. Continuing the figures the prophet represents the spiritual realm under Christ as one of satisfaction in its products. It has always been possible in a country to build houses and plant vineyards. But it often happens that some enemy will invade the land and destroy the houses and interfere with the use of the vineyards. In this perfect institution no fear of this kind will need be felt. Not that there will be no enemies of the citizens for there will be those who will persecute. But the actual "houses" and "vineyards" will be the spiritual blessings of the inhabitants and no power can take those away from a faithful servant of Christ.

Verse 22. The first part of this verse is the same in meaning as the preceding one except it is expressed in negative form. The long life of the inhabitants is compared to that of a tree because that most stately of all vegetable plants is known to live many times longer than the average life of man. *Mine elect* is a phrase to designate the citizens of the new creation who have become such by subjection to the laws of the country for the reception of new citizens.

Verse 23. The labor of the inhabitants will be protected from the ravages of the enemy as has previously been promised. However, even without the interference of outside parties, sometimes the earnest toil of the citizen proves unfruitful and disappointing from many of the uncertainties of life. It will not be so in this spiritual realm, but all the labor in the Lord will be a success (1 Cor. 15: 58).

Verse 24. Strictly speaking there could be no *answer* to a *call* before one has been made, so the expression must be understood as another figure of speech. The idea is that the Lord's care for his people will be such that he will not wait until they ask for blessings before bestowing them, for he already knows the things they need and deserve. Jesus taught this very thing in Matt. 6: 8. The last clause of this verse is just another form of the same prediction explained above.

Verse 25. The strong but beautiful figures continue. The mingling of these natural enemies in the beast creation in this manner illustrates the peaceable character of the spiritual citizens. A *serpent* figuratively means a wicked person and such a character will not have the privilege of partaking of the good things of life as will the faithful citizens, but will be compelled to live on the filth of the land; in the dust.

And regardless of the natural tendency of such a vile creature to take vengeance on the fortunate persons of the kingdom who may happen to be treading on the ground near him, he will not be permitted to harm the worthy inhabitants of the righteous institution. To speak in literal terms, in the kingdom of Christ there can be no actual harm come to the faithful child of God.

ISAIAH 66

Verse 1. The outstanding thought in this verse is the great power of God and his independence of all other beings. Moreover, even if the Lord needed anyone to "help him out," man would be unable to do so since he is himself the creature of God's making. And if God needed a place in which to dwell, it would be foolish for man to think he could build a house suitable for the purpose. It would be like a person who had erected a mansion that would house a million giants, then some man much smaller than a giant would think he ought to build a house in which this great builder could dwell. God is so great that his feet fill the universe and his person in general occupies the heaven as the place of his throne.

Verse 2. Since God has made all of the materials from which a man would have to build his proposed dwelling place for Him, he should not think God will expect him to obtain the divine favor by trying to do some great feat like building a showy mansion. No, we are told here the kind of person who will obtain the friendly attention of the Most High. It must be one who is poor and contrite in spirit, which means a man who is humble and who realizes his need for spiritual help. Jesus taught this same principle in Matt. 5: 3. A man whose attitude is opposite of this will not obtain the favor of God. This is not because the Lord just arbitrarily wills that it must be so; there is a logical basis for the conclusion. A man who is not humble and who does not feel the need of spiritual help will naturally not put forth any effort to obtain such help, which means he will not obey the commands of God. And if he will not obey the Lord's commands he need not expect him to *look* with favor upon him. One word in the lexicon definition of the original for *trembled* is "reverential." Thus if a man is humble of mind and has reverence for the word of God, he has the promise that he will be noticed by Him.

Verse 3. As a general comment on this verse it should be said the Israelites confounded the true with heathen religious practices. *Is as if* is not in the original Hebrew and the omission will make the thought clearer, which is that they classed the offering of an ox and the sacrificing of a human being as equally acceptable. The same conflicting action would be said of the offering of a lamb (a thing God desired) and that of a dog (a thing God abhorred). An *oblation* was a sacrifice of a clean animal while the blood of swine was unclean, yet these people made no difference between them. God called for the burning of incense, but these Jews replaced that service with the admiration of an idol. In general they placed the way of their own choosing on a par with the commandments that the Lord had instructed them to follow. Such corrupt practices as here described were so displeasing to God that he determined to exile them into the land of the heathen where their religious practice would be the unmixed kind, the pure idolatrous religion they had learned of those heathen.

Verse 4. *Will choose their delusions* means that God would "take them at their word" and just give them over, to these idolatrous practices which they seemed to like so well. *Fears* means the things they reverenced which was the idols of the heathen nations. Since the people of Israel had so much *fear* or reverence for the idols of the heathen, God determined to bring those very foreigners *upon them* which was done according to 2 Ki. 24 and 25. This treatment of these wayward Israelites would be just when their long period of rebellion is considered. When their true God called to them they did not even answer, while they not only answered the call of the heathen but yielded their services to them. *Did evil before mine eyes* means their practices were all seen by the eyes of God. This sinful manner of life was not merely through indifference or forgetfulness but it was deliberate; they *chose* to do so.

Verse 5. In all of this terrible history of rebellion there were some exceptions and God had a few men who remained true. (See the long note at 2 Ki. 22: 17 in Vol. 2 of the COMMENTARY.) These were the ones who would *tremble at his word* which means they had reverence for it (v. 2). *Brethren hated you* refers to the harsh treatment that was imposed on these righteous people by the wicked leaders (ch.

58: 3), who hypocritically said "Let the Lord be glorified." Now the "tables are turned" and he (the Lord) will appear to *you* (the mistreated Israelites) with *joy*, and *they* (the wicked leaders) *shall be ashamed*.

Verse 6. This verse is a prediction of the wrath of God against the wicked leaders of the nation who have been so cruel toward the common people. *City* means Jerusalem and *temple* is mentioned because it was built in the *city* as the earthly headquarters of the Lord. The determination of God to punish his corrupt people is appropriately represented as being announced in thundering tones *(voice of noise)* from this temple since that is the place where the law was to be executed.

Verse 7. Again the "telescope" (see the illustration at the beginning of this book) is extended and the prophet sees the birth of the church of Christ. The subject is illustrated by the circumstances connected with the facts of physical childbirth, only that the usual experiences are varied. It is the rule that a birth will be preceded by and accompanied with labor pains. The birth of the church is compared to a case where the child was born even before there had been any labor pains; *before she travailed*. This was literally true of the setting up of the church. That event took place as recorded in Acts 2, but there had not been any violence or public disturbances in connection with that wonderful day; there had been no labor pains.

Verse 8. This verse is a repetition of the preceding one with the addition of some inspired comments on the wonderful character of the great event; nothing like it had ever taken place. The earth had never been known to sprout and mature a plant in a day, but always required many days or weeks for the production. And no nation was ever born in a day, for even the great nation composed of the descendants of Abraham required a period of gestation that lasted 430 years in the womb of Egypt before the infant could be born. But here is a child that was destined to be the most important of all institutions the world had ever seen, and the birth was completed in one day and without any preceding labor throes.

Verse 9. The power of God to complete any work he starts is the thought in this verse. Again the prophet uses the subject of childbirth for his illustration. He supposes a case where a person is responsible, either personally or otherwise, for the pregnancy of a woman, and who cares for her during all the period previous to the time of birth. Then, when the critical hour has come when the expectant mother needs help the most, that person either deserts her or is unable to give her any assistance. It is predicted in question form that the Lord will not be that weak or unfaithful. He had been 4,000 years preparing for the birth of this great institution. The "prenatal" formation had been going on during that time and all the necessary parts of its structure were connected and everything was ready for the birth. The Lord proved his power and faithfulness by completing the great event and helping to deliver the infant church in one day; the day of Pentecost recorded in Acts 2. (See last verse of that chapter.)

Verse 10. When a child is born into a home there usually is great rejoicing, not only on the part of the members of that family but by the friends and neighbors. And continuing the line of comparison with the processes of reproduction in the natural realm, the prophet bids the world to congratulate Jerusalem upon the successful birth of this most important infant. *Love* and *mourn* are both used in connection with Jerusalem. The same friends who would sincerely rejoice over the good fortune of Jerusalem in this important birth, would be the ones who also would *mourn* with her in her many sorrows of the past. This is the same principle that Paul taught when he said: "Rejoice with them that do rejoice, and weep with them that weep" (Rom. 12: 15).

Verse 11. The prophet continues his use of the beautiful figures drawn from the circumstances of natural birth and nourishment. And, as is so frequently done in the use of figures, some exceptional performances are supposed and injected into the picture. The ordinary situation when an infant has been born is that the mother will be thereby enabled to supply the nourishment needed for the newborn infant. No others are supposed to need or desire to partake of this nourishment. Here is where the exception is introduced, for the friends are also invited to feed themselves at the breasts of this mother.

Verse 12. But it would be a heavy drain on the strength of this mother for so many others besides her infant to draw upon her supply that was originally intended only for her offspring.

The food she would be able to eat and digest would be what is generally required to nourish herself and her child. But the Lord will take care of that situation and see that the mother is provided with an extra amount of nourishment and of course will be given the ability to take in this added amount of food and she will also be enabled to convert it into nourishment for the use of others. We are to understand this all has a spiritual meaning in its fulfillment. The extra sustenance that is to be furnished this infant (the church) that is to be born in Jerusalem will be *the glory of the Gentiles*. Jerusalem originally had to live only on the services of the Jews, but after the church is born in that city, the services and support of the Gentiles will also be given her. With this additional strength this mother will be able not only to nurse her own offspring, but will be able to take others on her knees near her sides so they might nurse at her spiritual breasts.

Verse 13. God's people who were to be born in Jerusalem will be loved by Him and cared for on the same basis as a mother "stills her child" by her comforting words. The enemies of the people of God have always been on hand when there appeared to be an opportunity for oppressing them. And now, when the former people of the Lord who were restricted to a certain race, are merged with the races of the world to form a newborn offspring, the enemies will be on hand again to project their opposition and endeavor to destroy the child. But God will be attentive and see that all necessary protection is provided for his beloved.

Verse 14. This verse is the same in thought as the preceding one with some additional items on the assurances of divine oversight. It was to be so helpful and evident that all people would be aware of it. Not only would the favor for the righteous be known, but also the wrath of God would be realized against his enemies.

Verse 15. Let us not forget while passing along in our study of this prophetic book that the writer has his eye on both fleshly and spiritual Israel much of the time. Many of his passages are a blending of thoughts applicable to both. The book was written over a century before the captivity and that event was to come as a punishment on the nation for its unfaithfulness. Also, the vengeance upon the heathen whom God used as instruments for his purpose was predicted. All of the above is indicated in this verse, as well as a glimpse into the more distant future when the Lord would declare his intention of vengeance against the enemies of the church which was to be born in the mother city of Jerusalem.

Verse 16. The vengeance of God on behalf of fleshly Israel was manifested at the end of the captivity. (Dan. 5.) The spiritual fulfillment of this prediction is recorded in Acts 2 where the sword of the Spirit was used and thousands of sinners were brought under its power. *All flesh* is a prediction that Gentiles as well as Jews would be called upon to accept the law of the Lord. That fact is predicted in Joel 2: 28 and quoted by Peter at Jerusalem as recorded in Acts 2: 17.

Verse 17. The general comment on this verse is that it is a description of some idol worshipers, and there is a prediction of the wrath of God that was going to come upon them. I shall explain the various terms used, some of which are unusual as they are rendered in the A. V. A *garden* was an enclosed place that was well adapted to such activities as religious services. Smith's Bible Dictionary says that "the retirement of gardens rendered them favorite places of devotion." Naturally they could be thus used by both true and heathen worshipers. *Tree* is not in the original but the word *one* is. The idea is that these idolatrous worshipers followed behind each other in unison to practice the same iniquity, as if they all had a mind to serve the same idol god. *Mouse* is from a Hebrew word that refers to any kind of unclean rodent. Worshipers of idols glorified in defying the law of God which forbade the use of any unclean creature, either as food or in sacrifice. These wicked people showed their devotion to idols by eating such abominable things as swines' flesh and these filthy rodents here translated *mice*. *Sanctify* and *purify themselves* refers to their preparation for the participation in these heathen abnominations. All these *shall be consumed together* is the prediction of God's wrath upon the sinful nation, ending in their captivity by the Babylonians. This was to be fulfilled as recorded in 2 Ki. 24 and 25. But having made such a prediction against fleshly Israel, the prophet follows his usual style and jumps ahead to the time when spiritual Israel was to come into being and which was destined to include many people besides the Jews. This will be introduced in the next few verses and comments offered thereon.

Verse 18. The first clause is still in reference to the shortcomings of fleshly Israel. Then the scene shifts to the time of the Christian Dispensation when the Lord was to bring in the Gentiles. This idea of dropping the exclusive favors to the Jews when they proved unworthy, and in their place putting the Gentiles is a well established subject in the Bible. This verse makes the complete exchange of nations and thus spans several hundreds of years of time in making the change. It will be well for the reader to study chapters 9 and 11 of Romans in connection with the matter of the respective standing of the Jews and Gentiles before God.

Verse 19. In the case of fleshly Israel there was a remnant who survived the effects of the captivity, and they were sent to Palestine to restore the institutions of the Lord. In that of spiritual Israel there were to be some who would *escape* (would react favorably) the contact with the sword of the Spirit. (At least three thousand, Acts 2: 41.) These were to be sent back to their homes in various parts of the world (here figuratively called Tarshish, Pul and Lud) to *draw the bow*, which means to spread the good tidings of their new-found religion which they learned in Jerusalem. These new converts were to tell the story of the cross among the Gentiles.

Verse 20. From here to the close of the book the prophet will be writing on the same subject that has been running through much of the preceding portions of the book. The outstanding feature of the few remaining verses will be that they will pertain to spiritual Israel exclusively. The apparent references to fleshly Israel will be only for the purpose of obtaining some figures of speech to use as illustrations (either by comparison or contrast) of the new system of salvation under Christ. *All your brethren* and *out of all nations* is plainly a prediction that the Gentiles would finally be admitted into the services under Christ. However, the new system was to be offered to the Jews first and to the Gentiles a few years later. Hence the first application of this verse is to the events that are recorded in Acts 2. One of the annual feasts of the Jews (Pentecost) was at hand, and all able-bodied men were required to go to Jerusalem on such occasions. (Ex. 23: 15-17; Deut. 16: 16.) The men only were required to attend these feasts, but women were permitted and usually did come to Jerusalem on such occasions. The Lord took that occasion for the time of setting up the new institution since he wished to begin it with the services of the Jews only, and he knew that many of that race would be in the city, the place where the church was to be born. Thus our verse says the *children of Israel* will come to bring an offering *into the house of the Lord* which means the temple since that Jewish service will be still in force. These people literally traveled in such conveyances as are named here (see Acts 8: 27, 28), and Acts 2: 5 declares historically that many Jews were actually in Jerusalem at this time and that they had come from various nations.

Verse 21. Under the Mosaic system the tribe of Levi performed all of the general services about the tabernacle or temple. And the special services of the altars and other articles on the inside of these buildings were performed by the priests only, who also were of this tribe. This verse predicts that under Christ the people who will have become members of the new system, whether Jew or Gentile, will all be figuratively the priests and Levites. That means that under Christ there will not be any separate tribes nor any special class for priests. The whole brotherhood will form one tribe (with Christ as its head) and every member of it will be a priest. In other words, in the service of Christ there will be no class distinction but all will be expected to perform in the service according to ability and thus carry out the New Testament form of activities that will be genuine mutual ministry or mutual service. The religious priesthood under Christ is taught in 1 Pe. 2: 9; Rev. 1: 10; 5: 10.

Verse 22. This and the two following verses should be marked as a bracket and given the title "the kingdom of Christ." All of the many passages of the context go to show beyond any doubt that such title is a correct one. *New heavens and new earth* is the name of the system as a whole (see 2 Cor. 5: 17), and *your seed* refers to the individual Christians since they will have been begotten by the Word of God which is the seed of the kingdom (1 Pe. 1: 23). A wonderful truth and assurance may be seen in this verse. We have learned that the passage refers to the system of salvation under Christ and to the individuals living according to it. The prediction is made that all this *SHALL REMAIN*. This is the assurance that regardless of all the opposition and persecution that may be waged against the church, it will continue to live until Christ comes again to deliver it up to his Father. Christianity shall never die but will continue to the end of this world which should be a sweet thought for all who are interested in the greatest of all subjects, the salvation of man through Christ. He taught the same truth in Luke 18: 8 where he declares that notwithstanding the hard times that would come, when he comes to the earth again he shall find faith on it. And in 1 Cor. 15: 51 and 1 Thess 4: 17 Paul refers to the people of Christ by the pronoun "we" and speaks of them as being on the earth when Jesus comes.

Verse 23. Under the Mosaic system the *new moon* was a monthly date and the regular Sabbath was a weekly date. There are no special days as dates in the Christian Dispensation, so the terms are used figuratively. The thought is that Christians will be expected to render service to Christ constantly, and not only on some particular days that may be convenient.

Verse 24. No physical violence was to be used against those who resisted the claims of the Gospel, so the words are used figuratively because in former ages the Lord literally slew those who opposed his law. But Christians will be able to understand that men who refuse to bow to the will of Christ will be regarded as rebels in this life. If they continue in rebellion until death, they will be cast into the lake of fire where *their worm shall not die, neither shall their fire be quenched.* Jesus taught this same terrible truth in Mark 9: 43-48. *Shall be an abhorring unto all flesh.* There is no evidence that the saved in heaven will pay any attention to the thought of those who are in the lake of fire. Hence this prediction refers to the attitude that Christians will have toward those who are so disrespectful toward the God who gave them their existence as to live in sin. This great truth teaches that the followers of Christ have the right to be interested in the salvation of all men, but if they will persist in rebellion against the great Saviour of man, they should be looked upon as the wickedest of creatures and unworthy of the friendship of the faithful servants of the Son of God.

www.ingramcontent.com/pod-product-compliance
Lightning Source LLC
Chambersburg PA
CBHW070835160426
43192CB00012B/2195